T0094367

x64 Assembly Language Step-by-Step

4TH Edition

x64 Assembly Language Step-by-Step

Programming with Linux®

4TH Edition

Jeff Duntemann

WILEY

To the eternal memory of my father,

Frank W. Duntemann, Engineer

1922–1978

Who said, "When you build 'em right, they fly."

You did. And I do.

About the Author

Jeff Duntemann has had his technical nonfiction and science-fiction work professionally published since 1974. He worked as a programmer for Xerox Corporation and as a technical editor for Ziff-Davis Publishing and Borland International. He launched and edited two print magazines for programmers and has 20 technical books to his credit, including the bestselling *Assembly Language Step-by-Step*. He wrote the "Structured Programming" column in *Dr. Dobb's Journal* for four years and has published dozens of technical articles in many magazines. He has a longstanding interest in "strong" artificial intelligence, and most of his fiction explores the possibilities and consequences of strong AI. His other interests include electronics and amateur radio (callsign K7JPD), telescopes, and kites. Jeff lives in Phoenix, Arizona, with his wife Carol.

About the Technical Editor

David Stafford is an enthusiast of low-level programming in assembly language, from 8-bit processors to modern 64-bit multicore architectures. He lives in the Seattle area and works in the field of artificial intelligence for robotics.

Acknowledgments

Thanks are due to a number of people who helped me out as this edition took shape, in various ways. First, thanks to Jim Minatel and Pete Gaughan of Wiley, who got the project underway and made sure it went to completion. Also thanks to David Stafford, who acted as technical editor and provided a constant stream of invaluable advice.

The event shocked me to the core, but antony-jr of GitHub managed to create a working Linux appimage of the quirky and ancient but very accessible Insight debugger, which was pulled from Linux repositories soon after the third edition of this book hit print in 2009. A very big thanks to him for what was likely a *very* peculiar project. You can find his Insight appimage here: `https://appimage.github.io/Insight`.

Abundant thanks also to Dmitriy Manushin, who created SASM, a free assembly language IDE targeted at beginners: `https://dman95.github.io/SASM/english.html`.

When I ran into a weirdness in `glibc`, my wizard crew on Contrapositive Diary helped me figure it out:

- Jim Strickland
- Bill Buhler
- Jason Bucata
- Jonathan O'Neal
- Bruce and Keith (last names not given, and that's OK—the advice was golden)

Finally, and as always, a toast to Carol for her support and sacramental friendship that have enlivened me now for 54 years and enabled me to take on difficult projects like this and see them through to the end, no matter how nuts they made me along the way!

Contents at a Glance

Contents

Introduction

"Why Would You Want to Do That?"

It was 1985, and I was in a chartered bus in New York City, heading for a press reception with a bunch of other restless media egomaniacs. I was only beginning my tech journalist career (as technical editor for *PC Tech Journal*), and my first book was still months in the future. I happened to be sitting next to an established programming writer/guru, with whom I was impressed and to whom I was babbling about one thing or another. I would like to eliminate this statement; it adds little to the book, and as annoying as he is, even though we don't name him, I now understand why he's so annoying: He lives and works in a completely different culture than I do.

During our chat, I happened to let slip that I was a Turbo Pascal fanatic, and what I really wanted to do was learn how to write Turbo Pascal programs that made use of the brand new Microsoft Windows user interface. He wrinkled his nose and grimaced wryly, before speaking the Infamous Question:

"Why would you want to do *that*?"

I had never heard the question before (though I would hear it many times thereafter), and it took me aback. Why? Because, well, because. . .I wanted to know how it *worked*.

"Heh. That's what C is for."

Further discussion got me nowhere in a Pascal direction. But some probing led me to understand that you *couldn't* write Windows apps in Turbo Pascal. It was impossible. Or. . .the programming writer/guru didn't know how. Maybe both. I never learned the truth as it stood in 1985. (Delphi answered the question once and for all in 1995.) But I did learn the meaning of the Infamous Question.

Note well: When somebody asks you, "Why would you want to do *that*?" what it really means is this: "You've asked me how to do something that is either impossible using tools that I favor or completely outside my experience, but I don't want to lose face by admitting it. So. . .how 'bout those Blackhawks?"

I heard it again and again over the years:

Q: How can I set up a C string so that I can read its length without scanning it?

A: Why would you want to do *that?*

Q: How can I write an assembly language subroutine callable from Turbo Pascal?

A: Why would you want to do *that?*

Q: How can I write Windows apps in assembly language?

A: Why would you want to do *that?*

You get the idea. The answer to the Infamous Question is always the same, and if the weasels ever ask it of you, snap back as quickly as possible: *because I want to know how it works.*

That is a completely sufficient answer. It's the answer I've used every single time, except for one occasion a considerable number of years ago, when I put forth that I wanted to write a book that taught people how to program in assembly language as their *first* experience in programming.

Q: Good grief, why would you want to do *that?*

A: Because it's the best way there is to build the skills required to understand how *all the rest* of the programming universe works.

Being a programmer is one thing above all else: It is understanding how things work. Learning to be a programmer, furthermore, is almost entirely a process of learning how things work. This can be done at various levels, depending on the tools you're using. If you're programming in Visual Basic, you have to understand how certain things work, but those things are by and large confined to Visual Basic itself. A great deal of machinery is hidden by the layer that Visual Basic places between the programmer and the computer. (The same is true of Delphi, Lazarus, Java, Python, and many other very high-level programming environments.) If you're using a C compiler, you're a lot closer to the machine, so you see a lot more of that machinery—and must, therefore, understand how it works to be able to use it. However, quite a bit remains hidden, even from the hardened C programmer.

If, on the other hand, you're working in assembly language, you're as close to the machine as you can get. Assembly language hides *nothing*, and withholds no power. The flipside, of course, is that no magical layer between you and the machine will absolve any ignorance and "take care of" things for you. If you don't understand how something works, you're dead in the water—unless you know enough to be able to figure it out on your own.

That's a key point: My goal in creating this book is not entirely to teach you assembly language *per se*. If this book has a prime directive at all, it is to impart a certain disciplined curiosity about the underlying machine, along with some basic context from which you can begin to explore the machine at its very lowest levels—that, and the confidence to give it your best shot. This is difficult stuff, but it's nothing you can't master given some concentration, patience, and the time it requires—which, I caution, may be considerable.

In truth, what I'm really teaching you here is how to learn.

What You'll Need

To program as I intend to teach, you're going to need a 64-bit Intel computer running a 64-bit distribution of Linux. The one I used in preparing this book is Linux Mint Cinnamon V20. 3 Una. "Una" here is a code name for this version of Linux Mint. It's nothing more than a short way of saying "Linux Mint 20.3." I recommend Mint; it's thrown me fewer curves than any other distro I've ever used—and I've used Linux here and there ever since it first appeared. I don't think which graphical shell you use matters a great deal. I like Cinnamon, but you can use whatever you like or are familiar with.

You need to be reasonably proficient with Linux at the user level. I can't teach you how to install, configure, and run Linux in this book. If you're not already familiar with Linux, get a tutorial text and work through it. There are many such online.

You'll need a piece of free software called SASM, which is a simple interactive development environment (IDE) for programming in assembly. Basically, it consists of an editor, a build system, and a front end to the standard Linux debugger gdb. You'll also need a free assembler called NASM.

You don't have to know how to download, install, and configure these tools in advance because, at the appropriate times, I'll cover all necessary tool installation and configuration.

Do note that other Unix implementations not based on the Linux kernel may not function precisely the same way under the hood. BSD Unix uses different conventions for making system calls, for example, and other Unix versions like Solaris are outside my experience.

Remember that *this book is about the x64 architecture*. To the extent that x64 contains x86, I will also be teaching elements of the x86 architecture. The gulf between 32-bit x86 and 64-bit x64 is a *lot* narrower than the gulf between 16-bit x86 and 32-bit x86. If you already have a firm grounding in 32-bit x86, you'll breeze through most of this book at a gallop. If you can do that, cool—just please remember that the book is for those who are just starting out in programming on Intel CPUs.

Also remember that this book is limited in size by its publisher: Paper, ink, and cover stock aren't free. That means I have to narrow the scope of what I teach and explain within those limits. I wish I had the space to cover the AVX math subsystem. I don't. But I'll bet that once you go through this book, you can figure much of it out by yourself.

The Master Plan

This book starts at the beginning, and I mean the *beginning*. Maybe you're already there, or well past it. I respect that. I still think that it wouldn't hurt to start at the first chapter and read through all the chapters in order. Review is useful, and hey—you may realize that you didn't know *quite* as much as you thought you did. (Happens to me all the time!)

But if time is at a premium, here's the cheat sheet:

- If you already understand the fundamental ideas of computer programming, skip Chapter 1.

- If you already understand the ideas behind number bases other than decimal (especially hexadecimal and binary), skip Chapter 2.

- If you already have a grip on the nature of computer internals (memory, CPU architectures, and so on) skip Chapter 3.

- If you already understand x64 memory addressing, skip Chapter 4.

- No. Stop. Scratch that. Even if you already understand x64 memory addressing, *read Chapter 4*.

The last bullet is there, and emphatic, for a reason: *Assembly language programming is about memory addressing.* If you don't understand memory addressing, nothing else you learn in assembly will help you one. . .bit. So, don't skip Chapter 4 no matter what else you know or think you know. Start from there, and see it through to the end. Memory addressing comes up regularly throughout the rest of the book. It's really the heart of the topic.

Load every example program, assemble each one, and run them all. Strive to understand every single line in every program. Take nothing on faith. Furthermore, don't stop there. Change the example programs as things begin to make sense to you. Try different approaches. Try things that I don't mention. Be audacious. Nay, go nuts—bits don't have feelings, and the worst thing that can happen is that Linux throws a segmentation fault, which may hurt your program but does not hurt Linux. The only catch is that when you do try something, strive to understand why it *doesn't* work as clearly as you understand all the other things that do. Single-step your way through a program in the SASM debugger, even when the program works. *Take notes.*

That is, ultimately, what I'm after: to show you the way to understand what every however distant corner of your machine is doing and how all its many pieces work together. This doesn't mean I'll explain every corner of it myself—no one will live long enough to do that because computing isn't simple anymore—but if you develop the discipline of patient research and experimentation, you can probably work it out for yourself. Ultimately, that's the only way to learn it: by yourself. The guidance you find—in friends, on the Net, in books like this—is only guidance and grease on the axles. You have to decide who's to be the master, you or the machine, and make it so. Assembly programmers are the only programmers who can truly claim to be masters, which is a truth worth meditating on.

A Note on Capitalization Conventions

Assembly language is peculiar among programming languages in that there is no universal standard for case-sensitivity. In the C language, all identifiers are case-sensitive, and I have seen assemblers that do not recognize differences in case at all. NASM, the assembler I'm presenting in this book, is case-sensitive only for programmer-defined identifiers. The instruction mnemonics and the names of registers, however, are *not* case sensitive.

There are customs in the literature on assembly language, and one of those customs is to treat CPU instruction mnemonics as uppercase in the chapter text and in lowercase in source code files and code snippets interspersed within the text. I'll be following that custom here. Within discussion text, I'll speak of MOV and CALL and CMP. In example code, it will be `mov` and `call` and `cmp`. Code snippets and listings will be in a monospace Courier-style font. When mentioned in the text, registers will be in uppercase but not in the Courier font and lowercase in snippets and listings.

There are two reasons for this:

- In text discussions, the mnemonics need to stand out. It's too easy to lose track of them amid a torrent of ordinary mixed-case words.
- To read and learn from existing documents and source code outside of this one book, you need to be able to easily read assembly language whether it's in uppercase, lowercase, or mixed case. Getting comfortable with different ways of expressing the same things is important.

Remember Why You're Here

Anyway. Wherever you choose to start the book, it's time to get underway. Just remember that whatever gets in your face, be it the weasels, the machine, or your own inexperience, the thing to keep in the forefront of your mind is this: *You're in it to figure out how it works.*

Let's go.

Jeff Duntemann
Scottsdale, Arizona
May 24, 2023

x64 Assembly Language Step-by-Step

4TH Edition

It's All in the Plan

Understanding What Computers Really Do

Another Pleasant Valley Saturday

"Quick, Mike, get your sister and brother up; it's past 7. Nicky's got Little League at 9, and Dione's got ballet at 10. Give Max his heartworm pill! (We're out of them, Mom, remember?) Your father picked a great weekend to go fishing . . . . Here, let me give you 10 bucks and go get more pills at the vet's . . . . My God, that's right, Hank needed gas money and left me broke. There's a teller machine over by Kmart, and if I go there, I can take that stupid toilet seat back and get the right one. "I guess I'd better make a list . . . ."

It's another Pleasant Valley Saturday, and 30-odd million suburban home-makers sit down with a pencil and pad at the kitchen table to try to make sense of a morning that would kill and pickle any lesser being. In her mind she thinks of the dependencies and traces the route:

"Drop Nicky at Rand Park, go back to Dempster, and it's about 10 minutes to Golf Mill Mall. Do I have gas? I'd better check first—if not, stop at Del's Shell or I won't make it to Milwaukee Avenue. Milk the teller machine at Golf Mill; then cross the parking lot to Kmart to return the toilet seat that Hank bought last weekend without checking what shape it was. Gotta remember to throw the toilet seat in back of the van—write that at the top of the list.

"By then it'll be half past, maybe later. Ballet is all the way down Greenwood in Park Ridge. No left turn from Milwaukee—but there's the sneak path around behind the mall. I have to remember not to turn right onto Milwaukee like I always do—jot that down. While I'm in Park Ridge, I can check and see if Hank's new glasses are in—should call, but they won't even be open until 9:30. Oh, and groceries—can do that while Dione dances. On the way back I can cut over to Oakton and get the dog's pills."

In about 90 seconds flat the list is complete:

- Throw toilet seat in van.
- Check gas—if empty, stop at Del's Shell.
- Drop Nicky at Rand Park.
- Stop at Golf Mill teller machine.
- Return toilet seat at Kmart.
- Drop Dione at ballet (remember the sneak path to Greenwood).
- See if Hank's glasses are at Pearle Vision—if they are, make double sure they remembered the extra scratch coating.
- Get groceries at Jewel.
- Pick up Dione.
- Stop at vet for heartworm pills.
- Drop off groceries at home.
- If it's time, pick up Nicky. If not, collapse for a few minutes; then pick up Nicky.
- Collapse!

What we often call a "laundry list" (whether it involves laundry or not) is the perfect metaphor for a computer program. Without realizing it, our intrepid homemaker has written herself a computer program and then set out (with herself acting as the computer) to execute it and be done before noon.

Computer programming is nothing more than this: you the programmer write a list of steps and tests. The computer then performs each step and test in sequence. When the list of steps has been executed, the computer stops.

A computer program is a list of steps and tests, nothing more.

Steps and Tests

Think for a moment about what I call a test in the preceding laundry list. A *test* is the sort of either/or decision we make dozens or hundreds of times on even the most placid of days, sometimes nearly without thinking about it.

Our homemaker performed a test when she jumped into the van to get started on her adventure. She looked at the gas gauge. The gas gauge would tell her one of two things: (1) she has enough gas, or (2) she doesn't. If she has enough gas, she takes a right and heads for Rand Park. If she doesn't have enough gas, she takes a left down to the corner and fills the tank at Del's Shell. (Del takes credit cards.) Then, with a full tank, she continues the program by making a U-turn and heading for Rand Park.

In the abstract, a test consists of these two parts:

- First, you take a look at something that can go one of two ways.
- Then you do one of two things, depending on what you saw when you took a look.

Toward the end of the program, our homemaker got home, took the groceries out of the van, and looked at the clock. If it isn't time to get Nicky back from Little League, she has a moment to collapse on the couch in a nearly empty house. If it *is* time to get Nicky, there's no rest for the ragged: she sprints for the van and heads back to Rand Park.

(Any guesses as to whether she really gets to rest when the program finishes running?)

More Than Two Ways?

You might object, saying that many or most tests involve more than two alternatives. Sorry, you're wrong—in every case. Read this twice: except for totally impulsive or psychotic behavior, every human decision comes down to the choice between two alternatives.

What you have to do is look a little more closely at what goes through your mind when you make decisions. The next time you buzz down to Chow Now for fast Chinese, observe yourself while you're poring over the menu. The choice might seem, at first, to be of one item out of 26 Cantonese main courses. Not so—the choice, in fact, is between choosing one item and *not* choosing that one item. Your eyes rest on chicken with cashews. Naw, too bland. *That was a test.* You slide down to the next item. Chicken with black mushrooms. Hmmm, no, had that last week. *That was another test.* Next item: kung pao chicken. Yeah, that's it! *That was a third test.*

The choice was not among chicken with cashews, chicken with black mushrooms, and chicken with kung pao. Each dish had its moment, poised before the critical eye of your mind, and you turned thumbs up or thumbs down on it, individually. Eventually, one dish won, but it won in that same game of "to eat or not to eat."

Let me give you another example. Many of life's most complicated decisions come about because 99.99867 percent of us are not nudists. You've been there: you're standing in the clothes closet in your underwear, flipping through your rack of pants. The tests come thick and fast. This one? No. This one? No. This one? No. This one? Yeah. You pick a pair of blue pants, say. (It's a Monday, after all, and blue would seem an appropriate color.) Then you stumble over to your sock drawer and take a look. Whoops, no blue socks. *That was a test.* So you stumble back to the clothes closet, hang your blue pants back on the pants rack, and start over. This one? No. This one? No. This one? Yeah. This time it's brown pants, and you toss them over your arm and head back to the sock drawer to take another look. Nertz, out of brown socks, too. So it's back to the clothes closet . . . .

What you might consider a single decision, or perhaps two decisions inextricably tangled (like picking pants and socks of the same color, given stock on hand), is actually a series of small decisions, always binary in nature: pick 'em or don't pick 'em. Find 'em or don't find 'em. The Monday morning episode in the clothes closet is a good analogy of a programming structure called a *loop*: you keep doing a series of things until you get it right, and then you stop (assuming you're not the kind of geek who wears blue socks with brown pants). But whether you get everything right always comes down to a sequence of simple either/or decisions.

Computers Think Like Us

I can almost hear what you're thinking: "Sure, it's a computer book, and he's trying to get me to think like a computer." Not at all. Computers think like *us*. We designed them; how else could they think? No, what I'm trying to do is get you to take a long, hard look at how *you* think. We run on automatic for so much of our lives that we literally do most of our thinking without really thinking about it.

The best model for the logic of a computer program is the same logic we use to plan and manage our daily affairs. No matter what we do, it comes down to a matter of confronting two alternatives and picking one. What we might think of as a single large and complicated decision is nothing more than a messy tangle of many smaller decisions. The skill of looking at a complex decision and seeing all the little decisions in its tummy will serve you well in learning how to program. Observe yourself the next time you have to decide something. Count up the little decisions that make up the big one. You'll be surprised.

And, surprise! You'll be a programmer.

Had This Been the Real Thing . . .

Do not be alarmed. What you have just experienced was a metaphor. It was not the real thing. (The real thing comes later.)

I use metaphors a lot in this book. A metaphor is a loose comparison drawn between something familiar (such as a Saturday morning laundry list) and something unfamiliar (such as a computer program). The idea is to anchor the unfamiliar in terms of the familiar so that when I begin tossing facts at you, you'll have someplace comfortable to lay them down.

The most important thing for you to do right now is keep an open mind. If you know a little bit about computers or programming, don't pick nits. Yes, there are important differences between a homemaker following a scribbled laundry list and a computer executing a program. I'll mention those differences all in good time.

For now, it's still Chapter 1. Take these initial metaphors on their own terms. Later, they'll help a lot.

Assembly Language Programming As a Square Dance

Carol and I have a certain fondness for "called" dances, the most prevalent type being square dances. There are others, like New England contra dances, which are a lot like square dances but with better music. In a called dance, the caller person at the front of the hall calls out movements, and the dancers perform those movements. The music provides a beat, like the ticking of a clock. The sequence of movements taken together is the dance, and the dance usually has a name.

The first time Carol and I attended a contra dance, I was poleaxed: *this was like assembly language programming!* The caller called out "allemande left," and we performed the movement known as "allemande left." The caller called out "forward and back," and we executed the "forward and back" movement. The caller called out "box the gnat," and, well, we boxed the gnat. (I am not making this up!) There are a reasonable number of movements, and to be good at that sort of dancing, you have to memorize them all by name. Otherwise, if the caller calls a movement that you don't know, the dance might stumble or grind to a halt. (Bluescreen!)

At its deepest level, a computer understands a collection of individual operations called *instructions*. These perform arithmetic, execute logic like AND and OR, move data around, and do many other things. Each instruction is performed inside the CPU chip. Just as a set of dance movements are the individual atoms of motion making up a square dance, instructions are the atoms of a computer program. The program is like the dance as a whole: a sequence of instructions executed in order. The couples taking part in the dance execute the dance/program as the caller moves down the list of movements, calling out each one in turn. The couples, then, are the computer on which the dance runs.

That's about as far as the square dance metaphor goes. Once you get the knack of assembly language, hey, go take square dance or contra dance lessons somewhere and see if you don't come to the same conclusion that I did.

Assembly Language Programming As a Board Game

Board games were a really big deal when I was a kid, when board games were actually printed on a species of board. (OK, cardboard.) Monopoly was one that almost everybody had. There was a sort of pathway around the edge of the board divided into squares. You had a game piece that advanced from square to square according to dice throws, and when your piece landed on a square, you could do one of several things: buy property that hadn't been bought yet, pay rent on property owned by other players, pull a card from the Chance stack, or—eek!—go to jail. You had a pile of Monopoly money to spend, and when another player had to pay rent, you got more.

The specifics of the Monopoly game aren't important here. What matters is that you progress through a series of steps, and at each step, something happens. Your pile of money grows or shrinks. Assembly language is a little like that: a program is like the game board. Each step in the program does something. There are places where you can store numbers. The numbers change as you move through the program.

Now that you're thinking in terms of board games, take a look at Figure 1.1. What I've drawn is actually a fair approximation of assembly language as it was used on some of our simpler computers 50 or 60 years ago. The column marked "Program Instructions" is the main path around the edge of the board, of which only a portion can be shown here. This is the assembly language computer program, the actual series of steps and tests that, when executed, causes the computer to do something useful. Setting up this series of program instructions is what programming in assembly language actually *is*.

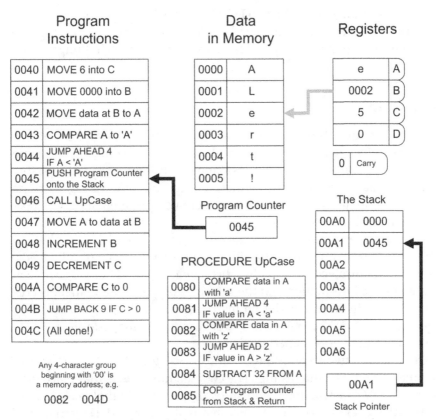

Figure 1.1: The Game of Assembly Language

Everything else is odds and ends in the middle of the board that serve the game in progress. Most of these are storage locations that contain your data. You're probably noticing (perhaps with sagging spirits) that there are a *lot* of numbers involved. (They're weird numbers, too. What, for example, does "004B" mean? I deal with that issue in Chapter 2, "Alien Bases.") I'm sorry, but that's simply the way the game is played. Assembly language, at its deepest level, is nothing *but* numbers, and if you hate numbers the way most people hate anchovies, you're going to have a rough time of it. (I like anchovies, which is part of my legend. Learn to like numbers. They're not as salty.) Higher-level programming languages such as Pascal or Python disguise the numbers by treating them symbolically. But assembly language, well, it's just you and the numbers.

I should caution you that the Game of Assembly Language in Figure 1.1 represents no real computer processor, like the Intel Core i5. Also, I've made the names of instructions more clearly understandable than the names of the instructions in Intel assembly language actually are. In the real world, instruction names are typically short things like **LAHF, STC, INC, SHRX,** and other crypticisms that cannot be understood without considerable explanation. We're easing into this stuff sidewise, and in this chapter I have to sugarcoat certain things a little to draw the metaphors clearly.

Code and Data

Like most board games, the assembly language board game consists of two broad categories of elements: game steps and places to store things. The "game steps" are the steps and tests I've been speaking of all along. The places to store things are just that: cubbyholes into which you can place numbers, with the confidence that those numbers will remain where you put them until you take them out or change them somehow.

In programming terms, the game steps are called *code*, and the numbers in their cubbyholes (as distinct from the cubbyholes themselves) are called *data*. The cubbyholes themselves are usually called *storage*. (The difference between the places you store information and the information you store in them is crucial. Don't confuse them.) Consider an instruction in the Game of Assembly Language that says **ADD 32 to A**. An **ADD** instruction in the code alters a data value stored in a cubbyhole named Register A.

Code and data are two very different kinds of critters, but they interact in ways that make the game interesting. The code includes steps that place data into storage (**MOVE** instructions) and steps that alter data that is already in storage (**INCREMENT** and **DECREMENT** instructions, and **ADD** instructions, among others). Most of the time you'll think of code as being the master of data, in that the code writes data values into storage. Data does influence code as well, however. Among the tests that the code makes are tests that examine data in storage, the **COMPARE** instructions. If a given data value exists in storage, the code may do one thing; if that value does not exist in storage, the code will do something else, as in the **JUMP BACK** and **JUMP AHEAD** instructions.

The short block of instructions marked **PROCEDURE** is a detour off the main stream of instructions. At any point in the program you can duck out into the procedure, perform its steps and tests, and then return to the very place from which you left. This allows a sequence of steps and tests that is generally useful and used frequently to exist in only one place rather than exist as separate copies everywhere it's needed.

Addresses

Another critical concept lies in the funny numbers at the left side of the program step locations and data locations. Each number is unique, in that a location tagged with that number appears only *once* inside the computer. This location is called an *address*. Data is stored and retrieved by specifying the data's address in the machine. Procedures are called by specifying the address at which they begin.

The little box (which is also a storage location) marked "Program Counter" keeps the address of the next instruction to be performed. The number inside the program counter is increased by one (*incremented*) each time an instruction is performed *unless the instruction tells the program counter to do something else*. For example, notice the **JUMP BACK 9** instruction at address 004B. When this instruction is performed, the program counter will "back up" by nine locations. This is analogous to the "go back three spaces" concept in most board games.

Metaphor Check!

That's about as much explanation of the Game of Assembly Language as I'm going to offer for now. This is still Chapter 1, and we're still in metaphor territory. People who have had some exposure to computers will recognize and understand some of what Figure 1.1 is doing. People with no exposure to computer innards at all shouldn't feel left behind for being utterly lost. I created the Game of Assembly Language solely to put across the following points:

- *The individual steps are very simple.* One single instruction rarely does more than move a single value from one storage cubbyhole to another, perform very elementary arithmetic like addition or subtraction, or compare the value contained in one storage cubbyhole to a value contained in another. This is good news, because it allows you to concentrate on the simple task accomplished by a single instruction without being overwhelmed by complexity. The bad news, however, is the next point.

- *It takes a lot of steps to do anything useful.* You can often write a useful program in such languages as Pascal or BASIC in five or six lines. You can actually create useful programs in visual programming systems like Visual Basic, Delphi, or Lazarus *without writing any code at all*. (The code is still there . . . but the code is "canned" and all you're really doing is choosing which chunks of canned code in a collection of many such chunks will run.) A useful assembly language program cannot be implemented in fewer than about 50 lines, and anything challenging takes hundreds or thousands—or tens of thousands—of lines. The skill of assembly language programming lies in structuring these hundreds or thousands of instructions so that the program both operates correctly and can still be read and understood by other programmers—and yourself—six months later.

- *The key to assembly language is understanding memory addresses.* In such languages as Pascal and BASIC, the compiler takes care of where something is located—you simply have to give that something a symbolic name and call it by that name whenever you want to look at it or change it.

In assembly language, you must always be cognizant of where things are in your computer's memory or register set. So, in working through this book, pay special attention to the concept of memory addressing, which is nothing more than the art of specifying where something is. The Game of Assembly Language is peppered with addresses and instructions that work with addresses (such as **MOVE data at B to C**, which means move the data stored at the address specified by register B to register C). Addressing is by far the trickiest part of assembly language, but master it and you've got most of the whole thing in your hip pocket.

Everything I've said so far has been orientation. I've tried to give you a taste of the big picture of assembly language and how its fundamental principles relate to the life you've been living all along. Life is a sequence of steps and tests, as are square dances and board games—and so is assembly language. Keep those metaphors in mind as we proceed to get real by confronting the nature of computer numbers.

Alien Bases

Getting Your Arms Around Binary and Hexadecimal

The Return of the New Math Monster

The year was 1966. Perhaps you were there. (I was 13 and in eighth grade.) New Math burst upon the grade-school curricula of the nation, and homework became a turmoil of number lines, sets, and alternate bases. Middle-class parents scratched their heads with their children over questions like, "What is 17 in Base 5?" and "Which sets does the Null Set belong to?" In very short order (I recall a period of about two months), the whole thing was tossed in the trash as quickly as it had been concocted by bored educrats with too little to do.

This was a pity actually. What nobody seemed to realize at the time was that, granted, we were learning New Math—except that *Old* Math had never been taught at the grade-school level either. We kept wondering of what possible use it was to know what the intersection of the set of squirrels and the set of mammals was. The truth, of course, was that it was no use at all. Mathematics in America has always been taught as *applied* mathematics—arithmetic—heavy on the word problems. If it won't help you balance your checkbook or proportion a recipe, it ain't real math, man. Little or nothing of the logic of mathematics has *ever* made it into the elementary classroom, in part because elementary school in America has historically been a sort of trade school for everyday life. Getting the little beasts fundamentally literate is difficult enough. Trying to get them to appreciate the beauty of alternate number systems simply went over the line for practical middle-class America.

Nerdball that I was, I actually enjoyed fussing with math in the New-Age style back in 1966, but I gladly laid it aside when the whole thing blew over. I didn't have to pick it up again until 1976, when, after working like a maniac with a wire-wrap gun for several weeks, I fed power to my COSMAC ELF micro-computer and was greeted by an LED display of a pair of numbers in *base 16!*

Mon dieu, New Math *redux.*

This chapter exists because at the assembly language level, your computer does not understand numbers in our familiar base 10. Computers, in a slightly schizoid fashion, work in base 2 *and* base 16—all at the same time. If you're willing to confine yourself to higher-level languages such as Basic or Pascal, you can ignore these alien bases altogether, or perhaps treat them as an advanced topic once you get the rest of the language down pat. Not here. *Everything* in assembly language depends on your thorough understanding of these two number bases. So before we do anything else, we're going to learn how to count all over again—in Martian.

Counting in Martian

There is intelligent life on Mars.

That is, the Martians are intelligent enough to know from watching our TV programs these past 90 years or so that a thriving tourist industry would not be to their advantage. So they've remained in hiding, emerging only briefly to carve big rocks into the shape of Elvis's face to help the *National Enquirer* ensure that no one will ever take Mars seriously again. The Martians do occasionally communicate with science fiction writers like me, knowing full well that nobody has *ever* taken *us* seriously. That's the reason for the information in this section, which involves the way Martians count.

Martians have three fingers on one hand, and only one finger on the other. Male Martians have their three fingers on the left hand, while females have their three fingers on the right hand. This makes waltzing and certain other things easier.

Like human beings and any other intelligent race, Martians started counting by using their fingers. Just as we used our 10 fingers to set things off in groups and powers of 10, the Martians used their four fingers to set things off in groups and powers of four. Over time, our civilization standardized on a set of 10 digits to serve our number system. The Martians, similarly, standardized on a set of four digits for their number system. The four digits follow, along with the names of the digits as the Martians pronounce them: Θ (xip), ⌈ (foo), ∩ (bar), ≡ (bas).

Like our zero, xip is a placeholder representing no items, and while Martians sometimes count from xip, they usually start with foo, representing a single item. So they start counting: *foo, bar, bas* . . . .

Now what? What comes after bas? Table 2.1 demonstrates how the Martians count to what we here on Earth would call 25.

Table 2.1: Counting in Martian, Base Fooby

MARTIAN NUMERALS	MARTIAN PRONUNCIATION	EARTH EQUIVALENT
Θ	Xip	0
⌠	Foo	1
∩	Bar	2
≡	Bas	3
⌠Θ	Fooby	4
⌠⌠	Fooby-foo	5
⌠∩	Fooby-bar	6
⌠≡	Fooby-bas	7
∩Θ	Barby	8
∩⌠	Barby-foo	9
∩∩	Barby-bar	10
∩≡	Barby-bas	11
≡Θ	Basby	12
≡⌠	Basby-foo	13
≡∩	Basby-bar	14
≡≡	Basby-bas	15
⌠ΘΘ	Foobity	16
⌠Θ⌠	Foobity-foo	17
⌠Θ∩	Foobity-bar	18
⌠Θ≡	Foobity-bas	19
⌠⌠Θ	Foobity-fooby	20
⌠⌠⌠	Foobity-fooby-foo	21
⌠⌠∩	Foobity-fooby-bar	22
⌠⌠≡	Foobity-fooby-bas	23
⌠∩Θ	Foobity-barby	24
⌠∩⌠	Foobity-barby-foo	25

With only four digits (including the one representing zero) the Martians can count only to bas without running out of digits. The number after bas has a new name, *fooby*. Fooby is the base of the Martian number system and probably the most important number on Mars. Fooby is the number of fingers a Martian has. We would call it *four*.

The most significant thing about fooby is the way the Martians write it out in numerals: ⌈ Θ. Instead of a single column, fooby is expressed in two columns. Just as with our decimal system, each column has a value that is a power of fooby. This only means that as you move from the rightmost column toward the left, each column represents a value fooby times the column to its right.

The rightmost column represents units, in counts of foo. The next column over represents fooby times foo, or (given that arithmetic works the same way on Mars as here, New Math notwithstanding) simply fooby. The next column to the left of fooby represents fooby times fooby, or foobity, and so on. This relationship should become clearer through Table 2.2.

Table 2.2: Powers of Fooby

⌈	Foo	x Fooby = ⌈ Θ	(Fooby)
⌈ Θ	Fooby	x Fooby = ⌈ ΘΘ	(Foobity)
⌈ ΘΘ	Foobity	x Fooby = ⌈ ΘΘΘ	(Foobidity)
⌈ ΘΘΘ	Foobidity	x Fooby = ⌈ ΘΘΘΘ	(Foobididity)
⌈ ΘΘΘΘ	Foobididity	x Fooby = ⌈ ΘΘΘΘΘ	(Foobidididity)
⌈ ΘΘΘΘΘ	Foobidididity	x Fooby = ⌈ ΘΘΘΘΘΘ	and so on . . .

Dissecting a Martian Number

Any given column may contain a digit from xip to bas, indicating how many instances of that column's value are contained in the number as a whole. Let's work through an example. Look at Figure 2.1, which is a dissection of the Martian number ∩ ≡ ⌈ Θ ≡, pronounced "Barbididity-basbidity-foobity-bas." (A visiting and heavily disguised Martian precipitated the doo-wop craze while standing at a Philadelphia bus stop in 1954, counting his change.)

The rightmost column tells how many units are contained in the number. The digit there is bas, indicating that the number contains bas units. The second column from the right carries a value of fooby times foo (fooby times 1) or fooby. A xip in the fooby column indicates that there are no foobies in the number. The xip digit in ⌈ Θ is a placeholder, just as zero is in our numbering system. Notice also that in the columnar sum shown to the right of the digit matrix, the foobies line is represented by a double xip. Not only is there a xip to tell us that there are no foobies, but also a xip holding the foos place as well. This pattern continues in the columnar sum as we move toward the more significant columns to the left.

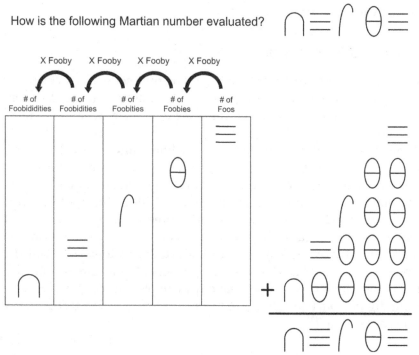

Figure 2.1: The anatomy of ∩≡⌈ Θ ≡

Fooby times fooby is foobity, and the ⌈ digit tells us that there is foo foobity (a single foobity) in the number. The next column, in keeping with the pattern, is foobity times fooby, or foobidity. In the columnar notation, foobidity is written as ⌈ ΘΘΘ. The ≡ digit tells us that there are bas foobidities in the number. Bas foobidities is a number with its own name, basbidity, which may be written as ≡ ΘΘΘ. Note the presence of basbidity in the columnar sum.

The next column to the left has a value of fooby times foobidity, or foobididity. The ∩ digit tells us that there are bar foobididities in the number. Bar foobididities (written ∩ ΘΘΘΘ) is also a number with its own name, barbididity. Note also the presence of barbididity in the columnar sum, as well as the four xip digits that hold places for the empty columns.

The columnar sum expresses the sense of the way a number is assembled: the number contains barbididity, basbidity, foobity, and bas. Roll all that together by simple addition, and you get ∩ ≡ ⌈ Θ ≡. The name is pronounced simply by hyphenating the component values: barbididity-basbidity-foobity-bas. Note that there is no part in the name representing the empty fooby column. In our own familiar base 10 we don't, for example, pronounce the number 401 as "four hundred, zero tens, one." We simply say, "four hundred one." In the same manner, rather than say "xip foobies," the Martians just leave it out.

As an exercise, given what I've told you so far about Martian numbers, figure out the Earthly value equivalent to $\cap \equiv \lceil \Theta \equiv$.

The Essence of a Number Base

Since tourist trips to Mars are unlikely to begin any time soon, of what Earthly use is knowing the Martian numbering system? Just this: it's an excellent way to see the sense in a number base without getting distracted by familiar digits and our universal base 10.

In a columnar system of numeric notation like both ours and the Martians', the *base* of the number system is the magnitude by which each column of a number exceeds the magnitude of the column to its right. In our base 10 system, each column represents a value 10 times the column to its right. In a base fooby system like the one used on Mars, each column represents a value fooby times that of the column to its right. (In case you haven't already caught on, the Martians are actually using base 4—but I wanted you to see it from the Martians' perspective first.) Each has a set of digit symbols, the number of which is equal to the base. In our base 10, we have 10 symbols, from 0 to 9. In base 4, there are four digits, from 0 to 3. *In any given number base, the base itself can never be expressed in a single digit!*

Octal: How the Grinch Stole Eight and Nine

Farewell to Mars. Aside from lots of iron oxide and some terrific *a capella* groups, they haven't much to offer us 10-fingered folk. There are some similarly odd number bases in use here, and I'd like to take a quick detour through one that occupies a separate world right here on Earth: the world of Digital Equipment Corporation, better known as DEC.

Back in the '60s, DEC invented the minicomputer as a challenger to the massive and expensive mainframes pioneered by IBM. (The age of minicomputers is long past, and DEC itself is now history.) To ensure that no software could possibly be moved from an IBM mainframe to a DEC minicomputer, DEC designed its machines to understand only numbers expressed in base *8*.

Let's think about that for a moment, given our experience with the Martians. In base 8, there must be eight digits. DEC was considerate enough not to invent its own digit symbols, so what it used were the traditional Earthly digits from 0 to 7. *There is no digit 8 in base 8!* That always takes a little getting used to, but it's part of the definition of a number base. DEC gave an appropriate name to its base 8 system: *octal*.

A columnar number in octal follows the rule we encountered in thinking about the Martian system: each column has a value *base* times that of the column to its right. (The rightmost column is always units.) In the case of octal, each column has a value eight times that of the next column to the right.

Who Stole Eight and Nine?

This shows better than it tells. Counting in octal starts out in a very familiar fashion: one, two, three, four, five, six, seven . . . 10.

This is where the trouble starts. In octal, 10 comes after seven. What happened to eight and nine? Did the Grinch steal them? (Or the Martians?) Hardly. They're still there—but they have different names. In octal, when you say "10," you mean "eight." Worse, when you say "11," you mean "nine."

Unfortunately, what DEC did *not* do was invent clever names for the column values. The first column is, of course, the units column. The next column to the left of the units column is the tens column, just as it is in our own decimal system. But there's the rub and the reason I dragged Mars into this: *octal's "tens" column actually has a value of 8.*

You may be getting a headache about now. Pop an aspirin. I'll wait.

A counting table will help. Table 2.3 counts up to 30 octal, which has a value of 24 decimal. I dislike the use of the terms *eleven*, *twelve*, and so on, in bases other than 10, but the convention in octal has always been to pronounce the numbers as we would in decimal, only with the word *octal* after them. Don't forget to say *octal*—otherwise, people get *really* confused!

Table 2.3: Counting in Octal, Base 8

OCTAL NUMERALS	OCTAL PRONUNCIATION	DECIMAL EQUIVALENT
0	Zero	0
1	One	1
2	Two	2
3	Three	3
4	Four	4
5	Five	5
6	Six	6
7	Seven	7
10	Ten	8
11	Eleven	9
12	Twelve	10

Continues

Table 2.3 (*continued*)

OCTAL NUMERALS	OCTAL PRONUNCIATION	DECIMAL EQUIVALENT
13	Thirteen	11
14	Fourteen	12
15	Fifteen	13
16	Sixteen	14
17	Seventeen	15
20	Twenty	16
21	Twenty-one	17
22	Twenty-two	18
23	Twenty-three	19
24	Twenty-four	20
25	Twenty-five	21
26	Twenty-six	22
27	Twenty-seven	23
30	Thirty	24

Remember, each column in a given number base has a value *base* times the column to its right, so the "tens" column in octal is actually the eights column. (They call it the tens column because it is written 10 and pronounced "ten.") Similarly, the column to the left of the tens column is the hundreds column (because it is written 100 and pronounced "hundreds"), but the hundreds column actually has a value of 8 times 8, or 64. The next column to the left has a value of 64 times 8, or 512, and the column left of that has a value of 512 times 8, or 4,096.

This is why if someone talks about a value of "ten octal," they mean 8; "one hundred octal," they mean 64; and so on. Table 2.4 summarizes the octal column values and their decimal equivalents.

Table 2.4: Octal Columns as Powers of Eight

OCTAL POWER OF 8		DECIMAL OCTAL
$1 = 8^0$	=	$1 \times 8 = 10$
$10 = 8^1$	=	$8 \times 8 = 100$
$100 = 8^2$	=	$64 \times 8 = 1000$
$1000 = 8^3$	=	$512 \times 8 = 10000$
$10000 = 8^4$	=	$4096 \times 8 = 100000$
$100000 = 8^5$	=	$32768 \times 8 = 1000000$
$1000000 = 8^6$	=	$262144 \times 8 = 10000000$

A digit in the first column (the units, or ones column) tells how many units are contained in the octal number. A digit in the next column to the left, the tens column, tells how many eights are contained in the octal number. A digit in the third column, the hundreds column, tells how many 64s are in the number, and so on. For example, 400 octal means that the number contains four 64s, which is 256 in decimal.

Yes, it's confusing, in spades. The best way to make it all gel is to dissect a middling octal number, just as we did with a middling Martian number. This is what's happening in Figure 2.2: the octal number 76225 is pulled apart into columns and added up again.

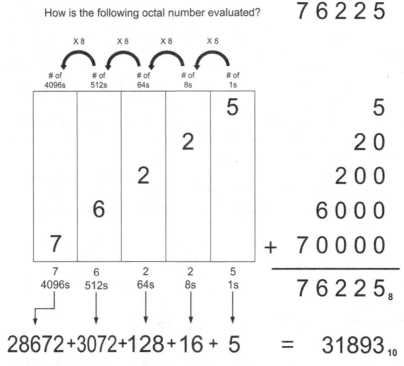

Figure 2.2: The anatomy of 76225 octal

It works here the same way it does in Martian or in decimal or in any other number base you could devise. In general (and somewhat formal) terms, each column has a value consisting of the number base raised to the power represented by the ordinal position of the column minus 1. For example, the value of the first column is the number base raised to the 1 minus 1, or zero, power. Since any number raised to the zero power is 1, the first column in *any* number base always has the value of one and is called the *units column*. The second column has the value of the number base raised to the 2 minus 1, or first power, which is the value of the number base itself. In octal this is 8; in decimal, 10; in Martian base fooby numbers, fooby. The third column has a value consisting of the number base raised to the 3 minus 1, or second power, and so on.

Within each column, the digit holding that column tells how many instances of that column's value is contained in the number as a whole. Here, the 6 in 76225 octal tells us that there are six instances of its column's value in the total value 76225 octal. The six occupies the fourth column, which has a value of 8^{4-1}, which is 8^3, or 512. This tells us that there are six 512s in the number as a whole.

You can convert the value of a number in any base to decimal (our base 10) by determining the value of each column in the alien (nondecimal) base, then multiplying the value of each column by the digit contained in that column (to create the decimal equivalent of each digit), and finally taking the sum of the decimal equivalent of each column. This is done in Figure 2.2, and the octal number and its decimal equivalent are shown side by side. Something to notice in Figure 2.2 is the small subscript numerals on the right side of the columnar sums. These subscripts are used in many technical publications to indicate a number base. The subscript in the value 76225_8, for example, indicates that the value 76225 is here denoting a quantity in octal, which is base 8. Unlike the obvious difference between Martian digits and our traditional decimal digits, there's really nothing about an octal number itself that sets it off as octal. (We encounter something of this same problem a little later on when we confront hexadecimal.) The value 31893_{10}, by contrast, is shown by its subscript to be a base 10, or decimal, quantity. This is mostly done in scientific and research writing. In most computer publications (including this one), other indications are used; more on that later.

Now that we've looked at columnar notation from both a Martian and an octal perspective, make sure you understand how columnar notation works in any arbitrary base before we go on.

Hexadecimal: Solving the Digit Shortage

Octal is unlikely to be of use to you unless you do what a friend of mine did and restore an ancient DEC PDP8 computer that he had purchased as surplus from his university, by the pound. (He said it was considerably cheaper than potatoes, if not quite as easy to fry. Not quite.) As I mentioned earlier, the *real* numbering system to reckon with in the microcomputer world is base 16, which we call *hexadecimal*, or (more affectionately) simply *hex*.

Hexadecimal shares the essential characteristics of any number base, including both Martian and octal. It is a columnar notation, in which each column has a value 16 times the value of the column to its right. It has 16 digits, running from 0 to . . . what?

We have a shortage of digits here. From zero through nine we're in fine shape. However, 10, 11, 12, 13, 14, and 15 need to be expressed with single symbols of some kind. Without any additional numeric digits, the people who developed hexadecimal notation in the early 1950s borrowed the first six letters of the alphabet to act as the needed digits.

Counting in hexadecimal, then, goes like this: 1, 2, 3, 4, 5, 6, 7, 8, 9, A, B, C, D, E, F, 10, 11, 12, 13, 14, 15, 16, 17, 18, 19, 1A, 1B, 1C, and so on. Table 2.5 restates this in a more organized fashion, with the decimal equivalents up to 32.

Table 2.5: Counting in Hexadecimal, Base 16

HEXADECIMAL NUMERALS	PRONUNCIATION (FOLLOW WITH "HEX")	DECIMAL EQUIVALENT
0	Zero	0
1	One	1
2	Two	2
3	Three	3
4	Four	4
5	Five	5
6	Six	6
7	Seven	7
8	Eight	8
9	Nine	9
A	A	10
B	B	11
C	C	12
D	D	13
E	E	14
F	F	15
10	Ten (or, One-oh)	16
11	One-one	17
12	One-two	18
13	One-three	19
14	One-four	20
15	One-five	21
16	One-six	22

Continues

Table 2.5 (*continued*)

HEXADECIMAL NUMERALS	PRONUNCIATION (FOLLOW WITH "HEX")	DECIMAL EQUIVALENT
17	One-seven	23
18	One-eight	24
19	One-nine	25
1A	One-A	26
1B	One-B	27
1C	One-C	28
1D	One-D	29
1E	One-E	30
1F	One-F	31
20	Twenty (or, Two-oh)	32

One of the conventions in hexadecimal that I much favor is the dropping of words such as *eleven* and *twelve* that are a little too tightly bound to our decimal system and only promote gross confusion. Confronted by the number 11 in hexadecimal (usually written 11H to let us know what base we're speaking), we would say, "one-one hex." Don't forget to say "hex" after a hexadecimal number, again to avoid gross confusion. This is unnecessary with the single digits 0 through 9, which represent the exact same values in both decimal and hexadecimal.

Some people still say things like "twelve hex," which is valid and means 18 decimal. But I don't care for it and advise against it. This business of alien bases is confusing enough without giving the aliens Charlie Chaplin masks.

Each column in the hexadecimal system has a value 16 times that of the column to its right. (The rightmost column, as in *any* number base, is the units column and has a value of 1.) As you might guess, the values of the individual columns go up frighteningly fast as you move from right to left. Table 2.6 shows the values of the first seven columns in hexadecimal. For comparison's sake, note that the seventh column in decimal notation has a value of 1 million, while the seventh column in hexadecimal has a value of 16,777,216.

Table 2.6: Hexadecimal Columns as Powers of 16

HEXADECIMAL	POWER OF 16	DECIMAL
1H	$= 16^0 =$	$1 \times 16 = 10H$
10H	$= 16^1 =$	$16 \times 16 = 100H$
100H	$= 16^2 =$	$256 \times 16 = 1000H$

Continues

Table 2.6 (*continued*)

HEXADECIMAL	POWER OF 16	DECIMAL
1000H	$= 16^3 =$	4096 x 16 = 10000H
10000H	$= 16^4 =$	65536 x 16 = 100000H
100000H	$= 16^5 =$	1048576 x 16 = 1000000H
1000000H	$= 16^6 =$	16777216 etc. . . .

To help you understand how hexadecimal numbers are constructed, I've dissected a middling hex number in Figure 2.3, in the same fashion that I dissected numbers earlier in both Martian base fooby, and in octal, base 8. Just as in octal, zero holds a place in a column without adding any value to the number as a whole. Note in Figure 2.3 that there are 0, that is, no, 256s present in the number 3C0A9H.

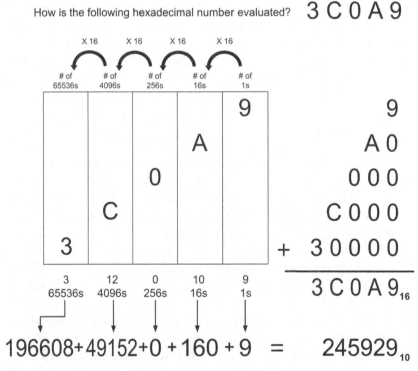

Figure 2.3: The anatomy of 3C0A9H

As in Figure 2.2, the decimal values of each column are shown beneath the column, and the sum of all columns is shown in both decimal and hex. (Note the subscripts!)

From Hex to Decimal and from Decimal to Hex

Most of the manipulation of hex numbers you'll be performing will be simple conversions between hex and decimal, in both directions. The easiest way to perform such conversions is by way of a hex calculator, either a "real" calculator like the venerable 1980s TI Programmer (which I still have, wretched battery-eater that it is) or a software calculator with hexadecimal capabilities. The Galculator (Gnome Calculator) app that you can install from most Linux repositories will do math in decimal, hex, octal, and binary if you select View ⇨ Scientific. The Windows calculator works the same way: the default view is basic, and you have to select the Programmer view to get into any alien bases. Speedcrunch is another calculator that works decimal, hex, octal, and binary from the get-go. Some may already be installed in your Linux distro. Check your software manager app to see if they are.

Using a calculator demands nothing of your gray matter, of course, and won't help you understand the hexadecimal number system any better. So while you're a relatively green student of alien bases, lay off anything that understands hex, be it hardware, software, or human associates.

In fact, the best tool while you're learning is a simple four-function memory calculator. The conversion methods I describe here all make use of such a calculator, since what I'm trying to teach you is number base conversion, not decimal addition or long division.

From Hex to Decimal

As you'll come to understand, converting hex numbers to decimal is a good deal easier than going the other way. The general method is to do what we've been doing all along in the number-dissection Figures 2.1, 2.2, and 2.3: derive the value represented by each individual column in the hex number, and then add up the total of all the column values in decimal.

Let's try an easy one. The hex number is 7A2. Start at the right column. This is the units column in any number system. You have 2 units, so enter 2 into your calculator. Now store that 2 into memory. (Or press the SUM button, if you have a SUM button.)

So much for units. Keep in mind that what you're really doing is keeping a running tally of the values of the columns in the hex number. Move to the next column to the left. Remember that in hex, each column represents a value 16 times the value of the column to its right. So, the second column from the right is the 16s column. (Refer to Table 2.6 if you lose track of the column values.) The 16s column has an A in it. A in hex is decimal 10. The total value of that column, therefore, is 16×10, or 160. Perform that multiplication on your calculator, and add the product to the 2 that you stored in memory. (Again, the SUM button is a handy way to do this if your calculator has one.)

Remember what you're doing: evaluating each column in decimal and keeping a running total. Now, move to the third column from the right. This one contains a 7. The value of the third column is 16×16, or 256. Perform 256×7 on your calculator, and add the product to your running total.

You're done. Retrieve the running total from your calculator memory. The total should be 1,954, which is the decimal equivalent of 7A2H.

Let's try it again, more quickly, with a little less natter and a much larger number: C6F0DBH.

1. First, evaluate the units column. $B \times 1 = 11 \times 1 = 11$. Start your running total with 11.

2. Evaluate the 16s column. $D \times 16 = 13 \times 16 = 208$. Add 208 to your running total.

3. Evaluate the 256s column. $0 \times 256 = 0$. Move on.

4. Evaluate the 4,096s column. $F \times 4,096 = 15 \times 4,096 = 61,440$. Add it to your running total.

5. Evaluate the 65,536s column. $6 \times 65,536 = 393,216$. Add it to the running total.

6. Evaluate the 1,048,576s column. $C \times 1,048,576 = 12 \times 1,048,576 = 12,582,912$. Add it to your total.

The running total should be 13,037,787.

Finally, do it yourself without any help for the following number: 1A55BEH.

From Decimal to Hex

The lights should be coming on about now. This is good, because going in the other direction, from our familiar decimal base 10 to hex, is *much* harder and involves more math. What we have to do is find the hex column values "within" a decimal number—and that involves some considerable use of that fifth-grade bogeyman, long division.

But let's get to it, again, starting with a fairly easy decimal number: 449. The calculator will be handy with a vengeance. Tap in the number 449 and store it in the calculator's memory.

What we need to do first is find the *largest* hex column value that is contained in 449 at least *once*. Remember grade-school "gazintas"? (12 *gazinta* 855 how many times?) Division is often introduced to students as a way of finding out how many times some number is present in—"goes into"—another. It's something like that. Looking back at Table 2.6, we can see that 256 is the largest power of

16, and hence the largest hex column value, that is present in 449 at least once. (The next largest power of 16—512—is obviously too large to be present in 449.)

So, we start with 256 and determine how many times 256 "gazinta" 449: 449 / 256 = 1.7539. At least once, but not quite twice. So, 449 contains only one 256. Write down a 1 on paper. *Don't enter it into your calculator.* We're not keeping a running total here; if anything, we could say we're keeping a running remainder. The 1 is the leftmost hex digit of the hex value that is equivalent to decimal 449.

We know that there is only one 256 contained in 449. What we must do now is *remove* that 256 from the original number, now that we've "counted" it by writing a 1 down on paper. Subtract 256 from 449. Store the difference, 193, into memory.

The 256 column has been removed from the number we're converting. Now we move to the next column to the right, the 16s. How many 16s are contained in 193? 193 / 16 = 12.0625. This means the 16s column in the hex equivalent of 449 contains a . . . 12? Hmmmm . . . remember the digit shortage, and the fact that in hex, the value we call 12 is represented by the letter C. From a hex perspective, we have found that the original number contains C in the 16s column. Write a C down to the right of your 1: 1C. So far, so good.

We've got the 16s column, so just as with the 256s, we have to remove the 16s from what's left of the original number. The total value of the 16s column is C × 16 = 12 × 16 = 192. Bring the 193 value out of your calculator's memory and subtract 192 from it. A lonely little 1 is all that's left.

So we're down to the units column. There is one unit in one, obviously. Write that 1 down to the right of the C in our hexadecimal number: 1C1. Decimal 449 is equivalent to hex 1C1.

Now perhaps you'll begin to understand why programmers like hexadecimal calculators so much.

Let's glance back at the big picture of the decimal-to-hex conversion. We're looking for the hexadecimal columns hidden in the decimal value. We find the largest column contained in the decimal number, find that column's value, and subtract that value from the decimal number. Then we look for the next smallest hex column, the next smallest, and so on, removing the value of each column from the decimal number as we go. In a sense, we're dividing the number by consecutively smaller powers of 16 and keeping a running remainder by removing each column as we tally it.

Let's try it again. The secret number is 988,664.

1. Find the largest column contained in 988,664 from Table 2.6: 65,536. 988,664 / 65,536 = 15 and change. Ignore the change. 15 = F in hex. Write down the F.

2. Remove F × 65,536 from 988,664. Store the remainder: 5,624.

3. Move to the next smallest column. 5,624 / 4,096 = 1 and change. Write down the 1.

4. Remove 1 × 4,096 from the remainder: 5,624 − 4096 = 1528. Store the new remainder: 1,528.

5. Move to the next smallest column. 1,528 / 256 = 5 and change. Write down the 5.

6. Remove 5 × 256 from the stored remainder, 1,528. Store 248 as the new remainder.

7. Move to the next smallest column. 248 / 16 = 15 and change. 15 = F in hex. Write down the F.

8. Remove F × 16 from stored remainder, 248. The remainder, 8, is the number of units in the final column. Write down the 8.

There you have it: 988,664 decimal = F15F8H.

Note the presence of the *H* at the end of the hex number. From now on, every hex number in the text of this book will have that H affixed to its hindparts. It's important, because not *every* hex number contains letter digits to scream out the fact that the number is in base 16. There is a 157H as surely as a 157 decimal, and the two are *not* the same number. (Quick, now: by how much are they different?) Don't forget that H in writing your assembly programs, as I'll be reminding you later.

Practice. Practice! PRACTICE!

The best (actually, the only) way to get a gut feel for hex notation is to use it lots. Convert *each* of the following hex numbers to decimal. Lay each number out on the dissection table and identify how many 1s, how many 16s, how many 256s, how many 4,096s, and so on, are present in the number, and then add them up in decimal.

```
CCH
157H
D8H
BB29H
7AH
8177H
A011H
99H
2B36H
FACEH
8DB3H
9H
```

That done, now turn it inside out, and convert each of the following decimal numbers to hex. Remember the general method: From Table 2.6, choose the largest power of 16 that is *less* than the decimal number to be converted. Find out how many times that power of 16 is present in the decimal number, and write it down as the leftmost hex digit of the converted number. Then subtract the total value represented by that hex digit from the decimal number. Then repeat the process, using the next smallest power of 16 until you've subtracted the decimal number down to nothing.

```
39
413
22
67,349
6,992
41
1,117
44,919
12,331
124,217
91,198
307
112,374,777
```

(Extra credit for that last one . . . .) If you need more practice, choose some decimal numbers and convert them to hex and then convert them back. When you're done, check your work with a calculator.

Arithmetic in Hex

As you become more and more skilled in assembly language, you'll be doing more and more arithmetic in base 16. You may even (good grief) come to do it *in your head*. Still, it takes some practice.

Addition and subtraction are basically the same as what we know in decimal, with a few extra digits tossed in for flavor. The trick is nothing more than knowing your addition tables up to 0FH. This is best done not by thinking to yourself, "Now, if C is 12 and F is 15, then C + F is 12 + 15, which is 27 decimal but 1BH." Instead, you should simply say inside your head, "C + F is 1BH."

Yes, that's asking a lot. But I ask you now, as I will ask you again on this journey, do you wanna hack assembly . . . or do you just wanna fool around? It takes practice to learn the piano, and it takes practice to drive the core skills of assembly language programming down into your synapses where they belong.

So let me sound like an old schoolmarm and tell you to memorize the following. Make flash cards if you must:

9	8	7	6	5
+1	+2	+3	+4	+5
0AH	0AH	0AH	0AH	0AH

```
   A      9      8      7      6
 + 1    + 2    + 3    + 4    + 5
 0BH    0BH    0BH    0BH    0BH

   B      A      9      8      7      6
 + 1    + 2    + 3    + 4    + 5    + 6
 0CH    0CH    0CH    0CH    0CH    0CH

   C      B      A      9      8      7
 + 1    + 2    + 3    + 4    + 5    + 6
 0DH    0DH    0DH    0DH    0DH    0DH

   D      C      B      A      9      8      7
 + 1    + 2    + 3    + 4    + 5    + 6    + 7
 0EH    0EH    0EH    0EH    0EH    0EH    0EH

   E      D      C      B      A      9      8
 + 1    + 2    + 3    + 4    + 5    + 6    + 7
 0FH    0FH    0FH    0FH    0FH    0FH    0EH

   F      E      D      C      B      A      9      8
 + 1    + 2    + 3    + 4    + 5    + 6    + 7    + 8
 10H    10H    10H    10H    10H    10H    10H    10H

   F      E      D      C      B      A      9
 + 2    + 3    + 4    + 5    + 6    + 7    + 8
 11H    11H    11H    11H    11H    11H    11H

   F      E      D      C      B      A      9
 + 3    + 4    + 5    + 6    + 7    + 8    + 9
 12H    12H    12H    12H    12H    12H    12H

   F      E      D      C      B      A
 + 4    + 5    + 6    + 7    + 8    + 9
 13H    13H    13H    13H    13H    13H

   F      E      D      C      B      A
 + 5    + 6    + 7    + 8    + 9    + A
 14H    14H    14H    14H    14H    14H

   F      E      D      C      B
 + 6    + 7    + 8    + 9    + A
 15H    15H    15H    15H    15H

   F      E      D      C      B
 + 7    + 8    + 9    + A    + B
 16H    16H    16H    16H    16H
```

```
   F      E      A      C
 + 8    + 9    + A    + B
 ─────  ─────  ─────  ─────
 17H    17H    17H    17H

   F      E      D      C
 + 9    + A    + B    + C
 ─────  ─────  ─────  ─────
 18H    18H    18H    18H

   F      E      D
 + A    + B    + C
 ─────  ─────  ─────
 19H    19H    19H

   F      E      D
 + B    + C    + D
 ─────  ─────  ─────
 1AH    1AH    1AH

   F      E
 + C    + D
 ─────  ─────
 1BH    1BH

   F      E
 + D    + E
 ─────  ─────
 1CH    1CH

   F
 + E
 ─────
 1DH

   F
 + F
 ─────
 1EH
```

If nothing else, this exercise should make you glad that computers don't work in base 64.

Columns and Carries

With all of these single-column additions committed (more or less) to memory, you can tackle multicolumn addition. It works pretty much the same way it does with decimal. Add each column starting from the right, and carry into the next column anytime a single column's sum exceeds 0FH.

For example:

```
    1          1
    2 F 3 1 A DH
 + 9 6 B A 0 7H
 ──────────────
  C 5 E B B 4H
```

Carefully work this one through, column by column. The sum of the first column (that is, the rightmost) is 14H, which cannot fit in a single column, so we must carry the one into the next column to the left. Even with the additional 1, however, the sum of the second column is 0BH, which fits in a single column and no carry is required.

Keep on adding toward the left. The second-to-last column will again over-flow, and you will need to carry the one into the last column. As long as you have your single-digit sums memorized, it's a snap.

Well, more or less.

Now, here's something you should take note of:

The most you can ever carry out of a single-column addition of two numbers is 1.

It doesn't matter what base you're in: 16, 10, fooby, or 2. You will either carry a 1 (in Martian, a foo) out of a column or carry nothing at all. This fact surprises people for some reason, so ask yourself: what two single digits in old familiar base 10 can you add that will force you to carry a 2? The largest digit is 9, and 9 + 9 = 18. Put down the 8 and carry the 1. Even if you have to add in a carry from a previous column, that will bring you up (at most) to 19. Again, you carry a 1 and no more. This is important when you add numbers on paper, or within the silicon of your CPU, as we'll learn a few chapters further on.

Subtraction and Borrows

If you have your single-column sums memorized, you can usually grind your way through subtraction with a shift into a sort of mental reverse: "If E + 6 equals 14H, then 14H – E must equal 6." The alternative is memorizing an even larger number of tables, and since I haven't memorized them, I won't ask you to.

But over time, that's what tends to happen. In hex subtraction, you should be able to dope out any given single-column subtraction by turning a familiar hexadecimal sum inside-out. And just as with base 10, multicolumn subtractions are done column by column, one column at a time:

```
 F76CH
-A05BH
 5711H
```

During your inspection of each column, you should be asking yourself: "What number added to the bottom number yields the top number?" Here, you should know from your tables that B + 1 = C, so the difference between B and C is 1. The leftmost column is actually more challenging: what number added to A gives you F? Chin up; even I have to think about it on an off day.

The problems show up, of course, when the top number in a column is smaller than its corresponding bottom number. Then (like the federal government on a bomber binge) you have no recourse but to borrow.

Borrowing is one of those grade-school rote-learned processes that few people really understand. (To understand it is tacit admittance that something of New

Math actually stuck, horrors.) From a height, what happens in a borrow is that one count is taken from a column and applied to the column on its right. I say *applied* rather than *added to* because in moving from one column to the column on its right, that single count is multiplied by 10, where 10 represents the number base. (Remember that 10 in octal has a value of 8, while 10 in hexadecimal has a value of 16.)

It sounds worse than it is. Let's look at a borrow in action, and you'll get the idea:

```
 9 2H
-4 FH
```

Here, the subtraction in the rightmost column can't happen as is, because F is larger than 2. So, we borrow from the next column to the left.

Nearly 60 years out of the past, I can still hear old Sister Marie Bernard toughing it out on the blackboard, albeit in base 10: "Cross out the 9; make it an 8. Make the 2 a 12. And 12 minus F is what, class?" It's 3, Sister. And that's how a borrow works. (I hope the poor dear will forgive me for putting hex bytes in her mouth . . . .)

Think about what happened there, functionally. *We subtracted 1 from the 9 and added 10H to the 2.* One obvious mistake is to subtract 1 from the 9 and add 1 to the 2, which (need I say it?) won't work. Think of it this way: we're moving part of one column's surplus value over to its right, where some extra value is needed. The *overall* value of the upper number doesn't change (which is why we call it a *borrow* and not a *steal*), but the recipient of the loan is increased by *10*, not *1*.

After the borrow, what we have looks something like this:

```
8¹2H
- 4 FH
```

(On Sister Marie Bernard's blackboard, we crossed out the 9 and made it an 8. I just made it an 8. Silicon has advantages over chalk—except that the 8's earlier life as a 9 is not so obvious.)

And of course, once we're here, the columnar subtractions all work out, and we discover that the difference is 43H.

People sometimes ask if you ever have to borrow more than 1. The answer, plainly, is *no*. If you borrow 2, for example, you would add 20 to the recipient column, and *20 minus any single digit remains a two-digit number*. That is, the difference won't fit into a single column. Subtraction contains an important symmetry with addition:

The most you ever need to borrow in any single-column subtraction of two numbers is 1.

Borrows Across Multiple Columns

Understanding that much about borrows gets you most of the way there. But, as life is wont, you will *frequently* come across a subtraction similar to this:

```
  F 0 0 0H
- 3 B 6 CH
```

Column 1 needs to borrow, but neither column 2 nor column 3 have anything at all to lend. Back in grade school, Sister Marie Bernard would have rattled out with machine-gun efficiency: "Cross out the F, make it an E. Make the 0 a 10. Then cross it out, make it an F. Make the next 0 a 10; cross it out, make it an F. Then make the last 0 a 10." Got that? (I got it. In Catholic school back in the early 60s, the consequences of *not* getting it were too terrible to consider.)

What happens is that the middle two 0s act as loan brokers between the F and the rightmost 0, keeping their commission in the form of enough value to allow their own columns' subtractions to take place. Each column to the right of the last column borrows 10 from its neighbor to the left and loans 1 to the neighbor on its right. After all the borrows trickle through the upper number, what we have looks like this (minus all of Sister's cross-outs):

```
  E F F¹0H
- 3 B 6 CH
```

At this point, each columnar subtraction can take place, and the difference is B494H.

In remembering your grade-school machinations, don't fall into the old decimal rut of thinking, "Cross out the 10, and make it a 9." In the world of hexadecimal, 10H − 1 = F. Cross out the 10, and make it an *F*.

What's the Point?

What is the point of all this if you have a hex calculator or a hex-capable screen calculator? The point is *practice*. Hexadecimal is the *lingua franca* of assemblers, to seriously mangle a metaphor. The more you burn a gut-level understanding of hex into your reflexes, the easier assembly language will be. Furthermore, understanding the internal structure of the machine itself will be *much* easier if you have that intuitive grasp of hex values. We're laying important groundwork here. Take it seriously now and you'll lose less hair later.

Binary

Hexadecimal is excellent practice for taking on the strangest number base of all: *binary*. Binary is base 2. Given what we've learned about number bases so far, what can we surmise about base 2?

- Each column has a value two times the column to its right.
- There are only two digits (0 and 1) in the base.

Counting is a little strange in binary, as you might imagine. It goes like this: 0, 1, 10, 11, 100, 101, 110, 111, 1,000 . . . . Because it sounds absurd to say, "Zero, one, 10, 11, 100, . . .," it makes more sense to simply enunciate the individual digits, followed by the word *binary*. For example, most people say "one zero one one one zero one binary" instead of "one million, eleven thousand, one hundred one binary" when pronouncing the number 1011101—which sounds enormous until you consider that its value in decimal is only 93.

Odd as it may seem, binary follows all of the same rules we've discussed in this chapter regarding number bases. Converting between binary and decimal is done using the same methods described for hexadecimal in an earlier section of this chapter.

Because counting in binary is as much a matter of counting columns as counting digits (since there are only two digits), it makes sense to take a long, close look at Table 2.7, which shows the values of the binary number columns out to 32 places. (Taking it out to 64 places would be problematic because of the size of the decimal equivalent, as I'll show you shortly.)

Table 2.7: Binary Columns as Powers of 2

BINARY	POWER OF 2	DECIMAL
1	$=2^0=$	1
10	$=2^1=$	2
100	$=2^2=$	4
1000	$=2^3=$	8
10000	$=2^4=$	16
100000	$=2^5=$	32
1000000	$=2^6=$	64
10000000	$=2^7=$	128
100000000	$=2^8=$	256
1000000000	$=2^9=$	512

Continues

Table 2.7 (*continued*)

BINARY	POWER OF 2	DECIMAL
10000000000	$=2^{10}=$	1024
100000000000	$=2^{11}=$	2048
1000000000000	$=2^{12}=$	4096
10000000000000	$=2^{13}=$	8192
100000000000000	$=2^{14}=$	16384
1000000000000000	$=2^{15}=$	32768
10000000000000000	$=2^{16}=$	65536
100000000000000000	$=2^{17}=$	131072
1000000000000000000	$=2^{18}=$	262144
10000000000000000000	$=2^{19}=$	524288
100000000000000000000	$=2^{20}=$	1048576
1000000000000000000000	$=2^{21}=$	2097152
10000000000000000000000	$=2^{22}=$	4194304
100000000000000000000000	$=2^{23}=$	8388608
1000000000000000000000000	$=2^{24}=$	16777216
10000000000000000000000000	$=2^{25}=$	33554432
100000000000000000000000000	$=2^{26}=$	67108864
1000000000000000000000000000	$=2^{27}=$	134217728
10000000000000000000000000000	$=2^{28}=$	268435456
100000000000000000000000000000	$=2^{29}=$	536870912
1000000000000000000000000000000	$=2^{30}=$	1073741824
10000000000000000000000000000000	$=2^{31}=$	2147483648
100000000000000000000000000000000	$=2^{32}=$	4294967296

One look at that imposing pyramid of zeros implies that it's hopeless to think of pronouncing the larger columns as strings of digits: "one zero zero zero zero zero zero zero . . ." and so on. There's a crying need for a shorthand notation here, so I'll provide you with one in a little while—and its identity will surprise you.

You might object that such large numbers as the bottommost in the table aren't likely to be encountered in ordinary programming. Sorry, but even antiquated 32-bit microprocessors such as the 386/486/Pentium can swallow numbers like that in one electrical gulp and eat billions of them for lunch. Now that mainstream PCs just about all use 64-bit CPUs, you *must* become accustomed to thinking in terms of such numbers as 2^{64}, even though the numbers themselves are immense:

$$2^{64} = 1.8 \times 10^{19} = 18,446,744,073,709,551,616$$

This figure can be imagined (by sheer coincidence) as (roughly) the number of stars in our observable universe. How astronomers calculated that is fascinating; see `https://bigthink.com/starts-with-a-bang/how-many-stars`.

Don't even ask what 2^{128} comes out to in decimal. The answer is more than I can imagine, and like Han Solo, I can imagine a *lot*.

Now, just as with octal and hexadecimal, there can be identity problems when using binary. The number 101 in binary is *not* the same as 101 in hex, or 101 in decimal. For this reason, always append the suffix "B" to your binary values to make sure people reading your programs (including you, six weeks after the fact) know what number base you're working from.

Values in Binary

Converting a value in binary to a value in decimal is done the same way it's done in hex—more simply, in fact, for the simple reason that you no longer have to count how many times a column's value is present in any given column. In hex, you have to see how many 16s are present in the 16s column, and so on. In binary, a column's value is either present (1 time) or not present (0 times).

Running through a simple example should make this clear. The binary number 11011010B is a relatively typical binary value in small-time computer work. (On the small side, actually—many common binary numbers are twice its size or more.) Converting 11011010B to decimal comes down to scanning it from right to left with the help of Table 2.7 and tallying any column's value where that column contains a 1, while ignoring any column containing a 0.

Clear your calculator and let's get started:

1. Column 0 contains a 0; skip it.
2. Column 1 contains a 1. That means its value, 2, is present in the value of the number. So we punch 2 into the calculator.
3. Column 2 is 0. Skip it.
4. Column 3 contains a 1. The column's value is 2^3, or 8; add 8 to our tally.
5. Column 4 also contains a 1; 2^4 is 16, which we add to our tally.
6. Column 5 is 0. Skip it.
7. Column 6 contains a 1; 2^6 is 64, so add 64 to the tally.

8. Column 7 also contains a 1. Column 7's value is 2^7, or 128. Add 128 to the tally, and what do we have? 218. That's the decimal value of 11011010B. It's as easy as that.

Converting from decimal to binary, while more difficult, is done *exactly* the same way as converting from decimal to hex. Go back and read that section again, searching for the *general method* used. In other words, see what was done and separate the essential principles from any references to a specific base like hex.

I'll bet by now you can figure it out without much trouble.

As a brief aside, perhaps you noticed that I started counting columns from 0 rather than 1. A peculiarity of the computer field is that we always begin counting things from 0. Actually, to call it a peculiarity is unfair; the computer's method is the reasonable one, because 0 is a perfectly good number and should not be discriminated against. The rift occurred because in our real, physical world, counting things tells us *how many* things are there, while in the computer world counting things is more generally done to *name* them. That is, we need to deal with bit number 0, and then bit number 1, and so on, far more than we need to know how many bits there are.

This is not a quibble, by the way. The issue will come up again and again in connection with memory addresses, which as I have said and will say again are the key to understanding assembly language.

In programming circles, always begin counting from 0!

A practical example of the conflicts this principle can cause grows out of the following question: What year began our new millennium? Most people would intuitively say the year 2000—and back during the runup to 2000 many people did—but technically, the twentieth century continued its plodding pace until January 1, 2001. Why? *Because there was no year 0.* When historians count the years moving from B.C. to A.D., they go right from 1 B.C. to 1 A.D. Therefore, the first century began with year 1 and ended with year 100. The second century began with year 101 and ended with year 200. By extending the sequence you can see that the 20th century began in 1901 and ended in 2000. On the other hand, if we had had the sense to begin counting years in the current era computer style, from year 0, the 20th century would indeed have ended at the end of 1999.

Now is a good point to get some practice in converting numbers from binary to decimal and back. Sharpen your teeth on these:

```
110
10001
11111
11
101
1100010111010010
11000
1011
```

When that's done, convert these decimal values to binary:

```
77
42
106
255
18
6309
121
58
18,446
```

Why Binary?

If it takes eight whole digits (11011010) to represent an ordinary three-digit number such as 218, binary as a number base would seem to be a bad intellectual investment. Certainly for us it would be a waste of mental bandwidth, and even aliens with only two fingers would probably have come up with a better system.

The problem is, either lights are on or they're off.

This is just another way of saying (as I will discuss in detail in Chapter 3) that at the bottom of it, *computers are electrical devices*. In an electrical device, either voltage is present or it isn't; either current flows or it doesn't. Very early in the game, computer scientists decided that the presence of a voltage in a computer circuit would indicate a 1 digit, while lack of a voltage at that same point in the circuit would indicate a 0 digit. This isn't many digits, but it's enough for the binary number system. This is the only reason we use binary, but it's a pretty compelling one, and we're stuck with it. However, you will not necessarily drown in ones and zeros, because I've already taught you a form of shorthand.

Hexadecimal as Shorthand for Binary

The number 218 expressed in binary is 11011010B. Expressed in hex, however, the same value is quite compact: DAH. The two hex digits comprising DAH merit a closer look. AH (or 0AH as your assembler will require it for reasons I will explain later) represents 10 decimal. Converting any number to binary simply involves detecting the powers of 2 within it. The largest power of 2 within 10 decimal is 8. Jot down a 1 digit and subtract 8 from 10. What's left is 2. Now, 4 is a power of 2, but there is no 4 hiding within 2, so we put a 0 to the right of the 1. The next smallest power of 2 is 2, and there is a 2 in 2. Jot down another 1 to the right of the 0. Two from 2 is 0, so there are no 1s left in the number. Jot down a final 0 to the right of the rest to represent the 1s column. What you have is this:

```
1 0 1 0
```

Look back at the binary equivalent of 218: 11011010. The last four digits are 1010—the binary equivalent of 0AH.

The same will work for the upper half of DAH. If you work out the binary equivalence for 0DH as we just did (and it would be good mental exercise), it is 1101. Look at the binary equivalent of 218 this way:

```
  218      decimal
1101 1010  binary
  D    A   hex
```

It should be dawning on you that you can convert long strings of binary 1s and 0s into more compact hex format by converting every four binary digits (starting from the right, *not* from the left!) into a single hex digit.

As an example, here is a 32-bit binary number that is not the least bit remarkable:

```
11110000000000001111101001101110
```

It is, however, a pretty obnoxious collection of bits to remember or manipulate, so let's split it up into groups of four from the right:

```
1111 0000 0000 0000 1111 1010 0110 1110
```

Each of these groups of four binary digits can be represented by a single hexadecimal digit. Do the conversion now. What you should get is the following:

```
1111 0000 0000 0000 1111 1010 0110 1110
 F    0    0    0    F    A    6    E
```

In other words, the hex equivalent of that mouthful is

```
F000FA6E
```

In use, of course, you would append the *H* on the end and also put a 0 at the beginning, so in any kind of assembly language work the number would actually be written 0F000FA6EH.

Suddenly, this business starts looking a little more graspable.

Hexadecimal is the programmer's shorthand for the computer's binary numbers.

This is why I said earlier that computers use base 2 (binary) and base 16 (hexadecimal) both at the same time in a rather schizoid fashion. What I didn't say is that the computer isn't really the schizoid one; *you* are. At their very hearts (as I will explain in Chapter 3) computers use *only* binary. Hex is a means by which you and I make dealing with the computer easier. Fortunately, every four binary digits may be represented by a hex digit, so the correspondence is clean and comprehensible, even when it's 64 bits—or 16 hexadecimal digits—long.

Prepare to Compute

Everything up to this point has been necessary groundwork. I've explained conceptually what computers *do* and have given you the tools to understand the slightly alien numbers that they use. But I've said nothing so far about what computers actually *are*, and it's well past time. We will return to hexadecimal numbers again and again in this book; I've said nothing thus far about hex multiplication or bit-banging. The reason is plain: before you can bang on a bit, you must know where the bits live. So, let's lift the hood and see if we can catch a few of them in action.

Lifting the Hood

Discovering What Computers Actually Are

RAXie, We Hardly Knew Ye

In January 1970, I was on the downwind leg of my senior year in high school, and the Chicago Public Schools had installed a computer somewhere. A truckful of these fancy IBM typewriter gadgets was delivered to Lane Tech, and a bewildered math teacher was drafted into teaching computer science (as they had the nerve to call it) to a high school full of rowdy (and mostly nerdy) males.

I figured it out fairly quickly. You pounded out a deck of these goofy computer cards on the card-punch machine, dropped them into the card hopper of one of the typewriter gadgets, and watched in awe as the typewriter danced its little golfball over the greenbar paper, printing out your inevitable list of error messages. It was fun. I got straight As. I even kept the first program I ever wrote that did something useful, astronomy being my passion at the time: a little deck of cards that generated a table of parabolic correction factors for hand-figuring telescope mirrors. (I still have the card deck, though the gummy mess left behind by disintegrating rubber bands would not be healthy for a card reader, assuming that one still exists.)

The question that kept gnawing at me was exactly what sort of beast RAX (the computer's wonderfully appropriate name) actually was. What we had were RAM-charged typewriters that RAX controlled over phone lines—that much I understood. But what was RAX itself?

I asked the instructor. In brief, the conversation went something like this:

ME: "Umm, sir, what exactly *is* RAX?"

HE: "Eh? Um, a computer. An electronic computer."

ME: "That's what it says on the course notes. But I want to know what RAX is made of and how it works."

HE: "Well, I'm sure RAX is all solid-state."

ME: "You mean, there's no levers and gears inside."

HE: "Oh, there may be a few. But no vacuum tubes."

ME: "I wasn't worried about tubes. I suppose it has a calculator in it somewhere. But what makes it remember that A comes before B? How does it know what FORMAT means? How does it tell time? What does it have to do to answer the phone?"

HE: "Now, come on, that's why computers are so great! They put it all together so that we don't have to worry about that sort of thing! Who cares what RAX is? RAX knows FORTRAN and will execute any correct FORTRAN program. That's what matters, isn't it?"

He was starting to sweat. So was I. End of conversation.

That June I graduated with 3 inches of debugged and working FORTRAN punch cards in my bookbag and still had absolutely no clue as to what RAX actually *was*.

It has bothered me to this day.

Gus to the Rescue

I was thinking about RAX 6 years later, while on Chicago's Devon Avenue bus heading for work, with the latest copy of *Popular Electronics* in my lap. The lead story described a do-it-yourself project called the COSMAC ELF, which consisted of a piece of perfboard full of integrated circuit chips, all wired together, plus some toggle switches and a pair of LED numeric displays.

It was a computer. (Said so right on the label, heh.) The article told us how to put it together, and that was about all. What did those chips do? What did the whole thing do? There was no fancy robotic typewriter anywhere in sight. It was driving me nuts.

As usual, my friend Gus Flassig got on the bus at Ashland Avenue and sat down beside me. I asked him what the COSMAC ELF did. He was the first human being to make the concept of a *physical* computer hang together for me:

"These are memory chips. You load numbers into the memory chips by flipping these toggle switches in different binary code patterns, where "up" means a 1-bit, and "down" means a 0-bit. Each number in memory means something to the CPU chip. One number makes it add; another number makes it subtract; another makes it write different numbers into memory, and lots of other things. A program consists of a bunch of these instruction numbers in a row in memory. The computer reads the first number, does

> what the number tells it to do, and then reads the second one, does what
> *that* number says to do, and so on, until it runs out of numbers."

If *you* don't find that utterly clear; don't worry. I had the advantage of being an electronics hobbyist (so I knew what some of the chips did) and had already written some programs in RAX's FORTRAN. But for me, my God, everything suddenly hit critical mass and exploded in my head until the steam started pouring out of my ears. I *got* it!

No matter what RAX was, I knew that it had to be something like the COS-MAC ELF, only on a larger scale. I built an ELF. It was quite an education and allowed me to understand the nature of computers at a very deep level. I don't recommend that anybody but total crazies wirewrap their own computers out of loose chips anymore, although it was a common enough thing to do in the mid-to-late 1970s.

In this chapter I will provide you with some of the insights that I obtained while assembling my own computer the hard way. (You wonder where the "hard" in "hardware" comes from? Not from the sound it makes when you bang it on the table, I promise.)

Switches, Transistors, and Memory

Switches remember.

Think about it: you flip the wall switch by the door, and the light in the middle of the ceiling comes on. It stays on. When you leave the room, you flip the switch down again, and the light goes out. It stays out. Poltergeists notwithstanding, the switch will remain in the position you last left it until you or someone else comes back and flips it to its other position. Even if the bulb burns out, you can look at the position of the switch handle and know if the light circuit is on or off.

In a sense, the switch remembers what its last command was until you change it and "overwrite" that earlier command with a new one. In this sense, a light switch represents a sort of rudimentary memory element.

Light switches are more mechanical than electrical. This does not prevent them from acting as memory. In fact, the very first computer (Babbage's 19th-century Difference Engine) was entirely mechanical. In fact, the far larger version he designed but never finished was to have been *steam-powered*. Babbage's machine had lots of little cams that could be flipped by other cams from one position to another. Numbers were encoded and remembered as patterns of cam positions.

One If by Land...

Whether a switch is mechanical, electrical, hydraulic, or something else is irrelevant. What counts is that a switch contains a two-way pattern: on or off; up or down; flow or no flow. To that pattern can be assigned a meaning. Paul Revere told his buddy to set up a code in the Old North Church: "One if by land, two if by sea." Once lit, the lamps in the steeple remained lit (and thus remembered that very important code) long enough for Paul to call out the militia and whup the British.

In general then, what we call *memory* is an aggregate of switches that will retain a pattern long enough for that pattern to be read and understood by a person or a mechanism. For our purposes, those switches will be electrical, but keep in mind that both mechanical and hydraulic computers have been proposed and built with varying degrees of success.

Memory consists of containers for alterable patterns that retain an entered pattern until someone or something alters the pattern.

Transistor Switches

One problem with building a computer memory system of light switches is that light switches are pretty specialized: they require fingers to set them, and their output is a current path for electricity. Ideally, a computer memory switch should be operated by the same force it controls. This allows the patterns stored in memory to be passed on to other memory storage locations. In the gross electromechanical world, such a switch is called a *relay*.

A relay is a mechanical switch that is operated by electricity for the purpose of controlling electricity. You "flip" a relay by feeding it a pulse of electricity, which powers a little hammer that whaps a lever to one side or another. This lever then opens or closes a set of electrical contacts, just as your garden-variety light switch does. Computers have been made out of relays, although as you might imagine, it was a long time ago, and (with a typical relay being about the size of an ice cube) they weren't especially powerful computers.

Fully electronic computers are made out of transistor switches. *Transistors* are tiny crystals of silicon that use the peculiar electrical properties of silicon to act as switches. I won't try to explain what those peculiar properties are, since that would take an entire book unto itself. Let's consider a transistor switch a sort of electrical black box and describe it in terms of inputs and outputs.

Figure 3.1 shows a transistor switch. (It is a *field-effect* transistor, which in truth is only one type of transistor, but it is the type that our current computers are made of.) When an electrical voltage is applied to pin 1, current flows between pins 2 and 3. When the voltage is removed from pin 1, current ceases to flow between pins 2 and 3.

In real life, a tiny handful of other components (typically diodes and capacitors) are necessary to make things work smoothly in a computer memory context. These are not necessarily little gizmos connected by wires to the outside of the transistor (although in early transistorized computers they were) but are now cut from the same silicon crystal the transistor itself is cut from and occupy almost no space at all. Taken together, the transistor switch and its support components are called a *memory cell*. I've hidden the electrical complexity of the memory cell within an appropriate black-box symbol in Figure 3.1.

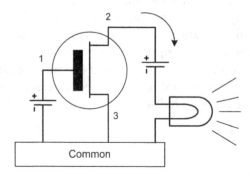

Transistor Switch

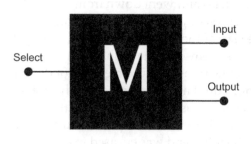

Memory Cell

Figure 3.1: Transistor switches and memory cells

A memory cell keeps current flow through it to a minimum because electrical current flow produces heat, and heat is the enemy of electrical components. The memory cell's circuit is arranged so that if you put a tiny voltage on its input pin and a similar voltage on its *select* pin, a voltage will appear *and remain* on its output pin. That output voltage will remain in its set state until you remove the voltage from the cell as a whole or else remove the voltage from the input pin while putting a voltage on the select pin.

The "on" voltage being applied to all of these pins is kept at a consistent level (except, of course, when it is removed entirely). In other words, you don't put 12 volts on the input pin and then change that to 6 volts or 17 volts. The computer designers pick a voltage and stick with it. The pattern is binary in nature: either you put a voltage on the input pin, or you take the voltage away entirely. The output pin echoes that: either it holds a fixed voltage or it holds no voltage at all.

We apply a code to that state of affairs: *the presence of voltage indicates a binary 1, and the lack of voltage indicates a binary 0.* This code is arbitrary. We could as well have said that the *lack* of voltage indicates a binary 1 and vice versa (and computers have been built this way for obscure reasons), but the choice is up to us. Having the *presence* of something indicate a binary 1 is more natural, and that is the way things have evolved in the computing mainstream.

A single computer memory cell, such as the transistor-based one we're speaking of here, holds one binary digit, either a 1 or a 0. This is called a *bit*. A bit is the indivisible atom of information. There is no half-a-bit, and no bit-and-a-half.

A bit is a single binary digit, either 1 or 0.

The Incredible Shrinking Bit

One bit doesn't tell us much. To be useful, we need to bring *lots* of memory cells together. Transistors started out fairly small (the originals from the 1950s looked a lot like stovepipe hats for tin soldiers) and went down from there. The first transistors were created from little chips of germanium or silicon crystal about an eighth of an inch square. The size of the crystal chip hasn't changed outrageously since then, but the transistors themselves have shrunk incredibly.

Where, in the beginning, one chip held one transistor, in time semiconductor designers crisscrossed the chip into four equal areas and made each area an independent transistor. From there it was an easy jump to adding the other minuscule components needed to turn a transistor into a computer memory cell.

The chip of silicon was a tiny and fragile thing and was encased in an oblong molded-plastic housing, like a small stick of gum with metal legs for the electrical connections.

What we had now was a sort of electrical egg carton: four little cubbyholes, each of which could contain a single binary bit. Then the shrinking process began. First 8 bits, then 16, then multiples of 8 and 16, all on the same tiny silicon chip. By the late 1960s, 256 memory cells could be made on one chip of silicon, usually in an array of 8 cells by 32. In 1976, my COSMAC ELF computer contained two memory chips. On each chip was an array of memory cells 4 wide and 256 long. (Picture a *really* long egg carton.) Each chip could thus hold 1,024 bits.

This was a pretty typical memory chip capacity at that time. We called them "1K RAM chips" because they held roughly 1,000 bits of *random-access memory* (RAM). The *K* comes from *kilobit*, that is, 1,000 bits. We'll get back to the notion of what *random access* means shortly.

Toward the mid-1970s, the great memory-shrinking act was kicking into high gear. One kilobyte chips were crisscross divided into 4K chips containing 4,096 bits of memory. The 4K chips were almost immediately divided into 16K chips

(16,384 bits of memory). These 16K chips were the standard when the IBM PC first appeared in 1981. By 1982, the chips had been divided once again, and 16K became 64K, with 65,536 bits inside that same little gumstick. Keep in mind that we're talking more than 65,000 transistors (plus other odd components) formed on a square of silicon about a quarter-inch on a side.

Come 1985 and the 64K chip had been pushed aside by its drawn-and-quartered child, the 256K chip (262,144 bits). Memory chips generally increase in capacity by a factor of 4 simply because the current-generation chip is divided into 4 equal areas, onto each of which is then placed the same number of transistors that the previous generation of chip had held over the whole silicon chip.

By 1990, the 256K chip was history, and the 1 megabit chip was state of the art. (*Mega* is Greek for million.) By 1992, the 4 megabit chip had taken over. The critter had a grand total of 4,194,304 bits inside it, still no larger than that little stick of cinnamon gum. About that time, the chips themselves grew small and fragile enough so that four or eight of them were soldered to tiny printed circuit boards so that they would survive handling by clumsy human beings. These "memory sticks" are what modern computers use. They have the advantage that you can in many cases remove and replace them with even bigger memory sticks as those become available.

The memory chip game has continued apace, and in 2022, 16 gigabit chips are mainstream. That's 16 *billion* bits per chip.

Will it stop here? Unlikely. More is better in this world of real-time animated video games and 4K video, and we're bringing some staggeringly powerful technology to bear on the creation of ever-denser memory systems. Some physicists warn that the laws of physics may soon call a time-out in the game, since the transistors are now so small that it gets hard pushing more than one electron at a time through them. At that point some truly ugly limitations of life called *quantum mechanics* begin to get in the way. We'll find a way around these limitations (we always do), but in the process the whole nature of computer memory may change.

If trying to keep track of what's "current" in the computer world makes your head hurt, well, you're not alone.

Random Access

Newcomers sometimes find *random* a perplexing and disturbing word with respect to memory, since it often connotes chaos or unpredictability. What the word really means here is "at random," indicating that you can reach into a random-access memory chip and pick out any of the bits it contains without disturbing any of the others, just as you might select one book at random from your public library's many shelves of thousands of books without sifting through them in order or disturbing the places of other books on the shelves.

Memory didn't always work this way. Before memory was placed on silicon chips, it was stored on electromagnetic machines of some kind, usually rotating drums or disks distantly related to the hard drives we use today. Rotating magnetic memory sends a circular collection of bits beneath a magnetic sensor. The bits pass beneath the sensor one at a time, and if you miss the one you want, like a Chicago bus in January, you simply have to wait for it to come by again. These are *serial-access devices*. They present their bits to you serially, in a fixed order, one at a time, and you have to wait for the one you want to come up in its order.

There's no need to remember that; we've long since abandoned serial-access devices for main computer memory. We still use such systems for *mass storage*, as I will describe a few pages down the road. (Your hard drive is at its heart a serial-access device.)

Random access works like this: inside the chip, each bit is stored in its own memory cell, identical to the memory cell diagrammed in Figure 3.1. Each of the however-many memory cells has a unique number. This number is a cell's (and hence a bit's) *address*. It's like the addresses on a street: the bit on the corner is number 0 Silicon Alley, and the bit next door is 1, and so on. You don't have to knock on the door of bit 0 and ask which bit it is and then go to the next door and ask there too, until you find the bit you want. If you have the address, you can zip right down the street and park square in front of the bit you intend to visit.

Each chip has a number of pins coming out of it. The bulk of these pins are called *address pins*. One pin is called a *data pin*. (See Figure 3.2.) The address pins are electrical leads that carry a binary address code. This address is a binary number, expressed in 1s and 0s only. You apply this address to the address pins by encoding a binary 1 as (say) 5 volts, and a binary 0 as 0 volts. Many other voltages have been used and are still used in computer hardware. What matters is that we all agree that a certain voltage on a pin represents a binary 1. Special circuits inside the RAM chip decode this address to one of the select inputs of the numerous memory cells inside the chip. For any given address applied to the address pins, only *one* select input will be raised to five volts, thereby selecting that memory cell.

Depending on whether you intend to read a bit or write a bit, the data pin is switched between the memory cells' inputs or outputs, as shown in Figure 3.2.

But that's all done internally to the chip. As far as you on the outside are concerned, once you've applied the address to the address pins, *voilà*! The data pin will contain a voltage representing the value of the bit you requested. If that bit contained a binary 1, the data pin will contain a 5-volt signal; otherwise, the binary 0 bit will be represented by 0 volts.

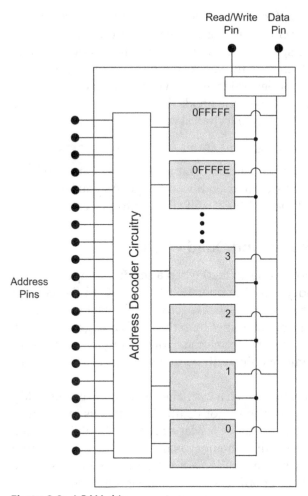

Figure 3.2: A RAM chip

Memory Access Time

Chips are graded by how long it takes for the data to appear on the data pin after you've applied the address to the address pins. Obviously, the faster the better, but some chips (for electrical reasons that again are difficult to explain) are faster than others.

Years ago, when computers used individual chips plugged into their motherboards, memory access time was (mostly) the time it took for data to appear after an address was applied to the chips. Even then, there were other issues that involved the speed of the CPU chip and how the memory system overall was designed.

Today, PC memory systems are focused on memory sticks (more on that later), which gang up several memory chips with a great deal of support circuitry. The sticks are sensitive to the CPU speed of the computer in which they work and to the sorts of sockets into which they fit. Memory timing has become hugely more complex in the last 20 years. Several factors govern how quickly memory chips can accept an address and deliver the goods. Here's a good explanation, given with fair warning that it's a *highly* technical presentation:

`https://appuals.com/ram-timings-cas-ras-trcd-trp-tras-explained`

I can reassure you that you do not need to completely understand the intricacies of PC memory hardware to learn assembly language. As you learn more about PC internals generally, little by little it will all fall into place.

Bytes, Words, Double Words, and Quad Words

The days are long gone (decades gone, in fact) when a serious computer could be made with only one memory chip. My poor 1976 COSMAC ELF needed at least two. Today's computers need many, irrespective of the fact that today's memory chips can hold billions of bits rather than the ELF's meager 2,048 bits.

Our memory system must store our information. How we organize a memory system out of a hatful of memory chips will be dictated largely by how we organize our information.

The answer begins with this thing called a *byte*. The fact that the granddaddy of all computer magazines took this word for its title indicates its importance in the computer scheme of things. (Alas, *Byte Magazine* ceased publishing late in 1998.) From a *functional* perspective, memory is measured in bytes. A byte is eight bits. Two bytes side by side are called a *word*, and two words side by side are called a *double word*. A *quad word*, as you might imagine, consists of two double words, for four words or eight bytes in all. Going the other direction, in the past some people referred to a group of four bits as a nybble—a *nybble* being half of a byte. (This term is now largely extinct.)

Here's the quick tour:

- A bit is a single binary digit, 0 or 1.
- A byte is 8 bits side by side.
- A word is 2 bytes side by side: 16 bits.
- A double word is 2 words side by side: 32 bits.
- A quad word is 2 double words side by side: 64 bits.

Computers were designed to store and manipulate human information. The basic elements of human discourse are built from a set of symbols consisting of letters of the alphabet (two of each for upper and lower case), digits, and symbols including commas, colons, periods, exclamation marks, and so on. Add to these the various international variations on letters such as *ä* and *ò* plus the more arcane mathematical symbols, and you'll find that human information requires a symbol set of well over 200 symbols. (The symbol set used in nearly all PC-style computers is given in Appendix C.)

Bytes are central to the scheme because one symbol out of that symbol set can be neatly expressed in one byte. A byte is 8 bits, and 2^8 is 256. This means that a binary number 8 bits in size can be one of 256 different values, numbered from 0 to 255. Because we use these symbols so much, most of what we do in computer programs is expressed in byte-sized chunks representing numbers or text. This doesn't mean computers act on only single bytes. Most computers today, in fact, can process information a quad word (eight bytes, or 64 bits) at a time. The 32-bit machines that seemed so unbeatable 20 years ago are rapidly fading into the mists of history.

To make internationalization and localization of software practical, there is a standard for character sets called Unicode, which itself is a collection of standards. Unicode character sets may be expressed in one to four bytes, the first byte of which is almost identical to the long-established ASCII standard character set. Explaining how Unicode encoding works is outside the mission of this book, but for programmers outside the United States it is well worth studying.

Pretty Chips All in a Row

One of the more perplexing things for beginners to understand is that a single RAM chip does not even contain *1* byte...though it might contain several *billion* bits. Most of the individual RAM chips that we use today have no more than eight data pins, and some only *one* data pin. Whole memory systems are created by combining individual memory chips electrically in clever ways.

A simple example will help. Consider Figure 3.3. I've drawn a memory system that distributes a single stored byte across eight separate RAM chips. Each of the black rectangles represents a RAM chip like the one shown in Figure 3.2. There is one bit from the byte stored within each of the eight chips, at the same address across all eight chips. The 20 address pins for all eight chips are connected together, "in parallel" as an electrician might say. When the computer applies a memory address to the 20 address lines, the address appears simultaneously on the address pins of all eight memory chips in the memory system. This way, a single address is applied simultaneously to the address pins of all eight chips, which deliver all eight bits simultaneously on the eight data lines, with one bit from each chip.

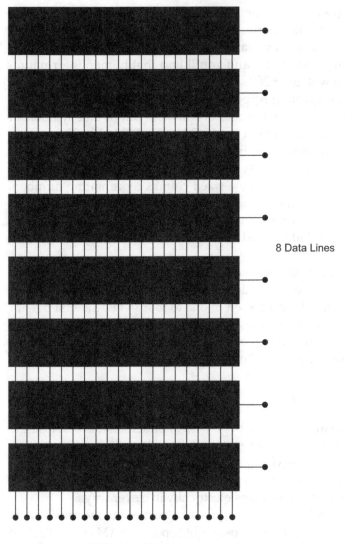

8 Data Lines

20 Address Lines

Figure 3.3: A simple 1-megabyte memory system

In the real world, such simple memory systems no longer exist, and there are many different ways of distributing chips (and their stored bits) across a memory system. All memory chips today do in fact store more than one bit at each address. Chips storing one, two, three, four, or eight bits per address are relatively common. How to design a fast and efficient computer memory system is an entire subdiscipline within electrical engineering, and as our memory chips are improved to contain more and more memory cells, the "best" way to design a physical memory system will change, perhaps radically.

It's been a long time, after all, since we've had to plug individual memory chips into our computers. Today, memory chips are nearly always gathered together into plug-in dual inline memory modules (DIMMs) of various capacities. These modules are little green-colored circuit boards about 5" long and 1" high. Since 1990 or so, all desktop PC-compatible computers use such modules, generally in pairs. Each module currently in use typically stores 64 bits at each memory address.

Today in 2022, there is a bewildering array of different DIMM memory modules, with different numbers of pins and different combinations of chips to cater to different types of computers. The important thing to remember is that the way memory chips are combined into a memory system does *not* affect the way your programs operate. When a program that you've written accesses a byte of memory at a particular address, the computer takes care of fetching it from the appropriate place in that jungle of chips and DIMM circuit boards. One memory system arranged a certain way might bring the data back from memory *faster* than another memory system arranged a different way, but the addresses are the same, and the data is the same. From the point of view of your program, there is no functional difference unless the speed at which your programs run is important.

To summarize, electrically, your computer's memory consists of one or more rows of memory chips on small (and generally removable) circuit boards, each chip containing a *large* number of memory cells made out of transistors and other minuscule electrical components. Most of the time, to avoid confusion, it's just as useful to forget about the transistors and even the rows of physical chips. (My high school FORTRAN teacher was not *entirely* wrong...but he was right for the wrong reasons.)

Over the years, memory systems have been accessed in different ways. Eight-bit computers (now ancient and almost extinct) accessed memory eight bits (one byte) at a time. Sixteen-bit computers access memory 16 bits (one word) at a time, and 32-bit computers access memory 32 bits (one double word) at a time. Modern computers based on x64 64-bit processors access memory 64 bits (one quad word) at a time. This can be confusing, so it's better in most cases to envision a very long row of byte-sized containers, each with its own unique address. Don't assume that in computers that process information a word at a time that only *words* have addresses. It's a convention within the PC architecture that *every* byte has its own unique numeric address, irrespective of how many bytes are pulled from memory in one operation.

Every byte of memory in the computer has its own unique address, even in computers that process 2, 4, or 8 bytes of information at a time.

If this seems counterintuitive, yet another metaphor will help. When you go to the library to take out the three volumes of Tolkien's massive fantasy *The Lord of the Rings*, you'll find that each of the three volumes has its own card catalog number (essentially that volume's address in the library) but that you take all three down at once and process them as a single entity. If you really *want* to, you can check only one of the books out of the library at a time, but doing so will require two more trips to the library later to get the other two volumes, which is wasteful of your time and effort.

So it is with 64-bit computers. Every byte has its own address, but when a 64-bit computer accesses a byte in main memory, it actually reads 64 bytes, with the requested byte somewhere within the block that was read. This block of 64 bytes is called a *cache line*. Cache is basically a block of memory locations *inside the CPU chip itself*, and not outside in DIMMs on the motherboard. Reading data or instructions from cache is hugely faster than reading them from external memory. As your program toodles along, reading, writing, and executing, most of what the program is using already exists in cache. The CPU has some extremely sophisticated machinery to manage cache. This machinery is constantly swapping in memory from outside the CPU, doing its best to predict what memory your program will be using next.

Describing how this cache-management machinery works involves other complicated things such as virtual memory, paging, and branch prediction, which are outside the scope of an introductory book like this. The good news is that all this machinery is controlled by a partnership between the CPU and the operating system. Your program will run the same way irrespective of what is in cache and what isn't. (Again, it may run faster or slower depending on how much the CPU has to bring in from external memory.) As a beginning programmer, you don't need to concern yourself with cache lines and all the rest. However, when you are enough of an assembly expert to understand how caching and other memory management mechanisms affect the speed of the program, you'll need to learn those mechanisms from top to bottom.

The Shop Supervisor and the Assembly Line

All of this talk about reading things from memory and writing things to memory has so far carefully skirted the question of *who* is doing the reading and writing. The who is almost always a single chip, and a remarkable chip it is, too: the *central processing unit*, or CPU. If you are the president and CEO of your personal computer, the CPU is your shop supervisor, who sees that your orders are carried out down among the chips where the work gets done.

Some would say that the CPU is what actually does the work, but while largely true, it's an oversimplification. Plenty of real work is done in the memory system and also in what are called *peripherals*, such as video display boards, USB and network ports, and so on. So, while the CPU does do a good deal of the work, it also parcels out quite a bit of the work to other components within the computer, largely to allow the CPU to do what it does best a lot more quickly.

Like any good manager, the shop supervisor delegates to other computer subsystems whatever it can.

Most of the CPU chips used in the machines we lump together as a group and call PCs were designed by a company called Intel, which pretty much invented the single-chip CPU way back in the early 1970s. Intel CPUs have evolved briskly since then, as I'll describe a little later in this chapter. There have been many changes in the details over the years, but from a high level, what any Intel or Intel-compatible CPU does is largely the same.

Talking to Memory

The CPU chip's most important job is to communicate with the computer's memory system. Like a memory chip, a CPU chip is a small square of silicon onto which a great many transistors—today, many *billions* of them!—have been placed. The fragile silicon chip is encased in a metal/ceramic housing with a large number of electrical connection pins protruding from its bottom surface or its edges. Like the pins of memory chips, the CPU's pins transfer information encoded as voltage levels, typically 3 to 5 volts. Five volts on a pin indicate a binary 1, and zero volts on a pin indicate a binary 0.

Like memory chips, the CPU chip has a number of pins devoted to memory addresses, and these pins are connected to the computer's system of memory chips. I've drawn this in Figure 3.4, and the memory system to the left of the CPU chip is the same one I drew in Figure 3.3, just tipped on its side. When the CPU desires to read a byte (or a word, double word, or quad word) from memory, it places the memory address of the byte to be read on its address pins, encoded as a binary number. Some vanishingly small fragment of a second later, the requested byte appears (also as a binary number) on the data pins of the memory chips. The CPU chip also has data pins, and it slurps up the byte presented by the memory chips through its own data pins.

The process, of course, also works in reverse. To write a byte into memory, the CPU first places the memory address where it wants to write onto its address pins. Some number of nanoseconds later (which varies from system to system depending on general system speed and how memory is arranged) the CPU places the byte it wants to write into memory on its data pins. The memory system obediently stores the byte inside itself at the requested address.

Figure 3.4 is, of course, purely conceptual. Modern memory systems are *hugely* more complex than what is shown in the figure, but from a height they all work the same way: the CPU passes an address to the memory system, and the memory system either accepts data from the CPU for storage at that address or places the data found at that address on the computer's data bus for the CPU to process.

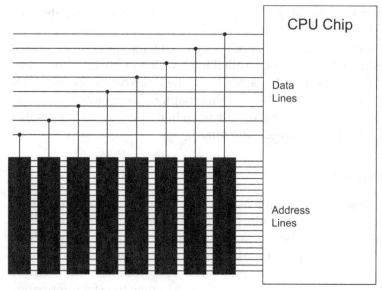

Figure 3.4: The CPU and memory

Riding the Data Bus

This give-and-take between the CPU and the memory system represents the bulk of what happens inside your computer. Information flows from memory into the CPU and back again. Information flows in other paths as well. Your computer contains additional devices called *peripherals* that are either sources or destinations (or both) for information.

Video display boards, disk drives, USB ports, and network ports are the most common peripherals in PC-type computers. Like the CPU and memory, they are all ultimately electrical devices. Most modern peripherals consist of one or two large chips and perhaps a couple of smaller chips that support the larger chips. Like both the CPU chip and memory chips, these peripheral devices have both address pins and data pins. Some peripherals, video boards in particular, have their own memory chips and, these days, their own dedicated CPUs. (Your modern high-performance video board is a high-powered computer in its own right, albeit one with a specific and limited job.)

Peripherals "talk" to the CPU (that is, they pass the CPU data or take data from the CPU) and sometimes to one another. These conversations take place across the electrical connections linking the address pins and data pins that all devices in the computer have in common. These electrical lines are called a *data bus* and form a sort of party line linking the CPU with all the other parts of the computer. There is an elaborate system of electrical arbitration that determines when and in what order the different devices can use this party line to talk with one another. But it happens in generally the same way: an address is placed on the bus, followed by some data. (How much data moves at once depends on the peripherals involved.) Special signals go out on the bus with the address to indicate whether the address is of a location in memory, or of one of the peripherals attached to the data bus. The address of a peripheral is called an *I/O address* to differentiate between it and a *memory address* such as those we've been discussing all along.

The data bus is the major element in the *expansion slots* present in a lot of PC-type computers, though fewer now than in decades past. Many peripherals (especially video display adapters) are printed circuit boards that plug into these slots. The peripherals talk to the CPU and to memory through the data bus connections brought out as electrical pins in the expansion slots.

As convenient as expansion slots are, they introduce delays into a computer system. More and more as time goes on, peripherals are simply a couple of chips on one corner of the main circuit board (the *motherboard*) inside the computer. Such peripherals are called *integrated* peripherals, the commonest being integral graphics, which consists of one or more special-purpose chips on the motherboard. There are modern PCs today in 2022 that are designed specifically for high-resolution real-time animated graphics (largely for games), and such machines generally have special expansion slots specifically designed to hold graphics boards.

The Shop Supervisor's Pockets

Every CPU contains a few data storage cubbyholes called *registers*. These registers are at once the shop supervisor's pockets and workbench. When the CPU needs a place to tuck something away for a short while, an empty register is just the place. The CPU could always store the data out in memory, but that takes considerably more time than tucking the data in a register. Because the registers are actually inside the CPU, placing data in a register or reading it back again from a register is *fast*.

But more important, registers are the supervisor's workbench. When the CPU needs to add two numbers, the easiest and fastest way is to place the numbers in two registers and add the two registers together. The sum (in usual CPU practice) replaces one of the two original numbers that were added, but after that the sum could then be placed in yet another register, be added to still another number in another register, be stored out in memory, or take part in any of a multitude of other operations.

> *The CPU's immediate work in progress is held in temporary storage containers called* registers.

Work involving registers is always fast because the registers are within the CPU and are specially connected to one another and to the CPU's internal machinery. Very little movement of data is necessary—and what data does move doesn't have to move very far.

Like memory cells and, indeed, like the entire CPU, registers are made out of transistors. But rather than having numeric addresses, registers have individual names such as RAX or RDI. To make matters even more complicated, while all CPU registers have certain common properties, some registers have unique special powers not shared by other registers. Understanding the ways and the limitations of CPU registers is something like following a world peace conference: there are partnerships, alliances, and always a bewildering array of secret agendas that each register follows. There's no general system describing such things; like irregular verbs, you simply have to memorize them.

Most peripherals also have registers, and peripheral registers are even more limited in scope than CPU registers. Their agendas are quite explicit and in no way secret. This does not prevent them from being confusing, as anyone who has tried programming a video board at the register level will attest. Fortunately, these days nearly all communication with peripheral devices is handled by the operating system, as I'll explain later in this book.

The Assembly Line

If the CPU is the shop supervisor, then the peripherals are the assembly-line workers, and the data bus is the assembly line itself. (Unlike most assembly lines, however, the supervisor works the line much harder than the rest of the crew!)

As an example, information enters the computer through a network port peripheral, which assembles bits received from a computer network cable into bytes of data representing characters and digits. The network port then places the assembled byte onto the data bus, from which the CPU picks it up, tallies it, or processes it in other ways, and then places it back on the data bus. The display board then retrieves the byte from the data bus and writes it into video memory so that you can see it on your screen.

This is a severely simplified description, but obviously, *a lot* is going on inside the box. Continuous furious communication along the data bus between CPU, memory, and peripherals is what accomplishes the work that the computer does. The question then arises: who tells the supervisor and crew what to do? *You* do. How do you do that? You write a program. Where is the program? It's in memory, along with all the rest of the data stored in memory. In fact, the program *is* data, and that is the heart of the whole idea of programming as we know it.

The Box That Follows a Plan

Finally, we come to the essence of computing: the nature of programs and how they direct the CPU to control the computer and get your work done.

We've seen how memory can be used to store bytes of information. These bytes are all binary codes, patterns of 1 bits and 0 bits stored as minute electrical voltage levels and collectively making up binary numbers. We've also spoken of symbols and how certain binary codes may be interpreted as meaning something to us human beings, things like letters, digits, punctuation, and so on.

Just as the alphabet and the numeric digits represent a set of codes and symbols that mean something to us humans, there is a set of codes that mean something to the CPU. These codes are called *machine instructions*, and their name is evocative of what they actually are: instructions to the CPU. When the CPU is executing a program, it picks a sequence of numbers off the data bus, one at a time. Each number tells the CPU to do something. The CPU knows how. When it completes executing one instruction, it picks the next one up and executes that. It continues doing so until something (a command in the program, or electrical signal like a reset button) tells it to stop.

Let's take an example or two drawn from older 32-bit CPU chips from Intel. (I'm using those as examples here because the point is that a machine instruction is a number acting as a command to the CPU. The specific machine instructions are not important in this particular discussion.)

The 8-bit binary code 01000000 (40H) means something to the CPU. It is an order: *Add 1 to register AX and put the sum back in AX*. That's about as simple as they get. Most machine instructions occupy more than a single byte. Many are two bytes in length, and no small number are four bytes in length. The longest among them, in fact, are 15 bytes in length. The binary codes 11010110 01110011 (0D6H 073H) comprise another order: *Load the value 73H into register DH*. On the other end of the spectrum, the binary codes 11110011 10100100 (0F3H 0A4H) direct the CPU to do the following (take a deep breath): *Begin moving the number of bytes specified in register CX from the 32-bit address stored in registers DS and SI to the 32-bit address stored in registers ES and DI, updating the address in both SI and DI after moving each byte, and also decreasing CX by one each time, and finally stopping when CX becomes zero*.

I'll come back to machine instruction specifics in later chapters when we get down to writing actual x64 assembly code. The point here is that machine instructions are numbers (or short sequences of numbers) that the CPU understands as commands to do something. There are instructions that perform arithmetic operations (addition, subtraction, multiplication, and division) and logical operations (AND, OR, XOR, etc.), and instructions that move information around memory. Some instructions serve to "steer" the path that program execution takes within the logic of the program being executed. Some instructions have highly arcane functions and don't turn up very often outside of operating system internals. The important thing to remember right now is that *each instruction tells the CPU to perform one generally small and limited task*. Many instructions handed to the CPU in sequence direct the CPU to perform far more complicated tasks. Writing that sequence of instructions is what assembly language programming actually *is*.

Let's talk more about that.

Fetch and Execute

A computer program is nothing more than a sequence of these machine instructions stored in memory. There's nothing special about the sequence, nor about where it is positioned in memory. It could be almost anywhere, and the bytes in the sequence are nothing more than binary numbers.

The binary numbers comprising a computer program are special only in the way that the CPU treats them. When a modern 64-bit CPU begins running a program, it starts by fetching bytes (not words, double words, or quad words) from an agreed-upon address in memory. (How this starting address is agreed upon is an operating system issue and doesn't matter right now.) These initial bytes are the start of a stream of instructions that come in from memory to be executed. The stream is loaded into a special memory system inside the CPU called the *instruction cache*, which the CPU can access very quickly. As the CPU works through the instructions in the cache, more instructions are automatically loaded from memory to keep the cache full (or close to it) at all times.

The crucial point to remember here is that *not all machine instructions are the same length*. In x64, an instruction can be anywhere from 1 to 15 bytes in length. The CPU examines the incoming stream of machine instruction bytes in cache to determine where each instruction begins and ends. When the CPU identifies an instruction in the stream, it executes that instruction and then continues examining the stream to identify the next instruction.

Inside the CPU is a special register called the *instruction pointer* that quite literally contains the address of the next instruction to be executed. In x64 CPUs the instruction pointer is named RIP. Each time an instruction is executed, the instruction pointer is updated to point to the next instruction in memory. There is some silicon magic afoot inside modern CPUs that "guesses" what's to be fetched next and keeps it on a side shelf so it'll be there when fetched, only much more quickly—but the process as I've described it is true in terms of the outcome.

All of this is done literally like clockwork. The computer has an electrical subsystem called a *system clock*, which is actually an oscillator that emits square-wave pulses at very precise intervals. The immense number of microscopic transistor switches inside the CPU coordinate their actions according to the pulses generated by the system clock. In years past, it often took several clock cycles (basically, pulses from the clock) to execute a single instruction. As computers became faster and their internal design more sophisticated, the majority of machine instructions executed in a single clock cycle. Modern CPUs can execute instructions in parallel, so multiple instructions can often execute in a single clock cycle.

So the process goes: fetch and execute; fetch and execute. The CPU works its way through memory, with the instruction pointer register leading the way. As it goes, it works: moving data around in memory, moving values around in registers, passing data to peripherals, crunching data in arithmetic or logical operations.

Computer programs are lists of binary machine instructions stored in memory. They are no different from any other list of data bytes stored in memory except in how they are interpreted when fetched by the CPU.

The Supervisor's Innards

I made the point earlier that machine instructions are *binary* codes. This is something we often gloss over, yet to understand the true nature of the CPU, we have to step away from the persistent image of machine instructions as *numbers*. They are *not* numbers. They are binary *patterns* designed to throw electrical switches. We refer to them as numbers so we don't have to learn to deal with (large) sequences of ones and zeros. 01010001 or 51H? You tell me.

Inside the CPU are a *very* large number of transistors. The Intel Core i5 Quad that I have on my desk contains 582 million transistors, and CPU chips with more than a billion transistors are now commonplace. The 10-core i7 Broadwell E introduced in 2016 has 3.3 *billion* transistors. It's only been going up from there.

A quick aside: why do I still use a 10-year-old machine with a piddling 582 million transistors? It does everything I need it to do, *and it runs cool*. Cool is *important*. All I need when it's Phoenix summer and 118 degrees outside is a box full of fans pumping heat into my office so that I can pay the electric company to pump it out again. If I were a video game developer or a scientist running significant computer models, well, I'd buy a CPU with all the transistors that I could afford and consider the power bills a cost of doing business. *What you need depends on what you do.* Computer power comes at a cost in both dollars and heat.

Some number of all those transistors goes into making up the supervisor's pockets: machine registers for holding information. In the x64 architecture, these registers are all 64 bits (8 bytes) in size. A significant number of transistors go into making up short-term storage called *cache* that I'll describe later. (For now, think of cache as a small set of storage shelves always right there at the supervisor's elbow, making it unnecessary for the supervisor to cross the room to get more materials.) The vast majority of CPU transistors, however, are switches connected to other switches, which are connected to still more switches in a mind-numbingly complex network.

This is one case where a "view from a height" example is essential. The extremely simple one-byte machine instruction 01010001 (51H) directs the CPU to push the value stored in the 64-bit register RCX onto the stack. The CPU breaks this down into two separate steps. First, the CPU subtracts 8 from the value in the stack pointer register (RSP) to make room for the 64-bit register on the stack. Next, the value in RCX is copied to the memory location now referenced by the stack pointer register. Then the job is done, and the CPU is ready to move on to the next instruction. You'll soon see how individual instructions are interpreted by the CPU as sequences of one or more fine-grained steps. It's very instructive of the true nature of computers to think about the execution of machine instruction 01010001 in this way.

Precisely how all this happens electrically is extremely difficult to explain, but you must remember that *any* number stored inside the CPU can also be looked upon as a binary code, including values stored in registers. Also, most switches within the CPU contain more than one handle. These switches are called *gates* and work according to the rules of logic. Perhaps two, or three, or even more "up" switch throws have to arrive at a particular gate at the same time in order for one "down" switch throw to pass through that gate.

These gates are used to build complex internal machinery within the CPU. Collections of gates can add two numbers in a device called an *adder*, which again is nothing more than a crew of hundreds of little switches working together first as gates and then as gates working together to form an adder. Other mechanisms exist within the CPU, all of them made of transistor switches and gates.

The supervisor of your computer, then, is made of switches—just like all the other parts of the computer. It contains a mind-boggling number of such switches, interconnected in even more mind-boggling ways. But the important thing is that whether you are boggled or (like me, on off-days) merely jaded by it all, the CPU, and ultimately the computer, *does exactly what we tell it to do*. We set up a list of machine instructions as a table in memory, and then, by gully, that mute silicon brick comes alive and starts earning its keep.

Changing Course

The first piece of genuine magic in the nature of computers is that a string of binary codes in memory tells the computer what to do, step by step. The second piece of that magic is really the jewel in the crown: *there are machine instructions that change the order in which machine instructions are fetched and executed.*

In other words, once the CPU has executed a machine instruction that does something useful, the next machine instruction may tell the CPU to go back and play it again—and again, and again, as many times as necessary. The CPU can keep count of the number of times that it has executed that particular instruction or list of instructions and keep repeating them until a prearranged count has been met.

Or it can arrange to skip certain sequences of machine instructions entirely if they don't need to be executed at all.

This means the list of machine instructions in memory does not necessarily begin at the top and run without deviation to the bottom. The CPU can execute the first 50 or 100 or 1,000 instructions and then jump to the end of the program—or jump back to the start and begin again. It can skip and bounce up and down the list like a stone tossed over a calm pond. It can execute a few instructions up here, then zip down somewhere else and execute a few more instructions, and then zip back and pick up where it left off, all without missing a beat or even wasting too much time.

How is this done? Recall that the CPU includes a special register that always contains the address of the next instruction to be executed. This register, the instruction pointer, is not essentially different from any of the other registers in the CPU. Just as a machine instruction can add one to register RCX, another machine instruction can add—or subtract—some number to or from the address stored in the instruction pointer. Add 100 (decimal) to the instruction pointer, and the CPU will *instantly* skip 100 bytes down the list of machine instructions before it continues. Subtract 100 from the address stored in the instruction pointer, and the CPU will *instantly* jump *back* 100 bytes up the machine instruction list.

Finally, the third whammy: *the CPU can change its course of execution based on the work it has been doing.* The CPU can decide whether to execute a given instruction or group of instructions, based on values stored in memory, or based on the individual state of several special one-bit CPU registers called *flags*. The CPU can count up how many times it needs to do something and then do that something that number of times. Or it can do something and then do it again, and again, and again, checking each time (by looking at some data somewhere) to see if it's finished yet or whether it has to take another run through the task.

So, not only can you tell the CPU what to do, you can tell it where to go. Better, you can sometimes let the CPU, like a faithful bloodhound, sniff out the best course forward in the interest of getting the work done in the quickest possible way.

In Chapter 1, I spoke of a computer program being a sequence of steps and tests. Most of the machine instructions understood by the CPU are steps, but others are tests. The tests are always two-way tests, and in fact the choice of what to do is always the same: jump or don't jump. *That's all.* You can test for any of numerous different conditions within the CPU, but the choice is *always* one of jumping to another place in the program or to just keep truckin' along.

What vs. How: Architecture and Microarchitecture

This book is really about programming in assembly language for Intel's 64-bit CPUs, as well as those CPUs made by other companies to be compatible with Intel's. There are *lots* of different Intel and Intel-compatible x86-family CPU chips. A full list would include the 8086, 8088, 80186, 80286, 80386, 80486, the Celeron, Pentium, Pentium Pro, Pentium MMX, Pentium II, Pentium D, Pentium III, Pentium 4, Pentium Xeon, Xeon, Core, Athlon, and literally dozens of others now in families with names such as Haswell and Coffee Lake. Furthermore, those are only the CPU chips designed and sold by Intel. Other companies (primarily AMD) have designed their own Intel-compatible CPU chips, which adds dozens more to the full list. And within a single CPU type are often another three or four variants, with exotic names such as Coppermine, Katmai, Conroe, Haswell, Coffee Lake, and so on.

How does anybody keep track of all this?

Quick answer: nobody really does. Why? For nearly all purposes, the great mass of details don't matter. The soul of a CPU is pretty cleanly divided into two parts: *what the CPU does*, and *how the CPU does it*. We as programmers see it from the outside: what the CPU does. Electrical engineers and system designers who create computer motherboards and other hardware systems incorporating Intel processors need to know some of the rest, but they are a small and hardy crew, and they know who they are.

Evolving Architectures

Our programmers' view from the outside includes the CPU registers, the set of machine instructions that the CPU understands, and special-purpose subsystems like fast math processors that generally include machine instructions and registers of their own. All of these things are defined at length by Intel, and published online and in largish books so that programmers can study and understand them. Taken together, these definitions are called the CPU's *architecture*.

A CPU architecture evolves over time, as vendors add new instructions, registers, and other features to the product line. Ideally, this is done with an eye toward *backward compatibility*, which means the new features do not generally replace, disable, or change the outward effects of older features. Intel has been very good about backward compatibility within its primary x86 product line, which began in 1978 with the 8086 CPU. Within certain limitations, even programs written for the ancient 8086 will run on the modern 64-bit Core i5 Quad CPU on my desk. Whatever incompatibilities arise are more often related to different operating systems than the details of the CPUs themselves.

The reverse, of course, is not true. New machine instructions creep slowly into Intel's product line over the years. A new machine instruction first introduced in 1996 will not be recognized by a CPU designed, say, in 1993. But a machine instruction first introduced in 1993 will almost always be present and operate identically in newer CPUs.

In addition to periodic additions to the instruction set, architectures occasionally make quantum leaps. Such quantum leaps typically involve a change in the "width" of the CPU. In 1986, Intel's 16-bit architecture expanded to 32 bits with the introduction of the 80386 CPU, which added numerous instructions and operational modes, and doubled the width of the CPU registers. In 2003, Intel's mainstream architecture expanded yet again, this time to 64 bits, with new instructions, modes of operation, and expanded registers. However, CPUs that adhere to the expanded 64-bit architecture will still run software written for the older 32-bit architecture.

Intel's 32-bit architecture is called IA-32 (Intel Architecture 32-bit). The newer 64-bit architecture is called x64 for peculiar reasons, chief of which is that *Intel did not originate it*. Intel's major competitor AMD created a backward-compatible 64-bit x86 architecture in the early 2000s, and it was so well done that Intel had to swallow its pride and adopt it. There was much pride to be swallowed: Intel's own 64-bit architecture, called IA-64 Itanium, was roundly rejected by the market for technical reasons that go well beyond what I can explain in this book.

With only minor glitches, the newer 64-bit Intel architecture *includes* the IA-32 architecture, which in turn includes the still older 16-bit x86 architecture. It's useful to know what CPUs have added what instructions to the architecture, keeping in mind that when you use a "new" instruction, your code will not run on CPU chips made before that new instruction appeared.

The Secret Machinery in the Basement

Because of the backward-compatibility issue, CPU designers do not add new instructions or registers to an architecture without *very* good reason. There are other, better ways to improve a family of CPUs. The most important of these is increased processor throughput, which is *not* a mere increase in CPU clock rates. The other is reduced power consumption. This is not even mostly a "green" issue. As I mentioned earlier, a certain amount of the power used by a CPU is wasted as heat, and waste heat, if not minimized, can cook a CPU chip and damage surrounding components. It also makes for noisy fan-filled boxes and higher utility bills. Designers are thus always looking for ways to reduce the power required to perform the same tasks.

Increasing processor throughput means increasing the number of instructions that the CPU executes over time. There are a lot of arcane tricks associated with increasing throughput, with names like prefetching, L1, L2, and L3 cache, branch prediction, hyper-pipelining, macro-ops fusion, along with plenty of others. Some of these techniques were created to reduce or eliminate bottlenecks within the CPU so that the CPU and the memory system can remain busy nearly all the time. Other techniques stretch the ability of the CPU to process multiple instructions at once.

Taken together, all of the mysterious electrical mechanisms by which the CPU does what its instructions tell it to do is called the CPU's *microarchitecture*. It's the machinery in the basement that you can't see. The metaphor of the shop supervisor breaks down a little here. Let me offer you another one.

Suppose that you own a company that manufactures automatic transmission parts for Ford. You have two separate plants. One is 40 years old, and one has just been built. Both plants make *precisely* the same parts—they have to because Ford puts them into its transmissions without knowing or caring which of your two plants manufactured them. A cam or a housing are thus identical within a 10/1000th of an inch, whether they were made in your old plant or in your new plant.

Your old plant has been around for awhile. Your new plant was designed and built based on everything you've learned while operating the old plant these past 40 years. It's got a more logical layout, better lighting, and modern automated tooling that requires fewer people to operate and goes longer without adjustment.

The upshot is that your new plant can manufacture those cams and housings much more quickly and efficiently, wasting less power and raw materials and requiring fewer people to do it. The day will come when you'll build an even more efficient third plant based on what you've learned running the second plant, and you'll shut the first plant down.

Nonetheless, the cams and housings are the same, no matter where they were made. Precisely *how* they were made is no concern of Ford's nor anyone else's. As long as the cams are built of the same materials and to the same specs and dimensional tolerance, the "how" doesn't matter.

All of the tooling, the assembly line layouts, and general structure of each plant may be considered that plant's microarchitecture. Each time you build a new plant, the new plant's microarchitecture is more efficient at doing what the older plants have been doing all along.

So it is with CPUs. Intel and AMD are constantly redesigning their CPU micro-architectures to make them more efficient. Driving these efforts are improved silicon fabrication techniques that allow more and more transistors to be placed on a single CPU die. More transistors mean more switches and more potential solutions to the same old problems of throughput and power efficiency.

The prime directive in improving microarchitectures, of course, is to avoid "breaking" existing programs by changing the way machine instructions or registers operate. That's why it's the *secret* machinery in the basement. CPU designers go to great lengths to maintain a very bright line between what the CPU does and how those tasks are actually accomplished down in the forest of those billions of transistors.

All the exotic code names like Conroe, Katmai, Haswell, or Coffee Lake actually indicate tweaks in the microarchitecture. Major changes in the microarchitecture also have names: P6, Netburst, Core, and so on. These are described in great detail online, but don't feel bad if you don't quite follow it all. Most of the time I'm hanging on by my fingernails too.

I say all this so that you as a newly minted programmer don't make more of Intel microarchitecture differences than you should. It is an *extremely* rare case (like, almost never) when a difference in microarchitecture details gives you an exploitable advantage in how you code your programs. Okay, microarchitecture is not kept secret (a boggling amount of information about it is available online), but for the sake of your sanity, you should probably treat it as a mystery for the time being. We have many more important things to learn right now.

Enter the Plant Manager

What I've described so far is less "a computer" than "computation." A CPU executing a program does not a computer make. The 8-bit COSMAC ELF device that I built in 1976 was an experiment, and at best a sort of educational toy.

The ELF was a CPU with some memory and just enough electrical support (through switches and LED digits) that I could enter binary machine instructions and see what was happening inside the registers and memory chips. I learned a great deal from it, but it was in no sense of the word *useful*.

My first useful computer came along a couple of years later. It had a keyboard, a CRT display (though not one capable of graphics), a pair of 8″ floppy disk drives, and a daisy-wheel printer. Retro-techies will appreciate that its beating heart was a *1 MHz* 8080 CPU! The machine was tremendously useful, and I wrote numerous magazine articles and my first three books with it. I had a number of simple application programs for it, like the primordial WordStar word processor. But what made it useful was something else: an operating system.

Operating Systems: The Corner Office

An *operating system* is a program that manages the operation of a computer system. It's like any other program in that it consists of a sequence of machine instructions executed by the CPU. Operating systems are different in that they have special powers not generally given to word processors and spreadsheet programs. If we continue the metaphor of the CPU as the shop supervisor, then the operating system is the plant manager. The entire physical plant is under its control. It oversees the bringing in of raw materials to the plant. It supervises the work that goes on inside the plant (including the work done by the shop supervisor) and packages up the finished products for shipment to customers.

In truth, our early microcomputer operating systems weren't very powerful and didn't do much. They "spun the disks" and handled the storage of data to the disk drives and brought data back from disks when requested. They picked up keystrokes from the keyboard and sent characters to the video display. With some fiddling, they could send characters to a printer. That was about it.

The CP/M operating system was "state of the art" for desktop microcomputers in 1979. If you entered the name of a program at the keyboard, CP/M would go out to disk, load the program from a disk file into memory, and then literally hand over all power over the machine to the loaded program. When

WordStar ran, it overwrote the operating system's command processor in memory because memory in that era was extremely expensive and there wasn't very much of it. When WordStar exited, the CP/M command processor would be reloaded from the floppy disk and would simply wait for another command from the keyboard.

BIOS: Software, Just Not as Soft

As our computer systems grew faster and memory cheaper, our operating systems improved right along with our word processors and spreadsheets. When the IBM PC appeared in 1981, PC DOS replaced CP/M almost overnight. The PC's much larger memory space (16 times that of CP/M) made many more things possible and most things faster. DOS could do a lot more than CP/M. This was possible because DOS had help.

IBM had taken the program code that handled the keyboard, the display, serial ports, and disk drives and burned it into a special kind of memory chip called *read-only memory* (ROM). Ordinary random-access memory goes blank when power to it is turned off. ROM retains its data whether it has power or not. The software on the ROM was called the Basic Input/Output System (BIOS) because it handled computer inputs (like the keyboard) and computer outputs (like the display and printer).

To be completely fair to CP/M, it also had a BIOS, but it was far more limited in scope than the DOS BIOS and had to be loaded into memory with the operating system. In a very real sense, the CP/M BIOS was part of the operating system, whereas the DOS BIOS was part of the computer itself.

Somewhere along the way, software like the BIOS, which existed on "nonvolatile" ROM chips, was nicknamed *firmware* because while it was still software, it was not quite as, well, *soft* as software stored in memory. All modern computers have a firmware BIOS, though the BIOS software does different things now than it did in 1981.

Multitasking Magic

PC DOS had a long reign. The first versions of Windows were not really whole new operating systems but were simply file managers and program launchers drawn on the screen in graphics mode. Down in the basement under the icons, DOS was still there, doing what it had always done.

It wasn't until 1995 that things changed radically. In that year Microsoft released Windows 95, which not only had a new graphical user interface but had something far more radical down in the basement. Windows 95 operated in 32-bit protected mode and required at least an 80386-class CPU to run. (I'll explain in detail what "protected mode" means in Chapter 4.) For the moment, think of protected mode as allowing the operating system to definitely be The Boss and no longer merely a peer of word processors and spreadsheets. Windows 95 did not make full use of protected mode because it still had DOS and DOS applications to deal with, and such "legacy" software was written long before protected mode was an option. Windows 95 did, however, have something not seen previously in the low-cost personal computer world: *pre-emptive multitasking*.

Memory had gotten cheap enough by 1995 so that it was possible to have not just one or two but several programs resident in memory at the same time. In an elaborate partnership with the CPU, Windows 95 created the convincing illusion that all of the programs in memory were running at once. This was done by giving each program loaded into memory a short "slice" of the CPU's time. A program would begin running on the CPU, and some number of its machine instructions would execute. However, after a set period of time (usually a small fraction of a second) Windows 95 would "pre-empt" that first program and give control of the CPU to the second program on the list. That program would execute instructions for a few milliseconds until it too was pre-empted. Windows 95 would go down the list, letting each program run for a little while. When it reached the bottom of the list, it would start again at the top and continue running through the list, round-robin fashion, letting each program run for a little while. The 32-bit CPUs of the era were fast enough so that a user sitting in front of the display would think that all the programs were running simultaneously.

The metaphor in Figure 3.5 may make this clearer. Imagine a rotary switch, in which a rotor turns continuously and touches each of several contacts in sequence, once per revolution. Each time it touches the contact for one of the programs, that program is allowed to run. When the rotor moves to the next contact, the previous program stops in its tracks, and the next program gets a little time to run.

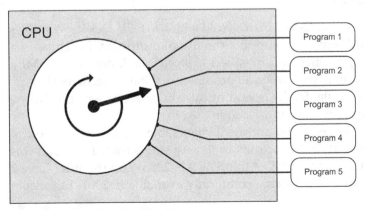

Figure 3.5: The idea of multitasking

The operating system can define a priority for each program on the list so that some get more time to run than others. High-priority tasks get more clock cycles to execute, whereas low-priority get fewer.

Promotion to Kernel

Much was made of Windows 95's ability to multitask, but in 1995 few people had heard of a Unix-like operating system called Linux, which a young Finn named Linux Torvalds had written almost as a lark and released in 1991.

That first release of Linux ran in text mode and did not have the elaborate graphical user interface that Windows 95 did, but it could handle multitasking and had a much more powerful structure internally. The core of Linux was a block of code called the *kernel*, which took full advantage of IA-32 protected mode. The Linux kernel was entirely separate from the user interface, and it was protected from damage due to malfunctioning programs elsewhere in the system. System memory was tagged as either *kernel space* or *user space*, and nothing running in user space could write to (nor generally read from) anything stored in kernel space. Communication between kernel space and user space was handled through strictly controlled system calls. (More on this later in the book.)

Direct access to physical hardware, including memory, video, and peripherals, was limited to software running in kernel space. Programs wanting to make use of system peripherals could get access only through kernel-mode device drivers.

Microsoft released its own Unix-inspired operating system in 1993. Windows NT had an internal structure a great deal like Linux, with kernel and device drivers running in kernel space and everything else running in user space. This basic design is still in use, for both Linux and Windows NT's successors from Windows 2000 to today's Windows 11. The general design for true protected-mode operating systems is shown schematically in Figure 3.6.

The Core Explosion

In the early 2000s, desktop PCs began to be sold with two CPU sockets. Windows 2000/XP/Vista and Linux both support the use of multiple CPU chips in a single system, through a mechanism called *symmetric multiprocessing* (SMP). Multiprocessing is "symmetric" when all processors are the same. In most cases, when two CPUs are available, the operating system runs its own code in one CPU, and user-mode applications are run in the other.

As technology improved, Intel and AMD were able to place two identical but entirely independent code execution units on a single chip. The result was the first dual-core CPUs, the AMD Athlon 64 X2 (2005) and the Intel Core 2 Duo (2006). Four-core CPUs became commonly available in 2007. Eight-core

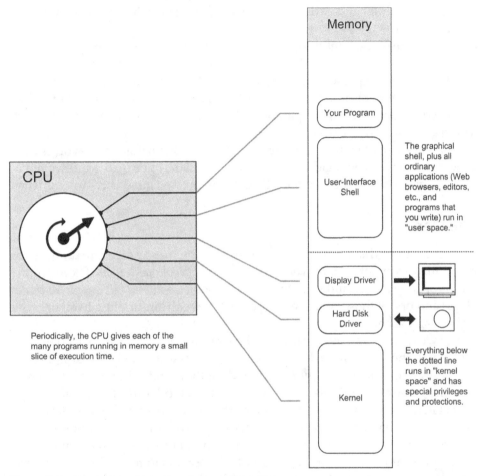

Figure 3.6: A mature protected-mode operating system

CPUs arrived in 2014, with the Haswell microarchitecture. In 2016, the i7-6950X entered the industry with 10 cores and the new Broadwell microarchitecture.

It's important to remember that *performance is not all about cores* but about processor throughput and to some extent cache. (More on cache later.) At this writing (2023) most business desktops have either four or eight cores. That's more than enough compute power for conventional word processors, spreadsheets, and web browsers.

What large numbers of cores mostly enable is the processing of many relatively simple things *in parallel*. In an Internet server farm, many server machines each having many many cores are doggedly handing out web pages to hordes of Internet users. Handing out a web page is not compute-intensive. The server receives the request, finds the HTML document and its components, and shoves them out through the port where the request came in. This is a computational specialty, and Intel and AMD are now designing specialty multicore CPUs to serve that market.

And oh, the cores. Intel shipped a 56-core CPU in 2022. Each core can run two threads, for a total of 112. AMD's Epyc Milan 7763 chip shipped a year earlier and has 64 cores capable of running a total of 128 threads.

Want one on your desk? It'll only cost you. . .$7,900. For the chip. But unless you need to run 128 things in parallel at top speed, it won't do you much good. These are data-center chips.

That microarchitecture machinery in the basement changes and evolves over time. There have been quad-core systems since 2007, but a quad-core system in 2022 is a *whole* lot faster and more efficient than the first quad-core systems were.

The Plan

I can sum all of this up by borrowing one of the most potent metaphors for computing ever uttered: *the computer is a box that follows a plan.* These are the words of Ted Nelson, author of the uncanny book *Computer Lib/Dream Machines* (1974) and one of those very rare people who have the infuriating habit of being right nearly all of the time.

You write the plan. The computer follows it by passing the instructions, byte by byte, to the CPU. At the bottom of it, the process is a hellishly complicated electrical chain reaction involving hundreds of thousands of switches composed of many hundreds of thousands, millions, or even billions of transistors. That part of it, however, is hidden from you so that you don't have to worry about it. Once you tell that mountain of transistors what to do, they'll know how to do it.

This plan, this list of machine instructions in memory, is your assembly language program. The secondary point of this book is to teach you to correctly arrange machine instructions in memory for the use of the CPU. The primary point of this book is to teach you to understand how the machine follows your programs to do the work you need it to do.

With any luck at all, by now you'll have a reasonable conceptual understanding of both what computers are and what they do. It's time to start looking more closely at the nature of the operations that machine instructions direct the CPU to perform. For the most part, as with everything in computing, this is about memory, both the pedestrian memory out on the motherboard and those emperors of remembrance, the CPU registers.

Location, Location, Location

Registers, Memory Addressing, and Knowing Where Things Are

I wrote this book in large part because I could not find a beginning text on assembly language that I respected in the least. Nearly all books on assembly start by introducing the concept of an instruction set and then begin describing machine instructions, one by one. This is moronic, and the authors of such books should be spanked. Hard. *Even if you've learned every single instruction in an instruction set, you haven't learned assembly language.*

You haven't even come close.

The naïve objection that a CPU exists to execute machine instructions can be disposed of pretty easily: it executes machine instructions once it has them in its electronic hands. The *real* job of a CPU, and the real challenge of assembly language, lies in locating the required instructions and data in memory. Any idiot can learn machine instructions. *The skill of assembly language consists of a deep comprehension of memory addressing.* Everything else is details—and easy details, at that.

The Joy of Memory Models

Memory addressing is a difficult business, made much more difficult by the fact that there are a fair number of different ways to address memory in the

Intel/AMD CPU family. Each of these ways is called a *memory model*. There are three major memory models that you can use with the more recent members of the Intel family, and a number of minor variations on those three, especially the one in the middle.

In programming for modern, 64-bit Linux, you're pretty much limited to one memory model, and once you understand memory addressing a little better, you'll be *very* glad of it. However, I'm going to describe all three in some detail here, even though the older two of the trio have become museum pieces. Don't skip over the discussion of those museum pieces. In the same way that studying fossils to learn how various living things evolved over time will give you a better understanding of living things as they exist today, knowing a little about older Intel memory models will give you a more intuitive understanding of the one memory model that you're likely to *use*.

The oldest and now ancient memory model is called *real mode flat model*. It's thoroughly fossilized but relatively straightforward. The elderly (and now retired) memory model is called a *real-mode segmented model*. It may be the most hateful thing you ever learn in *any* kind of programming, assembly or otherwise. (If you're just starting out in 2023, you will almost certainly be spared from having to learn it.) DOS programming at its peak used the real-mode segmented model, and much Pepto Bismol was sold as a result. The newest memory model is called a *protected-mode flat model*, which comes in two flavors: 32-bit and 64-bit. It's the memory model behind modern operating systems such as Windows 2000/XP/Vista/7/8/10/11 and Linux. Note that protected mode flat model is available *only* on the 386 and newer CPUs that support the IA-32 or x64 architecture. The 8086, 8088, and 80286 do not support it. Windows 9x falls somewhere between models, and I doubt anybody except the people at Microsoft really ever understood all the kinks in the ways it addressed memory—and maybe not even them. Mercifully, if not yet a fossil, it is certainly dead and in its grave.

I have a strategy in this book, and before we dive in, I'll lay it out: I will begin by explaining how memory addressing works under the real mode flat model, which was available under DOS. It's amazingly easy to learn. I will discuss the real-mode segmented model to some extent because you will keep stubbing your toe on it here and there and need to understand it, even if you never write a single line of code for it. Real work done today and going forward lies in 64-bit "long mode," for Windows, Linux, or any true 64-bit protected-mode operating system. The model itself is also amazingly easy to learn—the hard part is trying to think like a C compiler while your code calls into the libraries that support it, which has little or nothing to do with the memory model itself. Key to the whole business is this: *real mode flat model is very much like protected-mode flat model in miniature.*

There is a big flat model and a little flat model. If you grasp the real mode flat model, you will have no trouble with protected-mode flat model. That monkey in the middle is just the dues you have to pay to consider yourself a real master of memory addressing.

So let's go see how this crazy stuff works.

16 Bits'll Buy You 64 KB

In 1974, the year I graduated from college, Intel introduced the 8080 CPU and basically invented microcomputing. (Yes, I'm an old guy, but I've been blessed with a sense of history—by virtue of having lived through quite a bit of it.) The 8080 was a white-hot little item at the time. I had one that ran at 1 MHz, and it was a pretty effective word processor, which is mostly what I did with it.

The 8080 was an 8-bit CPU, meaning that it processed 8 bits of information at a time. However, it had 16 address lines coming out of it. The "bitness" of a CPU—how many bits wide its general-purpose registers are—is important, but to my view the far more important measure of a CPU's effectiveness is how many address lines it can muster in one operation. In 1974, 16 address lines was aggressive, because memory was *extremely* expensive, and most machines had 4K or 8 KB bytes (remember, that means 4,000 or 8,000 bytes) at very most—and some had a lot less.

Sixteen address lines will address 64 KB bytes. If you count in binary (which computers always do) and limit yourself to 16 binary columns, you can count from 0 to 65,535. (The colloquial "64 KB64 KB" is shorthand for the number 66,536.) This means that every one of 65,536 separate memory locations can have its own unique address, from 0 up to 65,535.

The 8080 memory-addressing scheme was very simple: you put a 16-bit address out on the address lines, and you got back the 8-bit value that was stored at that address. Note that there is *no* necessary relation between the number of address lines in a memory system and the size of the data stored at each memory location! The 8080 stored 8 bits at each location, but it could have stored 16 or even 32 bits at each location and still had 16 memory address lines.

By far and away, the operating system most used with the 8080 was CP/M-80. CP/M-80 was a little unusual in that it existed at the *top* of installed memory—sometimes so that it could be contained in ROM, but mostly just to get it out of the way and allow a consistent memory starting point for *transient programs*—those that (unlike the operating system) were loaded into memory and run only when needed. When CP/M-80 read a program in from disk to run it, it would load the program into low memory, at address 0100H—that is, 256 bytes from the very bottom of memory. The first 256 bytes of memory were called the *program segment prefix* (PSP) and contained various odd bits of information as well as a general-purpose memory buffer for the program's disk input/output (I/O). But the executable code itself did not begin until address 0100H.

I've drawn the 8080 and CP/M-80 memory model in Figure 4.1.

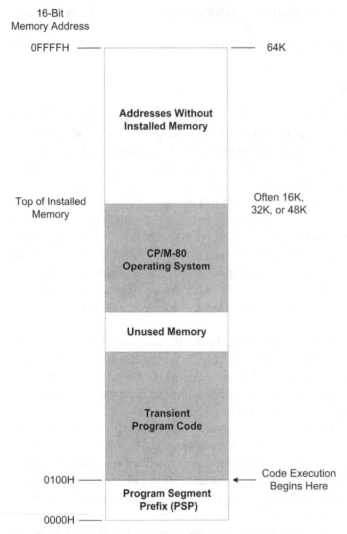

16-Bit
Memory Address

0FFFFH ———— 64K

Addresses Without
Installed Memory

Top of Installed   Often 16K,
Memory   32K, or 48K

CP/M-80
Operating System

Unused Memory

Transient
Program Code

0100H ————   ← Code Execution
                              Begins Here
Program Segment
Prefix (PSP)

0000H ————

Figure 4.1: The 8080 memory model

The 8080's memory model as used with CP/M-80 was simple, and people used it a lot. So, when Intel created its first 16-bit CPU, the 8086, it wanted to make it easy for people to translate older CP/M-80 software from the 8080 to the 8086—what we call *porting*. One way to do this was to make sure that a 16-bit addressing system such as that of the 8080 still worked. So, even though the 8086 could address 16 times as much memory as the 8080 (16 × 64 KB64 KB = 1 MB), Intel set up the 8086 so that a program could take some 64 KB byte segment within that megabyte of memory and run entirely inside it, just as though it were the smaller 8080 memory system.

This was done by the use of *segment registers*—which are basically memory pointers located in CPU registers that point to a place in memory where things begin, whether this be data storage, code execution, or anything else. I'll have more to say about segment registers very shortly. For now, it's enough to think of them as pointers indicating where, within the 8086's megabyte of memory, a program ported from the 8080 world would begin. See Figure 4.2.

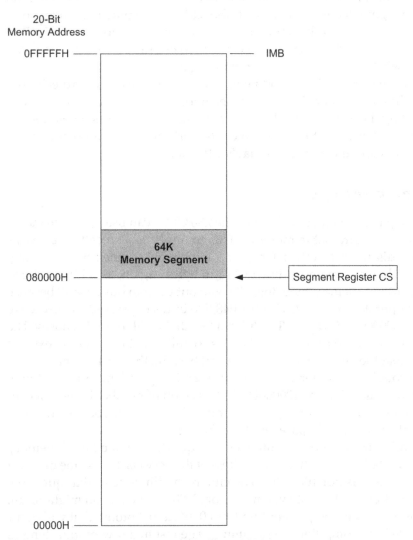

Figure 4.2: The 8080 memory model inside an 8086 memory system

When speaking of the 8086 and 8088, there are four segment registers to consider—and again, we'll be dealing with them in detail soon. But for the purposes of Figure 4.2, consider the register called CS—which stands for *code segment*. Again, it's a pointer pointing to a location within the 8086's megabyte of memory. This location acts as the starting point for a 64 KB region of memory, within which a quickly converted CP/M-80 program could run very happily.

This was very wise short-term thinking—and catastrophically bad long-term thinking. Any number of CP/M-80 programs were converted to the 8086 within a couple of years. The problems began in earnest when programmers attempted to create new programs from scratch that had never seen the 8080 and had no need for the segmented memory model. Too bad—the segmented model dominated the architecture of the 8086. Programs that needed more than 64 KB of memory at a time had to use memory in 64 KB chunks, switching between chunks by switching values into and out of segment registers.

This was a nightmare. The good news is that no one except retrotech hobbyists ever has to use it again. There is one good reason to learn it, however: Understanding the way real-mode segmented memory addressing works will help you understand how today's flat models work, and in the process you will come to understand the nature of today's CPUs a lot better.

The Nature of a Megabyte

When running in segmented real mode, the x86 CPUs can use up to one megabyte of directly addressable memory. This memory is also called *real mode memory*. As I discussed briefly in Chapter 3, a megabyte of memory is actually not 1 million bytes of memory, but 1,048,576 bytes. Again, as with the shorthand term "64 KB," a megabyte doesn't come out even in our base 10 because computers operate on base 2. Those 1,048,576 bytes expressed in base 2 are 100000000000000000000B bytes. That's 2^{20}, a fact that we'll return to shortly. The printed number 100000000000000000000B is so bulky that it's better to express it in the compatible (and much more compact) base 16, the hexadecimal system we went through in Chapter 2. The quantity 2^{20} is equivalent to 16^5 and may be written in hexadecimal as 100000H. (If the notion of number bases still confounds you, I recommend another trip through Chapter 2, if you haven't been through it already, or, perhaps, even if you have.)

Now, here's a tricky and absolutely critical question: in a bank of memory containing 100000H bytes, what's the address of the very last byte in the memory bank? The answer is not 100000H. The clue is the flip side to that question: what's the address of the first byte in memory? That answer, you might recall, is 0. Computers always begin counting from 0. It's a dichotomy that will occur again and again in computer programming. The last in a row of four items is item 3, because the first item in a row of four is item number 0. Count: 0, 1, 2, 3.

The address of a byte in a memory bank is just the number of that byte *starting from zero*. This means the last, or highest, address in a memory bank containing 1 megabyte is 100000H minus one, or 0FFFFFH. (The initial zero, while not mathematically necessary, is there for the convenience of your assembler and helps keep the assembler program from getting confused. Get in the habit of using an initial zero on any hex number beginning with the hex digits A through F.)

The addresses in a megabyte of memory, then, run from 00000H to 0FFFFFH. In binary notation, that is equivalent to the range of 00000000000000000000B to 11111111111111111111B. That's a lot of bits—20, to be exact. If you look back to Figure 3-3 in Chapter 3, you'll see that a megabyte memory bank has 20 address lines. One of those 20 address bits is routed to each of those 20 address lines so that any address expressed as 20 bits will identify one and only one of the 1,048,576 bytes contained in the memory bank.

That's what a megabyte of memory is: some arrangement of memory chips within the computer, connected by an address bus of 20 lines. A 20-bit address is fed to those 20 address lines to identify 1 byte out of the megabyte.

Backward Compatibility and Virtual 86 Mode

Modern CPUs can address hugely more memory than this, and I'll explain how shortly. With the original 8086 and 8088 CPUs, the 20 address lines and 1 megabyte of memory was literally all they had. The 386 and later Intel 32-bit CPUs could address 4 gigabytes of memory without carving it up into smaller segments. When a 32-bit CPU is operating in protected mode flat model, a segment *is* 4 gigabytes—so one segment is, for the most part, plenty, and more can be had if 8, 16, or 64 GB of memory is installed in your system. With x64 long mode, well, your one segment can be as long as you want it to be. How long that is may surprise you. We'll come back to that when the history lesson is over.

However, a huge pile of DOS software written to make use of segments was everywhere around and had to be dealt with. So, to maintain *backward compatibility* with the ancient 8086 and 8088, newer CPUs were given the power to limit themselves to what the older chips could address and execute. When a Pentium-class or better CPU needs to run software written for the real-mode segmented model, it pulls a neat trick that, temporarily, makes it *become* an 8086. This was called *virtual-86 mode*, and it provided excellent backward compatibility for DOS software.

When you launch an MS-DOS window or "DOS box" under Windows NT and later Windows versions, you're using virtual-86 mode to create what amounts to a little real-mode island inside the Windows protected mode memory system. It was the only good way to keep that backward compatibility, for reasons you will understand fairly soon.

16-Bit Blinders

In the real-mode segmented model, an x86 CPU can "see" a full megabyte of memory. That is, the CPU chips set themselves up so that they can use 20 of their 32 address pins and can pass a 20-bit address to the memory system. From that perspective, it seems pretty simple and straightforward. However, the bulk of the trouble you may have in understanding the real-mode segmented model stems from this fact: Whereas those CPUs can see a full megabyte of memory, they are constrained to look at that megabyte through 16-bit blinders.

The blinders metaphor is closer to literal than you might think. Look at Figure 4.3. The long rectangle represents the megabyte of memory that the CPU can address in the real-mode segmented model. The CPU is off to the right. In the middle is a piece of metaphorical cardboard with a slot cut in it. The slot is 1 byte wide and 65,536 bytes long. The CPU can slide that piece of cardboard up and down the full length of its memory system. However, *at any one time*, it can access only 65,536 bytes.

The CPU's view of memory in the real-mode segmented model is peculiar. It is constrained to look at memory in chunks, where no chunk is larger than 65,536 bytes in length—again, what we call "64 KB." Making use of those chunks— that is, knowing which one is currently in use and how to move from one to another—is the real challenge of real-mode segmented model programming. It's time to take a closer look at what they are and how they work.

The Nature of Segments

We've spoken informally of segments so far as chunks of memory within the larger memory space that the CPU can see and use. In the context of the real-mode segmented model, a *segment* is a region of memory that begins on a paragraph boundary and extends for some number of bytes. In the real-mode segmented model, this number is less than or equal to 64 KB (65,536). We've spoken of the number 64 KB before. But paragraphs?

Time out for a lesson in old-time 86-family trivia. A *paragraph* is a measure of memory equal to 16 bytes. It is one of numerous technical terms used to describe various quantities of memory. We've spoken of some of them before, and all of them are even multiples of 1 byte (except for the now-archaic "nybble," which is 4 bits, or half of a byte). Bytes are data atoms, remember; loose memory bits are more like subatomic particles and never exist in the absence of a byte (or more) of memory to contain them. Some of these terms are used more than others, but you should be aware of all of them, which are given in Table 4.1.

Some of these terms, such as 10 byte, occur rarely, and others, such as page, hardly ever occur. The term *paragraph* was never common and for the most part was used only in connection with the places in memory where segments may begin.

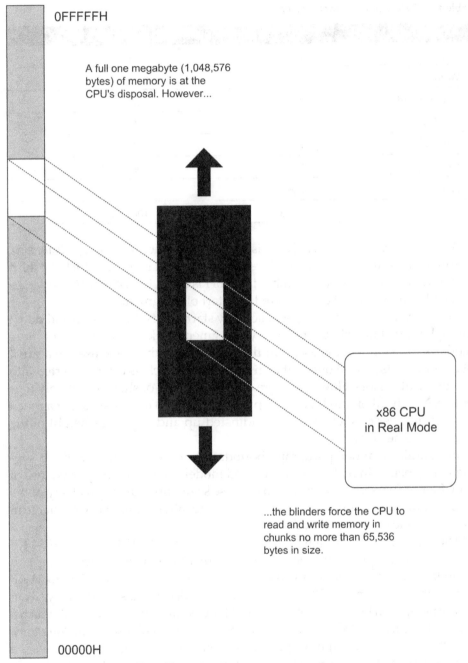

Figure 4.3: Seeing a megabyte through 64 KB blinders

Table 4.1: Collective Terms for Memory

NAME	# OF BYTES IN DECIMAL	# OF BYTES IN HEX
Byte	1	01H
Word	2	02H
Double word	4	04H
Quad word	8	08H
Ten byte	10	0AH
Paragraph	16	10H
Page	256	100H
Segment	65,536	10000H

Any memory address evenly divisible by 16 is called a *paragraph boundary*. The first paragraph boundary is address 0. The second is address 10H, the third address 20H, and so on. (Remember that 10H is equal to decimal 16.) Any paragraph boundary may be considered the start of a segment.

This *doesn't* mean that a segment actually starts every 16 bytes up and down throughout that megabyte of memory. A segment is like a shelf in one of those modern adjustable bookcases. On the back face of the bookcase are a great many little slots spaced one-half inch apart. Shelf brackets can be inserted into any of the little slots. However, there aren't hundreds of shelves, but only four or five. Nearly all of the slots are empty and unused. They exist so that a much smaller number of shelves may be adjusted up and down the height of the bookcase as needed.

In a similar manner, paragraph boundaries are little slots at which a segment may begin. In real-mode segmented model, a program may make use of only four or five segments, but each of those segments may begin at any of the 65,536 paragraph boundaries existing in the megabyte of memory available in the real-mode segmented model.

There's that number again: 65,536—our beloved 64 KB. There are 64 KB different paragraph boundaries where a segment may begin. Each paragraph boundary has a number. As always, the numbers begin from 0 and go to 64 KB minus one; in decimal 65,535, or in hex 0FFFFH. Because a segment may begin at any paragraph boundary, the number of the paragraph boundary at which a segment begins is called the *segment address* of that particular segment. We rarely, in fact, speak of paragraphs or paragraph boundaries at all. When you see the term *segment address* in connection with the real-mode segmented model, keep in mind that each segment address is 16 bytes (one paragraph) further along in memory than the segment address before it. See Figure 4.4. In the figure, each shaded bar is a segment address, and segments begin every 16 bytes. The highest segment address is 0FFFFH, which is 16 bytes from the very top of real mode's one megabyte of memory.

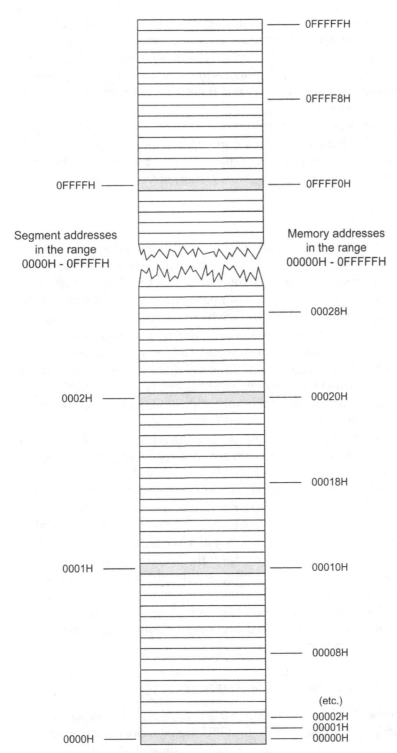

Figure 4.4: Memory addresses versus segment addresses

In summary, segments may begin at any segment address. There are 65,536 segment addresses evenly distributed across real mode's full megabyte of memory, 16 bytes apart. A segment address is more a permission than a compulsion; for all the 64 KB possible segment addresses, only five or six are ever actually used to begin segments at any one time. Think of segment addresses as slots where segments may be placed.

So much for segment addresses; now, what of segments themselves? The most important thing to understand is that a segment may be up to 64 KB bytes in size, but it doesn't *have* to be. A segment may be only 1 byte long, or 256 bytes long, or 21,378 bytes long, or any length at all short of 64 KB bytes.

A Horizon, Not a Place

You define a segment primarily by stating where it begins. What, then, defines how *long* a segment is? Nothing, really—and we get into some very tricky semantics here. A segment is more a *horizon* than a *place*. Once you define where a segment begins, that segment can encompass any location in memory between that starting place and the horizon—which is 65,536 bytes down the line.

Nothing says, of course, that a segment must use all of that memory. In most cases, when a segment is defined at some segment address, a program considers only the next few hundred or perhaps few thousand bytes as part of that segment, unless it's a really world-class program. Most beginners read about segments and think of them as some kind of memory allocation, a protected region of memory with walls on both sides, reserved for some specific use.

This is about as far from true as you can get. In real mode, nothing is protected within a segment, and segments are not reserved for any specific register or access method. Segments can overlap. (People often don't think about or realize this.) In a very real sense, segments don't really exist, *except* as horizons beyond which a certain type of memory reference cannot go. It comes back to that set of 64 KB blinders that the CPU wears, as I drew in Figure 4.3. Think of it this way: *a segment is the location in memory at which the CPU's 64 KB blinders are positioned*. In looking at memory through the blinders, you can see bytes starting at the segment address and going on until the blinders cut you off, 64 KB bytes down the way.

The key to understanding this admittedly metaphysical definition of a segment is knowing how segments are used, and coming to understand that finally requires a detailed discussion of registers.

Making 20-Bit Addresses Out of 16-Bit Registers

A *register*, as I've mentioned informally in earlier chapters, is a memory location *inside* the CPU chip rather than outside the CPU in a memory bank somewhere.

The 8086, 8088 and 80286 are often called 16-bit CPUs because their internal registers are almost all 16 bits in size. The 80386 and its 25 years' worth of successors are called 32-bit CPUs because most of their internal registers are 32 bits in size. Intel's last 32-bit CPU was the Lincroft Atom series, introduced in 2010 and targeted at portable devices. Their last 32-bit desktop CPU was a member of the Pentium 4 family introduced in 2002. The 32-bit era may be worth a close look, but now in 2023 it is well and truly over.

The x64 CPUs are 64 bits in design, with registers that are 64 bits wide. The Intel CPUs have a fair number of registers, and they are an interesting crew indeed.

Registers do many jobs, but perhaps their most important single job is holding addresses of important locations in memory. If you'll recall, the 8086 and 8088 have 20 address pins, and their megabyte of memory (which is the real-mode segmented memory we're talking about) requires addresses 20 bits in size.

How do you put a 20-bit memory address in a 16-bit register?

Easy. You don't.

You put a 20-bit address in *two* 16-bit registers.

What happens is this: All memory locations in real mode's megabyte of memory have not one address but *two*. Every byte in memory is assumed to reside in a segment. A byte's complete address, then, consists of the address of its segment, along with the distance of the byte from the start of that segment. The address of the segment is (as we said before) the byte's *segment address*. The byte's distance from the start of the segment is the byte's *offset address*. Both addresses must be specified to completely describe any single byte's location within the full megabyte of real-mode memory. When written out, the segment address comes first, followed by the offset address. The two are separated with a colon. Segment:offset addresses are always written in hexadecimal.

I've drawn Figure 4.5 to help make this a little clearer. A byte of data we'll call MyByte exists in memory at the location marked. Its address is given as 0001:0019. This means that MyByte falls within segment 0001H and is located 0019H bytes from the start of that segment. Note that it is a convention that when two numbers are used to specify an address with a colon between them, you do *not* end each of the two numbers with an *H* for hexadecimal.

The universe is perverse, however, and clever eyes will notice that MyByte can have two other perfectly legal addresses: 0:0029 and 0002:0009. How so? Keep in mind that a segment may start every 16 bytes throughout the full megabyte of real memory. A segment, once begun, embraces all bytes from its origin to 65,535 bytes further up in memory. There's nothing wrong with segments overlapping, and in Figure 4.5 we have three overlapping segments. MyByte is 29H bytes into the first segment, which begins at segment address 0000H. MyByte is 19H bytes into the second segment, which begins at segment address 0001H. It's not that MyByte is in two or three places at once. It's in only one place, but that one place may be described in any of three ways.

MyByte could have
any of three possible
addresses:
0000 : 0029
0001 : 0019
0002 : 0009

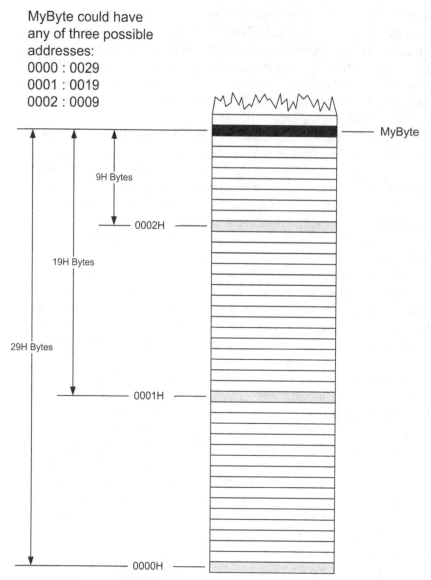

MyByte

9H Bytes

0002H

19H Bytes

29H Bytes

0001H

0000H

Figure 4.5: Segments and offsets

It's a little like Chicago's street-numbering system. Howard Street is 76 blocks north of Chicago's "origin," Madison Street. Howard Street is, however, only 4 blocks north of Touhy Avenue. You can describe Howard Street's location relative to either Madison Street or Touhy Avenue, depending on what you want to do.

An arbitrary byte somewhere in the middle of segmented real mode's mega-byte of memory may fall within literally thousands of different segments. Which segment the byte is *actually* in is strictly a matter of convention.

In summary, to express a 20-bit address in two 16-bit registers is to put the segment address into one 16-bit register and the offset address into another 16-bit register. The two registers taken together identify 1 byte among all 1,048,576 bytes in real mode's megabyte of memory.

Is this awkward? You have *no* idea. But it was the best we could do for a good many years.

Segment Registers

Think of the segment address as the starting position of real mode's 64 KB blinders. Typically, you would move the blinders to encompass the location where you want to work and then leave the blinders in one place while moving around within their 64 KB limits.

This is exactly how registers tend to be used in real mode segmented model assembly language. The 8086, 8088 and 80286 have exactly four segment registers specifically designated as holders of segment addresses. The 386 and later CPUs have two more that can also be used in real mode. (You need to be aware of the CPU model you're running on if you intend to use the two additional segment registers, because the older CPUs don't have them.) Each segment register is a 16-bit memory location existing within the CPU chip itself. No matter what the CPU is doing, if it's addressing some location in memory, the segment address of that location is present in one of the six segment registers.

The segment registers have names that reflect their general functions: CS, DS, SS, ES, FS, and GS. FS and GS exist only in the 386 and later Intel x86 32-bit CPUs—but are still 16 bits in size. *All segment registers are 16 bits in size, irrespective of the CPU.* This is true even of the modern 64-bit Intel CPUs, though there's a catch—more on that shortly.

- *CS stands for code segment.* Machine instructions exist at some offset into a code segment. The segment address of the code segment of the currently executing instruction is contained in CS.

- *DS stands for data segment.* Variables and other data exist at some offset into a data segment. There may be many data segments, but the CPU may use only one at a time, by placing the segment address of that segment in register DS.

- *SS stands for stack segment.* The *stack* is a very important component of the CPU used for temporary storage of data and addresses. I explain how the stack works a little later; for now simply understand that, like everything else within real mode's megabyte of memory, the stack has a segment address, which is contained in SS.

- *ES stands for extra segment.* The extra segment is exactly that: a spare segment that may be used for specifying a location in memory.

- *FS and GS are clones of ES.* They are both additional "extra" segments with no specific job or specialty. Their names come from the fact that they were created after ES. (Think, E, F, G.) Don't forget that they exist *only* in the 386 and later Intel CPUs.

Segment Registers and x64

Now, there's something odd about segment registers in the x64 architecture: *They're not used in application programs.* At all. Think about it: 64 bits can identify 2^{64} bytes of memory. In decimal scientific notation, that's 1.8×10^{19}. Out loud we'd say "18 exabytes." If that word is new to you, you're not alone. An *exabyte* is a billion gigabytes, i.e., a billion billion bytes. My none-too-new everyday work machine contains 16 gigabytes of RAM. Most new-build desktops today can take 64 GB, and that's about all. Even gamers understand that more than 64 GB of RAM won't improve their game play.

The whole point of segment registers was to allow 20 bits of address space to be addressed by two 16-bit registers. When one single 64-bit register can address almost as many bytes of memory as there are stars in the observable universe (I'm not exaggerating about that!), segment registers become useless, at least in application programming. Operating systems use two of them for purposes that are way beyond the scope of this book to explain. The others are there but may cause trouble if you try to use them. In short, when you move to x64 long mode, the familiar 16-bit segment registers simply go away.

So. . .do Intel's x64 CPUs have 64 address lines? No. There isn't even machinery inside the chips to support more than 48 bits of address on older x64 CPUs. (Intel raised this value to 52 bits for certain high-end CPUs a few years ago.) Why even that many? Looking ahead to memory technologies we can't yet imagine is part of it. The issue is not that simple, and there's not enough room for me to take it up in more detail in this book. But this is the money quote:

From a 64-bit perspective, segment registers are now history.

General-Purpose Registers

All Intel CPUs have a crew of generalist registers to do the bulk of the work of assembly language computing. These *general-purpose registers* hold values for arithmetic and logic manipulation, for bit-shifting (more on this later), and many other things, including holding memory addresses. They are truly the craftsperson's pockets inside the CPU.

But now we come to one of the biggest and most obvious differences between the different eons of Intel microcomputing: the width of the general-purpose registers. The primordial 8080 had 8-bit registers. The 16-bit x86 CPUs (the 8086, 8088, 80186, and 80286) had 16-bit registers. The 32-bit x86 CPUs starting with the 386 have 32-bit registers. And in the x64 world, CPUs have 14 general-purpose 64-bit registers. Two more registers, the stack pointer and base pointer registers, are specialists and exist in 16-bit, 32-bit, and 64-bit architectures. The stack pointer always points to the top of the stack. (I'll have much more to say about the stack in later chapters.) The base pointer is a bit like a bookmark and used to access data "further down" on the stack; again, we'll get to the stack eventually, and I'll explain this in more depth.

Like the segment registers, the x64 general-purpose registers are memory locations existing inside the CPU chip itself. The general-purpose registers really are generalists in that all of them share a large suite of capabilities. However, some of the general-purpose registers also have what I call a "hidden agenda:" a task or set of tasks that only they can perform. I'll explain all these hidden agendas as I go—keeping in mind that some of the hidden agendas are actually limitations of the older 16-bit CPUs. The newer 32-bit and 64-bit general-purpose registers are much more, well, *general*.

In our current 64-bit world, the general-purpose registers fall into four general classes: the 16-bit general-purpose registers, the 32-bit extended general-purpose registers, the 64-bit general-purpose registers, and the 8-bit register halves. These four classes do not represent four entirely distinct sets of registers at all. The 8-bit, 16-bit, and 32-bit registers are actually names of regions *inside* the 64-bit registers. Register growth in the vintage x86 CPU family came about by *extending* registers existing in older CPUs. Adding a room to your house doesn't make it two houses—just one bigger house. And so it has been with the x86 registers.

There are eight 16-bit general-purpose registers: AX, BX, CX, DX, BP, SI, DI, and SP. (SP and BP are a little less general than the others, but we'll get to that.) These all existed in the 8086, 8088, 80186, and 80286 CPUs. They are all 16 bits in size, and you can place any value in them that may be expressed in 16 bits or fewer. When Intel expanded the x86 architecture to 32 bits in 1985, it doubled the size of all eight registers and gave them new names by prefixing an E in front of each register name, resulting in EAX, EBX, ECX, EDX, EBP, ESI, EDI, and ESP.

Things changed once more in 2003, when Intel began adopting AMD's 64-bit backward-compatible x64 architecture. Again, Intel had its own 64-bit architecture by then, IA-64 Itanium, but Itanium had some subtle but important technical difficulties in its microarchitecture that I can't describe in an introductory book like this. Intel then swallowed its pride and did the smart thing by adopting AMD's successful 64-bit architecture. Alas, the 8080 stands alone. Backward compatibility can extend only so far back before it becomes more of a bug than a feature.

The x64 architecture expanded the general-purpose register lineup from 32 to 64 bits. This time the prefix became *R*. So now instead of the 32-bit EAX, we have RAX, and so on down the list of 32-bit registers. Intel also added eight new 64-bit registers that had never been part of their architecture before. Their names are mostly numbers: R8 through R15.

64-bit x64 registers are in truth registers inside registers. Like a lot of things, this shows better than it tells. Take a look at Figure 4.6, which lays out how this works with x64 registers RAX and R8.

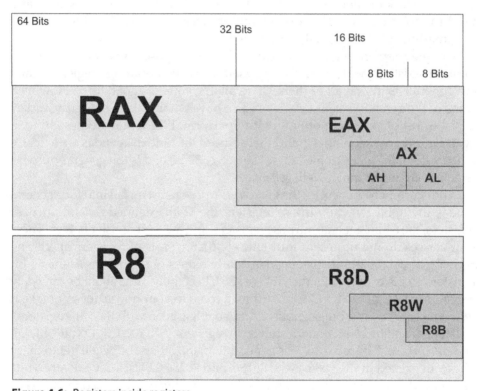

Figure 4.6: Registers inside registers

RAX contains EAX, AX, AH, and AL. EAX contains AX, AH, and AL. AX contains AH and AL. The names "RAX," "EAX," "AX," "AH," and "AL" are all valid in x64. You can use all of these names in your assembly language programs to access the 64 bits contained in RAX or certain smaller parts of it. Want to access the lower 32 bits of RAX? Use the name EAX. Want to access the lowest 16 bits of RAX? Use AX.

Register Halves

The same is true for the four general-purpose registers RAX, RBX, RCX, and RDX, but there's an additional twist: the low 16 bits are themselves divided into two named 8-bit halves. So, what we have are register names on four levels. The 16-bit registers AX, BX, CX, and DX are present as the lower 16-bit portions of EAX, EBX, ECX, and EDX, which in turn are the lower 32-bit portions of RAX, RBX, RCX, and RDX.

But AX, BX, CX, and DX are themselves divided into 8-bit halves, and assemblers recognize special names for the two halves. The A, B, C, and D are retained, but instead of the X, a half is specified with an H (for high half) or an L (for low half). Each register half is 1 byte (8 bits) in size. Thus, making up 16-bit register AX, you have byte-sized register halves AH and AL; within BX there is BH and BL, and so on.

The new x64 registers R8-R15 can be addressed as 64 bits, 32 bits, 16 bits, and 8 bits. However, the AH/AL scheme for the low 16 bits is a trick reserved for *only* RAX-RDX. The naming scheme for the R registers provides a mnemonic: D for double word, W for word, and B for byte. For example, if you want to deal with the lowest 8 bits of R8, you use the name R8B.

Don't make the beginner's mistake of assuming that R8, R8D, R8W, and R8B are four separate and independent registers! A better metaphor is to think of the register names as country/state/county/city. A city is a small portion of a county, which is a small portion of a state, and so on. If you write a value into R8B, you change the value stored in R8, R8D, and R8W.

Again, this can best be shown in a diagram. See Figure 4.7, which is an expansion of Figure 4.6 to include all of x64's general-purpose registers. These registers are a low-half kind of thing. Apart from AH, BH, CH, and DH, there is no name for the high half of any general-purpose register.

Of course, it's possible to access the high half of any register by using more than one machine instruction. You just can't do it by name in one swoop, unless you're dealing with the four 8-bit exceptions mentioned above.

Being able to treat the AX, BX, CX, and DX registers as 8-bit halves can be extremely handy in situations where you're manipulating a lot of 8-bit quantities. Each register half can be considered a separate register, leaving you twice the number of places to put things while your program works. As you'll see later, finding a place to stick a value in a pinch is one of the great challenges facing assembly-language programmers.

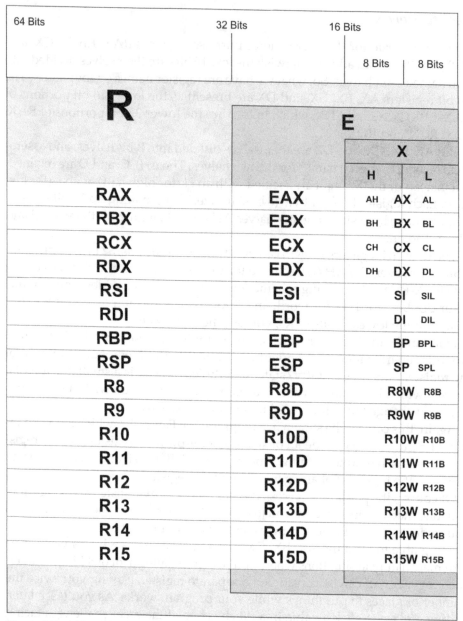

Figure 4.7: 8-bit, 16-bit, 32-bit, and 64-bit registers

The Instruction Pointer

Yet another type of register lives inside all Intel CPUs, including x64. The instruction pointer IP is in a class by itself. In 16-bit modes, the instruction pointer is called simply IP. In 32-bit modes, it's EIP. In x64, it's RIP. In all cases, however, this register is not directly accessible by the assembly programmer. Instead, it is indirectly accessed when performing a jump, conditional branch, procedure call, or interrupt. In general discussion not limited to a particular mode, I'll follow convention and call it IP.

In radical contrast to the gang of true general-purpose registers, IP is a specialist *par excellence*—more of a specialist than even the segment registers. It can do only one thing: it contains the offset address of the next machine instruction to be executed in the current code segment.

A *code segment* is an area of memory where machine instructions are stored. Depending on the memory model you're using, there may be many code segments in a program, or (most of the time) only one. The *current code segment* is that code segment whose segment address is currently stored in code segment register CS. At any given time, the machine instruction currently being executed exists within the current code segment. In the real-mode segmented model, the value in CS can change frequently. In the flat models (which includes x64 long mode), the value in CS (almost) never changes—and certainly never changes at the behest of an application program. Managing code segments and the instruction pointer is now the job of the operating system. This is especially true in x64 long mode, where there's only one segment that contains *everything*, and segment registers have so little to do in user space that they're basically invisible to user-space programs like those you write.

While executing a program, the CPU uses IP to keep track of where it is in the current code segment. Each time an instruction is executed, IP is *incremented* by some number of bytes. The number of bytes is the size of the instruction just executed. The net result is to bump IP further into memory so that it points to the start of the *next* instruction to be executed. Instructions come in different sizes, ranging typically from 1 to 15 bytes. The CPU knows the size of each instruction it executes. It's careful to increment IP by just the right number of bytes so that it does in fact end up pointing to the start of the next instruction and not merely into the middle of the last instruction or the middle of some other instruction entirely.

If IP contains the offset address of the next machine instruction, where is the segment address? The segment address is kept in the code segment register CS. Together, CS and IP contain the full address of the next machine instruction to be executed.

The nature of this address depends on what CPU you're using and what memory model you're using it for. In the 8086, 8088 and (usually) 80286, IP is 16 bits in size. In the 386 and later CPUs, IP (like all the other registers except the segment registers) graduates to 32 bits in size and becomes EIP.

In the real-mode segmented model, CS and IP working together give you a 20-bit address pointing to one of the 1,048,576 bytes in real-mode memory. In flat models (more on this shortly), CS is set by the operating system and held constant. IP does all the instruction pointing that you the programmer have to deal with. In the 16-bit flat model (real-mode flat model), this means IP can follow instruction execution all across a full 64 KB segment of memory. The 32-bit flat model does far more than double that; 32 bits can represent 4,294,967,290 different memory addresses. In 64-bit long mode, well, RIP can address as much memory as you could put into the machine in your lifetime and certainly mine. Opinion is divided on whether there will ever be 128-bit CPUs. I don't think so, for reasons I'll mention a little later in this chapter.

IP is notable in being the *only* register that can neither be read nor written to directly. There are tricks that may be used to obtain the current value in IP, but having IP's value is not as useful as you might think, and you won't have to do it very often.

The Flags Register

There is yet another type of register inside the CPU: what we generically call the *flags register*. It is 16 bits in size in the 8086, 8088, and 80286, and its formal name is FLAGS. It is 32 bits in size in the 32-bit CPUs, and its formal name in the 32-bit CPUs is EFLAGS. The RFLAGS register in x64 is 64 bits in size. Just under half of the bits in the RFLAGS register are used as single-bit registers called *flags*. (The rest are undefined.) Each of these individual flags has a name with a two-character abbreviation, such as CF, DF, OF, and so on, and each flag has a very specific meaning within the CPU.

Since a single bit may contain one of only two values, 1 or 0, testing a flag in assembly language is truly a two-way affair: either a flag's value is 1 or it isn't. When the flag's value is 1, we say that the flag is *set*. When the flag's value is 0, we say that the flag is *cleared*.

When your program performs a test, what it tests is one or occasionally two of the single-bit flags in the RFLAGS register. It then takes a separate path of execution depending on the state of the flag or flags. There are separate jump instructions for all the common flags, and a few more for testing specific pairs of flags.

The RFLAGS register is almost never dealt with as a unit unless the flags are being saved onto the stack. We're concentrating on memory addressing at the moment, so for now I'll simply promise to go into flag lore in more detail at more appropriate moments later in the book, when we discuss machine instructions that test the various flags in the RFLAGS register.

Math Coprocessors and Their Registers

Ever since the 32-bit 80486DX CPU, there has been a math coprocessor on the same silicon chip with the general-purpose CPU. In ancient times, the math chip was an entirely separate IC that plugged into its own socket on the motherboard. The x64 CPUs all have integrated math coprocessors, with their own registers and machine instructions. The x64 architecture uses the third generation of math coprocessor, AVX. (The MMX and SSE architectures are the first two generations and came before AVX.)

The question often comes up, *when will we have 128-bit CPUs? The truth is, we already have them*—for the things that count. The one place where 128-bit registers are essential is in advanced math applications, like 3D modeling, video processing, cryptography, data compression, and AI. All modern CPUs incorporating the SSE coprocessor have 128-bit registers for the math coprocessor's use. (The general-purpose CPU cannot use them directly.) And it doesn't stop there. The AVX coprocessor ups the ante to 256 bits. And AVX-512, introduced in 2021, largely for server CPUs, can do its math in 512-bit registers. With 128-, 256-, and 512-bit math registers available for crunching numbers, there's very little point in expanding the GP registers to 128 bits. 64 bits is widely seen as a sort of "sweet spot" for general-purpose computing and should remain so for a very long time.

It's *way* outside the scope of this book to explain how to use SSE, much less AVX. A good beginner's treatment can be found in *Beginning x64 Assembly Programming* by Jo Van Hoey (Apress, 2019). Math coprocessor programming is subtle and complex. I would recommend becoming reasonably fluent in ordinary x64 assembly before diving in on the math side.

The Four Major Assembly Programming Models

I mentioned earlier in this chapter that there are four major programming models available for use on the x64-bit Intel CPUs, though two of them are now considered archaic. The differences between them lie (mostly) in the use of registers to address memory. (And the other differences, especially on the high end, are for the most part hidden from you by the operating system.) In this section, I'm going to summarize the four models for historical reference. Only one of them, x64 long mode, will be treated in detail in the rest of the book.

Real-Mode Flat Model

In real mode, if you recall, the CPU can see only 1 megabyte (1,048,576) of memory. You can access every last one of those million-odd bytes by using the segment:offset register trick shown earlier to form a 20-bit address out of two 16-bit addresses contained in the segment and offset registers. Or...you can be content with 64 KB of memory and not fool with segments at all.

In real-mode flat model, your program and all the data it works on must exist within a single 64 KB block of memory. Sixty-four kilobytes! Pfeh! What could you possibly accomplish in only 64 KB bytes? Well, the first version of WordStar for the IBM PC fit in 64 KB. So did the first three major releases of Turbo Pascal—in fact, the Turbo Pascal program itself occupied a lot less than 64 KB because it compiled its programs into memory. The whole Turbo

Pascal package—compiler, text editor, and some odd tools—came to just over 39K. Thirty-nine kilobytes! You can't even write a letter to your mother with Microsoft Word in that little space these days!

Real-mode flat model is shown diagrammatically in Figure 4.8. There's not much to it. The segment registers are all set to point to the beginning of the 64 KB block of memory you can work with. (The operating system sets them when it loads and runs your program.) They all point to that same place and never change as long as your program is running. That being the case, you can simply forget about them. Poof! No segment registers, no fooling with segments, and none of the ugly complication that comes with them.

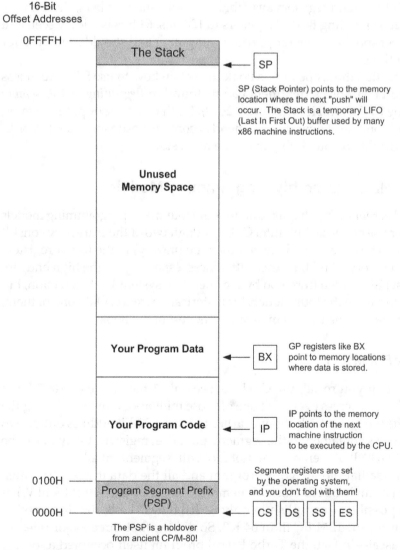

Figure 4.8: Real-mode flat model

Most of the general-purpose registers may contain addresses of locations in memory. You use them in conjunction with machine instructions to bring data in from memory and write it back out again.

At the top of the single segment that your program exists within, you'll see a small region called the *stack*. The stack is a last in, first out (LIFO) storage location with some very special properties and uses. I will explain what the stack is and how it works in considerable detail in a later chapter.

Real-Mode Segmented Model

The first two editions of this book focused entirely on real-mode segmented model, which was the mainstream programming model throughout the MS-DOS era. It's a complicated, ugly system that requires you to remember a lot of little rules and gotchas. I explained segments earlier in this chapter and won't go into a lot of detail here, especially considering how little the real-mode segmented model is used today.

In real-mode segmented model, your program can see the full 1 MB of memory available to the CPU in real mode. It does this by combining a 16-bit segment address with a 16-bit offset address. It doesn't just glom them together into a 32-bit address, however. You need to think back to my discussion of segments earlier in this chapter. A segment address is not really a memory address. A segment address specifies one of the 65,535 slots at which a segment may begin. One of these slots exists every 16 bytes from the bottom of memory to the top. Segment address 0000H specifies the first such slot, at the very first location in memory. Segment address 0001H specifies the next slot, which lies 16 bytes higher in memory. Jumping up-memory another 16 bytes gets you to segment address 0002H, and so on. You can translate a segment address to an actual 20-bit memory address by multiplying it by 16. Segment address 0002H is thus equivalent to memory address 0020H, which is the 32nd byte in memory.

The CPU handles the combination of segments and offsets into a full 20-bit address internally. *Your* job is to tell the CPU where the two different components of that 20-bit address are stored. The customary notation is to separate the segment register and the offset register by a colon. Here's an example:

```
SS : SP
SS : BP
ES : DI
DS : SI
CS : BX
```

Each of these five register combinations specifies a full 20-bit address. ES:DI, for example, specifies the address as the distance in DI from the start of the segment called out in extra segment register ES.

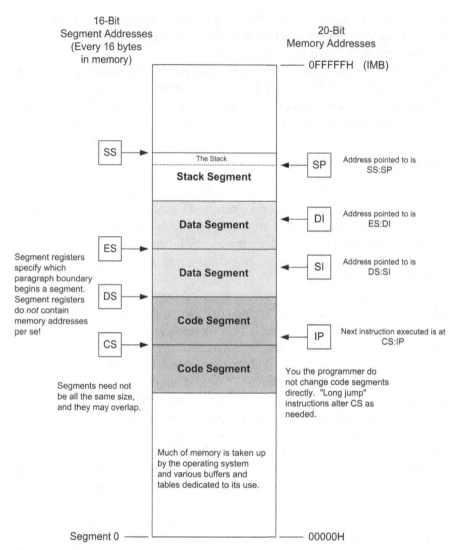

Figure 4.9: The real-mode segmented model

To visually sum up real-mode segmented model, I've drawn a diagram outlining the model in Figure 4.9. In contrast to the real-mode flat model (shown in Figure 4.8), the diagram here shows *all* of memory, not just the one little 64 KB chunk that your real-mode flat model program is allocated when it runs. A program written for real-mode segmented model can see all of real-mode memory.

The diagram shows two code segments and two data segments. In practice, you can have any reasonable number of code and data segments, not just two of each. You can access two data segments at the same time, because you have two segment registers available to do the job: DS and ES. (In the 386 and later processors, you have two additional segment registers, FS and GS.) Each can specify a data segment, and you can move data from one segment to another using any of several machine instructions. However, you have only one code segment register, CS. CS always points to the current code segment, and the next instruction to be executed is pointed to by the IP register. You don't load values directly into CS to change from one code segment to another. Your program can span several code segments, and when a jump instruction (of which there are several kinds) needs to take execution into a different code segment, it changes the value in CS for you.

There is only one stack segment for any single program, specified by the stack segment register SS. The stack pointer register SP points to the memory address (relative to SS, albeit in an upside-down direction) where the next stack operation will take place. The stack will require some considerable explaining, which I'll take up later.

You need to keep in mind that in real mode, there will be pieces of the operating system in memory with your program, along with important system data tables. You can destroy portions of the operating system by careless use of segment registers, which will cause the operating system to crash and take your program with it. This is the danger that prompted Intel to build new features into its 80386 and later CPUs to support a "protected" mode. In protected mode, application programs (that is, the programs that you write, as opposed to the operating system or device drivers) cannot destroy the operating system nor other application programs that happen to be running elsewhere in memory via multitasking. That's what the word *protected* means.

32-Bit Protected Mode Flat Model

Intel's CPUs have implemented a very good protected mode architecture since the 386 first appeared in 1985. However, application programs cannot make use of protected mode all by themselves. The operating system must set up and manage a protected mode before application programs can run within it. MS-DOS couldn't do this, and Microsoft Windows couldn't really do it either until Windows NT first appeared in 1994. Linux, having no real-mode "legacy" issues to deal with, has operated in protected mode since its first appearance in 1992.

Protected-mode assembly language programs may be written for both Linux and Windows releases from NT forward. I exclude Windows 9x for technical reasons. Its memory model is an odd proprietary hybrid of real mode and protected mode and very difficult to completely understand—and now almost entirely irrelevant. Note also that programs written for Windows need not be graphical in nature. The easiest way to program in protected mode under Windows is to create *console applications*, which are text-mode programs that run in a text-mode window called a *console*. The console is controlled through a command line similarly to the one in MS-DOS—with *lots* more available commands. Console applications use protected mode flat models and are fairly straightforward compared to writing Windows or Linux GUI applications, which I will not address in this book.

I've drawn the 32-bit protected mode flat model in Figure 4.10. Your program sees a single block of memory addresses running from zero to a little over 4 gigabytes. Each address is a 32-bit quantity. All of the general-purpose registers are 32 bits in size, so one GP register can point to any location in the full 4 GB address space. The instruction pointer is 32 bits in size as well, so EIP can indicate any machine instruction anywhere in the 4 GB of memory.

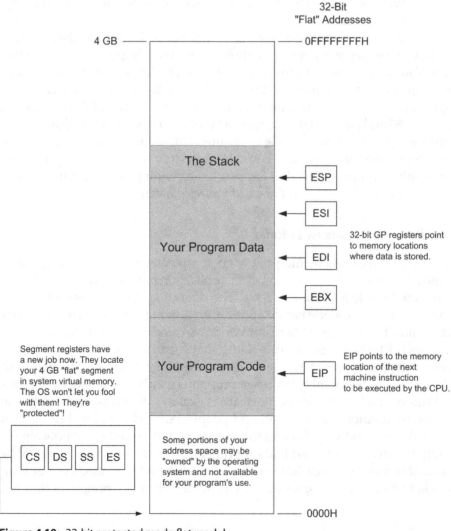

Figure 4.10: 32-bit protected mode flat model

The segment registers still exist, but they work in a radically different way. Not only don't you have to fool with them, you *can't*. The segment registers are now considered part of the operating system, and in almost all cases you can neither read nor change them directly. Their new job is to define where your 4 GB memory space exists in physical or virtual memory. Physical memory may be much larger than 4 GB, and at this writing, 4 GB of memory is not especially expensive. However, a 32-bit register can express only 4,294,967,296 different locations. If you have more than 4 GB of memory in your computer, the operating system must arrange a 4 GB region within memory, and your 32-bit programs are limited to operating in this region. Defining where in your larger memory system this 4 GB region falls is the job of the segment registers, and the operating system keeps them very close to its vest.

I won't say a great deal about virtual memory in this book. It's a system whereby a much larger memory space can be "mapped" onto disk storage, so that even with only 4 GB of physical memory in your machine, the CPU can address a "virtual" memory space billions of bytes larger. Again, this is handled by the operating system, and handled in a way that is almost completely transparent to the software that you write.

It's enough to understand that when your x86 program runs, it receives a 4 GB address space in which to play, and any 32-bit register can potentially address any of those 4 billion memory locations, all by itself. Yes, this is an oversimplification, especially for ordinary Intel-based desktop PCs. Not all of the 4 GB is at your program's disposal, and there are certain parts of the memory space that you can't use or even look at. Unfortunately, the rules are specific to the operating system you're running under, and I can't generalize too far without specifying Linux or Windows NT or some other protected mode OS.

But it's worth taking a look back at Figure 4.8 and comparing the real-mode flat model to the 32-bit protected-mode flat model. The main difference is that in the real-mode flat model, your program owns the full 64 KB of memory that the operating system hands it. In 32-bit protected-mode flat model, you are given a portion of 4 GB of memory as your own, while other portions will still belong to the operating system. Apart from that, the similarities are striking: A general-purpose (GP) register can *by itself* specify any memory location in the full memory address space, and the segment registers are the tools of the operating system and not you the application programmer.

64-Bit Long Mode

The previous summaries are historical context. The fourth programming mode is the one we'll be using for actual code examples in this book.

The x64 architecture defines three general modes: real mode, protected mode, and long mode. Real mode is a compatibility mode allowing the CPU to run older real-mode operating systems and software like DOS and Windows 3.1.

In real mode, the CPU works just like an 8086 or other 16-bit x86 CPU does in real mode and supports both real mode flat model and real mode segmented model. Protected mode is also a compatibility mode and makes the CPU "look like" a 32-bit CPU to software so that x64 CPUs can run Windows 2000/XP/Vista/7/8 and other 32-bit operating systems like older versions of Linux, plus their 32-bit drivers and applications. (Windows 10 and 11 are strictly 64-bit now in new-build 64-bit machines.)

But those are 16-bit and 32-bit compatibility modes included strictly for the sake of legacy software. Long mode is a true 64-bit mode. When the CPU is in long mode, all registers but the segment registers are 64 bits wide, and all machine instructions that act on 64-bit operands are available. There's only one segment, which is as large (for the time being) as you can afford. Everything that's a part of your program, or data on which your program acts, is fully contained within that one truly gigantic segment. X64 long mode is so conceptually simple that I haven't drawn a diagram. It's almost exactly like Figure 4.10, except that there is no 4 GB "ceiling."

Long mode is also a protected mode, and ordinary computing requires an operating system that understands protected mode and does its way-down-deep housework. In long mode, segment registers belong to the operating system, and you don't need to manipulate them nor even be aware of them, especially as a beginner.

There is a great deal more to x64 long-mode memory addressing that I can't explain without first explaining a little bit about the programming process itself—and the tools you use to do it.

The Right to Assemble

The Process of Creating Assembly Language Programs

The Nine and Sixty Ways to Code

Rudyard Kipling's poem "In the Neolithic Age" (1895) gives us a tidy little scold on tribal certainty. Having laid about himself successfully with his trusty diorite tomahawk, the poem's Neolithic narrator eats his former enemies while congratulating himself for following the One True Tribal Path. Alas, his totem pole has other thoughts and in a midnight vision puts our cocky narrator in his place.

> "There are nine and sixty ways of constructing tribal lays,
> And every single one of them is right!"

The moral of the poem is to trust your totem pole (and read more Kipling!). What's true of tribal lays is also true of programming methodologies. There are at *least* nine and sixty ways of making programs, and I've tried most of them over the years since I wrote my first line of FORTRAN in 1970. They're all different, but they all work in that they all produce programs that can be loaded and run—once the programmer figures out how to follow a particular method and use the tools that go with it.

Still, although all these programming techniques work, they are not interchangeable, and what works for one programming language or tool set will not apply to another programming language or tool set. In 1977, I learned to program in a language called APL (A Programming Language; how profound!) by typing in lines of code and watching what each one did. That was the way APL worked: Each line was mostly an independent entity, which performed a calculation or some sort of array manipulation, and once you pressed Enter, the line would crunch up a result and print it for you. (I learned it on an IBM Selectric printer/terminal.) You could string lines together to produce more complex programs, of course, and I did, but it was an intoxicating way to produce a program from an initial state of total ignorance, testing everything one single microstep at a time.

Later I learned BASIC almost the same way that I had learned APL, but there were other languages that demanded other, better techniques. Pascal and C both required significant study beforehand because you couldn't just hammer in one line and execute it independently. Much later still, when Microsoft Windows went mainstream, Visual Basic and especially Dephi changed the rules radically. Programming became a sort of stimulus-response mechanism, in which the operating system sent up stimuli called *events* (keystrokes, mouse clicks, and so on) and simple programs consisted mostly of responses to those events.

Assembly language is not constructed the same way that C, Java, or Pascal are. Very pointedly, you *cannot* write assembly language programs purely by trial and error, nor can you do it by letting other people do your thinking for you. It is a complicated and tricky process compared to BASIC or Perl or such visual environments as Delphi, Lazarus, or Gambas. You have to pay attention. You have to read the sheet music. Most of all, you have to practice.

In this chapter, I'll teach you assembly language's tribal lays as I've learned them.

Files and What's Inside Them

All programming is about processing files. Some programming methods hide some of those files, and all methods to some extent, strive to make it easier for human beings to understand what's inside those files. But at the bottom of it, you'll be creating files, processing files, reading files, and executing files.

Most people understand that a file is a collection of data stored on a medium, for example, a hard disk drive, a thumb drive or flash memory card, an optical disk, or the occasional exotic device of some kind. The collection of data is given a name and manipulated as a unit. Your operating system governs the management of files on storage media. Ultimately, it allows you to see data within a file and can write changes that you make back to the file or to a new file that you create with the assistance of the operating system.

Assembly language is notable in that it hides almost nothing from you, and to be good at it, you have to be willing to go inside any file that you deal with and understand it down to the byte and sometimes the bit level. This takes longer, but it pays a huge dividend in knowledge: *you will know how everything works.* APL and BASIC, by contrast, were and remain mysteries. I typed in a line, and the computer spat back a response. What happened in between was hidden very well. In assembly language, you see it *all.* The trick is to understand what you're looking at.

Binary vs. Text Files

The looking isn't always easy. If you've worked with Windows or Linux (and before that, DOS) for any length of time, you may have a sense for the differences between files in terms of how you "look at" them. A simple text file is opened and examined in a simple text editor. A word processor file is opened in the species of word processor that created it. A PowerPoint slideshow file is opened from inside the PowerPoint application. If you try to load it into Word or Excel, the application will display garbage or (more likely) politely refuse to obey the open command. Trying to open an executable program file in a word processor or other text editor will generally get you either nowhere or screenfuls of garbage.

Text files are files that can be opened and examined meaningfully in a text editor, like Notepad or Wordpad in Windows, or any of the many text editors available for Linux. *Binary files* are files containing values that do not display meaningfully as text. Most higher-end word processors confuse the issue by manipulating text and then mixing the text with formatting information that does not translate into text but instead dictates things such as paragraph spacing, line height, and so on. Open a Word or OpenOffice document in a simple text editor like Notepad, and you'll see what I mean.

Text files contain upper and lowercase letters and numeric digits, plus odd symbols such as punctuation. There are 94 such visible characters. Text files also contain a group of characters called *whitespace.* Whitespace characters give text files their structure by dividing them into lines and providing space within lines. These include the familiar space character, the tab character, the newline character that indicates a line end, and sometimes a couple of others. There are fossil characters like the BEL character, which was used many decades ago to ring the little mechanical brass bell in teletype machines, and while BEL is technically considered whitespace, most text editors simply ignore it.

Text files in the PC world are a little more complicated, because there are another 127 characters containing glyphs for mathematical symbols, characters with accent marks and other modifiers, Greek letters, and "box draw" characters that were widely used for drawing screen forms on text screens in ancient times before graphical user interfaces like Windows and Cinnamon. How these additional characters display in a text editor or terminal window depends entirely on the text editor or terminal window and how it is configured.

Text files become even more complex when you introduce non-Western alphabets through the Unicode standard. Explaining Unicode in detail is beyond the scope of this book, but a good introduction is available on Wikipedia.

Text files are easy to display, edit, and understand. Alas, there's a *lot* more to the programming world than text files. In previous chapters, I defined what a computer program is, from the computer's perspective. A program is, metaphorically, a long journey in very small steps. These steps are a list of binary values representing machine instructions that direct the CPU to do what it must to accomplish the job at hand. These machine instructions, even in their hexadecimal shorthand form, are gobbledygook to human beings. Here's a short sequence of binary values expressed in hexadecimal:

```
FE FF A2 37 4C 0A 29 00 91 CB 60 61 E8 E3 20 00 A8 00 B8 29 1F FF 69 55
```

Is this part of a real program or isn't it? You'd probably have to ask the CPU to find out, unless you were a binary machine-code maniac of the kind that hasn't been seen since 1978. (Spoiler: it isn't.)

But the CPU has no trouble with programs presented in this form. In fact, the CPU can't handle programs in any other way. The CPU itself simply isn't equipped to understand and obey a string of characters such as

```
LET X = 42
```

or even something that we humans would call assembly language:

```
mov rax,42
```

To the CPU, it's binary-only. The CPU just *might* interpret a sequence of text characters as binary machine instructions, but if this happened, it would be pure coincidence, and the coincidence would not go on longer than three or four characters' worth. Nor would the sequence of instructions be likely to do anything useful.

From a high level, the process of assembly language programming (or programming in many other languages) consists of taking human-readable text files and translating them somehow into files containing sequences of binary machine instructions that the CPU can understand. You, as an assembly language programmer, need to understand which files are which (lots more on this later) and how each is processed. Also, you will need to be able to "open" an executable binary file and examine the binary values that it contains.

Looking at Binary File Internals with the GHex Hex Editor

Fortunately, there are utilities that can open, display, and allow you to change characters or binary bytes inside *any* kind of file. These are called *binary editors* or *hexadecimal editors*, and the best of them, in my experience (at least for the 64-bit Linux world), is the GHex hex editor. It was designed to operate under graphical user interfaces such as Cinnamon and is easy to figure out by exploring the menus.

GHex is not automatically installed by default under Linux Mint. How applications are installed under Linux differs across major distros. I've been a Linux Mint user since the Maya release. What installation instructions I include here will be for Linux Mint 20.3 Una Cinnamon, which is a Long Term Support (LTS) release as I write this in 2023.

To install GHex under Linux Mint, bring up the Software Manager and search for *GHex*. There will be both a Debian package and a Flatpack. I recommend the Debian package. (I don't have space here to explain the differences.) Choose the Debian package and click Install. When the dust settles, close the Software Manager. Click the Mint menu button and select the Programming category. The GHex icon will be there. If you want it as an icon on your desktop as well, right-click GHex and select Add To Desktop.

A good way to demonstrate GHex will also demonstrate why it's necessary for programmers to understand even text files at the byte level. In the listings archive for this book (see the introduction for the URL) are two files, `samwindows` `.txt` and `samlinux.txt`. Extract them both. Launch GHex, and using the File ⇨ Open command open `samlinux.txt`.

Figure 5.1 shows the GHex window in its smallest size to save space here on the printed page; after all, the file itself is only 15 bytes long. For larger files, you can enlarge GHex both horizontally and vertically.

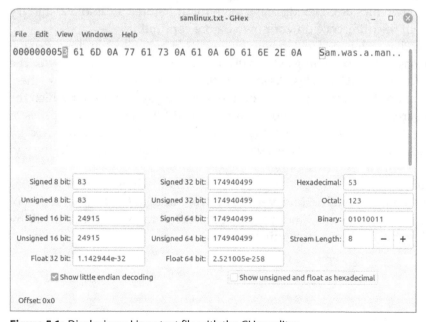

Figure 5.1: Displaying a Linux text file with the GHex editor

The display pane is divided into three parts. The left column is the offset column. It contains the offset from the beginning of the file for the first byte displayed on that line in the center column. The offset is given in hexadecimal. If you're at the beginning of the file, the offset column will be 00000000H. The center column is the hex display column. It displays a line of data bytes from the file in hexadecimal format. How many bytes will be shown depends on how you size the GHex window. In the center column the display is always in hexadecimal, with each byte separated from adjacent bytes by a space. The right column is the same line of data with any "visible" text characters displayed as text. Nondisplayable binary values are represented by period characters.

If you open the `samwindows.txt` tab, GHex will create a new window, and you'll see the same display for the other file, which was created using the Windows Notepad text editor. The `samwindows.txt` file is a little longer, and you have a second line of data bytes in the center column. The offset for the second line is 00000010. This is the offset in hex of the first byte in the second line.

Now, why are the two files different? Bring up a terminal window and navigate to whatever folder you're using for your assembly learning files. Use the `cat` command to display both files. The display in either case will be identical.

```
Sam
was
a
man.
```

Figure 5.2 shows the GHex editor displaying `samwindows.txt`. Look carefully at the two files as GHex displays them (or at Figures 5.1 and 5.2) and try to figure out the difference on your own before continuing.

At the end of each line of text in both files is a 0AH byte. The Windows version of the file has a little something extra: a 0DH byte preceding each 0AH byte. The Linux file lacks the 0DH bytes. As standardized as "plain" text files are, there can be minor differences depending on the operating system under which the files were created. As a convention, Windows text files (and DOS text files in older times) mark the end of each line with two characters: 0DH followed by 0AH. Linux (and nearly all Unix-descendent operating systems) marks the end of each line with a 0AH byte only.

As you've seen in using `cat` on the two files, Linux displays both versions identically and accurately. However, if you were to take the Linux version of the file and load it into the Windows Notepad text editor, you'd see something a little different, as shown in Figure 5.3.

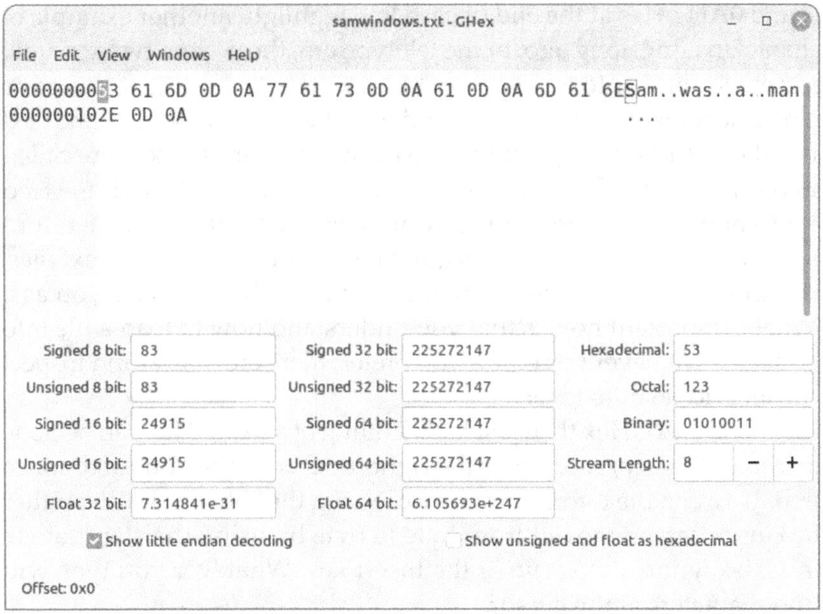

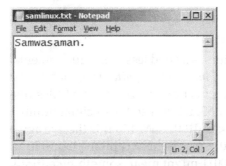

Figure 5.2: Displaying a Windows text file with the GHex editor

Figure 5.3: A Linux text file displayed under Windows

Notepad expects to see *both* the 0DH and the 0AH at the end of each text line and doesn't understand a lonely 0AH value as an end-of-line (EOL) marker. So, it ignores the 0AH characters, and the words all run together on the same line. (Remember from the GHex display that there are no space characters in `samlinux.txt`.) Not all Windows software is that fussy. Many or most other Windows utilities understand that 0AH is a perfectly good EOL marker.

The 0DH and 0AH bytes at the end of each line highlight another example of a "fossil" character. Long, long ago, in the teletype era, there were two separate electrical commands built into teletype machines to handle the end of a text line when printing a document: one command indexed the paper upward to the next line, and the other returned the print head to the left margin. These were called *line feed* and *carriage return*. Carriage return was encoded as 0DH and line feed as 0AH. Many computer systems and software now ignore the carriage return code, though a few (like Notepad) still require it for proper display of text files.

This small difference in text file standards won't be a big issue for you as a beginner. What's important now is that you understand how to load a file into the GHex editor (or whatever hex editor you prefer; there are many) and inspect the file at the individual byte level.

You can do more with GHex than just look. Editing of a loaded file can be done in either the center (binary) column or the right (text) column. You can bounce the edit cursor between the two columns by pressing the Tab key. Within either column, the cursor can be moved from byte to byte by using the stand-alone arrow keys. GHex ignores the state of the Insert key. Whatever you type will overwrite the characters at the cursor.

I shouldn't have to say that once you've made useful changes to a file, save it back to disk by clicking the Save button.

Interpreting Raw Data

Seeing a text file as a line of hexadecimal values is a good lesson in a fundamental principle of computing: *everything is made of bits, and bit patterns mean what we agree they mean*. The capital letter *S* that begins both of the two text files displayed in GHex is the hexadecimal number 53H. It is also the decimal number 83. At the bottom, it is a pattern of eight bits: 01010011. Within this file, we agree among ourselves that the bit pattern 01010011 represents a capital letter *S*. In an executable binary file, the bit pattern 01010011 might mean something entirely different, depending on where in the file it happened to be and what other bit patterns existed nearby in the file.

This is why the lower pane of the GHex editor exists. It takes the sequence of bytes that begins at the cursor and shows you all the various ways that those bytes may be interpreted. Remember that you won't always be looking at text files in a hex editor like GHex. You may be examining a data file generated by a program you're writing and that data file may represent a sequence of 32-bit signed integers. Or that data file may represent a sequence of unsigned 16-bit integers. Or that data file may represent a sequence of 64-bit floating-point numbers. Or it may be a mixture of any or all of the above. All you'll see in the center pane is a series of hexadecimal values. What those values represent depends on what program wrote those values to the file and what those values stand for by convention in the "real" world. Are they dollar amounts? Measurements? Data points generated by some sort of instrument? That's up to you—and to the software that you use. The file, as with all files, is simply a sequence of binary patterns stored somewhere that we display (using GHex) as hexadecimal values to make them easier to understand and manipulate.

Bounce the cursor around the list of hex values in the center column, and watch how the interpretations in the bottom pane change. Note that some of the interpretations look at only one byte (8 bits); others two bytes (16 bits), four bytes (32 bits), or eight bytes (64 bits). In every case the sequence of bytes being interpreted begins at the cursor and goes toward the right. For example, with the cursor at the first position in the file:

- 53H may be interpreted as decimal value 83.
- 53 61H may be interpreted as decimal 21345.
- 53 61 6D 0AH may be interpreted as decimal 1398893834.
- 53 61 6D 0A 77 61 73 0AH may be interpreted as the floating-point number 4.54365038640977[93].

(The differences between a signed value and an unsigned value will have to wait until later in this book.) The important thing to understand is that in all cases it's the same sequence of bytes at the same location within the file. All that changes is how many bytes we look at and what kind of value we choose to agree that sequence of bytes represent.

This may become clearer later when we begin writing programs that work on numbers. And, speaking of numbers. . .

"Endianness"

In the lower-left corner of the bottom pane of the GHex editor is a check box marked "Show little endian decoding." By default the box is not checked, but in almost all cases, it should be. The box tells GHex whether to interpret sequences of bytes as numeric values in "big endian" order or in "little endian" order. If you click and unclick the check box, the values displayed in the lower pane will change radically, even if you don't move the cursor at all. When you change the state of that check box, you are changing the way that the GHex editor interprets a sequence of bytes in a file as some sort of number.

If you recall from Chapter 4, a single byte can represent numbers from 0 to 255. If you want to represent a number larger than 255, you must use more than one byte to do it. A sequence of two bytes in a row can represent any number from 0 to 65,535. However, once you have more than one byte representing a numeric value, *the order of the bytes becomes crucial.*

Let's go back to the first two bytes in either of the two files we loaded earlier into GHex. They're nominally the letters *S* and *a*, but that is simply another interpretation. The hexadecimal sequence 53 61H may also be interpreted as a number. The 53H appears first in the file. The 61H appears after it. (See Figures 5-1 and 5-2.) So, taken together as a single 16-bit value, the two bytes become the hex number 53 61H.

Or do they? Perhaps a little weirdly, it's not that simple. See Figure 5.4. The left part of the figure is a little excerpt of the information shown in the GHex hex display pane for our example text file. It shows only the first two bytes and their offsets from the beginning of the file. The right portion of the figure is the same information but reversed left for right, as though seen in a mirror. It's the same bytes in the same order, but we see them differently. What we assumed at first was that the 16-bit hex number 53 61H now appears to be 61 53H.

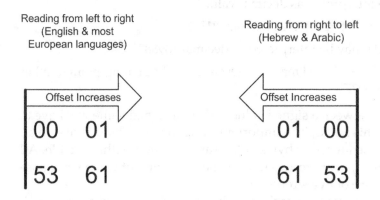

So is it "53 61H" or "61 53H" ?

Figure 5.4: Differences in display order versus differences in evaluation order

Did the number change? Not from the computer's perspective. All that changed was the way we printed it on the page of this book. By custom, people reading English start at the left and read toward the right. The layout of the GHex hex editor display reflects that. But certain other languages in the world, including Hebrew and Arabic, start at the right margin and read toward the left. An Arabic programmer's first impulse might be to see the two bytes as 61 53H, especially if they are using software designed for the Arabic language conventions, displaying file contents from right to left.

It's actually even more confusing than that. Western languages (including English) are a little schizoid, in that they read *text* from left to right, but evaluate numeric columns from right to left. The number 426 consists of four hundreds, two tens, and six ones, not four ones, two tens, and six hundreds. By convention here in the West, the least significant column is at the right, and the values of the columns increase from right to left. The most significant column is the leftmost. (I covered columnar numbers in depth in Chapter 2.)

Confusion is a bad idea in computing. So whether a sequence of bytes is displayed from left to right or from right to left, we all have to agree on which of those bytes represents the least and which is the most significant figure in a multibyte number. In a computer, we have two choices.

- We can agree that the least significant byte of a multibyte value is at the lowest offset and that the most significant byte is at the highest offset.

- We can agree that the most significant byte of a multibyte is at the lowest offset and the least significant byte is at the highest offset.

These two choices are mutually exclusive. A computer must operate using one choice or the other; they cannot both be used at the same time at the whim of a program. Furthermore, this choice is not limited to the operating system or to a particular program. The choice is baked right into the silicon of the CPU and its instruction set. A computer architecture that stores the least significant byte of a multibyte value at the lowest offset in memory or registers is called *little endian*. A computer architecture that stores the most significant byte of a multibyte value at the lowest offset is called *big endian*.

Figure 5.5 should make this clearer. In big-endian systems, a multibyte value begins with its *most* significant byte. In little-endian systems, a multibyte value begins with its *least* significant byte. Think: big endian, big end first. Little endian, little end first.

There are *big* differences at stake here! The two bytes that begin our example text file represent the decimal number 21,345 in a big endian system but 24,915 in a little endian system.

It's possible to do quite a bit of programming without being aware of a system's "endianness." If you program in higher-level languages like Visual Basic, Pascal, or C, most of the consequences of endianness are hidden by the language and the language compiler—at least until something goes wrong at a low level. Once you start reading files at a byte level, you have to know how to read them. And if you're programming in assembly language, you had better be comfortable with endianness going in.

Reading hex displays of numeric data in big-endian systems is easy because the digits appear in the order that Western people expect, with the most significant digits on the left. In little-endian systems, everything is reversed, and the more bytes used to represent a number, the more confusing it can become. Figure 5.6 shows the endian differences between evaluations of a 32-bit value. Little-endian programmers have to read hex displays of multibyte values as though they were reading Hebrew or Arabic, from right to left.

I won't present a figure for a 64-bit quantity here because its complexity might obscure its meaning. If you can "see" a 32-bit quantity in little-endian terms, 64 bits will be a short jump if it's any jump at all.

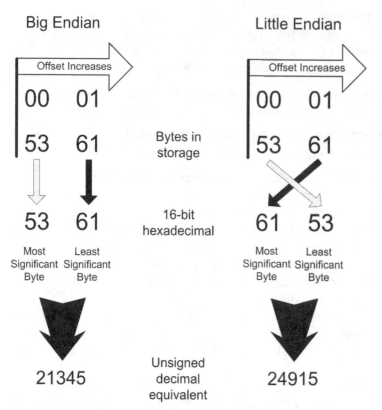

Figure 5.5: Big endian versus little endian for a 16-bit value

Remember that endianness differences apply not only to bytes stored in files but also to bytes stored in memory. When (as I'll explain later) you inspect numeric values stored in memory with a debugger, all the same rules apply.

So, which "endianness" do Linux systems use? Both! (Though not at the same time.) Again, it's not about operating systems. The entire Intel x86/x64 hardware architecture, from the lowly 8086 up to the latest Core i9, is little endian. Other hardware architectures, like Motorola's 68000 and the original PowerPC, and most IBM mainframe architectures like System/370, are big endian. More recent hardware architectures have been designed as "bi-endian," meaning that they can be configured (with some difficulty) to interpret numeric values one way or the other at the hardware level. Alpha, MIPS, and Intel's Itanium IA-64 architecture are bi-endian.

If (as required for this book) you're running Linux on an ordinary Intel or AMD x64 CPU, you'll be little endian, and you should check the box on the GHex editor labeled "Show little-endian decoding." Other programming tools may offer you the option of selecting big-endian display or little-endian display. Make sure that whatever tools you use, you have the correct option selected.

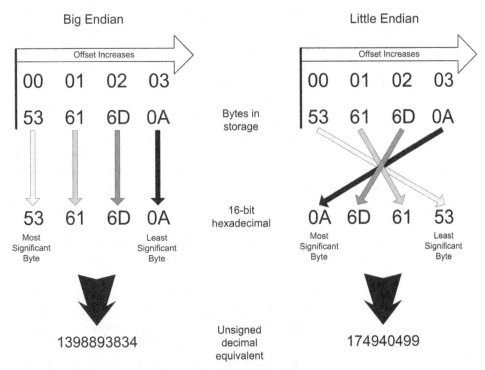

Figure 5.6: Big endian versus little endian for a 32-bit value

Linux, of course, can be made to run on *any* hardware architecture. So, using Linux doesn't guarantee that you will be facing a big-endian or little-endian system, and that's one reason I've gone on at some length about endianness here. You have to know from studying the system what endianness is currently in force, though you can learn it by inspection: store a 32-bit integer to memory and then look at it with a debugger. If you know your hex (and you had *better*!), the system's endianness will jump right out at you.

Text In, Code Out

From a high level, all programming is a matter of processing files. The goal is to take one or more human-readable text files and process them to create an executable program file that you can load and run under whatever operating system and hardware architecture that you're using. For this book, that would be Linux on an Intel x64 CPU, but the general process that I'll describe in this section applies to almost any kind of programming under almost any operating system.

Programming as a process varies wildly by language and by the set of tools that support the language. In modern graphical interactive development environments such as Visual Basic, Delphi, and Lazarus, much of file processing is done "behind the scenes," while you, the programmer, are staring at one or more files on display and pondering your next move. In assembly language that's not the case. Most assembly language programmers use a much simpler tool set and explicitly process the files as sequences of discrete steps entered from a command line or from a script file.

However it's done, the general process of converting text files to binary files is one of translation, and the programs that do it are as a class called translators. A *translator* is a program that accepts human-readable source files and generates some kind of binary file. The output binary file could be an executable program file that the CPU can understand, or it could be a font file, a compressed binary data file, or any of a hundred other types of binary file.

Program translators are translators that generate machine instructions that the CPU can understand. A program translator reads a source code file line by line and writes a binary file of machine instructions that accomplishes the computer actions that the source code file describes. This binary file is called an *object code file*.

A *compiler* is a program translator that reads in source code files written in higher-level languages such as C or Pascal and writes out object code files.

An *assembler* is a special type of compiler. It, too, is a program translator that reads source code files and outputs object code files for execution by the CPU. However, an assembler is a translator designed specifically to translate what we call *assembly language* into object code. In the same sense that a language compiler for Pascal or C compiles a source code file to an object code file, we say that an assembler *assembles* an assembly language source code file to an object code file. The process, one of translation, is similar in both cases. Assembly language, however, has an overwhelmingly important characteristic that sets it apart from compilers: *total control over the object code*.

Assembly Language

Some people define assembly language as a language in which one line of source code generates one machine instruction. This has never been literally true since some lines in an assembly language source code file are instructions to the translator program (rather than to the CPU) and do not generate machine instructions at all.

Here's a better definition:

Assembly language is a translator language that allows total control over every individual machine instruction generated by the translator program. Such a translator program is called an *assembler*.

Pascal or C compilers, on the other hand, make a multitude of invisible and inalterable decisions about how a given language statement will be translated into a sequence of machine instructions. For example, the following single Pascal statement assigns a value of 42 to a numeric variable called I:

```
I := 42;
```

When a Pascal compiler reads this line, it outputs a series of four or five machine instructions that take the literal numeric value 42 and store it in memory at a location encoded by the name I. Normally, you the Pascal programmer have *no idea* what these four or five instructions actually are, and you have utterly no way of changing them, even if you know a sequence of machine instructions that is faster and more efficient than the sequence that the compiler uses. The Pascal compiler has its own way of generating machine instructions, and you have no choice but to accept what it writes to its object code file to accomplish the work of the Pascal statements you wrote in the source code file.

To be fair, modern high-level language compilers generally implement something called *in-line assembly*, which allows a programmer to "take back" control from the compiler and "drop in" a sequence of machine instructions of their own design. A fair amount of modern assembly language work is done this way, but it's actually considered an advanced technique because you first have to understand how the compiler generates its own code before you can "do better" using in-line assembly. (And don't assume, as many do, that you can do better than the compiler without a great deal of study and practice! Twenty-first century compilers are *mighty* good at generating efficient code!)

An assembler sees *at least* one line in the source code file for every machine instruction that it generates. It sees more lines than that, and the additional lines handle various other things, but *every* machine instruction in the final object code file is controlled by a corresponding line in the source code file.

Each of the CPU's many machine instructions has a corresponding *mnemonic* in assembly language. As the word suggests, these mnemonics began as devices to help programmers remember a particular binary machine instruction. For example, the mnemonic for binary machine instruction FCH, which clears the direction flag, is CLD—which is a country mile easier to remember than FCH. And that's for a 1-byte machine instruction. Many machine instructions with simple mnemonics assemble to four or more bytes.

When you write your source code file in assembly language, you will arrange a series of mnemonics, typically one mnemonic per line in the source code text file. A portion of an x64 source code file might look like this:

```
mov rax,1             ; 01H specifies the sys_write kernel call
mov rdi,1             ; 01H specifies file descriptor stdout
mov rsi,Message       ; Load starting address of display string into RSI
mov rdx,MessageLength ; Load the number of chars to display into RDX
syscall               ; Make the kernel call
```

Here, the words mov and syscall at the left margin are the mnemonics. The numbers and textual items to the immediate right of each mnemonic are that mnemonic's *operands*. There are various kinds of operands for various machine instructions, and a few instructions (such as CLD or SYSCALL) use no operands at all.

Taken together, a mnemonic and its operands are called an *instruction*. (Words to the right of the semicolons are comments and are not parts of the instructions.) Instruction is the word I'll be using most of the time in this book to indicate the human-readable proxy of one of the CPU's pure binary machine code instructions. To talk about the binary code specifically, we'll always refer to a *machine instruction*.

The assembler's most important job is to read lines from the source code file and write machine instructions to an object code file. See Figure 5.7.

Mnemonic Operands   Comment

mov rax,rbx   ;Copy sum in rbx into rax

The assembler reads a line like this from the source code file, and writes the equivalent machine instruction to an object code file:

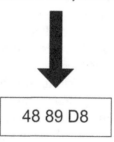

48 89 D8

Figure 5.7: What the assembler does

Comments

To the right of each instruction (see Figure 5.7) is text starting with a semicolon. This text is called a *comment*, and its purpose should be obvious: to cast some light on what the associated assembly language instruction is for. The instruction MOV RAX,RBX places the current value of register RBX into register RAX—but *why*? What is the instruction accomplishing in the context of the assembly language program that you're writing? Comments provides the why—and *you* provide the comments.

Structurally, a comment begins with the first semicolon on a line and continues toward the right to the EOL marker at the end of that line. A comment does not need to be on the same line with an instruction. A lot of useful description in assembly language programs exists in *comment blocks*, which are sequences of lines consisting solely of comment text. Each line in a comment block begins with a semicolon at the left margin.

Far more than in any other programming language, comments are critical to the success of your assembly language programs. My own recommendation is that *every* instruction in your source code files should have a comment to its right. Furthermore, every group of instructions that act together in some way should be preceded by a comment block that explains that group of instructions "from a high level" and how they work together.

Comments are one area where understanding how a text file is structured is important—because in assembly language, comments end at the ends of lines. In most other languages such as Pascal and C, comments are placed *between* pairs of comment delimiters like (* and *), and EOL markers at line ends are ignored.

In short, *comments begin at semicolons and end at EOL.*

Slightly weird note: As I wrote this edition in 2022, I encountered a bug in the SASM IDE that violated the "rules" of comments. The word *section* in a comment would sometimes cause SASM to crash. That's a bug, I reported it, and eventually it will be fixed. If you're using SASM and it crashes, check to see if you use the word *section* in a comment somewhere.

Beware "Write-Only" Source Code!

This is as good a time as any to point out a serious problem with assembly language. The instructions themselves are almost vanishingly terse, and doing anything useful takes a *lot* of them. And whereas each instruction states (tersely) what it does, there is very little in the source code itself to indicate a context within which that instruction operates. Name things with an eye toward hinting at what those named items do. This includes procedure names, code labels, variables, and equates. `TheBuffer` tells us nothing about what that buffer is up to. `CharInputBuffer` at least suggests that it's involved in character input.

Indicative naming (as I call it) helps a little, but comments do most of the heavy lifting when it comes to creating context. Without context, assembly language starts to turn into what we call "write-only" code. It can happen like this: On November 1, in the heat of creation, you crank out about 300 instructions in a short utility program that does something important. You go back on January 1 to add a feature to the program—and discover that *you no longer remember how it works.* The individual instructions are all correct, and the program assembles and runs as it should, but knowledge of how it all came together and how it works from a high level have vanished under the weight of Christmas memories and eight weeks of doing other things. In other words, you *wrote* it, but you can no longer *read* it nor change it. *Voilà!* Write-only code.

Although it's true that comments do take up room in your source code disk files, they are *not* copied into your executable code files, and a program with loads of comments in its source code runs *exactly* as fast as the same program with no comments at all.

You will be making a considerable investment in time and energy when you write assembly language programs—far more than in "halfway to heaven" languages like C and Pascal and unthinkably more than in "we do it all for you" IDEs like Delphi and Lazarus. It's more difficult than just about any other way of writing programs, and if you don't comment, you may end up having to simply toss out hundreds of lines of inexplicable code and write it again, *from scratch*.

Work smart. Comment till you drop.

Object Code, Linkers, and Libraries

Assemblers read your source code files and generate an object code file containing the machine instructions that the CPU understands, plus any data you've defined in the source code.

There's no reason at all why an assembler could not read a source code file and write out a finished, executable program as its object code file, but this is almost never done. The assembler I'm teaching in this book, NASM, can do that for DOS programs and can write out COM executable files for the real mode flat model. More modern operating systems like Linux and Windows are too complex for that, and in truth, there's no real payoff in such one-step assembly except when you're first learning to write assembly language.

So, the object code files produced by modern assemblers are a sort of intermediate step between source code and executable program. This intermediate step is a type of binary file called an *object module* or simply an object code file.

Object code files cannot themselves be run as programs. An additional step, called *linking*, is necessary to turn object code files into executable program files.

The reason for object code files as intermediate steps is that a single large source code file may be cut up into numerous smaller source code files to keep the files manageable in size and complexity. The assembler assembles the various fragments separately, and the several resulting object code files are then woven together by the linker into a single executable program file. This process is shown in Figure 5.8.

When you're first learning assembly programming, it's unlikely that you'll be writing programs spread out across several source code files. This may make the linker seem extraneous, since there's only one piece to your program and thus nothing to link together. As with much else in programming (especially assembly programming) it's not that simple. The linker handles a critical step on the path from source code to executable program: It converts object code generated by the assembler into an executable program. For simple programs there may be only one object code file to convert. For larger and more sophisticated programs, there are likely to be several; nay, many.

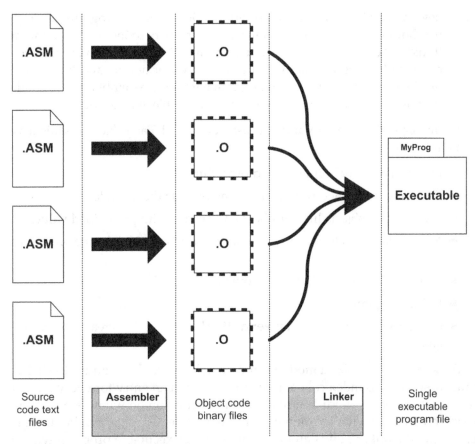

Figure 5.8: The assembler and linker

Remember that *the linker does more than link*. It doesn't just stitch lumps of object code together into a single executable file. It makes sure that function calls out of one object module will arrive at the target object module and that all the many memory references actually reference what they're supposed to reference. The assembler's job is obvious; the linker's job is subtle. Both are necessary to produce a finished, working executable file.

Besides, you'll quickly get to the point where you begin extracting frequently used portions of your programs into your own personal code libraries. There are two reasons for doing this.

- You can move tested, proven routines into separate libraries and link them into any program you write that might need them. This way, you can reuse code over and over again and not build the same old wheels every time you begin a new programming project in assembly language.

- Once portions of a program are tested and found to be correct, there's no need to waste time assembling them over and over again along with newer, untested portions of a program. Once a major program gets into the thousands of lines of code (and you'll get there sooner than you might think!), you can save a significant amount of time by assembling only the portion of a program that you are currently working on and linking the finished portions into the final program without re-assembling *every* single part of the whole thing every time you assemble *any* part of it.

The linker's job is complex and not easily described. Each object module may contain the following:

- Program code including named procedures
- References to named procedures lying outside the module
- Named data objects like numbers and strings with predefined values
- Named data objects that are just empty space "set aside" for the program's use later
- References to data objects lying outside the module
- Debugging information
- Other, less common odds and ends that help the linker create the executable file

To process several object modules into a single executable module, the linker must first build an index called a *symbol table*, with an entry for every named item in every object module it links, with information on what name (called a *symbol*) refers to what location within the module. Once the symbol table is complete, the linker builds an image of how the executable program will be arranged in memory when the operating system loads it. This image is then written to disk as the executable file.

The most important thing about the image that the linker builds relates to addresses. Object modules are allowed to refer to symbols in other object modules. During assembly, these *external references* are left as holes to be filled later—naturally enough, because the module in which these external symbols exist may not have been assembled or even written yet. As the linker builds an image of the eventual executable program file, it learns where all of the symbols are located within the image and thus can drop real addresses into all of the external reference holes.

Debugging information is, in a sense, a step backward. Portions of the source code, which was all stripped out early in the assembly process, are put back into the object module by the assembler. These portions of the source code are mostly the names of data items and procedures, and they're embedded in the object file to make it easier for the programmer (you!) to see the names of data items when you debug the program. (I'll go into the debugging concept more deeply later.) Debugging information is optional; that is, the linker does not need it to build a proper executable file. You choose to embed debugging information in the object file while you're still working on the program. Once the program is finished and debugged to the best of your ability, you run the linker one more time, without requesting debugging information. Linking a thoroughly debugged program without debugging information is more like "tidying up" by making the finished executable file smaller and thus easier to distribute to others.

Relocatability

Primordial microcomputers like 8080 systems running CP/M-80 had a simple memory architecture. Programs were written to be loaded and run at a specific physical memory address. For CP/M, this was 0100H. The programmer could assume that any program would start at 0100H and go up from there. Memory addresses of data items and procedures were actual physical addresses, and every time the program ran, its data items were loaded and referenced at *precisely* the same place in memory.

This all changed with the arrival of the 8086, and 8086-specific operating systems such as CP/M-86 and PC DOS. Improvements in the Intel architecture introduced with the 8086 made it unnecessary for the program to be assembled for running at any specific physical memory address. This feature is called *relocatability* and is a necessary part of any modern operating system, especially when multiple programs may be running at once. Handling relocatability is complex, and I don't have room to explain it in depth here. Once you're more comfortable with the assembly language process, it will become a worthy topic for further research.

The Assembly Language Development Process

As you can see, there are a lot of different file types and a fair number of programs involved in the process of writing, assembling, and testing an assembly language program. The process itself sounds more complex than it is. I've drawn you a map to help you keep your bearings during the discussions in the rest of this chapter. Figure 5.9 shows the most common form that the assembly language development process takes, in a "view from a height." At first glance it may look like a map of the LA freeway system, but in reality the flow is fairly straightforward, and you'll do it enough so that it will become second nature in just a couple of evenings spent hammering at a program or two.

In a nutshell, the process cooks down to this:

1. Create your assembly language source code file in a text editor.

2. Use your assembler to create an object module from your source code file.

3. Use your linker to convert the object module (and any previously assembled object modules that are part of the project) into a single executable program file.

4. Test the program file by running it, using a debugger if necessary.

5. Go back to the text editor in step 1, fix any mistakes you may have made earlier, and write new code as necessary.

6. Repeat steps 1–5 until done.

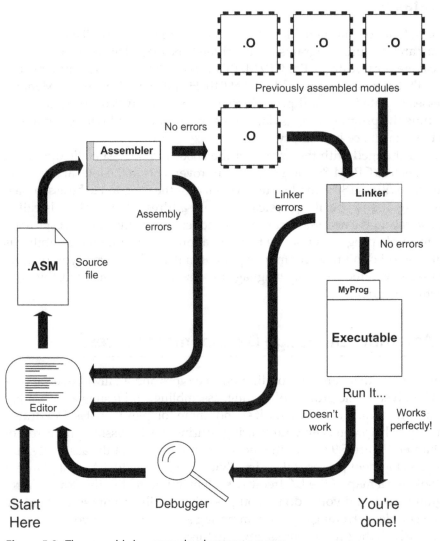

Figure 5.9: The assembly language development process

The Discipline of Working Directories

Programmers generally count from 0, and if we're counting steps in the assembly language development process, step 0 consists of setting up a system of directories on your Linux PC to manage the files you'll be creating and processing as you go.

There's a rule here that you need to understand and adopt right up front: *store only one project in a directory*. That is, when you want to write a Linux program called TextCaser, create a directory called TextCaser (or something else that won't confuse you) and keep nothing in that directory but files directly related to the TextCaser project. If you have another project in the works called TabExploder, give that project its own separate directory. This is good management practice, first of all, and prevents your makefiles from getting confused (more on this later when I take up make and makefiles).

I recommend that you establish a directory scheme for your assembly development projects, and my experience suggests something like this: Create a directory under your Linux Home directory called Assembly (or make up some other suitably descriptive name), and create your individual project directories as subdirectories under that overall assembly language directory.

By the way, it's okay to make the name of a directory the same as the name of the main ASM file for the project; that is, `textcaser.asm` is perfectly happy living in a directory called `textcaser`.

At this point, if you haven't already downloaded and unpacked the listings archive for this book, I suggest you do that—we're going to need one of the files in the archive for the demonstration in this section. The file is called `asmsbs4e .zip`, and it can be found here:

`www.copperwood.com/pub`

or, alternatively, here:

`www.junkbox.com/pub`

(I have these two domains on two different Internet hosting services so that at least one of them will always be up and available. The file is identical, whichever site you download it from.)

When unpacked, the listings archive will create individual project directories under whatever parent directory you choose. I recommend unpacking it under your Assembly directory, or whatever you end up naming it.

A short warning to Windows users coming to Linux for the first time: *Linux identifiers are case-sensitive*. That means `textcaser` and `Textcaser` are two different directories and could be used to hold two entirely separate projects.

As you might imagine, that's a bad idea. Choose folder names and filenames so that they follow some sort of schema, like CamelCase. Or just leave everything in lowercase, which is how it's generally done throughout the Unix world.

Editing the Source Code File

You begin the actual development process by typing your program code into a text editor. *Which* text editor doesn't matter very much, and there are dozens of them to choose from. In this book I'm going to recommend an interactive development environment (IDE) that contains a text editor, a make facility, and a front end to gdb, the Linux debugger. The only important thing to keep in mind is that word processors like Microsoft Word and Open Office Writer embed a lot of extra binary data in their document files, above and beyond the text that you type. This binary data controls things such as line spacing, fonts and font size, page headers and footers, and many other things that your assembler has no need for and no clue about. Assemblers are not always good at ignoring such data, which may cause errors at assembly time.

As for how you come up with what you type in, well, that's a separate question and one that I give most of a short chapter to later. You will certainly have a pile of notes, probably some pseudocode, some diagrams, and perhaps a formal flowchart. These can all be done on your screen with software utilities or with a pencil on a paper quadrille pad.

Assembly language source code files are almost always saved to disk with an .asm file extension. In other words, for a program named MyProg, the assembly language source code file would be named MyProg.asm.

Assembling the Source Code File

As you can see from the flow in Figure 5.9, the text editor produces a source code text file with an .asm extension. This file is then passed to the assembler program itself for translation to an object module file. Under Linux and with the NASM assembler that I'm focusing on in this book, the file extension for the object code file will be .o.

When you invoke the assembler from the command line, you provide it with the name of the source code file that you want it to process. Linux will load the assembler from disk and run it, and the assembler will open the source code file that you named on the command line. Almost immediately afterward (especially for the small learning programs that you'll be poking at in this book), it will create an object file with the same name as the source file, but with an .o file extension.

As the assembler reads lines from the source code file, it will examine them, build a symbol table summarizing any named items in the source code file, construct the binary machine instructions that the source code lines represent, and then write those machine instructions and symbol information to the object module file. When the assembler finishes and closes the object module file, its job is done, and it terminates. On modern PCs and with programs representing fewer than 500 lines of code, this happens in a second or (sometimes much) less.

Assembler Errors

Note that the previous paragraphs describe what happens if the .asm file is *correct*. By correct, I mean that the file is completely comprehensible to the assembler and can be translated into machine instructions without the assembler getting confused. If the assembler encounters something it doesn't understand when it reads a line from the source code file, we call the misunderstood text an *error*, and the assembler displays an *error message*.

For example, the following line of assembly language will confuse the assembler and prompt an error message:

```
mov rax,rvx
```

The reason is simple: there's no such thing as rvx. What came out as rvx was actually intended to be rbx, which is the name of a CPU register. (The *V* key is right next to the *B* key and can be struck by mistake without your fingers necessarily knowing that they erred. Done that!)

Typos like this are by far the easiest kind of error to spot. Others that take some study to find involve transgressions of the assembler's many rules—which in most cases are the CPU's rules. For example:

```
mov eax,rbx
```

At first glance this looks like it should be correct, since EAX and RBX are both real registers. However, on second thought, you may notice that EAX is a 32-bit register, and RBX is a 64-bit register. You are not allowed to copy a 64-bit register into a 32-bit register.

You don't have to remember the instruction operand details here; we'll go into the rules later when we discuss the individual instructions themselves in more detail. For now, simply understand that some things that may look reasonable to you (especially as a beginner) are simply against the rules for technical reasons and are considered errors.

And these are easy ones. There are much, *much* more difficult errors that involve inconsistencies between two otherwise legitimate lines of source code. I won't offer any examples here, but I wanted to point out that errors can be truly ugly, hidden things that can take a lot of study and torn hair to find. Toto, we are definitely *not* in BASIC anymore....

The error messages vary from assembler to assembler, and they may not always be as helpful as you might hope. The error NASM displays upon encountering the evx typo follows:

```
testerr.asm:20: symbol 'evx' undefined
```

This is pretty plain, assuming that you know what a "symbol" is. And it tells you where to look: the "20" is the line number where it noticed the error.

The error message NASM offers when you try to load a 64-bit register into a 32-bit register is far less helpful.

```
testerr.asm:22: invalid combination of opcode and operands
```

This lets you know you're guilty of performing illegal acts with an opcode and its operands, but that's it. *You* have to know what's legal and what's illegal to really understand what you did wrong. As in running a stop sign, ignorance of the law is no excuse, and unlike the local police department, the assembler will catch you *every* time.

Assembler error messages do not absolve you from understanding the CPU's or the assembler's rules.

This will become clear the first time you sit down to write your own assembly code. I hope I don't frighten you too terribly by warning you that for more abstruse errors, the error messages may be almost no help at all.

You may make (or *will* make—let's get real) more than one error in writing your source code files. The assembler will display more than one error message in such cases, but it may not necessarily display an error for *every* error present in the source code file. At some point, multiple errors confuse the assembler so thoroughly that it cannot necessarily tell right from wrong anymore. While it's true that the assembler reads and translates source code files line by line, there is a cumulative picture of the final assembly language program that is built up over the course of the whole assembly process. If this picture is shot too full of errors, in time the whole picture collapses.

The assembler will terminate, having printed numerous error messages. *Start at the first one*, make sure you understand it (take notes!), and keep going. If the errors following the first one don't make sense, fix the first one or two and assemble again.

Back to the Editor

The way to fix errors is to load the offending source code file back into your text editor and start hunting up errors. This loopback is shown in Figure 5.9. It may well be the highway you see the most of on this particular road map.

The assembler error message will almost always contain a line number. Move the cursor to that line number and start looking for the false and the fanciful. If you find the error immediately, fix it and start looking for the next. Assuming that you're using a Linux graphical desktop like Cinnamon, it's useful to keep the terminal window open at the same time as your editor window so that you don't have to scribble down a list of line numbers on paper or redirect the compiler's output to a text file. With a 20-inch monitor or better, there's plenty of room for multiple windows at once.

There is a way to make the NASM assembler write its error messages to a text file during the assembly process, and we'll talk about that in Chapter 6.

Assembler Warnings

As taciturn a creature as an assembler may appear to be, it will sometimes display *warning messages* during the assembly process. These warning messages are a monumental puzzle to beginning assembly language programmers: are they errors, or aren't they? Can I ignore them, or should I fool with the source code until they go away?

Alas, there's no crisp answer. Sorry about that.

Assembly-time warnings are the assembler acting as experienced consultant and hinting that something in your source code is a little dicey. This something may not be serious enough to cause the assembler to stop assembling the file, but it may be serious enough for you to take note and investigate. For example, NASM will sometimes flag a warning if you define a named label but put no instruction after it. That may not be an error, but it's probably an omission on your part, and you should take a close look at that line and try to remember what you were thinking when you wrote it. (This may not always be easy, when it's 3 a.m. or three weeks after you originally wrote the line in question.)

If you're a beginner doing ordinary, 100-percent-by-the-book sorts of things, you should crack your assembler reference manual and figure out why the assembler is tut-tutting you. Ignoring a warning *may* cause peculiar bugs to occur later during program testing. Or, ignoring a warning message may have no undesirable consequences at all. I feel, however, that it's always better to know what's going on. Follow this rule:

Ignore an assembler warning message only if you know exactly what it means.

In other words, until you understand why you're getting a warning message, treat it as though it were an error message. Only once you fully understand why it's there and what it means should you try to make the decision whether to ignore it.

In summary, the first part of the assembly language development process (as shown in Figure 5.9) is a loop. You must edit your source code file, assemble it, and return to the editor to fix errors until the assembler spots no further errors. *You cannot continue until the assembler gives your source code file a clean bill of health,* that is, without errors. I also recommend studying any warnings offered by the assembler until you understand them clearly. Fixing the condition that triggered the warning is always a good idea, especially when you're first starting out.

When no further errors are found, the assembler will write an .o file to disk, and you will be ready to go on to the next step.

Linking the Object Code File

As I explained a little earlier in this chapter, the linking step is nonobvious and a little mysterious to newcomers, especially when you have only one object code module in play, like the simple examples in this book. It is nonetheless crucial, and whereas it was possible in ancient times to assemble a simple DOS assembly language program direct to an executable file without a linking step, the nature of modern operating systems like Linux and Windows makes this impossible.

The linking step is shown on the right half of Figure 5.9. In the upper-right corner is a row of .o files. These .o files were assembled earlier from correct .asm files, yielding object module files containing machine instructions and data objects. When the linker links the .o file produced from your in-progress .asm file, it adds in the previously assembled .o files. The single executable file that the linker writes to disk contains the machine instructions and data items from all of the .o files that were handed to the linker when the linker was invoked.

Once the in-progress .asm file is completed and made correct, its .o file can be put up on the rack with the others and added to the *next* in-progress .asm source code file that you work on. Little by little you construct your application program out of the modules you build and test one at a time.

An important bonus is that some of the procedures in an .o module may be used in a future assembly language program that hasn't even been started yet. Creating such libraries of "toolkit" procedures can be an extraordinarily effective way to save time by reusing code over and over, without even passing it through the assembler again!

There are numerous assemblers in the world (though only a few really good ones) and plenty of linkers as well. Linux comes with its own linker, called ld. (The name is actually short for "load," and "loader" was what linkers were originally called, in the First Age of Unix, back in the 1970s.) We'll use ld for some of the simplest programs in this book, but in later chapters, we're going to take up a Linux peculiarity and use a C compiler for a linker. . .sort of.

Like I said, we're not doing BASIC anymore.

As with the assembler, invoking the linker is generally done from the Linux terminal command line. Linking multiple files involves naming each file on the command line, along with the desired name of the output executable file. You may also need to enter one or more command-line switches, which give the linker additional instructions and guidance. Few of these will be of interest while you're a beginner, and I'll discuss the ones you need along the way.

You need to know how invoking the ld linker works, but once we get to the IDE called SASM, the IDE will invoke the linker behind the scenes and make it unnecessary to do so much typing into the terminal window command line.

Linker Errors

As with the assembler, the linker may discover problems as it weaves multiple .o files together into a single executable program file. Linker errors are subtler than assembler errors and are usually harder to find. Fortunately, they are less common and not as easy to make.

As with assembler errors, linker errors are "fatal;" that is, they make it impossible to generate the executable file, and when the linker encounters one, it will terminate immediately. When you're presented with a linker error, you have to return to the editor and figure out what the problem is. Once you've identified the problem (or *think* you have) and changed something in the source code file to fix the problem, you must re-assemble and then re-link the program to see if the linker error went away. Until it does, you have to loop back to the editor, try something else, and assemble/link once more.

If possible, avoid doing this by trial and error. Read your assembler and linker documentation. Understand what you're doing. The more you understand about what's going on within the assembler and the linker, the easier it will be to determine what's giving the linker fits.

(Hint: It's almost always *you!*)

Testing the EXE File

If you receive no linker errors, the linker will create a single executable file that contains all the machine instructions and data items present in all of the .o files named on the linker command line. The executable file is your program. You can run it to see what it does by simply typing its path on the terminal command line and pressing Enter.

Again, if you're familiar with Linux, you already know this, but executable programs in Linux do *not* have an .exe suffix nor any other suffix at all. It's just the name of the program.

The Linux path comes into play here, though if you have any significant experience with Linux at all, you already know this. The terminal window is a purely textual way of looking at your working directory, and all of the familiar command-line utilities will operate on whatever is in your working directory. However, remember that your working directory is *not* in your path unless you explicitly put it there, and although people argue about this and always have, there are good reasons for not putting your working directory into your path.

When you execute a program from the terminal window command line, you must tell Linux where the program is by prefixing the name of the program with the ./ specifier, which simply means "in the working directory." This is unlike DOS, in which whatever directory is current is also on the search path for executable programs. A command-line invocation of your program under Linux might look like this:

```
./myprogram
```

This is when the fun *really* starts.

Errors vs. Bugs

When you launch your program in this way, one of two things will happen: the program will work as you intended it to, or you'll be confronted with the effects of one or more program bugs. A *bug* is anything in a program that doesn't work the way you intended. This makes a bug somewhat more subjective than an error. One person might think red characters displayed on a blue background is a bug, while another might consider it a clever New Age feature and be quite pleased. Settling bug-versus-feature conflicts like this is up to you. You should have a clear idea of what the program is supposed to do and how it works, backed up by a written spec or other documentation of some kind, and this is the standard by which you judge a bug.

Characters in odd colors are the least of it. When working in assembly language, it is *extremely* common for a bug to abort the execution of a program with little or no clue on the display as to what happened. If you're lucky, the operating system will spank your executable and display an error message. Just as an example, this is one you will see sooner or later, probably *much* sooner than later:

```
Segmentation Fault
```

Such an error is called a *runtime error* to differentiate it from assembler errors and linker errors. Most often, your program will not annoy the operating system. It just won't do what you expect it to do, and it may not say much in the course of its failure.

Fortunately, Linux is a rugged operating system designed to take buggy programs into account, and it is *extremely* unlikely that one of your programs will "blow the machine away," as happened so often in the DOS era decades ago.

All that being said, and in the interest of keeping the Babel effect at bay, I think it's important here to carefully draw the distinction between errors and bugs. An *error* is something wrong with your source code file that either the assembler or the linker kicks out as unacceptable. An error prevents the assembly or link process from going to completion and will thus prevent a final executable file from being produced.

A *bug*, by contrast, is a problem discovered during the *execution* of a program. Bugs are not detected by either the assembler or the linker. Bugs can be benign, such as a misspelled word in a screen message or a line positioned on the wrong screen row; or a bug can force your program to abort prematurely. If your program attempts to do certain forbidden things, Linux will terminate it and present you with a message. We call these *runtime errors*, but they are actually caused by bugs.

Both errors and bugs require that you go back to the text editor and change something in your source code file. The difference here is that most errors from the assembler are reported with a line number telling you precisely where to go in your source code file to fix the problem. Bugs, on the other hand, are left as an exercise for the student. You have to hunt them down, and neither the assembler nor the linker will give you many clues.

Are We There Yet?

Figure 5.9 announces the exit of the assembly language development process as happening when your program works perfectly. A serious question is this: how do you know when it works perfectly? Simple programs assembled while learning the language may be easy enough to test in a minute or two. But any program that accomplishes anything useful at all will take *hours* of testing at *minimum*. A serious and ambitious application could take weeks—or months—to test thoroughly. A program that takes various kinds of input values and produces various kinds of output should be tested with as many different combinations of input values as possible, and you should examine every possible output every time.

Even so, finding every last bug in a nontrivial program is considered by some to be an impossible ideal. Perhaps—but you should strive to come as close as you can, in as efficient a fashion as you can manage. I'll have more to say about bugs and debugging in the following section and throughout the rest of this book.

Debuggers and Debugging

The final—and almost certainly the most painful—part of the assembly language development process is debugging. *Debugging* is simply the systematic process by which bugs are located and corrected. A *debugger* is a utility program designed specifically to help you locate and identify bugs.

Debuggers are among the most mysterious and difficult-to-understand of all classes of software. Debuggers are part X-ray machine and part magnifying glass. A debugger loads into memory *with* your program and remains in memory, side by side with your program. The debugger then puts tendrils down into your program and enables some truly peculiar things to be done.

One of the problems with debugging computer programs is that they operate so quickly. Millions—and sometimes billions—of machine instructions can be executed in a single second, and if one of those instructions isn't quite right, it's past and gone long before you can identify which one it was by staring at the screen. A debugger allows you to execute the machine instructions in a program *one at a time*, allowing you to pause indefinitely between each instruction to examine the effects of the last instruction that executed. The debugger also lets you look at the contents of named data items, as well as the values stored in any CPU registers, during that pause between instructions. Some debuggers will give you a "hexdump-style" window showing the memory in which your program is running.

Debuggers can do all of this mysterious stuff because they are necessary, and the CPU has special features baked into its silicon to make debuggers possible. How they work internally is outside the scope of this book, but it's a fascinating business, and once you're comfortable with x64 CPU internals, I encourage you to research it further. The more you know, the better you'll do.

Most debuggers have the ability to display the source code with the machine instructions so that you can see which lines of source code text correspond to which binary opcodes. Others allow you to locate a program variable by name rather than simply by memory address.

Many operating systems are shipped with a debugger. DOS and early versions of Windows were shipped with DEBUG, and in earlier editions of this book I explained DEBUG in detail. Linux has a powerful debugger called gdb, and I'll introduce it in Chapter 6.

Taking a Trip Down Assembly Lane

You can stop asking, "Are we there yet?" where "there" means "ready to build an actual working program." We are indeed there, and for the rest of this chapter we're going to take a simple program and run it through the process that I drew out graphically in Figure 5.9.

You don't have to write the program yourself. I've explained the process, but I haven't gone into any of the machine instructions or the CPU registers in detail. So I'll provide you with a simple example program and give you enough explanation of its workings so that it's not a total mystery. In the chapters that follow, we'll look at machine instructions and their operation in great detail. In the meantime, you must understand the assembly language development process, or knowing how the instructions work won't help you in the slightest.

Installing the Software

One of the fantastic things about Linux is the boggling array of software that can be had for it, nearly all of it completely free of charge. If you've used Linux for any length of time, you've probably encountered products such as LibreOffice,

Gimp, Scribus, and Calibre. A few of these are preinstalled when you install the operating system. The rest are obtained through the use of a *package manager*. A package manager is a catalog program that lives on your PC and maintains a list of all the free software packages that are available for Linux. You choose the ones you want, and the package manager will then go online, download them from their online homes (called *repositories* in the Linux universe), and then install them for you.

On recent versions of Linux Mint, the package manager is called Software Manager. You open it by clicking its icon when you click the Mint icon in the lower-left corner of the display. The Software Manager icon is a rounded white square with a circle at its center and nine dots inside the circle. Figure 5.10 shows Software Manager's initial window. As you can see, most of it could be considered "advertising," though in this case for completely free products.

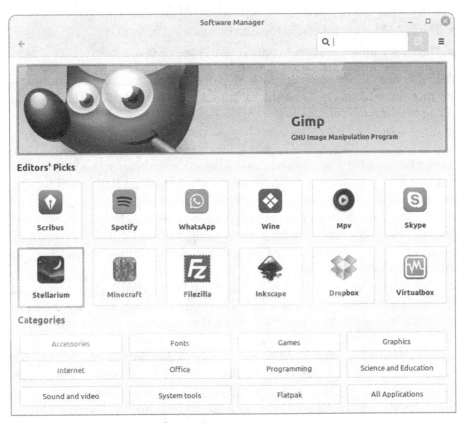

Figure 5.10: The Linux Mint Software Manager

Needless to say, you need an active Internet connection to use Linux Mint Software Manager. If you're coming from the Windows world, it's good to understand that under Linux you don't have to worry about where software is being installed. Almost all software is installed in the /usr directory hierarchy, in a place that's on your file search path. Once installed on your search path, you can run a program simply by naming it on a terminal window command line.

Running a program that isn't on your search path requires a little extra typing. Open a terminal window and navigate to any directory as your working directory, and then launch a program located in that directory by naming it on the command line preceded by the current directory specifier, like this:

```
./eatsyscall
```

The ./ prefix specifies the current directory.

In this chapter, we're going to need a number of things to take a quick tour through the assembly language development process: an editor, an assembler, and a linker.

- The Xed editor is preinstalled with Linux Mint 20.
- The NASM assembler will have to be installed.
- The Linux linker ld is preinstalled with Linux Mint 20.

We'll also need a debugger for later exploration. The debugger situation is a little more complex. The canonical Linux debugger, gdb, is preinstalled in nearly all versions of Linux. However, gdb is more of a debugger "engine" than a complete debugger. It's extraordinarily powerful but command-line driven, with an *immense* learning curve. To make it truly useful (especially to beginners), we have to download something to make its controls easier to handle and its output easier to understand. This function is built into an IDE called SASM, which (among other things) contains a "front end" to gdb. I'll explain how to install SASM and how to use it (including its front end to gdb) in the next chapter. For now, just take it on faith that debuggers are useful and necessary in assembly language work. (I have some suggestions relating to the debugger question in Appendix A.)

Note that Xed is referred to as "Text Editor" on Linux Mint 20. It can be found in the Accessories category, on the menu that jumps up when you click the Mint button in the lower-left corner of the display. If you select Help ➪ About, you'll see its true name in the About dialog box.

Installing NASM is dirt simple. In the search field at the top of the Software Manager window, type **NASM**. Software Manager will begin searching its repositories immediately. It will display a list of any package that is or mentions NASM. NASM itself will be the first search hit, and its entry will be highlighted in green. Click the NASM entry. This will take you to a dialog that allows you to read more about the assembler. The dialog will have a green Install button. Click it. Software Manager will download NASM from its repository and ask for your Linux password before installing it. After you enter your password, it will complete the install.

Note that Software Manager will *not* place an icon for NASM in the Programming category. NASM does not have its own user interface window and thus does not qualify for a desktop icon to run it. You have to run it from a terminal window as I'll explain next, or via SASM, as I'll explain in the next chapter.

Step 1: Edit the Program in an Editor

A great many text editors are available for Linux Mint, and the easiest of them to understand is probably Xed. You can launch Xed from the Accessories menu, in which it's called "Text Editor." (You can place its icon on the desktop by right-clicking the Text Editor icon in Accessories and selecting Add to Desktop.) Later we'll be using SASM as our text editor, but for the moment bring up Xed.

With Xed's File ➪ Open dialog, navigate to the directory where you placed the eatsyscall.asm file from the book listings archive. I use a directory called Assembly under the Home directory and create project directories under the Assembly directory. Double-click the eatsyscall.asm file in that directory. Xed will display the file, which I show here in Listing 5.1. Read it over. You don't have to understand it completely, but it's simple enough so that you should be able to understand what it does in general terms.

Listing 5.1: eatsyscall.asm

```
;   Executable name  : EATSYSCALL
;   Version          : 1.0
;   Created date     : 4/25/2022
;   Last update      : 4/25/2022
;   Author           : Jeff Duntemann
;   Architecture     : x64
;   From             : Assembly Language Step By Step, 4th Edition
;   Description      : A simple program in assembly for x64 Linux, using
;                       ; NASM 2.14,
;                         demonstrating the use of the syscall instruction to
display text.
;
;   Build using these commands:
;     nasm -f elf64 -g -F stabs eatsyscall.asm
;     ld -o eatsyscall eatsyscall.o
;
SECTION .data          ; Section containing initialized data
    EatMsg: db "Eat at Joe's!",10
    EatLen: equ $-EatMsg
SECTION   .bss          ; Section containing uninitialized data
SECTION   .text         ; Section containing code
global    .start        ; Linker needs this to find the entry point!
start:
    mov rbp, rsp        ; for correct debugging
    nop                 ; This no-op keeps gdb happy...
```

```
mov rax,1          ; 1 = sys_write for syscall
mov rdi,1          ; 1 = fd for stdout; i.e., write to the
                   ; terminal window
mov rsi,EatMsg     ; Put address of the message string in rsi
mov rdx,EatLen     ; Length of string to be written in rdx
syscall            ; Make the system call
mov rax,60         ; 60 = exit the program
mov rdi,0          ; Return value in rdi 0 = nothing to return
syscall            ; Call syscall to exit
```

Step 2: Assemble the Program with NASM

The NASM assembler does not have a user interface as nontechnical people understand "user interface" today. It doesn't put up a window, and there's no place for you to enter filenames or select options in check boxes. NASM works via text only, and you communicate with it through a terminal and a Linux console session. It's like those old DOS days when everything had to be entered on the command line. (How soon we forget!)

So, open up a terminal window. Many different terminal utilities are available for Ubuntu Linux. The one I use most of the time is called Konsole, but they will all work here. Terminal windows generally open with your home directory as the working directory. Once you have the command prompt, navigate to the eatsyscall project directory using the cd command.

```
myname@mymachine:~$ cd assembly/eatsyscall
```

If you're new to Linux, make sure you're in the right directory by checking the directory contents with the ls command. The file eatsyscall.asm should at least be there, either extracted from the listings archive for this book or entered by you in a text editor.

Assuming that the file eatsyscall.asm is present, assemble it by (carefully) entering the following command and pressing Enter:

```
nasm -f elf64 -g -F dwarf eatsyscall.asm
```

When NASM finds nothing wrong, it will say nothing, and you will simply get the command prompt back. That means the assembly worked! If you entered the eatsyscall.asm file yourself and typed something incorrectly, you may get an error. Make sure the file matches Listing 5.1.

Now, what did all that stuff that you typed into the terminal mean? I've dissected the command line you just entered in Figure 5.11. A NASM invocation begins with the name of the program itself. Everything after that are parameters that govern the assembly process. The ones shown here are nearly all of the ones you're likely to need while first learning the assembly language development process. There are others with more arcane purposes, and all of them are summarized in the NASM documentation. Let's go through the ones used here, in order.

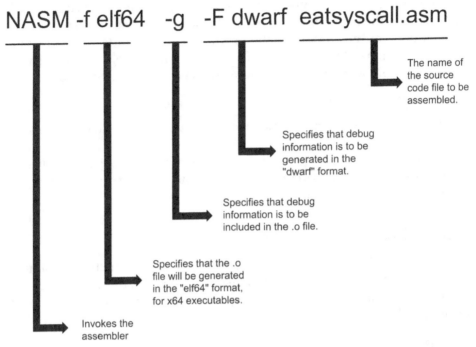

Figure 5.11: The anatomy of a NASM command line

- `-f elf64`: There are a fair number of useful object file formats, and each one is generated differently. The NASM assembler is capable of generating most of them, including other formats like bin, aout, and coff, that you probably won't need, at least for awhile. The `-f` command tells NASM which format to use for the object code file it's about to generate. The elf64 format is what you want for x64 executables.

- `-g`: While you're still working on a program, you want to have debugging information embedded in the object code file so that you can use a debugger to spot problems. (You'll learn more about how this is done in Chapter 6.) The `-g` command tells NASM to include debugging information in the output file. This will increase the size of the output file a little, but for small practice projects not enough to be a problem.

- `-F dwarf`: As with the output file, there are different formats in which NASM can generate debug information. Again, as with the output file format, if you're working in x64 Linux, you'll probably be using the DWARF format for debug information, at least while you're starting out. Remember that Linux commands are case-sensitive. The `-f` command and the `-F` command are two different commands, so watch that shift key!

- `eatsyscall.asm`: The last item on the NASM command line shown is the name of the file to be assembled. Again, as with everything in Linux, the filename is case-sensitive. `EATSYSCALL.ASM` and `EatSysCall.asm` (as well as all other case variations) are considered entirely different files.

Unless you give NASM other orders, it will generate an object code file and name it using the name of the source code file and the file extension .o. The "other orders" are given through the -o option. If you include an -o command in a NASM command line, it must be followed by a filename, which is the name you want NASM to give to the generated object code file. For example:

```
nasm -f elf64 -g -F dwarf eatsyscall.asm -o eatsyscall.o
```

Here, NASM will assemble the source file eatsyscall.asm to the object code file eatdemo.o.

Now, before moving on to the link step, verify that the object code file has been created by using the ls command to list your working directory contents. The file eatsyscall.o should be there.

Step 3: Link the Program with ld

So far so good. Now we have to create an executable program file by using the Linux linker utility, ld. After making sure that the object code file eatsyscall.o is present in your working directory, type the following linker command into the terminal:

```
ld -o eatsyscall eatsyscall.o
```

If the original program assembled without errors or warnings, the object file should link without any errors as well. As with NASM, when ld encounters nothing worth mentioning, it says nothing at all. No news is good news in the assembly language world—and, in truth, throughout the programming world as a whole.

The command line for linking is simpler than the one for assembling. I've drawn it out in Figure 5.12. The ld command runs the linker program itself. The -o command specifies an output filename, which here is eatsyscall. In the DOS and Windows world, executable files almost always use the .exe file extension. In the Linux world, executables generally have no file extension at all.

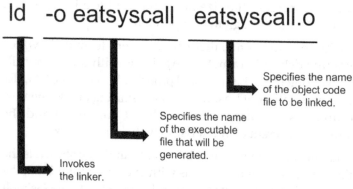

Figure 5.12: The anatomy of an ld command line

Note that if you do *not* specify an executable filename with the -o command, ld will create a file with the default name a.out. If you ever see a mysterious file named a.out in one of your project directories, it probably means you ran the linker without the -o command.

The last things you enter on the ld command line are the names of the object files to be linked. In this case there is only one, but once you begin using assembly language code libraries (whether your own or those written by others), you'll have to enter the names of any libraries you're using on the command line. The order you enter them doesn't matter. Just make sure that they're all there.

Step 4: Test the Executable File

Once the linker completes an error-free pass, your finished executable file will be waiting for you in your working directory. It's error-free if the assembler and linker digested it without displaying any error messages. However, error-free does not imply bug-free. To make sure it works, just name it on the terminal command line:

```
./eatsyscall
```

Linux newcomers need to remember that *your working directory is not automatically on your search path*, and if you simply type the name of the executable on the command line (without the "working directory" prefix ./), Linux will not find it. But when named with the prefix, your executable will load and run and print out its 13-character advertisement:

```
Eat at Joe's!
```

Victory!

Step 5: Watch It Run in the Debugger

Assuming that you entered Listing 5.1 correctly (or unpacked it from the listings archive), there are no bugs in eatsyscall.asm. That's an uncommon circumstance for programmers, especially those just starting out. Most of the time you'll need to start bug hunting almost immediately. The easiest way to do this is to load your executable file into a debugger so that you can single-step it, pausing after the execution of each machine instruction so that you can see what effect each instruction has on the registers and any variables defined in memory.

The canonical debugger under Linux is gdb, the Gnu Debugger. We're going to use gdb in this book, but to keep the tutorial simple we're going to use it from within an IDE, a subject I'll take up in Chapter 6.

I can teach barely a smidgen of gdb in an absolute beginner's book like this. There is a reference guide for gdb that has 800 pages of fine print and weighs

5 pounds. I encourage you to explore gdb as your skills improve. You need to be aware that it's a long, steep slope to a very high mountaintop. All commands to gdb (and there are *lots*) must be entered on a terminal command line. There are no menus and (as with NASM and ld) no graphical user interface at all.

This doesn't mean that no graphical user interface for gdb exists. Several do. The trick is that they're not part of gdb. It's possible to create a windowed interface to GDB by setting up menus and dialogs specifying what you want gdb to do and then allowing the windowed interface to pass the commands as pure text to gdb. This is done "behind the scenes" and out of sight. It looks like you're debugging with gdb and you are—just through a sort of GUI middleman.

The 2009 edition of this book discussed two such interfaces: one called Kdbg and the other called Insight. Kdbg exists but does not work under Linux Mint Cinnamon, and Insight, alas, was removed from Linux distributions and all repositories that I'm aware of, way back in 2009. Insight can be downloaded from websites and installed under Linux, but it's a fair bit of fussy work. (I've written some advice about installing and using Insight in Appendix A.)

Mostly, it doesn't matter. Today in 2023, we have something better. Turn the page, and let's meet an assembly language IDE called SASM.

A Place to Stand, with Access to Tools

Linux and the Tools That Shape the Way You Work

Integrated Development Environments

Archimedes, the primordial engineer, had a favorite saying: "Give me a lever long enough, and a place to stand, and I will move the Earth." The old guy was not much given to metaphor and was speaking literally about the mechanical advantage of *really* long levers, but behind his words there is a larger truth about work in general: To get something done, you need a place to stand, with access to tools. My radio bench out in the small garage is set up that way: a large, flat space to lay ailing transmitters down on and a shelf above where my oscilloscope, VTVM, frequency counter, signal generator, signal tracer, and dip meter are within easy reach. On the opposite wall, just two steps away, is a long line of shelves where I keep parts, raw materials like sheet metal, circuit board stock, and scrap plastic, plus test equipment I don't need very often.

In some respects, an operating system is your place to stand while getting your computational work done. All the tools you need should be right there within easy reach, and there should be a standard, comprehensible way to access them. Storage for your data should be "close by" and easy to browse and search. The Linux operating system meets this need like almost nothing else in the desktop computing world today.

Ancient operating systems like DOS gave us our "place to stand" in a limited way. DOS provided access to disk storage and a standard way to load and run software, and not much more. The tool set was small, but it was a good start, and about all that we could manage on 6 MHz 8088 machines that were mainstream in the mid-to-late 1980s.

In some ways, the most interesting thing about DOS 2.0 was that it was created as a "dumbed-down" version of a much more powerful operating system, Unix, which had been developed by AT&T's research labs in the 1960s and 1970s. At the time that the IBM PC appeared, Unix ran only on large, expensive mainframes and minicomputers. The PC didn't have the raw compute power to run Unix itself, but DOS 2.0 was created with a hierarchical filesystem very much like the Unix filesystem, and its command line provided access to a subset of tools that worked very much like Unix tools.

The x86 PC grew up over the years, and by 1990 or so Intel's CPUs were powerful enough to run an operating system modeled on Unix. Meanwhile, Unix "grew down" until the two met somewhere in the middle. In 1991 the young Finnish programmer Linus Torvalds wrote a Unix "lookalike" that would run on an inexpensive 386-based PC. It was modeled on an implementation of Unix called Minix, which had been written in the Netherlands in the late 1980s as a Unix lookalike capable of running on small computers. Torvalds' Linux operating system eventually came to dominate the Unix world.

Linux is our place to stand, and it's a good one. But in terms of access to tools, it also helps to have a sort of software workbench designed specifically for the type of work we're doing at the moment. Word processors are workbenches for writing and printing (mostly) textual content. PowerPoint and its clones are workbenches for creating presentations, and so on.

The NASM assembler is powerful but taciturn, and inescapably tied to the command line, as are ld, gdb, and most of the venerable Unix tools that you'll find in the Linux tool chest. In Chapter 5, we ran through a simple development project the old hard way, by typing commands at the terminal command line. Beginners need to know how that works, but it's by no means the best we can do. Also, you may eventually outgrow the interactive development environment you're using. Special circumstances could also force you back to the Linux command line to get the job done.

The legendary success of Turbo Pascal for DOS in the 1980s was largely because it integrated an editor and a compiler together. It presented a menu allowing easy and fast movement among the editor, to write code; the compiler, to compile code into executable files; and DOS, where those files could be run and tested. Programming in Turbo Pascal was easier to grasp and much faster than traditional methods that involved constantly issuing commands from the command line.

Turbo Pascal was the first really successful commercial product to provide an interactive development environment (IDE) for small-system programmers.

Others had appeared earlier (particularly the primordial UCSD P-system, which was used mostly in colleges), but Turbo Pascal put the idea on the map for all-time.

In the previous edition of this book (the third edition, 2009), I presented a toolset including the Kate editor, the Konsole terminal, and the powerful if unconventional Insight front end for the gdb debugger. In our 2009 run-through in Chapter 5, I presented a simpler debugger front end called Kdbg.

Times change. Insight was removed from Linux distros and repositories in late 2009, not long after the third edition was published. It's been abandonware since 2009, and the product is extremely tricky to install on modern Linux distros. Somewhere along the road to 2022, Kdbg also vanished from the Linux scene and cannot be installed on most recent distributions. I liked both products, but I think I understand why they fell out of use. Kate and Konsole are still very much with us. I will describe Konsole at some length later in this chapter, in the section The Linux Console.. You can use Kate if you want, but for simple text editing I prefer the Xed editor. As for a debugger, see Appendix A. Insight is back.

Mostly.

In preparing this edition, however, I found something remarkable: an IDE designed specifically for assembly-language work, with an emphasis on beginning programmers. Simple ASM (SASM) was written by Dmitriy Manushin. It's still maintained and still being actively developed. It's powerful enough to handle most of the simple programs I present in this book. It's also a good way to introduce debugging.

Now, as good as it is in some respects, SASM was designed for beginners and lacks some advanced features. It is an excellent place to start, and it will give you an idea of what an IDE is. Certainly, once you start writing large-scale assembly programs or start mixing assembly with C, SASM will not be enough. I'm also going to cover the Make utility that comes with Linux so that when you outgrow SASM, you'll know how to create your own makefiles. And while SASM contains its own terminal window, I'm going to explain the more powerful Konsole terminal, as I did in 2009.

The old Insight debugger has been given another run. See Appendix A. It's not perfect, but it's still more beginner-friendly than any other stand-alone free debugger for Linux.

There are other, more powerful IDEs in the Linux universe, such as KDevelop, Geany, and Eclipse. Trying to usefully explain any one of those here would take more room than I have in this book. Once you understand the basic principles of IDEs, you can install and learn them as your needs and skills require. In the meantime, we'll begin with SASM and move on to Make and Konsole.

I've tested SASM on Linux Mint Cinnamon and Kubuntu Plasma. It works on both distros and can be installed using each platform's package manager. My guess is that it will run on any modern distro.

Introducing SASM

SASM is a simple IDE designed specifically for assembly language programming. These are its major features:

- Support for the NASM, FASM, MASM, and gas assemblers. (MASM works only under Windows.)
- Support for sessions, so you can have multiple projects open at one time.
- A source-code editor with full-color syntax highlighting.
- Separate terminal windows for standard input and standard output.
- A source-code debugger allowing you to use breakpoints and single-stepping in your assembly language projects.
- Register display during debugging, and a useful if limited display of memory.

Installing it is done from the package manager on whatever Linux distro you're using. Mint's package manager is called Software Manager. Under Kubuntu it's called Discover. (Kubuntu has a more advanced version of Discover called Muon Discover, but plain-vanilla Discover will do just fine.)

Both package managers give you a search field. Just type in **SASM** and hit Enter. You'll probably get a lot of search hits that have nothing to do with assembly language (or programming, for that matter), but right at the top you should see a line for SASM. Click that line. The package manager will show you a description of SASM.

As with all installs, you'll be asked for your Linux password. But once you enter that, SASM will be installed on your hard drive. In the software menu it will reside in the Programming category. I recommend that you create an icon on your desktop. Just right-click SASM's entry in the Programming category and select Add To Desktop.

Configuring SASM

There's not much to configure. All configuration is done from the Settings dialog. Here's the list:

- On the Settings ➪ Common tab, pull down On Start and select "Restore Previous Session." You don't want to see the Get Started" dialog every time you run SASM.
- Click the radio button No, Show Only General-Purpose for register display. We won't be discussing the x64 AVX math features, so displaying the math registers just clutters up SASM's window.

- On the Settings ⇨ Build tab (see Figure 6.1), click the x64 radio button for 64-bit coding. SASM also supports x86 32-bit code, and the x86 option is the default. *This is important.* You're going to be writing x64 code, and SASM will not correctly deal with x64 source code if you have x86 selected.

- Also on the Settings ⇨ Build tab, check the Build In Current Directory box.

- Everything else you can leave alone for the time being.

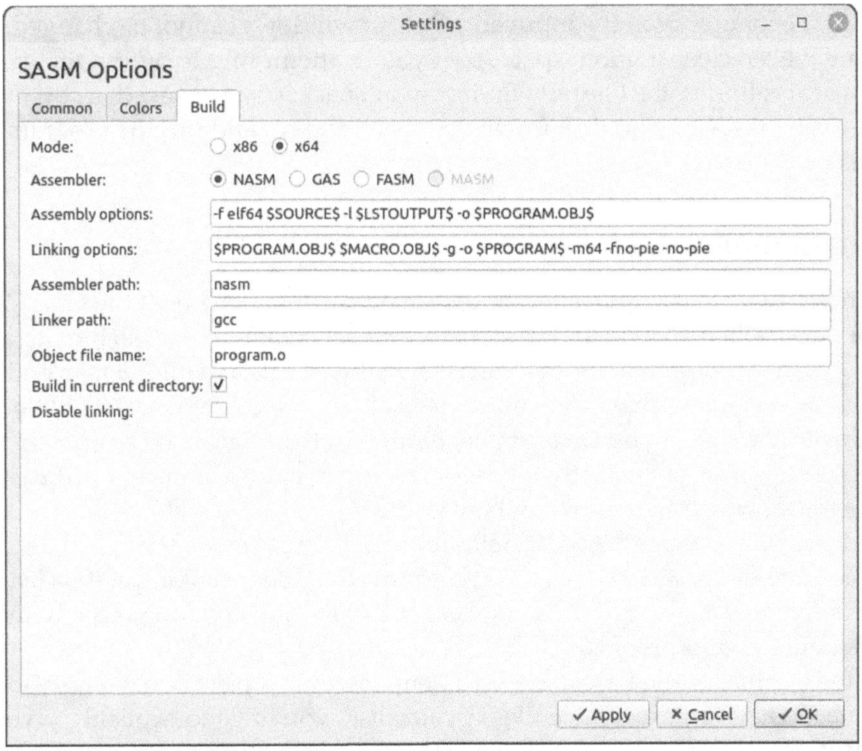

Figure 6.1: The SASM Build dialog

Take note of the version number, as shown in Help ⇨ About. As I write this in early 2023, the current version is 3.12.2. It will almost certainly be higher by the time you read this. The version number is important for this reason: A search for SASM packages may show up with more than one SASM package. Choose the one with the most recent release number. Then click the Install button.

SASM's Fonts

At this writing (2023), there is a rough edge to SASM's use of fonts. Most people who program do so in a purely monospace font like Courier. With Courier and other monospace fonts, all your columns will line up vertically because every character is the same width.

SASM's default font is Liberation Mono, which is not true monospace like Courier. You can change the editor window font in Settings ➪ Common. Change the font to Courier 10 Pitch. It's a true monospace font and a little bolder (and thus easier to read) than any of the several other monospace fonts that SASM presents.

Another font shortcoming is that you can specify a font only for the editor window. The font for both the Input and Output windows cannot be changed. It's nothing even close to monospace, so if you're attempting to output text or digits in neat columns, the Output window won't hack it. For testing that sort of output, save the EXE file to disk from SASM, exit SASM, and run the program from inside Konsole.

Using a Compiler to Link

SASM has a twist that you need to be aware of: By default, it uses the Gnu C compiler gcc rather than ld to link assembly object code into executable files. The gcc compiler doesn't do the linking itself. Rather, it acts as a middleman and calls ld after gcc determines what all ld needs to link to create the executable. This adds to the size of your executable, though not enough to be a problem. What it complicates are the instructions for assembling and linking in the Build tab of Settings, which I've shown in Figure 6.1.

The downside to using SASM's default build parameters is that you can't assemble and link the eatsyscall.asm program we've been looking at thus far. It takes a few minor changes to eatsyscall.asm to make it compatible with SASM's default build process.

Like the original Turbo Pascal, SASM assembles your project into memory to save time. To have an executable file on your disk, you have to explicitly save the executable as a disk file using the File ➪ Save .exe menu option.

In keeping with my advice to store only one project per directory, create a new directory under your assembly directory called eatsyscallgcc. Extract Listing 6.1 (the file eatsyscallgcc.asm) from the listings archive and place it in the new directory.

One last note about SASM before we get started: It includes a 64-bit I/O function include library called io64.inc. Although the library is useful, I won't be discussing it in this book. I encourage you to explore it as time permits.

Listing 6.1: eatsyscallgcc.asm

```
;   Executable name : eatsyscallgcc (For linking with gcc)
;   Version         : 1.0
;   Created date    : 4/25/2022
;   Last update     : 4/10/2023
;   Author          : Jeff Duntemann
;   Architecture    : x64
```

```
;   From            : x64 Assembly Language Step By Step, 4th Edition
;   Description:
;     A simple program in assembly for x64 Linux, using NASM 2.14,
;     demonstrating the use of the syscall instruction to display text.
;     This eatsyscall links via gcc, the default linker
;     for use with SASM. The entry point MUST be "main" to link with gcc.
;
;     Build using the default build configuration in SASM
;

SECTION .data             ; Section containing initialized data

 EatMsg: db "Eat at Joe's!",10
 EatLen: equ $-EatMsg

SECTION .bss         ; Section containing uninitialized data

SECTION .text             ; Section containing code

global   main  ; Linker needs this to find the entry point!
main:
     mov rbp,rsp          ; SASM may add another copy of this in debug
mode!

     mov rax,1            ; 1 = sys_write for syscall
     mov rdi,1            ; 1 = fd for stdout; write to the terminal window
     mov rsi,EatMsg       ; Put address of the message string in rsi
     mov rdx,EatLen       ; Length of string to be written in rdx
     syscall              ; Make the system call

     mov rax,60           ; 60 = exit the program
     mov rdi,0            ; Return value in rdi 0 = nothing to return
     syscall              ; Call syscall to exit
```

A Quick Tour of SASM

So let's take a look at what SASM can do, and then I'll explain it in more detail. With the Listing 6.1 source code file in its directory, use File ⇨ Open to navigate to the directory, and click Select when the source file is highlighted. SASM will load the source file into its source window.

A brief aside: SASM's window can get mighty busy when you're in debug mode, so I powerfully recommend you always maximize SASM when you use it.

The first step is to build the executable. "Build" here includes both the assemble and the link process, which SASM does in one step. The hammer icon in the toolbar starts the build process. Click it.

The build will take less than a second on a fast PC. In the log pane at the bottom of the SASM window, you'll see "Built successfully" in green. Green means all is well. Any build errors will appear in red.

To run the program, click the Run icon, which is the green triangle to the right of the Build icon. The log window will report that the program began running and finished normally. In the Output window, the message "Eat at Joe's!" will appear.

Yes, it's that simple—if your program works correctly. If it doesn't, you'll need to start debugging. The Debug icon is a green triangle with a little gray bug in front of it. (You may have to look closely to tell that it's a bug.) Click the Debug icon. Again, if you haven't maximized SASM's window already, do so now, because once you're in debug mode, there's a whole lot more going on in the window's several panes, and you'll need all the screen real estate that you can get.

Two Debug menu options will become available once you're in Debug mode. Click Show Registers and Show Memory. On the right side of the window a new pane will be open. That's the registers pane, and it will show the contents of all of the general-purpose x64 registers. (The math coprocessor registers will not be there if you configured SASM correctly for this book's demos.) Note: *You can see the registers pane only while in debug mode.* Furthermore, until you begin single-stepping, the register window won't always "fill."

The Memory pane will appear across the top of SASM's window. Using it can be tricky, as I'll explain a little later.

The SASM window at this point will look like Figure 6.2.

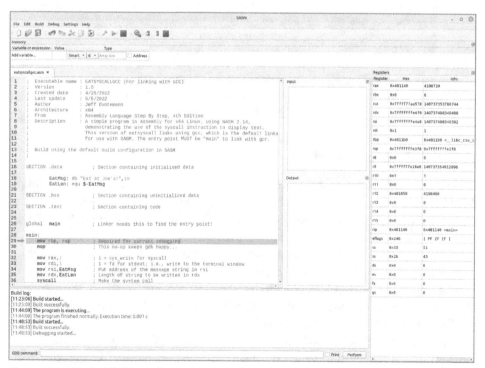

Figure 6.2: The full SASM window in debug mode

There will be a yellow highlight bar on the first line of executable code (not comments or labels) in the source pane. Execution is paused at that line. We call such a pause a *breakpoint*. With SASM, the first line of code will always be a de facto breakpoint when you enter debug mode. I say "de facto" because you can set your own breakpoint on any line of code by clicking that line's number, at the left margin of the source pane. For now, click the line number for this line:

```
mov rax,1
```

A red dot will appear to the right of the line number. That tells you there's a breakpoint at that line.

Now click the Debug icon. Once you're in debug mode, the Debug icon tells SASM to continue execution. The highlight will move down to your breakpoint. This is important: Execution stops at a breakpoint *before* the breakpoint's line is executed. The highlighted MOV instruction has not executed yet.

This is a good time to see the registers pane at work. The RAX register is the first on the list. It will contain a value of some sort. This value isn't important. It's what I call "leftovers" from whatever SASM was doing with RAX before your program began execution.

With execution awaiting your command, click the Step Over icon, which is immediately to the right of the Debug icon. The highlight will move down to the next code line. If you look at the contents of RAX in the registers pane, you'll see that it now contains the value 1.

If you click the Step Over icon again, the highlight will move down another line, and the instruction MOV RDI,1 will execute. You can check the value of RDI in the registers pane to see that it, too, now contains the value 1.

You can step through the execution of your program one instruction at a time by clicking the Step Over icon. Once you execute the final SYSCALL instruction, your program will exit, and debug mode will be over. The registers and memory panes will both go away.

You've probably noticed that there are two Step icons, one Step Over and the other Step Into. What's the difference? For very simple programs like this one, none. The two diverge once you create procedures and procedure libraries for your assembly programs. You call a procedure with the CALL instruction. But suppose your procedure already works well. You don't have to step through it. So by clicking the Step Over button, you skip the procedure call and continue. If you click Step Into instead, SASM allows you to step through the procedure's machine instructions, before returning to the place in the program where the procedure call is.

I'll take this up again in more detail when we get to procedures later in the book.

To sum up, the debugger allows you to "see inside" assembly code in two ways: by allowing you to set breakpoints and run the code at full speed until execution hits a breakpoint; or by stepping one instruction at a time, pausing after each step to watch registers or memory. Of course, you can use both, using a breakpoint to get to the point of interest quickly and then stepping through the area of interest to see what it's up to.

SASM's Editor

SASM's editor is pretty basic. It offers most of the common text editor commands used in source code editors: Open, Save, Save As, Close, Select All, Cut, Copy, Paste, and Find/Replace. The only one I miss is Delete Line, via the venerable Ctrl+Y shortcut. To delete a line, you must select it with the mouse and then press the Delete key. I admit that this may count as a safety feature, at least while you're first starting out.

What SASM Demands of Your Code

If you look closely at the `eatsyscallgcc.asm` demo program, you may spot a couple of differences between it and the `eatsyscall.asm` program we looked at earlier. SASM has two requirements due to its use of `gcc` as a link manager.

- The program's entry point *must* be `main` rather than `_start`, and `main` must be in lowercase; see below.
- The first line in a program's body must be `MOV RBP,RSP`. NASM is not case-sensitive by default, and the lowercase form `mov rbp,rsp` is what you'll see in the editor window. This is deliberate: You need to be comfortable with both all-lowercase source code and all-caps source code. In the book text, code will be in uppercase; in the listings, it will be lowercase.

Why these requirements? SASM automatically links your programs to the standard C library, `libc`. In a way, what you're writing with SASM is a C program without writing C code. There are conventions necessary in a C program that apply even if the program isn't written in C. One of those conventions is that the body of a C program is always called `main`. Another is to save the stack pointer register RSP in register RBP before anything else happens. This allows the program to access data on the stack without destroying the original value of the stack pointer RSP.

One odd feature of SASM that I don't care for is that whether or not you place `MOV RBP,RSP` as the first instruction in a program, *SASM will add it when you enter debug mode.* So if you place the `MOV` instruction at the beginning of the program, you'll have *two* instances of `MOV RBP,RSP` as soon as you enter debug mode. That won't hurt anything, but it is peculiar. (Note that this may be a bug, and by the time you read this book, it may have been eliminated in a newer release.) It also goes against something called the *standard prolog* that I'll discuss in Chapters 11 and 12.

SASM is a good way to learn simple assembly techniques. It's especially good at visual debugging, because you see your source code—and your comments—while you're stepping through a program. You'll probably upgrade to a more powerful IDE as your skills improve. While you're just breaking into assembly language, the SASM IDE will be more than good enough.

That's the quick demo of what SASM can do. It's time to talk about a couple of other tools that are useful in assembly language work.

Linux and Terminals

Unix people hated to admit it at the time, but when it was created, Unix really was a mainframe operating system like IBM's, and it supported multiple simultaneous users via timesharing. Each user communicated with the central computer through separate, stand-alone terminals, especially those from the Digital Equipment Corporation's VT series.

These terminals did *not* display the graphical desktops we've come to see as essential since 1995 or so. They were text-only devices, typically presenting 25 lines of 80 characters without icons or windows. Some applications used the full screen, presenting numbered menus and fill-in fields for data entry. The bulk of the Unix software tools, especially those used by programmers, were controlled from the command line and sent back scroll-up-from-the-bottom output.

Linux works the same way. Put most simply, Linux *is* Unix. Linux does not use external "dumb terminals" like the 1970s DEC VT100, but the DEC-style terminal-oriented software machinery is still there inside Linux and still functioning, in the form of terminal emulation.

The Linux Console

There are any number of terminal emulator programs for Linux and other Unix implementations like BSD. Ubuntu and Kubuntu come with one called GNOME Terminal, and you can download and install many others from your distro's package manager. The one that I use for the discussions in this book and recommend generally is called Konsole. Do install it if you haven't already.

When you open a terminal emulator program under Linux, you get a text command line with a flashing cursor, much like the old DOS command line or the Command Prompt utility in Windows. The terminal program does its best to act like one of those old DEC CRT serial terminals from the First Age of Unix. By default, a terminal emulator program uses the PC keyboard and display for its input and output. And what it connects to is a special Linux device called *dev/console*, which is a predefined device that provides communication with the Linux system itself.

It's useful to remember that a terminal program is just a program, and you can have several different varieties of terminal program installed on your Linux machine, with multiple instances of each running, all at the same time. However, there is only *one* Linux console, by which I mean the device named dev/ console that channels commands to the Linux system and returns the system's responses. By default, a terminal emulator program connects to dev/console when it launches. If you want, you can use a Linux terminal emulator to connect to other things through a network, though how that works and how to do it are outside the scope of this book.

The simplest way of communicating with a Linux program is through a terminal emulator like the Konsole program, which is the one I'll refer to in this book. The alternative to a terminal emulator is to write your programs for a windowing system of some kind. Describing Linux desktop managers and the X Window system that operates beneath them would alone take a whole book (or several) and involves layers of complexity that really have nothing to do with assembly language. So in this book the example programs will operate strictly from the terminal emulator command line.

Character Encoding in Konsole

There's not much to configure in a terminal emulator program, at least while taking your first steps in assembly language. One thing that does matter for the example programs in this book is *character encoding*. A terminal emulator has to put characters into its window, and one of the configurable options in a terminal emulator has to do with what glyphs correspond to which 8-bit character code. Note well that this has nothing directly to do with fonts. A glyph is a specific recognizable symbol, like the letter *A* or the @ sign. How that symbol is rendered graphically depends on what font you use. Rendered in different fonts, a particular glyph might be fatter or thinner or have little feet or flourishes of various kinds. You can display an *A* in any number of fonts, but assuming that the font is not excessively decorative (and such fonts exist), you can still tell that a particular glyph is an *A*.

Character encoding maps a numeric value to a particular glyph. In our familiar Western ASCII standard, the decimal number 65 is associated with the glyph we recognize as an uppercase *A*. In a different character encoding, one created to render an entirely different, non-Roman alphabet (like Hebrew, Arabic, or Thai), the number 65 might be associated with an entirely different glyph.

This book is being written in a Roman alphabet for a Western and mostly English-speaking audience, so our terminal emulator's default glyphs for the alphabet will do just fine. However, the ASCII character set really goes only from character 0 up to character 127. Eight bits can express values up to 256, so there are another 128 "high" characters beyond the top end of the ASCII standard. There's no standard nearly as strong as ASCII on which glyphs to encode for those 128 characters. Different character encoding schemes include many different glyphs, most of them Roman characters with modifiers (umlaut, circumflex, tilde, accents, and so on), the major Greek letters, and symbols from mathematics and logic.

When IBM released its original PC in 1981, it included glyphs that it had created for its mainframe terminals years earlier to allow boxes to be rendered on terminal screens that were text-only and could not display pixel graphics. These glyphs turned out to be useful for delimiting fill-in forms and other things. The PC's ROM-based character set eventually came to be called Code Page 437, which includes a lot of other symbols like the four card suits.

A similar character encoding scheme was later used in IBM's Unix implementation, AIX, and came to be called IBM-850. IBM-850 includes a subset of the box-draw characters in CP437, plus a lot of Roman alphabet characters with modifiers, to allow correct rendering of text in languages other than English.

Linux terminal emulators do not encode either the CP437 encoding scheme or the IBM-850 scheme (and thus its box-border characters) by default. The IBM-850 encoding scheme is available, but you have to select it from the menus. By the way, at this writing I have never seen a Linux terminal emulator capable of displaying IBM's original CP437 character set. Such may exist, but CP437 is considered obsolete, and requiring it to run a program you've written will annoy users.

Launch Konsole and pull down the Settings ⇨ Manage Profiles item. Konsole comes with one profile, named Default. In the Manage Profiles dialog that appears, select New Profile, and give the new profile a name like **Shell Box**. Save it. In the Edit Profile dialog, select the Advanced tab, and look for the Default Character Encoding drop-down in the pane. Click Select, and from the list presented, hover over Western European until the list of encodings appears. Select IBM850, and click OK (see Figure 6.3).

To use the IBM-850 character encoding, you need to make the new Shell Box profile Konsole's default profile. This is done by selecting Settings ⇨ Manage Profiles and clicking the check box immediately to the left of the profile's name. When the Shell Box profile is in force, the IBM box-border characters will be available for the use of your programs. We'll use them a few chapters down the road.

Figure 6.3: Changing Konsole's character encoding to IBM-850

The Three Standard Unix Files

Computers have been described as machines that move data around, and that's not a bad way to see it. That said, the best way to get a grip on program input and output via terminal emulators is to understand one of Unix's fundamental design principles: *Everything is a file*. A file can be a collection of data on disk, as I explained in some detail in Chapter 5. But in more general terms, *a file is an endpoint on a path taken by data*. When you write to a file, you're sending data along a path to an endpoint. When you read from a file, you are accepting data from an endpoint. The path that the data takes between files may be entirely within a single computer, or it may be between computers along a network of some kind. Data may be processed and changed along the path, or it may simply move from one endpoint to another without modification. No matter. Everything is a file, and all files are treated more or less identically by Unix's internal file machinery.

The "everything is a file" dictum applies to more than collections of data on disk. Your keyboard is a file: It's an endpoint that generates data and sends it somewhere. Your display is a file: It's an endpoint that receives data from somewhere and puts it up where you can see it. Unix files do not have to be text files. Binary files (like the executables created by SASM) are handled the same way.

Three standard files are defined by Unix and are always open to your programs while the programs are running. I've listed them in Table 6.1.

Table 6.1: The Three Standard Unix Files

FILE	C IDENTIFIER	FILE DESCRIPTOR	DEFAULTS TO
Standard Input	stdin	0	Keyboard
Standard Output	stdout	1	Display
Standard Error	stderr	2	Display

At the bottom of it, a file is known to the operating system by its file descriptor, which is just a number. The first three such numbers belong to the three standard files. When you open an existing file or create a new file from within a program, Linux will return a file descriptor value specific to the file you've opened or created. To manipulate the file, you call into the operating system and pass it the file descriptor of the file you want to work with. Table 6.1 also provides the conventional identifiers by which the standard files are known in the C world. When people talk about "stdout," for example, they're talking about file descriptor 1.

If you look back to Listing 5-1, the short example program I presented in Chapter 5 during our walk-through of the assembly language development process, you'll see this line:

```
mov rdi,1 ; 1 = fd for stdout; write to the terminal window
```

When we sent the little slogan "Eat at Joe's!" to the display, we were in fact writing it to file descriptor 1, standard output. By changing the value to 2, we could have sent the slogan to standard error instead. It wouldn't have been displayed any differently on the screen. Standard error is identical in all ways to standard output in terms of how data is handled. By custom, programs like NASM send their error messages to standard error, but the text written to standard error isn't marked as an "error message" or displayed in a different color or character set. Standard error and standard output exist so that we can keep our program's output separate from our program's errors and other messages relating to how and what the program is doing.

This will make a lot more sense once you understand one of the most useful basic mechanisms of all Unix-descended operating systems: I/O redirection.

I/O Redirection

By default, standard output goes to the display. (This is generally a terminal emulator window.) But that's just the default. You can change the endpoint for a data stream coming from standard output. The data from standard output can be sent to a file on disk instead. A file is a file; data traffic between files is handled the same way by Linux, so switching endpoints is no big trick. Data from standard output can be sent to an existing file, or it can be sent to a new file created when your program is run.

Input to your programs by default comes from the keyboard, but all the keyboard sends is text. This text could as well come from another text file. Switching the source of data sent to your programs is no more difficult than switching the destination of its output. The mechanism is called *I/O redirection*, and we're going to use it for a lot of the example programs later in this book.

You've probably already used I/O redirection in your Linux work, even if you didn't know it by name. All of Linux's basic shell commands send their output to standard output. The `ls` command, for example, sends a listing of the contents of the working directory to standard output. You can capture that listing by redirecting the text emitted by `ls` into a Linux disk file, by entering this command at the command line:

```
ls > dircontents.txt
```

The file `dircontents.txt` is created if it doesn't already exist, and the text emitted by ls is stored in `dircontents.txt`. You can then print the file or load it into a text editor.

The > symbol is one of two redirection operators. The < symbol works the other way and redirects standard input away from the keyboard and to another file, typically a text file stored on disk. This is less useful for handing keyboard commands to a program than it is for providing the raw material on which the program is going to work.

Let's say you want to write a program to force all the lowercase text in a file to uppercase characters. (This is a wonderfully contrarian thing to do, as uppercase characters make some Unix people half-nuts.) You can write the program to obtain its text from standard input and send its text to standard output. This is easy to do from a programming standpoint—and in fact, we'll be doing it a little further along in the book.

You can test your program by typing this line of text at the keyboard:

```
i want live things in their pride to remain.
```

Your program will process this line of text and send the processed text to standard output, where it will be posted to the terminal emulator display:

```
I WANT LIVE THINGS IN THEIR PRIDE TO REMAIN.
```

Well, the test was a success: It looks like things work inside the program. So, the next step is to test `uppercaser` on some real files. You don't have to change the `uppercaser` program at all. Just enter this at the shell prompt:

```
uppercaser < santafetrail.txt > vachelshouting.txt
```

By the magic of I/O redirection, your program will read all the text from a disk file called `santafetrail.txt`, force any lowercase characters to uppercase, and then write the uppercased text to the disk file `vachelshouting.txt`.

The redirection operators can be thought of as arrows pointing in the direction that data is moving. Data is being taken from the file `santafetrail.txt` and sent to the `uppercaser` program; hence, the symbol < points from the input file to the program where it's going. The `uppercaser` program is sending data to the output file `vachelshouting.txt`, and thus the redirection operator points away from the name of the program and toward the name of the output file.

From a height, what's going on looks like what I've drawn in Figure 6.4. I/O redirection acts as a sort of data switch, steering streams of data away from the standard files to named source and destination files of your own choosing.

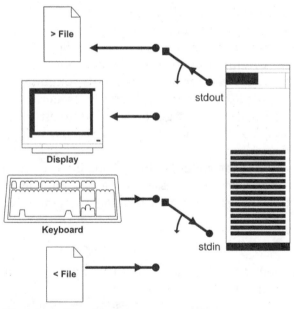

Figure 6.4: I/O redirection

Simple Text Filters

We're actually going to create a little program called `uppercaser` later, and that's exactly what it's going to do: read text from a text file, process the text, and write the processed text to an output file. Inside the program, we'll be reading from standard input and writing to standard output. This makes it unnecessary for the program to prompt the user for input and output filenames, create the output file, and so on. Linux will do all that for us, which makes for a *much* easier programming task.

Programs that work this way represent a standard mechanism in the greater Unix world, called a *filter*. You've already met a couple of them. The NASM assembler itself is a filter: It takes text files full of assembly language source code, processes them, and writes out a binary file full of object code and symbol information. The Linux linker reads in one or more files full of object code and symbol information and writes out an executable program file. NASM and the linker operate on more than simple text, but that's OK. A file is a file is a file, and the machinery that Linux uses to operate on files doesn't distinguish between text and binary files.

Filter programs don't always use I/O redirection to locate their inputs and outputs. NASM and most linkers pick their source and destination filenames off the command line, which is a useful trick that we'll discuss later in this book. Still, I/O redirection makes programming simple text filter programs *much* easier.

Once you grasp how filter programs work, you'll begin to understand why the standard error file exists and what it does. A filter program processes input data into output data. Along the way, it may need to post an error message or simply confirm to us that it's still plugging along and hasn't fallen into an endless loop. For that, we need a communication channel independent of the program's inputs and outputs. Standard error provides such a communication channel. Your program can post textual status and error messages to the terminal emulator display by writing those messages to the standard error file, all during the time that it's working and the standard output file is busy writing program output to disk.

Standard error can be redirected just as standard output is, and if you wanted to capture your programs status and/or error messages to a disk file named `joblog.txt`, you would launch the program from the terminal command line this way:

```
uppercaser < santafetrail.txt > vachelshouting.txt 2> joblog.txt
```

Here, the `2>` operator specifies that file descriptor 2 (which, if you recall, is standard error) is what's being redirected to `joblog.txt`.

If you redirect output (from whatever source) to an existing disk file, redirection will replace whatever may already be in the file with new data, and the old data will be overwritten and lost. If you want to append redirected data to the end of an existing file that already contains data, you must use the `>>` append operator instead.

Using Standard Input and Standard Output from Inside SASM

Most of the simple demo programs in this book use Linux standard input (stdin) and standard output (stdout). SASM has a dedicated window for both. When your program sends characters to stdout (as the eatsyscall program and most of the others do), the characters will appear in the Output window.

How to use the Input window is less obvious. Typically, stdin reads characters from a text file on disk. When you invoke a program that uses stdin on a terminal command line, you would use stdin like this:

```
hexdump2 < texttestfile.txt
```

Here, the program hexdump2 (which we'll look at later in this book) takes data from a file called texttestfile.txt and sends a formatted hex dump of the file to stdout.

That's using the terminal command line. So, how do you use stdin from *inside* SASM?

It's simple: Copy the text you want your program to process from some file or other text source and paste it into SASM's Input window. The paste command is on the right-click context menu when the mouse is in the Input window. The text will appear in the Input window. When your program needs text from stdin, it will use system call 0 to read the text in one character at a time, until all the text has been read. You can also simply type text from the keyboard into the Input window before your program begins running. Typed text will be treated the same as text pasted into the window.

To clear the Input window, put the mouse in the window, right-click, and select Select All (shortcut Ctrl+A) followed by the Delete key.

Note that reading text from the Input window will *not* remove that text from the window. It all stays there until you clear it manually.

Terminal Control with Escape Sequences

By default, output to a terminal emulator window enters at the left end of the bottom line, and previously displayed lines scroll up with the addition of each new line at the bottom. This is perfectly useful, but it's not pretty and certainly doesn't qualify as a "user interface" in any honest sense. There were plenty of "full-screen" applications written for the Unix operating system in ancient times, and they wrote their data entry fields and prompts all over the screen. When color display terminals became available, text could be displayed in different colors, on fields with backgrounds set to white or to some other color to contrast with the text.

How was this done? The old DEC VT terminals like the VT100 could be controlled by way of special sequences of characters embedded in the stream of data sent to the terminal from standard output or standard error. These sequences of characters were called *escape sequences*, because they were an "escape" (albeit a temporary one) from the ordinary stream of data being sent up to be displayed.

The VT terminals watched the data streams that they were displaying and picked out the characters in the escape sequences for separate interpretation. One escape sequence would be interpreted as a command to clear the display. Another escape sequence would be interpreted as a command to display the next characters on the screen starting five lines from the top of the screen and thirty characters from the left margin. There were dozens of such recognized escape sequences, and they allowed the relatively crude text terminals of the day to present neatly formatted text to the user a full screen at a time.

A Linux terminal emulator like Konsole is a program written to "look like" one of those old DEC terminals, at least in terms of how it displays data on our 21st century LCD computer monitors. Send the character sequence "Eat at Joe's!" to Konsole, and Konsole puts it up obediently in its window, just like the old VT100s did. We've already seen that with Listing 5-1. Konsole, however, watches the stream of characters that we send to it, and it knows those escape sequences as well. The key to Konsole's vigilance lies in a special character that is normally invisible: Esc, the numeric equivalent of which is 27 decimal, or 01Bh. When Konsole sees an Esc character come in on the stream of text that it is displaying, it looks very carefully at the next several characters. If the first three characters after the Esc character are "[2J," Konsole recognizes that as the escape sequence that commands it to clear its display. If, however, the four characters after the Esc are "[11H," then Konsole sees an escape sequence commanding it to move the cursor to the home position in the upper-left corner of the display.

There are literally dozens of different escape sequences, all of them representing commands to move the cursor around; to change the foreground and background colors of characters; to switch fonts or character encodings; to erase lines, portions of lines, or portions of the entire screen; and so on. Programs running in a terminal window can take complete control over the display by sending carefully crafted escape sequences to standard output. (We'll do some of this a little later, so keep in mind that there are caveats, and the whole business is not as simple as it sounds.) Prior to the era of graphical user interface (GUI) applications, sending escape sequences to terminals (or terminal emulators) was precisely how display programming under Unix was done.

Note that SASM's Output window does *not* understand character escape sequences! If your program emits text formatted via escape sequences, save the EXE file to disk, exit SASM, and test it under Konsole, which does understand simple escape sequences.

So Why Not GUI Apps?

That brings us to an interesting question. This book has been in print now for more than 35 years (since the spring of 1990), and I get a lot of mail about it. The number-one question is this: How can I write GUI apps? Most of my correspondents mean Windows apps, but here and there people ask about writing assembly apps for GNOME or KDE as well. I learned my lesson years ago and never respond by saying "Why would you want to do *that?*" but instead respond with the honest truth: It's a project that represents a *huge* amount of research and effort, for relatively little payoff.

On the other hand, if you *do* learn to write GUI apps for Windows or Linux, you will understand how those operating systems' UI mechanisms work. And that can certainly be valuable, if you have the time and energy to devote to it.

The problem is that there is an *enormous* barrier to entry. Before you can write your first GUI app in assembly, you have to know how it *all* works, for very large values of "all." GUI apps require managing "signals" (in Windows, "events") sent up by the operating system, indicating that keys have been pressed or mouse buttons clicked, etc. GUI apps have to manage a large and complex "widget set" of buttons and menus and fill-out fields and a mind-boggling number of application programming interface (API) calls. There is memory to manage and redrawing to do when a part of an app's screen display area gets "dirty" (that is, overwritten by something else or updated by the app) or when the user resizes the app's window or windows.

The internals of Windows GUI programming is one of the ugliest things I've ever seen. (Linux is just as complex, though not as ugly.) Fortunately, it's a standardized sort of ugliness and easily encapsulated within code libraries that don't change much from one application to another. This is why graphical IDEs and very high-level programming language products are so popular: They hide most of the ugliness of interfacing to the operating system's GUI machinery behind a set of standard class libraries working within an application framework. You can write very good apps in Delphi or Visual Basic (for Windows) or Lazarus or Gambas for Linux, with only a sketchy understanding of what's going on way down deep. If you want to work in assembly, you basically have to know it all before you even start.

This means you have to start somewhere else. If you genuinely want to write assembly language GUI apps for one of the Linux desktop managers, approach it this way:

1. Study Linux programming in a capable native-code high-level language like Pascal, C, or C++. Intermediate language systems like Python, Basic, or Perl won't help you much here.

2. Get good at that language. Study the code that it generates by loading it into a debugger, or compile to assembly language source and study the generated assembly source code files.

3. Learn how to write and link assembly language functions to programs written in your chosen high-level language.

4. Study the underlying windowing mechanism. For Linux, this would be the X Window technology, on which several good books have been written. (My favorite is *The Joy of X* by Niall Mansfield; Addison-Wesley, 1994.)

5. Study the details of a particular desktop environment and widget set, be it GNOME, KDE, xfce, or some other. The best way to do this is to write apps for it in your chosen high-level language and study the assembly language code that the compiler emits.

6. Finally, try creating your own assembly code by imitating what the compiler generates.

Don't expect to find a lot of help online. Unix (and thus Linux) is heavily invested in the culture of portability, which requires that the bulk of the operating system and all apps written for it be movable to a new hardware platform by a simple recompile. Assembly language is the hated orphan child in the Unix world (almost as hated as my own favorite high-level language, Pascal) and many cultural tribalists will try to talk you out of doing anything ambitious in assembly. Resist—but remember that you will be very much on your own.

If you're simply looking for a more advanced challenge in assembly language, look into writing network apps using Unix sockets. This involves *way* less research, and the apps you produce may well be useful for administering servers or other "in the background" software packages that do not require graphical user interfaces. Several books exist on sockets programming, most of them by W. Richard Stevens. Read up; it's a fascinating business.

Using Linux Make

If you've done any programming in C at all, you're almost certainly familiar with the concept of the Make utility. The Make mechanism grew up in the C world, and although it's been adopted by many other programming languages and environments, it's never been adopted quite as thoroughly as in the C world.

What the Make mechanism does is build executable program files from their component parts. The Make utility is a puppet master that executes other programs according to a master plan, which is a simple text file called a makefile. The *makefile* is a little like a computer program in that it specifies how something is to be done. But unlike a computer program, it doesn't specify the precise sequence of operations to be taken. What it does is specify what pieces of a program are required to build other pieces of the program and in doing so ultimately defines what it takes to build the final executable file. It does this by specifying certain rules called *dependencies*.

Dependencies

Throughout the rest of this book we'll be looking at teeny, little programs, generally with 100 lines of code or less. In the real world, useful programs can take thousands, tens of thousands, or even millions of lines of source code. Managing such an immense quantity of source code is *the* central problem in software engineering. Writing programs in a modular fashion is the oldest and most-used method of dealing with program complexity. Cutting up a large program into smaller chunks and working on the chunks separately helps a great deal. In ambitious programs, some of the chunks are further cut into even smaller chunks, and sometimes the various chunks are written in more than one programming language. Of course, that creates the additional challenge of knowing how the chunks are created and how they all fit together. For that you really need a blueprint.

A makefile is such a blueprint.

In a modular program, each chunk of code is created somehow, generally by using a compiler or an assembler. Compilers, assemblers, and linkers take one or more files and create new files from them. An assembler, as you've learned, takes an ASM file full of assembly language source code and uses it to create a linkable object code file. You can't create the object code file without having and working with the source code file. The object code file *depends* on the source code file for its very existence.

Similarly, a linker connects multiple object code files together into a single executable file. The executable file depends on the existence of the object code files for its existence. The contents of a makefile specify which files are necessary to create which other files and what steps are necessary to accomplish that creation. The Make utility looks at the rules (called *dependencies*) in the makefile and invokes whatever compilers, assemblers, and other utilities it sees are necessary to build the final executable or library file.

There are numerous flavors of Make utilities, and not all makefiles are comprehensible to all Make utilities everywhere. The Unix Make utility is pretty standard, however, and the one that comes with Linux is the one we'll be discussing here.

Let's take an example that actually makes a simple Linux assembly program. Typically, in creating a makefile, you begin by determining which file or files are necessary to create the executable program file. The executable file is created in the link step, so the first dependency you have to define is which files the linker requires to create the executable file. The dependency itself can be pretty simply stated.

```
eatsyscall: eatsyscall.o
```

All this line says is that to generate the executable file eatsyscall (which is presented in Chapter 5 as Listing 5.1) we first need to have the file eatsyscall.o. The previous line is actually a dependency line written as it should be for inclusion in a makefile. In any but the smallest programs (such as this one) the linker will have to link more than one .o file. So this is probably the simplest possible sort of dependency: One executable file depends on one object code file. If there are additional files that must be linked to generate the executable file, they are placed in a list, separated by spaces:

```
linkbase: linkbase.o linkparse.o linkfile.o
```

This line tells us that the executable file linkbase depends on *three* object code files, and all three of these files must exist before we can generate the executable file that we want.

Lines like these tell us what files are required, but not what must be done with them. That's an essential part of the blueprint, and it's handled in a line that follows the dependency line. The two lines work together. Here are both lines for our simple example:

```
eatsyscall: eatsyscall.o
    ld -o eatsyscall.o eatsyscall
```

At least for the Linux version of Make, *the second line must be indented by a single tab character at the beginning of the line.* I emphasize this because Make will hand you an error if there is no tab character at the beginning of the second line. *Using space characters to indent will not work.* A typical "missing tab" error message (which beginners see a lot) looks like this:

```
Makefile:2: *** missing separator. Stop.
```

Here, a tab was missing at the beginning of line 2.

The two lines of the makefile taken together should be pretty easy to understand: The first line tells us what file or files are required to do the job. The second line tells us how the job is to be done: in this case, by using the ld linker to link eatsyscall.o into the executable file eatsyscall.

Nice and neat: We specify which files are necessary and what has to be done with them. The Make mechanism, however, has one more very important aspect: knowing whether the job as a whole actually has to be done at all.

When a File Is Up-to-Date

It may seem idiotic to have to come out and say so, but once a file has been compiled or linked, it's been done, and it doesn't have to be done again. . .*until we modify one of the required source or object code files*. The Make utility knows this. It can tell when a compile or a link task needs to be done at all, and if the job doesn't have to be done, Make will refuse to do it.

How does Make know if the job needs doing? Consider this dependency:

```
eatsyscall: eatsyscall.o
```

Make looks at this and understands that the executable file `eatsyscall` depends on the object code file `eatsyscall.o` and that you can't generate `eatsyscall` without having `eatsyscall.o`. It also knows when both files were last changed, and if the executable file `eatsyscall` is *newer* than `eatsyscall.o`, it deduces that any changes made to `eatsyscall.o` are already reflected in `eatsyscall`. (It can be absolutely sure of this because the only way to generate `eatsyscall` is by processing `eatsyscall.o`.)

The Make utility pays close attention to Linux timestamps. Whenever you edit a source code file or generate an object code file or an executable file, Linux updates that file's timestamp to the moment that the changes were finally completed. And even though you may have created the original file six months ago, by convention we say that a file is *newer* than another if the time value in its timestamp is more recent than that of another file, even one that was created only 10 minutes ago.

(In case you're unfamiliar with the notion of a *timestamp*, it's simply a value that an operating system keeps in a filesystem directory for every file in the directory. A file's timestamp is updated to the current clock time whenever the file is changed.)

When a file is newer than all of the files that it depends upon (according to the dependencies called out in the makefile), that file is said to be *up-to-date*. Nothing will be accomplished by generating it again, because all information contained in the component files is reflected in the dependent file.

Chains of Dependencies

So far, this may seem like a lot of fuss to no great purpose. But the real value in the Make mechanism begins to appear when a single makefile contains *chains* of dependencies. Even in the simplest makefiles, there will be dependencies that depend on other dependencies. Our completely trivial example program requires two dependency statements in its makefile.

Consider that the following dependency statement specifies how to generate an executable file from an object code (.o) file:

```
eatsyscall: eatsyscall.o
    ld -o eatsyscall.o eatsyscall
```

The gist here is that to build the eatsyscall file, you start with eatsyscall.o and process it according to the recipe in the second line. So where does eatsyscall.o come from? That requires a second dependency statement.

```
eatsyscall.o: eatsyscall.asm
    nasm -f elf64 -g -F dwarf eatsyscall.asm
```

Here we explain that to generate eatsyscall.o, we need eatsyscall.asm, and to generate it, we follow the recipe in the second line. The full makefile would contain nothing more than these two dependencies:

```
eatsyscall: eatsyscall.o
    ld -o eatsyscall.o eatsyscall
eatsyscall.o: eatsyscall.asm
    nasm -f elf64 -g -F dwarf eatsyscall.asm
```

These two dependency statements define the two steps that we must take to generate an executable program file from our very simple assembly language source code file eatlinux.asm. However, it's not obvious from the two dependencies I show here that all the fuss is worthwhile. Assembling eatlinux .asm pretty much requires that we link eatlinux.o to create eatlinux. The two steps go together in virtually all cases.

But consider a real-world programming project, in which there are hundreds of separate source code files. Only some of those files might be "on the rack" in an editor and undergoing changes on any given day. However, to build and test the final program, *all* of the files are required. But...are all the compilation steps and assembly steps required? Not at all.

An executable program is knit together by the linker from one or more—often *many* more—object code files. If all but (let's say) two of the object code files are up-to-date, there's no reason to assemble the other 147 source code files. You just assemble the two source-code files that have been changed and then link all 149 object code files into the executable.

The challenge, of course, is correctly remembering *which* two files have changed—and being sure that *all* changes that have been recently made to *any* of the 149 source code files are reflected in the final executable file. That's a lot of remembering, or referring to notes. And it gets worse when more than one person is working on the project, as will be the case in nearly all commercial software development shops. The Make utility makes remembering any of this unnecessary. Make figures it out and does only what must be done—no more, no less.

The Make utility looks at the makefile, and it looks at the timestamps of all the source code and object code files called out in the makefile. If the executable file is newer than all of the object code files, nothing needs to be done. However, if *any* of the object code files are newer than the executable file, the executable file must be relinked. And if one or more of the source code files are newer than either the executable file or their respective object code files, some assembling or compiling must be done before any linking is done.

What Make does is start with the executable file and looks for chains of dependency moving away from that. The executable file depends on one or more object files, which in turn depend on one or more source code files. Make walks the path up the various chains, taking note of what's newer than an executable file and what must be done to put it all right. Make then executes the compiler, assembler, and linker selectively to be sure that the executable file is ultimately newer than all of the files that it depends on. Make ensures that all work that needs to be done gets done. Furthermore, Make avoids spending unnecessary time compiling and assembling files that are already up-to-date and do not need to be compiled or assembled. Given that a full build (by which I mean the recompilation/reassembly and relinking of every single file in the project) can take hours on an ambitious program, Make saves an enormous amount of idle time when all you need to do is test changes made to one small part of the program.

There is actually a lot more to the Unix Make facility than this, but what I've described are the fundamental principles. You have the power to make assembling and compilation conditional, inclusion of files conditional, and much more. You won't need to fuss with such things on your first forays into assembly language (or C programming, for that matter), but it's good to know that the power is there as your programming skills improve and you take on more ambitious projects.

Invoking Make

Running Make is about as easy as anything you'll ever do in programming: You type **make** on the terminal command line and hit Enter. Make will handle the rest. There is only one command-line option of interest to beginners, and that is -k. The -k option instructs Make to stop building any file in which an error occurs and leave the previous copy of the target file undisturbed. (It continues building any other files that need building.) Absent the -k option, Make may overwrite your existing object code and executable files with incomplete copies, which isn't the end of the world but is sometimes a nuisance, as well as confusing. If this doesn't make total sense to you right now, don't worry—it's a good idea to use -k until you're *really* sure you don't need to.

That said, for simple projects where there is one project per directory and an appropriate makefile named makefile in each directory, navigate to the project directory you want to work on, and type this command:

```
make -k
```

Any time you make *any* change to one of your source code files, no matter how minor, you will have to run Make to test the consequences of that change. As a beginner you will probably be learning by the "tweak and try" method, which means you might change only one machine instruction on one line of your source code file and then "see what that does."

If you do tend to learn this way (I do, and there's nothing wrong with it!), you're going to be running Make a *lot*. All Linux IDEs and a lot of Linux text editors allow you to run Make without leaving the program. Unfortunately, SASM does not have that feature. It has its own build system, which is not as powerful as Make. But when you graduate from SASM to a full-blown IDE like KDevelop or Eclipse, you'll find ways to launch Make from a menu item or a key binding.

And if you use a customizable terminal emulator like Konsole, you don't need an IDE. You can launch Make from a single keystroke. Konsole allows you to create custom key bindings. A *key binding* is an association between a keystroke or combination keystroke and a text string entered at the terminal console.

Creating a Custom Key Binding for Make

To give yourself a Make key, you have to add a key binding to Konsole. Interestingly, Konsole is embedded in some text editors like the Kate editor. Adding the key binding to Konsole automatically adds it to Kate. In fact, any program that uses Konsole for its terminal emulator will inherit your Make key binding.

Here's how to create a key binding in Konsole. The option is buried deep in Konsole's menu tree, so read carefully.

1. Launch Konsole from the desktop, *not* from within some other program.

2. Select Settings ⇨ Manage profiles from Konsole's main menu.

3. Create a new profile if you haven't already. Earlier in this chapter I described how to create a new profile for Konsole to provide the IBM-850 character encoding (for the sake of the old box-border character set), and if you created a new profile back then, select the new profile and open it.

4. When the Edit Profile dialog appears, click the Keyboard tab.

5. When the Key Bindings dialog appears, make sure that xFree 4 is selected. This is the default set of key bindings used by Konsole. Click the Edit button.

6. When the Edit Key Binding List dialog appears, scroll down the list of bindings to see if there is already a key binding for the ScrollLock key in the Key Combination column. We're going to hijack the ScrollLock key, which I consider the most expendable key in the standard PC keyboard. If ScrollLock already has a key binding for something, you may have to choose a different key—or change whatever output the current binding specifies.

7. If there's no existing key binding for Scroll Lock, create one: Click the Add button. A blank line will appear at the bottom of the bindings table. Type ScrollLock (no space!) in the Key Combination column.

8. Click in the Output column to the right of ScrollLock. This allows us to enter a string that will be emitted to standard output by Konsole any time the ScrollLock key is pressed when Konsole has the focus. Type the following string, minus quotes: make -k\r (see Figure 6.5).

9. Click OK in the Edit Key Bindings List dialog, and click OK in the Key Bindings dialog. Then click Close in the Manage Profiles dialog. You're done!

Figure 6.5: Adding a key binding to Konsole

Test the new key binding by bringing up Konsole and pressing the ScrollLock key. Konsole should type `make -k` on the command line, followed by Enter. (That's what the `\r` means in the key binding string.) Make will be invoked, and depending on whether Konsole was open to a project directory with a makefile in it, Make will then build your project.

Note that if you invoke Make successfully on a given project, Make will not repeat the action if you immediately press ScrollLock (or whatever key you chose for the key binding) again, without editing the source code or deleting the object code file. Make will instead say, "'eatsyscall' is up to date.'"

Using Touch to Force a Build

As I said earlier, if your executable file is newer than all of the files that it depends on, Make will refuse to perform a build—after all, in its own understanding of the process, when your executable file is newer than everything it depends on, there's no work to do.

However, there is the occasional circumstance when you want Make to perform a build even when the executable is up-to-date. The one you'll most likely encounter as a beginner is when you're tinkering with the makefile itself. If you've changed your makefile and want to test it but your executable is up-to-date, you need to engage in a little persuasion. Linux has a command called Touch that has one job only: to update the timestamp in a file to the current clock time. If you invoke Touch on your source code file, it will magically become "newer" than the executable file, and Make will obediently do the build.

Invoke `touch` in a terminal window, followed by the name of the file to be "touched."

```
touch eatsyscall.asm
```

Then invoke Make again, and the build will happen—assuming that your makefile exists and is correct!

Debugging with SASM

SASM's debugging features aren't enabled until you explicitly enter debug mode by selecting Debug ➪ Debug from the menu, press F5 on the keyboard, or click the Debug icon in the toolbar. SASM will highlight the first line of code in the program, which for SASM's build features must be as follows:

```
mov rbp,rsp
```

The program pauses at the highlighted line. At this point you can do one of three things.

- Execute to a breakpoint.
- Single-step.
- End debugging and go back to editing the source code.

Setting a breakpoint is done by clicking the line number in the code where you want execution to pause. A red circle will appear to the right of the line number. The circle tells you that a breakpoint is in force at that line. To execute code up to the breakpoint, you can select Debug ➢ Continue from the menu, click the Debug icon in the toolbar, or press F5. All three of those actions are toggles: When in edit mode, they put SASM in debug mode, and when in debug mode, they continue execution up to the next breakpoint. If there are no further breakpoints, execution continues until the program exits. When the program exits, the log window will say "Debugging finished," and SASM will return to edit mode.

It's important to remember that *you can't edit the source code when in debug mode*, as handy as that might seem at times. The two modes are mutually exclusive. Get back into edit mode first—and it's as simple as clicking the red Stop button.

Single-stepping is straightforward. You can select the two step options from the Debug menu or click the step buttons on the toolbar. The two step buttons are Step Over and Step Into. While you're working with very simple programs, Step Over is the command you'll use. Each time you click Step Over, the highlighted instruction will be executed, and the highlight will move to the next machine instruction. Remember, *an instruction under the highlight has not yet executed*. You have to step to the next instruction to execute the highlighted instruction.

The Step Into option does the same thing as Step Over until the instruction to be executed next is a CALL instruction. When a CALL instruction is highlighted, you have three choices.

- Click Step Over and skip past the CALL instruction.
- Click Step Into and follow the CALL instruction into the subroutine named by CALL. Execution will move into the subroutine until a RET (return) instruction is executed. Then the instruction immediately after the CALL instruction will be highlighted. (More on subroutines later in this book.)
- As always, you can get out of debug mode by clicking the red Stop icon in the toolbar.

While single-stepping, watch the registers in the Registers window. When something in your code changes a register, that change will appear immediately in the window. Register names are displayed in the left column of the Registers window in hexadecimal. The right column is the Info column. Most of the time, the Info column displays registers in decimal.

The biggest exception is the EFlags register. We'll talk about flags in detail in Chapter 7. For now, think of EFlags as a collection of 1-bit registers that indicate a binary (one of two ways) state. You can test the state of each of the flags and branch to another part of the program depending on which way a given flag bit goes.

One aside: In x64, EFlags has expanded to 64 bits and become RFlags, as you might expect. However, at this writing, the high 32 bits of RFlags have not been given any responsibilities and are reserved for Intel's future use. For this reason, SASM's Registers window displays EFlags rather than RFlags. That doesn't mean you're missing any flags. All the flags that exist are in EFlags.

The Registers window displays the names of flags that are set (equal to 1) by name, within square brackets. In the Info pane, EFlags will look something like this:

```
[ PF ZF IF ]
```

(This is just an example; you may see more or fewer flags.) There are many branch instructions that test individual flags, and it's handy to see which flags are set (or not set) before you execute a branch instruction.

Now, compared to most debuggers, SASM's memory display option is extremely limited. In Chapter 7 I describe how to display data items. Displaying runs of memory is sufficiently complex that I'll point you to a more powerful (though much less accessible) debugger that does a better job of showing you what's in a region of memory (see Appendix A).

Pick up Your Tools. . .

At this point, you have the background you need and the tools that you need. It's time (finally!) to sit down and begin looking at the x64 instruction set in detail and then begin writing programs in earnest.

Following Your Instructions

Meeting Machine Instructions Up Close and Personal

After a long monolog, a famous comedian once said, I told you *that* story so I could tell you *this* one...." We're a third of the way through this book, and I haven't even begun describing in detail the principal element in PC assembly language: the 64-bit x64 instruction set. Most books on assembly language, even those targeted at beginners, assume that the instruction set is as good a place as any to start their story, without considering the mass of groundwork without which most beginning programmers get totally lost and give up.

Orientation is crucial. That's why I began at the *real* beginning and took 200 pages to get to where the other guys start.

Keep in mind that this book was created to supply that essential groundwork and orientation for your first steps in assembly language itself. It is *not* a complete course in x64 assembly language. Once you run off the end of this book, you'll have one leg up on any of the multitude of other books on assembly language from other authors and publishers.

And it's high time that we got to the heart of things, way down where software meets the silicon.

Build Yourself a Sandbox

The best way to get acquainted with the x64 instruction set is to build yourself a sandbox and just have fun. An assembly language program doesn't need to run correctly from Linux. It doesn't even need to be complete, as programs go. All it has to be is comprehensible to NASM and the linker, and that in itself doesn't take a lot of doing.

In my personal techie jargon, a *sandbox* is a program intended to be run *only* in a debugger. If you want to see what effects an instruction has on memory or one of the registers, single-stepping it in SASM's debugger will show you vividly. The program doesn't need to return visible results on the command line. It simply has to contain correctly formed instructions.

In practice, my sandbox idea works this way: You assemble and link a program called newsandbox.asm. You create a minimal NASM program in source code and save it to disk as sandbox.asm. Any time you want to play around with machine instructions, you open newsandbox.asm in SASM and save it again as SANDBOX.ASM, overwriting any earlier version of sandbox.asm that may exist. (If for some reason you want to keep a particular sandbox program, save it under a different name.) You can add instructions for observation.

It's possible that your experiments will yield a useful combination of machine instructions that's worth saving. In that case, save the sandbox file as EXPERIMENT1 .ASM (or whatever descriptive name you want to give it), and you can build that sequence into a "real" program whenever you're ready.

A Minimal NASM Program for SASM

So what does a program require to be assembled by NASM within the SASM IDE? In truth, not much. Listing 7.1 is the source code for what I use as a starter sandbox in SASM. Listing 7.1 presents more, in fact, than NASM technically requires but nothing more than it needs to be useful as a sandbox.

Listing 7.1: newsandbox.asm

```
section .data
section .text

global main

main:
     mov rbp, rsp ;Save stack pointer for debugger
     nop
; Put your experiments between the two nops...
```

```
; Put your experiments between the two nops...
    nop

section .bss
```

NASM will in fact assemble a source code file that contains no instruction mnemonics at all—though in fairness, the instructionless executable will not be run by Linux. What we *do* need is a starting point that is marked as global—here, the label `main`. (Using `main` is a requirement of SASM, not NASM.) We also need to define a data section and text section as shown. The data section holds named data items that are to be given initial values when the program runs. The old "Eat at Joe's" ad message from Listing 5.1 was a named data item in the data section. The text section holds program code. Both of these sections are needed to create an executable, even if one or both are empty.

The section marked `.bss` isn't strictly essential, but it's good to have if you're going to be experimenting. The `.bss` section holds uninitialized data, that is, space saved for data items that are given no initial values when the program begins running. These are empty buffers, basically, for data that will be generated or read from somewhere while the program is running. By custom, the `.bss` section is located after the `.text` section. (I'll have a lot more to say about the `.bss` section and uninitialized data in upcoming chapters.)

There are two NOP instructions in `sandbox.asm`. Remember that NOP instructions do nothing but take up a little time. They are there to make it easier to watch the program in the SASM debugger. To play around with machine instructions, place the instructions of your choice between the two comments. Build the program, click the Debug button, and have fun!

Set a breakpoint at the first instruction you place between the comments, and click Debug. Execution will begin and stop at your breakpoint. To observe the effects of that instruction, click the Step Over button. Here's why the second NOP instruction is there: When you single-step an instruction, there has to be an instruction *after* that instruction for execution to pause on. If the first instruction in your sandbox is the last instruction, execution will "run off the edge" on your first single step, and your program will terminate. When that happens, SASM's Registers and Memory panes will go blank, and you won't be able to see the effects of that one instruction!

The notion of running off the edge of the program is an interesting one. If you click the Debug button or press its shortcut key F5, you'll see what happens when you don't properly end the program: Linux will hand up a segmentation fault, which can have a number of causes. However, what happened in this case is that your program attempted to execute a location *past* the end of the `.text` section. Linux knows how long your program is, and it won't allow you to execute any instructions that were not present in your program when it was loaded.

There's no lasting harm in that, of course. Linux is *very* good at dealing with misbehaving and malformed programs (especially simple ones), and nothing you're likely to do by accident will have any effect on the integrity of Linux itself. You can avoid generating the segmentation fault by clicking the red Stop button before you send execution off the end of your little experimental program. SASM will move from Debug mode to Edit mode. Keep in mind that if you exit Debug mode, you will no longer be able to see the registers or memory items.

Of course, if you want to just let a program run, you can add a few lines making a SYSCALL to the x64 Exit routine at the end of your sandbox. That way, if execution runs off the bottom of your experiments, the SYSCALL will gracefully cease execution. The following is the code for the Exit SYSCALL:

```
mov rax,60    ; Code for Exit Syscall
mov rdi,0     ; Return a code of zero
syscall       ; Make kernel call
```

Place this code *after* the second NOP, and you're covered. Note that I have *not* done this to the newsandbox.asm file in the listings archive.

Instructions and Their Operands

The single most common activity in assembly language work is getting data from here to there. There are several specialized ways to do this, but only one truly general way: the MOV instruction. MOV can move a byte, word (16 bits), double word (32 bits), or quad word (64 bits) of data from one register to another, from a register into memory, or from memory into a register. What MOV *cannot* do is move data directly from one address in memory to a different address in memory. (To do that, you need two separate MOV instructions: first from memory to a register and second from that register back out to a different place in memory.)

The name MOV is a bit of a misnomer, since what actually happens is that data is *copied* from a source to a destination. Once copied to the destination, however, the data does not vanish from the source but continues to exist in both places. This conflicts a little with our intuitive notion of moving something, which usually means that something disappears from a source location and reappears at a destination location.

Source and Destination Operands

Most machine instructions, MOV included, have one or more *operands*. (Some instructions have no operands or operate on registers or memory implicitly.

When this is the case, I'll make a point of mentioning it in the text.) Consider this machine instruction:

```
mov rax,1
```

There are two operands in the previous instruction. The first is RAX, and the second is the digit 1. By convention in assembly language, the first (leftmost) operand belonging to a machine instruction is the *destination operand*. The second operand from the left is the *source operand*.

With the mov instruction, the sense of the two operands is pretty literal: The source operand is copied to the destination operand. In the previous instruction, the source operand (the literal value 1) is copied into the destination operand RAX. The sense of source and destination is not nearly so literal in other instructions, but a rule of thumb is this: Whenever a machine instruction causes a new value to be generated, that new value is placed in the destination operand.

There are three different flavors of data that may be used as operands. These are *memory data*, *register data*, and *immediate data*. I've laid out some example mov instructions on the dissection pad in Table 7.1 to give you a flavor for how the different types of data are specified as operands to the mov instruction.

Table 7.1: MOV and Its Operands

MACHINE INSTRUCTION	DESTINATION OPERAND	SOURCE OPERAND	OPERAND NOTES
MOV	RAX,	42h	Source is immediate data.
MOV	RBX,	RDI	Both are 64-bit register data.
MOV	BX,	CX	Both are 16-bit register data.
MOV	DL,	BH	Both are 8-bit register data.
MOV	[RBP],	RDI	Destination is 64-bit memory data at the address stored in RBP.
MOV	RDX,	[RSI]	Source is 64-bit memory data at the address stored in RSI.

Immediate Data

The mov RAX, 42h instruction in Table 7.1 is a good example of using what we call *immediate data*, accessed through an addressing mode called *immediate addressing*. Immediate addressing gets its name from the fact that the item being addressed is data built right into the machine instruction itself. The CPU does not have to go anywhere to find immediate data. It's not in a register, nor is it stored in a data item somewhere out there in memory. Immediate data is always right inside the instruction being fetched and executed.

Immediate data must be of an appropriate size for the operand. For example, you can't move a 16-bit immediate value into an 8-bit register section such as AH or DL. NASM will not allow you to assemble an instruction like this:

```
mov cl,067EFh
```

CL is an 8-bit register, and 067EFh is a 16-bit quantity. Won't go!

Because it's built right into a machine instruction, you might think that immediate data would be quick to access. This is true only up to a point: Fetching *anything* from memory takes more time than fetching anything from a register, and instructions are, after all, stored in memory. So, while addressing immediate data is somewhat quicker than addressing ordinary data stored in memory, neither is anywhere near as quick as simply pulling a value from a CPU register.

Also keep in mind that *only* the source operand may be immediate data. The destination operand is the place where data *goes*, not where it comes from. Since immediate data consists of literal constants (numbers such as 1, 0, 42, or 07F2Bh), trying to copy something *into* immediate data rather than *from* immediate data simply has no meaning and is always an error.

NASM allows some interesting forms of immediate data. For example, the following is perfectly legal, if not necessarily as useful as it looks at first glance:

```
mov eax,'WXYZ'
```

This is a good instruction to load into your sandbox and execute in the debugger. Look at the contents of register EAX in the registers view:

```
0x5a595857
```

This may seem weird, but look close: The numeric equivalents of the upper-case ASCII characters W, X, Y, and Z have been loaded nose-to-tail into EAX. If you're not up on your ASCII, take a look at the chart in Appendix C. W is 57h, X is 58h, Y is 59h, and Z is 5Ah. Each character equivalent is 8 bits in size, so four of them fit snugly into 32-bit register EAX. However, they're backward!

Well, no. Recall the concept of "endianness" that I introduced early in Chapter 5, and if you don't recall, do go back and read that section again. The x86/x64 architecture is "little endian," meaning that the least significant byte in a multibyte sequence is stored at the lowest address. This applies to registers as well and makes sense once you understand how we refer to units of storage within a register.

The confusion comes about because of our schizoid habit of reading text from left to right, while reading numbers from right to left. Take a look at Figure 7.1.

(This example uses 32-bit register EAX to make the figure less complex and easier to understand.) Treated as a sequence of text characters, the *W* in WXYZ is considered the least significant element. EAX, however, is a container for numbers, where the least significant column is always (for Western languages) on the right. The least significant byte in EAX we call AL, and that's where the *W* goes. The second-to-least significant byte in EAX we call AH, and that's where the *X* goes. The two most significant bytes in EAX do not have separate names and may not be addressed individually, but they are still 8-bit bytes and may contain 8-bit values like ASCII characters. The most significant character in the sequence WXYZ is the *Z*, and it's stored in the most significant byte of EAX.

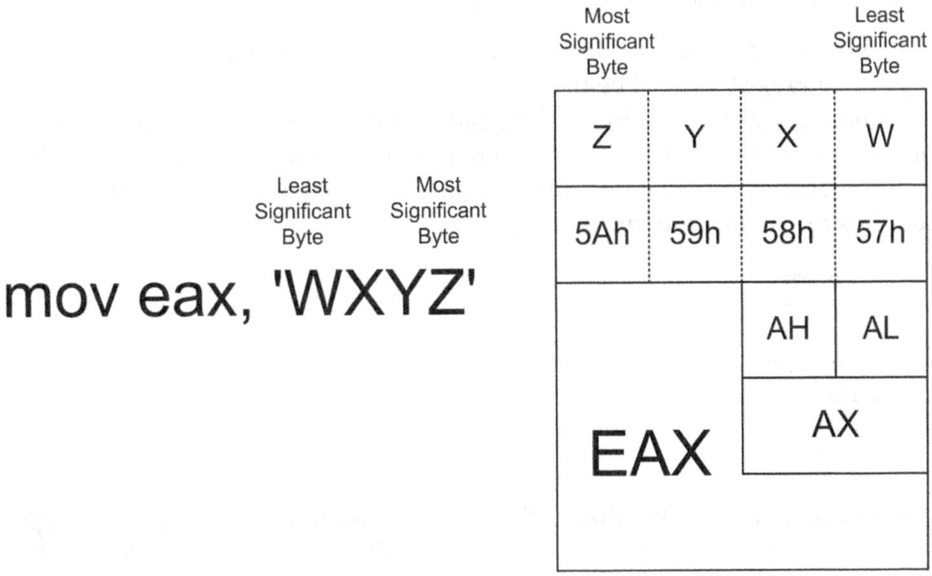

Figure 7.1: Character strings as immediate data

Register Data

Data stored inside a CPU register is known as *register data*, and accessing register data directly is an addressing mode called *register addressing*. Register addressing is done by simply naming the register we want to work with. Here are some entirely legal examples of register data and register addressing:

```
mov rbp,rsi    ; 64-bit
add ecx,edx    ; 32-bit
add di,ax      ; 16-bit
mov bl,ch      ; 8-bit
```

We're not speaking *only* of the mov instruction here. The ADD instruction does just what you might expect and adds the source and destination operands.

The sum replaces whatever was in the destination operand. Irrespective of the instruction, register addressing happens any time data in a register is acted on directly.

The assembler keeps track of certain things that don't make sense, and one such situation is naming a 16-bit register half and a full 64-bit register within the same instruction. Such operations are not legal—after all, what would it mean to move an 8-byte source into a 2-byte destination? And while moving a 2-byte source into an 8-byte destination might seem possible and sometimes even reasonable, the CPU does not support it, and it cannot be done directly. If you try, NASM will hand you this error:

```
error: invalid combination of opcode and operands
```

In other words, if you're moving data from register to register, the source and destination registers *must* be the same size.

Watching register data in the debugger is a good way to get a gut sense for how this works, especially when you're just starting out. Let's practice a little. Enter these instructions into your sandbox, build the executable, and load the sandbox executable into the debugger:

```
xor rbx,rbx
xor rcx,rcx

mov rax,067FEh
mov rbx,rax
mov cl,bh
mov ch,bl
```

Set a breakpoint on the first of the instructions, and then click Run. Single-step through the instructions, watching carefully what happens to RAX, RBX, and RCX. Keep in mind that SASM's Registers window does *not* show the 8-bit, 16-bit, or 32-bit register sections separately and individually. EAX is part of RAX, AX is part of EAX, and CL is part of ECX, etc. Anything you place in RAX is already in EAX, AX, and AL.

Once you're done single-stepping, click the red Stop icon to terminate the program. Remember that if you select Debug ⇨ Continue or try to step past the end of the program, Linux will hand you a segmentation fault for not terminating the program properly. Nothing will be harmed by the fault; remember that the sandbox is not expected to be a complete and proper Linux program. It's good practice to "kill" the program via Stop rather than generate the fault, however.

Note the first two instructions. When you want to put the value 0 into a register, the fastest way is to use the xor instruction, which performs a bitwise xor operation on the source and destination operands. As we'll see a little later, XORing a value against itself yields 0. Yes, you could use

```
mov rbx,0
```

instead, but that has to go out to memory to load the immediate value 0. XORing a register against itself does not go out to memory for either the source or the destination operand and is thus a little faster.

Once you've zeroed out RBX and RCX, this is what happens: The first MOV instruction is an example of immediate addressing using 64-bit registers. The 16-bit hexadecimal value 067FEH is moved into the RAX register. (Note here that you *can* MOV a 16-bit or any other size *immediate* value that will fit in the destination register.) The second instruction uses register addressing to copy register data from EAX into EBX.

The third and fourth MOV instructions both move data between 8-bit register segments rather than 16-, 32-, or 64-bit registers. These two instructions accomplish something interesting. Look at the last register display, and compare the value of RBX and RCX. By moving the value from BX into CX a byte at a time, it's possible to reverse the order of the two bytes making up BX. The high half of BX (what we sometimes call the *most significant byte,* or MSB, of BX) was moved into the low half of CX. Then the low half of BX (what we sometimes call the *least significant byte,* or LSB, of BX) was moved into the high half of CX. This is just a sample of the sorts of tricks you can play with the general-purpose registers.

Just to disabuse you of the notion that the MOV instruction should be used to exchange the two halves of a 16-bit register, let me suggest that you do the following: Go back to SASM and add this instruction to the end of your sandbox:

```
xchg cl,ch
```

Rebuild the sandbox and head back into the debugger to see what happens. The XCHG instruction exchanges the values contained in its two operands. What was interchanged before is interchanged again, and the value in RCX will match the values already in RAX and RBX. A good idea while writing your first assembly language programs is to double-check the instruction set periodically to see that what you have cobbled together with four or five instructions is not possible using a single instruction. The Intel instruction set is very good at fooling you in that regard.

There is one caution here: Sometimes a "special case" is faster in terms of machine execution time than a more general case. Dividing by a power of 2 can be done using the DIV instruction, but it can also be done by using the SHR (Shift Right) instruction. DIV is more general (you can use it to divide by any unsigned integer, not simply powers of 2), but it is a great deal slower. (I'll have more to say about DIV later in this chapter.) The speed of individual instructions matters far less now than it did 30 years ago. That said, for programs with complex repetitive functions that are executed thousands or hundreds of thousands of times in a loop, instruction speed may well make a difference.

Memory Data and Effective Addresses

Immediate data is built right into its own machine instruction. Register data is stored in one of the CPU's collection of internal registers. In contrast, *memory data* is stored somewhere in the sliver of system memory "owned" by a program, at a 64-bit memory address.

With one or two important exceptions (the string instructions, which I cover to a degree—but not exhaustively—later), only *one* of an instruction's two operands may specify a memory location. In other words, you can move an immediate value to memory, a memory value to a register, or some other similar combination, but you *can't* move a memory value directly to another memory value. This is an inherent limitation of the Intel CPUs of all generations (not just x64), and we have to live with it, inconvenient as it might be at times.

To specify that we want the data at the memory location contained in a register rather than the data in the register itself, we use square brackets around the name of the register. In other words, to move the quadword in memory at the address contained in RBX into register RAX, we would use the following instruction:

```
mov rax, [rbx]
```

The square brackets may contain more than the name of a single 64-bit register, as we'll learn in detail later. For example, you can add a literal constant to a register within the brackets, and NASM will do the math.

```
mov rax, [rbx+16]
```

Ditto adding two general-purpose registers, like so:

```
mov rax, [rbx+rcx]
```

And as if that weren't enough, you can add two registers plus a literal constant.

```
mov rax, [rbx+rcx+11]
```

Not everything goes, of course. Whatever is inside the brackets is called the *effective address* of a data item in memory, and there are rules dictating what can be a valid effective address and what cannot. At the current evolution of the Intel hardware, two registers may be added together to form the effective address, but not three or more. In other words, these are *not* legal effective address forms:

```
mov rax, [rbx+rcx+rdx]
mov rax, [rbx+rcx+rsi+rdi]
```

The more complicated forms of effective addresses are easier to demonstrate than explain, but we have to learn a few other things first. They're especially useful when you're dealing with lookup tables, and I'll go into that at some length later. For the time being, the most important thing to do is *not* confuse a data item with where it exists!

Confusing Data and Its Address

This sounds banal, but trust me, it's an easy enough thing to do. Back in Listing 5.1, we had this data definition and this instruction:

```
EatMsg: db "Eat at Joe's!"
  .    .    .    .
mov rsi,EatMsg
```

If you've had any exposure to high-level languages like Pascal, your first instinct might be to assume that whatever data is stored in EatMsg will be copied into RSI. Assembly doesn't work that way. That MOV instruction actually copies the *address* of EatMsg, not what's stored *in* (actually, at) EatMsg.

In assembly language, variable names represent addresses, not data!

So, how do you actually "get at" the data represented by a variable like EatMsg? Again, it's done with square brackets.

```
mov rdx,[EatMsg]
```

What this instruction does is go out to the location in memory specified by the address represented by EatMsg, pulls in the first 64 bits' worth of data from that address, and loads that data into RDX starting with the least significant byte in RDX. Given the contents we've defined for EatMsg, that would be the eight characters *E*, *a*, *t*, a space, *a*, *t*, a space, and *J*.

The Size of Memory Data

But what if you want to work with only a single character and not the first eight? What if you don't want all 64 bits? Basically, if you want to use one byte of data, you need to load it into a byte-sized container. The register RAX is 64 bits in size. However, we can address the least-significant byte of RAX as AL. AL is one byte in size, and by making AL the destination operand, we can bring back the first byte of EatMsg this way:

```
mov al,[EatMsg]
```

AL, of course, is contained *within* RAX—it's not a separate register. (Look back to Figure 7.1 if this isn't immediately clear to you.) But the name "AL" allows us to fetch only one byte at a time from memory.

We can perform a similar trick using the name EAX to refer to the lower 4 bytes (32 bits) of RAX:

```
mov eax, [EatMsg]
```

This time, the characters *E*, *a*, *t*, and a space are read from memory and placed in the four least significant bytes of RAX.

Where the size issue gets tricky is when you write data in a register out to memory. NASM does not "remember" the sizes of variables, like higher-level languages do. It knows where EatMsg *starts* in memory, and that's it. You have to tell NASM how many bytes of data to move. This is done by a *size specifier*. Here's an example:

```
mov byte [EatMsg],'G'
```

Here, we tell NASM that we want to move only a single byte out to memory by using the BYTE size specifier. Other size specifiers include WORD (16 bits), DWORD (32 bits), and QWORD (64 bits).

The Bad Old Days

Be glad you're learning Intel assembly in the current day. It was a *lot* more complicated in years past. In real mode under DOS, there were several restrictions on the components of an effective address that just don't exist today, in either 32-bit protected mode or 64-bit long mode. In real mode, only certain x86 general-purpose registers could hold a memory address: BX, BP, SI, and DI. The others, AX, CX, and DX, could not.

Worse, every address had two parts, as we learned in Chapter 4. You had to be mindful of which segment an address was in, and you had to make sure you specified the segment where the segment was not obvious. You had to use constructs like [DS:BX] or [ES:BP]. You had to fool with diabolical things called ASSUMEs, about which the less said, the better. (If you are for some reason forced to program in real mode for the x86, try to find a copy of the second edition of this book, from 2000, in which I take on the whole mess in gruesome detail.)

In so many ways, life is just *better* now.

Rally Round the Flags, Boys!

Although I mentioned it in the overview of the x64 architecture, we haven't yet studied the RFlags register in any detail. RFlags is a veritable junk drawer of disjointed little bits of information, and it's tough (and perhaps misleading) to just sit down and describe all of them in detail at once. What I will do is describe the CPU flags briefly here and then in more detail as we encounter them while discussing the various instructions that change the values of flags or use them while branching.

A *flag* is a single bit of information whose meaning is independent from any other bit. A bit can be *set* to 1 or *cleared* to 0 by the CPU as its needs require. The idea is to tell you, the programmer, the state of certain conditions inside the CPU so that your program can test for and act on the states of those conditions. Much more rarely, you the programmer set a flag as a way of signaling something to the CPU.

I often imagine a row of country mailboxes, each with its own little red flag on the side. Each flag can be up or down, and if the Smiths' flag is up, it tells the mail carrier that the Smiths have placed mail in their box to be picked up. The mail carrier looks to see if the Smiths' flag is raised (a test) and, if so, opens the Smiths' mailbox and picks up the waiting outbound mail.

RFlags as a whole is a single 64-bit register buried inside the CPU. It's the 64-bit extension of the 32-bit EFlags register, which in turn is the 32-bit extension of the 16-bit Flags register present in the ancient 8086/8088 CPUs. Only 18 bits of the RFlags register are actually flags. The rest are reserved for later use in future generations of Intel CPUs. Even among the defined flags, only a few are commonplace, and fewer still are useful when you're just learning your way around. Some are used only inside system software like operating systems and are not available at all in userspace programs.

It's a bit of a mess, but take a look at Figure 7.2, which summarize all flags currently defined in the x64 architecture. The flags I've put against a gray background are the arcane ones that you can safely ignore for the moment. Spaces and lines colored black are considered reserved and do not contain defined flags.

Each of the RFlags register's flags has a two-, three-, or four-letter symbol by which most programmers know them. I use those symbols in this book, and you should become familiar with them. The most common flags, their symbols, and brief descriptions of what they stand for follows:

- OF—The Overflow flag is set when the result of an arithmetic operation on a signed integer quantity becomes too large to fit in the operand it originally occupied. OF is generally used as the "carry flag" in signed arithmetic.

- DF—The Direction flag is an oddball among the flags in that it tells the *CPU* something that *you* want it to know, rather than the other way around. It dictates the direction that activity moves (up-memory or down-memory) during the execution of string instructions. When DF is set, string instructions proceed from high memory toward low memory. When DF is cleared, string instructions proceed from low memory toward high memory.

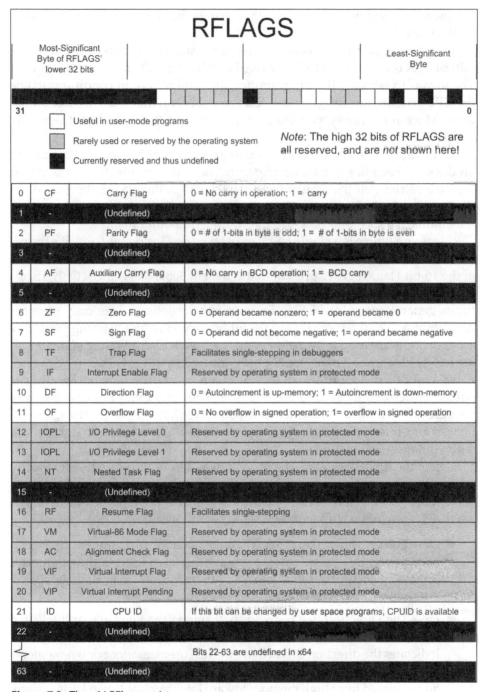

Figure 7.2: The x64 RFlags register

- IF—The Interrupt Enable flag is a two-way flag. The CPU sets it under certain conditions, and you can set it yourself using the STI and CLI instructions—though you probably won't; see below. When IF is set, interrupts are enabled and may occur when requested. When IF is cleared, interrupts are ignored by the CPU. Ordinary programs could set and clear this flag with impunity in Real Mode, back in the DOS era. Under Linux (whether 32-bit or 64-bit) IF is reserved for the use of the operating system and sometimes its drivers. If you try to use the STI and CLI instructions within one of your programs, Linux will hand you a general protection fault, and your program will be terminated. Consider IF off-limits for userspace programming like we're discussing in this book.

- TF—When set, the Trap flag allows debuggers to manage single-stepping, by forcing the CPU to execute only a single instruction before calling an interrupt routine. This is not an especially useful flag for ordinary programming, and I won't have anything more to say about it in this book.

- SF—The Sign flag becomes set when the result of an operation forces the operand to become negative. By *negative*, we mean only that the highest-order bit in the operand (the *sign bit*) becomes 1 during a signed arithmetic operation. Any operation that leaves the sign of the result positive will clear SF.

- ZF—The Zero flag becomes set when the results of an operation become zero. If the destination operand instead becomes some nonzero value, ZF is cleared. You'll be using this one a lot for conditional jumps.

- AF—The Auxiliary Carry flag is used only for BCD arithmetic. BCD arithmetic treats each operand byte as a pair of 4-bit "nybbles" and allows something approximating decimal (base 10) arithmetic to be done directly in the CPU hardware by using one of the BCD arithmetic instructions. These instructions are considered obsolete and are not present in x64. I do not cover them in this book.

- PF—The Parity flag will seem instantly familiar to anyone who understands serial data communications and utterly bizarre to anyone who doesn't. PF indicates whether the number of set (1) bits in the low-order byte of a result is even or odd. For example, if the result is 0F2H, PF will be cleared because 0F2H (11110010) contains an odd number of 1 bits. Similarly, if the result is 3AH (00111100), PF will be set because there is an even number (four) of 1 bits in the result. This flag is a carryover from the days when all computer communications were done through a serial port, for which a system of error detection called *parity checking* depends on knowing whether a count of set bits in a character byte is even or odd. PF is used very rarely, and I won't be describing it further.

- CF—The Carry flag is used in unsigned arithmetic operations. If the result of an arithmetic or shift operation "carries out" a bit from the operand, CF becomes set. Otherwise, if nothing is carried out, CF is cleared.

Flag Etiquette

What I call "flag etiquette" is the way a given instruction affects the flags in the RFlags register. You *must* remember that the descriptions of the flags on the previous pages are generalizations *only* and are subject to specific restrictions and special cases imposed by individual instructions. Flag etiquette for individual flags varies widely from instruction to instruction, even though the *sense* of the flag's use may be the same in every case.

For example, some instructions that cause a zero to appear in an operand set ZF, while others do not. Sadly, there's no system to it and no easy way to keep it straight in your head. When you intend to use the flags in testing by way of conditional jump instructions, you have to check each individual instruction to see how the various flags are affected.

> *Flag etiquette is a highly individual matter. Check an instruction reference for each instruction to see if it affects the flags. Assume nothing!*

Watching Flags from SASM

The RFlags register is a register, just as RAX is, and when you're in debug mode, its value is displayed in SASM's Registers view. The values of the flags are shown between square brackets. When you start to debug userspace code, SASM will typically show the names of the PF, ZF, and IF flags.

```
[ PF ZF IF ]
```

This means that for whatever reason, when Linux allows you to begin debugging, the Parity flag, Zero flag, and Interrupt Enable flag are set. These initial values are "leftovers" from code executed earlier and are not in any way caused by your code in the debugger. Their values, furthermore, don't carry any meaning into your debug session and thus don't need interpretation.

When you execute an instruction that affects the flags in a debug session, SASM will show a flag's name if that flag is set or will erase the flag's name if that flag is cleared.

Adding and Subtracting One with INC and DEC

A simple lesson in flag etiquette involves the two instructions INC and DEC. Several x86 machine instructions come in pairs, INC and DEC among them. They increment and decrement an operand by one, respectively.

Adding one to something or subtracting one from something are actions that happen a *lot* in computer programming. If you're counting the number of times that a program is executing a loop, counting bytes in a table, or doing something that advances or retreats one count at a time, INC or DEC can be very quick ways to make the actual addition or subtraction happen.

Both INC and DEC take only one operand. An error will be flagged by the assembler if you try to use either INC or DEC with two operands or without any operands. Neither will work on immediate data.

Try both by adding the following instructions to your sandbox. Build the sandbox as usual, go into debug mode, and step through it:

```
mov eax,0FFFFFFFFh
mov ebx,02Dh
dec ebx
inc eax
```

Watch what happens to the EAX and EBX registers. Decrementing EBX predictably turns the value 2DH into value 2CH. Incrementing 0FFFFFFFFH, on the other hand, rolls over the EAX register over to 0, because 0FFFFFFFFH is the largest unsigned value that can be expressed in a 32-bit register. (I used EAX in the example here because filling 64-bit register RAX with bits takes a *lot* of Fs!) Adding 1 to it rolls it over to zero, just as adding 1 to 99 rolls the rightmost two digits of the sum to zero in creating the number 100. The difference with INC is that *there is no carry*. The Carry flag is not affected by INC, so don't try to use it to perform multidigit arithmetic.

- The Overflow flag (OF) was cleared because the operand, interpreted as a signed integer, did not become too large to fit in EBX. This may not help you if you don't know what makes a number "signed," so let's leave it at that for the moment.

- The Sign flag (SF) was cleared because the high bit of EBX did not become 1 as a result of the operation. Had the high bit of EBX become 1, the value in EBX, interpreted as a signed integer value, would have become negative, and SF is set when a value becomes negative. As with OF, SF is not very useful unless you're doing signed arithmetic.

- The Zero flag (ZF) was cleared because the destination operand did not become zero. Had it become zero, ZF would have been set to 1.

- The Auxiliary Carry flag (AF) was cleared because there was no BCD carry out of the lower four bits of EBX into the next higher four bits. (BCD instructions were removed from the x64 instruction set, so AF is of no use today and can be ignored.)

- The Parity flag (PF) was cleared because the number of 1-bits in the operand after the decrement happened was three, and PF is cleared when the number of bits in the destination operand is odd. Check it yourself: The value in EBX after the DEC instruction is 02Ch. In binary, this is 00101100. There are three 1-bits in the value, and thus PF is cleared.

The DEC instruction does not affect the IF flag, which remained set. In fact, almost nothing changes the IF flag, and userspace applications like the sandbox (and everything else you're likely to write while learning assembly) are forbidden to change IF.

Now, execute the INC EAX instruction, and re-display the registers in the Console view. Boom! Lots of action this time:

- The Parity flag PF was set because the number of 1-bits in EAX is now zero, and PF is set when the number of 1-bits in the operand becomes even. Zero is considered an even number.

- The Auxiliary Carry flag AF was set because the lower four bits in EAX went from FFFF to 0000. This implies a carry out of the lower four bits to the upper four bits, and AF is set when a carry out of the lower four bits of the operand happens. (Again, you can't use AF in x64 programming.)

- The Zero flag ZF was set because EAX became zero.

- As before, the IF flag doesn't change and remains set at all times. Remember that IF belongs exclusively to Linux and is not affected by userspace code.

How Flags Change Program Execution

Watching the flags change value after instructions execute is a good way to learn flag etiquette. However, the purpose and real value of the flags doesn't lie in their values, per se, but in how they affect the flow of machine instructions in your programs.

There is a whole category of machine instructions that "jump" to a different location in your program based on the current value in one or more of the flags. These instructions are called *conditional jump* instructions, and most of the flags in RFLAGS have one or more associated conditional jump instructions. They're listed in Appendix B.

Think back to the notion of "steps and tests" that I introduced in Chapter 1. Most machine instructions are steps taken in a list that runs generally from top to bottom. The conditional jump instructions are the tests. They test the condition of one of the flags and either keep on going or jump to a different location in your program.

The simplest example of a conditional jump instruction, and the one you're likely to use the most, is JNZ, Jump If Not Zero. The JNZ instruction tests the value of the Zero flag. If ZF is set (that is, equal to 1), nothing happens, and the CPU goes on to execute the next instruction in sequence. However, if ZF is *not* set (that is, if it's cleared and equal to 0), then execution travels to a new destination in your program.

This sounds worse than it is. You don't have to worry about adding or subtracting anything. In nearly all cases, the destination is given as a *label*. Labels are descriptive names given to locations in your programs. In NASM, a label is a character string followed by a colon, generally placed on a line containing an instruction.

Like so many things in assembly language, this will become clearer with a simple example. Load up a fresh sandbox, and type in the following instructions:

```
        mov rax,5
DoMore: dec rax
        jnz DoMore
```

Build the sandbox and go into debug mode. Watch the value of RAX in the Registers view as you step through these instructions. In particular, watch what happens in the source code window when you execute the JNZ instruction. JNZ jumps to the label named as its operand if ZF is 0. If ZF = 1, it "falls through" to the next instruction.

The DEC instruction decrements the value in its operand; here, RAX. As long as the value in RAX does not change to 0, the Zero flag remains cleared. And as long as the Zero flag is cleared, JNZ jumps back to the label DoMore. So for five passes, DEC takes the value in RAX down a notch, and JNZ jumps back to DoMore. But as soon as DEC takes RAX down to 0, the Zero flag becomes set, and JNZ "falls through" to the NOP instruction at the end of the sandbox.

Constructs like this are called *loops* and are common in all programming, not just assembly language. The loop shown earlier isn't useful, but it demonstrates how you can repeat an instruction as many times as you need to, by loading an initial count value in a register and decrementing that value once for each pass through the loop. The JNZ instruction tests ZF each time through and knows to exit the loop when the count register goes to 0.

We can make the loop a little more useful without adding a lot of complication. What we do need to add is a data item for the loop to work on. Load Listing 7.2 into a SASM sandbox, build it, and then enter debug mode.

Listing 7.2: kangaroo.asm

```
section .data
        Snippet db "KANGAROO"

section .text
        global main
main:
        mov rbp,rsp ;Save stack pointer for debugger
        nop

; Put your experiments between the two nops...

        mov rbx,Snippet
        mov rax,8
DoMore: add byte [rbx],32
        inc rbx
        dec rax
        jnz DoMore

; Put your experiments between the two nops...
        nop
```

How to Inspect Variables in SASM

The program KANGAROO.ASM defines a variable and then changes it. So how do we see what changes are being made? SASM has the ability to display named variables in debug mode. I should note here that at this writing, SASM 3.11.2 does *not* have the ability to display arbitrary regions of memory, hexdump-style. More advanced debuggers will do that, and I discuss such a debugger in Appendix A.

What SASM does is display named variables. To use this feature, you have to select the Show Memory check box *when you're in debug mode*. (The check box is grayed out in edit mode.) By default, the Show Memory window is at the top of SASM's display. To show the contents of a named variable in a program or sandbox you've built, you must do this:

1. Enter debug mode.
2. In the Variable Or Expression field, enter **Snippet**.
3. In the Type field, select Smart in the leftmost pull-down menu.
4. In the next field, select b from the pull-down menu.
5. In the next field, type the length of the variable you want to see, in bytes. For this example, since the contents of Snippet are eight characters long, enter **8**.

Once you do that, you'll see "KANGAROO" in the Value field. That's what's in Snippet. With that done, step through the program with Snippet on display.

After eight passes through the loop, "KANGAROO" has become "kangaroo"—how? Look at the ADD instruction located at the label DoMore. Earlier in the program, we had copied the memory address of Snippet into register RBX. The ADD instruction adds the literal value 32 to whatever number is at the address stored in RBX. If you look at the ASCII charts in Appendix C, you'll notice that the difference between the value of ASCII uppercase letters and ASCII lowercase letters is 32. A capital *K* has the value 4Bh, and a lowercase *k* has the value 6Bh. 6Bh–4Bh is 20h, which in decimal is 32. So if we treat ASCII letters as numbers, we can add 32 to an uppercase letter and transform it into a lowercase letter.

What the loop does is make eight passes, one for each letter in "KANGAROO." After each ADD, the program increments the address in RBX, which puts the next character of "KANGAROO" in the crosshairs. It also decrements RAX, which had been loaded with the number of characters in the variable Snippet before the loop began. So within the same loop, the program is counting up along the length of Snippet in RBX, while counting down the length of the remaining letters in RAX. When RAX goes to zero, it means that we've gone through all of the characters in Snippet, and we're done.

The operands of the ADD instruction are worth a closer look. Putting RBX inside square brackets references the contents of Snippet, rather than its address. But more important, the BYTE size specifier tells NASM that we're writing only a single byte to the memory address in RBX. NASM has no way to know otherwise. It's possible to write one byte, two bytes, four bytes, or eight bytes to memory at once, depending on what we need to accomplish. However, we have to tell NASM how many bytes we want it to use, with a size specifier.

Don't forget that KANGAROO.ASM is still a sandbox program, suitable only for single-stepping in the SASM debugger. If you just "let it run," it will generate a segmentation fault when execution moves past the final NOP instruction. Once you single-step to that final NOP, kill the program and either begin execution again or exit debug mode.

Signed and Unsigned Values

In assembly language we can work with both signed and unsigned numeric values. Signed values, of course, are values that can become negative. An unsigned value is always positive. There are instructions for the four basic arithmetic operations in the basic x64 instruction set, and these instructions can operate on both signed and unsigned values. (With multiplication and division, there are separate instructions for signed and unsigned calculations, as I'll explain later.)

The key to understanding the difference between signed and unsigned numeric values is knowing where the CPU puts the sign. It's not a dash character but actually a bit in the binary pattern that represents the number. The highest bit in the most significant byte of a signed value is the *sign bit*. If the sign bit is a 1-bit, the number is negative. If the sign bit is a 0-bit, the number is positive.

Keep in mind through all of this that whether a given binary pattern represents a signed or an unsigned value depends on how we choose to use it. If we intend to perform signed arithmetic, the high bit of a register value or memory location is considered the sign bit. If we do not intend to perform signed arithmetic, the high bits of the very same values in the very same places will simply be the most significant bits of unsigned values. The signed nature of a value lies in how we treat the value, not in the nature of the underlying bit pattern that represents the value. For example, does the binary number 10101111 represent a signed or an unsigned value? The question is meaningless without context: If we need to treat the value as a signed value, we treat the high-order bit as the sign bit, and the value is -81. If we need to treat the value as an unsigned value, we treat the high bit as just another digit in a binary number, and the value is 175.

Two's Complement and NEG

One mistake beginners sometimes commit is assuming that you can make a value negative by setting the sign bit to 1. Not so! You can't simply take the value 42 and make it -42 by setting the sign bit. The value you get will certainly be negative, but it will *not* be -42.

One way to get a sense for the way negative numbers are expressed in assembly language is to decrement a positive number down into negative territory. Bring up a clean sandbox and enter these instructions:

```
        mov eax,5
DoMore: dec eax
        jmp DoMore
```

(I'm using 32-bit register EAX here because a "full" 64-bit register is a handful to display on the printed page. The takeaway is the same.) Build the sandbox as usual and enter debug mode. Note that we've added a new instruction here, and a hazard: The JMP instruction does *not* look at the flags. When executed, it *always* jumps to its operand; so, execution will bounce back to the label DoMore each and every time that JMP executes. If you're sharp, you'll notice that there's no way out of this particular sequence of instructions, and, yes, this is the legendary "endless loop" that you'll fall into now and then.

So, make sure that you set a breakpoint on the initial MOV instruction, and don't just let the program rip. Or. . .go ahead! (Nothing will be harmed.) If you click the red square, SASM will stop the program. Under DOS, you would have been stuck and had to reboot the PC. Linux makes for a much more robust programming platform, one that doesn't go down in flames on your tiniest mistake.

Start single-stepping the sandbox, and watch EAX in the Registers view. The starting value of 5 will count down to 4, then 3, then 2, then 1, then 0, and then. . .0FFFFFFFFh! That's the 32-bit expression of the simple value -1. If you keep on decrementing EAX, you'll get a sense for what happens:

```
0FFFFFFFFh  (-1)
0FFFFFFFEh  (-2)
0FFFFFFFDh  (-3)
0FFFFFFFCh  (-4)
0FFFFFFFBh  (-5)
0FFFFFFFAh  (-6)
0FFFFFFF9h  (-7)
```

. . .and so on. When negative numbers are handled in this fashion, we call it *two's complement*. In Intel assembly language, negative numbers are stored as the two's complement form of their absolute value, which if you remember from eighth-grade math is the distance of a number from 0, in either the positive or negative direction.

The mathematics behind two's complement is surprisingly subtle, and I refer you to Wikipedia for a fuller treatment than I can afford in this (already long) book.

```
en.wikipedia.org/wiki/Two's_complement/
```

The magic of expressing negative numbers in two's complement form is that the CPU doesn't really need to subtract at the level of its transistor logic. It simply generates the two's complement of the subtrahend and adds it to the minuend. This is relatively easy for the CPU, and it all happens transparently to your programs, where subtraction is done about the way you'd expect.

The good news is that you almost never have to calculate a two's complement value manually. There is a machine instruction that will do it for you: NEG. The NEG instruction will take a positive value as its operand and negate that value, that is, make it negative. It does so by generating the two's complement form of the positive value. Load the following instructions into a clean sandbox and single-step though them. Watch EAX in the Registers view:

```
mov eax,42
neg eax
add eax,42
```

In one swoop, 42 becomes 0FFFFFFD6h, the two's complement hexadecimal expression of -42. Add 42 to this value, and watch EAX go to 0.

At this point, the question may arise: What are the largest positive and negative numbers that can be expressed in one, two, four, or eight bytes? Those two values, plus all the values in between, constitute the *range* of a value expressed in a given number of bits. I've laid this out in Table 7.2.

Table 7.2: The Ranges of Signed Values

| VALUE SIZE | GREATEST NEGATIVE VALUE | | GREATEST POSITIVE VALUE | |
	DECIMAL	HEX	DECIMAL	HEX
8 Bits	-128	80h	127	7Fh
16 Bits	-32768	8000h	32767	7FFFh
32 Bits	-2147483648	80000000h	2147483647	7FFFFFFFh

64 Bits:

Greatest Negative Value, Decimal: -9223372036854775808

Greatest Negative Value, Hex: 8000000000000000h

Greatest Positive Value, Decimal: 9223372036854775807

Greatest Positive Value, Hex: 7FFFFFFFFFFFFFFFh

If you're sharp and know how to count in hex, you may notice something here from the table: The greatest positive value and the greatest negative value for a given value size are *one count apart*. That is, if you're working in 8 bits and add one to the greatest positive value, 7Fh, you get 80h, the greatest negative value.

You can watch this happen in SASM by executing the following two instructions in a sandbox and watching RAX in the Registers display:

```
mov rax,07FFFFFFFFFFFFFFFh
inc rax
```

(Make sure you get the number of *F*s correct! It's one 7 and 15 F's.) After the MOV instruction executes, RAX will show the decimal value 9223372036854775807. That's the highest signed value expressible in 64 bits. Increment the value by 1 with the INC instruction, and instantly the value in RAX becomes -9223372036854775808.

Sign Extension and MOVSX

There's a subtle gotcha to be avoided when you're working with signed values in different sizes. The sign bit is the high bit in a signed byte, word, or double word. But what happens when you have to move a signed value into a larger register or memory location? What happens, for example, if you need to move a signed 16-bit value into a 32-bit register? If you use the MOV instruction, nothing good. Try this:

```
mov ax,-42
mov ebx,eax
```

The hexadecimal form of -42 is 0FFD6h. If you have that value in a 16-bit register like AX and use MOV to move the value into a larger register like EBX or RBX, *the sign bit will no longer be the sign bit*. In other words, once -42 travels from a 16-bit container into a 32-bit container, it changes from -42 to 65494. The sign bit is still there. It hasn't been cleared to zero. However, in a larger register, the old sign bit is now just another bit in a binary value, with no special meaning.

This example is a little misleading. First, we can't literally move a value from AX into EBX. The MOV instruction will handle only register operands of the same size. However, remember that AX is simply the lower two bytes of EAX. We can move AX into EBX by moving EAX into EBX, and that's what we did in the previous example.

Alas, SASM is not capable of showing us signed 8-bit, 16-bit, or 32-bit values. Its debugger can display only RAX, and we can see AL, AH, AX, or EAX only by seeing them inside RAX. That's why, in the previous example, SASM shows the value we thought was -42 as 65494. SASM's Registers view has no concept of a sign bit except in the highest bit of a 64-bit value.

Modern Intel CPUs provides us with a way out of this trap, in the form of the MOVSX instruction. MOVSX means "Move with Sign Extension," and it is one of many instructions that were not present in the original 8086/8088 CPUs. MOVSX was introduced with the 386 family of CPUs, and because Linux will not run on anything older than a 386, you can assume that any Linux PC supports the MOVSX instruction.

Load this into a sandbox and try it:

```
xor rax,rax
mov ax,-42
movsx rbx,ax
```

The first line is simply to zero out RAX to make sure there are no "leftovers" stored in it from code executed earlier. Remember that SASM cannot display AX individually, and so will show RAX as containing 65494. However, when you move AX into RBX with MOVSX, the value of RBX will then be shown as -42. What happened is that the MOVSX instruction performed *sign extension* on its operands, taking the sign bit from the 16-bit quantity in AX and making it the sign bit of the 64-bit quantity in RBX.

MOVSX is significantly different from MOV in that *its operands may be of different sizes*. MOVSX has several possible variations, which I've summarized in Table 7.3.

Table 7.3: The MOVSX Instruction

INSTRUCTION	DESTINATION	SOURCE	OPERAND NOTES
MOVSX	r16	r/m8	8-bit signed to 16-bit signed
MOVSX	r32	r/m8	8-bit signed to 32-bit signed
MOVSX	r64	r/m8	8-bit signed to 64-bit signed
MOVSX	r32	r/m16	16-bit signed to 32-bit signed
MOVSX	r64	r/m16	16-bit signed to 64-bit signed
MOVSX	r64	r/m32	32-bit signed to 64-bit signed

Note that the destination operand can *only* be a register. The notation here is one you'll see in many assembly language references in describing instruction operands. The notation "r16" is an abbreviation for "any 16-bit register." Similarly, "r/m" means "register or memory" and is followed by the bit size. For example, "r/m16" means "any 16-bit register or 16-bit memory location."

With all that said, you may find after solving some problems in assembly language that signed arithmetic is used less often than you think. It's good to know how it works, but don't be surprised if you go months or even years without ever needing it.

Implicit Operands and MUL

Most of the time, you hand values to machine instructions through one or two operands placed right there on the line beside the mnemonic. This is good, because when you say MOV RAX, RBX, you know *precisely* what's moving, where it comes from, and where it's going. Alas, that isn't always the case. Some instructions act on registers or even memory locations that are not stated in a list of operands. These instructions do in fact have operands, but they represent assumptions made by the instruction. Such operands are called *implicit operands*, and they do not change and cannot be changed. To add to the confusion, most instructions that have implicit operands have explicit operands as well.

The best examples of implicit operands in the x64 instruction set are the multiplication and division instructions. The x64 instruction set has two sets of multiply and divide instructions. One set, MUL and DIV, handle unsigned calculations. The other, IMUL and IDIV, handle signed calculations. MUL and DIV are used much more frequently than their signed-math alternates, and they're what I'll discuss in this section.

The MUL instruction does what you'd expect: It multiplies two values and returns a product. Among the basic math operations, however, multiplication has a special problem: It generates output values that are often *hugely* larger than the input values. This makes it impossible to follow the conventional pattern in Intel instruction operands, where the value generated by an instruction goes into the destination operand.

Consider a 32-bit multiply operation. The largest unsigned value that will fit in a 32-bit register is 4,294,967,295. Multiply that even by two and you've got a 33-bit product, which will no longer fit in any 32-bit register. This problem has plagued the Intel architectures (all architectures, in fact) since the beginning. When the x86 was a 16-bit architecture, the problem was where to put the product of two 16-bit values, which can easily overflow a 16-bit register.

Intel's designers solved the problem the only way they could: by using *two* registers to hold the product. It's not immediately obvious to non-mathematicians, but it's true (try it on a calculator!) that the largest product of two binary numbers can be expressed in no more than twice the number of bits required by the larger factor. Simply put, any product of two 16-bit values will fit in 32 bits, and any product of two 32-bit values will fit in 64 bits. So while two registers may be needed to hold the product, no *more* than two registers will ever be needed.

That brings us to the MUL instruction. MUL is an odd bird from an operand standpoint: It takes only one operand, which contains one of the factors to be multiplied. The other factor is implicit, as is the pair of registers that receives the product of the calculation. MUL thus looks deceptively simple.

```
mul rbx
```

Obviously, if multiplication is going on, more is involved here than just RBX. The implicit operands depend on the size of the explicit one. This gives us four variations, which I've summarized in Table 7.4.

Table 7.4: The MUL Instruction

INSTRUCTION	EXPLICIT OPERAND (FACTOR 1)	IMPLICIT OPERAND (FACTOR 2)	IMPLICIT OPERAND (PRODUCT)
MUL r/m8	r/m8	AL	AX
MUL r/m16	r/m16	AX	DX : AX
MUL r/m32	r/m32	EAX	EDX : EAX
MUL r/m64	r/m64	RAX	RDX : RAX

The first factor is given in the single explicit operand, which can be a value either in a register or in a memory location. The second factor is implicit and always in the "A" general-purpose register appropriate to the size of the first factor. If the first factor is an 8-bit value, the second factor is always in 8-bit register AL. If the first factor is a 16-bit value, the second factor is always in the 16-bit register AX, and so on. Once the product requires more than 16 bits, the

DX registers are drafted to hold the high-order portion of the product. By "high-order" here I mean the portion of the product that won't fit in the "A" register. For example, if you multiply two 16-bit values and the product is 02A456Fh, register AX will contain 0456Fh, and the DX register will contain 02Ah.

Note that when a product is small enough to fit entirely in the first of the two registers holding the product, the high-order register (whether AH, DX, EDX, or RDX) is zeroed out. Registers often get scarce in assembly work, but even if you're *sure* that your multiplications always involve small products, you can't use the high-order register for anything else while a MUL instruction is executed.

Also, note that immediate values cannot be used as operands for MUL; that is, you can't do this, as useful as it would often be to state the first factor as an immediate value:

```
mul 42
```

MUL and the Carry Flag

Not all multiplications generate large enough products to require two registers. Most of the time you'll find that 64 bits is more than enough. So how can you tell whether there are significant figures in the high-order register? MUL very helpfully sets the Carry flag CF when the value of the product overflows the low-order register. If, after a MUL, you find CF set to 0, you can ignore the high-order register, secure in the knowledge that the entire product is in the lower-order of the two registers.

This is worth a quick sandbox demonstration. First, try a "small" multiplication where the product will easily fit in a single 32-bit register.

```
mov eax,447
mov ebx,1739
mul ebx
```

Remember that we're multiplying EAX by EBX here. Step through the three instructions, and after the MUL instruction has executed, look at the Registers view to see the product in EDX and EAX. EAX contains 777333, and EDX contains 0. Look next at the current state of the various flags. No sign of CF, meaning that CF has been cleared to 0.

Next, add the following instructions to your sandbox, after the three shown earlier:

```
mov eax,0FFFFFFFFh
mov ebx,03B72h
mul ebx
```

Step through them as usual, watching the contents of EAX, EDX, and EBX in the Registers view. After the MUL instruction, look at the flags in the Registers view. The Carry flag CF will be set to 1 (so have the Overflow flag OF, Sign flag SF, Interrupt enable flag IF, and Parity flag PF, but those are not generally useful in unsigned arithmetic). What CF basically tells you here is that there are significant figures in the high-order portion of the product, and these are stored in EDX for 32-bit multiplies, RDX for 64-bit multiplies, and so on.

Unsigned Division with DIV

As a third grader, I recall stating flatly in class that division is multiplication done backward, and I was closer to the truth than poor Sister Agnes Eileen was willing to admit at the time. It's certainly true enough for there to be a strong resemblance between the unsigned multiply instruction MUL and the unsigned division instruction DIV. DIV does what you'd expect from your third-grade training: It divides one value by another and gives you a quotient and a remainder. Remember, we're doing integer and not decimal arithmetic here, so there is no way to express a decimal quotient like 17.76 or 3.14159. These require the "floating-point" machinery of the CPU architecture, which is a vast and subtle subject that I won't be covering in this book.

In division, you don't have the problem that multiplication has, of generating large output values for some input values. If you divide a 16-bit value by another 16-bit value, you will never get a quotient that will not fit in a 16-bit register. On the other hand, it would be useful to be able to divide very large numbers, and so Intel's engineers created something very like a mirror image of MUL: For 64-bit division, you place a dividend value in RDX and RAX, which means that it may be up to 128 bits in size. The divisor is stored in DIV's only explicit operand, which may be a register or in memory. (As with MUL, you cannot use an immediate value as the operand.) The quotient is returned in RAX, and the remainder in RDX.

That's the situation for a full, 64-bit division. As with MUL, DIV's implicit operands depend on the size of the single explicit operand, here acting as the divisor. There are four "sizes" of DIV operations, depending on the size of the explicit operand, the divisor. This is summarized in Table 7.5.

Table 7.5: The DIV Instruction

INSTRUCTION	EXPLICIT OPERAND (DIVISOR)	IMPLICIT OPERAND (DIVIDEND)	RESULT (QUOTIENT)	RESULT (REMAINDER)
DIV r/m8	r/m8	AX	AL	AH
DIV r/m16	r/m16	DX : AX	AX	DX
DIV r/m32	r/m32	EDX : EAX	EAX	EDX
DIV r/m64	r/m64	RDX : RAX	RAX	RDX

I won't even try to print out what integer number you can store in 128 bits using two 64-bit registers. In scientific notation, it's 3.4×10^{38}. Given that 64 bits can hold 1.8×10^{19} and that's just short of the estimated number of stars in the observable universe, I suggest treating the number as an undisplayed abstraction.

Let's give DIV a spin. Put the following code in a fresh sandbox:

```
mov rax,250    ; Dividend
mov rbx,5      ; Divisor
div rbx        ; Do the DIV
```

The explicit operand is the divisor, stored in RBX. The dividend is in RAX. Step through it. After DIV executes, the quotient will be placed in RAX, replacing the dividend. There is no remainder, so RDX is zero. Plug in a new dividend and divisor that don't divide evenly; 247 and 17 will work. Once you execute DIV with the new operands, look at RDX. It should contain 9. That's your remainder.

The DIV instruction does not place useful data in any of the flags. In fact, DIV will leave OF, SF, ZF, AF, PF, and CF in undefined states. Don't try to test any of those flags in a jump instruction following DIV.

As you might expect, dividing by zero will trigger an error that will terminate your program: an arithmetic exception. It's a good idea to test your divisor values to make sure no zeros end up in the divisor. Now, dividing zero by a nonzero number does not trigger an error; it will simply place 0 values in the quotient and remainder registers. Just for fun, try both cases in your sandbox to see what happens.

MUL and DIV Are Slowpokes

A common beginner's question about MUL and DIV concerns the two "smaller" versions of both instructions. (See Tables 7.4 and 7.5.) If a 64-bit multiply or divide can handle anything the x64 architecture can stuff in registers, why are the smaller versions even necessary? Is it all a matter of backward compatibility with older 16-bit CPUs?

Not entirely. In many cases, it's a matter of speed. The DIV and MUL instructions are close to the slowest instructions in the entire x64 instruction set. They're certainly not as slow as they used to be, but compared to other instructions like MOV or ADD, they're goop. Furthermore, both the 32-bit and 64-bit versions of both instructions are slower than the 16-bit version, and the 8-bit version is the fastest of all. DIV is slower than MUL, but both are slowpokes.

Now, speed optimization is a *very* slippery business in the x86/x64 world— and not something beginners should be concerned with. Having instructions in the CPU cache versus having to pull them from memory is a speed difference that swamps most speed differences among the instructions themselves. Other factors come into play in the most recent CPUs that make generalizations about instruction speed almost impossible, and certainly impossible to state with any precision.

If you're doing only a few isolated multiplies or divides, don't let any of this bother you. Where instruction speed may become important is inside loops where you're doing a *lot* of calculations constantly, as in data encryption or physics simulations. My own personal heuristic is to use the smallest version of MUL and DIV that the input values allow—tempered by the even stronger heuristic that most of the time, *instruction speed doesn't matter*. When you become experienced enough at assembly to make performance decisions at the instruction level, you will know it. Until then, concentrate on making your programs bug-free and leave speed up to the CPU.

Reading and Using an Assembly Language Reference

Assembly language programming is about details. Good grief, is it about details. There are broad similarities among instructions, but it's the differences that get you when you start feeding programs to the unforgiving eye of the assembler.

Remembering a host of tiny, tangled details involving several dozen different instructions is brutal and unnecessary. Even the Big Guys don't try to keep it all between their ears at all times. Most keep some other sort of reference document handy to jog their memories about machine instruction details.

Memory Joggers for Complex Memories

This problem has existed for a long time. Back in 1975, when I first encountered microcomputers, a complete and useful instruction set memory jogger document could be printed on two sides of a trifold card that could fit in your shirt pocket. Such cards were common, and you could get them for almost any microprocessor. For reasons unclear, they were called "blue cards," though most were printed on ordinary white cardboard.

By the early to mid-1980s, what had once been a single card was now an 89-page booklet, sized to fit in your pocket. The Intel *Programmer's Reference Pocket Guide* for the 8086 family of CPUs was shipped with Microsoft's Macro Assembler, and everybody I knew had one. (I still have mine.) It really did fit in your shirt pocket, as long as nothing else fatter than a grocery list tried to share the space.

The power and complexity of the x86 architecture exploded in the mid-1980s, and a full summary of all instructions in all their forms, plus all the necessary explanations, became book-sized material and, as the years passed, required not one but several books to cover completely. Intel provides PDF versions of its processor documentation as free downloads, and you can get them here:

`www.intel.com/content/www/us/en/developer/articles/technical/`
`intel-sdm.html`

They're worth having—but forget cramming them in your pocket. The instruction set reference alone represents *more than 2,300 pages* in a single PDF, and there are several other related books to round out the set. The one you want is Volume 2. The good news is that you can download the PDF files for free and browse them on your PC or print out only the sections that you might find handy for a particular project. (Printed books are available through `lulu.com`, but they are expensive.) I definitely suggest that you become at least reasonably familiar with the common x64 instructions before tackling Intel's exhaustive (and exhausting!) reference.

Thirty-odd years ago there were excellent book-sized reference guides for the x86 family of CPUs, the best of them being Robert L. Hummel's *PC Magazine Technical Reference: The Processor and Coprocessor* (Ziff-Davis Press, 1992). Although I see it regularly on used book sites, it will take you only as far as the 486. I still consider it a good thing to have on your shelf if you spot it somewhere and can get it cheap.

An Assembly Language Reference for Beginners

As I described, the problem with assembly language references is that to be complete, they cannot be small. However, a great deal of the complexity of the x86/x64 instruction sets in the modern day rests with instructions and memory addressing machinery that are of use only to operating systems and drivers. For smallish applications running in user mode, they simply do not apply.

So in deference to people just starting out in assembly language, I have put together a beginner's reference to the most common x86/x64 instructions, in Appendix B. It contains at least a page on every instruction I cover in this book, plus a few additional instructions that everyone ought to know. It does *not* include descriptions on *every* instruction, but only the most common and most useful. Once you've gotten skillful enough to use the more arcane instructions, you should be able to read Intel's x64 documentation and run with it.

Some of the instructions from 32-bit x86 were removed from the x64 instruction set, and I have not included those in Appendix B.

Below is a sample entry from Appendix B. Refer to it during the following discussion.

The instruction's mnemonic is at the top of the page at the left margin. To the mnemonic's right is the name of the instruction, which is a little more descriptive than the naked mnemonic.

Flags

Immediately beneath the mnemonic is a minichart of CPU flags in the RFlags register. As I described earlier, the RFlags register is a collection of 1-bit values that retain certain essential information about the state of the machine for short periods of time. Many (but by no means all) x64 instructions change the values of one or more flags. The flags may then be individually tested by one of the Jump On Condition instructions, which change the course of the program depending on the states of the flags.

Each of the flags has a name, and each flag has a symbol in the flags minichart. You'll come to know the flags by their two-character symbols in time, but until then, the full names of the flags are shown to the right of the minichart. The majority of the flags are not used often (if at all) in beginning assembly language work. Most of what you'll be paying attention to, flags-wise, are the Zero flag (ZF) and the Carry flag (CF).

There will be an asterisk (*) beneath the symbol of any flag affected by the instruction. *How* the flag is affected depends on what the instruction does. You'll have to divine that from the Notes section. When an instruction affects no flags at all, the word <none> will appear in the flags minichart.

In the example page here, the minichart indicates that the NEG instruction affects the Overflow flag, the Sign flag, the Zero flag, the Auxiliary Carry flag, the Parity flag, and the Carry flag. The ways that the flags are affected depend on the results of the negation operation on the operand specified. These ways are summarized in the second paragraph of the Notes section.

NEG Negate (Two's Complement; i.e., Multiply by −1)

Flags Affected

```
O D I T S Z A P C   OF: Overflow flag  TF: Trap flag AF: Aux carry
F F F F F F F F F   DF: Direction flag SF: Sign flag PF: Parity flag
*       * * * *   IF: Interrupt flag ZF: Zero flag CF: Carry flag
```

Legal Forms

```
NEG r8
NEG m8
NEG r16
NEG m16
NEG r32      386+
NEG m32      386+
NEG r64      x64
NEG m64      x64
```

Examples

```
NEG AL
NEG DX
NEG ECX
NEG RCX
NEG BYTE [BX]    ; Negates BYTE quantity at [BX]
NEG WORD [DI]    ; Negates WORD quantity at [BX]
NEG DWORD [EAX]  ; Negates DWORD quantity at [EAX]
NEG QWORD [RCX]  ; Negates QWORD quantity at [RCX]
```

Notes

This is the assembly language equivalent of multiplying a value by − 1. Keep in mind that negation is *not* the same as simply inverting each bit in the operand. (Another instruction, NOT, does that.) The process is also known as generating the *two's complement* of a value. The two's complement of a value added to that value yields zero: 1 = $FF; 2 = $FE; 3 = $FD; and so on.

If the operand is 0, CF is cleared, and ZF is set; otherwise, CF is set, and ZF is cleared. If the operand contains the maximum negative value for the operand size, the operand does not change, but OF and CF are set. SF is set if the result is negative, or else SF is cleared. PF is set if the low-order 8 bits of the result contain an even number of set (1) bits; otherwise, PF is cleared.

Note: You *must* use a size specifier (BYTE, WORD, DWORD, QWORD) with memory data!

```
r8 = AL AH BL BH CL CH DL DH     r16 = AX BX CX DX BP SP SI DI
sr = CS DS SS ES FS GS           r32 = EAX EBX ECX EDX EBP
                                 ESP ESI EDI
m8 = 8-bit memory data           m16 = 16-bit memory data
m32 = 32-bit memory data         i8 = 8-bit immediate data
i16 = 16-bit immediate data      i32 = 32-bit immediate data
d8 = 8-bit signed displacement   d16 = 16-bit signed displacement
d32 = 32-bit unsigned displacement
```

Legal Forms

A given mnemonic represents a single machine instruction, but each instruction may include more than one legal form. The form of an instruction varies by the type and order of the operands passed to it.

What the individual forms actually represent are different binary number opcodes. For example, beneath the surface, the POP RAX instruction is the number 058h, whereas the POP RSI instruction is the number 05Eh. Most x64 opcodes are not single 8-bit values, and most are at least two bytes long, and often four or more.

When you want to use an instruction with a certain set of operands, make sure you check the Legal Forms section of the reference guide for that instruction to make sure that the combination is legal. More forms are legal now than they were in the bad old DOS days, and many of the remaining restrictions involve segment registers, which you will not be able to use anyway when writing ordinary 64-bit long-mode user applications.

In the example reference page on the NEG instruction, you see that a segment register cannot be an operand to NEG. (If it could, there would be a NEG sr item in the Legal forms list.)

Operand Symbols

The symbols used to indicate the nature of the operands in the Legal Forms section are summarized at the bottom of every instruction's page in Appendix A. They're close to self-explanatory, but I'll take a moment to expand upon them slightly here:

- **r8**—An 8-bit register half, one of AH, AL, BH, BL, CH, CL, DH, or DL.
- **r16**—A 16-bit general-purpose register, one of AX, BX, CX, DX, BP, SP, SI, or DI.
- **r32**—A 32-bit general-purpose register, one of EAX, EBX, ECX, EDX, EBP, ESP, ESI, or EDI.
- **r64**—A 64-bit general-purpose register, one of RAX, RBX, RCX, RDX, RBP, RSP, RSI, RDI, or one of R8-R15.
- **sr**—One of the segment registers, CS, DS, SS, ES, FS, or GS.
- **m8**—An 8-bit byte of memory data.
- **m16**—A 16-bit word of memory data.
- **m32**—A 32-bit word of memory data.
- **m64**—A 64-bit word of memory data.
- **i8**—An 8-bit byte of immediate data.

- **i16**—A 16-bit word of immediate data.

- **i32**—A 32-bit word of immediate data.

- **i64**—A 64-bit word of immediate data.

- **d8**—An 8-bit signed displacement. We haven't covered these yet, but a *displacement* is a distance between the current location in the code and another place in the code to which we want to jump. It's *signed* (that is, either negative or positive) because a positive displacement jumps you higher (forward) in memory, whereas a negative displacement jumps you lower (back) in memory. We'll examine this notion in detail later.

- **d16**—A 16-bit signed displacement. Again, for use with jump and call instructions.

- **d32**—A 32-bit signed displacement.

- **d64**—A 64-bit signed displacement.

Examples

Whereas the Legal Forms section shows what combinations of operands are legal for a given instruction, the Examples section shows examples of the instruction in actual use, just as it would be coded in an assembly language program. I've tried to put a good sampling of examples for each instruction, demonstrating the range of different possibilities with the instruction. Not every single legal form will be present in the examples.

Notes

The Notes section of the reference page describes the instruction's action briefly and provides information on how it affects the flags, how it may be limited in use, and any other detail that needs to be remembered, especially things that beginners would overlook or misconstrue.

What's Not Here. . .

I have omitted any instruction from Appendix B that no longer exists in the x64 instruction set.

Appendix B differs from most detailed assembly language references in that it does not include the binary opcode encoding information, nor indications of how many machine cycles are used by each form of the instruction.

The binary encoding of an instruction is the actual sequence of binary bytes that the CPU digests and recognizes as the machine instruction. What we would call POP RAX, the machine sees as the binary number 58h. What we call ADD RSI,07733h, the machine sees as the 7-byte sequence 48h 81h 0C6h 33h 77h 00h 00h. Machine instructions are encoded into anywhere from one to as many as

15 bytes depending on what instruction they are and what their operands are. Laying out the system for determining what the encoding will be for any given instruction is extremely complicated, in that its component bytes must be set up bit-by-bit from several large tables. I've decided that this book is not the place for that particular discussion and have left encoding information out of Appendix B. (This issue is one thing that makes the Intel instruction reference books as big as they are.)

Finally, I've included nothing anywhere in this book that indicates how many machine cycles are expended by any given machine instruction. A *machine cycle* is one pulse of the master clock that makes the PC perform its magic. Each instruction uses some number of those cycles to do its work, and the number varies all over the map depending on criteria that I won't be explaining in this book. Worse, the number of machine cycles used by a given instruction differs from one model of Intel processor to another. An instruction may use fewer cycles on the Pentium than on the 486, or perhaps more. (In general, Intel machine instructions have come to use fewer clock cycles over the years, but this is not true of every single instruction.)

Furthermore, as Michael Abrash explains in his immense book *Michael Abrash's Graphics Programming Black Book* (Coriolis Group Books, 1997), knowing the cycle requirements for individual instructions is rarely sufficient to allow even an expert assembly language programmer to calculate how much time a given series of instructions will take to execute. The CPU cache, prefetching, branch prediction, hyperthreading, and any number of other factors combine and interact to make such calculations almost impossible except in broad terms. He and I both agree that it is no fit subject for beginners, but if you'd like to know more at some point, I suggest hunting down his book and seeing for yourself.

Our Object All Sublime

Creating Programs That Work

The Bones of an Assembly Language Program

They don't call it "assembly" for nothing. Facing the task of writing an assembly language program brings to mind images of Christmas morning: You've spilled 1,567 small metal parts out of a large box marked "Land Shark HyperBike (Some Assembly Required)" and now you have to somehow put them all together with nothing left over. (In the meantime, the kids seem more than happy playing in the box....)

I've actually explained just about all you absolutely *must* understand to create your first assembly language program. Still, there is a nontrivial leap from here to there; you are faced with many small parts with sharp edges that can fit together in an infinity of different ways, most wrong, some workable, but only a few that are ideal.

So here's the plan: In this chapter, I'll present you with the completed and operable Land Shark HyperBike—which I will then tear apart before your eyes. This is the best way to learn to assemble: by pulling apart programs written by those who know what they're doing. Over the rest of this chapter, we'll pull a few more programs apart, in the hope that by the time it's over you'll be able to move in the other direction all by yourself.

In Listing 5.1 in Chapter 5, I presented perhaps the simplest correct program for Linux that will do anything visible and still be comprehensible and expandable. Since then we've been looking at instructions in a sandbox through SASM's debugger. That's a good way to become familiar with individual instructions, but in very little time a sandbox just isn't enough. Now that you have a grip on the most common x64 instructions (and know how to set up a sandbox to experiment with and get to know the others), we need to move on to complete programs.

As you saw when you ran it, the program EASTSYSCALL.ASM displays one (short) line of text on your display screen.

```
Eat at Joe's!
```

For that, you had to feed 35 lines of text to the assembler! Many of those 35 lines are comments and unnecessary in the strictest sense, but they serve as internal documentation to allow you to understand what the program is doing (or, more important, *how* it's doing it) six months or a year from now.

Listing 8.1 is the same program you saw in Listing 5.1, but it's short, and I'm going to reprint it here so that you don't have to flip back and forth during the discussion on the following pages.

Listing 8.1: eatsyscall.asm

```
;   Executable name  : eatsyscall
;   Version          : 1.0
;   Created date     : 4/25/2022
;   Last update      : 5/10/2023
;   Author           : Jeff Duntemann
;   Architecture     : x64
;   From             : x64 Assembly Language Step By Step, 4th Edition
;   Description      : A simple program in assembly for x64 Linux
;                      using NASM
;                      2.14, demonstrating the use of the syscall
;                      instruction
;                      to display text. Not for use within SASM.
;
;   Build using these commands:
;     nasm -f elf64 -g -F dwarf eatsyscall.asm
;     ld -o eatsyscall eatsyscall.o
;

SECTION .data          ; Section containing initialized data

    EatMsg: db Eat at Joe's!",10
    EatLen: equ $-EatMsg

SECTION .bss           ; Section containing uninitialized data

SECTION .text          ; Section containing code
```

```
    global  _start      ; Linker needs this to find the entry point!

_start:
    push rbp
    mov rbp,rsp

    mov rax,1           ; 1 = sys_write for syscall
    mov rdi,1           ; 1 = fd for stdout; i.e., write to the
                        ;   terminal window
    mov rsi,EatMsg      ; Put address of the message string in rsi
    mov rdx,EatLen      ; Length of string to be written in rdx
    syscall             ; Make the system call

    mov rax,60          ; 60 = exit the program
    mov rdi,0           ; Return value in rdi 0 = nothing to return
    syscall             ; Call syscall to exit
```

The Initial Comment Block

One of the aims of assembly language coding is to use as few instructions as possible to get the job done. This does *not* mean creating as short a source code file as possible. The size of the source file has *nothing* to do with the size of the executable file assembled from it! The more comments you put in your file, the better you'll remember how things work inside the program the next time you pick it up. I think you'll find it amazing how quickly the logic of a complicated assembly language program goes cold in your head. After no more than 48 hours of working on other projects, I've come back to assembly projects and had to struggle to get back to flank speed on development.

Comments are neither time nor space wasted. IBM used to say, "One line of comments per line of code." That's good—and should be considered a *minimum* for assembly language work. A better course (that I will in fact follow in the more complicated examples later in the chapter) is to use one short line of commentary to the right of each line of code, along with a comment block at the start of each sequence of instructions that work together in accomplishing some discrete task.

At the top of every program should be a sort of standardized comment block, containing some important information.

- The name of the source code file.
- The name of the executable file.
- The date you created the file.
- The date you last modified the file.
- The name of the person who wrote it.
- The name and version of the assembler used to create it.

- An "overview" description of what the program or library does. Take as much room as you need. It doesn't matter to the size or speed of the executable program.

- A copy of the commands used to build the file, taken from the make file if you use a make file or from SASM's Build dialog if you use SASM.

The challenge with an initial comment block is updating it to reflect the current state of your project. None of your tools is going to do that automatically. It's up to you.

The .data Section

Ordinary user-space programs written in NASM for Linux are divided into three sections. The order in which these sections fall in your program really isn't important, but by convention the .data section comes first, followed by the .bss section and then the .text section.

The .data section contains data definitions of initialized data items. Initialized data is data that has a value before the program begins running. These values are part of the executable file. They are loaded into memory when the executable file is loaded into memory for execution. You don't have to load them with their values, and no machine cycles are used in their creation beyond what it takes to load the program as a whole into memory.

The important thing to remember about the .data section is that the more initialized data items that you define, the larger the executable file will be, and the longer it will take to load it from disk into memory when you run it.

We'll talk in detail about how initialized data items are defined shortly.

The .bss Section

Not all data items need to have values before the program begins running. When you're reading data from a disk file, for example, you need to have a place for the data to go after it comes in from disk. Data buffers like that are defined in the Block Start Symbol (.bss) section of your program. I've heard it called a few other things down the years, like Buffer Start Symbol. The acronym doesn't matter in the slightest. In the .bss section, you allocate blocks of memory to be used later and give those blocks names.

All assemblers have a way to set aside some number of bytes for a buffer and give that buffer a name, but you don't specify what values are to be stored in the buffer. (More on this later.) Those values will appear due to program action while the program is running.

There's a crucial difference between data items defined in the .data section and data items defined in the .bss section: Data items in the .data section add to the size of your executable file. Data items in the .bss section do not. A buffer that takes up 16,000 bytes (or more, sometimes *much* more) can be defined in .bss and add almost nothing (about 50 bytes for the description) to the executable file size.

This is possible because of the way the Linux loader brings the program into memory. When you build your executable file, the Linux linker adds information to the file describing all the symbols you've defined, including symbols naming data items. The loader knows which data items do not have initial values, and it allocates space in memory for them when it brings the executable in from disk. Data items with initial values are read in along with their values.

The very simple program eatsyscall.asm does not need any buffers or other uninitialized data items and technically does not require that a .bss section be defined at all. I put one in simply to show you how one is defined. Having an empty .bss section does not increase the size of your executable file, and deleting an empty .bss section does not make your executable file any smaller.

The .text Section

The actual machine instructions that make up your program go into the .text section. Ordinarily, there are no data items defined in .text. The .text section contains symbols called *labels* that identify locations in the program code for jumps and calls, but beyond your instruction mnemonics, that's about it.

All global labels must be declared in the .text section, or the labels cannot be "seen" outside your program, either by the Linux linker or by the Linux loader. Let's look at the labels issue a little more closely.

Labels

A *label* is a sort of bookmark, describing a place in the program code and giving it a name that's easier to remember than a naked memory address. Labels are used to indicate the places where jump instructions should jump to and give names to callable assembly language procedures. I'll explain how that's all done in later chapters.

In the meantime, here are the most important things to know about labels:

▪ *Labels must begin with a letter or else with an underscore, period, or question mark.* These last three have special meanings to the assembler, so don't use them until you know how NASM interprets them.

▪ *Labels must be followed by a colon when they are defined.* This is basically what tells NASM that the identifier being defined is a label. NASM will punt if no colon is there and will not flag an error, but the colon nails it and prevents a mistyped instruction mnemonic from being mistaken for a label. So use the colon!

▪ *Labels are case sensitive.* For example, *yikes:*, *Yikes:*, and *YIKES:* are three completely different labels. This is a convention in the C language but differs from practice in a lot of other languages (Pascal particularly) where labels and other identifiers are *not* case-sensitive. Keep it in mind if you have experience in other high-level languages beyond C.

Later, we'll see such labels used as the targets of jump and call instructions. For example, the following machine instruction transfers the flow of instruction execution to the location marked by the label GoHome:

```
jmp GoHome
```

Notice that the colon is *not* used here. The colon is placed only where the label is *defined*, not where it is *referenced*. Think of it this way: Use the colon when you're *marking* a location, not when you're *going* there.

There is only one label in eatsyscall.asm, and it's a little bit special. The _start label indicates where the program begins. (It's case-sensitive, so don't try using _START or _Start.) This label must be marked as global at the top of the .text section, as shown.

SASM changes things a little. When you're compiling an assembly language program in SASM, the _start label becomes main. SASM uses the Gnu C compiler gcc to act as a middleman between NASM and the Linux linker, ld. What SASM does, in a sense, is create a C program without any C code in it. All C programs have to have a starting point, and in a C program that starting point is always main. There are reasons for doing this that involve linking functions written in C to your assembly program, as I'll explain how to do later.

Remember this: When assembling from a make file, use _start. When assembling from within SASM, use main.

Variables for Initialized Data

The identifier EatMsg in the .data section defines a *variable*. Specifically, EatMsg is a string variable (more on which shortly), but still, as with all variables, it's one of a class of items we call *initialized data*: something that comes with a value and not just an empty box into which we can place a value at some future time. A variable is defined by associating an identifier with a *data definition directive*. Data definition directives look like this:

```
MyByte      db 07h                  ; 8 bits in size
MyWord      dw 0FFFFh               ; 16 bits in size
MyDouble    dd 0B8000000h           ; 32 bits in size
MyQuad      dq 07FFFFFFFFFFFFFFFh    ; 64 bits in size
```

Think of the DB directive as "Define Byte." DB sets aside one byte of memory for data storage. Think of the DW directive as "Define Word." DW sets aside one word (16 bits, or two bytes) of memory for data storage. Think of the DD directive as "Define Double." DD sets aside a double word in memory for storage. DQ means "Define Quad," that is, a quad word, which is 64 bits in size.

String Variables

String variables are an interesting special case. A *string* is just that: a sequence or string of characters, all in a row in memory. One string variable is defined in eatsyscall.asm:

```
EatMsg: db "Eat at Joe's!",10
```

Strings are an exception to the general rule that a data definition directive sets aside a particular quantity of memory. The DB directive ordinarily sets aside one byte only. However, a string may be any length you like. Because there is no data directive that sets aside 17 bytes, or 42, strings are defined simply by associating a label with the place where the string *starts*. The EatMsg label and its DB directive specify one byte in memory as the string's starting point. The number of characters in the string is what tells the assembler how many bytes of storage to set aside for that string.

Either single quote (') or double quote (") characters may be used to delineate a string, and the choice is up to you, *unless* you're defining a string value that itself contains one or more quote characters. Notice in eatsyscall.asm that the string variable EatMsg contains a single-quote character used as an apostrophe. Because the string contains a single-quote character, you *must* delineate it with double quotes. The reverse is also true: If you define a string that contains one or more double-quote characters, you must delineate it using single-quote characters:

```
Yukkh: db 'He said, "How disgusting!" and threw up.',10
```

You may combine several separate substrings into a single string variable by separating the substrings with commas. This is a perfectly legal (and sometimes useful) way to define a string variable:

```
TwoLineMsg: db "Eat at Joe's...",10,
"...Ten million flies can't ALL be wrong!",10
```

So, what's with the numeric literal 10 tucked into the previous example strings? In Linux text work, the end of line (EOL) character has the numeric value of 10 decimal, or 0Ah. It tells the operating system where a line submitted for display to the console ends. Any subsequent text displayed to the console will be shown on the next line down, at the left margin. In the variable TwoLineMsg, the EOL character in between the two substrings will direct Linux to display the first substring on one line of the console, and the second substring on the next line of the console below it:

```
Eat at Joe's!
Ten million flies can't ALL be wrong!
```

You can concatenate such individual numbers within a string, but you must remember that, as with EOL, *they will not appear as numbers*. A string is a string of *characters*. A number appended to a string will be interpreted by most operating system routines as an ASCII character. The correspondence between numbers and ASCII characters is shown in Appendix C. To show numbers in a string, you must represent them as ASCII characters, either as character literals, like the digit character 7, or as the numeric equivalents to ASCII characters, like 37h.

In ordinary assembly work, nearly all string variables are defined using the DB directive and may be considered strings of bytes. (An ASCII character is one byte in size.) You can define string variables using DW, DD, or DQ, but they're handled a little differently than those defined using DB. Consider these variables:

```
WordString:   dw 'CQ'
DoubleString: dd 'Stop'
QuadString:   dq 'KANGAROO'
```

The DW directive defines a word-length variable, and a word (16 bits) may hold two 8-bit characters. Similarly, the DD directive defines a double word (32-bit) variable, which may hold four 8-bit characters. The DQ directive defines a quad word variable, which may contain eight 8-bit characters. The different handling comes in when you load these named strings into registers. Consider these three instructions:

```
mov ax, [WordString]
mov edx, [DoubleString]
mov rax, [QuadString]
```

Remember here that to move the data in a variable into a register, you must place the name of the variable (which is its address) between square brackets. Without the brackets, what you move into the register is the variable's address in memory, *not* what data exists at that address.

In the first MOV instruction, the characters *CQ* are placed into register AX, with the *C* in AL and the *Q* in AH. In the second MOV instruction, the characters *Stop* are loaded into EDX in little-endian order, with the *S* in the lowest order byte of EDX, the *t* in the second lowest byte, and so on. If you look at the string QuadString loaded into RAX from SASM, you'll see that it contains "KANGAROO" spelled backward.

Loading strings into a single register this way (assuming that they fit!) is a lot less common (and less useful) than using DB to define character strings, and you won't find yourself doing it very often.

Because `eatsyscall.asm` does not define any uninitialized data in its `.bss` section, I'll hold off discussing such definitions until we look at the next example program.

Deriving String Length with EQU and $

Beneath the definition of EatMsg in the `eatsyscall.asm` file is an interesting construct.

```
EatLen: equ $-EatMsg
```

This is an example of a larger class of things called *assembly-time calculations*. What we're doing here is calculating the length of the string variable EatMsg and making that length value accessible to program code through the label EatLen. At any point in your program, if you need to use the length of EatMsg, you can use the label EatLen.

A statement containing the directive EQU is called an *equate*. An equate is a way of associating a value with a label. Such a label is then treated very much like a named constant in Pascal. Any time the assembler encounters an equate during assembly, it will swap in the equate's value for its name. Here's an example:

```
FieldWidth: equ 10
```

Here, we're telling the assembler that the label FieldWidth stands for the numeric value 10. Once that equate is defined, the following two machine instructions are *exactly* the same:

```
mov eax,10
mov eax,FieldWidth
```

There are two advantages to this.

- An equate makes the instruction easier to understand by using a descriptive name for a value. We know what the value 10 is for; it's the width of a field.

- An equate makes programs easier to change down the road. If the field width changes from 10 to 12 at some point, we need only change the source code file at *one* line rather than everywhere we access the field width.

Don't underestimate the value of this second advantage. Once your programs become larger and more sophisticated, you may find yourself using a particular value dozens or hundreds of times within a single program. Either you can make that value an equate and change one line to alter a value used 267 times, or you can go through your code and change all 267 uses of the value individually—except for the five or six that you miss, causing havoc when you next assemble and run your program.

Combining assembly language calculation with equates allows some wonderful things to be done very simply. As I'll explain shortly, to display a string in Linux, you need to pass both the address of the string and its length to the operating system. You can make the length of the string an equate this way:

```
EatMsg: db "Eat at Joe's!",10
EatLen: equ 14
```

This works, because the `EatMsg` string is in fact 14 characters long, including the EOL character. But suppose Joe sells his diner to Ralph, and you swap in "Ralph" for "Joe." You have to change not only the ad message but also its length.

```
EatMsg: db "Eat at Ralph's!",10
EatLen: equ 16
```

What are the chances that you're going to forget to update the `EatLen` equate with the new message length? Do that sort of thing often enough, and you *will*. With an assembly-time calculation, you simply change the definition of the string variable, and its length is automatically calculated by NASM at assembly time.

How? This way:

```
EatLen: equ $-EatMsg
```

It all depends on the magical "here" token, expressed by the humble dollar sign. As I explained earlier, at assembly time NASM chews through your source code files and builds an intermediate file with a `.o` extension. The $ token marks the spot where NASM is in building the intermediate file (*not* the source code file!). The label `EatMsg` marks the beginning of the advertising slogan string. Immediately after the last character of `EatMsg` is the label `EatLen`. Labels, remember, are not data, but *locations*—and in the case of assembly language, addresses. When NASM reaches the label `EatLen`, the value of $ is the location immediately after the last character in `EatMsg`. The assembly-time calculation is to take the location represented by the $ token (which when the calculation is done contains the location just past the end of the `EatMsg` string) and subtract from it the location of the beginning of the `EatMsg` string. End – Beginning = Length.

This calculation is performed every time you assemble the file, so any time you change the contents of `EatMsg`, the value `EatLen` will be recalculated automatically. You can change the text within the string any way you like and never have to worry about changing a length value anywhere in the program.

Assembly-time calculation has other uses, but this is the most common one and the only one you're likely to use as a beginner.

Last In, First Out via the Stack

The little program `eatsyscall.asm` doesn't do much: It displays a short text string in the Linux console. Explaining how it does that one simple thing, however, will take some doing, and before I can even begin, I have to explain one of the key concepts of not only the x86/x64 architecture but in fact all computing: the *stack*.

The stack is a storage mechanism built right into the CPU hardware. Intel didn't invent it; the stack has been an integral part of computer hardware since the 1950s. The name is appropriate, and for a usable metaphor I can go back to my high school days, when I was a dishwasher for Resurrection Hospital on Chicago's Northwest Side.

Five Hundred Plates an Hour

There were a lot of different jobs in the hospital kitchen back then, but what I did most of the time was pull clean plates off a moving conveyor belt that emerged endlessly from the steaming dragon's mouth of a 180° dishwashing machine. This was hot work, but it was a lot less slimy than stuffing the dirty plates into the other end of the machine.

When you pull 500 plates an hour out of a dishwashing machine, you had better have some place efficient to stash them. Obviously, you could simply stack them on a table, but stacked ceramic plates in any place habituated by rowdy teenage boys is asking for tableware mayhem. What the hospital had instead was an army of little wheeled stainless steel cabinets equipped with one or more spring-loaded circular plungers accessed from the top. When you had a handful of plates, you pushed them down into the plunger. The plunger's spring was adjusted such that the weight of the added plates pushed the whole stack of plates down just enough to make the new top plate flush with the top of the cabinet.

Each plunger held about 50 plates. We rolled one up next to the dragon's mouth, filled it with plates, and then rolled it back into the kitchen where the clean plates were used at the next meal shift to set patient trays.

It's instructive to follow the path of the first plate out of the dishwashing machine on a given shift. That plate got into the plunger first and was subsequently shoved down into the bottom of the plunger by the remaining 49 plates that the cabinet could hold. After the cabinet was rolled into the kitchen, the kitchen ladies pulled plates out of the cabinet one by one as they set trays for patients. The *first* plate out of the cabinet was the *last* plate to go in. The *last* plate out of the cabinet had been the *first* plate to go in.

The Intel stack (and most other stacks in other computer architectures) is like that. We call it a last in, first out (*LIFO*) stack. Instead of plates, we push chunks of data onto the top of the stack, and they remain on the stack until we pull them off in reverse order.

The stack doesn't exist in some separate alcove of the CPU. It exists in ordinary memory, and in fact what we call "the stack" is really a way of managing data in memory. The stack is a place where we can tuck away one or two (or however many) values for the time being and come back to them a little later. The stack's primary virtue is that it does not require that we give the stored data a name. We put that data on the stack, and we retrieve it later by its position, or in some cases by accessing the stack using ordinary memory addressing relative to a fixed point in the stack's memory. (More on the second method a little later, after we get all the basics down.)

The jargon involving use of the stack reflects my dishwasher's metaphor: When we place something on the stack, we say that we *push* it; when we retrieve something from the stack, we say that we *pop* it. The stack grows or shrinks as data is pushed onto it or popped off of it. The most recently pushed item on the stack is said to be at the top of the stack. When we pop an item from the stack, what we get is the item at the top of the stack. I've drawn this out conceptually in Figure 8.1.

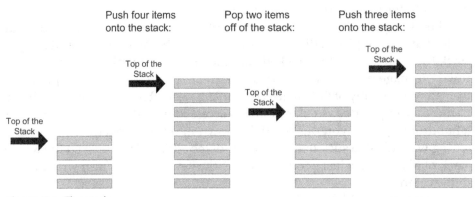

Figure 8.1: The stack

In the x64 architecture, the top of the stack is marked by a register called the *stack pointer*, with the formal name RSP. It's a 64-bit register, and it holds the memory address of the last item pushed onto the stack.

Stacking Things Upside Down

Making things a little trickier to visualize is the fact that the Intel stack is basically upside-down. If you picture a region of memory with the lowest address at the bottom and the highest address at the top, the stack begins up at the ceiling, and as items are pushed onto the stack, the stack grows downward, toward low memory.

Figure 8.2 shows in broad terms how Linux organizes the memory that it gives to your program when it runs. At the bottom of memory are the three sections that you define in your program: .text at the lowest addresses, followed by .data, followed by .bss. The stack is located all the way at the opposite end of your program's memory block. In between the end of the .bss section and the top of the stack is basically empty memory. C programs routinely use this free memory space to allocate variables "on the fly" in a region called the *heap*. Assembly programs can do that as well, though it's not as easy as it sounds, and I don't have space to cover it in this book. I drew the heap in Figure 8.2 because it's important to know where it lies in the user-space memory map. Like the stack, the heap grows or shrinks as data structures are created (by allocating memory) or destroyed (by releasing memory).

The important thing to remember (especially if you've had previous experience writing assembly for DOS) is that we're not in real mode anymore. When your app begins running, Linux reserves a contiguous range of virtual memory for the stack that defaults to something like 8 gigabytes. (The exact amount of virtual memory depends on how Linux is configured and may vary.) Of this, only a few pages are actually committed at the top of the virtual address space. When the stack grows downward and runs out of physical memory, a page fault occurs, and more physical memory is mapped into the virtual address space by the OS and then becomes available for the stack's use. This continues until the entire virtual space is exhausted—which basically never happens unless the program is ravenously eating stack space due to a bug.

Virtual memory is a wonderful but complicated thing, and I can't go into it in detail in this book. The takeaway here is that your app's stack can pretty much have all the memory it needs thanks to virtual memory, and you no longer have to worry about running out.

The only caution I should offer on Figure 8.2 is that the relative sizes of the program sections versus the stack shouldn't be seen as literal. You may have thousands of bytes of program code and tens of thousands of bytes of data in a middling assembly program, but compared to that, the stack is still quite small: a few hundred bytes at most and generally less than that.

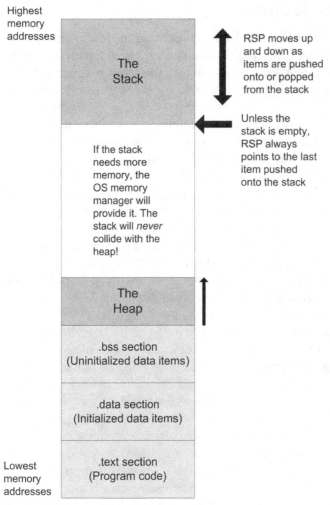

Figure 8.2: The stack in program memory

Push-y Instructions

You can place data onto the stack in several ways, but the most straightforward way involves two related machine instructions, PUSH and PUSHFQ. The two are similar in how they work, and they differ mostly as to what they push onto the stack:

- PUSH pushes a 16-bit or 64-bit register or memory value that is specified by you in your source code. Note that *you can't push an 8-bit nor a 32-bit value onto the stack!* You'll get an error if you try.

- PUSHFQ pushes the full 64-bit RFlags register onto the stack. (The Q means "quadword" here.) This even though more than half of the flags in RFlags are reserved and have no use. You won't use PUSHFQ often, but it's there if you need it.

Here are some examples of the PUSH family of instructions in use:

```
pushfq        ; Push the RFlags register
push rax      ; Push the RAX register
push bx       ; Push the 16-bit register BX
push [rdx]    ; Push the quadword in memory at RDX
```

Note that PUSHFQ takes no operands. You'll generate an assembler error if you try to hand PUSHFQ operands; the instruction pushes the 64-bit RFlags register onto the stack, and that's all it's capable of doing.

PUSH works this way, for 64-bit operands: First RSP is decremented by 64 bits (eight bytes) so that it points to an empty area of stack memory that is eight bytes long. Then whatever is to be pushed onto the stack is written to memory at the address in RSP. *Voilà!* The data is safe on the stack, and RSP has crawled eight bytes closer to the bottom of memory. PUSH can also push 16-bit values onto the stack, and when it does, the only difference is that RSP moves by two bytes instead of eight.

All memory between RSP's initial position and its current position (the top of the stack) contains real data that was explicitly pushed on the stack and will presumably be popped from the stack later. Some of that data was pushed onto the stack by the operating system before running your program, and we'll talk about that a little later in the book.

What can and cannot be pushed onto the stack in x64 long mode is reasonably simple: Any of the 16-bit and 64-bit general-purpose registers may be pushed individually onto the stack. You can't push AL or BH or any other of the 8-bit registers. 16-bit and 64-bit immediate data can be pushed onto the stack. User-space Linux programs cannot push the segment registers onto the stack under any circumstances. With x64, segment registers belong to the OS and are unavailable to user-space programs.

As odd as it might seem, 32-bit values (including all 32-bit registers) may *not* be pushed onto the stack.

POP Goes the Opcode

In general, what gets pushed must get popped, or you can end up in any of several different kinds of trouble. Getting an item of data *off* the stack is most easily done with another duet of instructions, POP and POPFQ. As you might expect, POP is the general-purpose one-at-a-time popper, while POPFQ is dedicated to popping the flags off of the stack and into RFlags.

```
popfq         ; Pop the top 8 bytes from the stack into RFlags
pop rcx       ; Pop the top 8 bytes from the stack into RCX
pop bx        ; Pop the top 2 bytes from the stack into BX
pop [rbx]     ; Pop the top 8 bytes from the stack into memory at EBX
```

As with PUSH, POP operates only on 16-bit or 64-bit operands. Don't try to pop data from the stack into an 8-bit or 32-bit register such as AH or ECX.

POP works pretty much the way PUSH does, but in reverse. As with PUSH, how much comes off the stack depends on the size of the operand. Popping the stack into a 16-bit register takes the top two bytes off the stack. Popping the stack into a 64-bit register takes the top eight bytes off the stack.

Note that nothing in the CPU nor in Linux remembers the sizes of the data items that you place on the stack. *It's up to you to know the size of the last item pushed onto the stack.* If the last item you pushed onto the stack was a 16-bit register, popping the stack into a 64-bit register will take six more bytes off the stack than you pushed. This is called *misaligning* the stack, and it's nothing but trouble—which is one reason why you should work with 64-bit registers and memory values whenever you can and avoid using the stack with 16-bit values.

When a POP instruction is executed, things work in this order: First, the data at the address currently stored in RSP is copied from the stack and placed in POP's operand, whatever you specified that to be. After that, RSP is incremented (rather than decremented) by the size of the operand—either 16 bits or 64 bits—so that in effect RSP moves either two or eight bytes up the stack, away from low memory.

It's significant that RSP is decremented *before* placing a word on the stack at push time but incremented *after* removing a word from the stack at pop time. Certain other CPUs outside the x86 universe work in the opposite manner, which is fine—just don't get them confused. For x86/x64, this is always true: *Unless the stack is completely empty, RSP points to real data, not empty space.* Ordinarily, you don't have to remember that fact, as PUSH and POP handle it all for you, and you don't have to manually keep track of what RSP is pointing to.

PUSHA and POPA Are Gone

Just about everything you had in 32-bit assembly is still there in x64 assembly. Some things have changed, but very little was removed when x86 became x64.

Some sacrifices were in fact made. Four instructions are gone completely: PUSHA, PUSHAD, POPA, and POPAD. In earlier architectures, these instructions were used to push or pop all of the general-purpose registers at once.

So, why did they go away? I've never found an authoritative explanation, but I have a theory: There are a *lot* more general-purpose registers in x64. Pushing 15 64-bit registers onto the stack rather than 7 32-bit registers takes a big chunk of stack space. (Stack pointer ESP was not acted on by PUSHA/POPA for the obvious reason that ESP defines the stack!)

If you want to preserve general-purpose registers on the stack for some reason, you'll have to push and pop them individually.

Pushing and Popping in Detail

If you're still a little iffy on how the stack works, allow me to present an example that shows how the stack operates in detail, with real values. For clarity's sake in the associated diagram, I'm going to use 16-bit registers rather than 64-bit registers. This will allow me to show individual bytes on the stack. It works the same way with 64-bit values. The difference, again, is that eight bytes are pushed or popped rather than two.

Figure 8.3 shows how the stack looks after each of four instructions is executed. (I'm using 16-bit values in the figure for clarity. The mechanism is the same for 64-bit values.) The values of the four 16-bit x general-purpose registers at some hypothetical point in a program's execution are shown at the top of the figure. AX is pushed first on the stack. Its least significant byte is at RSP, and its most significant byte is at RSP+1. (Remember that both bytes are pushed onto the stack at once, as a unit!)

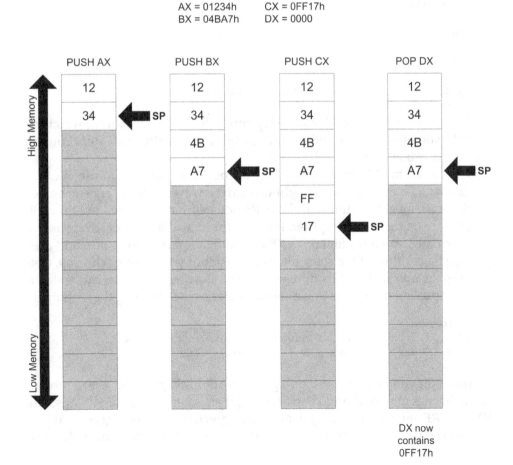

Figure 8.3: How the stack works

Each time one of the 16-bit registers is pushed onto the stack, RSP is decremented two bytes, moving down toward low memory. The first three columns show AX, BX, and CX being pushed onto the stack, respectively. But note what happens in the fourth column, when the instruction POP DX is executed. The stack pointer is incremented by two bytes and moves away from low memory. DX now contains a copy of the contents of CX. In effect, CX was pushed onto the stack and then immediately popped off into DX.

If you want to try Figure 8.3 in a SASM sandbox, bring up a new sandbox and add these machine instructions:

```
xor rax,rax   ;We first zero out all 4 64-bit "x" registers
xor rbx,rbx   ;so there are no "leftovers" in the high bits
xor rcx,rcx
xor rdx,rdx

mov ax,01234h   ;Place values in AX, BX, and CX
mov bx,04ba7h
mov cx,0ff17h

push ax         ;Push AX,BX,& CX onto the stack
push bx
push cx

pop dx          ;Pop the top of the stack into DX.
```

Go into debug mode and single-step through these instructions, watching both the stack pointer RSP and the four 16-bit registers after each step. You can follow the action in Figure 8.3 as well.

Yes, that's a mighty roundabout way to copy the value of CX into DX. MOV DX,CX is a lot faster and more straightforward. However, moving register values via the stack must sometimes be done. Remember that the MOV instruction will *not* operate on the RFlags register. If you want to load a copy of RFlags into a 64-bit register, you must first push RFlags onto the stack with PUSHFQ and then pop the flags value off the stack into the register of your choice with POP. Getting RFlags into RBX is thus done with the following code. You can watch it work by putting these lines into a sandbox and single-stepping through them:

```
xor rbx,rbx     ; Clear rbx
pushfq          ; Push the RFlags register onto the stack
pop qword rbx   ; ...and pop it immediately into RBX
```

Although you can restore the flag values into RFlags using POPFQ, not all bits of RFlags may be changed by popping them off the stack into RFlags. Bits VM and RF are not affected by POPFQ. Little gotchas like this suggest that you should not try saving and restoring the flags until you know *precisely* what you're doing.

Storage for the Short Term

The stack should be considered a place to stash things for the short term. Items stored on the stack have no names and in general must be taken off the stack in the reverse order that they were put on. Last in, first out, remember. LIFO!

One excellent use of the stack allows the all-too-few registers to do multiple duty. If you need a register to temporarily hold some value to be operated on by the CPU and all the registers are in use, push one of the busy registers onto the stack. Its value will remain safe on the stack while you use the register for other things. When you're finished using the register, pop its old value off the stack—and you've gained the advantages of an additional register without really having one. (The cost, of course, is the time you spend moving that register's value onto and off of the stack. It's not something you want to do in the middle of an often-repeated loop!)

Short-term storage during your program's execution is the simplest and most obvious use of the stack, but its most important use is probably in calling procedures and Linux kernel services. And now that you understand the stack, we can take on the mysterious matter of Linux system calls.

Using Linux Kernel Services Through Syscall

Everything else in `eatsyscall.asm` is preparation for the single instruction that performs the program's only real work: displaying a line of text in the Linux console. At the heart of the program is a call into the Linux operating system. A second call into Linux is at the end, when the program finishes up and needs to tell Linux that it's all done.

As I explained in Chapter 6, an operating system is something like a god and something like a troll, and Linux is no different. It controls all the most important elements of the machine in godlike fashion: memory, the disk drives, the printer, the keyboard, various ports (Ethernet, USB, serial, Bluetooth, etc.), and the display. At the same time, Linux is like a troll living under a bridge to all those parts of your machine: You tell the troll what you want done, and the troll will go off and do it for you. There are several hundred Linux kernel services available. Here's where you can find a good list of x64 Linux system calls:

`soliduscode.com/linux-system-calls`

One of the services that Linux provides is simple text-mode access to your PC's display. For the purposes of `eatsyscall.asm`—which is just a lesson in getting your first assembly language program written and operating—simple services are enough.

So—how do we use Linux's services? If you looked closely at `eatsyscall.asm`, you should recall two instances of the machine instruction `SYSCALL`.

In x64 instances of Linux, the SYSCALL instruction is how you access Linux kernel services.

X64 Kernel Services via the SYSCALL Instruction

In 32-bit versions of Linux, software interrupt INT 80h was the way to reach the kernel services dispatcher. INT 80h is no longer used. The x64 architecture gives us something a *whole* lot better: the SYSCALL instruction.

The challenge in accessing kernel services is this: passing execution to a code library without having any idea where that library is. The SYSCALL instruction looks in a CPU register that user-space programs can't access. When the Linux kernel starts up, it places the address of its services dispatcher in this register. One of the first things that the SYSCALL instruction does is escalate its privilege level from level 3 (user) to level 0 (kernel). It then reads the address in the services dispatch register and jumps to that address to invoke the dispatcher.

Most x64 system calls using SYSCALL have parameters, which are passed in CPU registers. Which registers? It's not random. In fact, there's something called the System V Application Binary Interface (ABI) for Linux, which lays out a whole system for passing parameters to Linux via SYSCALL. It does more than that, but what's of interest to us here is the machinery that allows you to call kernel services using SYSCALL. The best online presentation of those calls is here:

soliduscode.com/category/technology/assembly

ABI vs. API?

This is a good spot for a short digression. If you have any programming experience at all, you've probably heard of "API calls" or "the Windows API." What, then, is the difference between an ABI and an API? API stands for *application programming interface*. An API is a collection of callable functions to be used primarily by high-level programming languages like Pascal or C. It's possible for an assembly language program to call an API function, and I'll show you how a little later.

An application binary interface, by contrast, is a detailed description of what happens down at the machine-code level when one piece of binary machine code talks to another or to CPU hardware like registers. It's a layer "below" the API. The ABI defines a collection of fundamental callable functions, generally supplied by the operating system, as is done in Linux. This definition describes how to pass parameters to the many kernel service functions. An ABI also defines how linkers link compiled or assembled modules into a single executable binary program and much else that's beyond what I can discuss in this book.

The ABI's Register Parameter Scheme

Let's take a closer look at the `eatsyscall.asm` program I included in the first few pages of this chapter. The following code writes a textual message to the Linux console:

```
mov rax,1          ; 1 = sys_write for syscall
mov rdi,1          ; 1 = fd for stdout; i.e., write to the
                     terminal window
mov rsi,EatMsg     ; Put address of the message string in rsi
mov rdx,EatLen     ; Length of string to be written in rdx
syscall            ; Make the system call
```

In a nutshell, this code places certain values in certain registers and then executes the `SYSCALL` instruction. The Linux services dispatcher grabs the values placed in those registers and then calls the function specified in RAX.

There's a system for specifying which registers are used for which service and which parameters (if any) for that service. The best way to explain is to show you the first two lines of the System V ABI system call table, in Table 8.1.

Table 8.1: System Call Conventions for the System V ABI

RAX SYSTEM CALL		RDI	RSI	RDX	R10	R8	R9
0	sys_read	File descriptor	Address of buf.	Length of buf.	n/a	n/a	n/a
1	sys_write	File descriptor	Address of text	Length of text	n/a	n/a	n/a

All of the columns except for System Call are registers. System Call is the human-readable name of the system call, which is the name used by high-level languages like Pascal and C to make system calls via the `SYSCALL` instruction. Because Linux is written mostly in C, the verbiage you'll see in system call tables will be C verbiage. I've massaged that verbiage a little to make the table easier to understand for beginners.

Register RAX is dedicated to the numeric code specifying the system call to be made. The name of system call 1 is `sys_write`. The registers after the system call name contain parameters. The ABI specifies six registers to be used for parameters. Not all system calls require six parameters. The `sys_write` call used in `eatsyscall.asm` has only three. The list of parameters always begins with RDI and uses registers in the order given in the table.

RDI, RSI, RDX, R10, R8, R9

After a system call's parameters have all been assigned to registers, any registers remaining unused for the system call do not apply to the system call and are left blank.

The parameters for sys_write are these:

- **RDI:** The file descriptor to which text will be written. In Linux (and all flavors of Unix) the file descriptor for sys_write is 1.
- **RSI:** The address of the text to be written to the console.
- **RDX:** The length (number of characters) in the text to be written to the console.

If any system call needs to return a numeric value, that value is returned by the system in RAX.

Exiting a Program via SYSCALL

There is a second SYSCALL instruction in eatsyscall.asm, and it has a humble but crucial job: to shut down the program and return control to Linux. This sounds simpler than it is, and once you understand Linux internals a little more, you'll come to appreciate the work that must be done both to launch a process and to shut one down.

From your own program's standpoint, however, it's dirt-simple: You place the number of the sys_exit service in RAX, place a return code in RDI, and then execute SYSCALL:

```
mov rax,60          ; 60 = sys_exit to exit the program gracefully
mov rdi,0           ; Return value in rdi 0 = nothing to return
syscall             ; Call syscall to exit this program
```

The return code is a numeric value that you can define however you want. Technically there are no restrictions on what it is (aside from having to fit in a 64-bit register), but by convention, a return value of 0 means "everything worked OK; shutting down normally." Return values other than 0 typically indicate an error of some sort. Keep in mind that in larger programs, you have to watch out for things that don't work as expected: A disk file cannot be found, a disk drive is full, and so on. If a program can't do its job and must terminate prematurely, it should have some way of telling you (or in some cases, another program) what went wrong. The return code is a good way to do this.

Exiting this way is not just a nicety. *Every* x64 program you write *must* exit by making a call to sys_exit through the kernel services dispatcher. If a program just "runs off the edge," it will in fact end, but Linux will hand up a segmentation fault, and you'll be none the wiser as to what happened. This is why your "sandbox" programs are used only for debugging within SASM. They're program snippets and will generate a segmentation fault if you just let them run.

Programs written in SASM use elements of the Standard C Library, which gives programs a "shutdown code" section that actually makes the exit system call. Such programs end by executing a RET instruction, as I'll explain later.

Which Registers Are Trashed by SysCall?

Although x64 gives you twice the number of general-purpose registers as x86, not all of those "general-purpose" registers are free for you to use anywhere, at any time. From one to six of those registers are required to make a Linux system call with SYSCALL. Those six are called out in Table 8.1, and in the text a little later. The number of registers used varies by system call, and you'll have to look them up in a table of system calls to see how many. If a system call doesn't need all of the six SYSCALL parameter registers (sys_read and sys_write use only three), you can use any of those not required for that system call in your own code.

The SYSCALL instruction itself makes use of RAX, RCX, and R11 internally. After the SYSCALL returns, you can't assume that RAX, RCX, or R11 will have the same values they did before the SYSCALL.

Designing a Nontrivial Program

At this point, you know most of what you need to know to design and write small utilities that perform significant work—work that may even be useful. In this section, we'll approach the challenge of writing a utility program from the engineering standpoint of solving a problem. This involves more than just writing code. It involves stating the problem, breaking it down into the problem's component parts, and then devising a solution to the problem as a series of steps and tests that may be implemented as an assembly language program.

There's a certain "chicken-and-egg" issue with this section: It's difficult to write a nontrivial assembly program without conditional jumps and difficult to explain conditional jumps without demonstrating them in a nontrivial program. I've touched on jumps a little in previous chapters and will take them up in detail in Chapter 9. The jumps I'm using in the demo program in this section are pretty straightforward, and if you're a little fuzzy on the details, read Chapter 9 and then come back and go through this section and its examples again.

Defining the Problem

Years ago, I was on a team that was writing a system that gathered and validated data from field offices around the world and sent that data to a large central computing facility, where it would be tabulated, analyzed, and used to generate status reports. This sounds easy enough, and in fact gathering the data itself out at the field offices was not difficult. What made the project difficult was that it involved several separate and very different types of computers that saw data in entirely different and often incompatible ways. The problem was related to the issue of data encoding that I touched on briefly in Chapter 6. We had to deal with three different encoding systems for data characters. A character that was interpreted one way on one system would not be considered the same character on one of the other systems.

To move data from one system to one of the others, we had to create software that translated data encoding from one scheme to another. One of the schemes used a database manager that did not digest lowercase characters well, for reasons that seemed peculiar back then and are probably inconceivable today. We had to translate any lowercase characters into uppercase before we could feed data files into that system. There were other encoding issues but that was an important one, and because it's a simple problem to describe and then solve, it's a good first exercise in genuine assembly language program design.

At the very highest level, the problem to be solved here can be stated this way: *Convert any lowercase characters in a data file to uppercase.*

With that in mind, it's a good idea to take notes on the problem. In particular, take notes on the limitations of any proposed solution. We used to call these notes the "bounds" of the solution, and they need to be kept in mind while thinking about the program that will solve the problem.

- We'll be working under Linux.
- The data exists in disk files.
- We do not know ahead of time how large any of the files will be.
- There is no maximum nor minimum size for the files.
- We will use I/O redirection to pass filenames to the program.
- All the input files are in the same encoding scheme. The program can assume that an *a* character in one file is encoded the same way as an *a* in another file. (In our case, this is ASCII.)
- We must preserve the original file in its original form, rather than reading data from the original file and then writing it back to the original file. (Why? If the process crashes, we've destroyed the original file without completely generating an output file.)

In a real-world project there might be pages and pages of these notes, but just a few facts here will serve to shape our simple solution to the character-case problem. Note that these notes expand on what must be done, and to some extent put limits on the nature of the eventual solution, but do not attempt to say *how* it must be done. That's what we do in the next step.

Starting with Pseudocode

Once we understand the nature of the problem as thoroughly as possible, we can begin crafting a solution. At the outset, this much resembles the process I describe in Chapter 1, where someone makes a "do it" list of tasks for running the day's errands. You state a solution in a broad form and in as few statements as possible. Then, little by little, you refine the stated solution by breaking down the larger steps into the smaller steps that the larger steps contain.

In our case, the solution is fairly easy to state in broad terms. To get started, here's one form that the statement might take:

```
Read a character from the input file.
Convert the character to uppercase (if necessary)
Write the character to the output file.
Repeat until done.
```

This really is a solution, if perhaps an extreme "view from a height." It's short on *details*, but not short on function. If we execute the steps listed, we'll have a program that does what we need it to do. Note also that the statements given are not statements written in any programming language. They're certainly not assembly language instructions. They're descriptions of several actions, independent of any particular system for accomplishing those actions. Lists of statements like this, because they are deliberately *not* written as code for a particular programming environment, are called *pseudocode*.

Successive Refinement

From our first complete but detail-challenged statement of the solution, we move toward a more detailed statement of the solution. We do this by refining the pseudocode statements so that each is more specific about how the action being described is to be done. We repeat this process, adding more details every time, until what we have can be readily translated into actual assembly language instructions. This process, called *successive refinement*, is not specific to assembly language. It's used with all programming languages to one degree or another, but it works peculiarly well with assembly.

Let's stare at the pseudocode given earlier and create a new version with additional details. We know we're going to be using Linux for the program—it's part of the spec and one of the bounds of any solution—so we can begin adding details specific to the Linux way of doing such things. The next refinement might look like this:

```
Read a character from standard input (stdin)
Test the character to see if it's lowercase.
If the character is lowercase, convert it to uppercase by
subtracting 20h.
Write the character to standard output (stdout).
Repeat until done.
Exit the program by calling sys_exit.
```

At each pass, look long and hard at each action statement to see what details it may hide, and expand those details in the next refinement. Sometimes this will be easy; sometimes, well, not so easy. In the previous version, the statement "Repeat until done" sounds pretty plain and obvious at first, until you think about what "done" means here: running out of data in the input file. How do we know when the input file is out of characters? This may require some research, but in most operating systems (including Linux) the routine that you call to read data from a file returns a value. This value can indicate a successful read, a read error, or special-case results like "end of file" (EOF). The precise details can come later; what matters here is that we have to test for EOF when we read characters from the file. An expanded (and slightly rearranged) version of the solution pseudocode might look like this:

```
Read a character from standard input (stdin)
Test if we have reached End Of File (EOF)
If we have reached EOF, we're done, so jump to exit
Test the character to see if it's lowercase.
If the character is lowercase, convert it to uppercase by subtracting 20h.
Write the character to standard output (stdout).
Go back and read another character.
Exit the program by calling sys_exit.
```

And so we go, adding detail each time. Notice that this is starting to look a little more like program code now. So be it: As the number of statements increases, it helps to add labels to those statements that represent jump targets so that we don't get the jump targets mixed up, even in pseudocode. It also helps to break the pseudocode up into blocks, with related statements grouped together. Sooner or later we'll get to something like the following:

```
Read:  Set up registers for the sys_read kernel call.
Call sys_read to read from stdin.
Test for EOF.
If we're at EOF, jump to Exit.

Test the character to see if it's lowercase.
If it's not a lowercase character, jump to Write.
Convert the character to uppercase by subtracting 20h.

Write: Set up registers for the Write kernel call.
Call sys_write to write to stdout.
Jump back to Read and get another character.

Exit:  Set up registers for terminating the program via sys_exit.
Call sys_exit.
```

This is a good example of "bending" the pseudocode statement in the direction of the operating system and programming language that you're going to use. All programming languages have their quirks, their limitations, and a general "shape" to them. If you keep this shape in mind while you craft your pseudo-code, making the final transition to real code will be easier.

At some point, your pseudocode will have all the details it can contain and still remain pseudocode. To go further, you will have to begin turning your pseudocode into real assembly code. This means you have to take each state-ment and ask yourself: Do I know how to convert this pseudocode statement into one or more assembly language statements? It's especially true while you're a beginner, but even after you've earned your chops as an assembly language programmer, you may not know everything that there is to be known. In most programming languages (including assembly), there are often several or some-times many different ways to implement a particular action. Some may be faster than others; some may be slower but easier to read and modify. Some solutions may be limited to a subset of the full line of Intel CPUs. Does your program need to run on older x86 CPUs? Or can you assume that everyone will have a system with a 64-bit CPU? (Your original sheets of notes should include such bounding conditions for any usable solution to the original problem.)

The jump from pseudocode to instructions may seem like a big one, but the good news is that once you've converted your pseudocode to instructions, you can make the text an assembly language source code file and turn SASM loose on it to spot your syntactic booboos. Expect to spend some time fixing assembly errors and then program bugs, but if you've gone through the refinement pro-cess with a clear head and reasonable patience, you may be surprised at how good a program you have on your first attempt.

A competent translation of the previous pseudocode to real assembly is shown in Listing 8.2. (This is the version that links via gcc rather than ld. Open it and build it in SASM.) Read through it and see if you can follow the translation from the pseudocode, knowing what you already know about assembly language. The code shown will work but is not "finished" in any real sense. It's a "first cut" for real code in the successive refinement process. It needs some hard thinking about how good and how complete a solution it is to the original problem. *A working program is not necessarily a finished program.*

Listing 8.2: uppercaser1gcc.asm

```
section .bss
    Buff resb 1

section .data

section .text
global   main

main:
    mov rbp, rsp    ; for correct debugging
```

```
Read:
      mov rax,0        ; Specify sys_read call
      mov rdi,0        ; Specify File Descriptor 0: Standard Input
      mov rsi,Buff     ; Pass address of the buffer to read to
      mov rdx,1        ; Tell sys_read to read one char from stdin
      syscall          ; Call sys_read

      cmp rax,0        ; Look at sys_read's return value in RAX
      je Exit          ; Jump If Equal to 0 (0 means EOF) to Exit:
                       ; or fall through to test for lowercase

      cmp byte [Buff],61h  ; Test input char against lowercase 'a'
      jb Write             ; If below 'a' in ASCII chart, not lowercase
      cmp byte [Buff],7Ah  ; Test input char against lowercase 'z'
      ja Write             ; If above 'z' in ASCII chart, not lowercase

                           ; At this point, we have a lowercase character
      sub byte [Buff],20h  ; Subtract 20h from lowercase to give uppercase
                           ; and then write out the char to stdout:
Write:
      mov rax,1        ; Specify sys_write call
      mov rdi,1        ; Specify File Descriptor 1: Standard output
      mov rsi,Buff     ; Pass address of the character to write
      mov rdx,1        ; Pass number of chars to write
      syscall          ; Call sys_write
      jmp Read         ; The go to the beginning to get another char

Exit:    ret             ; End program
```

This looks scary, but it consists almost entirely of instructions and concepts that we've already discussed. Here are a few notes on things you might not completely understand at this point:

▪ Buff is an uninitialized variable and therefore located in the .bss section of the program. It's reserved space with an address. Buff has no initial value and contains nothing until we read a character from stdin and store it there.

▪ When a call to sys_read returns a 0, sys_read has reached the end of the file it's reading from. If it returns a positive value, this value is the number of characters it has read from the file. In this case, since we requested only one character, sys_read will return either a count of 1 or a 0 indicting that we're out of characters.

▪ The CMP instruction compares its two operands and sets the flags accordingly. The conditional jump instruction that follows each CMP instruction takes action based on the state of the flags. (More on this in Chapter 9.)

- The JB (Jump If Below) instruction jumps if the preceding CMP's left operand is lower in value than its right operand.

- The JA (Jump If Above) instruction jumps if the preceding CMP's left operand is higher in value than its right operand.

- Because a memory address (like Buff) simply points to a location in memory of no particular size, you must place the qualifier BYTE between CMP and its memory operand to tell the assembler that you want to compare two 8-bit values. In this case, the two 8-bit values are an ASCII character like *w* and a hex value like 7Ah.

- Because programs written in SASM use the Standard C Library, they generally end with a RET instruction rather than the SYSCALL Exit function.

Running the executable program is done by using I/O redirection. The command line for uppercaser1 looks like this:

```
./uppercaser1 > outputfile < inputfile
```

Both inputfile and outputfile can be any text file. Here's one thing to try:

```
./uppercaser1 > allupper.txt < uppercaser1.asm
```

The file allupper.txt will be created when you run the program, and it will be filled with the source code for the program, with all characters forced to uppercase.

Note that if you're working within SASM, you can place text to be converted in the Input window. (Load up a pure text file into a text editor and lift out some text via the Copy command and then drop it into the Input window via Paste.) When you run the program, it will read text from the Input window, force it to uppercase, and then write the converted text into the Output window. SASM maps the Input window to stdin, and the Output window to stdout.

Those Inevitable "Whoops!" Moments

Especially while you're a beginner, you may discover as you attempt this last step going from pseudocode to machine instructions that you've misunderstood something or forgotten something and that your pseudocode isn't complete or correct. (Or both!) You may also realize that there are better ways to do something in assembly statements than what a literal translation of the pseudocode might give you. Learning is a messy business, and no matter how good you think you are, you will always be learning.

A good example, and one that may actually have occurred to you while reading the previous assembly code, is this: *The program has no error detection.* It just assumes that whatever input file name the user enters for I/O redirection is an existing and not corrupt file with data in it, that there will be room on the current drive for the output file, and so on. That's a dangerous way to operate, though heaven knows it's been done. File-related Linux system calls return error values, and any program that uses them should examine those error values and take action accordingly.

So there will be times when you have to seriously rearrange your pseudocode partway through the process, or even scrap it entirely and begin again. These insights have an annoying habit of occurring when you're in that final stage of converting pseudocode to machine instructions. Be ready.

And there's another issue that may have occurred to you, if you know anything at all about low-level file I/O: The Linux `sys_read` kernel call isn't limited to returning a single character at one go. You pass the address of a buffer to `sys_read`, and `sys_read` will attempt to fill that buffer with as many characters from the input file as you tell it to. If you set up a buffer 500 bytes in size, you can ask `sys_read` to bring in 500 characters from `stdin` and put them in that buffer. A single call to `sys_read` can thus give you 500 characters (or 1,000, or 16,000) to work on, all at once. This reduces the amount of time that Linux spends chasing back and forth between its filesystem and your program, but it also changes the shape of the program in significant ways. You fill the buffer, and then you have to step through the buffer one character at a time, converting whatever is there in lowercase to uppercase.

Yes, you should have known that up front, while refining a pseudocode solution to your problem—and after you've been at it for a while, you will. There is a daunting number of such details that you have to have at your mental fingertips, and you won't commit them all to indelible memory in an afternoon. Now and then, such a revelation may force you to "back up" an iteration or two and recast some of your pseudocode.

Scanning a Buffer

That's the case with the current example. The program needs error handling, which in this case mostly involves testing the return values from `sys_read` and `sys_write` and displaying meaningful messages on the Linux console. There's no technical difference between displaying error messages and displaying slogans for greasy-spoon diners, so I may let you add error handling yourself as an exercise. (Don't forget about `stderr`.)

The more interesting challenge, however, involves buffered file I/O. The Unix read and write kernel calls are buffer-oriented and not character-oriented, so we have to recast our pseudocode to fill buffers with characters and then process the buffers.

Let's go back to pseudocode and give it a try:

```
Read:   Set up registers for the sys_read kernel call.
        Call sys_read to read a buffer full of characters from stdin.
```

```
         Test for EOF.
         If we're at EOF, jump to Exit.

         Set up registers as a pointer to scan the buffer.
   Scan: Test the character at buffer pointer to see if it's lowercase.
         If it's not a lowercase character, skip conversion.
         Convert the character to uppercase by subtracting 20h.
         Decrement buffer pointer.
         If we still have characters in the buffer, jump to Scan.

  Write: Set up registers for the Write kernel call.
         Call sys_write to write the processed buffer to stdout.
         Jump back to Read and get another buffer full of characters.

   Exit: Set up registers for terminating the program via sys_exit.
         Call sys_exit.
```

This adds everything you need to read a buffer from disk, scan and convert the characters in the buffer, and then write the buffer back out to disk. (Of course, the buffer has to be enlarged from one character to some useful size, like 1024 characters.) The gist of the buffer trick is to set up a pointer into the buffer and then examine and (if necessary) convert the character at the address expressed by the pointer. Then we move the pointer to the next character in the buffer and do the same thing, repeating the process until we've dealt with all the characters in the buffer.

Scanning a buffer is a very good example of an assembly language loop. At each pass through the loop we have to test something to see if we're finished and should exit the loop. The "something" in this case is the pointer. We can set the pointer to the beginning of the buffer and test to see when it reaches the end, or we could set the pointer to the end of the buffer and work our way forward, testing to see when we reach the beginning of the buffer.

Both approaches will work. However, starting at the end and working our way forward toward the beginning of the buffer can be done a little more quickly and with fewer instructions. (I'll explain why shortly.) Our next refinement should start talking specifics: which registers do what, and so on.

```
   Read: Set up registers for the sys_read kernel call.
         Call sys_read to read a buffer full of characters from stdin.
         Store the number of characters read in RSI
         Test for EOF (rax = 0).
         If we're at EOF, jump to Exit.

         Put the address of the buffer in rsi.
         Put the number of characters read into the buffer in rdx.
```

```
Scan:   Compare the byte at [r13+rbx] against 'a'.
        If the byte is below 'a' in the ASCII sequence, jump to Next.
        Compare the byte at [r13+rbx] against 'z'.
        If the byte is above 'z' in the ASCII sequence, jump to Next.
        Subtract 20h from the byte at [r13+rbx].
Next:   Decrement rbx by one.
        Jump if not zero to Scan.

Write:  Set up registers for the Write kernel call.
        Call sys_write to write the processed buffer to stdout.
        Jump back to Read and get another buffer full of characters.
Exit:   Set up registers for terminating the program via sys_exit.
        Call sys_exit.
```

This refinement recognizes that there is not one test to be made, but two. Lowercase characters represent a range in the ASCII sequence, and ranges have beginnings and ends. We have to determine if the character under examination falls within the range. Doing that requires testing the character to see if it's either below the lowest character in the lowercase range (*a*) or above the highest character in the lowercase range (*z*). If the character in question is not lowercase, no processing is required, and we jump to the code that bumps the pointer to the next character.

Navigating within the buffer involves two registers. The address of the beginning of the buffer is placed in R13. The number of characters in the buffer is placed in the RBX register. If you add the two registers, you'll get the address of the last character in the buffer. If you decrement the character counter in RBX, the sum of R13 and RBX will point to the second-to-last character in the buffer. Each time you decrement RBX, you'll have the address to a character one closer to the start of the buffer. When RBX is decremented to zero, you'll be at the beginning of the buffer, and all the characters will have been processed.

"Off by One" Errors

But wait. . .that's not entirely true. There's a bug in the pseudocode, and it's one of the most common beginner bugs in all assembly language: the legendary "off by one" error. The sum of R13 and RBX will point one address *past* the end of the buffer. And when the count in RBX goes to zero, one character—the one at the very beginning of the buffer—will remain unexamined and (if it's lowercase) untouched. The easiest way to explain where this bug comes from is to draw it out, as I've done in Figure 8.4.

There's a very short text file in the listings archive for this book called gazabo .txt. It contains only the single nonsense word *gazabo* and the EOL marker, for a total of seven characters. Figure 8.4 shows the gazabo.txt file as it would look after Linux loads it into a buffer in memory. The address of the buffer has

Before DEC R13:

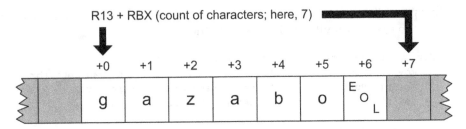

After DEC R13:

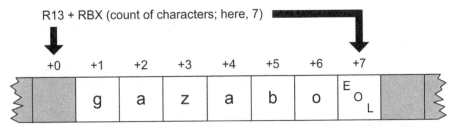

Figure 8.4: The "off by one" error

been loaded into register R13, and the number of characters (here, 7) has been loaded into RBX. If you add R13 and RBX, the resulting address goes past the end of the buffer into unused (you hope!) memory.

This kind of problem can occur any time you begin mixing address offsets and counts of things. Counts begin at 1, and offsets begin at 0. Character #1 is actually at offset 0 from the beginning of the buffer, character #2 is at offset 1, and so on. We're trying to use a value in RBX as *both* a count and an offset, and if the offsets into the buffer are assumed to begin with 0, an off-by-one error is inevitable.

The solution is simple: Decrement the address of the buffer (which is stored in R13) by 1 before beginning the scan. R13 now points to the memory location immediately *before* the first character in the buffer. With R13 set up this way, we can use the count value in R13 as both a count *and* an offset. By the time the value in R13 is decremented to 0, we've processed the *g* character, and we exit the loop.

An interesting experiment is to "comment out" the DEC R13 machine instruction and then run the program. This is done by simply putting a semicolon at the beginning of the line containing DEC R13 and rebuilding. Type **gazabo** or anything else in all lowercase in the Input window and then run the program.

From Pseudocode to Assembly Code

At this point I'm going to take that scary jump to actual machine instructions, but for the sake of brevity, will show only the loop itself:

```
; Set up the registers for the process buffer step:
      mov rbx,rax           ; Place the number of bytes read into rbx
      mov r13,Buff          ; Place address of buffer into r13
      dec r13               ; Adjust r13 to offset by one

; Go through the buffer and convert lowercase to uppercase characters:

Scan:
      cmp byte [r13+rbx],61h  ; Test input char against lowercase 'a'
      jb Next                 ; If below 'a' in ASCII, not lowercase
      cmp byte [r13+rbx],7Ah  ; Test input char against lowercase 'z'
      ja Next                 ; If above 'z' in ASCII, not lowercase

                              ; At this point, we have a lowercase char
      sub byte [r13+rbx],20h  ; Subtract 20h to give uppercase...

Next:
      dec rbx               ; Decrement counter
      jnz Scan              ; If characters remain, loop back
```

The state of the buffer and the pointer registers before beginning the scan is shown in the second part of Figure 8.4. The first time through, the value in RBX is the count of characters in the buffer. The sum R13 + RBX points at the EOL character at the buffer's end. The next time through, RBX is decremented to 6, and R13 + RBX points at the *o* in *gazabo*. Each time we decrement RBX, we look at the Zero flag by using the JNZ instruction, which jumps back to the Scan label when the Zero flag is *not* set. On the last pass through the loop, RBX contains 1, and R13 + RBX points to the *g* in the very first location in the buffer. Only when RBX is decremented to zero does JNZ "fall through" and the loop end.

Purists may think that decrementing the address in R13 before the loop begins is a dicey hack. They're half-right: After being decremented, R13 points to a location in memory outside the bounds of the buffer. If the program tried to write to that location, another variable might be corrupted, or a segmentation fault might result. The logic of the loop doesn't require writing to that particular address, but it could easily be done by mistake.

Listing 8.3 shows the completed program, fully commented with all pseudocode converted to assembly code.

Listing 8.3: uppercaser2gcc.asm

```
;   Executable name  : uppercaser2gcc
;   Version          : 2.0
```

```
;   Created date     : 6/17/2022
;   Last update      : 5/8/2023
;   Author           : Jeff Duntemann
;   Description      : A simple program in assembly for Linux, using NASM
;                      2.15.05, demonstrating simple text file I/O
;                      (through redirection) for reading an input file to
;                      a buffer in blocks, forcing lowercase characters to
;                      uppercase, and writing the modified buffer to
;                      an output file.
;
;   Run it this way in a terminal window:
;
;     uppercaser2 > (output file) < (input file)
;
;   Build in SASM using the default make lines and x64 checked
;

SECTION .bss            ; Section containing uninitialized data

    BUFFLEN   equ 128        ; Length of buffer
    Buff:     resb BUFFLEN   ; Text buffer itself

SECTION .data           ; Section containing initialised data

SECTION .text           ; Section containing code

global main             ; Linker needs this to find the entry point

main:
    mov rbp,rsp         ; for correct debugging

; Read a buffer full of text from stdin:
Read:
    mov rax,0           ; Specify sys_read call
    mov rdi,0           ; Specify File Descriptor 0: Standard Input
    mov rsi,Buff        ; Pass offset of the buffer to read to
    mov rdx,BUFFLEN     ; Pass number of bytes to read at one pass
    syscall             ; Call sys_read to fill the buffer
    mov r12,rax         ; Copy sys_read return value to r12 for later
    cmp rax,0           ; If rax=0, sys_read reached EOF on stdin
    je Done             ; Jump If Equal (to 0, from compare)

; Set up the registers for the process buffer step:
    mov rbx,rax         ; Place the number of bytes read into rbx
    mov r13,Buff        ; Place address of buffer into r13
    dec r13             ; Adjust count to offset

; Go through the buffer and convert lowercase to uppercase characters:
Scan:
    cmp byte [r13+rbx],61h  ; Test input char against lowercase 'a'
    jb .Next                ; If below 'a' in ASCII, not lowercase
```

```
        cmp byte [r13+rbx],7Ah   ; Test input char against lowercase 'z'
        ja .Next                 ; If above 'z' in ASCII, not lowercase
                                 ; At this point, we have a lowercase char
        sub byte [r13+rbx],20h   ; Subtract 20h to give uppercase...
.Next:
        dec rbx                  ; Decrement counter
        cmp rbx,0
        jnz Scan                 ; If characters remain, loop back

; Write the buffer full of processed text to stdout:
Write:
        mov rax,1                ; Specify sys_write call
        mov rdi,1                ; Specify File Descriptor 1: Standard output
        mov rsi,Buff             ; Pass offset of the buffer
        mov rdx,r12              ; Pass # of bytes of data in the buffer
        syscall                  ; Make kernel call
        jmp Read                 ; Loop back and load another buffer full

; All done! Let's end this party:
Done:
        ret
```

The SASM Output Window Gotcha

There is a shortcoming in SASM that you may stumble upon, if you're testing programs like uppercaser2gcc within SASM, using the Input and Output windows. The problem is that the Output window will hold only so much text. If you fill the Output window's buffer, further output will not cause any errors, but the last bit of text will push the first bit of text off the top edge of the Output window.

Once you have a reasonably functional program in SASM, save the EXE file to disk. Then exit SASM, bring up a terminal window, navigate to the project directory, and execute your program there. I don't know if Linux places a limit on how much text it will pass through stdout, but I've passed some pretty big files to stdout without any of the text getting lost.

Going Further

This general process will serve you well no matter what language you program in. Here are some notes as you proceed, on this project and on all your future projects:

■ Keep in mind that there's nothing that says you have to convert everything from pseudocode to machine instructions in one pass. Successive refinement is, well, *successive*. A perfectly reasonable statement for the problem could include a mixture of instructions and pseudocode. Over time you'll evolve a technique that works for you, and as you become more confident as a programmer, you'll make fewer refinement passes, and better ones.

■ Don't be afraid to draw pictures. Pencil sketches of pointers, buffers, and so on, scribbled on a quadrille pad, can be enormously helpful when trying to get a handle on a complicated loop or any process with a lot of moving parts.

■ *Save your notes*, no matter how ugly. Memories of the programming process get stale. If you write a utility and use it for six months, you may need a refresher on how its innards operate before attempting to enhance it. Toss everything in a (real-world) file folder, including paper printouts of pseudocode written to disk files.

The program we developed in this chapter is a simple example of a Unix *text filter*. Filters are common in Unix work, and I'll be returning to the concept in later chapters. In the meantime, go back and add error checking to the uppercaser program, on both read and write. Yes, you'll need a system call reference, one of which I cited earlier in the book. Others are online. Research may be the single toughest part of programming, and that's not going to get any easier; trust me.

Bits, Flags, Branches, and Tables
Easing Into Mainstream Assembly Coding

As you've seen by now, my general method for explaining things starts with the "view from a height" and then moves down toward the details. That's how I do things because that's how people learn: by plugging individual facts into a larger framework that makes it clear how those facts relate to one another. It's possible (barely) to move from details to the big picture, but across 60-odd years of banging my head against various subjects in the pursuit of knowledge, it's become very clear that having the overall framework in place first makes it a *lot* easier to establish all those connections between facts. It's like carefully placing stones into a neat pile before shoveling them into a box. If the goal is to get the stones into a box, it's much better to have the box in place before starting to pick up the stones.

And so it is here. The big picture is mostly in place. From now on in this book, we'll be looking at the details of assembly code and seeing how they fit into that larger view.

Bits Is Bits (and Bytes Is Bits)

Assembly language is big on bits. Bits, after all, are what bytes are made of, and one essential assembly language skill is building bytes and taking them apart again. A technique called bit mapping is widely used in assembly language. *Bit mapping* assigns special meanings to individual bits within a byte to save space and squeeze the last little bit of utility out of a given amount of memory.

There is a family of instructions in the x64 instruction set that allows you to manipulate the bits within the bytes by applying Boolean logical operations between bytes on a bit-by-bit basis. These are the *bitwise logical instructions*: AND, OR, XOR, and NOT. Another family of instructions allows you to slide bits back and forth within a single byte or word. These are the most-used shift/rotate instructions: ROL, ROR, RCL, RCR, SHL, and SHR. (There are a few others that I will not be discussing in this book.)

Bit Numbering

Dealing with bits requires that we have a way of specifying which bits we're dealing with. By convention, bits in assembly language are numbered, starting from 0, at the *least-significant bit* in the byte, word, double word, or other item we're using as a bit map. The *least-significant bit* is the one with the least value in the binary number system. It's also the bit on the far right, if you write the value down as a binary number in the conventional manner.

I've shown this in Figure 9.1, for a 16-bit word. Bit numbering works exactly the same way no matter how many bits you're dealing with: bytes, words, double words, or quadwords. Bit 0 is *always* on the right-hand end, and the bit numbers increase toward the left.

15	14	13	12	11	10	9	8	7	6	5	4	3	2	1	0

Most significant bit   Least significant bit

Figure 9.1: Bit numbering

When you count bits, start with the bit on the right-hand end, and number them leftward from 0.

"It's the Logical Thing to Do, Jim. . ."

The term *Boolean logic* sounds arcane and forbidding, but remarkably, it reflects the realities of ordinary thought and action. The Boolean operator AND, for instance, pops up in many of the decisions you make every day of your life. For example, to write a check that doesn't bounce, you must have money in your checking account AND checks in your checkbook. Neither alone will do the job. You can't write a check that you don't have, and a check without money behind it will bounce. People who live out of their checkbooks use the AND operator frequently.

When mathematicians speak of Boolean logic, they manipulate abstract values called True and False. The AND operator works like this: Condition1

AND Condition2 will be considered True if *both* Condition1 and Condition2 are True. If either condition is False, the result will be False.

There are in fact four different combinations of the two input values, so logical operations between two values are usually summarized in a form called a *truth table*. The truth table for the logical operator AND (*not* the AND instruction yet; we'll get to that shortly) is shown in Table 9.1.

Table 9.1:   The AND Truth Table for Formal Logic

CONDITION1	OPERATOR	CONDITION2	RESULT
False	AND	False =	False
False	AND	True =	False
True	AND	False =	False
True	AND	True =	True

There's nothing mysterious about the truth table. It's just a summary of all possibilities of the AND operator as applied to two input conditions. The important thing to remember about AND is that *only* when both input values are True will the result also be True.

That's the way mathematicians see AND. In assembly language terms, the AND instruction looks at two bits and yields a third bit based on the values of the first two bits. By convention, we consider a 1 bit to be True and a 0 bit to be False. The *logic* is identical; we're just using different symbols to represent True and False. Keeping that in mind, we can rewrite AND's truth table to make it more meaningful for assembly language work. See Table 9.2.

Table 9.2:   The AND Truth Table for Assembly Language

BIT 1	OPERATOR	BIT 2	RESULT BIT
0	AND	0 =	0
0	AND	1 =	0
1	AND	0 =	0
1	AND	1 =	1

The AND Instruction

The AND instruction embodies this concept in the x64 instruction set. The AND instruction performs the AND logical operation on two like-sized operands and replaces the destination operand with the result of the operation as a whole.

(Remember that the destination operand is the operand closest to the mnemonic.) In other words, consider this instruction:

```
and al,bl
```

What will happen here is that the CPU will perform a gang of eight bitwise AND operations on the eight bits in AL and BL. Bit 0 of AL is ANDed with bit 0 of BL, bit 1 of AL is ANDed with bit 1 of BL, and so on. Each AND operation generates a result bit, and that bit is placed in the destination operand (here, AL) *after* all eight AND operations occur. This is a common thread among machine instructions that perform some operation on two operands and produce a result: The result replaces the first operand (the destination operand) and *not* the second!

Masking Out Bits

A major use of the AND instruction is to isolate one or more bits out of a byte, word, dword, or qword value. *Isolate* here simply means to set all *unwanted* bits to a reliable 0 value. As an example, suppose we are interested in testing bits 4 and 5 of a value to see what those bits are. To do that, we have to be able to ignore the other bits (bits 0 through 3 and 6 through 7), and the only way to safely ignore bits is to set them to 0.

AND is the way to go. We set up a *bit mask* in which the bit numbers that we want to inspect and test are set to 1, and the bits we wish to ignore are set to 0. To mask out all bits but bits 4 and 5, we must set up a mask in which bits 4 and 5 are set to 1, with all other bits at 0. This mask in binary is 00110000B, or 30H. (To verify it, count the bits from the right-hand end of the binary number, starting with 0.) This bit mask is then ANDed against the value in question. Figure 9.2 shows this operation in action, with the 30H bit mask just described and an initial value of 9DH.

The three binary values involved are shown laid out vertically, with the least-significant bit (that is, the right-hand end) of each value at the top. You should be able to trace each AND operation and verify it by looking at Table 9.2.

The end result is that all bits except bits 4 and 5 are *guaranteed* to be 0 and can thus be safely ignored. Bits 4 and 5 could be either 0 or 1. (That's why we need to test them; we don't *know* what they are.) With the initial value of 9DH, bit 4 turns out to be a 1, and bit 5 turns out to be a 0. If the initial value were something else, bits 4 and 5 could both be 0, both be 1, or some combination of the two.

Don't forget: The result of the AND instruction replaces the destination operand after the operation is complete.

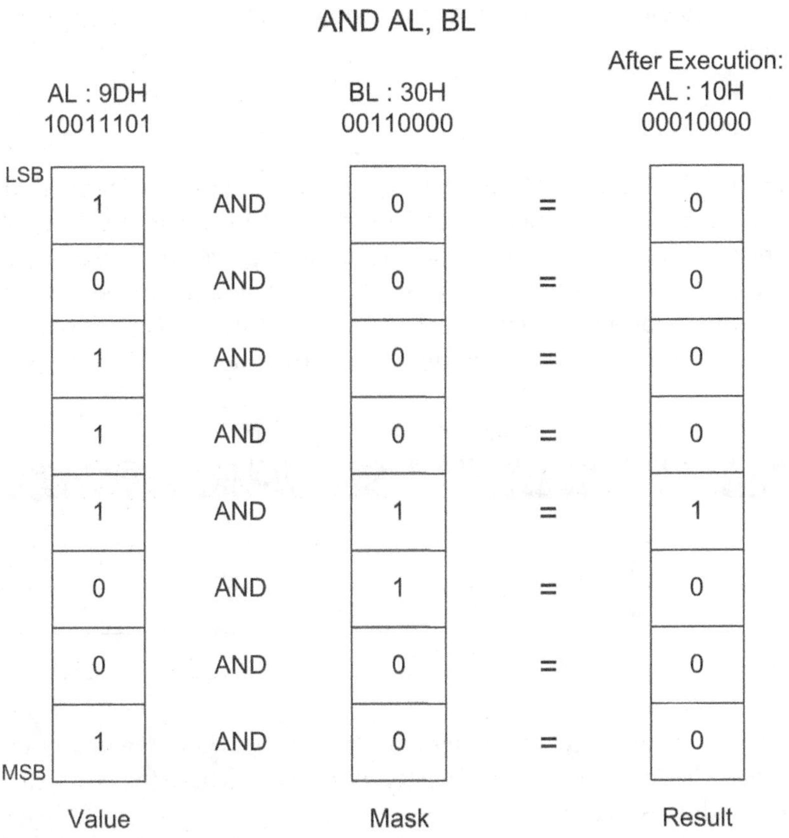
AND AL, BL
AL : 9DH
10011101
BL : 30H
00110000
After Execution:
AL : 10H
00010000
LSB
MSB
1 AND 0 = 0
0 AND 0 = 0
1 AND 0 = 0
1 AND 0 = 0
1 AND 1 = 1
0 AND 1 = 0
0 AND 0 = 0
1 AND 0 = 0
Value
Mask
Result

Figure 9.2: The anatomy of an AND instruction

The OR Instruction

Closely related to the AND logical operation is OR, which, like the AND logical operation, has an embodiment with the same name in the x86/x64 instruction set. Structurally, the OR instruction works identically to AND. Only its truth table is different: While AND requires that both its operands be 1 for the result to be 1, OR is satisfied that at least *one* operand has a 1 value. The truth table for OR is shown in Table 9.3.

Table 9.3: The OR Truth Table for Assembly Language

BIT 1	OPERATOR	BIT 2	RESULT BIT
0	OR	0 =	0
0	OR	1 =	1
1	OR	0 =	1
1	OR	1 =	1

Because it's unsuitable for isolating bits, the OR instruction is used much more rarely than AND.

The XOR Instruction

In a class by itself is the exclusive OR operation, embodied in the XOR instruction. XOR, again, does in broad terms what AND and OR do: It performs a bit-by-bit logical operation on its two operands, and the result replaces the destination operand. The logical operation, however, is *exclusive or*, meaning that the result is 1 only if the two operands are *different* (that is, 1 and 0 or 0 and 1). The truth table for XOR (see Table 9.4) should make this slightly slippery notion a little clearer.

Table 9.4:   The XOR Truth Table for Assembly Language

BIT 1	OPERATOR	BIT 2	RESULT BIT
0	XOR	0 =	0
0	XOR	1 =	1
1	XOR	0 =	1
1	XOR	1 =	0

Look Table 9.4 over carefully! In the first and last cases, where the two operands are the *same*, the result is 0. In the middle two cases, where the two operands are *different*, the result is 1.

Some interesting things can be done with the XOR instruction, but most of them are a little arcane for a beginners' book like this. One nonobvious but handy use of XOR is this: XORing any value against *itself* yields 0. In other words, if you execute the XOR instruction with both operands as the same register, that register will be cleared to 0:

```
xor rax,rax   ; Zero out the rax register
```

In the old days, this was faster than loading a 0 into a register from immediate data using MOV. Although that's no longer the case, it's an interesting trick to know. How it works should be obvious from reading the truth table, but to drive it home I've laid it out in Figure 9.3.

Follow each of the individual exclusive OR operations across the figure to its result value. Because each bit in AL is XORed against itself, in every case the XOR operations happen between two operands that are identical. Sometimes both are 1, sometimes both are 0, but in every case the two are the same. With the XOR operation, when the two operands are the same, the result is always 0. *Voilà!* Zero in a register.

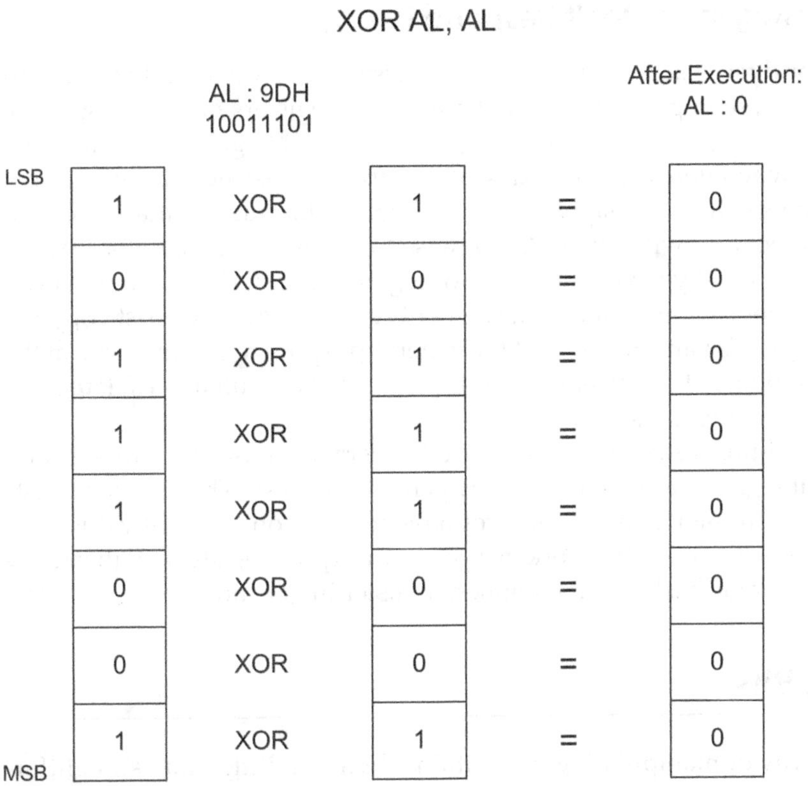

XOR AL, AL

AL : 9DH
10011101

After Execution:
AL : 0

LSB

1	XOR	1	=	0
0	XOR	0	=	0
1	XOR	1	=	0
1	XOR	1	=	0
1	XOR	1	=	0
0	XOR	0	=	0
0	XOR	0	=	0
1	XOR	1	=	0

MSB

Figure 9.3: Using XOR to zero a register

The NOT Instruction

Easiest to understand of all the bitwise logical instructions is NOT. The truth table for NOT is simpler than the others we've looked at because NOT takes only one operand. And what it does is simple as well: NOT takes the state of each bit in its single operand and changes that bit to its opposite state. What was 1 becomes 0, and what was 0 becomes 1. I show this in Table 9.5.

Table 9.5: The NOT Truth Table for Assembly Language

BIT	OPERATOR	RESULT BIT
0	NOT	1
1	NOT	0

Segment Registers Don't Respond to Logic!

You won't be directly accessing the segment registers until you get into the depths of operating-system programming. The segment registers now belong to the OS for its own use, and user-space programs cannot change them in any way.

But even when you begin working at the operating-system level, the segment registers come with significant limitations. One such limitation is that they cannot be used with any of the bitwise logic instructions. If you try, the assembler will hand you an "Illegal use of segment register" error. If you need to perform a logical operation on a segment register, you must first copy the segment register's value into one of the general-purpose registers, perform the logical operation on the GP register, and then copy the result in the GP register back into the segment register.

The general-purpose registers are called "general purpose" for a reason, and the segment registers are not in any way general-purpose. They are specialists in memory addressing, and if you ever have to work on segment values, the general approach is to do the work in a general-purpose register and then copy the modified value back into the segment register in question.

Shifting Bits

The other way of manipulating bits within a byte is a little more straightforward: You *shift* them toward one side or the other. There are a few wrinkles to the process, but the simplest shift instructions are pretty obvious: SHL SHifts its operand Left, whereas SHR SHifts its operand Right.

All of the shift instructions (including the slightly more complex ones I'll describe a little later) have the same general form, illustrated here by the SHL instruction:

```
shl <register/memory>,<count>
```

The first operand is the target of the shift operation, that is, the value that you're going to be shifting. It can be register data or memory data, but not immediate data. The second operand specifies the number of bits by which to shift.

Shift by What?

This <count> operand has a peculiar history. On the ancient 8086 and 8088, it could be one of two things: the immediate digit 1, or else the register CL. (*Not* CX!) If you specified the count as 1, then the shift would be by one bit. If you wanted to shift by more than one bit at a time, you had to first load the shift count into register CL. In the days before the x86 general-purpose registers became truly general-purpose, counting things used to be CX's (and hence CL's) "hidden agenda." It would count shifts, passes through loops, string elements, and a few other things. That's why it's sometimes called the *count register* and can be remembered by the *C* in *count*. Starting with the 286 and for all more recent x86/x64 CPUs, the <count> operand may be any immediate value from 0 to 255. The shift count may also be passed in CL if you prefer. Note that you cannot specify RCX for the count, even though it "contains" CL. Even in x64, the shift instructions really do require either an immediate value from 0–255 or CL. Any other register specified for the count value will trigger an assembler error.

Obviously, shifting by 0 bits is pointless, but it's possible and not considered an error. *Watch your typing.*

Now, there's an important asterisk to the previous paragraph: *You can't shift more positions than the destination register has.* In 64-bit long mode, you can't shift (or rotate; see the next section) more than 63 counts. Attempting to do so won't trigger an error. It just won't work. It won't work because before the instruction is executed, the CPU masks the count value to the six lowest bits. Those low six bits can count only to 63. It takes seven bits to express 64.

A literal value of 146 won't cause an error, but you'll only shift the destination operand by 18 positions.

In 32-bit protected mode, the CPU masks the count value to the five lowest bits, because five bits can count to 31.

How Bit Shifting Works

Understanding the shift instructions requires that you think of the numbers being shifted as *binary* numbers, and not hexadecimal or decimal numbers. (If you're fuzzy on binary notation, again, take another focused pass through Chapter 2.) A simple example would start with register AX containing a value of 0B76FH. (I'm using AX for the example here to keep the binary numbers short and graspable, but the shift instructions may be used on any size register.) Expressed as a binary number (and hence as a bit pattern), 0B76FH is as follows:

```
1011011101101111
```

Keep in mind that each digit in a binary number is one bit. If you execute an SHL AX, 1 instruction, what you'd find in AX after the shift is the following:

```
0110111011011110
```

A 0 has been inserted at the right-hand end of the number, and the whole shebang has been bumped toward the left by one digit. Notice that a 1 bit has been bumped off the left end of the number into cosmic nothingness.

You can even use the shift instructions on CL, with CL containing the count. This is legal, even if it looks peculiar, and may not be the best idea:

```
mov cl,1
shl cl,cl
```

What happens in this example is that the count value in CL is shifted left by the value CL contains. Here the 1 bit in CL is shifted to become a 2 bit. If this still seems strange, put it in a sandbox and watch the registers.

Bumping Bits into the Carry Flag

Shifting a bit off the left end of a binary value doesn't *exactly* send that bit into cosmic nothingness. A bit shifted out of the left end of a binary value is bumped into a temporary bucket for bits called the Carry flag (CF). The Carry flag is one of those informational bits gathered together as the RFlags register, which I described in Chapter 7. You can test the state of the Carry flag with a branching instruction, as I'll explain a little later in this chapter.

However, keep in mind when using shift instructions that a *lot* of different instructions use the Carry flag—not only the shift instructions. If you bump a bit into the Carry flag with the intent of testing that bit later to see what it is, test it *before* you execute another instruction that affects the Carry flag. That list includes all the arithmetic instructions, all the bitwise logical instructions, a few other miscellaneous instructions—and, of course, all the other shift instructions.

If you shift a bit into the Carry flag and then immediately execute another shift instruction, the bit bumped into the Carry flag earlier *will* be bumped off the end of the world into cosmic nothingness.

The Rotate Instructions

That said, if a bit's destiny is *not* to be lost in cosmic nothingness, you need to use the rotate instructions RCL, RCR, ROL, and ROR instead. The rotate instructions are almost identical to the shift instructions, but with a crucial difference: A bit bumped off one end of the operand reappears at the opposite end of the operand. As you rotate an operand by more than one bit, the bits march steadily in one direction, falling off the end and immediately reappearing at the opposite end. The bits thus "rotate" through the operand as the rotate instruction is executed.

Like so many things, this shows better than it tells. Take a look at Figure 9.4. The example shown here is the ROL (Rotate Left) instruction, but the ROR instruction works the same way, with the bits moving in the opposite direction. An initial binary value of 10110010 (0B2h) is placed in AL. When an ROL AL,1 instruction is executed, all the bits in AL march toward the left by one position. The 1-bit in bit 7 exits AL stage left but runs around and reappears immediately from stage right.

Again, ROR works exactly the same way, but the movement of bits is from left to right instead of (as with ROL) right to left. The number of bits by which an operand is rotated can be either an immediate value or a value in CL.

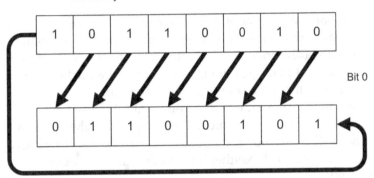

The binary value 10110010 in AL before ROL AL,1:
1 0 1 1 0 0 1 0
Bit 0
0 1 1 0 0 1 0 1
ROL shifts all bits left and moves bit 7 to bit 0.
What was 10110010 is now 01100101.

Figure 9.4: How the rotate instructions work

Rotating Bits Through the Carry Flag

There is a second pair of rotate instructions in the x86/x64 instruction set: RCR (Rotate Carry Right) and RCL (Rotate Carry Left). These operate as ROL and ROR do, but with a twist: The bits that are shifted out the end of an operand and re-enter the operand at the beginning travel by way of the Carry flag. The path that any single bit takes in a rotate through CF is thus one bit longer than it would be in ROL and ROR. I've shown this graphically in Figure 9.5.

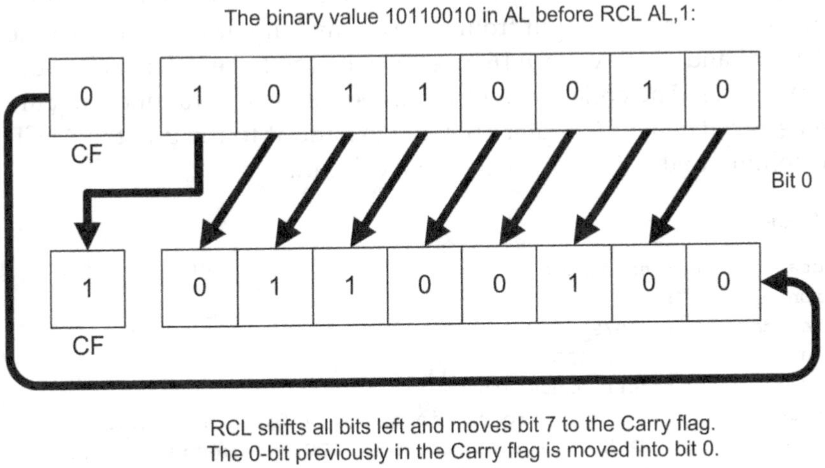

The binary value 10110010 in AL before RCL AL,1:
0
CF
1 0 1 1 0 0 1 0
Bit 0
1
CF
0 1 1 0 0 1 0 0
RCL shifts all bits left and moves bit 7 to the Carry flag.
The 0-bit previously in the Carry flag is moved into bit 0.

Figure 9.5: How the rotate through carry instructions work

Setting a Known Value into the Carry Flag

It's also useful to remember that previous instructions can leave values in CF, and those values will be rotated into an operand during an RCL or RCR instruction. Some people have the mistaken understanding that CF is forced to 0 before a shift or rotate instruction, and that's just not true. If another instruction leaves a 1-bit in CF immediately before an RCR or RCL instruction, that 1-bit will obediently enter the destination operand, whether you want it to or not.

If starting out a rotate with a known value in CF is important, there is a pair of x86 instructions that will do the job for you: CLC and STC. CLC clears the Carry flag to 0. STC sets the Carry flag to 1. Neither instruction takes an operand and neither has any other effects.

Bit-Bashing in Action

As we saw in earlier chapters, Linux has a fairly convenient method for displaying text to your screen. The problem is that it displays only *text*—if you want to display a numeric value from a register as a pair of hex digits, Linux won't help. You first have to convert the numeric value into its string representation and then display the string representation by calling the sys_write kernel service via syscall.

Converting hexadecimal numbers to hexadecimal digits isn't difficult, and the code that does the job demonstrates several of the new concepts we're exploring in this chapter. The code in Listing 9.1 is the bare-bones core of a hex-dump utility. When you redirect its input from a file of any kind, it will read that file 16 bytes at a time and display those 16 bytes in a line, as 16 hexadecimal values separated by spaces. The code contains a number of new techniques that are worth discussing. Then, in Chapter 10, we'll expand it to include the ASCII equivalent column to the right of the hexdump column.

Listing 9.1: hexdump1gcc.asm

```
;   Executable name : hexdump1gcc
;   Version         : 2.0
;   Created date    : 5/9/2022
;   Last update     : 5/8/2023
;   Author          : Jeff Duntemann
;   Description     : A simple program in assembly for Linux, using
;                     NASM 2.15 under the SASM IDE, demonstrating the
;                     conversion of binary values to hexadecimal
;                     strings. It acts as a very simple hex dump utility
;                     for files, without the ASCII equivalent column.
;
;   Run it this way:
;       hexdump1gcc < (input file)
```

```
;
;   Build using SASM's default build setup for x64
;
SECTION .bss                    ; Section containing uninitialized data

    BUFFLEN  equ 16             ; We read the file 16 bytes at a time
    Buff:    resb BUFFLEN       ; Text buffer itself, reserve 16 bytes


SECTION .data                   ; Section containing initialised data

    HexStr: db " 00 00 00 00 00 00 00 00 00 00 00 00 00 00 00 00",10
    HEXLEN equ $-HexStr

    Digits: db "0123456789ABCDEF"


SECTION .text                   ; Section containing code

global  main                    ; Linker needs this to find the entry point!

main:
    mov rbp,rsp                 ; SASM Needs this for debugging

; Read a buffer full of text from stdin:
Read:
    mov rax,0                   ; Specify sys_read call 0
    mov rdi,0                   ; Specify File Descriptor 0: Standard Input
    mov rsi,Buff                ; Pass offset of the buffer to read to
    mov rdx,BUFFLEN             ; Pass number of bytes to read at one pass
    syscall                     ; Call sys_read to fill the buffer
    mov r15,rax                 ; Save # of bytes read from file for later
    cmp rax,0                   ; If rax=0, sys_read reached EOF on stdin
    je Done                     ; Jump If Equal (to 0, from compare)


; Set up the registers for the process buffer step:parm
    mov rsi,Buff                ; Place address of file buffer into esi
    mov rdi,HexStr              ; Place address of line string into edi
    xor rcx,rcx                 ; Clear line string pointer to 0

; Go through the buffer and convert binary values to hex digits:
Scan:
    xor rax,rax                 ; Clear rax to 0

; Here we calculate the offset into the line string, which is rcx X 3
    mov rdx,rcx                 ; Copy the pointer into line string into rdx
;   shl rdx,1                   ; Multiply pointer by 2 using left shift
;   add rdx,rcx                 ; Complete the multiplication X3
    lea rdx,[rdx*2+rdx]         ; This does what the above 2 lines do!
                                ; See discussion of LEA later in Ch. 9
```

```
; Get a character from the buffer and put it in both rax and rbx:
    mov al,byte [rsi+rcx] ; Put a byte from the input buffer into al
    mov rbx,rax           ; Duplicate byte in bl for second nybble

; Look up low nybble character and insert it into the string:
    and al,0Fh                 ; Mask out all but the low nybble
    mov al,byte [Digits+rax]   ; Look up the char equivalent of nybble
    mov byte [HexStr+rdx+2],al ; Write the char equivalent to
                               ;   the line string

; Look up high nybble character and insert it into the string:
    shr bl,4                   ; Shift high 4 bits of char into low 4 bits
    mov bl,byte [Digits+rbx]   ; Look up char equivalent of nybble
    mov byte [HexStr+rdx+1],bl ; Write the char equivalent to
                               ;   the line string

; Bump the buffer pointer to the next character and see if we're done:
    inc rcx        ; Increment line string pointer
    cmp rcx,r15    ; Compare to the number of characters in the buffer
    jna Scan       ; Loop back if rcx is <= number of chars in buffer

; Write the line of hexadecimal values to stdout:
    mov rax,1      ; Specify syscall call 1: sys_write
    mov rdi,1      ; Specify File Descriptor 1: Standard output
    mov rsi,HexStr ; Pass address of line string in rsi
    mov rdx,HEXLEN ; Pass size of the line string in rdx
    syscall        ; Make kernel call to display line string
    jmp Read       ; Loop back and load file buffer again

; All done! Let's end this party:
Done:
    ret            ; Return to the glibc shutdown code
```

The hexdump1 program is at its heart a filter program and has the same general filter machinery I used in the uppercaser2 program from Chapter 8. The important parts of the program for this discussion are the parts that read 16 bytes from the input buffer and convert them to a string of characters for display to the Linux console. This is the code between the Scan label and the RET instruction. I'll be referring to that block of code in the discussion that follows.

If you read Listing 9.1, you'll see that two of the lines of code are commented out. This was not a mistake, and I'll come back to it.

Splitting a Byte into Two Nybbles

Remember that the values read by Linux from a file are read into memory as binary values. Hexadecimal is a way of displaying binary values, and for you to display binary values as displayable ASCII hexadecimal digits, you have to do some converting.

Displaying a single 8-bit binary value requires two hexadecimal digits. The bottom four bits in a byte are represented by one digit (the least-significant, or rightmost, digit), and the top four bits in the byte are represented by another digit (the most significant, or leftmost, digit). The binary value 11100110, for example, is the equivalent of E6 in hex. (I went over all this in detail in Chapter 2.) Converting an 8-bit value into two 4-bit digits must be done one digit at a time, which means that we have to separate the single byte into two 4-bit quantities, which are often called *nybbles*, especially in assembly work.

In the hexdump1 program, a byte is read from `Buff` and is placed in two registers, RAX and RBX. This is done because separating the high from the low nybble in a byte is destructive, in that we basically zero out the nybble that we don't want.

To isolate the low nybble in a byte, we need to *mask out* the unwanted high nybble. This is done with an AND instruction:

```
and al,0Fh
```

The immediate constant 0Fh expressed in binary is 00001111. If you follow the operation through the AND truth table (Table 9.2) you'll see that any bit ANDed against 0 is 0. We AND the high nybble of register AL with 0000, which zeros out anything that might be there. ANDing the low nybble against 1111 leaves the bits of the low nybble precisely as they were.

When we're done, we have the low nybble of the byte read from `Buff` in AL.

Shifting the High Nybble into the Low Nybble

Masking out the high nybble from the input byte in AL destroys it. We need that high nybble, but we have a second copy in RBX, and that's the copy from which we'll extract the high nybble. As with the low nybble, we'll actually work with the least significant eight bits of RBX, as BL. Remember that BL is just a different way of referring to the lowest eight bits of RBX. It's not a different register. If a value is loaded into RBX, its least-significant eight bits are in BL.

We could mask out the low nybble in BL with an AND instruction, leaving behind the high nybble, but there's a catch: Masking out the low four bits of a byte does not make the high four bits a nybble. We have to somehow move the high four bits of the input byte into the low four bits.

The fastest way to do this is simply to shift BL to the right by four bits. This is what the SHR BL, 4 instruction does. The low nybble is simply shifted off the edge of BL, into the Carry flag, and then out into cosmic nothingness. After the shift, what was the high nybble in BL is now the low nybble.

At this point, we have the low nybble of the input byte in AL, and the high nybble of the input byte in BL. The next challenge is converting the four-bit binary number in a nybble (for example, 1110) into its displayable ASCII hex digit; in this example, that's the "E" character.

Using a Lookup Table

In the .data section of the program is the definition of a very simple *lookup table*. The Digits table has this definition:

```
Digits db '0123456789ABCDEF'
```

The important thing to note about the Digits table is that each digit occupies a position in the string whose offset from the start of the string is the value it represents. In other words, the ASCII character 0 is at the very start of the string, offset zero bytes from the string's beginning. The character 7 lies seven bytes from the start of the string, and so on.

We "look up" a character in the Digits table using a memory reference:

```
mov al,byte [Digits+rax]
```

As with most of assembly language, everything here depends on memory addressing. The first hex digit character in the lookup table is at the address in Digits. To get at the desired digit, we must *index* into the lookup table. We do this by adding an offset into the table to the address inside the brackets. This offset is the nybble in AL.

Adding the offset in AL to the address of Digits (using RAX) takes us right to the character that is the ASCII equivalent of the value in AL. I've drawn this out graphically in Figure 9.6.

There are two possibly confusing things about the MOV instruction that fetches a digit from Digits and places it in AL:

- We must use RAX in the memory reference rather than AL, because *AL cannot take part in effective address calculations*. Don't forget that AL is "inside" RAX! (More on effective address calculations a little later in this chapter.)

- We are replacing the nybble in AL with its character equivalent. The instruction first fetches the character equivalent of the nybble from the table and then stores the character equivalent back into AL. The nybble that had been in AL is overwritten and thus gone.

So far, we've read a character from the lookup table into AL. The conversion of that nybble is done. The next task sounds simple but is actually surprisingly tricky: Writing the ASCII hex digit character now stored in AL into the display string at HexStr.

MOV AL, BYTE [Digits+RAX]

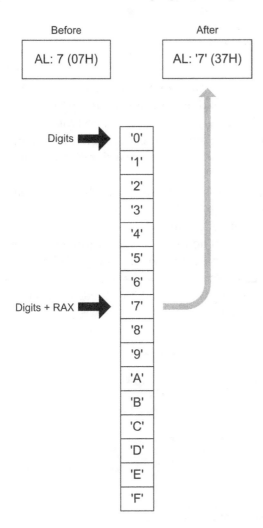

Note: Here, 'Digits' is the address of a
16-byte table in memory, containing
ASCII hex digits from 0-F.

Figure 9.6: Using a lookup table

Multiplying by Shifting and Adding

The hexdump1 program reads bytes from a file and displays them in lines, with
16 bytes represented in hex in each line. A sample of the output from hexdump1
is shown here:

```
3B 20 20 45 78 65 63 75 74 61 62 6C 65 20 6E 61
6D 65 20 3A 20 45 40 54 53 59 53 43 40 4C 4C 0D
0A 3B 20 20 56 65 72 73 69 6F 6E 20 20 20 20 20
```

```
20 20 20 20 3A 20 30 2E 30 0D 0A 3B 20 20 43 72
65 60 74 65 64 20 64 60 74 65 20 20 20 20 3A 20
30 2F 37 2F 32 30 30 39 0D 0A 3B 20 20 4C 60 73
74 20 75 70 64 60 74 65 20 20 20 20 20 3A 20 32
2F 30 38 2F 32 30 30 39 0D 0A 3B 20 20 40 75 74
68 6F 72 20 20 20 20 20 20 20 20 20 3A 20 4A
```

Each of these lines is a display of the same data item: HexStr, a string of 48 characters with an EOL value (0ah) on the end. Each time hexdump1 reads a block of 16 bytes from the input file, it formats them as ASCII hex digits and inserts them into HexStr. In a sense, this is another type of table manipulation, except that instead of looking up something in a table, we're writing values *into* a table based on an index.

One way to think about HexStr is as a table of 16 entries, each entry three characters long. (See Figure 9.7.) In each entry, the first character is a space, and the second and third characters are the hex digits themselves. The space characters are already there, as part of the original definition of HexStr in the .data section. The original "empty" HexStr has 0 characters in all hex digit positions. To "fill" HexStr with "real" data for each line's display, we have to scan through HexStr in an assembly language loop, writing the low nybble character and the high nybble character into HexStr separately.

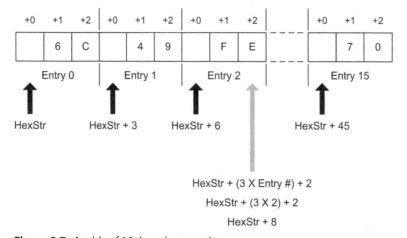

Figure 9.7: A table of 16 three-byte entries

The tricky business here is that for each pass through the loop, we have to "bump" the index into HexStr by three instead of just by one. The offset of one of those 3-byte entries in HexStr is the index of the entry multiplied by three. I've already described the MUL instructions, which handle arbitrary unsigned multiplication in the x86/x64 instruction set. MUL, however, is slow as instructions go.

It has other limitations as well, especially the ways it requires specific registers for its implicit operands.

Fortunately, with a little cleverness, there are other, faster ways to multiply in assembly. These ways are based on the fact that it's very easy and very fast to multiply by powers of two, using the SHL (Shift Left) instruction. It may not be immediately obvious to you, but each time you shift a quantity one bit to the left, you're multiplying that quantity by two. Shift a quantity two bits to the left, and you're multiplying it by four. Shift it three bits to the left, and you're multiplying by eight, and so on.

You can take my word for it, or you can actually watch it happen in a sandbox. Set up a fresh sandbox in SASM and enter the following instructions:

```
mov al,3
shl al,1
shl al,1
shl al,2
```

Build the sandbox and go into debug mode. Then step through the instructions, watching the value of RAX change in the Registers view for each step.

The first instruction loads the value 3 into AL. The next instruction shifts AL to the left by one bit. The value in AL becomes 6. The second SHL instruction shifts AL left by one bit again, and the 6 becomes 12. The third SHL instruction shifts AL by two bits, and the 12 becomes 48. I've shown this graphically in Figure 9.8.

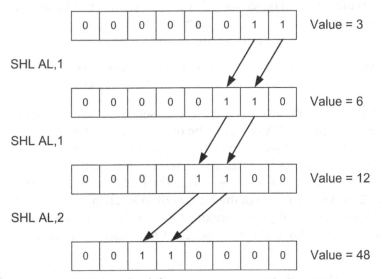

Figure 9.8: Multiplying by shifting

But what if you want to multiply by three? Easy: You multiply by 2 and then add one more copy of the multiplicand to the product. In the hexdump1 program, it's done this way:

```
mov rdx,rcx    ; Copy the character counter into edx
shl rdx,1      ; Multiply pointer by 2 using left shift
add rdx,rcx    ; Complete the multiplication X3
```

Here, the multiplicand is loaded from the loop counter RCX into RDX. RDX is then shifted left by one bit to multiply it by 2. Finally, RCX is added once to the product RDX to make it multiplication by 3.

Multiplication by other numbers that are not powers of two may be done by combining an SHL and one or more ADDs. To multiply a value in RCX by seven, you would do this:

```
mov rdx,rcx    ; Keep a copy of the multiplicand in rcx
shl rdx,2      ; Multiply rdx by 4
add rdx,rcx    ; Makes it X 5
add rdx,rcx    ; Makes it X 6
add rdx,rcx    ; Makes it X 7
```

This may look clumsy, but remarkably enough, it's still faster than using MUL! (And there's an even faster way to multiply by three that I'll show you a little later in this chapter.)

Once you understand how the string table HexStr is set up, writing the hex digits into it is straightforward. The least significant hex digit is in AL, and the most significant hex digit is in BL. Writing both hex digits into HexString is done with a three-part effective memory address:

```
mov byte [HexStr+rdx+2],al ; Write LSB char digit to line string
mov byte [HexStr+rdx+1],bl ; Write MSB char digit to line string
```

Refer back to Figure 9.7 to work this out for yourself: You begin with the address of HexStr as a whole. RDX contains the offset of the first character in a given entry. To obtain the address of the entry in question, you add HexStr and RDX. However, that address is of the first character in the entry, which in HexStr is always a space character. The position of the LSB digit in an entry is the entry's offset +2, and the position of the MSB digit in an entry is the entry's offset +1. The address of the LSB digit is therefore HexStr + the offset of the entry + 2. The address of the MSB digit is therefore HexStr + the offset of the entry + 1.

Flags, Tests, and Branches

From a height, the idea of conditional jump instructions is simple, and withou it, you won't get much done in assembly. I've been using conditional jum informally in the last few example programs without saying much about th because the sense of the jumps was pretty obvious from context, and they were necessary to demonstrate other things. But underneath the simplicity of the idea of assembly language jumps lies a great deal of complexity. It's time to get down and cover that in detail.

Unconditional Jumps

A *jump* is just that: an abrupt change in the flow of instruction execution. Ordinarily, instructions are executed one after the other, in order, moving from low memory toward high memory. *Jump instructions* alter the address of the next instruction to be executed. Execute a jump instruction, and *zap!* All of a sudden you're somewhere else. A jump instruction can move execution forward in memory or backward. It can bend execution back into a loop (and it can tie your program logic in knots).

There are two kinds of jumps: conditional and unconditional. An *unconditional* jump is a jump that *always* happens. It takes this form:

```
jmp <label>
```

When this instruction executes, the sequence of execution moves to the instruction located at the label specified by `<label>`. It's just that simple.

Conditional Jumps

A *conditional* jump instruction is one of those fabled tests I introduced in Chapter 1. When executed, a *conditional jump* tests something, usually one, occasionally two, or far more rarely three of the flags in the RFlags register. If the flag or flags being tested happen to be in a particular state, execution will jump to a label somewhere else; otherwise, it simply falls through to the next instruction in sequence.

This two-way nature is important. Either a conditional jump instruction jumps or it falls through. Jump or no jump. It can't jump to one of two places, or three. Whether it jumps or not depends on the current value of a very small set of bits within the CPU.

As I mentioned earlier in this book while discussing the RFlags register as a whole, there is a flag that is set to 1 by certain instructions when the result of that instruction is zero: the Zero flag ZF. The DEC (DECrement) instruction is a good example. DEC subtracts 1 from its operand. If by that subtraction the operand becomes zero, ZF is set to 1. One of the conditional jump instructions, JZ (Jump if Zero) tests ZF. If ZF is found set to 1, a jump occurs, and execution transfers to the label after the JZ mnemonic. If ZF is found to be 0, execution falls through to the next instruction in sequence. This may be the most common conditional jump in the entire x86/x64 instruction set. It's often used when you're counting a register down to zero while executing a loop, and when the register counting passes through the loop goes to zero by virtue of the DEC instruction, the loop ends, and execution picks up again at the instruction right after the loop.

Here's a simple (if nonoptimal) example, using instructions you should already understand:

```
        mov [RunningSum],0 ; Clear the running total
        mov rcx,17          ; We're going to do this 17 times

WorkLoop:
        add [RunningSum],3 ; Add three to the running total
        dec rcx             ; Subtract 1 from the loop counter
        jz SomewhereElse    ; If the counter is 0, we're done!
        jmp WorkLoop
```

The variable RunningSum was defined earlier with the DQ specifier, making it 64 bits in size. Before the loop begins, we set up a value in RCX, which acts as the count register and contains the number of times we're going to run through the loop. The body of the loop is where something gets done on each pass through the loop. In this example it's a single ADD instruction, but the body could be dozens or hundreds of instructions long.

After the work of the loop is accomplished, the count register is decremented by 1 with a DEC instruction. Immediately afterward, the JZ instruction tests the Zero flag. Decrementing RCX from 17 to 16, or from 4 to 3, does not set ZF, and the JZ instruction simply falls through. The instruction after JZ is an unconditional jump instruction, which obediently and consistently takes execution back to the WorkLoop label every time.

Now, decrementing RCX from 1 to 0 *does* set ZF. . .and that's when the loop ends. JZ finally takes us out of the loop by jumping to SomewhereElse (a label in the larger program that is not shown here), and execution leaves the loop.

You may be sharp enough (or experienced enough) to think that this is a lousy way to set up a loop, and you're right. (That doesn't mean it's never been done, nor that you yourself may not do it in a late-night moment of impatience.) What we're really looking for each time through the loop is when a condition—the Zero flag—*isn't* set, and there's an instruction for that too.

Jumping on the Absence of a Condition

There are quite a few conditional jump instructions, of which I'll discuss several but not all in this book. Their number is increased by the fact that almost every conditional jump instruction has an alter ego: a jump when the specified condition is *not* set to 1.

The JZ instruction provides a good example of jumping on a condition. JZ jumps to a new location in the code segment if the Zero flag (ZF) is set to 1.

JZ's alter ego is JNZ (Jump if Not Zero). JNZ jumps to a label if ZF is 0 and falls through if ZF is 1.

This may be confusing at first, because JNZ jumps when ZF is equal to 0. Keep in mind that the name of the instruction applies to the *condition* being tested and not necessarily the binary bit value of the flag. In the previous code example, JZ jumped when the DEC instruction decremented a counter to zero. The condition being tested is something connected with an earlier instruction, *not* simply the state of ZF.

Think of it this way: A condition raises a flag. "Raising a flag" means setting the flag to 1. When one of numerous instructions forces an operand to a value of zero (which is the condition), the Zero flag is raised. The logic of the instruction refers to the condition, *not* to the flag.

As an example, let's improve the little loop shown earlier by changing the loop logic to use JNZ:

```
mov word [RunningSum],0   ; Clear the running total
mov ecx,17                ; We're going to do this 17 times

WorkLoop:
add word [RunningSum],3   ; Add 3 to the running total
dec ecx                   ; Subtract 1 from the loop counter
jnz WorkLoop              ; If the counter is 0, we're done!
```

The JZ instruction has been replaced with a JNZ instruction. That makes much more sense, since to close the loop we have to jump, and we close the loop only while the counter is greater than 0. The jump back to label WorkLoop will happen only while the counter is greater than 0.

Once the counter decrements to 0, the loop is considered finished. JNZ "falls through," and the code that follows the loop (which I don't show here) executes. The point is that if you can position the program's next task immediately after the JNZ instruction, you don't need to use the unconditional JMP instruction *at all*. Instruction execution will just flow naturally into the next task that needs performing. The program will have a more natural and less-tangled top-to-bottom flow and will be easier to read and understand.

Flags

In Chapter 7, I explained the RFlags register and briefly described the purposes of all the flags it contains. RFlags is sparse; more than half of it is reserved for future use and thus undefined. Most of the flags that are defined are not terribly useful, especially when you're first starting out as an assembly programmer. The Carry flag (CF) and the Zero flag (ZF) will be 90 percent of your involvement in flags as a beginner, with the Direction flag (DF), Sign flag (SF), and

Overflow flag (OF) together making up an additional 9.998 percent. It might be a good idea to reread that part of Chapter 7 now, just in case your grasp of flag etiquette has gotten a little rusty.

As I explained earlier, JZ jumps when ZF is 1, whereas JNZ jumps when ZF is 0. Most instructions that perform some operation on an operand (such as AND, OR, XOR, INC, DEC, and all arithmetic instructions) set ZF according to the results of the operation. On the other hand, instructions that simply move data around (such as MOV, XCHG, PUSH, and POP) do not affect ZF nor any of the other flags at all. (Obviously, POPF affects the flags by popping the top-of-stack value into them.) One irritating exception is the NOT instruction, which performs a logical operation on its operand but does *not* set any flags—even when it causes its operand to become 0. Before you write code that depends on flags, *check your instruction reference* to make sure that you have the flag etiquette down correctly for that particular instruction. The x86/x64 instruction set is nothing if not quirky.

Comparisons with CMP

One major use of flags is in controlling loops. Another is in comparisons between two values. Your programs will often need to know whether a value in a register or memory is equal to some other value. Further, you may want to know if a value is greater than a value or less than a value if it is not equal to that value. There is a jump instruction to satisfy every need, but something has to set the flags for the benefit of the jump instruction. The CMP (CoMPare) instruction is what sets the flags for comparison tasks.

CMP's use is straightforward and intuitive. The second operand is compared with the first, and several flags are set accordingly:

```
cmp <op1>,<op2>    ; Sets OF, SF, ZF, AF, PF, and CF
```

The sense of the comparison can be remembered if you simply recast the comparison in arithmetic terms:

```
Result = <op1> - <op2>
```

CMP is very much a subtraction operation where the result of the subtraction is thrown away, and only the flags are affected. The second operand is subtracted from the first. Based on the results of the subtraction, the flags it affects are set to appropriate values.

After a CMP instruction, you can jump based on several arithmetic conditions. People who have a reasonable grounding in math, and FORTRAN or Pascal programmers, will recognize the conditions: *Equal, Not equal, Greater than, Less than, Greater than or equal to,* and *Less than or equal to.* The sense of these operators follows from their names and is exactly like the sense of the equivalent operators in most high-level languages.

A Jungle of Jump Instructions

There is a bewildering array of jump instructions, but those dealing with arithmetic relationships sort out well into just six categories, one category for each of the six conditions I just listed. Complication arises out of the fact that there are *two* mnemonics for each machine instruction, for example, JLE (Jump if Less than or Equal) and JNG (Jump if Not Greater than). These two mnemonics are *synonyms* in that the assembler generates the identical binary opcode when it encounters either mnemonic. The synonyms are a convenience to you the programmer in that they provide two alternate ways to think about a given jump instruction. In the preceding example, *Jump if Less than or Equal to* is logically identical to *Jump if Not Greater than*. (Think about it!) If the importance of the preceding compare was to see if one value is less than or equal to another, you'd use the JLE mnemonic. On the other hand, if you were testing to be sure one quantity was not greater than another, you'd use JNG. The choice is yours.

Another complication is that there is a separate set of instructions for signed and unsigned arithmetic comparisons. I haven't spoken much about assembly language math in this book and thus haven't said much about the difference between signed and unsigned quantities. A *signed* quantity is one in which the high bit of the quantity is considered a built-in flag indicating whether the quantity is negative. If that bit is 1, the quantity is considered negative. If that bit is 0, the quantity is considered positive.

Signed arithmetic in assembly language is complex and subtle and not as useful as you might immediately think. I won't be covering it in detail in this book, though most assembly language books treat it to some extent. All you need to know to get a high-level understanding of signed arithmetic is that in signed arithmetic, negative quantities are legal and the most significant bit of a value is treated as the sign bit. (If the sign bit is set to 1, the value is considered negative.) Unsigned arithmetic, on the other hand, does not recognize negative numbers, and the most significant bit is just one more bit in the binary number expressing the value being tested.

"Greater Than" Versus "Above"

To tell the signed jumps apart from the unsigned jumps, the mnemonics use two different expressions for the relationship between two values:

- *Signed values* are thought of as being *greater than* or *less than*. For example, to test whether one signed operand is greater than another, you would use the JG (Jump if Greater) mnemonic after a CMP instruction.

- *Unsigned values* are thought of as being *above* or *below*. For example, to tell whether one unsigned operand is greater than (above) another, you would use the JA (Jump if Above) mnemonic after a CMP instruction.

Table 9.6 summarizes the arithmetic jump mnemonics and their synonyms. Any mnemonics containing the words *above* or *below* are for unsigned values, whereas any mnemonics containing the words *greater* or *less* are for signed values. Compare the mnemonics with their synonyms and see how the two represent opposite viewpoints from which to look at identical instructions.

Table 9.6:   Jump Instruction Mnemonics and Their Synonyms

MNEMONICS		SYNONYMS	
JA	Jump if Above	JNBE	Jump if Not Below or Equal
JAE	Jump if Above or Equal	JNB	Jump if Not Below
JB	Jump if Below	JNAE	Jump if Not Above or Equal
JBE	Jump if Below or Equal	JNA	Jump if Not Above
JE	Jump if Equal	JZ	Jump if result is Zero
JNE	Jump if Not Equal	JNZ	Jump if result is Not Zero
JG	Jump if Greater	JNLE	Jump if Not Less than or Equal
JGE	Jump if Greater or Equal	JNL	Jump if Not Less
JL	Jump if Less	JNGE	Jump if Not Greater or Equal
JLE	Jump if Less or Equal	JNG	Jump if Not Greater

Table 9.6 simply serves to expand the mnemonics into a more comprehensible form and associate a mnemonic with its synonym. Table 9.7, on the other hand, sorts the mnemonics out by logical condition and according to their use with signed and unsigned values. Also listed in Table 9.7 are the flags whose values are tested by each jump instruction. Notice that some of the jump instructions require one of two possible flag values to take the jump while others require *both* of two flag values.

Several of the signed jumps compare two of the flags against one another. JG, for example, will jump when either ZF is 0 or when the Sign flag (SF) is equal to the Overflow flag (OF). (See Table 9.7.) I won't spend any further time explaining the nature of the Sign flag or Overflow flag. As long as you have the sense of each instruction under your belt, understanding exactly how the instructions test the flags can wait until you've gained some programming experience.

Table 9.7: Arithmetic Tests Useful After a CMP Instruction

CONDITION	PASCAL OPERATOR	UNSIGNED VALUES	JUMPS WHEN	SIGNED VALUES	JUMPS WHEN
Equal	=	JE	ZF=1	JE	ZF=1
Not Equal	<>	JNE	ZF=0	JNE	ZF=0
Greater Than	>	JA	CF=0 and ZF=0	JG	ZF=0 or SF=OF
Not Less than or Equal to		JNBE	CF=0 and ZF=0	JNLE	ZF=0 or SF=OF
Less than	<	JB	CF=1	JL	SF<>OF
Not Greater than or equal to		JNAE	CF=1	JNGE	SF<>OF
Greater than or equal to	>=	JAE	CF=0	JGE	SF=OF
Not Less than		JNB	CD=0	JNL	SF=OF
Less than or Equal to	<=	JBE	CF=1 or ZF=1	JLE	ZF=1 or SF<>OF
Not Greater Than		JNA	CF=1 or ZF=1	JNG	ZF=1 or SF<>OF

Some people have trouble understanding how it is that the JE and JZ mnemonics are synonyms, as are JNE and JNZ. Think again of the way a comparison is done within the CPU: The second operand is subtracted from the first, and if the result is 0 (indicating that the two operands were in fact equal), the Zero flag ZF is set to 1. That's why JE and JZ are synonyms: Both are simply testing the state of the Zero flag.

Looking for 1-Bits with TEST

The x86/x64 instruction set recognizes that bit testing is done a lot in assembly language, and it provides what amounts to a CMP instruction for bits: TEST. TEST performs an AND logical operation between two operands and then sets the flags as the AND instruction would, *without* altering the destination operand, as AND would. Here's the TEST instruction syntax:

```
test <operand>,<bit mask>
```

The bit mask operand should contain a 1 bit in each position where a 1 bit is to be sought in the operand, and 0 bits in all the other bits.

What TEST does is perform the AND logical operation between the instruction's destination operand and the bit mask and then set the flags as the AND instruction would do. The result of the AND operation is discarded, and the destination operand doesn't change. For example, if you want to determine if bit 3 of RAX is set to 1, you could use this instruction:

```
test rax,08h      ; Bit 3 in binary is 00001000B, or 08h
```

Bit 3, of course, does not have the numeric value 3—you have to look at the bit pattern of the mask and express it as a binary or hexadecimal value. (Bit 3 represents the value 8 in binary.) Using binary for literal constants is perfectly legal in NASM and is often the clearest expression of what you're doing when you're working with bit masks:

```
test rax,00001000B ; Bit 3 in binary is 00001000B, or 08h
```

Destination operand RAX doesn't change as a result of the operation, but the AND truth table is asserted between RAX and the binary pattern 00001000. If bit 3 in RAX is a 1 bit, then the Zero flag is cleared to 0. If bit 3 in RAX is a 0 bit, then the Zero flag is set to 1. Why? If you AND 1 (in the bit mask) with 0 (in RAX), you get 0. (Look it up in the AND truth table, which I showed in Table 9.2.) And if all eight bitwise AND operations come up 0, the result is 0, and the Zero flag is raised to 1, indicating that the result is 0.

Key to understanding TEST is thinking of TEST as a sort of Phantom of the Opcode, where the Opcode is AND. TEST puts on a mask (as it were) and *pretends* to be AND but then doesn't follow through with the results of the operation. It simply sets the flags *as though* an AND operation had occurred.

The CMP instruction we spoke of earlier is another Phantom of the Opcode and bears the same relation to SUB as TEST bears to AND. CMP subtracts its second operand from its first but doesn't follow through and store the result in the destination operand. It just sets the flags *as though* a subtraction had occurred. As we've already seen, this can be mighty useful when combined with conditional jump instructions.

Here's something important to keep in mind: *TEST is only useful for finding 1 bits*. If you need to identify 0 bits, you must first flip each bit to its opposite state with the NOT instruction. NOT changes all 1 bits to 0 bits and changes all 0 bits to 1 bits. Once all 0 bits are flipped to 1 bits, you can test for a 1 bit where you need to find a 0 bit. (Sometimes it helps to draw it out on paper to keep it all straight in your head.)

Finally, TEST will *not* reliably test for two or more 1 bits in the operand *at the same time*. TEST doesn't check for the presence of a bit pattern; *it checks for the presence of a single 1 bit*. In other words, if you need to check to make sure that *both* bits 4 and 5 are set to 1, TEST won't hack it.

Looking for 0-Bits with BT

As I explained, TEST has its limits: It's not cut out for determining when a bit is set to 0. TEST has been with us since the very earliest X86 CPUs, but the 386 and newer processors have an instruction that allows you to test for either 0 bits or 1 bits. BT (Bit Test) performs a very simple task: It copies the specified bit from the first operand into the Carry flag CF. In other words, if the selected bit was a 1 bit, the Carry flag becomes set. If the selected bit was a 0 bit, the Carry flag is cleared. You can then use any of the conditional jump instructions that examine and act on the state of CF.

BT is easy to use. It takes two operands: The destination operand is the value containing the bit in question. The source operand is the ordinal number of the bit that you want to test, *counting from 0*:

```
bt <value containing bit>,<bit number>
```

Once you execute a BT instruction, you should immediately test the value in the Carry flag and branch based on its value. Here's an example:

```
bt   rax,4   ; Test bit 4 of RAX
jnc quit     ; We're all done if bit 4 = 0
```

Something to be careful of, especially if you're used to using TEST, is that *you are not creating a bit mask*. With BT's source operand you are specifying the ordinal number of a bit. The literal constant 4 shown in the previous code is the bit's *number*, not the bit's *value*, and that's a crucial difference.

Also note in the previous code that we're branching if CF is *not* set; that's what JNC (Jump if Not Carry) does.

X64 Long Mode Memory Addressing in Detail

In so many ways, life is *better* now. And I'm not just talking about modern dentistry, plug-and-play networking, and eight-core CPUs. I used to program in assembly for the real-mode 8088 CPUs in the original IBM PC. And I remember real-mode memory addressing.

Like dentistry in the 1950s, 8088-based real-mode memory addressing was just...painful. It was a hideous ratbag of restrictions and gotchas and limits and Band-Aids, all of which veritably screamed out that the CPU was *desperately* hungry for more transistors on the die. Addressing memory, for example, was limited to BX and BP in most instructions, which meant a lot of fancy footwork when several separate items had to be addressed in memory all at the same time. And thinking about segment management still makes me shudder.

Well, over the past 40 years our Intel-family CPUs got pretty much all the transistors they wanted, and the bulk of those infuriating 16-bit memory addressing limitations have simply gone away. You can address memory with *any* of the general-purpose registers. You can even address memory directly with the stack pointer RSP, something that its 16-bit ancestor SP could not do. (You shouldn't *change* the value in RSP without considerable care, but RSP can now take part in addressing modes from which the stack pointer was excluded in 16-bit real-mode land.)

32-bit protected mode on the 386 CPU family introduced a general-purpose memory-addressing scheme in which all the GP registers could participate equally. Memory addressing in x64 long mode implements the same scheme with very few changes. I've sketched it out in Figure 9.9, which may well be the single most important figure in this entire book. *Memory addressing is the key skill in assembly language work.* If you don't understand how the CPU addresses memory, nothing else matters.

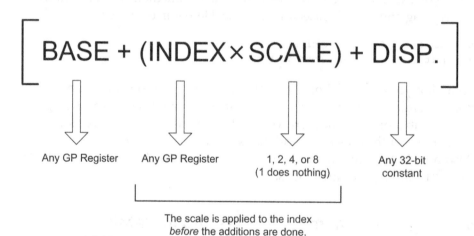

Figure 9.9: x64 long mode memory addressing

When I first studied and understood this scheme, wounds still bleeding from 16-bit 8088 segmented memory addressing, it looked too good to be true. But true it is! Here are the rules:

- The base and index registers may be any of the 64-bit general-purpose registers, including RSP.

- The displacement may be any 32-bit constant, either a literal value or a named value. Obviously, 0, while legal, isn't useful.

- The scale must be one of the values 1, 2, 4, or 8. That's it! The value 1 is legal, but given that the scale is used to multiply another value, 1 doesn't do anything useful.

- The index register is multiplied by the scale before the additions are done. In other words, it's not (base + index) × scale. Only the index register may be multiplied by the scale.

- All of the elements are optional and may be used in almost any combination.

- Both 32-bit and 64-bit registers may be used, but *you may not mix register sizes in a single address*. That is, the registers in a single memory addressing operation must be all 32-bit or all 64-bit.

- 16-bit and 8-bit registers may *not* be used in memory addressing.

Within those rules, there are several different ways you can address memory, by gathering the address components shown in Figure 9.9 in different combinations. Examples are shown in Table 9.8.

Table 9.8: 64-Bit Long Mode Memory-Addressing Schemes

SCHEME	EXAMPLE	DESCRIPTION
[BASE]	[rdx]	Base only
[DISPLACEMENT]	[0F3h] or [<variable>]	Displacement, either literal or named constant
[BASE + DISPLACEMENT]	[rcx + 033h]	Base plus displacement
[BASE + INDEX]	[rax + ecx]	Base plus index
[INDEX x SCALE]	[rbx * 4]	Index times scale
[INDEX x SCALE + DISPLACEMENT]	[rax * 8 + 65]	Index times scale plus displacement
[BASE + INDEX x SCALE]	[rsp + rdi * 2]	Base plus index times scale
[BASE + INDEX x SCALE + DISP.]	[rsi + rbp * 4 + 9]	Base plus index times scale plus displacement

Effective Address Calculations

Each of the lines in Table 9.8 summarizes a method of expressing a memory address in 64-bit long mode. All but the first two involve a little arithmetic among two or more terms within the brackets that signify an address. This arithmetic is called *effective address calculation*, and the result of the calculation is the *effective address*. This term means the address that will ultimately be used to read or write memory, irrespective of how it is expressed. Effective address calculation is done by the instruction, when the instruction is executed.

The effective address in the Base scheme is simply the 64-bit value stored in the GP register between the brackets. No calculation is involved, but what we see in the source code is not a literal or symbolic address. So although the instruction is coded with a register name between the brackets, the address that will be sent out to the memory system when the code executes is stored inside the register.

In most cases when you're dealing with an effective address, there's some arithmetic going on. In the Base + Index scheme, for example, the contents of the two GP registers between the brackets are added when the instruction is executed to form the effective address.

Displacements

Among the several components of a legal x64 long mode address, the displacement term is actually the slipperiest to understand. As I indicated in the previous paragraph, the displacement term can be a literal address, but in all my years of protected-mode assembly programming I've never done it nor seen anyone else do it. The reason? *You almost never know the literal address of something at assembly time.* There's another reason not to use literal addresses, which I'll come to shortly.

When the displacement term stands alone, it is virtually always a symbolic address. By that I mean a named data item that you've defined in your .data or .bss sections, like the HexStr variable from the hexdump1 program in Listing 9.1:

```
mov rax,HexStr
```

What is placed in RAX here is the address given to the variable HexStr when the program is loaded into memory by the OS. Like all addresses, it's just a number, but it's determined when the program is loaded rather than at assembly time, as a literal constant numeric address would be. Also note that the previous bit of source code loads an address into RAX, *not* the value in memory at that address. For that you need brackets:

```
mov rax, [HexStr]
```

A lot of beginners get confused when they see what looks like two displacement terms in a single address. The confusion stems from the fact that if NASM sees two (or more) constant values in a memory reference, it will combine them at assembly time into a single displacement value, which is placed in RAX by the MOV instruction. That's what's done here:

```
mov rax,HexStr+3
```

Note the lack of brackets. The address referred to symbolically by the variable named HexStr is simply added to the literal constant 3 to form a single displacement value.

The key characteristic of a displacement term is that it is not stored in a register.

The x64 Displacement Size Problem

Now, there's an x64-specific gotcha with respect to displacements: A displacement value must not be more than 32 bits in size. Why? As I sometimes have to say. . .it's complicated. And it's got nothing to do with the number of address bits supported in the silicon of a given x64 CPU. Put as simply as I can manage, limiting displacements to 32 bits was a design decision at AMD at the dawn of x64 time that "stuck." It may be fixed someday—or it may not. But, hey, never say "never."

In the meantime, we just have to live with it.

Base Addressing

When you exclude Displacement addressing, all x64 memory addressing is based on registers. The Base addressing scheme simply uses a single register into which an address has been loaded. It's called *Base* because all the more complex addressing schemes start with Base and extend it. Here's an example of Base addressing:

```
mov qword rax, [rcx]
```

This instruction takes whatever 64-bit value is stored in memory at the address contained in register RCX and loads it into register RAX.

Base + Displacement Addressing

A simple and common addressing scheme is Base + Displacement, and I demonstrated it in the `hexdump1` program in Listing 9.1. The instruction that inserts an ASCII character into the output line looks like this:

```
mov byte [HexStr+rdx+2],al
```

What happens here is that an 8-bit character value stored in register AL is written to the byte in memory addressed as `HexStr+RDX+2`. This is a perfect example of a case where there are two displacement terms that NASM combines into one. The variable name `HexStr` resolves to a number (the address of `HexStr`), and it is easily added to the literal constant 2. So, there is in truth only one base term (RDX) and one displacement term.

It's also a good example of how even 8-bit registers still have their uses, especially when you're dealing with 8-bit values like ASCII characters. Note too that the order of the terms in an address does not matter. The effective address could as well have been `RDX+HexStr+2`.

Base + Index Addressing

Perhaps the most common single addressing scheme is Base + Index, in which the effective address is calculated by adding the contents of two GP registers within the brackets. I demonstrated this addressing scheme in Chapter 8, in the uppercaser2 program in Listing 8.2. Converting a character in the input buffer from lowercase to uppercase is done by subtracting 20h from it:

```
sub byte [r13+rbx],20h
```

The address of the buffer was earlier placed in RBP, and the number in RCX is the offset from the buffer start of the character being processed during any given pass through the loop. Adding the address of the buffer with an offset into the buffer yields the effective address of the character acted upon by the SUB instruction.

But wait. . .why not use Base + Displacement addressing? This instruction would be legal:

```
sub byte [Buff+rbx],20h
```

However, if you remember from the program (and it would be worth looking back and reading the associated text), we had to decrement the address of Buff by 1 before beginning the loop. But wait some more. . .could we have NASM do that little tweak by adding a second displacement term of -1? Indeed we could, and it would work. The central loop of the uppercaser2 program would then look like this:

```
; Set up the registers for the process buffer step:

        mov rbx,rax         ; Place the number of bytes read into rbx
        mov r13,Buff        ; Place address of buffer into r13
;       dec r13             We don't need this instruction anymore!


; Go through the buffer and convert lowercase to uppercase characters:

Scan:
        cmp byte [r13-1+rbx],61h  ; Test input char against lowercase 'a'
        jb Next                   ; If below 'a' in ASCII, not lowercase
        cmp byte [r13-1+rbx],7Ah  ; Test input char against lowercase 'z'
        ja Next                   ; If above 'z' in ASCII, not lowercase

                                  ; Now we have a lowercase char
        sub byte [r13-1+rbx],20h  ; Subtract 20h to give uppercase...

Next:
        dec rbx             ; Decrement counter
        jnz Scan            ; If characters remain, loop back
```

The DEC R13 instruction in the first block is no longer necessary, and in the previous code that line is commented out. NASM does the math, and the address of Buff is decremented by 1 within the effective address expression when the program loads. This is actually the correct way to code this particular loop, and I thought long and hard about whether to show it back in Chapter 8 or wait until I could explain memory addressing schemes in detail.

Some people find the name "Base + Displacement" confusing, because in most cases, the Displacement term contains an address, and the Base term is a register containing an offset into a data item at that address. The word *displacement* resembles the word *offset* in most people's experience, which can lead to confusion. This is one reason I don't emphasize the names of the various memory addressing schemes in this book and certainly don't recommend memorizing the names. *Understand how effective address calculation works*, and ignore the names of the schemes.

Index X Scale + Displacement Addressing

Base + Index addressing is what you'll typically use to scan through a buffer in memory byte by byte. But what if you need to access a data item in a buffer or table where each data item is not a single byte, but a word or double word? This requires slightly more powerful memory addressing machinery.

As a side note here, the word *array* is the general term for what I've been calling a buffer or a table. Other writers may call a table an array, especially when the context of the discussion is a high-level language. But all three terms cook down to the same definition: a sequence of data items in memory, all of the same size and same internal definition. In the programs I've shown you so far, we've spoken only of very simple tables and buffers consisting of a sequence of 1-byte values all in a row. The Digits table in the hexdump1 program in Listing 9.1 is such a table:

```
Digits: db "0123456789ABCDEF"
```

It consists of 16 single-byte ASCII characters in a row in memory, starting at the address represented by Digits. You can access the "C" character within Digits this way, using Base + Displacement addressing:

```
mov rcx,12
mov rdx,[Digits+rcx]
```

But what if you have a table containing 64-bit numeric values? Such a table is easy enough to define:

```
Sums: dq "15,12,6,0,21,14,4,0,0,19"
```

The DQ qualifier tells NASM that each item in the table Sums is a 64-bit quad word quantity. The literal constants plug a numeric value into each element of the table. The address of the first element (here, 15) in Sums is just the address of the table as a whole. So what is the address of the second element, 12? And how do you access it from assembly code?

Keep in mind that memory is addressed byte-by-byte, and not double word-by-double word or quad word-by-quad word. The second entry in the table is at an offset of 8 bytes into the table. If you tried to reference the second entry in the table using an address [Sums+1], you would get one of the bytes inside the first table element's quad word, and that would *not* be useful.

This is where the concept of *scaling* comes in. An address may include a Scale term, which is a multiplier and may be any of the literal constants 2, 4, or 8. (The literal constant 1 is technically legal, but since the scale is a multiplier, 1 is not a useful scale value.) The product of the index and the scale terms is added to the displacement to give the effective address. This is known as the Index × Scale + Displacement addressing scheme. Keep in mind that the Scale term can only be used with the Index term.

Typically, the scale term is the size of the individual elements in the table. If your table consists of 2-byte word values, the scale would be 2. If your table consists of 4-byte double word values, the scale would be 4. If your table consists of 8-byte quad word values, the scale would be 8.

The best way to explain this is with a diagram. In Figure 9.10, we're confronted with the address [DQTable+ECX*8]. DQTable is a table of quad word (64-bit) values. DQTable's address is the displacement. The RCX register is the index, and for this example it contains 2, which is the number of the table element that you want to access. Because it's a table of 8-byte quad words, the scale value is 8. Note also that the multiplication symbol is not an "x" but an asterisk. The multiplication symbol "×" is not part of the ASCII character set, so like most high-level languages, assembly uses the asterisk as the multiplication operator symbol.

Because each table element is 8 bytes in size, the offset of element #2 from the start of the table is 16. The effective address of the element is calculated by first multiplying the index by the scale and then adding the product to the address of DQTable. There it is!

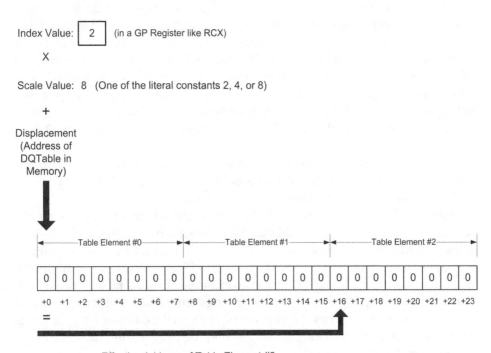

Figure 9.10: How address scaling works

Other Addressing Schemes

Any addressing scheme that includes scaling works just this way. The differences lie in what other terms are figured into the effective address. The Base + Index × Scale scheme adds a scaled index to a base value in register rather than a displacement:

```
mov rcx,2          ; Index is in rcx
mov rbp,DDTable    ; Table address is in rbp
mov rdx,[rbp+rcx*8] ; Put the selected element into rdx
```

You won't always be working with the address of a predefined variable like DDTable. Sometimes the address of the table will come from somewhere else, most often a two-dimensional table consisting of a number of subtables in memory, each subtable containing some number of elements. Such tables are accessed in two steps: First you derive the address of the inner table in the outer table, and then you derive the address of the desired element within the inner table.

The most familiar example of this sort of two-dimensional table is something I presented in earlier editions of this book, written for DOS. The 25-line × 80-character text video memory buffer under DOS was a two-dimensional table. Each of the 25 lines was a table of 80 characters, and each character was represented by a 2-byte word. (One byte was the ASCII value, and the other byte specified attributes such as color, underlining, and so on.) So, the buffer as a whole was an overall table of 24 smaller tables, each containing 80 2-byte word values.

That sort of video access system died with DOS; Linux does not allow you direct access to PC video memory. It was done a lot in the DOS era, however, and is a good example of a two-dimensional table.

Scaling will serve you well for tables with 2-byte, 4-byte, or 8-byte elements. So what if your table consists of 3-byte elements? Or 5-byte elements? Or 17-byte elements? Alas, in such cases you will have to do some additional calculations to zero in on one particular element. Effective address calculation won't do the whole job itself. I've already given you an example of such a table in Listing 9.1. The line display string is a table of 3-byte elements. Each element contains a space character followed by the two hex digit characters. Because the elements are each three characters long, scaling cannot be done within the instruction and must be handled separately.

It's not difficult. Scaling for the 3-byte elements in the HexStr table in the hexdump1 program is done like this:

```
mov rdx,rcx    ; Copy the character counter into rdx
shl rdx,1      ; Multiply counter by 2 using left shift
add rdx,rcx    ; Complete the multiplication X3
```

The calculation to multiply a value in RDX by 3 is done with a combination of an SHL instruction to multiply by 2, followed by an ADD instruction that adds a third copy of the index value to the shifted index value, effectively multiplying the original count value by 3.

Scaling for other index values can be done the same way. Scaling by 5 would be done by shifting the index value left by 2 bits, thus multiplying it by 4, followed by adding another copy of the index value to complete the multiplication by 5. In general terms, to scale an index value by X:

1. Find the largest power of 2 less than X.

2. Shift the index value left by that power of 2.

3. Add a copy of the original index value to the shifted copy as many times as it takes to complete the multiplication by X.

For example, if X is 11, the scale calculation would be done this way:

```
mov rdx,rcx ; Copy the index into rdx
shl rdx,3   ; Multiply index X 8 by shifting index left 3X
add rdx,rcx ; Add first of 3 additional copies of index
add rdx,rcx ; Add second of 3 additional copies of index
add rdx,rcx ; Add third of 3 additional copies of index
```

This works best for relatively small-scale values; once you get past 20, there will be a lot of ADD instructions. At that point, the answer is not to calculate the scale but look up the scale in a table specially defined for a given scale value. For example, suppose your table elements are each 25 bytes long. You could define a table with multiples of 25:

```
ScaleValues: dd 0,25,50,75,100,125,150,175,200,225,250,275
```

To scale an index value of 6 for an entry size of 25, you would look up the product of 6 × 25 in the table this way:

```
mov rcx,6
mov rax,[ScaleValues+rcx*4]
```

The value in RAX now contains the effective address of the first byte of element 6, counting elements (as usual) from 0.

LEA: The Top-Secret Math Machine

But wait, there's *more*. One of the oddest and in some respects the most wonderful instructions in the Intel architecture is LEA, Load Effective Address. On the surface, what it does is simple: It calculates an effective address using the terms between the brackets of its source operand and loads that address into any 64-bit general-purpose register given as its destination operand.

Look back to the code shown just before this section begins. The MOV instruction looks up the element with index 6 in the table ScaleValues. To look up the item at index 6, it has to first calculate the effective address of the item at index 6. This address is then used to access memory.

But what if you'd like to save that address in a register to use it later without having to calculate it all over again? That's what LEA does. Here's LEA in action:

```
lea rbx,[ScaleValues+rcx*4]
```

What happens here is that the CPU calculates the effective address given inside the brackets and loads that address into the RBX register. Keep in mind that the individual entries in a table do not have labels and thus cannot be referenced directly. LEA gives you the ability to calculate the effective address of any element in a table (or any calculable address at all!) and drop that address in a register.

In itself this is very useful. However, LEA has an "off-label" purpose: doing fast math without shifts, adds, or MUL. If you remember, there is a calculation in the hexdump1gcc program that multiplies by 3 using a shift and an add:

```
mov rdx,rcx    ; Copy the character counter into rdx
shl rdx,1      ; Multiply pointer by 2 using left shift
add rdx,rcx    ; Complete the multiplication X3
```

This works. But look at what we can use that does exactly the same thing:

```
mov rdx,rcx           ; Copy the character counter into rdx
lea rdx,[rdx*2+rdx]   ; Multiply rdx X 3
```

Not only is this virtually always faster than shifts combined with adds, it's also clearer from your source code what sort of calculation is actually being done. The fact that what ends up in RDX may not in fact be the legal address of anything is unimportant. LEA *does not try to reference the address it calculates*. It does the math on the stuff inside the brackets and drops the result in the destination operand. Job over. Memory is not touched, and the flags are not affected.

Of course, you're limited to what calculations can be done that yield effective addresses. But right off the top, you can multiply any GP register by 2, 3, 4, 5, 8, and 9. It's not arbitrary math, but multiplying by 2, 3, 4, 5, 8, and 9 comes up regularly in assembly work, and you can combine LEA with shifts and adds to do more complex math and "fill in the holes." You can also use multiple LEA instructions in a row. Two consecutive LEA instructions can multiply a value by 10, which is useful indeed:

```
lea rbx,[rbx*2]       ; Multiply rbx X 2, put product in RBX
lea rbx,[rbx*4+rbx]   ; Multiply rbx X 5 for a total of X 10
```

Some people consider this use of LEA a scurvy trick, but in all the years I've worked in x86/x64 assembly I've never seen a downside. Before throwing five or six instructions into the pot to cook up a particular multiplication, see if two or three LEAs can do it instead. LEA does its work in one machine cycle, and CPU math doesn't get any faster than that!

Character Table Translation

There is a type of table lookup that is (or perhaps was) so common that Intel's engineers baked a whole instruction into the x86 architecture to do nothing but. The type of table lookup is what I was alluding to toward the end of Chapter 8: character conversion. In the early 1980s I needed to convert character sets in various ways, the simplest of which was forcing all lowercase characters to uppercase. And so in Chapter 8 we built a simple program that went through a file a buffer at a time, bringing in characters, converting all lowercase characters to uppercase, and then writing them all back out again to a new file.

The conversion itself was simple: By relying on the ASCII chart for the relationship between all uppercase characters and their associated lowercase, we could convert a lowercase character to uppercase by simply subtracting 20h (32) from the character. That's reliable, but is very much a special case. It just so happens that ASCII lowercase characters are always 32 higher on the chart than their equivalent uppercase characters. What do you do if you need to convert all "vertical bar" (ASCII 124) characters to exclamation points? (I had to do this once, because one of the doddering old mainframes couldn't digest vertical bars.) You can write special code for each individual case that you have to deal with. . .

. . .or you can use a translation table.

Translation Tables

A translation table is a special type of table, and it works the following way: You set up a table of values, with one entry for every possible value that must be translated. A number (or a character, treated as a numeric value) is used as an index into the table. At the index position in the table is a value that is used to replace the original value that was used as the index. In short, the original value indexes into the table and finds a new value that replaces the original value, thus translating the old value to a new one.

We've done this once before, in the hexdump1gcc program in Listing 9.1. Recall the Digits table:

```
Digits: db "0123456789ABCDEF"
```

This is a translation table, though I didn't call it that at the time. The idea, if you recall, was to separate the two 4-bit halves of an 8-bit byte and convert those 4-bit values into ASCII characters representing hexadecimal digits. The focus at the time was separating the bytes into two nybbles via bitwise logical operations, but there was translation going on there as well.

The translation was accomplished by these three instructions:

```
mov al,byte [rsi+rcx]    ; Put a byte from the input buffer
                         ; into al
and al,0Fh               ; Mask out all but the low nybble
mov al,byte [Digits+rax] ; Look up the char equivalent of nybble
```

The first instruction loads a byte from the input buffer into the 8-bit AL register. The second instruction masks out all but the low nybble of AL. The third instruction does a memory fetch: It uses the value in AL to index into the Digits table and brings back whatever value was in the ALth entry in the table. (This has to be done using RAX between the brackets, because AL cannot take part in effective address calculations. Just remember that AL is the lowest-order byte in the RAX register.) If AL held 0, the effective address calculation added 0 to the address of Digits, bringing back the 0th table entry, which is the ASCII character for 0. If AL held 5, effective address calculation added 5 to the address of Digits, bringing back the 5th table entry, which is the ASCII character for 5. And so it would go for all 16 possible values that may be expressed in a 4-bit nybble. Basically, the code is used to translate a number to the ASCII character equivalent of that number.

There are only 16 possible hexadecimal digits, so the conversion table in hexdump1gcc only needs to be 16 bytes long. A byte contains enough bits to represent 256 different values, so if we're going to translate byte-sized values, we're going to need a table with 256 entries. Technically, the ASCII character set uses only the first 128 values, but as I described earlier in this book, the "high" 128 values have often been assigned to special characters like non-English letters, "box-draw" characters, mathematical symbols, and so on. One common use of character translation is to convert any characters with values higher than 128 to something lower than 128 to avoid havoc in older systems that can't deal with extended ASCII values.

Such a table is easy enough to define in an assembly language program:

```
UpCase:
    db  20h,20h,20h,20h,20h,20h,20h,20h,20h,09h,0Ah,20h,20h,20h,20h,20h
    db  20h,20h,20h,20h,20h,20h,20h,20h,20h,20h,20h,20h,20h,20h,20h,20h
    db  20h,21h,22h,23h,24h,25h,26h,27h,28h,29h,2Ah,2Bh,2Ch,2Dh,2Eh,2Fh
    db  30h,31h,32h,33h,34h,35h,36h,37h,38h,39h,3Ah,3Bh,3Ch,3Dh,3Eh,3Fh
    db  40h,41h,42h,43h,44h,45h,46h,47h,48h,49h,4Ah,4Bh,4Ch,4Dh,4Eh,4Fh
    db  50h,51h,52h,53h,54h,55h,56h,57h,58h,59h,5Ah,5Bh,5Ch,5Dh,5Eh,5Fh
    db  60h,41h,42h,43h,44h,45h,46h,47h,48h,49h,4Ah,4Bh,4Ch,4Dh,4Eh,4Fh
    db  50h,51h,52h,53h,54h,55h,56h,57h,58h,59h,5Ah,7Bh,7Ch,7Dh,7Eh,20h
    db  20h,20h,20h,20h,20h,20h,20h,20h,20h,20h,20h,20h,20h,20h,20h,20h
    db  20h,20h,20h,20h,20h,20h,20h,20h,20h,20h,20h,20h,20h,20h,20h,20h
    db  20h,20h,20h,20h,20h,20h,20h,20h,20h,20h,20h,20h,20h,20h,20h,20h
    db  20h,20h,20h,20h,20h,20h,20h,20h,20h,20h,20h,20h,20h,20h,20h,20h
    db  20h,20h,20h,20h,20h,20h,20h,20h,20h,20h,20h,20h,20h,20h,20h,20h
    db  20h,20h,20h,20h,20h,20h,20h,20h,20h,20h,20h,20h,20h,20h,20h,20h
    db  20h,20h,20h,20h,20h,20h,20h,20h,20h,20h,20h,20h,20h,20h,20h,20h
    db  20h,20h,20h,20h,20h,20h,20h,20h,20h,20h,20h,20h,20h,20h,20h,20h
```

The UpCase table is defined in 16 lines of 16 separate hexadecimal values. The fact that it's split across 16 lines in the code listing is purely for readability on the screen or printed page and does not affect the binary table that NASM generates in the output .o file. Once it's in binary, it's 256 8-bit values in a row.

A quick syntactic note here: When defining tables (or any data structure containing multiple predefined values), commas are used to separate values within a single definition. There is no need for commas at the ends of the lines of the DB definitions in the previous table. Each DB definition is separate and independent, but because they are adjacent in memory, we can treat the 16 DB definitions as a single 256-byte table.

Any translation table can be thought of as expressing one or more "rules" governing what happens during the translation process. The UpCase table shown earlier expresses these translation rules:

- All lowercase ASCII characters are translated to uppercase.
- All printable ASCII characters less than 127 that are *not* lowercase are translated to themselves. (They're not precisely "left alone" but are still translated, just to the same characters.)
- All "high" character values from 127 through 255 are translated to the ASCII space character (32, or 20h).
- All nonprintable ASCII characters (basically, values 0–31, plus 127) are translated to spaces *except* for values 9 and 10.
- Character values 9 and 10 (tab and EOL) are translated as themselves.

Not bad for a single data item, eh? (Just imagine how much work it would be to do all that fussing purely with machine instructions!)

Translating with MOV or with XLAT

So, how do we use the UpCase table? The obvious way would be this:

- Load the character to be translated into AL.
- Create a memory reference using AL as the base term and UpCase as the displacement term, and MOV the byte at the memory reference into AL, replacing the original value used as the base term.

The hypothetical MOV instruction would look like this:

```
mov al, byte [UpCase+al]
```

There's only one problem: *NASM won't let you do this.* In 32-bit protected mode and x64 long mode, the AL register can't take part in effective address calculations, nor can any other of the 8-bit registers. Enter XLAT.

The XLAT instruction is hard-coded to use certain registers in certain ways. Its two operands are both implicit:

- The address of the translation table must be in RBX.
- The character to be translated must be in AL.
- The translated character will be returned in AL, replacing the character originally placed in AL.

With the registers set up, the XLAT instruction has no operands and is used all by its lonesome:

```
xlat
```

I'll be honest here: XLAT is less of a win than it used to be. In x64 long mode, the same thing can be done with the following instruction:

```
mov al, byte [UpCase+rax]
```

The 64-bit register RAX can stand in for little 8-bit AL when calculating an effective address of the character used to translate the character in AL. There's only one catch: You must clear out any "leftover" values in the high 56 bits of RAX, or you could accidentally index far beyond the bounds of the translation table. The problem doesn't arise with XLAT since the XLAT instruction uses *only* AL for the index, ignoring whatever else might be in the higher bits of RAX.

Clearing RAX before loading the value to be translated into AL is done in either of these two common ways:

```
xor rax,rax
mov rax,0
```

In truth, given XLAT's requirement that it use AL and RBX, it's a wash, but the larger topic of character translation via tables is really what I'm trying to present here. Listing 9.2 puts it all into action. The program as shown does exactly what the uppercaser2 program in Listing 8.2 does: It forces all lowercase characters in an input file to uppercase and writes them to an output file. I didn't call it "uppercaser3" because it is a general-purpose character translator. In this particular example, with the UpCase table, it translates lowercase characters to uppercase; however, that's simply one of the rules that the UpCase table expresses. Change the table, and you change the rules. You can translate any or all of the 256 different values in a byte to any 8-bit value or values.

I've added a second table to the program for you to experiment with. The Custom table expresses these rules:

- All printable ASCII characters less than 127 are translated to themselves. (They're not precisely "left alone" but are still translated, just to the same characters.)

- All "high" character values from 127 through 255 are translated to the ASCII space character (32, or 20h.)

- All non-printable ASCII characters (basically, values 0–31, plus 127) are translated to spaces *except* for values 9 and 10.

- Character values 9 and 10 (tab and EOL) are translated as themselves.

Basically, it leaves all printable characters (plus tab and EOL) alone and converts all other character values to 20h, the space character. You can substitute the label Custom for UpCase in the program, make changes to the Custom table, and try it out. Convert that pesky vertical bar to an exclamation point. Change all "Z" characters to "Q." Changing the rules is done by changing the table. The code does not change at all!

As with earlier programs, xlat1gcc reads from standard input and writes to standard output. Copy some text to the clipboard and drop it into SASM's Input window. Then run the program, and see what it writes to the Output window.

Listing 9.2: xlat1gcc.asm

```
;   Executable name : xlat1gcc
;   Version         : 2.0
;   Created date    : 8/21/2022
;   Last update     : 7/17/2023
;   Author          : Jeff Duntemann
;   Description     : A simple program in assembly for Linux,
;                   : using NASM 2.15, demonstrating the XLAT
;                   : instruction to translate characters using
;                   : translation tables.
;
;   Run it either in SASM or using this command in the Linux terminal:
;
;       xlat1gcc < input file > output file
;
;          If an output file is not specified, output goes to stdout
;
;   Build using SASM's default build setup for x64
;   To test from a terminal, save out the executable to disk.

SECTION .data         ; Section containing initialised data

        StatMsg: db "Processing...",10
        StatLen: equ $-StatMsg
        DoneMsg: db "...done!",10
        DoneLen: equ $-DoneMsg

; The following translation table translates all lowercase characters
; to uppercase. It also translates all non-printable characters to
; spaces, except for LF and HT. This is the table used by default in
; this program.
        UpCase:
        db 20h,20h,20h,20h,20h,20h,20h,20h,20h,09h,0Ah,20h,20h,20h,20h,20h
        db 20h,20h,20h,20h,20h,20h,20h,20h,20h,20h,20h,20h,20h,20h,20h,20h
        db 20h,21h,22h,23h,24h,25h,26h,27h,28h,29h,2Ah,2Bh,2Ch,2Dh,2Eh,2Fh
        db 30h,31h,32h,33h,34h,35h,36h,37h,38h,39h,3Ah,3Bh,3Ch,3Dh,3Eh,3Fh
        db 40h,41h,42h,43h,44h,45h,46h,47h,48h,49h,4Ah,4Bh,4Ch,4Dh,4Eh,4Fh
        db 50h,51h,52h,53h,54h,55h,56h,57h,58h,59h,5Ah,5Bh,5Ch,5Dh,5Eh,5Fh
        db 60h,41h,42h,43h,44h,45h,46h,47h,48h,49h,4Ah,4Bh,4Ch,4Dh,4Eh,4Fh
        db 50h,51h,52h,53h,54h,55h,56h,57h,58h,59h,5Ah,7Bh,7Ch,7Dh,7Eh,20h
```

```
        db 20h,20h,20h,20h,20h,20h,20h,20h,20h,20h,20h,20h,20h,20h,20h,20h
        db 20h,20h,20h,20h,20h,20h,20h,20h,20h,20h,20h,20h,20h,20h,20h,20h
        db 20h,20h,20h,20h,20h,20h,20h,20h,20h,20h,20h,20h,20h,20h,20h,20h
        db 20h,20h,20h,20h,20h,20h,20h,20h,20h,20h,20h,20h,20h,20h,20h,20h
        db 20h,20h,20h,20h,20h,20h,20h,20h,20h,20h,20h,20h,20h,20h,20h,20h
        db 20h,20h,20h,20h,20h,20h,20h,20h,20h,20h,20h,20h,20h,20h,20h,20h
        db 20h,20h,20h,20h,20h,20h,20h,20h,20h,20h,20h,20h,20h,20h,20h,20h
        db 20h,20h,20h,20h,20h,20h,20h,20h,20h,20h,20h,20h,20h,20h,20h,20h

; The following translation table is "stock" in that it translates all
; printable characters as themselves, and converts all non-printable
; characters to spaces except for LF and HT. You can modify this to
; translate anything you want to any character you want. To use it,
; replace the default table name (UpCase) with Custom in the code below.
        Custom:
        db 20h,20h,20h,20h,20h,20h,20h,20h,20h,09h,0Ah,20h,20h,20h,20h,20h
        db 20h,20h,20h,20h,20h,20h,20h,20h,20h,20h,20h,20h,20h,20h,20h,20h
        db 20h,21h,22h,23h,24h,25h,26h,27h,28h,29h,2Ah,2Bh,2Ch,2Dh,2Eh,2Fh
        db 30h,31h,32h,33h,34h,35h,36h,37h,38h,39h,3Ah,3Bh,3Ch,3Dh,3Eh,3Fh
        db 40h,41h,42h,43h,44h,45h,46h,47h,48h,49h,4Ah,4Bh,4Ch,4Dh,4Eh,4Fh
        db 50h,51h,52h,53h,54h,55h,56h,57h,58h,59h,5Ah,5Bh,5Ch,5Dh,5Eh,5Fh
        db 60h,61h,62h,63h,64h,65h,66h,67h,68h,69h,6Ah,6Bh,6Ch,6Dh,6Eh,6Fh
        db 70h,71h,72h,73h,74h,75h,76h,77h,78h,79h,7Ah,7Bh,7Ch,7Dh,7Eh,20h
        db 20h,20h,20h,20h,20h,20h,20h,20h,20h,20h,20h,20h,20h,20h,20h,20h
        db 20h,20h,20h,20h,20h,20h,20h,20h,20h,20h,20h,20h,20h,20h,20h,20h
        db 20h,20h,20h,20h,20h,20h,20h,20h,20h,20h,20h,20h,20h,20h,20h,20h
        db 20h,20h,20h,20h,20h,20h,20h,20h,20h,20h,20h,20h,20h,20h,20h,20h
        db 20h,20h,20h,20h,20h,20h,20h,20h,20h,20h,20h,20h,20h,20h,20h,20h
        db 20h,20h,20h,20h,20h,20h,20h,20h,20h,20h,20h,20h,20h,20h,20h,20h
        db 20h,20h,20h,20h,20h,20h,20h,20h,20h,20h,20h,20h,20h,20h,20h,20h
        db 20h,20h,20h,20h,20h,20h,20h,20h,20h,20h,20h,20h,20h,20h,20h,20h

SECTION .bss                ; Section containing uninitialized data

        READLEN      equ 1024        ; Length of buffer
        ReadBuffer: resb READLEN     ; Text buffer itself

SECTION .text               ; Section containing code

global  main

main:
        mov rbp,rsp      ; This keeps gdb happy...

; Display the "I'm working..." message via stderr:
        mov rax,1        ; Specify sys_write call
        mov rdi,2        ; Specify File Descriptor 2: Standard error
        mov rsi,StatMsg  ; Pass address of the message
```

```
    mov rdx,StatLen   ; Pass the length of the message
    syscall           ; Make kernel call

; Read a buffer full of text from stdin:
read:
    mov rax,0         ; Specify sys_read call
    mov rdi,0         ; Specify File Descriptor 0: Standard Input
    mov rsi,ReadBuffer ; Pass address of the buffer to read to
    mov rdx,READLEN   ; Pass number of bytes to read at one pass
    syscall
    mov rbp,rax       ; Copy sys_read return value for safekeeping
    cmp rax,0         ; If rax=0, sys_read reached EOF
    je done           ; Jump If Equal (to 0, from compare)

; Set up the registers for the translate step:
    mov rbx,UpCase    ; Place the address of the table into rbx
    mov rdx,ReadBuffer ; Place the address of the buffer into rdx
    mov rcx,rbp       ; Place number of bytes in the buffer into rcx

; Use the xlat instruction to translate the data in the buffer:
translate:
    xor rax,rax             ; Clear rax
    mov al,byte [rdx-1+rcx] ; Load character into AL for translation
    xlat                    ; Translate character in AL via table
    mov byte [rdx-1+rcx],al ; Put the xlated character back in buffer
    dec rcx                 ; Decrement character count
    jnz translate     ; If there are more chars in the buffer, repeat

; Write the buffer full of translated text to stdout:
write:
    mov rax,1         ; Specify sys_write call
    mov rdi,1         ; Specify File Descriptor 1: Standard output
    mov rsi,ReadBuffer ; Pass address of the buffer
    mov rdx,rbp       ; Pass the # of bytes of data in the buffer
    syscall           ; Make kernel call
    jmp read          ; Loop back and load another buffer full

; Display the "I'm done" message via stderr:
done:
    mov rax,1         ; Specify sys_write call
    mov rdi,2         ; Specify File Descriptor 2: Standard error
    mov rsi,DoneMsg   ; Pass address of the message
    mov rdx,DoneLen   ; Pass the length of the message
    syscall           ; Make kernel call

; All done! Let's end this party:
    ret               ; Return to the glibc shutdown code
```

Tables Instead of Calculations

Standardization among computer systems has made character translation a lot less common than it used to be, but translation tables can be extremely useful in other areas. One of them is to perform faster math. Consider the following table:

```
Squares: db 0,1,4,9,16,25,36,49,64,81,100,121,144,169,196,225
```

No mystery here: Squares is a table of the squares of the numbers from 0–15. If you needed the square of 14 in a calculation, you could use MUL, which is slower than most instructions and requires two GP registers. Or you could simply fetch down the result from the Squares table:

```
mov rcx,14
mov al,byte [Squares+rcx]
```

Voilà! RAX now contains the square of 14. You can do the same trick with XLAT, though it requires that you use certain registers. Also remember that XLAT is limited to 8-bit quantities. The Squares table shown here is as large a squares value table as XLAT can use, because the next square value (of 16) is 256, which cannot be expressed in 8 bits, and thus a lookup table containing it cannot be used by XLAT.

Making the entries of a squares value lookup table 16 bits in size will allow you to include the squares of all integers up to 255. And if you give each entry in the table 32 bits, you can include the squares of integers up to 65,535, but that would be a *very* substantial table!

I don't have the space in this book to go into floating-point math, but using tables to look up values for things such as square roots was once done very frequently. Modern CPUs with math systems like AVX make such techniques a lot less compelling. Still, when confronted with a math calculation challenge, you should always keep the possibility of using table lookups somewhere in the corner of your mind.

Dividing and Conquering

Using Procedures and Macros to Battle Program Complexity

Complexity kills—programs, at least. This was one of the first lessons I ever learned as a programmer, and it has stuck with me all these intervening 40-odd years.

So listen well: There is a programming language called APL (an acronym for *A Programming Language*, how clever) that has more than a little Martian in it. APL was the second computer language I ever learned (on a major IBM mainframe), and when I learned it, I learned a little more than just APL.

APL uses a compact notation, including its very own character set (many of which are Greek letters), which bears little resemblance to our familiar ASCII. The character set has dozens of odd little symbols, each of which is capable of some astonishing power such as matrix inversion. You can do more in one line of APL than you can in one line of anything else I have ever learned since. The combination of the strange symbol set and the vanishingly compact notation makes it very hard to read and remember what a line of code in APL actually *does*.

So it was in 1977. Having mastered (or so I thought) the whole library of symbols, I set out to write a text formatter program. The program would take a plain-text file and generate a printout that was justified right and left, with centered headers, plus a few other things of a sort that we take for granted today but that were still very exotic in the '70s.

The program grew over a period of a week to about 600 lines of squirmy little APL symbols. I got it to work, and it worked fine—as long as I didn't try to format a column that was more than 64 characters wide. Then everything came out scrambled.

Whoops. I printed the whole thing out and sat down to do some serious debugging. Then I realized with a feeling of sinking horror that, having finished the last part of the program, *I had no idea how the first part worked anymore.*

The special APL symbol set was only part of the problem. I soon came to realize that the most important mistake I had made was writing the whole thing as one 600-line monolithic block of code. There were no functional divisions, nothing to indicate what any 10-line portion of the code was trying to accomplish.

The Martians had won. I did the only thing possible: I scrapped it. And I settled for ragged margins in my text. Like I said, complexity kills. This is as true of assembly language as it is of APL, Java, C, Pascal, or any other programming language that has ever existed. Now that you can write reasonably complex programs in assembly, you had better learn how to manage that complexity, or you will find yourself abandoning a great deal of code simply because you can no longer remember (or figure out) how it works.

Boxes within Boxes

Managing complexity is the great challenge in programming. Key to the skill is something that sounds like Eastern mysticism but that is really just an observation from life: *Within any action is a host of smaller actions.* Look inside your common activities. When you brush your teeth, you do the following:

1. Pick up your toothpaste tube.
2. Unscrew the cap.
3. Place the cap on the sink counter.
4. Pick up your toothbrush.
5. Squeeze toothpaste onto the brush from the middle of the tube.
6. Put your toothbrush into your mouth.
7. Work it back and forth vigorously for 2 minutes.
8. Rinse out your mouth.

And so on. When you brush your teeth, you perform every one of those actions. However, when you think about the sequence, you don't run through the whole list. You bring to mind the simple concept called "brushing my teeth."

Furthermore, when you think about what's behind the action we call "getting up in the morning," you might assemble a list of activities like this:

1. Shut off the clock radio.
2. Climb out of bed.

3. Put on your robe.

4. Let the dogs out.

5. Make breakfast.

6. Eat breakfast.

7. Brush your teeth.

8. Shave.

9. Shower.

10. Get dressed.

Brushing your teeth is certainly on the list, but within the activity you call "brushing your teeth" is a whole list of smaller actions, as I demonstrated earlier. The same can be said for most of the activities shown in the preceding list. How many individual actions, for example, does it take to put a reasonable breakfast together? And yet in one small, if sweeping, phrase, "getting up in the morning," you embrace that whole host of small and still smaller actions without having to laboriously trace through each one.

What I'm describing is the "Chinese boxes" method of fighting complexity. Getting up in the morning involves hundreds of little actions, so we divide the mass into coherent chunks and set the chunks into little conceptual boxes. "Making breakfast" is in one box, "brushing teeth" is in another, "getting dressed" in still another, and so on. Closer inspection of any single box shows that its contents can be divided further into numerous boxes, and those smaller boxes into even smaller boxes.

This process doesn't (and can't) go on forever, but it should go on as long as it needs in order to satisfy this criterion: *The contents of any one box should be understandable with only a little scrutiny.* No single box should contain anything so subtle or large and involved that it takes hours of staring and hair-pulling to figure it out.

Procedures as Boxes for Code

The mistake I made in writing my APL text formatter is that I threw the whole collection of 600 lines of APL code into one huge box marked "text formatter."

While I was writing it, I should have been keeping my eyes open for sequences of code statements that worked together on some identifiable task. When I spotted such sequences, I should have set them off as *procedures* and given each a descriptive name. Each sequence would then have a memory tag (its name) for the sequence's function. If it took 10 statements to justify a line of text, those 10 statements should have been gathered together and named `JustifyLine`, and so on.

Xerox's legendary APL programmer Jim Dunn later told me that I shouldn't ever write an APL procedure that wouldn't fit on a single 25-line terminal screen.

"More than 25 lines and you're doing too much in one procedure. Split it up," he said. Whenever I worked in APL after that, I adhered to that sage rule of thumb. The Martians still struck from time to time, but when they did, it was no longer a total loss.

All computer languages in common use today implement procedures in one form or another, and assembly language is no exception. Your assembly language program may have numerous procedures. In fact, there's no limit to the *number* of procedures you can include in a program, as long as the total number of bytes of code contained by all the procedures together, plus whatever data they use, will fit in the memory that Linux allocates to it. These days, with cheap memory available in multi-gigabyte chunks, writing code that won't fit in Linux's allocation is vanishing unlikely.

Whatever complexity you can generate in assembly language can be managed with procedures.

Let's start early with an example of procedures in action. Read Listing 10.1 closely and let's look at what makes it work and (more to the point) what helps it remain comprehensible.

Listing 10.1: hexdump2gcc.asm

```
;   Executable name  : hexdump2gcc
;   Version          : 2.0
;   Created date     : 5/9/2022
;   Last update      : 5/8/2023
;   Author           : Jeff Duntemann
;   Description      : A simple hexdump utility demonstrating the use of
;                    : assembly language procedures
;
;
;   Build with SASM's x64 build setup, which uses gcc & requires "main"
;   To run, type or paste some text into SASM's Input window and click
;   Run. The hex dump of the input text will appear in SASM's Output
;   window.

SECTION .bss          ; Section containing uninitialized data

        BUFFLEN       EQU 10h
        Buff:         resb BUFFLEN


SECTION .data         ; Section containing initialised data

; Here we have two parts of a single useful data structure, implementing
; the text line of a hex dump utility. The first part displays 16 bytes
; in hex separated by spaces. Immediately following is a 16-character
; line delimited by vertical bar characters. Because they are adjacent,
; the two parts can be referenced separately or as a single contiguous
; unit. Remember that if DumpLine is to be used separately, you must
; append an EOL before sending it to the Linux console.
```

```
DumpLine:         db " 00 00 00 00 00 00 00 00 00 00 00 00 00 00 00 00 "
DUMPLEN           EQU $-DumpLine
ASCLine:          db "|...............|",10
ASCLEN            EQU $-ASCLine
FULLLEN           EQU $-DumpLine
```

```
; The HexDigits table is used to convert numeric values to their hex
; equivalents. Index by nybble without a scale: [HexDigits+eax]
HexDigits:        db "0123456789ABCDEF"
```

```
; This table is used for ASCII character translation, into the ASCII
; portion of the hex dump line, via XLAT or ordinary memory lookup.
; All printable characters "play through" as themselves. The high 128
; characters are translated to ASCII period (2Eh). The non-printable
; characters in the low 128 are also translated to ASCII period, as is
; char 127.
DotXlat:
    db 2Eh,2Eh,2Eh,2Eh,2Eh,2Eh,2Eh,2Eh,2Eh,2Eh,2Eh,2Eh,2Eh,2Eh,2Eh,2Eh
    db 2Eh,2Eh,2Eh,2Eh,2Eh,2Eh,2Eh,2Eh,2Eh,2Eh,2Eh,2Eh,2Eh,2Eh,2Eh,2Eh
    db 20h,21h,22h,23h,24h,25h,26h,27h,28h,29h,2Ah,2Bh,2Ch,2Dh,2Eh,2Fh
    db 30h,31h,32h,33h,34h,35h,36h,37h,38h,39h,3Ah,3Bh,3Ch,3Dh,3Eh,3Fh
    db 40h,41h,42h,43h,44h,45h,46h,47h,48h,49h,4Ah,4Bh,4Ch,4Dh,4Eh,4Fh
    db 50h,51h,52h,53h,54h,55h,56h,57h,58h,59h,5Ah,5Bh,5Ch,5Dh,5Eh,5Fh
    db 60h,61h,62h,63h,64h,65h,66h,67h,68h,69h,6Ah,6Bh,6Ch,6Dh,6Eh,6Fh
    db 70h,71h,72h,73h,74h,75h,76h,77h,78h,79h,7Ah,7Bh,7Ch,7Dh,7Eh,2Eh
    db 2Eh,2Eh,2Eh,2Eh,2Eh,2Eh,2Eh,2Eh,2Eh,2Eh,2Eh,2Eh,2Eh,2Eh,2Eh,2Eh
    db 2Eh,2Eh,2Eh,2Eh,2Eh,2Eh,2Eh,2Eh,2Eh,2Eh,2Eh,2Eh,2Eh,2Eh,2Eh,2Eh
    db 2Eh,2Eh,2Eh,2Eh,2Eh,2Eh,2Eh,2Eh,2Eh,2Eh,2Eh,2Eh,2Eh,2Eh,2Eh,2Eh
    db 2Eh,2Eh,2Eh,2Eh,2Eh,2Eh,2Eh,2Eh,2Eh,2Eh,2Eh,2Eh,2Eh,2Eh,2Eh,2Eh
    db 2Eh,2Eh,2Eh,2Eh,2Eh,2Eh,2Eh,2Eh,2Eh,2Eh,2Eh,2Eh,2Eh,2Eh,2Eh,2Eh
    db 2Eh,2Eh,2Eh,2Eh,2Eh,2Eh,2Eh,2Eh,2Eh,2Eh,2Eh,2Eh,2Eh,2Eh,2Eh,2Eh
    db 2Eh,2Eh,2Eh,2Eh,2Eh,2Eh,2Eh,2Eh,2Eh,2Eh,2Eh,2Eh,2Eh,2Eh,2Eh,2Eh
    db 2Eh,2Eh,2Eh,2Eh,2Eh,2Eh,2Eh,2Eh,2Eh,2Eh,2Eh,2Eh,2Eh,2Eh,2Eh,2Eh
```

```
SECTION .text        ; Section containing code
```

```
;-----------------------------------------------------------------
; ClearLine:   Clear a hex dump line string to 16 0 values
; UPDATED:     5/9/2022
; IN:          Nothing
; RETURNS:     Nothing
; MODIFIES:    Nothing
; CALLS:       DumpChar
; DESCRIPTION: The hex dump line string is cleared to binary 0 by
;              calling DumpChar 16 times, passing it 0 each time.

ClearLine:
    push rax        ; Save all caller's r*x GP registers
    push rbx
    push rcx
    push rdx
```

```
        mov  rdx,15      ; We're going to go 16 pokes, counting from 0
.poke:
        mov rax,0        ; Tell DumpChar to poke a '0'
        call DumpChar    ; Insert the '0' into the hex dump string
        sub rdx,1        ; DEC doesn't affect CF!
        jae .poke         ; Loop back if RDX >= 0

        pop rdx          ; Restore caller's r*x GP registers
        pop rcx
        pop rbx
        pop rax
        ret              ; Go home


;-------------------------------------------------------------------
; DumpChar:      "Poke" a value into the hex dump line string.
; UPDATED:       5/9/2022
; IN:            Pass the 8-bit value to be poked in RAX.
;                Pass the value's position in the line (0-15) in RDX
; RETURNS:       Nothing
; MODIFIES:      RAX, ASCLine, DumpLine
; CALLS:         Nothing
; DESCRIPTION: The value passed in RAX will be put in both the hex dump
;              portion and in the ASCII portion, at the position passed
;              in RDX, represented by a space where it is not a
;              printable character.

DumpChar:
        push rbx    ; Save caller's RBX
        push rdi    ; Save caller's RDI

; First we insert the input char into the ASCII part of the dump line
        mov bl,[DotXlat+rax]       ; Translate nonprintables to '.'
        mov [ASCLine+rdx+1],bl     ; Write to ASCII portion

; Next we insert the hex equivalent of the input char in the hex
; part of the hex dump line:
        mov rbx,rax                ; Save a second copy of the input char
        lea rdi,[rdx*2+rdx]        ; Calc offset into line string (RDX X 3)

; Look up low nybble character and insert it into the string:
        and rax,000000000000000Fh ; Mask out all but the low nybble
        mov al,[HexDigits+rax]     ; Look up the char equiv. of nybble
        mov [DumpLine+rdi+2],al    ; Write the char equiv. to line string

; Look up high nybble character and insert it into the string:
        and rbx,00000000000000F0h ; Mask out all the but 2nd-lowest nybble
        shr rbx,4                  ; Shift high 4 bits of byte into low 4 bits
        mov bl,[HexDigits+rbx]     ; Look up char equiv. of nybble
        mov [DumpLine+rdi+1],bl    ; Write the char equiv. to line string
```

```
; Done! Let's return:
    pop rdi       ; Restore caller's RDI
    pop rbx       ; Restore caller's RBX
    ret           ; Return to caller


;-------------------------------------------------------------------
; PrintLine:    Displays DumpLine to stdout
; UPDATED:      5/8/2023
; IN:           DumpLine, FULLEN
; RETURNS:      Nothing
; MODIFIES:     Nothing
; CALLS:        Kernel sys_write
; DESCRIPTION:  The hex dump line string DumpLine is displayed to
;                stdout using syscall function sys_write. Registers
;                used are preserved.

PrintLine:

    push rax          ; Alas, we don't have pushad anymore.
    push rbx
    push rcx
    push rdx
    push rsi
    push rdi

    mov rax,1         ; Specify sys_write call
    mov rdi,1         ; Specify File Descriptor 1: Standard output
    mov rsi,DumpLine  ; Pass address of line string
    mov rdx,FULLLEN   ; Pass size of the line string
    syscall           ; Make kernel call to display line string

    pop rdi           ; Nor popad.
    pop rsi
    pop rdx
    pop rcx
    pop rbx
    pop rax
    ret               ; Return to caller


;-------------------------------------------------------------------
; LoadBuff:     Fills a buffer with data from stdin via syscall sys_read
; UPDATED:      5/8/2023
; IN:           Nothing
; RETURNS:      # of bytes read in R15
; MODIFIES:     RCX, R15, Buff
; CALLS:        syscall sys_read
; DESCRIPTION:  Loads a buffer full of data (BUFFLEN bytes) from stdin
;                using syscall sys_read and places it in Buff. Buffer
;                offset counter RCX is zeroed, because we're starting in
```

```
;                     on a new buffer full of data. Caller must test value in
;                     R15: If R15 contains 0 on return, we've hit EOF on stdin.
;                     < 0 in R15 on return indicates some kind of error.

LoadBuff:
     push rax        ; Save caller's RAX
     push rdx        ; Save caller's RDX
     push rsi        ; Save caller's RSI
     push rdi        ; Save caller's RDI

     mov rax,0       ; Specify sys_read call
     mov rdi,0       ; Specify File Descriptor 0: Standard Input
     mov rsi,Buff      ; Pass offset of the buffer to read to
     mov rdx,BUFFLEN   ; Pass number of bytes to read at one pass
     syscall         ; Call syscall's sys_read to fill the buffer
     mov r15,rax     ; Save # of bytes read from file for later
     xor rcx,rcx     ; Clear buffer pointer RCX to 0

     pop rdi         ; Restore caller's RDI
     pop rsi         ; Restore caller's RSI
     pop rdx         ; Restore caller's RDX
     pop rax         ; Restore caller's RAX
     ret             ; And return to caller

GLOBAL main ; You need to declare "main" here because SASM uses gcc
            ; to do builds.


; ------------------------------------------------------------------
; MAIN PROGRAM BEGINS HERE
;-------------------------------------------------------------------


main:
     mov rbp, rsp; for correct debugging

; Whatever initialization needs doing before loop scan starts is here:
     xor r15,r15     ; Zero out r15,rsi, and rcx
     xor rsi,rsi
     xor rcx,rcx
     call LoadBuff   ; Read first buffer of data from stdin
     cmp r15,0       ; If r15=0, sys_read reached EOF on stdin
     jbe Exit

; Go through the buffer and convert binary byte values to hex digits:
Scan:
     xor rax,rax               ; Clear RAX to 0
     mov al,[Buff+rcx]         ; Get a byte from the buffer into AL
     mov rdx,rsi               ; Copy total counter into RDX
     and rdx,000000000000000Fh ; Mask out lowest 4 bits of char counter
     call DumpChar             ; Call the char poke procedure
```

```
; Bump the buffer pointer to the next char and see if buffer's done:
    inc rsi             ; Increment total chars processed counter
    inc rcx             ; Increment buffer pointer
    cmp rcx,r15         ; Compare with # of chars in buffer
    jb .modTest         ; If we've processed all chars in buffer...
    call LoadBuff       ; ...go fill the buffer again
    cmp r15,0           ; If r15=0, sys_read reached EOF on stdin
    jbe Done            ; If we get EOF, we're done

; See if we're at the end of a block of 16 and need to display a line:
.modTest:
    test rsi,000000000000000Fh ; Test 4 lowest bits in counter for 0
    jnz Scan            ; If counter is *not* modulo 16, loop back
    call PrintLine      ; ...otherwise print the line
    call ClearLine      ; Clear hex dump line to 0's
    jmp Scan            ; Continue scanning the buffer

; All done! Let's end this party:
Done:
    call PrintLine      ; Print the final "leftovers" line
Exit:
    mov rsp,rbp
    pop rbp
    ret
```

I admit, that looks a little scary. It's more than 200 lines of code and by a significant fraction the largest program in this book so far. What it does, however, is fairly simple. It's a straightforward extension of the `hexdump1gcc` program from Listing 9.1. If you recall, a hex dump program takes a file of any kind (text, executable, binary data, whatever) and displays it on the screen (here, on the Linux console) such that each byte in the program is given in hexadecimal. Listing 9.1 did that much. What `hexdump2gcc` adds is a second display column in which any printable ASCII characters (letters, numbers, symbols) are shown in their "true" form, with nonprintable characters represented by a space-holder character. This space-holder character is typically an ASCII period character, but that's merely a convention, and it could be anything at all.

If you save the executable file to disk from SASM, you can display a hex dump of any Linux file using `hexdump2gcc`, invoking it this way:

```
$./hexdump2gcc < filename
```

The I/O redirection operator < takes whatever data exists in the file you name to its right and pipes that data into standard input. The `hexdump2gcc` program takes data from standard input and prints it out in hex dump format, 16 bytes to a line, for as many lines as it takes to show the entire file.

For example, a hex dump of a typical makefile is shown here:

```
68 65 78 64 75 6D 70 32 3A 20 68 65 78 64 75 6D |hexdump2: hexdum|
70 32 2E 6F 0A 09 6C 64 20 2D 6F 20 68 65 78 64 |p2.o..ld -o hexd|
```

```
75 6D 70 32 20 68 65 78 64 75 6D 70 32 2E 6F 0A  |ump2 hexdump2.o.|
68 65 78 64 75 6D 70 32 2E 6F 3A 20 68 65 78 64  |hexdump2.o: hexd|
75 6D 70 32 2E 61 73 6D 0A 09 6E 61 73 6D 20 2D  |ump2.asm..nasm -|
66 20 65 6C 66 20 2D 67 20 2D 46 20 73 74 61 62  |f elf -g -F stab|
73 20 68 65 78 64 75 6D 70 32 2E 61 73 6D 0A 00  |s hexdump2.asm..|
```

Makefiles are pure text, so there aren't a lot of nonprintable characters in the dump. Notice, however, that tab and EOL, the two nonprintable characters generally present in Linux text files, are clearly visible, both in hex form in the left column and as periods in the right column. This is useful, because when the file is shown as pure text on the console, tab characters and EOL characters are invisible. (They have visible *effects*, but you can't see the characters themselves.) Having a hex dump of a file shows you precisely where any tab and EOL characters fall in the file and how many of them there are in any particular place.

Given the complexity of hexdump2gcc, it may be useful to show you how the program works through pseudocode before we get too deeply into the mechanics of how a procedure mechanism operates internally. Here is how the program works, from a (high) height:

```
As long as there is data available from stdin, do the following:
    Read data from stdin
    Convert data bytes to a suitable hexadecimal/ASCII display form
    Insert formatted data bytes into a 16-byte hex dump line
    Every 16 bytes, display the hex dump line
```

This is a good example of an early pseudocode iteration, when you know roughly what you want the program to do but are still a little fuzzy on exactly how to do it. It should give you a head-start understanding of the much more detailed (and *how*-oriented) pseudocode shown here:

```
Zero out the byte count total (RSI) and offset counter (RCX)
Call LoadBuff to fill a buffer with first batch of data from stdin
    Test number of bytes fetched into the buffer from stdin
        If the number of bytes was 0, the file was empty; jump to Exit
Scan:
    Get a byte from the buffer and put it in AL
    Derive the byte's position in the hex dump line string
    Call DumpChar to poke the byte into the line string
    Increment the total counter and the buffer offset counter
    Test and see if we've processed the last byte in the buffer:
        If so, call LoadBuff to fill the buffer with data from stdin
        Test number of bytes fetched into the buffer from stdin
            If the number of bytes was 0, we hit EOF; jump to Exit
    Test and see if we've poked 16 bytes into the hex dump line
        If so, call PrintLine to display the hex dump line
  Loop back to Scan
Exit:
    Shut down the program gracefully per Linux requirements
```

Unlike the examples of pseudocode I presented in Chapter 8, there are explicit references to procedures here. I think that they may be almost self-explanatory from context, which is the sign of a good procedure. For example, CALL LoadBuff means "execute a procedure that loads the buffer." That's what LoadBuff does, and that's *all* LoadBuff does. You don't have to confront all the details of how LoadBuff does its work. This makes it easier to grasp the larger flow of logic expressed by the program as a whole.

Look through the Listing 10.1 code proper and see if you can understand how the previous pseudocode relates to the actual machine instructions. Once you have a grip on that, we can begin talking about procedures in more depth.

Calling and Returning

Right near the beginning of the main program block in hexdump2gcc is a machine instruction I haven't used before in this book:

```
call LoadBuff
```

The label LoadBuff refers to a procedure. As you might have gathered (especially if you've programmed in an older language such as BASIC or FORTRAN), CALL LoadBuff simply tells the CPU to go off and execute a procedure named LoadBuff and then come back when LoadBuff finishes running. LoadBuff is defined earlier in Listing 10.1, but for clarity's sake in the following discussion I'll reproduce it here.

LoadBuff is a good first example of a procedure, because it's fairly straightline in terms of its logic, and it uses instructions and concepts that we've already discussed. Like assembly language programs generally, a procedure like LoadBuff starts executing at the top, runs sequentially through the instructions in its body, and at some point ends. The end does not necessarily have to be at the very bottom of the sequence of instructions, but the "end" of a procedure is always the place where the procedure goes back to the part of the program that called it. This place is wherever you see CALL's alter ego, RET (for RETurn).

```
LoadBuff:
    push rax        ; Save caller's RAX
    push rdx        ; Save caller's RDX
    push rsi        ; Save caller's RSI
    push rdi        ; Save caller's RDI
    mov rax,0       ; Specify sys_read call
    mov rdi,0       ; Specify File Descriptor 0: Standard Input
    mov rsi,Buff    ; Pass offset of the buffer to read to
    mov rdx,BUFFLEN   ; Pass number of bytes to read at one pass
    syscall         ; Call syscall's sys_read function fill the buffer
    mov r15,rax     ; Save # of bytes read from file for later
    xor rcx,rcx     ; Clear buffer pointer RCX to 0
```

```
pop rdi          ; Restore caller's RDI
pop rsi          ; Restore caller's RSI
pop rdx          ; Restore caller's RDX
pop rax          ; Restore caller's RAX
ret              ; And return to caller
```

In a very simple example like LoadBuff, RET is at the very end of the sequence of instructions in the procedure. However, RET may be anywhere in the procedure, and there are situations where you may find it simplest to have more than one RET instruction in a procedure. Which of the several RET instructions actually takes execution back to the caller depends on what the procedure does and what circumstances it encounters, but that's immaterial. Each RET is an "exit point" back to the code that called the procedure, and (more importantly) all RET instructions within a procedure take execution back to the very same location: the instruction immediately after the CALL instruction that invoked the procedure.

The important points of procedure structure are these:

- A procedure must begin with a label, which is (as you should recall) an identifier followed by a colon.

- Somewhere within the procedure, there must be at least one RET instruction.

- There may be more than one RET instruction. Execution has to come back from a procedure by way of a RET instruction, but there can be more than one exit door from a procedure. Which exit is taken depends on the procedure's flow of execution, but with conditional jump instructions you can have exits anywhere it satisfies the requirements of the procedure's logic. All those exits lead to the same place: the instruction after the CALL instruction that called the procedure.

- A procedure may use CALL to call another procedure. (More on this shortly.)

The means by which CALL and RET operate may sound familiar: CALL first pushes the address of the *next* instruction after itself onto the stack. Then CALL transfers execution to the address represented by the label that names the procedure, in this case LoadBuff. The instructions contained in the procedure execute. Finally, the procedure is terminated by the instruction RET. The RET instruction pops the return address off the top of the stack and transfers execution to that address. Since the address pushed was the address of the first instruction *after* the CALL instruction, execution continues as though CALL had not changed the flow of instruction execution at all. See Figure 10.1.

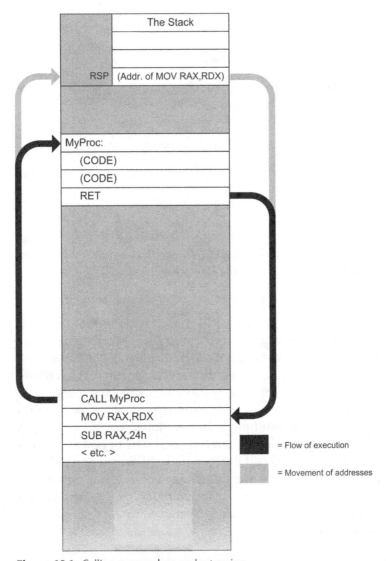

Figure 10.1: Calling a procedure and returning

Calls Within Calls

Within a procedure you can do anything that you can do within the main program itself. This includes calling other procedures from within a procedure and making SYSCALL calls to Linux kernel services.

There's a simple example in hexdump2gcc: The ClearLine procedure calls the DumpChar procedure to "clear" the hex dump line variable DumpLine:

```
ClearLine:
     push rax        ; Save all caller's r*x GP registers
```

```
        push rbx
        push rcx
        push rdx
        mov rdx,15     ; We're going to go 16 pokes, counting from 0
.poke:
        mov rax,0      ; Tell DumpChar to poke a '0'
        call DumpChar  ; Insert the '0' into the hex dump string
        sub rdx,1      ; DEC doesn't affect CF!
        jae .poke      ; Loop back if RDX >= 0
        pop rdx        ; Restore all caller's r*x registers
        pop rcx
        pop rbx
        pop rax
        ret            ; Go home
```

Basically, what `ClearLine` does is make a special-case use of the `DumpChar` procedure, which I'll explain in detail shortly. When filled with data and displayed to the console, the `DumpLine` variable looks like this:

```
75 6D 70 32 2E 61 73 6D 0A 09 6E 61 73 6D 20 2D |ump2.asm..nasm -|
```

Each two-character hex value, and each ASCII character in the ASCII column on the right, was inserted by a single call to `DumpChar`. It takes 16 calls to `DumpChar` to "fill" the `DumpLine` variable. At that point it can be displayed. After `DumpLine` is displayed to the console, `hexdump2gcc` continues its loop and begins filling `DumpLine` again. Every 16 calls to `DumpChar`, `hexdump2gcc` displays `DumpLine` to the console. . .except for the *last* time. A file being dumped to the console might not be (and usually isn't) a precise multiple of 16 bytes long. So the final display of `DumpLine` may be of a partial line of two, three, nine, eleven, or however many characters less than sixteen, which I call the "leftovers." When a partial line is displayed, the last several bytes in the line dump may be "old" data sent to the console on the previous display of `DumpLine`. To avoid this, `DumpLine` is cleared to zero values immediately after each time it is displayed in the terminal. This is what `ClearLine` does. After a call to `ClearLine`, `DumpLine` looks like this:

```
00 00 00 00 00 00 00 00 00 00 00 00 00 00 00 00 |................|
```

`ClearLine` does the simple and obvious thing: It calls `DumpChar` 16 times, each time passing `DumpChar` the value 0 in RAX. `DumpChar` "pokes" an ASCII equivalent of both the hex value 00 and an ASCII period to represent the 0 value in all positions in the ASCII column. 00 is not a displayable ASCII character and, as with all non-displayable characters, is represented by a period in the hexdump output.

The Dangers of Accidental Recursion

Calling procedures from within procedures requires you to pay at least a little attention to one thing: stack space. Remember that each procedure call pushes a 64-bit return address onto the stack. This return address is not removed from the stack until the RET instruction for that procedure executes. If you execute another CALL instruction before returning from a procedure, the second CALL instruction pushes another return address onto the stack. If you keep calling procedures from within procedures, one return address will pile up on the stack for each CALL until you start returning from all those *nested* procedures.

This used to be a real issue under DOS, when memory was scarce and programs might allocate only a few hundred bytes of memory to the stack, sometimes less. Each address pushed onto the stack makes the stack grow down toward the .data and .text sections of the program. Calling too "deep" could make the stack collide with data or code, causing a program crash that as often as not took DOS down with it. Under x64 Linux you have a *great* deal more memory, plus a virtual memory manager in the OS, and you would have to nest procedures literally millions deep to get into trouble, and that would be an ambitious program indeed.

However...you can still get in a similar sort of trouble by misusing an advanced programming technique called *recursion*. In recursion, a procedure calls *itself* to get its work done. This often seems peculiar to beginners, but it's a respected and legitimate way of expressing a certain kind of program logic. The trick with recursion, of course, is knowing when to stop. For every CALL to itself, a recursive procedure must eventually execute a RET. Even if the recursive procedure calls itself dozens or hundreds of times, as long as the CALL instructions balance the RET instructions, nothing bad will happen.

Problems begin when you write a recursive procedure badly and the logic that determines when to use that all-important RET instruction is miscoded. When to return is generally governed by a conditional jump instruction. Get the sense or the flag etiquette of that instruction wrong, and the procedure never returns but continues calling itself again and again and again. On a modern PC, an assembly language procedure can call itself a million times in a second or less. At some point, the stack reaches the extreme limit of its growth (set by the operating system) where it runs out of memory space. When that happens, Linux hands you a segmentation fault.

As I said, recursion is an advanced topic, and I'm not going to be explaining how to use it correctly in this book. I mention it here only because it's possible to use recursion *accidentally*. In keeping with our current example, suppose you were coding up ClearLine late at night, and at the point where ClearLine calls

DumpChar, you muddleheadedly write CALL ClearLine where you intended to write CALL DumpChar. Don't shake your head; I've been programming since 1970 and I've done it more than once. Sooner or later you'll do it too. Clearline was not designed to be recursive, so it will go into a not-quite-endless loop, calling itself until it runs out of stack memory and triggers a segmentation fault.

Add "accidental recursion" to the list of bugs you look for when Linux hands you a segmentation fault. It belongs to the category of bugs I call "uncommon but inevitable."

A Flag Etiquette Bug to Beware Of

And while we're talking bugs, the ClearLine procedure is pretty simple and does a simple job. It also provides a useful teaching moment about a flags-related bug that trips up beginners regularly. Take a look at the following alternate way of coding ClearLine:

```
ClearLine:
    push rax        ; Save all caller's r*x GP registers
    push rbx
    push rcx
    push rdx

    mov  rdx,15      ; We're going to go 16 pokes, counting from 0

.poke:
    mov  rax,0       ; Tell DumpChar to poke a '0'
    call DumpChar   ; Insert the '0' into the hex dump string
    sub  rdx,1      ; DEC doesn't affect CF!
    jae  .poke       ; Loop back if RDX >= 0

    pop  rdx        ; Restore caller's r*x GP registers
    pop  rcx
    pop  rbx
    pop  rax
    ret             ; Go home
```

Would this work? If you think so, think again. Yes, we're counting down from 15 to 0, making 16 passes through a simple loop. Yes, the DEC instruction is used a lot in loops, when we're counting down to zero. But this loop is a little different, as we need to do some work when the counter value in RDX is 0 and then decrement one more time. The conditional jump shown is JAE, Jump Above or Equal. It must jump back to Poke when the value in EDX goes *below* zero. DEC will count a counter down to zero and then below zero just fine. . .so why won't JAE jump after DEC? The sense is right.

The flag etiquette, however, is wrong. If you check the instruction reference in Appendix B for JAE, you'll see that it jumps when CF=0. The CPU doesn't understand the "sense" in JAE. It's not a mind; it's just a very small pile of very clean sand. All it understands is that the JAE instruction jumps when CF=0. Now, if you look up the DEC instruction in Appendix B and scrutinize the flags list, you'll see that DEC *doesn't affect CF at all*, and CF is what JAE examines before it decides whether to jump or not jump.

This is why we use the SUB instruction to decrement the counter register in this case, because SUB *does* affect CF and allows the JAE instruction to work correctly. There are no speed issues; SUB is precisely as fast as DEC. The lesson here is that you need to understand the ways that the conditional jump instructions interpret the various flags. The sense of a jump can be deceptive. It's the flag etiquette that matters.

Procedures and the Data They Need

Programs get their work done by acting on data: data in buffers, data in named variables, and data in registers. Procedures are often created to do a single type of manipulation on a particular type of data. Programs that call such procedures treat them as data meat-grinders: Data of one sort goes in, and transformed data of another sort comes out.

In addition, data is often handed to a procedure to control or direct the work that it does. A procedure may need a count value to know how many times to execute an operation, for example, or it may need a bit mask to apply to some data values for some reason, and it may not be precisely the same bit mask every time.

When you write procedures, you need to decide what data the procedure needs to do its work and how that data will be made available to the procedure. There are two general classes of data in assembly work (and in most programming in non-exotic languages) by method of access: global and local.

Global data is very common in pure assembly work, especially for smallish programs like the ones I'm presenting in this book. Global data is accessible to any code anywhere in the program. A global data item is defined in the .data or .bss sections of the program. CPU registers are also containers for global data, because the registers are part of the CPU and may be accessed from anywhere in a program.

The notion of global data gets more complex when you separate a program into a main program and multiple groups of procedures called *libraries*, as I'll explain a little later in this chapter.

But for simple programs, the obvious way to pass data to a procedure is often the best: Place the data in one or more registers and then call the procedure.

We've seen this mechanism at work already, in making calls to Linux kernel services through the SYSCALL instruction. For console input, you place the service number in RAX, the file descriptor in RDI, the address of a string in RSI, and the length of the string in RDX. Then you make the call with SYSCALL.

It's no different for ordinary procedures. You write a procedure under the assumption that when the procedure begins running, the values that it needs will be in particular registers. You have to make sure that the code calling the procedure places the right values in the right registers before calling the procedure, but it's really no more complex than that.

Tables, buffers, and other named data items are accessed from procedures just as they are from any other part of the program, via memory addressing expressions "between the brackets."

Saving the Caller's Registers

Once you start writing significant programs in assembly, you'll realize that you can never have enough registers, and (unlike higher-level languages like C and Pascal) you can't just create more when you need them. Registers have to be used carefully, and you'll find that within any program of significant complexity, all registers are generally in use all of the time.

Ducking out into a procedure from inside your main program (or from inside another procedure) carries a specific and subtle problem. You can call a procedure from anywhere—which means that *you won't always know what registers are already in use when the procedure is called*.

Or will you?

There is a convention for which registers must be preserved within a procedure and which do not. This convention is part of the x86-x64 System V ABI application binary interface) and I will explain it in detail in Chapters 11 and 12. Some registers are considered "volatile," meaning that they can be changed by a procedure, and others are "nonvolatile," which means they must be preserved. Hang on; it's coming.

If a procedure only examines a register value (but doesn't change it), preserving it doesn't need to be done. For example, a procedure may assume that a certain register contains a counter value that it needs to index into a table, and it can use that register freely as long as no changes to its value are made. However, whenever a register is changed by a procedure (unless the caller explicitly expects a return value in a register), it should be saved and restored before the procedure executes RET to go back to the caller.

Saving the register values is done with PUSH:

```
push rbx
push rsi
push rdi
```

Each PUSH instruction pushes a 64-bit register value onto the stack. Those values will remain safely on the stack until they are popped back into the same registers just prior to returning to the caller:

```
pop rdi
pop rsi
pop rbx
ret
```

There's an absolutely crucial detail here, one that causes a multitude of very peculiar program bugs: *The caller's values must be popped from the stack in the reverse order from how they were pushed.* In other words, if you push RBX, followed by RSI, followed by RDI, you must pop them from the stack as RDI followed by RSI followed by RBX. The CPU will obediently pop values stored on the stack into any registers in any order that you write. But if you get the order wrong, you will essentially be *changing* the caller's registers instead of saving them. What had been in RBX may now be in RDI, and the caller's program logic may simply go berserk.

I showed how this happens when I originally explained the stack in Chapter 8, but it may not have sunk in at the time. Take a quick flip back to Figure 8.3 and see what happens in the rightmost column. The value of CX had been pushed onto the stack, but the next instruction was POP DX. What had been in CX was now in DX. If that's what you want, fine—and sometimes it may be the best way to solve a particular problem. But if you're pushing register values to preserve them, the order of the pushes and pops is absolutely critical.

The best way to approach preserving registers is to push/pop any register changed by the procedure within the procedure. This excludes registers that pass values to the procedure: they were changed deliberately by the caller just before the procedure call. Consider that a procedure is defined once but called many times from many other places in your code. If you try to save registers and the procedure changes *before* calling the procedure, you're going to have a whole lot more pushing and popping going on than if you preserve registers that a procedure uses *inside* the procedure.

Also, if a procedure passes a value back to the caller in a register, the caller assumes that the register's value will change and will make use of the new value in that register.

Oh, there's yet another wrinkle: Your procedures aren't the only ones that use—and change—registers. Linux has a hand in it too.

Preserving Registers Across Linux System Calls

Linux uses registers too. It does this pretty transparently to your own code. The only serious issue is knowing what registers are changed during system calls via the SYSCALL instruction and which registers are left alone. Alas, there's no simple answer. It depends completely on *which* system call you make.

But first and above all, the SYSCALL instruction itself makes use of two registers:

- SYSCALL stores the return address in the RCX register.
- SYSCALL stores RFlags in the R11 register.

This is the functional equivalent of SYSCALL pushing RCX and R11 on the stack. However, saving values in registers is *much* faster than pushing values on the stack. Popping values off the stack is also slow, so SYSCALL doesn't restore anything. Every time you execute SYSCALL, RCX and R11 will be clobbered.

And that's not all the clobbering involved in making a system call. Register usage during a system call falls into three categories:

- You need to pass parameters to the system call code in registers.
- The system call code itself makes use of some additional registers.
- The system call may return values in registers that your code might need.

The definition of SYSCALL system calls includes the specifics. This definition is part of the x86-64 System V ABI. If the larger body of your code makes use of a register that gets clobbered during a system call, you must either choose another register for use in the program body or save it to the stack with a PUSH instruction before setting up parameters and executing SYSCALL. After the system call, you must restore it via a POP instruction. Using the stack in this way may cause problems with stack alignment unless you understand what makes the stack aligned and how to keep it that way. I'll take that up in detail in Chapters 11 and 12.

There is also the issue of volatile versus nonvolatile registers, which I also cover in Chapters 11 and 12.

The process of making a system call via SYSCALL is not complex. However, the last time I looked, there were 335 of them. Each system call requires that certain things be passed to it in specific registers. That's a *lot* to remember. Mostly you'll need to look up the details of making system calls in a printed reference or online. One reference I recommend is here:

https://hackeradam.com/x86-64-linux-syscalls

Another is here:

https://blog.rchapman.org/posts/Linux_System_Call_Table_for_x86_64

Both are very large tables resembling spreadsheets, with columns for register usage and values required for each system call number.

Now, web pages do come and go and if you're using this book some years after it was published in 2023, the web pages cited may simply be gone. Do a web search on "system call table x64" and you'll find several. Make sure the table you use is for system calls and not userspace calls. Userspace calls are calls into the `glibc` code library used in C programming, which is a whole different story. Calling `glibc` from assembly is possible and often very useful. I'll have more to say about that in Chapter 12.

One serious caution if you've already done some Linux assembly work in 32-bit protected mode: *The x64 system call parameters are not the same as those in 32-bit x86*. In most cases, they're not even close.

In x64 Linux, there is a system for register usage: The system call number (in other words, which system call you're calling) is always in RAX. A system call will accept up to six parameters. The registers used to pass parameters are in this order: RDI, RSI, RDX, R10, R8, and R9. In other words, the first parameter is passed in RDI. The second parameter is passed in RSI, and so on.

No system call requires any parameters be passed to it on the stack.

Note: Whether or not a register (like R9, say) is used to pass a parameter to a system call, *that register is not preserved*. Only seven registers are preserved by Linux across a system call: R12, R13, R14, R15, RBX, RSP, and RBP.

After a SYSCALL, RAX will contain a return value. If RAX is negative, it indicates an error occurred during the call. For most system calls, a 0 value indicates success.

PUSHAD and POPAD Are Gone

I mentioned this in Chapter 8, but it's worth repeating: There are cases where a procedure uses most or all of the general-purpose registers. Prior to x64, there was a pair of instructions that could push and pop *all* 32-bit GP registers at one go. These are PUSHAD and POPAD. (Another instruction pair, PUSHA and POPA, would push and pop all 16-bit GP registers. They're gone too.)

Now that x64 has 15 GP registers, with each register requiring eight bytes on the stack, isn't this wasteful of stack space? Not necessarily. Yes, it takes time to push a register on the stack, but remember: In *every* case where you weigh whether one instruction takes more time to execute than another, you must consider how many times that instruction is executed. If an instruction lies within a tight loop that executes sequentially tens of thousands or millions of times, instruction speed is important. On the other hand, if an instruction is executed only a few times over the course of a program's run, its speed is at best a minor consideration and can usually be ignored.

Yes, PUSHAD and POPAD were convenient shortcuts. They're gone. You must now think carefully about what registers a procedure modifies and then individually push those registers onto the stack and individually pop them off the stack when the procedure returns.

For a good example, let's look at the `LoadBuff` procedure shown earlier in this chapter in `hexdump2gcc`. `LoadBuff` preserves four of the caller's registers:

RAX, RDX, RSI, and RDI. However, it makes changes to two other registers, RCX and R15, without preserving them.

Why? The RCX register contains a "global" value: the position of the next character to be processed in the file buffer variable Buff. LoadBuff is called when one buffer full of data has been completely processed, and a new load of data must be brought in from stdin. When the buffer is refilled, the buffer counter has to be reset to 0 so that the processing can begin again and work through the new data from its beginning. LoadBuff does this, and the cleared RCX is passed back to the caller.

R15 has a mission, too: It carries back the number of bytes loaded into Buff by the SYSCALL call to sys_read. The call to sys_read requests the number of bytes specified by the BUFFLEN equate near the beginning of the program. However, because few files will be exact multiples of BUFFLEN long, the number of bytes in the last batch of data brought from stdin will be less than BUFFLEN. This value is also considered global and is used by the main program to determine when the current buffer has been completely processed.

LoadBuff preserves registers on the stack and restores them before it returns to the code that called it. Now, there's no reason that the pushing and popping to preserve registers must always be done inside the procedure.

The calling code can preserve its own registers, and this is occasionally done. For example, consider this (fictional) sequence of instructions:

```
push rbx
push rdx
call CalcSpace
pop  rdx
pop  rbx
```

There is only one difference between preserving registers outside the procedure rather than inside: The code calling the procedure can choose which of its registers are in use and thus in need of preserving. Saving all registers would be a waste if not all registers are in use by the caller's code.

Now, there may be more than one call to CalcSpace within the program. Each such call requires this sequence of five instructions instead of only one. If preserving registers is done inside the procedure, the preservation requires only four instructions, period, irrespective of how many places in the code call the procedure. With modern x64 PCs, the difference in code size and speed will not be significant. The advantage to putting register preservation inside the procedure is that your main program code will be less cluttered.

There are no hard and fast rules for which registers to preserve, though there are strong recommendations in the x86-64 System V ABI. I'll discuss those recommendations in detail in Chapters 11 and 12. Some registers are *volatile* and do not need to be preserved. Some are *nonvolatile*, and should be preserved. Again, I'll come back to this in the next two chapters, which also take up important issues like stack alignment.

You need to know how the registers are being used at any given point in the program and code accordingly. (Taking good notes on register use as you design the program is important.) The only advice I would offer is conservative and errs on the side of avoiding bugs: Preserve any registers that you know are not being used globally nor being used to pass values back to the caller. The time taken by register preservation is minor compared to the aggravation of bugs caused by register conflicts.

Local Data

Local data, in contrast to global data, is data that is accessible (we say "visible") only to a particular procedure or in some cases a library. (Again, let's postpone the library discussion for the time being.) When procedures have local data, it's almost always data that is data placed on the stack when a procedure is called.

The PUSH instructions place data on the stack. When part of your code calls a procedure with the CALL instruction, it can pass data down to that procedure by using PUSH one or more times before the CALL instruction. The procedure can then access these PUSHed data items on the stack. However, a word of warning: The procedure can't just pop those data items off the stack into registers, because *the return address is in the way.*

Remember that the first thing CALL does is push the address of the next machine instruction onto the stack. When your procedure gets control, that return address is at the top of the stack (TOS, as we say) ready for the inevitable RET instruction to use to go home. Anything pushed onto the stack by the caller before the CALL instruction is *above* the return address. These items can still be accessed using ordinary memory addressing and the stack pointer RSP. You cannot, however, use POP to get at them without popping and re-pushing the return address. This works, and I've done it a time or two, but it's slow and also unnecessary, once you understand the nature of a "stack frame" and how to address memory within one. Again, I'll take up the notion of stack frames later in this book, as it is absolutely crucial once you begin calling library procedures written in C or other higher-level languages. For now, simply understand that global data is almost always defined in the .data and .bss sections of your program, whereas local data is placed on the stack for the "local" use of a particular call to a particular procedure. Local data takes some care and discipline to use safely, for reasons I'll explain later.

Placing Constant Data in Procedure Definitions

By now you're used to thinking of code as living in the `.text` section, and data as living in the `.data` or `.bss` sections. In almost all cases this is a good way to organize things, but there's no absolute demand that you separate code and data in this way. It's possible to define data within a procedure using NASM's pseudoinstructions, which include DB, DW, DD, and DQ. I've created a useful procedure that shows how this is done, and it's a good example of when to do it.

The `newlines` procedure allows you to issue some number of newline characters to `stdout`, specified by a value passed to the subroutine in RDX:

```
;-------------------------------------------------------------------
; Newlines: Sends between 1-15 newlines to the Linux console
; VERSION:  2.0
; UPDATED:  8/27/2022
; IN: EDX:  # of newlines to send, from 1 to 15
; RETURNS:  Nothing
; MODIFIES: RAX, RDI
; CALLS:    Kernel sys_write
; DESCRIPTION: The number of newline chareacters (0Ah) specified
; in RDX is sent to stdout using using SYSCALL sys_write. This
; procedure demonstrates placing constant data in the
; procedure definition itself, rather than in the .data or
; .bss sections.

newlines:

        cmp rdx,15      ; Make sure caller didn't ask for more than 15
        ja .exit        ; If so, exit without doing anything
        mov rsi,EOLs    ; Put address of EOLs table into ECX
        mov rax,1       ; Specify sys_write
        mov rdi,1       ; Specify stdout
        syscall         ; Make the kernel call
.exit:
        Ret             ; Go home!

EOLs db 10,10,10,10,10,10,10,10,10,10,10,10,10,10,10
```

The table EOLs contains 15 EOL characters. If you recall, when the EOL character is sent to `stdout`, the console interprets it as a newline, in which the cursor position of the console is bumped downward one line. The caller passes the desired number of newlines in RDX. The `newlines` procedure first checks to make sure that the caller hasn't requested more newlines than there are EOL characters in the table and then plugs the address of the EOLs table and the requested number into a conventional call to `sys_write` using SYSCALL. Basically, `sys_write` displays the first RDX characters of the EOLs table to the console, which interprets the data as RDX newlines.

Having the data right in the procedure means that it's easy to cut and paste the procedure definition from one program into another without leaving the essential table of EOL characters behind. Because the only code that ever uses the EOLs table is the newlines procedure itself, there's no benefit to placing the EOLs table in the more centrally visible .data section. And although the EOLs table is not local in the technical computer-science sense (it is not placed on the stack by a caller to newlines), it "looks" local and keeps your .data and .bss sections from becoming a little more cluttered with data that is referenced from within a single procedure only.

There is a complete program source file called newlinestest.asm ready to assemble in the listings archive for this book. (Build it with SASM.) It contains the newlines procedure, which will allow you to play around with it.

More Table Tricks

The hexdump2gcc program works very much like the hexdump1gcc program from Listing 9.1, but it has a few more tricks in its black bag. One worth noting lies in the definition of the hex dump line variable DumpLine:

```
DumpLine:    db " 00 00 00 00 00 00 00 00 00 00 00 00 00 00 00 00 "
DUMPLEN      EQU $-DumpLine
ASCLine:     db "|................|",10
ASCLEN       EQU $-ASCLine
FULLLEN      EQU $-DumpLine
```

What we have here is a variable declared in two parts. Each part may be used separately, or (as is usually done) the two parts may be used together. The first section of DumpLine is the string containing 16 hex digits. Its length is defined by the DUMPLEN equate. (Note that my personal convention is to place the names of equates in uppercase. Equates are not the same species of animal as variables, and I find it makes programs more readable to set equates off so that they can be told from variables at a glance. This is not a NASM requirement; you can name equates in lower or mixed case as you choose.)

The second section of DumpLine is the ASCII column, and it has its own label, ASCLine. A program that needed only the ASCII column could use the ASCLine variable all by itself, along with its associated length equate, ASCLEN. Now, because the two sections of DumpLine are adjacent in memory, referencing DumpLine allows you to reference both sections as a unit, say, when you want to send a line to stdout via SYSCALL. In this case, the equate that calculates the length of the whole line is FULLLEN.

It's useful to have a separate name for the two-line sections, because data is not written to nor read from the two sections in anything like the same ways. Take a look at the DumpChar procedure from hexdump2gcc:

```
DumpChar:
     push rbx     ; Save caller's RBX
     push rdi     ; Save caller's RDI

; First we insert the input char into the ASCII portion of the dump line
     mov bl,[DotXlat+rax]        ; Translate nonprintables to '.'
     mov [ASCLine+rdx+1],bl      ; Write to ASCII portion

; Next we insert the hex equivalent of the input char in the hex portion
; of the hex dump line:
     mov rbx,rax                 ; Save a second copy of the input char
     lea rdi,[rdx*2+rdx]         ; Calc offset into line string (RDX X 3)

; Look up low nybble character and insert it into the string:
     and rax,000000000000000Fh ; Mask out all but the low nybble
     mov al,[HexDigits+rax]      ; Look up the char equiv. of nybble
     mov [DumpLine+rdi+2],al     ; Write the char equiv. to line string

; Look up high nybble character and insert it into the string:
     and rbx,00000000000000F0h ; Mask out all the but 2nd-lowest nybble
     shr rbx,4                   ; Shift high 4 bits of byte into low 4 bits
     mov bl,[HexDigits+rbx]      ; Look up char equiv. of nybble
     mov [DumpLine+rdi+1],bl     ; Write the char equiv. to line string

; Done! Let's return:
     pop rdi      ; Restore caller's RDI
     pop rbx      ; Restore caller's RBX
     ret          ; Return to caller
```

Writing to the ASCII column is very simple, because each character in the ASCII column is a single byte in memory, and the effective address of any one position in ASCLine is easy to calculate:

```
mov [ASCLin+rdx+1],bl    ; Write to ASCII portion
```

Each position in the hex dump portion of the line, however, consists of three characters: a space followed by two hex digits. Considered as a table, addressing a specific entry in DumpLine requires a scale of 3 in the effective address calculation:

```
lea rdi,[rdx*2+rdx]    ; Calc offset into line string (RDX × 3)
```

Note here that RDX*2+RDX is equivalent to RDX × 3 as cited in the line's comment. The two parts of the hex dump line are dealt with very differently from a data manipulation standpoint, and they act together only when they are sent to stdout. It's useful, then, to give each of the two sections its own label. Structs in C and records in Pascal are handled very much the same way "under the skin."

The `DotXlat` table from `hexdump2gcc` is another example of character translation and, as with all such translation tables, expresses the rules needed to display all 256 different ASCII values consistently in a text line:

- All printable characters translate as themselves.

- All nonprintable characters (which include all control characters, and all characters from 127 and up) translate as ASCII periods.

Local Labels and the Lengths of Jumps

Sooner or later, as your programs get longer and more complex, you're going to accidentally reuse a label. I won't be presenting any particularly long or complex programs in this book, so having problems with code labels conflicting with one another won't be a practical issue here. But as you begin to write more serious programs, you'll eventually be writing hundreds or even (with some practice and persistence) thousands of lines of assembly code in a single source code file. You will soon find that duplicate code labels will be a problem. How will you always remember that you've already used the label `Scan` on line 187 of a 2,732-line program?

You won't. And sooner or later (especially if you're crunching buffers and tables a lot), you'll try and use the label `Scan` again. NASM will call you on it with an error.

This is a common enough problem (especially with obviously useful labels such as `Scan`) that NASM's authors created a feature to deal with it: *local labels*. Local labels are based on the fact that nearly all labels in assembly work (outside of names of subroutines and major sections) are "local" in nature, by which I mean that they are only referenced by jump instructions that are *very* close to them—perhaps only two or three instructions away. Such labels are usually parts of tight loops and are not referenced from far away in the code and are often referenced from only one place.

Here's an example, from the main body of `hexdump2gcc`:

```
; Go through the buffer and convert binary byte values to hex digits:
Scan:
    xor rax,rax                    ; Clear RAX to 0
    mov al,[Buff+rcx]              ; Get a byte from the buffer into AL
    mov rdx,rsi                    ; Copy total counter into RDX
    and rdx,000000000000000Fh      ; Mask out lowest 4 bits of char counter
    call DumpChar                  ; Call the char poke procedure

; Bump the buffer pointer to the next char and see if buffer's done:
    inc rsi            ; Increment total chars processed counter
```

```
    inc rcx               ; Increment buffer pointer
    cmp rcx,r15           ; Compare with # of chars in buffer
    jb .modTest           ; If we've processed all chars in buffer...
    call LoadBuff         ; ...go fill the buffer again
    cmp r15,0             ; If r15=0, sys_read reached EOF on stdin
    jbe Done             ; If we get EOF, we're done

; See if we're at the end of a block of 16 and need to display a line:
.modTest:
    test rsi,000000000000000Fh ; Test 4 lowest bits in counter for 0
    jnz Scan             ; If counter is *not* modulo 16, loop back
    call PrintLine       ; ...otherwise print the line
    call ClearLine       ; Clear hex dump line to 0's
    jmp Scan             ; Continue scanning the buffer
```

Note that the label .modTest has a period in front of it. This period marks it as a *local label*. A local label is local to the first *nonlocal* label (that is, the first label not prefixed by a period; we call these *global*) that precedes it in the code. In this particular case, the global label to which .modTest belongs is Scan. The previous block is the portion of the main body of the program that scans the input file buffer, formats the input data into lines of 16 bytes, and displays those lines to the console.

In what way does a global label "own" a local label? It's a question of visibility within the source code: A local label cannot be referenced from higher in the source code file than the global label that owns it, which, again, is the first global label above it in the file.

In this case, the local label .modTest cannot be referenced above the global label Scan. This means there could conceivably be a second label .modTest in the program, on the "other side" of Scan. As long as a global label exists between two local labels with the same name, NASM has no trouble distinguishing them.

Local labels may also exist within procedures. In another example from hexdump2gcc, there is a local label .poke in the ClearLine procedure. It belongs to the ClearLine label and thus cannot be referenced from any other procedure elsewhere in the program or library. (Don't forget that procedure names are global labels.) This isolation within a single procedure isn't immediately obvious, but it's true and stems from the fact that "below" a procedure in a program or library there is always either another procedure or the _start or main label that marks the beginning of the main program. It's obvious once you see it drawn out, as I've done in Figure 10.2.

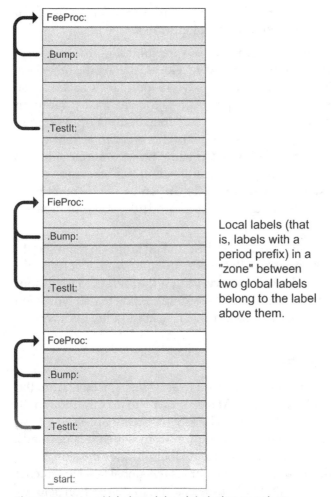

Figure 10.2: Local labels and the globals that own them

Here are some notes on local labels:

- Local labels within procedures are *at least* local to the procedures in which they are defined. (This is the whole point of Figure 10.2.) You may, of course, have global labels within procedures. Keep in mind that this will limit the visibility of local labels even further.

- It may seem peculiar, but it's perfectly legal and often helpful to define global labels that are never referenced, simply to provide ownership of local labels. If you're writing a simple-ish utility program that executes in straight-through fashion without a lot of jumping or long-distance looping back, you may go a long way without needing to insert a global label. I like to use global labels to set off major functional parts of a program, whether those labels are ever called or not. This allows me to use local labels freely within those major functional modules.

■ If you're writing dense code with a lot of intermixed global and local labels, be careful that you don't try to JMP to a local label on the other side of a global label. This is one reason *not* to have 15 local labels called .scan or .loopback within one part of a program—you can easily get them confused, and in trying to jump to one five instructions up, you may unknowingly be jumping to one seven instructions *down*. NASM won't warn you if there is a local label with the same name on your side of a global label and you try to jump to a local label on the other side of the global label. Bugs like this can be insanely difficult to find sometimes. Like any tool, local labels have to be used mindfully to be of greatest benefit.

■ Here's a rule of thumb that I use: Local labels and all jumps to them should occur within a single screen's worth of code. In other words, you should be able to see both a local label and everything that refers to it without scrolling your program editor. This is just a rough guide to help you keep sense in your programs, but I've found it very useful in my own work.

"Forcing" Local Label Access

Every so (not very) often, you may find the need to access a local label from the "other side" of its global label owner. NASM offers a way to do this, though I'll admit that I've never had the need to do it. The key to forcing access to a local label outside of its scope (the area of your program from which it is normally visible) is understanding how NASM treats local labels "under the skin."

A local label has an implicit definition that includes the global label to which it belongs. The local label .modTest that I discussed earlier in this section belongs to the global label Scan. Internally, NASM knows .modtest as Scan.modTest. If there were another .modtest local label elsewhere in the program (belonging, let's say, to a global label Calc), you could force a jump to it by including the name of its owner in the jump instruction:

```
jne Calc.modTest
```

In a sense, under the covers, a local label is just the "tail" of a global label. If you need to, you can access a local label by prepending the label of its global owner and thereby treating it as a global label.

Again, I've never had to do this and I don't consider it good practice, but it's good to know the ability is there if the need ever arises.

Short, Near, and Far Jumps

One of the oddest assembler errors you may ever encounter can appear in a completely correct program, and if you work with NASM long enough and create programs large enough, you *will* encounter it. Here it is:

```
error: short jump is out of range
```

This error occurs when a conditional jump instruction is too far from the label that it references, where "too far" means too many locations away in memory. This applies *only* to conditional jumps; the unconditional jump instruction JMP is not subject to this error.

The problem arises because of the different ways that NASM can generate a binary opcode for a particular conditional jump instruction. There are two different kinds of conditional jumps, based on how far away the jump target label is. A jump target that lies within 127 bytes of the conditional jump instruction is called a *short jump*. A jump target that is further away than 127 bytes but still within the current code segment is called a *near jump*.

There is a third kind of jump called a *far jump*, which involves leaving the current code segment entirely for whatever reason. In the old DOS real-mode world, this meant specifying both a segment address and an offset address for the jump target. Far jumps were not used very often, though I used them a time or two back in the DOS era. Don't forget that segments now belong to the operating system for its own use. In the 32-bit protected mode and 64-bit long mode, far jumps are *extremely* rare and involve all sorts of operating system complexity that I can't go into in this book. For userspace programming they're completely unnecessary.

The problem really lies with the difference between short and near jumps. A short conditional jump instruction generates a short—and hence compact—binary opcode. Short jump opcodes are always two bytes in size, no more. Near jump opcodes are either four or six bytes in size, depending on various factors. Compact code means fast code, and taking a short jump is (slightly) faster in most cases than taking a near jump. Furthermore, if you use short jumps most of the time, your executable files will be a little smaller.

Given that 90 percent or more of the conditional jump instructions you'll write target program locations only a few instructions away, it makes sense for NASM to generate opcodes for short jumps by default. In fact, *NASM generates opcodes for short jumps unless you explicitly tell it to use near jumps*. A near jump is specified using the NEAR qualifier:

```
jne Scan      ; Jump within 127 bytes in either direction
jne near Scan ; Jump anywhere in the current code segment
```

Beginners tend to run into the "short jump out of range" error this way: You begin a program and put a label like Exit: at the end, expecting to jump to the Exit: label from several different parts of the program. When the program is new and still fairly small, it may work fine. However, eventually code added to the middle of the program forces conditional jumps near the beginning of the program more than 127 bytes away from the Exit: label at the end. Bang! NASM hands you the "short jump out of range" error.

The fix is easy: For any jump that NASM calls "out of range," insert the NEAR qualifier between the conditional jump instruction mnemonic and the target label. Leave the others alone.

Building External Procedure Libraries

You'll notice that the hexdump2gcc program given in Listing 10.1 has most of its code separated out into procedures. This is as it should be, for the sake of keeping the program comprehensible and maintainable. However, the procedures declared within the file hexdump2gcc.asm are usable only by the hexdump2gcc program itself. If you were to write a more powerful program that for whatever reason needed to display a hex/ASCII dump of some data, those procedures could be used again—just not while they're still inside the file hexdump2gcc.asm.

The answer is to move hexdump2gcc's procedures out of hexdump2gcc.asm entirely and place them in a separate source code file called a *library*. It may be full of procedures, but it has no main program portion and thus no _start: or main: label to indicate where execution begins. All it contains are procedures (and maybe some data definitions) so it cannot be translated by the linker into its own executable program.

Once you create library files containing procedures, there are two ways to use them:

- A library file can be assembled separately to a .o file, which in turn can be linked by the Linux linker into other programs that you may write in the future.

- A library file can be included in the source code file of the main program, using a directive called %INCLUDE. (I'll tell you how to use %INCLUDE very shortly.) This is what you must do to use libraries from programs written within SASM.

When Tools Reach Their Limits

As easy as it is for assembly language beginners to learn and use SASM (which is what SASM was created for), the SASM IDE has its shortcomings, and we're about to run into a significant one: *SASM cannot link multiple assembly object code files together into a single executable file*. Basically, except in very limited cases, it can't perform separate assembly.

I described the separate assembly process briefly back in Chapter 5 and show it pictorially in Figures 5.8 and 5.9. A single program might consist of three or four separate .asm source code files, each of which is assembled separately to a separate .o file. To produce the final executable file, the Linux linker ld weaves all of the .o files together, resolving all of the references from one to the other, finally creating the executable file.

Separate assembly is not fully supported by SASM.

I'm going to describe separate assembly of library files in detail later in this chapter. The examples will have to be built without SASM, using makefiles. Absent SASM, debugging will also be a challenge, and we'll talk about that as well. In the meantime, there is one trick that SASM has that will allow you to create separate libraries of procedures.

Using Include Files in SASM

NASM includes a directive that allows you to "include" a file into another file during an assembly operation. The %INCLUDE directive is followed by the name of a text file, in double quotes:

```
%INCLUDE "%textlibgcc.asm"
```

(Don't forget the double quotes!) Only source code text files can be used here. You can't include a binary file of any kind. What happens is that when NASM is assembling a source code file and encounters an %INCLUDE directive, it opens the file named by the %INCLUDE directive and begins pulling in text from the include file, line-by-line.

Note that the include file is *not* inserted into your main assembly language source file. Basically, when NASM encounters %INCLUDE, it stops assembling your main source file and begins assembling the include file. Once it has processed all the lines in the include file, it picks up right where it left off after the %INCLUDE directive and continues assembling your main source file.

Multiple include files are no problem; you can have as many %INCLUDE directives in a program source file as you want. You can also have %INCLUDE directives in a library file that is itself an include file, though done enough, your source code will get very messy, and I don't recommend it unless you have a very good reason to do so.

No special declarations are necessary in an include file, since in a utilitarian sense it's part of the source file that contains the %INCLUDE directive. For an example of an include file, see Listing 10.2, which is an include file library of procedures that are used in Listing 10.3 (hexdump3gcc.asm) to write text to the Linux console.

Listing 10.2: textlibgcc.asm

```
;  Library name     : textlibgcc
;  Version          : 2.0
;  Created date     : 5/9/2022
;  Last update      : 5/9/2023
;  Author           : Jeff Duntemann
;  Description      : A simple include library demonstrating the use of
;                   : the %INCLUDE directive within SASM
;
;  Note that this file cannot be assembled by itself, as SASM does not
;  support separate assembly. It can only be used as the target of an
;  %INCLUDE directive.
;


SECTION .bss              ; Section containing uninitialized data

     BUFFLEN    EQU 10h
     Buff       resb BUFFLEN


SECTION .data             ; Section containing initialised data

; Here we have 2 parts of a single useful data structure, implementing
; the text line of a hex dump utility. The first part displays 16 bytes
; in hex separated by spaces. Immediately following is a 16-character
; line delimited by vertical bar characters. Because they are adjacent,
; the 2 parts can be referenced separately or as a single contiguous
; unit. Remember that if DumpLine is to be used separately, you must
; append an EOL before sending it to the Linux console.

DumpLine:  db " 00 00 00 00 00 00 00 00 00 00 00 00 00 00 00 00 "
DUMPLEN     EQU $-DumpLine
ASCLine:   db "|................|",10
ASCLEN      EQU $-ASCLine
FULLLEN     EQU $-DumpLine


; The HexDigits table is used to convert numeric values to their hex
; equivalents. Index by nybble without a scale: [HexDigits+eax]
HexDigits: db "0123456789ABCDEF"


; This table is used for ASCII character translation, into the ASCII
; portion of the hex dump line, via XLAT or ordinary memory lookup.
; All printable characters "play through" as themselves. The high 128
; characters are translated to ASCII period (2Eh). The non-printable
; characters in the low 128 are also translated to ASCII period, as is
; char 127.
DotXlat:
     db 2Eh,2Eh,2Eh,2Eh,2Eh,2Eh,2Eh,2Eh,2Eh,2Eh,2Eh,2Eh,2Eh,2Eh,2Eh,2Eh
     db 2Eh,2Eh,2Eh,2Eh,2Eh,2Eh,2Eh,2Eh,2Eh,2Eh,2Eh,2Eh,2Eh,2Eh,2Eh,2Eh
     db 20h,21h,22h,23h,24h,25h,26h,27h,28h,29h,2Ah,2Bh,2Ch,2Dh,2Eh,2Fh
     db 30h,31h,32h,33h,34h,35h,36h,37h,38h,39h,3Ah,3Bh,3Ch,3Dh,3Eh,3Fh
```

```
        db 40h,41h,42h,43h,44h,45h,46h,47h,48h,49h,4Ah,4Bh,4Ch,4Dh,4Eh,4Fh
        db 50h,51h,52h,53h,54h,55h,56h,57h,58h,59h,5Ah,5Bh,5Ch,5Dh,5Eh,5Fh
        db 60h,61h,62h,63h,64h,65h,66h,67h,68h,69h,6Ah,6Bh,6Ch,6Dh,6Eh,6Fh
        db 70h,71h,72h,73h,74h,75h,76h,77h,78h,79h,7Ah,7Bh,7Ch,7Dh,7Eh,2Eh
        db 2Eh,2Eh,2Eh,2Eh,2Eh,2Eh,2Eh,2Eh,2Eh,2Eh,2Eh,2Eh,2Eh,2Eh,2Eh,2Eh
        db 2Eh,2Eh,2Eh,2Eh,2Eh,2Eh,2Eh,2Eh,2Eh,2Eh,2Eh,2Eh,2Eh,2Eh,2Eh,2Eh
        db 2Eh,2Eh,2Eh,2Eh,2Eh,2Eh,2Eh,2Eh,2Eh,2Eh,2Eh,2Eh,2Eh,2Eh,2Eh,2Eh
        db 2Eh,2Eh,2Eh,2Eh,2Eh,2Eh,2Eh,2Eh,2Eh,2Eh,2Eh,2Eh,2Eh,2Eh,2Eh,2Eh
        db 2Eh,2Eh,2Eh,2Eh,2Eh,2Eh,2Eh,2Eh,2Eh,2Eh,2Eh,2Eh,2Eh,2Eh,2Eh,2Eh
        db 2Eh,2Eh,2Eh,2Eh,2Eh,2Eh,2Eh,2Eh,2Eh,2Eh,2Eh,2Eh,2Eh,2Eh,2Eh,2Eh
        db 2Eh,2Eh,2Eh,2Eh,2Eh,2Eh,2Eh,2Eh,2Eh,2Eh,2Eh,2Eh,2Eh,2Eh,2Eh,2Eh
        db 2Eh,2Eh,2Eh,2Eh,2Eh,2Eh,2Eh,2Eh,2Eh,2Eh,2Eh,2Eh,2Eh,2Eh,2Eh,2Eh


SECTION .text          ; Section containing code


;-------------------------------------------------------------------
; ClearLine:    Clear a hex dump line string to 16 0 values
; UPDATED:      5/9/2023
; IN:           Nothing
; RETURNS:      Nothing
; MODIFIES:     Nothing
; CALLS:        DumpChar
; DESCRIPTION:  The hex dump line string is cleared to binary 0 by
;               calling DumpChar 16 times, passing it 0 each time.

ClearLine:
    push rax        ; Save all caller's r*x GP registers
    push rbx
    push rcx
    push rdx

    mov rdx,15      ; We're going to go 16 pokes, counting from 0
.poke:
    mov rax,0       ; Tell DumpChar to poke a '0'
    call DumpChar   ; Insert the '0' into the hex dump string
    sub rdx,1       ; DEC doesn't affect CF!
    jae .poke       ; Loop back if RDX >= 0

    pop rdx         ; Restore all caller's GP registers
    pop rcx
    pop rbx
    pop rax
    ret             ; Go home


;-------------------------------------------------------------------
; DumpChar:     "Poke" a value into the hex dump line string.
; UPDATED:      5/9/2023
; IN:           Pass the 8-bit value to be poked in RAX.
;               Pass the value's position in the line (0-15) in RDX
```

```
; RETURNS:       Nothing
; MODIFIES:      RAX, ASCLine, DumpLine
; CALLS:         Nothing
; DESCRIPTION:   The value passed in RAX will be put in both the hex dump
;                portion and in the ASCII portion, at the position passed
;                in RDX, represented by a space where it is not a
;                printable character.

DumpChar:
    push rbx     ; Save caller's RBX
    push rdi     ; Save caller's RDI

; First we insert the input char into the ASCII portion of the dump line
    mov bl,[DotXlat+rax]    ; Translate nonprintables to '.'
    mov [ASCLine+rdx+1],bl    ; Write to ASCII portion

; Next we insert the hex equivalent of the input char in the hex portion
; of the hex dump line:
    mov rbx,rax              ; Save a second copy of the input char
    lea rdi,[rdx*2+rdx]      ; Calc offset into line string (RDX X 3)

; Look up low nybble character and insert it into the string:
    and rax,000000000000000Fh ; Mask out all but the low nybble
    mov al,[HexDigits+rax]     ; Look up the char equiv. of nybble
    mov [DumpLine+rdi+2],al    ; Write the char equiv. to line string

; Look up high nybble character and insert it into the string:
    and rbx,00000000000000F0h ; Mask out all the but 2nd-lowest nybble
    shr rbx,4                  ; Shift high 4 bits of rbx into low 4 bits
    mov bl,[HexDigits+rbx]     ; Look up char equiv. of nybble
    mov [DumpLine+rdi+1],bl    ; Write the char equiv. to line string

;Done! Let's go home:
    pop rdi      ; Restore caller's RDI
    pop rbx      ; Restore caller's RBX
    ret          ; Return to caller


;-----------------------------------------------------------------
; PrintLine:     Displays DumpLine to stdout
; UPDATED:       5/9/2022
; IN:            DumpLine, FULLEN
; RETURNS:       Nothing
; MODIFIES:      Nothing
; CALLS:         Kernel sys_write
; DESCRIPTION:   The hex dump line string DumpLine is displayed to stdout
;                using syscall function sys_write. Registers used
;                are preserved, along with RCX & R11.
```

```
PrintLine:
    ; Alas, we don't have pushad anymore.
    push rax
    push rbx
    push rcx         ; syscall clobbers
    push rdx
    push rsi
    push rdi
    push r11         ; syscall clobbers

    mov rax,1        ; Specify sys_write call
    mov rdi,1        ; Specify File Descriptor 1: Standard output
    mov rsi,DumpLine ; Pass address of line string
    mov rdx,FULLLEN  ; Pass size of the line string
    syscall          ; Make kernel call to display line string

    pop r11          ; syscall clobbers
    pop rdi
    pop rsi
    pop rdx
    pop rcx          ; syscall clobbers
    pop rbx
    pop rax
    ret              ; Return to caller


;-------------------------------------------------------------------
; LoadBuff:    Fills a buffer with data from stdin via syscall sys_read
; UPDATED:     5/9/2023
; IN:          Nothing
; RETURNS:     # of bytes read in R15
; MODIFIES:    RCX, R15, Buff
; CALLS:       syscall sys_read
; DESCRIPTION: Loads a buffer full of data (BUFFLEN bytes) from stdin
;              using syscall sys_read and places it in Buff. Buffer
;              offset counter RCX is zeroed, because we're starting in
;              on a new buffer full of data. Caller must test value in
;              R15: If R15 contains 0 on return, we've hit EOF on stdin.
;              < 0 in R15 on return indicates some kind of error.

LoadBuff:
    push rax         ; Save caller's RAX
    push rdx         ; Save caller's RDX
    push rsi         ; Save caller's RSI
    push rdi         ; Save caller's RDI

    mov rax,0        ; Specify sys_read call
    mov rdi,0        ; Specify File Descriptor 0: Standard Input
    mov rsi,Buff     ; Pass offset of the buffer to read to
```

```
        mov rdx,BUFFLEN  ; Pass number of bytes to read at one pass
        syscall          ; Call syscall's sys_read to fill the buffer
        mov r15,rax      ; Save # of bytes read from file for later
        xor rcx,rcx      ; Clear buffer pointer RCX to 0

        pop rdi          ; Restore caller's RDI
        pop rsi          ; Restore caller's RSI
        pop rdx          ; Restore caller's RDX
        pop rax          ; Restore caller's RAX
        ret              ; And return to caller
```

A program that uses a procedure library will be a lot smaller than one containing all the machinery in its single source code file. Listing 10.3 is basically hexdump2gcc.asm with its procedures taken out and gathered into the include file I presented as Listing 10.2.

Listing 10.3: hexdump3gcc.asm

```
; Executable name   : hexdump3gcc
; Version           : 2.0
; Created date       : 9/5/2022
; Last update       : 5/9/2023
; Author            : Jeff Duntemann
; Description        : A simple hex dump utility demonstrating the use
;                    : of code libraries by inclusion via %INCLUDE
;
; Build using SASM's standard x64 build setup
;
; Type or paste some text into Input window and click Build & Run.
;

SECTION .bss        ; Section containing uninitialized data

SECTION .data       ; Section containing initialised data

SECTION .text       ; Containing code

%INCLUDE "textlibgcc.asm"

GLOBAL main     ; You need to declare "main" here because SASM uses gcc
                ; to do builds.


;-------------------------------------------------------------------
; MAIN PROGRAM BEGINS HERE
;-------------------------------------------------------------------

main:
    mov rbp, rsp; for correct debugging
```

```
; Whatever initialization needs doing before loop scan starts is here:
    xor r15,r15     ; Zero out r15,rsi, and rcx
    xor rsi,rsi
    xor rcx,rcx
    call LoadBuff   ; Read first buffer of data from stdin
    cmp r15,0       ; If r15=0, sys_read reached EOF on stdin
    jbe Exit

; Go through the buffer and convert binary byte values to hex digits:
Scan:
    xor rax,rax                 ; Clear RAX to 0
    mov al,[Buff+rcx]           ; Get a byte from the buffer into AL
    mov rdx,rsi                 ; Copy total counter into RDX
    and rdx,000000000000000Fh   ; Mask out lowest 4 bits of char counter
    call DumpChar               ; Call the char poke procedure

; Bump the buffer pointer to the next char and see if buffer's done:
    inc rsi         ; Increment total chars processed counter
    inc rcx         ; Increment buffer pointer
    cmp rcx,r15     ; Compare with # of chars in buffer
    jb .modTest     ; If we've processed all chars in buffer...
    call LoadBuff   ; ...go fill the buffer again
    cmp r15,0       ; If r15=0, sys_read reached EOF on stdin
    jbe Done        ; If we get EOF, we're done

; See if we're at the end of a block of 16 and need to display a line:
.modTest:
    test rsi,000000000000000Fh ; Test 4 lowest bits in counter for 0
    jnz Scan                    ; If counter is *not* modulo 16, loop back
    call PrintLine              ; ...otherwise print the line
    call ClearLine              ; Clear hex dump line to 0's
    jmp Scan                    ; Continue scanning the buffer

; All done! Let's end this party:
Done:
    call PrintLine   ; Print the final "leftovers" line

Exit:
    ret
```

Where SASM's Include Files Must Be Stored

One of the issues in any programming language that supports include files is where the assembler or compiler will look for those include files. With SASM you have two choices:

1. You can create and use include file libraries in the current working directory, that is, the directory where your primary source file lives. This is

what you should do when you're developing the library that will later be used as an include file.

2. You can use include file libraries that live in a directory created by SASM for that purpose when SASM is installed. Here's the directory:

```
/usr/share/sasm/include
```

No big deal, right? Well, there's a catch: You need to be logged in as root to drop an include file into SASM's include directory. It's outside the scope of this book to explain Linux commands in detail, so if you're fuzzy on getting root permissions, do a web search. The root account is automatically created when you install Linux; you have to "claim" it by giving it a password. Again, there are too many details for these pages, but there are tutorials online, and it's a skill you will need if you're going to do any kind of serious Linux programming.

So why bother with that hard-to-reach include directory? Simply this: if you keep your libraries in the working directories of several projects, a change made to one project's copy of a library will not happen to all the other copies of the same library elsewhere among your various projects. If you're careless about this, the copies of a given library will gradually "evolve" away from one another, and the procedures in that library will start to behave differently or cause bugs.

The temptation to apply "quick 'n' dirty" fixes to small problems in a source code file is strong. Don't do it—especially for include file libraries. Create and perfect an include file library as a project or part of a project, and then, with root permissions, drop it into SASM's include directory. That way, all your projects will use the very same copy of the include library.

The Best Way to Create an Include File Library

If you're going to develop an include-style procedure library from scratch with SASM, here's a tried-and-true process to use:

1. Design your procedures. I simply create a text document and type up descriptions of what the library's procedures must do, gradually refining the descriptions until the descriptions are actually code.

2. Open the sandbox program I described earlier, and enter your procedures' source code. If you've already written them as parts of other programs, copy/paste their source code into the new file.

3. Create simple "exercise" code in the body of the sandbox program that calls your procedures and puts them through their paces. Debug as you always do with the SASM debugger. This will reveal relatively simple booboos like pushing and popping registers in the wrong order, trashing the caller's registers, and so on.

4. Once the easy debugging is done, include the library source code into a "real" program and test the library procedures more thoroughly.

5. When you're satisfied that all the procedures work as designed, gather them together into a file *without* the sandbox framework, and drop them into SASM's include files directory.

6. Keep a copy of the new library somewhere else, somewhere you back up regularly.

7. If at any point you make *any* changes to the library source code, test the changes thoroughly and then drop the modified file into SASM's include directory, replacing the earlier version that's already there.

At this point we're going to set SASM aside for a while and talk about using separate assembly to link preassembled .o object code files into a single executable file. It's easy to become "spoiled" using SASM, because it places so many useful tools within one IDE—an IDE created specifically for a student's first steps in assembly language programming.

I will continue to present example code for use within SASM in this book, which is an introduction to computing and assembly language concepts. But you will need to know how separate assembly works, once you "graduate" from SASM to more complex IDEs and sophisticated programming techniques.

Separate Assembly and Modules

From the standpoint of the assembly process, each separate .asm file is considered a *module*, whether it contains a _start: or main: label and is thus a program or simply contains procedures. Each module contains code and possibly some data definitions. When all the declarations are done correctly, all of the modules may freely "talk" to one another via procedure calls, and any procedure may refer to any data definition anywhere among the files that the linker combines. (Local labels are still visible only to the global labels that own them.) Each executable file may contain only one _start: or main: label, so among the several modules linked into an executable file, only one may contain a _start: or main: label and thus be the program proper.

This sounds harder than it is. The trick is simply to get all the declarations right.

Global and External Declarations

And it's *much* less of a trick than it used to be. Back in the bad old DOS days, you had to define code segments and data segments for the use of your separately assembled libraries and make sure that those segments were marked as PUBLIC, and on and on and on. For 32-bit protected-mode and x64 long mode user-space programs under Linux, there is only *one* segment, containing code, data, and stack—literally everything that a program has. Most of the manual "connecting" that we used to have to do is now done automatically by NASM, the linker, and the Linux loader. Creating libraries is now a snap, no more complex than creating programs and in some ways even easier.

The very heart of programming in modules is "putting off" resolution of addresses until link time. You may already have experienced the problem of address resolution if you've begun writing your own programs in assembly. It can happen by accident: If you intend to write a procedure in a program but in your manic enthusiasm write the code that references that (as yet unwritten) procedure's label first, NASM will gleefully give you an error message:

```
error: symbol 'MyProc' undefined
```

In modular programming, you're frequently going to be calling procedures that don't exist anywhere in the source code file that you're actually working on. How to get past the assembler's watchdogs?

The answer is to declare a procedure *external*. This works very much like it sounds: The assembler is told that a given label will have to be found outside the program somewhere, in another module, later. Once told that, NASM is happy to give you a pass on an undefined label, for now. You've promised NASM that you'll provide it later, and NASM accepts your promise. (The linker will hold you to that promise during the link step.) NASM will flag the reference as external and keep going without calling foul on the undefined label.

The promise that you make to NASM looks like this:

```
EXTERN MyProc
```

Here, you've told the assembler that the label MyProc represents a procedure and that it will be found somewhere external to the current module. That's all the assembler needs to know to withhold its error message.

And having done that, the assembler's part in the bargain is finished. It leaves in place an empty socket in your program where the address of the external procedure may be plugged in later. I sometimes think of it as an eyelet where the external procedure will later hook in.

Over in the other module where procedure MyProc is actually defined, it isn't enough just to define the procedure. An eyelet needs a hook. You have to warn the assembler that MyProc will be referenced from outside the module. The assembler needs to forge the hook that will hook into the eyelet. You forge the hook by declaring the procedure *global*, meaning that other modules anywhere else in the program may freely reference the procedure. Declaring a procedure global is no more complex than declaring it external:

```
GLOBAL MyProc
```

A procedure that is declared as GLOBAL where it is defined may be referenced from anywhere its label is declared as EXTERN.

With both the hook and the eyelet in place, who actually connects them? The linker does that during the link operation. At link time, the linker takes the two .o files generated by the assembler, one from your program and the other from the module containing MyProc, and combines them into a single executable binary file. The number of .o files isn't limited to two; you can have almost any number of separately assembled external modules in a single program. (Again, only one of them—the program proper—can have a _start: or main: label.) When the executable file created by the linker is loaded and run, the program can call MyProc as cleanly and quickly as though both had been declared in the same source code file.

This process is summarized graphically in Figure 10.3.

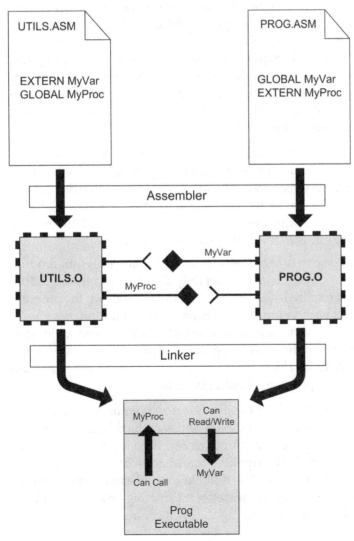

Figure 10.3: Connecting globals and externals

What works for procedures works for data as well, and it can work in either direction. Your program can declare any named variable as GLOBAL, and that variable may then be used by any module in which the same variable name is declared as external with the EXTERN directive. Finally, procedure libraries themselves may share data and procedures among one another in any combination, as long as all of the global and external declarations are handled correctly.

A program or module containing procedures or variables declared as global *exports* those items. Also, we say that a program or module that uses procedures or variables that are external to it *imports* those items.

The Mechanics of Globals and Externals

The hexdump2gcc program in Listing 10.1 contains several procedures. Let's pull those procedures out of the main program module and create a separately assembled library module from them so that we can see how it all works.

I've described the source code requirements of assembly language programs in detail in the last few chapters. Separately assembled library modules are similar to programs and may have all three of the sections (.text, .data, and .bss) that program modules may have. There are two major differences, however, concerning things that library modules lack:

- *External modules do not contain a main program and hence have no start address.* That is, no label _start: or main: exists in a library to indicate to the linker that this is the point at which code execution is to begin. Library modules are not intended to be run by themselves, so a _start: or main: label in a library module is both unnecessary and grounds for a fatal linker error if _start: already exists in the main program module.

- *External modules do not return to Linux.* If only the main program module contains a _start: or main: label, then only the main program module should contain the required sys_exit SYSCALL shutting down the program and giving control back to Linux. As a general rule of thumb, *never make a call to* sys_exit *from within a procedure,* whether it's a procedure located in the same module as the main program or a procedure located in an external library module. The main program gets permission to run from the OS, and the main program should give it back.

First, take a look at Listing 10.4. It's basically the same program as hexdump2gcc, but with its procedures gathered into a separately assembled library file called textlib.asm. It does precisely the same things as hexdump2gcc. It's smaller than hexdump2gcc from a source code standpoint, because most of its machinery has been outsourced. Outsourced where? You don't know yet—and you don't have to. NASM will put off resolving the addresses of the missing procedures as long as you list all the missing procedures using the EXTERN directive.

Listing 10.4: hexdump3.asm

```
;   Executable name : hexdump3
;   Version         : 2.0
;   Created date    : 9/14/2022
;   Last update     : 5/17/2023
;   Author          : Jeff Duntemann
;   Description     : A simple hex dump utility demonstrating the
;                   : use of eparately assembled code libraries via
;                   : EXTERN & GLOBAL
;
;   Build using these commands:
;     nasm -f elf64 -g -F dwarf hexdump3.asm
;     ld -o hexdump3 hexdump3.o <path>/textlib.o
;
SECTION .bss           ; Section containing uninitialized data

SECTION .data          ; Section containing initialised data

SECTION .text          ; Section containing code

EXTERN ClearLine, DumpChar, LoadBuff, PrintLine
EXTERN Buff, BuffLength

GLOBAL _start:

_start:
    push rbp           ;Alignment prolog
    mov rbp,rsp
    and rsp,-16

; Whatever initialization needs doing before the loop scan starts
;    is here:
    xor r15,r15        ; Clear registers to initial 0
    xor rsi,rsi
    xor rcx,rcx
    call LoadBuff      ; Read first buffer of data from stdin
    cmp r15,0          ; If r15=0, sys_read reached EOF on stdin
    jbe Exit

; Go through the buffer and convert binary values to hex digits:
Scan:
    xor rax,rax               ; Clear RAX to 0
    mov al,[Buff+rcx]         ; Get a char from the buffer into AL
    mov rdx,rsi               ; Copy total counter into RDX
    and rdx,000000000000000Fh ; Mask out lowest 4 bits of char counter
    call DumpChar             ; Call the char poke procedure

; Bump the buffer pointer to the next character and see if the buffer
; is done:
    inc rsi                   ; Increment buffer pointer
```

```
    inc rcx                     ; Increment total chars processed counter
    cmp rcx,r15                 ; Compare with # of chars in buffer
    jb modTest                  ; If we've processed all chars in buffer
    call LoadBuff               ; go fill the buffer again
    cmp r15,0                   ; If r15=0, sys_read reached EOF on stdin
    jbe Done                    ; If we get EOF, we're done

; See if we're at the end of a block of 16 and need to display a line:
modTest:
    test rsi,000000000000000Fh ; Test 4 lowest bits in counter for 0
    jnz Scan                    ; If counter is *not* modulo 16, loop back
    call PrintLine              ; ...otherwise print the line
    call ClearLine              ; Clear hex dump line to 0's
    jmp Scan                    ; Continue scanning the buffer

; All done! Let's end this party:
Done:
    call PrintLine              ; Print the "leftovers" line

Exit:
    mov rsp,rbp                 ; Epilog
    pop rbp

    mov rax,60                  ; Code for Exit system call
    mov rdi,0                   ; Return a code of zero
    syscall                     ; Make system call
```

External declarations of multiple items may be put on a single line, separated by commas, as in hexdump3:

```
EXTERN ClearLine, DumpChar, PrintLine
```

There does not have to be a single EXTERN directive. Several may exist in a module; each external identifier, in fact, may have its own EXTERN directive. It's up to you. When you have a longish list of external identifiers, however, don't make this mistake, which is an error:

```
EXTERN InitBlock, ReadBlock, ValidateBlock, WriteBlock, CleanUp,
ShowStats, PrintSummary          ; ERROR!
```

EXTERN declarations cannot span line boundaries. (In fact, almost nothing in assembly language can span line boundaries, especially with NASM. Pascal and C programmers run up against this peculiarity fairly often when they're assembly language first-timers.) If you have too many external declarations to fit on a single line with a single EXTERN, place additional EXTERN directives on following lines.

To link hexdump3 into a functioning executable program, we have to create an external library module for each of its procedures. All that's needed are the

procedures and their data in the proper sections and the necessary GLOBAL declarations. That's what's in Listing 10.5.

Listing 10.5: textlib.asm

```
;  Module name      : textlib.asm
;  Version          : 2.0
;  Created date     : 9/14/2022
;  Last update      : 5/9/2023
;  Author           : Jeff Duntemann
;  Description      : A simple procedure library demonstrating the use
;                   : of separately assembled code libraries via EXTERN
;
;  Build using this command:
;    nasm -f elf64 -g -F dwarf textlib.asm
;
;


SECTION .bss                 ; For containing uninitialized data

    BUFFLEN  EQU 10h          ; We read the input file 16 bytes at a time
    Buff:    resb BUFFLEN     ; Reserve memory for the input file read
                             ; buffer

SECTION .data                ; For containing initialised data

; Here we have two parts of a single useful data structure, implementing
; the text line of a hex dump utility. The first part displays 16 bytes
; in hex separated by spaces. Immediately following is a 16-character
; line delimited by vertical bar characters. Because they are adjacent,
; they can be referenced separately or as a single contiguous unit.
; Remember that if DumpLine is to be used separately, you must append an
; EOL before sending it to the Linux console.

DumpLine:    db " 00 00 00 00 00 00 00 00 00 00 00 00 00 00 00 00 "
DUMPLEN      EQU $-DumpLine
ASCLine:     db "|................|",10
ASCLEN       EQU $-ASCLine
FULLLEN      EQU $-DumpLine

; The equates shown above must be applied to variables to be exported:
DumpLength: dq DUMPLEN
ASCLength:  dq ASCLEN
FullLength: dq FULLLEN
BuffLength: dq BUFFLEN

; The HexDigits table is used to convert numeric values to their hex
; equivalents. Index by nybble without a scale, e.g.: [HexDigits+rax]
HexDigits:   db "0123456789ABCDEF"
```

```
; This table allows us to generate text equivalents for binary numbers.
; Index into the table by the nybble using a scale of 4:
; [BinDigits + rcx*4]
BinDigits:  db "0000","0001","0010","0011"
            db "0100","0101","0110","0111"
            db "1000","1001","1010","1011"
            db "1100","1101","1110","1111"


; Exported data items and procedures:
GLOBAL  Buff, DumpLine, ASCLine, HexDigits, BinDigits
GLOBAL  ClearLine, DumpChar, NewLines, PrintLine, LoadBuff


; This table is used for ASCII character translation, into the ASCII
; portion of the hex dump line, via XLAT or ordinary memory lookup.
; All printable characters "play through" as themselves. The high 128
; characters are translated to ASCII period (2Eh). The non-printable
; characters in the low 128 are also translated to ASCII period, as is
; char 127.
    DotXlat:
    db 2Eh,2Eh,2Eh,2Eh,2Eh,2Eh,2Eh,2Eh,2Eh,2Eh,2Eh,2Eh,2Eh,2Eh,2Eh,2Eh
    db 2Eh,2Eh,2Eh,2Eh,2Eh,2Eh,2Eh,2Eh,2Eh,2Eh,2Eh,2Eh,2Eh,2Eh,2Eh,2Eh
    db 20h,21h,22h,23h,24h,25h,26h,27h,28h,29h,2Ah,2Bh,2Ch,2Dh,2Eh,2Fh
    db 30h,31h,32h,33h,34h,35h,36h,37h,38h,39h,3Ah,3Bh,3Ch,3Dh,3Eh,3Fh
    db 40h,41h,42h,43h,44h,45h,46h,47h,48h,49h,4Ah,4Bh,4Ch,4Dh,4Eh,4Fh
    db 50h,51h,52h,53h,54h,55h,56h,57h,58h,59h,5Ah,5Bh,5Ch,5Dh,5Eh,5Fh
    db 60h,61h,62h,63h,64h,65h,66h,67h,68h,69h,6Ah,6Bh,6Ch,6Dh,6Eh,6Fh
    db 70h,71h,72h,73h,74h,75h,76h,77h,78h,79h,7Ah,7Bh,7Ch,7Dh,7Eh,2Eh
    db 2Eh,2Eh,2Eh,2Eh,2Eh,2Eh,2Eh,2Eh,2Eh,2Eh,2Eh,2Eh,2Eh,2Eh,2Eh,2Eh
    db 2Eh,2Eh,2Eh,2Eh,2Eh,2Eh,2Eh,2Eh,2Eh,2Eh,2Eh,2Eh,2Eh,2Eh,2Eh,2Eh
    db 2Eh,2Eh,2Eh,2Eh,2Eh,2Eh,2Eh,2Eh,2Eh,2Eh,2Eh,2Eh,2Eh,2Eh,2Eh,2Eh
    db 2Eh,2Eh,2Eh,2Eh,2Eh,2Eh,2Eh,2Eh,2Eh,2Eh,2Eh,2Eh,2Eh,2Eh,2Eh,2Eh
    db 2Eh,2Eh,2Eh,2Eh,2Eh,2Eh,2Eh,2Eh,2Eh,2Eh,2Eh,2Eh,2Eh,2Eh,2Eh,2Eh
    db 2Eh,2Eh,2Eh,2Eh,2Eh,2Eh,2Eh,2Eh,2Eh,2Eh,2Eh,2Eh,2Eh,2Eh,2Eh,2Eh
    db 2Eh,2Eh,2Eh,2Eh,2Eh,2Eh,2Eh,2Eh,2Eh,2Eh,2Eh,2Eh,2Eh,2Eh,2Eh,2Eh
    db 2Eh,2Eh,2Eh,2Eh,2Eh,2Eh,2Eh,2Eh,2Eh,2Eh,2Eh,2Eh,2Eh,2Eh,2Eh,2Eh


SECTION .text               ; For code


;-------------------------------------------------------------------
; ClearLine:    Clear a Full-Length hex dump line to 16 0 values
; UPDATED:      5/8/2023
; IN:           Nothing
; RETURNS:      Nothing
; MODIFIES:     Nothing
; CALLS:        DumpChar
; DESCRIPTION: The hex dump line string is cleared to binary 0.

ClearLine:
    push rax        ; Save all caller's r*x GP registers
    push rbx
```

```
        push rcx
        push rdx

        mov rdx,15       ; We're going to go 16 pokes, counting from 0
.poke:
        mov rax,0        ; Tell DumpChar to poke a '0'
        call DumpChar    ; Insert the '0' into the hex dump string
        sub rdx,1        ; DEC doesn't affect CF!
        jae .poke        ; Loop back if RDX >= 0

        pop rdx          ; Restore caller's r*x GP registers
        pop rcx
        pop rbx
        pop rax
        ret              ; Go home


;------------------------------------------------------------------
; DumpChar:      "Poke" a value into the hex dump line string DumpLine.
; UPDATED:       5/1/2023
; IN:            Pass the 8-bit value to be poked in RAX.
;                Pass the value's position in the line (0-15) in RDX
; RETURNS:       Nothing
; MODIFIES:      RAX
; CALLS:         Nothing
; DESCRIPTION:   The value passed in RAX will be placed in both the hex
;                dump portion and in the ASCII portion, at the position
;                passed in RCX, represented by a space where it is not a
;                printable character.

DumpChar:
        push rbx     ; Save caller's RBX
        push rdi     ; Save caller's RDI

; First we insert the input char into the ASCII portion of the dump line
        mov bl,[DotXlat+rax]        ; Translate nonprintables to '.'
        mov [ASCLine+rdx+1],bl      ; Write to ASCII portion

; Next we insert the hex equivalent of the input char in the hex portion
; of the hex dump line:
        mov rbx,rax                 ; Save a second copy of the input char
        lea rdi,[rdx*2+rdx]         ; Calc offset into line string (RDX X 3)

; Look up low nybble character and insert it into the string:
        and rax,000000000000000Fh ; Mask out all but the low nybble
        mov al,[HexDigits+rax]      ; Look up the char equivalent of nybble
        mov [DumpLine+rdi+2],al     ; Write the char equivalent to line string

; Look up high nybble character and insert it into the string:
        and rbx,00000000000000F0h ; Mask out all the but second-lowest nybble
        shr rbx,4                   ; Shift high 4 bits of char into low 4 bits
```

```
        mov bl,[HexDigits+rbx]     ; Look up char equivalent of nybble
        mov [DumpLine+rdi+1],bl    ; Write the char equiv. to line string

;Done! Let's go home:
        pop rdi        ; Restore caller's EDI register value
        pop rbx        ; Restore caller's EBX register value
        ret            ; Return to caller

;-------------------------------------------------------------------
; Newlines:     Sends between 1-15 newlines to the Linux console
; UPDATED:      5/9/2023
; IN:           # of newlines to send, from 1 to 15
; RETURNS:      Nothing
; MODIFIES:     Nothing
; CALLS:        Kernel sys_write
; DESCRIPTION:  The number of newline chareacters (0Ah) specified in
;               RDX is sent to stdout using using SYSCALL sys_write.
;               This procedure demonstrates placing constant data in
;               the procedure definition itself, rather than in .data
;               or .bss

Newlines:
        push rax       ; Push caller's registers
        push rsi
        push rdi
        push rcx       ; Used by syscall
        push rdx
        push r11       ; Used by syscall

        cmp rdx,15     ; Make sure caller didn't ask for more than 15
        ja .exit       ; If so, exit without doing anything
        mov rcx,EOLs   ; Put address of EOLs table into ECX
        mov rax,1      ; Specify sys_write call
        mov rdi,1      ; Specify File Descriptor 1: Standard output
        syscall        ; Make the system call

.exit:
        pop r11        ; Restore all caller's registers
        pop rdx
        pop rcx
        pop rdi
        pop rsi
        pop rax
        ret            ; Go home!

EOLs db 10,10,10,10,10,10,10,10,10,10,10,10,10,10,10
```

```
;------------------------------------------------------------------
; PrintLine:    Displays the hex dump line string via SYSCALL sys_write
; UPDATED:      5/9/2023
; IN:           Nothing
; RETURNS:      Nothing
; MODIFIES:     RAX RCX RDX RDI RSI
; CALLS:        SYSCALL sys_write
; DESCRIPTION:  The hex dump line string DumpLine is displayed to stdout
;                   using SYSCALL sys_write.


PrintLine:
    ; Alas, we don't have pushad anymore.
    push rax            ; Push caller's registers
    push rbx
    push rcx            ; Used by syscall
    push rdx
    push rsi
    push rdi
    push r11            ; Used by syscall

    mov rax,1           ; Specify sys_write call
    mov rdi,1           ; Specify File Descriptor 1: Standard output
    mov rsi,DumpLine    ; Pass offset of line string
    mov rdx,FULLLEN     ; Pass size of the line string
    syscall             ; Make system call to display line string

    pop r11             ; Restore callers registers
    pop rdi
    pop rsi
    pop rdx
    pop rcx
    pop rbx
    pop rax
    ret                 ; Go home!

;------------------------------------------------------------------
; LoadBuff:     Fills a buffer w. data from stdin via syscall sys_read
; UPDATED:      5/9/2023
; IN:           Nothing
; RETURNS:      # of bytes read in R15
; MODIFIES:     RAX, RDX, RSI, RDI, RCX, R15, Buff
; CALLS:        syscall sys_read
; DESCRIPTION:  Loads a buffer full of data (BUFFLEN bytes) from stdin
;                   using syscall sys_read and places it in Buff. Buffer
;                   oin on a new buffer full of data. Caller must test value
;                   in R15: If R15 contains 0 on return, we've hit EOF on
;                   stdin. Less than 0 in R15 on return indicates some kind
;                   of error.
```

```
LoadBuff:
     push rax          ; Save caller's RAX
     push rdx          ; Save caller's RDX
     push rsi          ; Save caller's RSI
     push rdi          ; Save caller's RDI

     mov rax,0         ; Specify sys_read call
     mov rdi,0         ; Specify File Descriptor 0: Standard Input
     mov rsi,Buff      ; Pass offset of the buffer to read to
     mov rdx,BUFFLEN   ; Pass number of bytes to read at one pass
     syscall           ; Call syscall's sys_read to fill the buffer
     mov r15,rax       ; Save # of bytes read from file for later
     xor rcx,rcx       ; Clear buffer pointer RCX to 0

     pop rdi           ; Restore caller's RDI
     pop rsi           ; Restore caller's RSI
     pop rdx           ; Restore caller's RDX
     pop rax           ; Restore caller's RAX
     ret               ; And return to caller
```

There are two lines of global identifier declarations, each line with its own
GLOBAL directive. As a convention in my own work, I separate declarations of
procedures and named data items and give each their own line. (Of course,
since GLOBAL declarations can't cross a text line, you may need more than just
two lines if you have lots of globals to export.)

```
GLOBAL  Buff, DumpLine, ASCLine, HexDigits, BinDigits
GLOBAL  ClearLine, DumpChar, NewLines, PrintLine, LoadBuff
```

Any procedure or data item that is to be exported (that is, made available
outside the module) must be declared on a line after a GLOBAL directive. You
don't have to declare everything in a module global. In fact, one way to manage
complexity and prevent certain kinds of bugs is to think hard about and strictly
limit what other modules can "see" inside their fellow modules. A module can
have "private" procedures and named data items that can be referenced only
inside the module. Making these items private is in fact the default: Just don't
declare them global.

Note well that all items declared global must be declared global *before* they
are defined in the source code. In practice, this means that you need to declare
global procedures at the top of the .text section, before any of the procedures
are actually defined. Similarly, all global named data items must be declared
in the .data section before the data items are defined.

Equates can be exported from modules, though this is an innovation of the
NASM assembler and not necessarily true of all assemblers. I think it's risky,

and instead of exporting equates, I define named variables to contain values defined by equates:

```
DumpLength:      dq DUMPLEN
ASCLength:       dq ASCLEN
FullLength:      dq FULLLEN
BuffLength:      dq BUFFLEN
```

If you want them to be exported, declare the variables GLOBAL. Note that the examples shown are *not* exported from textlib.asm and are just intended to illustrate the technique.

Linking Libraries into Your Programs

For all the previous example programs presented in this book, the makefiles are fairly simple. Here, for example, is the makefile for the hexdump2 program:

```
hexdump2: hexdump2.o
        ld -o hexdump2 hexdump2.o
hexdump2.o: hexdump2.asm
        nasm -f elf64 -g -F dwarf hexdump2.asm
```

The linker invocation converts HEXDUMP2.o into the executable file hexdump2, and that's all it has to do. Adding a library file complicates the picture slightly. The linker must now do some actual linking of multiple files. Additional library files in the .o format are added to the linker invocation after the name of the main program's linkable file. There can be any (reasonable) number of .o files in a link step. To build hexdump3, we need only two. Here is the makefile for hexdump3:

```
hexdump3: hexdump3.o
        ld -o hexdump3 hexdump3.o ../textlib/textlib.o
hexdump3.o: hexdump3.asm
        nasm -f elf64 -g -F dwarf hexdump3.asm
```

The textlib.o file is simply placed on the linker invocation line after the .o file for the program itself. There is one wrinkle in the previous makefile: The library file is on a path relative to the directory containing the hexdump3 project. Placing ../textlib/ in front of the textlib.o filename allows the linker to reach "up, across, and down" through the Linux file system into the project directory for the library. Otherwise, you'd have to place textlib.o in the same directory as hexdump3.o, or else copy it to a directory under usr/lib, which is on the default search path.

A directory under `usr/lib` would actually be a very good place for it, *once it's finished and thoroughly tested*—for large values of "thoroughly." While you're still actively working on a library, it's best to keep it in a project directory of its own within the same directory tree as all your other project directories so you can fix bugs and add features that don't occur to you until you've used it for a while building other programs.

The Dangers of Too Many Procedures and Too Many Libraries

In assembly programming as in life, there can be too much of a good thing. I've seen code libraries that consist of hundreds of files, each file containing a single procedure. These are not procedures that stand alone, either. They call one another right and left, in a thick web of execution that is very difficult to trace at the source code level, especially if you've inherited such a library from someone else and must get a grip (often very quickly) on how the mechanisms implemented by the library actually work. Absent very detailed text documentation, there's no "view from a height" to help you grasp what calls what from where. If the library came from somewhere else and is used like a "black box," that may not be a catastrophe, though I still like to know how any libraries that I use work.

There is, alas, a valid reason for creating single-procedure libraries like this: When you link a library to a program, *the whole library is added to the executable file*, even those procedures and data definitions that are never referenced from the main program. If every procedure is assembled separately into its own cozy little `.o` file, the linker will add *only* those procedures to your program that will actually be called by (and thus executed by) the program.

Much depends on where your code ends up. If your goal is the smallest possible executable file, this is significant, and there are some continents in the assembly language world (especially those relating to embedded systems) where every byte counts and "dead code" that never runs adds needless cost to the low-end hardware on which the code must run.

Assembly language code size won't be an issue on ordinary Linux PCs with 16 gigabytes of memory and a terabyte of disk. If that's where your code will run, you may be better off having fewer libraries and more comprehensible source code, even if you end up with a few thousand bytes of code in your executable files that never actually meet the CPU face-to-face.

The Art of Crafting Procedures

There's a little more to creating procedures than simply slicing out a section of code from one of your programs and making a CALL and RET sandwich out of it. The primary purpose of the whole idea of procedures is to make your code more maintainable, by gathering together instructions that serve a common purpose into named entities. Don't forget about the Martians and how they abducted my hapless APL text formatter in 1977. Maintainability is probably the single toughest nut to crack in software design, and maintainability depends utterly on comprehensibility. The whole idea in crafting libraries of procedures is to make your code comprehensible—primarily to you but very possibly to other people who may inherit or will attempt to use your code.

So in this section, I'm going to talk a little bit about how to think about procedures and the process of their creation, with code maintainability in mind.

Maintainability and Reuse

The single most important purpose of procedures is to manage complexity in your programs by replacing a sequence of machine instructions with a descriptive name. The close runner-up is code reuse. There's no point in writing the same common mechanisms from scratch every time you begin a new project. Write 'em once, write 'em well, and use 'em forever.

The two purposes interact. Code reuse aids code maintainability in several ways:

- Reuse means that there is less code in total to maintain across the breadth of all your projects.

- Reuse maintains your time and effort invested in debugging.

- Reuse forces you to maintain certain coding conventions across your projects over time (because your libraries require it), which gives your projects a "family resemblance" to one another that makes them easier to grasp after you've been away from them for a while.

- Reuse means that you will have fewer code sequences that do pretty much the same thing but in slightly different ways.

This last point is subtle but important. When you're debugging, what you're constantly referring to in the back of your head is an understanding of how each section of your program works. You'd like this understanding to be unique to every program that you write, but it doesn't work that way. Memory is imprecise, and memories of separate but very similar things tend to blur together after a period of time. (Quick: Is that a 2001 Toyota 4Runner or a 2003 Toyota 4Runner?) In programming, details matter crucially, and in assembly language programming, there are *lots* of details. If you scratch-wrote a RefreshText procedure three times for three different programs that differ in only minor ways, you may be relying on an understanding of one RefreshText implementation while staring at another. The further back in time these similar-but-not-identical procedures go, the more likely you are to confuse them and waste time sorting out the little quirks of how each one operates.

If there's only one `RefreshText` procedure, however, there's only one understanding of `RefreshText` to be had. All of the reuse advantage points mentioned cook down to this: managing complexity by simply reducing the amount of complexity that must be managed.

Deciding What Should Be a Procedure

So when should a block of instructions be pulled out and made a procedure? There are no hard-and-fast rules, but here are some useful heuristics that are worth discussing:

- Look for actions that happen a lot within a program.
- Look for actions that may not happen a lot within any single program but that tend to happen in the same ways in many or most programs.
- When programs get large (and by "large" I mean beyond the tutorial book demo class; let's say 1,000 lines or so), look for functional blocks that can be made into procedures so that the overall flow of execution in the main program becomes shorter, simpler, and thus easier to understand. (More on this in a moment.)
- Look for actions within a program that may change over time in response to forces outside your control (data specifications, third-party libraries, things like that) and isolate those actions in procedures.

In short: Think big, and think long-term. You aren't going to be a beginner forever. Try to anticipate your programming efforts "down the road" and create procedures of general usefulness. "General" here means not only useful within the single program you happen to be working on right now, but also useful in programs that you will be writing in the future.

There's no "minimum size" for procedures if they're called frequently enough. Extremely simple procedures—even ones with as few as four or five instructions—don't themselves hide a great deal of complexity. They *do* give certain frequently used actions descriptive names, which is valuable in itself. They can also provide standard basic building blocks for the creation of larger and more powerful procedures. That said, a short code sequence (5 to 10 instructions) that is called only once or perhaps twice within a middling program of several hundred machine instructions is a poor candidate for being a procedure, unless it is a candidate for reuse in future programs. Then it belongs in a code library, and code can't be in a library unless it's in a procedure.

There isn't any "maximum size" for procedures either, and there are circumstances where very large procedures make sense, if they serve some well-defined purpose. Remember that procedures don't always need to be in libraries. You may find it useful to define large procedures that are called only once when your program becomes big enough to require breaking it down into functional chunks for comprehensibility's sake. A thousand-line assembly language program might split well into a sequence of seven or eight largish procedures. Each procedure is meant to be called only once from the main program, but this allows your main program to be short, easily graspable, and very indicative of what the program is doing:

```
Start:  call Initialize     ; Open spec files, create buffers
        call OpenFile        ; Open the target data file
Input:  call GetRec          ; Fetch a record from the open file
        cmp rax,0            ; Test for EOF on file read
        je Done             ; If we've hit EOF, time to shut 'er down
        call ProcessRec      ; Crunch the rec
        call VerifyRec       ; Validate the modified data against the spec
        call WriteRec        ; Write the modified record out to the file
        jmp Input           ; Go back and do it all again
Done:   call CloseFile       ; Close the opened file
        call CleanUp         ; Delete the temp files
        mov rax,60          ; Code for Exit system call
        mov rdi,0           ; Return a code of zero
        syscall             ; Make system call
```

This (imaginary) program body is clean and readable and provides a necessary view from a height when you begin to approach a thousand-line assembly language program. Remember that the Martians are always hiding somewhere close by, anxious to turn your programs into unreadable hieroglyphics.

There's no weapon against them with half the power of procedures.

Use Comment Headers!

As time goes on, you'll find yourself creating dozens or even hundreds of procedures in the cause of managing complexity. The libraries of "canned" procedures that most high-level language vendors supply with their compilers just don't exist with NASM. By and large, when you need some function or another, you'll have to write it yourself.

Keeping such a list of routines straight is no easy task when you've written them all yourself. You *must* document the essential facts about each individual procedure or you'll forget them, or you'll remember them incorrectly and act on bad information. (The resultant bugs are often devilishly hard to find because you're *sure* you remember everything there is to know about that procedure! After all, you *wrote* it!)

I powerfully recommend adding a comment header to every procedure you write, no matter how simple. Such a header should at the very least contain the following information:

- The name of the procedure
- The date it was last modified

- The name of each entry point, if the procedure has multiple entry points
- What the procedure does
- What data items the caller must pass to it to make it work correctly
- What data (if any) is returned by the procedure, and where that data is returned (for example, in register RCX)
- What registers or data items the procedure modifies
- What other procedures, if any, are called by the procedure
- Any "gotchas" that need to be kept in mind while writing code that uses the procedure
- In addition to that, other information is sometimes helpful in comment headers:

  - The version of the procedure, if you use versioning
  - The date it was created
  - The name of the person who wrote the procedure, if you're dealing with code shared within a team

A typical workable procedure header might look something like this:

```
;--------------------------------------------------------------------
; LoadBuff:    Fills a buffer with data from stdin via syscall sys_read
; UPDATED:     10/9/2022
; IN:          Nothing
; RETURNS:     # of bytes read in RAX
; MODIFIES:    RCX, R15, Buff
; CALLS:       syscall sys_read
; DESCRIPTION: Loads a buffer full of data (BUFFLEN bytes) from stdin
;              using syscall sys_read and places it in Buff. Buffer
;              offset counter RCX is zeroed, because we're starting in
;              on a new buffer full of data. Caller must test value in
;              RAX: If RAX contains 0 on return, we hit EOF on stdin.
;              < 0 in RAX on return indicates some kind of error.
```

A comment header does *not* relieve you of the responsibility of commenting the individual lines of code within the procedure! As I've said many times, it's a good idea to put a short comment to the right of every line that contains a machine instruction mnemonic, and also (in longer procedures) a comment block describing every major functional block within the procedure.

Simple Cursor Control in the Linux Console

As a segue from assembly language procedures into assembly language macros, I'd like to spend a little time on the details of controlling the Linux console display from within your programs. Let's return to our little greasy-spoon advertising display for Joe's diner. Let's goose it up a little, first clearing the Linux console and then centering the ad text on the cleared display. I'm going to present the same program twice, first with several portions expressed as procedures and later with the same portions expressed as macros.

Procedures first, as shown in Listing 10.6.

Listing 10.6: eattermgcc.asm

```
;   Executable name : eattermgcc
;   Version         : 2.0
;   Created date    : 6/18/2022
;   Last update     : 5/10/2023
;   Author          : Jeff Duntemann
;   Description     : A simple program in assembly for Linux, using
;                   : NASM 2.15, demonstrating the use of escape
;                   : sequences to do simple "full-screen" text output
;                   : to a terminal like Konsole.
;
;   Build using SASM's x64 build configuration.
;
;   Run by executing the executable binary file.
;

section .data       ; Section containing initialised data

        SCRWIDTH        equ 80                  ; Default is 80 chars wide
        PosTerm:        db 27,"[01;01H"         ; <ESC>[<Y>;<X>H
        POSLEN          equ $-PosTerm           ; Length of term position string
        ClearTerm:      db 27,"[2J"             ; <ESC>[2J
        CLEARLEN        equ $-ClearTerm         ; Length of term clear string
        AdMsg:          db "Eat At Joe's!"      ; Ad message
        ADLEN           equ $-AdMsg             ; Length of ad message
        Prompt:         db "Press Enter: "      ; User prompt
        PROMPTLEN       equ $-Prompt            ; Length of user prompt

; This table gives us pairs of ASCII digits from 0-80. Rather than
; calculate ASCII digits to insert in the terminal control string,
; we look them up in the table and read back two digits at once to
; a 16-bit register like DX, which we then poke into the terminal
; control string PosTerm at the appropriate place. See GotoXY.
; If you intend to work on a larger console than 80 X 80, you must
; add additional ASCII digit encoding to the end of Digits. Keep in
; mind that the code shown here will only work up to 99 X 99.
        Digits: db "00010203040506070809101112131415161718 19"
                db "20212223242526272829303132333435363738 39"
                db "40414243444546474849505152535455565758 59"
                db "60616263646566676869707172737475767778 7980"

SECTION .bss        ; Section containing uninitialized data
```

```
    SECTION .text        ; Section containing code


;--------------------------------------------------------------------
; ClrScr:      Clear the Linux console
; UPDATED:     9/13/2022
; IN:          Nothing
; RETURNS:     Nothing
; MODIFIES:    Nothing
; CALLS:       SYSCALL sys_write
; DESCRIPTION: Sends the predefined control Estring <ESC>[2J to the
;              console, which clears the full display

ClrScr:
    push rax         ; Save pertinent registers
    push rbx
    push rcx
    push rdx
    push rsi
    push rdi

    mov rsi,ClearTerm ; Pass offset of terminal control string
    mov rdx,CLEARLEN  ; Pass the length of terminal control string
    call WriteStr     ; Send control string to console

    pop rdi          ; Restore pertinent registers
    pop rsi
    pop rdx
    pop rcx
    pop rbx
    pop rax
    ret              ; Go home


;--------------------------------------------------------------------
; GotoXY:      Position the Linux Console cursor to an X,Y position
; UPDATED:     9/13/2022
; IN:          X in AH, Y in AL
; RETURNS:     Nothing
; MODIFIES:    PosTerm terminal control sequence string
; CALLS:       Kernel sys_write
; DESCRIPTION: Prepares a terminal control string for the X,Y
;              coordinates passed in AL and AH and calls sys_write
;              to position the console cursor to that X,Y position.
;              Writing text to the console after calling GotoXY will
;              begin display of text at that X,Y position.

GotoXY:
    push rax                 ; Save caller's registers
    push rbx
    push rcx
```

```
        push rdx
        push rsi

        xor rbx,rbx             ; Zero RBX
        xor rcx,rcx             ; Ditto RCX

; Poke the Y digits:
        mov bl,al               ; Put Y value into scale term RBX
        mov cx,[Digits+rbx*2]   ; Fetch decimal digits to CX
        mov [PosTerm+2],cx      ; Poke digits into control string

; Poke the X digits:
        mov bl,ah               ; Put X value into scale term EBX
        mov cx,[Digits+rbx*2]   ; Fetch decimal digits to CX
        mov [PosTerm+5],cx      ; Poke digits into control string

; Send control sequence to stdout:
        mov rsi,PosTerm         ; Pass address of the control string
        mov rdx,POSLEN          ; Pass the length of the control string
        call WriteStr           ; Send control string to the console

; Wrap up and go home:
        pop rsi                 ; Restore caller's registers
        pop rdx
        pop rcx
        pop rbx
        pop rax
        ret                     ; Go home


;-------------------------------------------------------------------
; WriteCtr:     Send a string centered to an 80-char wide Linux console
; UPDATED:      5/10/2023
; IN:           Y value in AL, String addr. in RSI, string length in RDX
; RETURNS:      Nothing
; MODIFIES:     PosTerm terminal control sequence string
; CALLS:        GotoXY, WriteStr
; DESCRIPTION:  Displays a string to the Linux console centered in an
;               80-column display. Calculates the X for the passed-in
;               string length, then calls GotoXY and WriteStr to send
;               the string to the console

WriteCtr:
        push rbx                ; Save caller's RBX
        xor rbx,rbx             ; Zero RBX
        mov bl,SCRWIDTH         ; Load the screen width value to BL
        sub bl,dl               ; Take diff. of screen width and string length
        shr bl,1                ; Divide difference by two for X value
        mov ah,bl               ; GotoXY requires X value in AH
        call GotoXY             ; Position the cursor for display
        call WriteStr           ; Write the string to the console
```

```
        pop rbx              ; Restore caller's RBX
        ret                  ; Go home


;----------------------------------------------------------------
; WriteStr:     Send a string to the Linux console
; UPDATED:      5/10/2023
; IN:           String address in RSI, string length in RDX
; RETURNS:      Nothing
; MODIFIES:     Nothing
; CALLS:        Kernel sys_write
; DESCRIPTION:  Displays a string to the Linux console through a
;               sys_write kernel call

WriteStr:
        push rax     ; Save pertinent registers
        push rdi
        mov rax,1    ; Specify sys_write call
        mov rdi,1    ; Specify File Descriptor 1: Stdout
        syscall      ; Make the kernel call
        pop rdi      ; Restore pertinent registers
        pop rax
        ret          ; Go home

global  main

main:
        push rbp        ; Prolog
        mov rbp, rsp    ; for correct debugging

; First we clear the terminal display...
        call ClrScr

; Then we post the ad message centered on the 80-wide console:
        xor rax,rax     ; Zero out RAX.
        mov al,12
        mov rsi,AdMsg
        mov rdx,ADLEN
        call WriteCtr

; Position the cursor for the "Press Enter" prompt:
        mov rax,0117h   ; X,Y = 1,23 as a single hex value in AX
        call GotoXY     ; Position the cursor

; Display the "Press Enter" prompt:
        mov rsi,Prompt      ; Pass offset of the prompt
        mov rdx,PROMPTLEN   ; Pass the length of the prompt
        call WriteStr       ; Send the prompt to the console
```

```
; Wait for the user to press Enter:
    mov rax,0       ; Code for sys_read
    mov rdi,0       ; Specify File Descriptor 0: Stdin
    syscall         ; Make kernel call

; And we're done!
Exit:
    pop rbp
    ret
```

There's some new machinery here. All the programs I've presented so far in this book simply send lines of text sequentially to standard output, and the console displays them sequentially, each line on the next line down, scrolling up from the bottom.

This can be very useful, but it isn't the best we can do. Back in Chapter 6, I briefly describe the way that the Linux console can be controlled by sending it "escape sequences" embedded in the stream of text traveling from your program to stdout. It would be useful to reread that "Terminal Control with Escape Sequences" section if it's been a while, as I won't recap deeply here.

The simplest example of an escape sequence for controlling the console clears the entire console display to blanks. (Basically, space characters.) In the eattermgcc program, this sequence is a string variable called ClearTerm:

```
ClearTerm:      db 27,"[2J"   ; <ESC>[2J
```

The escape sequence is four characters long. It begins with ESC, a nonprintable character that we usually describe by its decimal value in the ASCII table, 27. (Or hex, which is 1Bh.) Immediately following the ESC character are the three printable characters: [2J. They're printable, but they're not printed because they follow ESC. The console watches for ESC characters and interprets any characters following ESC in a special way, according to a large and very complicated scheme. Particular sequences represent particular commands to the console, like this one, which clears the display.

There is no marker at the end of an escape sequence to indicate that the sequence is finished. The console knows each and every escape sequence to the letter, including how long each is, and there are no ambiguities. In the case of the ClearTerm sequence, the console knows that when it sees the "J" character, the sequence is complete. It then clears its display and resumes displaying characters that your program sends to stdout.

Nothing special has to be done in terms of sending an escape sequence to the console. The escape sequence goes to stdout by way of SYSCALL, just as all other text does. You can embed escape sequences in the middle of printable text by careful arrangement of DB directives in the .text sections of your programs. This is important: Even though escape sequences are not shown on the console display, they must still be counted when you pass the length of a text sequence to sys_write via SYSCALL.

The escape sequence to clear the display is easy to understand, because it's always the same and always does the same thing. The sequence that positions the cursor is a lot trickier, because it takes parameters that specify the X,Y position to which the cursor is to be moved. Each of these parameters is a two-digit textual decimal number in ASCII that must be embedded in the sequence by your program before the sequence is sent to stdout. All of the trickiness in moving the cursor around the Linux console involves embedding those X and Y parameters in the escape sequence.

The default sequence as defined in eattermgcc is called PosTerm:

```
PosTerm:        db 27,"[01;01H"      ; <ESC>[<Y>;<X>H
```

As with ClearTerm, it begins with an ESC character. Sandwiched between the [character and the H character are the two parameters. The Y value comes first and is separated from the X value by a semicolon. Note well that these are *not* binary numbers, but two ASCII characters representing decimal numeric digits, in this case, ASCII 48 (0) and ASCII 49 (1). You can't just poke the binary value 1 into the escape sequence. The console doesn't understand the binary value 1 as ASCII 49. Binary values for the X and Y positions must be converted to their ASCII equivalents and then inserted into the escape sequence.

This is what the GotoXY procedure does. Binary values are converted to their ASCII equivalents by looking up the ASCII characters in a table. The Digits table presents two-digit ASCII representations of numeric values from 0 through 80. Values less than 10 have leading zeros, as in 01, 02, 03, and so on. Here's where the magic happens inside GotoXY:

```
; Poke the Y digits:
    mov bl,al                   ; Put Y value into scale term RBX
    mov cx,[Digits+rbx*2]       ; Fetch decimal digits to CX
    mov [PosTerm+2],cx          ; Poke digits into control string

; Poke the X digits:
    mov bl,ah                   ; Put X value into scale term EBX
    mov cx,[Digits+rbx*2]       ; Fetch decimal digits to CX
    mov [PosTerm+5],cx          ; Poke digits into control string
```

The X,Y values are passed in the two 8-bit registers AL and AH. Each is placed in a cleared RBX that becomes a term in an effective address starting at Digits. Because each element of the Digits table is two characters in size, we have to scale the offset by two.

The trick (if there is one) is bringing down both ASCII digits with one memory reference and placing them in 16-bit register CX. With the two ASCII digits in CX, we then poke them both simultaneously into their proper position in the escape sequence string. The Y value begins at offset 2 into the string, and the X value begins at offset 5.

Once the `PosTerm` string has been modified for a particular X,Y coordinate pair, the string is sent to `stdout` and interpreted by the console as an escape sequence that controls the cursor position. The next character sent to the console will appear at the new cursor position, and subsequent characters will follow at subsequent positions until and unless another cursor control sequence is sent to the console.

Make sure when you run programs that issue cursor control codes that your console window is larger than the maximum X and Y values that your cursor will take on, or else the lines will fold, and nothing will show up quite where you intend it to. The `eattermgcc` program has a `Digits` table good up to 80 × 80. If you want to work across a larger display, you'll have to expand the `Digits` table with ASCII equivalents of two-digit values up to 99. Because of the way the table is set up and referenced, you can only fetch two-digit values, and thus with the code shown here you're limited to a 99 × 99 character console.

This isn't a serious problem, since text-mode screens in Linux generally respect the ancient text-terminal standard of 80 × 24.

Console Control Cautions

This all sounds great—but it isn't quite as great as it sounds. The very fundamental control sequences like clearing the display and moving the cursor are probably universal and will likely work identically on any Linux console you might find. Certainly they work on GNOME Terminal and Konsole, the two most popular console terminal utilities for Debian-based Linux distros.

Unfortunately, the history of Unix terminals and terminal control is a very spotted story, and for the more advanced console control functions, the sequences may not be supported or may be different from one console implementation to another. To ensure that everything works, your programs would have to probe the console to find out what terminal spec it supports, and then issue escape sequences accordingly.

This is a shame. In Konsole, the following escape sequence turns the console background green:

```
GreenBack:    db 27,"[42m"
```

At least it does in Konsole. How universal this sequence and others like it are, I just don't know. Ditto the multitude of other console control commands, through which you can turn the PC keyboard LEDs on and off, alter foreground colors, display with underlining, and so on. More on this (in the terse Unix style) can be found in the Linux man pages under the keyword "console_codes." I encourage you to experiment, keeping in mind that different consoles (especially those on non-Linux Unix implementations) may react in different ways to different sequences.

Still, controlling console output isn't the worst of it. The holy grail of console programming is to create full-screen text applications that "paint" a form on the console, complete with data entry fields, and then allow the user to tab from one field to another, entering data in each field. This is made diabolically difficult in Linux by the need to access individual keystrokes at the console keyboard, through something called *raw mode*. Even explaining how raw mode works would take most of a chapter and involve a lot of fairly advanced Linux topics, for which I don't have space in this book.

The standard Unix way to deal with the console is a C library called ncurses, and while ncurses may be called from assembly, it's a fat and ugly thing indeed. A better choice for assembly programmers is a much newer library written specifically for NASM assembly, called LinuxAsmTools. It was originally written by Jeff Owens and does nearly all of what ncurses does without C's brute-force calling conventions and other boatloads of C cruft. LinuxAsmTools is free and open-source. Alas, you may have to hunt for it. Do a Google search for "Linux ASM Tools" and you should find a link, most likely to GitHub. The library has moved several times since I first discovered it in the mid-oughts, and I suspect it will move again.

Creating and Using Macros

There is more than one way to split an assembly language program into more manageable chunks. Procedures are the most obvious way and certainly the easiest to understand. The mechanism for calling and returning from procedures is built right into the CPU and is independent of any given assembler product.

Today's major assemblers provide another complexity-management tool: *macros*. Macros are a different breed of cat entirely. Whereas procedures are implemented by the use of the CALL and RET instructions built right into the instruction set, macros are a trick of the assembler and do not depend on any particular instruction or group of instructions.

Most simply put, a macro is a label that stands for some sequence of text lines. This sequence of text lines can be (but is not necessarily) a sequence of instructions. When the assembler encounters the macro label in a source code file, it replaces the macro label with the text lines that the macro label represents. This is called *expanding* the macro, because the name of the macro (occupying one text line) is replaced by several lines of text, which are then assembled just as though they had appeared in the source code file all along. (Of course, a macro doesn't have to be several lines of text. It can be only one—but then there's a lot less advantage to using them!)

Macros bear some resemblance to include files, like those I explained earlier in this chapter. You might think of a macro as an include file that's built into the source code file. It's a sequence of text lines that is defined once, given a descriptive name, and then dropped into the source code again and again as needed by simply using the macro's name.

This process is shown in Figure 10.4. The source code as stored on disk has a definition of the macro, bracketed between the %MACRO and %ENDMACRO directives. Later in the file, the name of the macro appears several times. When the assembler processes this file, it copies the macro definition into a buffer somewhere in memory. As it assembles the text read from disk, the assembler drops the statements contained in the macro into the text wherever the macro name appears. The disk file is not affected; the expansion of the macros occurs *only* in memory.

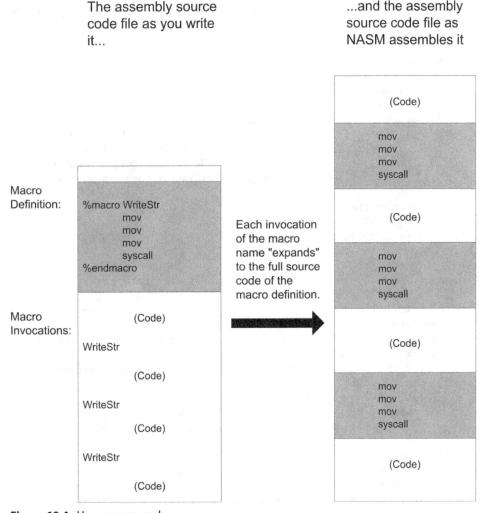

Figure 10.4: How macros work

The Mechanics of Macro Definition

A macro definition looks a little like a procedure definition, framed between a pair of special NASM directives: %MACRO and %ENDMACRO. Note that the %ENDMACRO directive is on the line *after* the last line of the macro. Don't make the mistake of treating %ENDMACRO like a label that marks the macro's last line.

One minor shortcoming of macros vis-à-vis procedures is that macros can have only *one* entry point. A macro, after all, is a sequence of code lines that are inserted into your program in the midst of the flow of execution. You don't call a macro, and you don't return from it. The CPU runs through it just as the CPU runs through any sequence of instructions.

Many or most procedures may be expressed as macros with a little care. In Listing 10.7, I've taken the program from Listing 10.6 and converted all the procedures to macros so that you can see the differences between the two approaches.

Listing 10.7: eatmacro.asm

```
;   Executable name : eatmacro
;   Version         : 2.0
;   Created date    : 10/11/2022
;   Last update     : 5/10/2023
;   Author          : Jeff Duntemann
;   Description     : A simple program in assembly for Linux, using
;                   : NASM 2.14.2, demonstrating the use of escape
;                   : escape sequences to do simple "full-screen" text
;                   ; output through macros rather than procedures
;
;   Build using these commands:
;      nasm -f elf -g -F dwarf eatmacro.asm
;      ld -o eatmacro eatmacro.o
;
;
section .data         ; Section containing initialised data

    SCRWIDTH:   equ 80              ; By default 80 chars wide
    PosTerm:    db 27,"[01;01H"     ; <ESC>[<Y>;<X>H
    POSLEN:     equ $-PosTerm       ; Length of term position string
    ClearTerm:  db 27,"[2J"         ; <ESC>[2J
    CLEARLEN:   equ $-ClearTerm     ; Length of term clear string
    AdMsg:      db "Eat At Joe's!"  ; Ad message
    ADLEN:      equ $-AdMsg         ; Length of ad message
    Prompt:     db "Press Enter: "  ; User prompt
    PROMPTLEN:  equ $-Prompt        ; Length of user prompt

; This table gives us pairs of ASCII digits from 0-80. Rather than
; calculate ASCII digits to insert in the terminal control string,
; we look them up in the table and read back two digits at once to
; a 16-bit register like DX, which we then poke into the terminal
; control string PosTerm at the appropriate place. See GotoXY.
```

```
; If you intend to work on a larger console than 80 X 80, you must
; add additional ASCII digit encoding to the end of Digits. Keep in
; mind that the code shown here will only work up to 99 X 99.
    Digits: db "00010203040506070809101112131415161718 19"
            db "20212223242526272829303132333435363738 39"
            db "40414243444546474849505152535455565758 59"
            db "60616263646566676869707172737475767778 7980"

SECTION .bss        ; Section containing uninitialized data

SECTION .text       ; Section containing code


;-------------------------------------------------------------------
; ExitProg:    Terminate program and return to Linux
; UPDATED:     10/11/2022
; IN:          Nothing
; RETURNS:     Nothing
; MODIFIES:    Nothing
; CALLS:       Kernel sys_exit
; DESCRIPTION: Calls syscall sys_edit to terminate the program and
;              return control to Linux

%macro  ExitProg 0
    mov rsp,rbp     ; Stack alignment epilog
    pop rbp

    mov rax,60      ; 60 = exit the program
    mov rdi,0       ; Return value in rdi 0 = nothing to return
    syscall         ; Call syscall sys_exit to return to Linux
%endmacro



;-------------------------------------------------------------------
; WaitEnter:   Wait for the user to press Enter at the console
; UPDATED:     10/11/2022
; IN:          Nothing
; RETURNS:     Nothing
; MODIFIES:    Nothing
; CALLS:       Kernel sys_read
; DESCRIPTION: Calls sys_read to wait for the user to type a newline
;              at the console

%macro WaitEnter 0
    mov rax,0       ; Code for sys_read
    mov rdi,0       ; Specify File Descriptor 0: Stdin
    syscall         ; Make kernel call
%endmacro
```

```
;-------------------------------------------------------------------
; WriteStr:      Send a string to the Linux console
; UPDATED:       5/10/2023
; IN:            String address in %1, string length in %2
; RETURNS:       Nothing
; MODIFIES:      Nothing
; CALLS:         Kernel sys_write
; DESCRIPTION:   Displays a string to the Linux console through a
;                sys_write kernel call

%macro WriteStr 2    ; %1 = String address; %2 = string length
    push r11     ; Save pertinent registers
    push rax
    push rcx
    mov rax,1    ; 1 = sys_write for syscall
    mov rdi,1    ; 1 = fd for stdout; i.e., write to the terminal window
    mov rsi,%1   ; Put address of the message string in rsi
    mov rdx,%2   ; Length of string to be written in rdx
    syscall      ; Make the system call
    pop rcx
    pop rax
    pop r11
%endmacro


;-------------------------------------------------------------------
; ClrScr:        Clear the Linux console
; UPDATED:       5/10/2023
; IN:            Nothing
; RETURNS:       Nothing
; MODIFIES:      Nothing
; CALLS:         Kernel sys_write
; DESCRIPTION:   Sends the predefined control string <ESC>[2J to the
;                console, which clears the full display

%macro ClrScr 0
    push rax     ; Save pertinent registers
    push rbx
    push rcx
    push rdx
    push rsi
    push rdi
; Use WriteStr macro to write control string to console:
    WriteStr ClearTerm,CLEARLEN
    pop rdi      ; Restore pertinent registers
    pop rsi
    pop rdx
    pop rcx
    pop rbx
    pop rax
%endmacro
```

```
;------------------------------------------------------------------
; GotoXY:       Position the Linux Console cursor to an X,Y position
; UPDATED:      10/11/2022
; IN:           X in %1, Y in %2
; RETURNS:      Nothing
; MODIFIES:     PosTerm terminal control sequence string
; CALLS:        Kernel sys_write
; DESCRIPTION:  Prepares a terminal control string for the X,Y
;               coordinates passed in AL and AH and calls sys_write to
;               position the console cursor to that X,Y position.
;               Writing text to the console after calling GotoXY will
;               begin display of text at that X,Y position.

%macro GotoXY 2 ; %1 is X value; %2 id Y value
    push rdx             ; Save caller's registers
    push rcx
    push rbx
    push rax
    push rsi
    push rdi
    xor rdx,rdx          ; Zero EDX
    xor rcx,rcx          ; Ditto ECX
; Poke the Y digits:
    mov dl,%2                ; Put Y value into offset term EDX
    mov cx,[Digits+rdx*2]    ; Fetch decimal digits to CX
    mov [PosTerm+2],cx       ; Poke digits into control string
; Poke the X digits:
    mov dl,%1                ; Put X value into offset term EDX
    mov cx,[Digits+rdx*2]    ; Fetch decimal digits to CX
    mov [PosTerm+5],cx       ; Poke digits into control string
; Send control sequence to stdout:
    WriteStr PosTerm,POSLEN
; Wrap up and go home:
    pop rdi              ; Restore caller's registers
    pop rsi
    pop rbx
    pop rcx
    pop rdx
%endmacro


;------------------------------------------------------------------
; WriteCtr:     Send a string centered to an 80-char wide Linux console
; UPDATED:      5/10/2023
; IN:           Y value in %1, String addr. in %2, string length in %3
; RETURNS:      Nothing
; MODIFIES:     PosTerm terminal control sequence string
; CALLS:        GotoXY, WriteStr
; DESCRIPTION:  Displays a string to the Linux console centered in an
;               80-column display. Calculates the X for the passed-in
;               string length, then calls GotoXY and WriteStr to send
;               the string to the console
```

```
%macro WriteCtr 3   ; %1 = row; %2 = String addr; %3 = String length
    push rbx         ; Save caller's RBX
    push rdx         ; Save caller's RDX
    mov rdx,%3       ; Load string length into RDX
    xor rbx,rbx      ; Zero RBX
    mov bl,SCRWIDTH  ; Load the screen width value to BL
    sub bl,dl        ; Calc diff. of screen width and string length
    shr bl,1         ; Divide difference by two for X value
    GotoXY bl,%1     ; Position the cursor for display
    WriteStr %2,%3   ; Write the string to the console
    pop rdx          ; Restore caller's RDX
    pop rbx          ; Restore caller's RBX
%endmacro


global  _start       ; Linker needs this to find the entry point!

_start:
    push rbp         ; Alignment prolog
    mov rbp,rsp
    and rasp,-16

; First we clear the terminal display...
    ClrScr
; Then we post the ad message centered on the 80-wide console:
    WriteCtr 12,AdMsg,ADLEN
; Position the cursor for the "Press Enter" prompt:
    GotoXY 1,23
; Display the "Press Enter" prompt:
    WriteStr Prompt,PROMPTLEN
; Wait for the user to press Enter:
    WaitEnter
; Aand we're done!
    ExitProg
```

Compare the macros in `eatmacro` with their procedure equivalents in `eattermgcc`. They've shed their RET instructions (and for those macros that invoke other macros, their CALL instructions) but for the most part consist of almost precisely the same code.

Macros are invoked simply by naming them. Again, don't use the CALL instruction. Just place the macro's name on a line:

```
ClrScr
```

The assembler will handle the rest.

Defining Macros with Parameters

Macros are for the most part a straight text-substitution trick, but text substitution has some interesting and sometimes useful wrinkles. One of these is the ability to pass parameters to a macro when the macro is invoked.

For example, in `eatmacro` there's an invocation of the macro `WriteCtr` with three parameters:

```
WriteCtr 12,AdMsg,ADDLEN
```

The literal constant 12 is passed "into" the macro and used to specify the screen row on which the centered text is to be displayed; in this case, line 12 from the top. You could replace the 12 with 3 or 16 or any other number less than the number of lines currently displayed in the Linux console. (If you attempt to position the cursor to a line that doesn't exist in the console, the results are hard to predict. Typically the text shows up on the bottom line of the display.) The other two parameters are passed the address and length of the string to be displayed.

Macro parameters are, again, artifacts of the assembler. They are not pushed on the stack or set into a shared memory area or anything like that. The parameters are simply placeholders for the actual values (called *arguments*) that you pass to the macro through its parameters.

Let's take a closer look at the `WriteCtr` macro to see how this works:

```
%macro WriteCtr 3   ; %1 = row; %2 = String addr; %3 = String length
    push rbx         ; Save caller's RBX
    push rdx         ; Save caller's RDX
    mov rdx,%3       ; Load string length into RDX
    xor rbx,rbx        ; Zero RBX
    mov bl,SCRWIDTH    ; Load the screen width value to BL
    sub bl,dl        ; Calc diff. of screen width and string length
    shr bl,1         ; Divide difference by two for X value
    GotoXY bl,%1     ; Position the cursor for display
    WriteStr %2,%3 ; Write the string to the console
    pop rdx          ; Restore caller's RDX
    pop rbx          ; Restore caller's RBX
%endmacro
```

So, where are the parameters? This is another area where NASM differs radically from Microsoft's MASM. MASM allows you to use symbolic names—such as the word `Row` or `StringLength`—to stand for parameters. NASM relies on a simpler system that declares the number of parameters in the definition of the macro and then refers to each parameter by number within the macro, rather than by some symbolic name.

In the definition of macro `WriteCtr`, the number 3 after the name of the macro indicates that the assembler is to look for three parameters. This number must be present—as 0—even when you have a macro like `ClrScr` with no parameters at all. *Every macro must have a parameter count.* Down in the definition of the macro, the parameters are referenced by number. `%1` indicates the first parameter used after the invocation of the macro name `WriteCtr`. `%2` indicates the second parameter, counting from left to right. `%3` indicates the third parameter, and so on.

The actual values passed into the parameters are referred to as *arguments*. Don't confuse the actual values with the parameters. If you understand Pascal, it's *exactly* like the difference between formal parameters and actual parameters. A macro's parameters correspond to Pascal's formal parameters, whereas a macro's arguments correspond to Pascal's actual parameters. The macro's parameters are the labels following the name of the macro in the line in which it is *defined*. The arguments are the values specified on the line where the macro is *invoked*.

Macro parameters are a kind of label, and they may be referenced anywhere *within* the macro—but *only* within the macro. In `WriteCtr`, the `%3` parameter is referenced as an operand to a `MOV` instruction. The argument passed to the macro in `%3` is thus loaded into register RDX.

Macro arguments may be passed as parameters to other macros. This is what happens within `WriteCtr` when `WriteCtr` invokes the macro `WriteStr`. `WriteStr` takes two parameters, and `WriteCtr` passes its parameters `%2` and `%3` to `WriteStr` as its arguments.

The Mechanics of Invoking Macros

You can pass a literal constant value as an argument to a macro, as the row value is passed to the macro `WriteCtr` in the `eatmacro` program. You can also pass a register name as an argument. This is legal and a perfectly reasonable invocation of `WriteCtr`:

```
mov al,4
WriteCtr al,AdMsg,ADLEN
```

Inside the `WriteCtr` macro, NASM substitutes the name of the AL register for the `%1` parameter:

```
GotoXY bl,%1  ; Position the cursor for display
```

becomes

```
GotoXY bl,al
```

Note well that all the usual rules governing instruction operands apply. Parameter `%1` can hold only an 8-bit argument, because ultimately `%1` is loaded into an 8-bit register inside `GotoXY`. You cannot legally pass register RBP or CX to `WriteCtr` in parameter `%1`, because you cannot directly move a 64-bit, 32-bit, or 16-bit register into an 8-bit register.

Similarly, you can pass a bracketed address as an argument:

```
WriteCtr [RowValue],AdMsg,ADLEN
```

This assumes, of course, that `RowValue` is a named variable defined as an 8-bit data item. If a macro parameter is used in an instruction requiring a 64-bit argument (as are `WriteCtr`'s parameters `%2` and `%3`), you can also pass labels representing 64-bit addresses or 64-bit numeric values.

When a macro is invoked, its arguments are separated by commas. NASM drops the arguments into the macro's parameters in order, from left to right. If you pass only two arguments to a macro with three parameters, you're likely to get an error message from the assembler, depending on how you've referenced the unfilled parameter. If you pass *more* arguments to a macro than there are parameters to receive the arguments, the extraneous arguments will be ignored.

Local labels Within Macros

The macros I included in `eatmacro.asm` were designed to be simple and fairly obvious. None of them contains any jump instructions at all, but code in macros can use conditional and unconditional jumps just as code in procedures or program bodies can. There is, however, an important problem with labels used inside macros: Labels in assembly language programs must be unique, and yet a macro is essentially duplicated in the source code as many times as it is invoked. This means there will be error messages flagging duplicate labels . . . unless a macro's labels are treated as local. *Local* items have no meaning outside the immediate framework within which they are defined. Labels local to a macro are not visible outside the macro definition, meaning that they cannot be referenced except from code within the `%MACRO`. . .`%ENDMACRO` bounds.

All labels defined within a macro are considered local to the macro and are handled specially by the assembler. Here's an example; it's a macro adaptation of a piece of code I presented earlier, for forcing characters in a buffer from lowercase to uppercase:

```
%macro UpCase 2       ; %1 = Address of buffer; %2 = Chars in buffer
        mov rdx,%1    ; Place the offset of the buffer into rdx
        mov rcx,%2    ; Place the number of bytes in the buffer into rcx
%%IsLC:cmp byte [rdx+rcx-1],'a'   ; Below 'a'?
        jb %%Bump                 ; Not lowercase. Skip
        cmp byte [rdx+rcx-1],'z'  ; Above 'z'?
        ja %%Bump                 ; Not lowercase. Skip
        sub byte [rdx+rcx-1],20h  ; Force byte in buffer to uppercase
%%Bump:dec rcx                    ; Decrement character count
        jnz %%IsLC                ; If more chars in the buffer, repeat
%endmacro
```

A label in a macro is made local by beginning it with two percent symbols: %%. When marking a location in the macro, the local label should be followed by a colon. When used as an operand to a jump or call instruction (such as JA, JB, and JNZ in the preceding), the local label is *not* followed by a colon. The important thing is to understand that unless the labels IsLC and Bump were made local to the macro by adding the prefix %% to each, there would be multiple instances of a label in the program (assuming that the macro was invoked more than once), and the assembler would generate a duplicate label error on the second and every subsequent invocation.

Because labels must in fact be unique within your program, NASM takes a local label such as %%Bump and generates a label from it that will be unique in your program. It does this by using the prefix ..@ plus a four-digit number and the name of the label. Each time your macro is invoked, NASM will change the number and thus generate unique synonyms for each local label within the macro. The label %%Bump, for example, might become ..@1771.Bump for a given invocation, and the number would be different each time the macro is invoked. This happens behind the scenes, and you'll rarely be aware that it's going on unless you read the code dump listing files generated by NASM.

Macro Libraries as Include Files

Just as procedures may be gathered into library modules external to your program, so may macros be gathered into macro libraries. A *macro library* is really nothing but a text file that contains the source code for the macros in the library. Unlike procedures gathered into a module, macro libraries are not separately assembled and must be passed through the assembler each time the program is assembled. This is a problem with macros in general, not only with macros that are gathered into libraries. Programs that manage complexity by dividing code up into macros will assemble more slowly than programs that have been divided up into separately assembled modules. Given the speed of 2020-era PCs, this is far less of a problem today than it was back in 1989 when I wrote the first edition of this book, but for very large projects it can affect the speed of the build.

Macro libraries are used by "including" them into your program's source code file. The means to do this is the %INCLUDE directive. The %INCLUDE directive precedes the name of the macro library:

```
%include "mylib.mac"
```

Technically this statement may be anywhere in your source code file, but you must keep in mind that all macros must be fully defined before they are invoked. For this reason, it's a good idea to use the %INCLUDE directive up near the top of your source code file's .text section, before any possible invocation of one of the library macros could occur.

If the macro file you want to include in a program is not in the same directory as your program, you may need to provide a fully qualified pathname as part of the %INCLUDE directive:

```
%include "../macrolibs/mylib.mac"
```

Otherwise, NASM may not be able to locate the macro file and will hand you an error message. (Do some research if you don't know how to create a fully qualified pathname in Linux, as it's not really a programming topic.)

Macros vs. Procedures: Pros and Cons

There are advantages to macros over procedures. One of them is speed. It takes time to execute the CALL and RET instructions that control entry to and exit from a procedure. In a macro, neither instruction is used. Only the instructions that perform the actual work of the macro are executed, so the macro's work is performed as quickly as possible.

There is a cost to this speed, and the cost is in extra memory used, especially if the macro is invoked a great many times. Notice in Figure 10.4 that three invocations of the macro WriteStr generate a total of 18 instructions in memory. If the macro had been set up as a procedure, it would have required the six instructions in the body of the procedure, plus one RET instruction and three CALL instructions to do the same work. This would require a total of eight instructions for the procedure implementation, and eighteen for the macro implementation. And if the macro were called five or seven times or more, the difference would grow. *Each time that a macro is called, all of its instructions are duplicated in the program yet another time.*

In short programs, this may not be a problem, and in situations where the code must be as fast as possible—as in graphics drivers—macros have a lot going for them, by eliminating the procedure overhead of calls and returns. It's a simple trade-off to understand: Think macros for speed and procedures for compactness.

On the other hand, unless you really *are* writing something absolutely performance-dependent—such as graphics drivers—this trade-off is minor to the point of insignificance. For ordinary software, the difference in size between a procedure-oriented implementation and a macro-oriented implementation might be only 2,000 or 3,000 bytes, and the speed difference would probably not be detectable. On modern CPUs, the performance of any given piece of software is *very* difficult to predict, and massive storage devices and memory systems make program size far less important than it was a generation ago. If you're trying to decide whether to go procedure or macro in any given instance, other factors than size or speed will predominate.

For example, I've always found macro-intensive software much more difficult to debug. Software tools don't necessarily deal well with macros. As an example, the Insight component of the Gdb debugger doesn't show expanded macro text in its source-code window. Insight wasn't designed with pure assembly debugging in mind (Gdb, like most Unix tools, has a powerful C bias), and when you step into a macro, *the source code highlighting simply stops*, until execution emerges from the macro. You thus can't step through a macro's code as you can step through procedure or program code. Gdb will still debug as always from the console window, but console debugging is a very painful process compared to the visual perspective available from SASM or Insight.

Finally, there's another issue connected with macros that's much harder to explain, but it's the reason I am famously uncomfortable with them: *Use macros too much, and your code will no longer look like assembly language*. Let's look again at the main program portion of the eatmacro.asm program, without its comments:

```
ClrScr
WriteCtr 12,AdMsg,ADLEN
GotoXY 1,23
WriteStr Prompt,PROMPTLEN
WaitEnter
ExitProg
```

That's the whole main program. The entire thing has been subsumed by macro invocations. Is this assembly language, or is it—good grief!—a dialect of BASIC?

I admit, I replaced the entire main program with macro invocations here to make the point, but it's certainly possible to create so many macros that your assembly programs begin to look like some odd high-level language. I actually used something similar to this back in the late 1970s when I was a programmer for Xerox. They had an in-house language that was basically an 8080 assembler with loads of macros for use on early (very slow; would you believe 1 megahertz?) 8080-based microcomputers. It worked. It *had* to, with that little computational power to do its processing.

The difficult truth is that macros can clarify what a program is doing, or, used to excess, they can totally obscure how things actually work "under the skin." In my projects, I use macros solely to reduce the clutter of very repetitive instruction sequences, especially things like setting up registers before making Linux system calls. The whole point of assembly programming, after all, is to foster a complete understanding of what's happening down where the software meets the CPU. Anything that impedes that understanding should be used carefully, expertly, and (most of all) *sparingly*—or you might just as well learn C.

Strings and Things

Those Amazing String Instructions

Most people, having learned a little assembly language, grumble about the seemingly huge number of instructions it takes to do anything useful. By and large, this is a legitimate gripe—and the major reason people write programs in higher-level languages such as Pascal and BASIC. The x64 instruction set, on the other hand, is full of surprises, and the surprise most likely to make apprentice assembly programmers gasp is the instruction group we call *string instructions*.

They alone, of all the instructions in the x64 instruction set, have the power to deal with long sequences of bytes, words, double words, or quad words at one time. Keep in mind that in assembly language, any contiguous sequence of bytes or larger units in memory may be considered a string—*not* simply sequences of human-readable characters. More amazingly, the string instructions deal with these large sequences of bytes or larger units in an extraordinarily compact way: by executing an instruction loop entirely *inside* the CPU! A string instruction is, in effect, a complete instruction loop baked into a single machine instruction.

The string instructions are subtle and complicated, and I won't be able to treat them exhaustively in this book. Much of what they do qualifies as an advanced topic. Still, you can get a good start on understanding the string instructions by using them to build some simple tools to add to your video toolkit.

Besides, for my money, the string instructions are easily the single most fascinating aspect of assembly language work.

The Notion of an Assembly Language String

Words fail us sometimes by picking up meanings as readily as a magnet picks up iron filings. The word *string* is a major offender here. It means roughly the same thing in all computer programming, but there are a multitude of small variations on that single theme. If you learned about strings in Pascal (as I did), you'll find that what you know isn't totally applicable when you program in C/C++, Python, BASIC, or (especially) assembly.

So here's the Big View: A *string* is any contiguous group of bytes in memory, containing any kind of data, of any arbitrary size that your operating system allows. (For modern Linux, that can be a *lot*.) The primary defining concept of an assembly language string is that its component bytes are right there in a row, with no interruptions.

That's pretty fundamental. Most high-level languages build on the string concept in several ways. Pascal implementations that descend from UCSD (and later Turbo) Pascal treat strings as a separate data type, with a length counter at the start of the string to indicate how many bytes are in the string. In C, a string has no length byte in front of it. Instead, a C string is said to end when a byte with a binary value of 0 is encountered. This will be important in assembly work, much of which relates intimately to C and the standard C library, where C's string-handling machinery lives. In BASIC, strings are stored in something called *string space*, which has a lot of built-in code machinery associated with it, to manage string space and handle the way-down-deep manipulation of string data.

When you begin working in assembly, you have to give up all that high-level language stuff. Assembly strings are just contiguous regions of memory. They start at some specified address, go for some number of bytes, and stop. There is no length counter to tell you how many bytes are in the string, with no standard boundary characters such as binary 0 to indicate where a string starts or ends. You can certainly write assembly language routines that allocate Pascal–style strings or C-style strings and manipulate them. To avoid confusion, however, you must then think of the data operated on by your routines to be Pascal or C strings rather than assembly language strings.

Turning Your "String Sense" Inside-Out

Assembly strings have no boundary values or length indicators. They can contain any values at all, including binary 0. In fact, you really have to stop thinking of strings in terms of specific regions in memory. You should instead think of strings in terms of the register values that define them.

It's slightly inside-out compared to how you think of strings in such languages as Pascal, but it works: You've got a string when you set up a register to point to one. And once you point to a string, the length of that string is defined by the value that you place in register RCX.

This is key, and at the risk of repeating myself I'll say it again: *Assembly strings are wholly defined by values you place in registers.* There is a set of assumptions about strings and registers baked into the silicon of the CPU. When you execute one of the string instructions (as I will describe shortly), the CPU uses those assumptions to determine which area of memory it reads from or writes to.

Source Strings and Destination Strings

There are two kinds of strings in x64 assembly work. *Source strings* are strings that you read from. *Destination strings* are strings that you write to. The difference between the two is *only* a matter of registers; source strings and destination strings can overlap. In fact, the very same region of memory can be *both* a source string and a destination string, all at the same time.

Here are the assumptions that the CPU makes about strings when it executes a string instruction in 64-bit long mode:

- A source string is pointed to by RSI.
- A destination string is pointed to by RDI.
- The length of both kinds of strings is the value you place in RCX. How this length is acted upon by the CPU depends on the specific instruction and how it's being used.
- Data coming from a source string or going to a destination string must begin the trip from, end the trip at, or pass through register RAX.

The CPU can recognize both a source string and a destination string simultaneously, because RSI and RDI can hold values independent of one another. However, because there is only one RCX register, the length of source and destination strings must be identical when they are used simultaneously, as in copying a source string to a destination string.

One way to remember the difference between source strings and destination strings is by their offset registers. The "SI" in RSI means "source index," and the "DI" in RDI means "destination index." The "R," as you know by now, is the convention by which the general-purpose registers are marked as 64 bits in size.

A Text Display Virtual Screen

The best way to cement all that string background information in your mind is to see some string instructions at work. In Listing 11.1 I've implemented an interesting mechanism using string instructions: a simple virtual text display for the Linux console.

Back in the days of real-mode programming under DOS on PC-compatible machines, we had unhampered access to the actual video display refresh buffer memory on the PC's graphics adapter. If we wrote an ASCII character or string of characters to the region of memory comprising the card's display buffer, *Wham!* The associated text glyphs appeared on the screen instantaneously. In earlier editions of this book that covered DOS, I took advantage of that direct-access display machinery and presented a suite of useful display routines that demonstrated the Intel architecture's string instructions.

Under Linux, that's no longer possible. The graphics display buffer is still there, but it's now the property of the Linux operating system, and user-space applications can't write to it or even read from it directly.

Writing text-mode applications in assembly for the Linux console is nowhere near as easy as it was under DOS. In Chapter 10, I explained how (very) simple console terminal control could be done by writing escape sequences to the console via the `sys_write` SYSCALL. However, except for the two or three simplest commands, variations in terminal implementation makes using "naked" escape sequences a little dicey. A given sequence might mean one thing to one terminal and something entirely different to another. Code libraries like `ncurses` go to great lengths to detect and adapt to the multitude of terminal specs that are out there. Code to do that is not something you can cobble up in an afternoon, and in fact, it's too large a topic to treat in detail in an introductory book like this.

However. . .we can pull a few scurvy tricks and learn a few things by pulling them. One is to allocate our own text video refresh buffer in memory as a named variable and periodically write the entire buffer out to the Linux console via a single SYSCALL instruction. Our PCs have gotten *extremely* fast since the DOS era, and text video buffers are not large. A 25 × 80 text display buffer is only 2,000 characters long, and the whole thing can be sent to the Linux console with a single SYSCALL `sys_write` call. The buffer appears on the console instantaneously, at least as far as any human observer can discern.

Placing text in the buffer is a simple matter of calculating the address of a given row and column position in the buffer and writing ASCII character values into the buffer variable starting at that address. After each modification of the buffer variable, you can update the console display by writing the entire buffer to the console via SYSCALL. Jaded experts might call this "brute force" (and yes, it's nowhere near as versatile as the `ncurses` library), but it's easy to understand. It doesn't give you control over character color or attributes (underlining, blinking, and so on), but it'll give you a good basic understanding of the x86 string instructions.

Look over the code in Listing 11.1. In the following sections, I'll go through it piece by piece. Note that a separate file is available for building via SASM, called `vidbuff1gcc.asm`. The two files are almost identical and differ almost entirely in the global start addresses `_start` versus `main`, which SASM requires.

Listing 11.1: vidbuff1.asm

```
;   Executable name : vidbuff1
;   Version         : 2.0
;   Created date    : 10/12/2022
;   Last update     : 5/13/2023
;   Author          : Jeff Duntemann
;   Description     : A simple program in assembly for Linux, using NASM
;                   : 2.14.02, demonstrating string instruction operation
;                   : by "faking" : full-screen memory-mapped text I/O.
;
;       Build with this makefile, adding the required tabs where needed:
;
;       vidbuff1: vidbuff1.o
;           ld -o vidbuff1 vidbuff1.o
;       vidbuff1.o: vidbuff1.asm
;           nasm -f elf64 -g -F dwarf vidbuff1.asm
;
;       Note that output to the console from this program will NOT display
;       correctly unless you have enabled the IBM850 character encoding in
;       the terminal program being used to display the console!
;

SECTION .data               ; Section containing initialized data
    EOL      equ 10          ; Linux end-of-line character
    FILLCHR  equ 32          ; ASCII space character
    HBARCHR  equ 196         ; Use dash char if this won't display
    STRTROW  equ 2           ; Row where the graph begins

; We use this to display a ruler across the screen.
    TenDigits   db 31,32,33,34,35,36,37,38,39,30
    DigitCount  db 10
    RulerString db
"12345678901234567890123456789012345678901234567890123456789012345678901234
5678901234567890"
    RULERLEN    equ $-RulerString

; The dataset is just a table of byte-length numbers:
    Dataset db 9,17,71,52,55,18,29,36,18,68,77,63,58,44,0
    Message db "Data current as of 5/13/2023"
    MSGLEN  equ $-Message

; This escape sequence will clear the console terminal and place the
; text cursor to the origin (1,1) on virtually all Linux consoles:
    ClrHome db 27,"[2J",27,"[01;01H"
    CLRLEN  equ $-ClrHome    ; Length of term clear string

SECTION .bss                ; Section containing uninitialized data

    COLS     equ 81          ; Line length + 1 char for EOL
    ROWS     equ 25          ; Number of lines in display
    VidBuff resb COLS*ROWS   ; Buffer size adapts to ROWS & COLS
```

```
        SECTION .text          ; Section containing code

        global  _start         ; Linker needs this to find the entry point!

        ClearTerminal:
            push r11           ; Save all modified registers
            push rax
            push rcx
            push rdx
            push rsi
            push rdi

            mov rax,1          ; Specify sys_write call
            mov rdi,1          ; Specify File Descriptor 1: Standard Output
            mov rsi,ClrHome    ; Pass address of the escape sequence
            mov rdx,CLRLEN     ; Pass the length of the escape sequence
            syscall            ; Make system call

            pop rdi            ; Restore all modified registers
            pop rsi
            pop rdx
            pop rcx
            pop rax
            pop r11
            ret

; -----------------------------------------------------------------
; Show:        Display a text buffer to the Linux console
; UPDATED:     5/10/2023
; IN:          Nothing
; RETURNS:     Nothing
; MODIFIES:    Nothing
; CALLS:       Linux sys_write
; DESCRIPTION: Sends the buffer VidBuff to the Linux console via
;              sys_write. The number of bytes sent to the console
;              calculated by multiplying the COLS equate by the
;              ROWS equate.

Show:
            push r11           ; Save all registers we're going to change
            push rax
            push rcx
            push rdx
            push rsi
            push rdi
            mov rax,1          ; Specify sys_write call
            mov rdi,1          ; Specify File Descriptor 1: Standard Output
            mov rsi,VidBuff    ; Pass address of the buffer
```

```
        mov rdx,COLS*ROWS  ; Pass the length of the buffer
        syscall            ; Make system call
        pop rdi            ; Restore all modified registers
        pop rsi
        pop rdx
        pop rcx
        pop rax
        pop r11
        ret


;----------------------------------------------------------------
; ClrVid:      Clears buffer to spaces and replaces EOLs
; UPDATED:     5/10/2023
; IN:          Nothing
; RETURNS:     Nothing
; MODIFIES:    VidBuff, DF
; CALLS:       Nothing
; DESCRIPTION: Fills the buffer VidBuff with a predefined character
;              (FILLCHR) and then places an EOL character at the end
;              of every line, where a line ends every COLS bytes in
;              VidBuff.

ClrVid:
        push rax             ; Save registers that we change
        push rcx
        push rdi
        cld                  ; Clear DF; we're counting up-memory
        mov al,FILLCHR       ; Put the buffer filler char in AL
        mov rdi,VidBuff      ; Point destination index at buffer
        mov rcx,COLS*ROWS    ; Put count of chars stored into RCX
        rep stosb            ; Blast byte-length chars at the buffer

; Buffer is cleared, now re-insert the EOL char after each line:
        mov rdi,VidBuff      ; Point destination at buffer again
        dec rdi              ; Start EOL position count at VidBuff char 0
        mov rcx,ROWS         ; Put number of rows in count register
.PtEOL:
        add rdi,COLS         ; Add column count to RDI
        mov byte [rdi],EOL   ; Store EOL char at end of row
        loop .PtEOL          ; Loop back if still more lines
        pop rdi              ; Restore caller's registers
        pop rcx
        pop rax
        ret                  ; and go home!


;----------------------------------------------------------------
; WrtLn:       Writes a string to a text buffer at a 1-based X,Y
; UPDATED:     5/10/2023
```

```
; IN:            The address of the string is passed in RSI
;                The 1-based X position (row #) is passed in RBX
;                The 1-based Y position (column #) is passed in RAX
;                The length of the string in chars is passed in RCX
; RETURNS:       Nothing
; MODIFIES:      VidBuff, RDI, DF
; CALLS:         Nothing
; DESCRIPTION: Uses REP MOVSB to copy a string from the
;                address in RSI to an X,Y location in the
;                text buffer VidBuff.

WrtLn:
    push rax        ; Save registers we will change
    push rbx
    push rcx
    push rdi
    cld             ; Clear DF for up-memory write
    mov rdi,VidBuff ; Load destination index with buffer address
    dec rax         ; Adjust Y value down by 1 for address
                    ;   calculation
    dec rbx         ; Adjust X value down by 1 for address
                    ;   calculation
    mov ah,COLS     ; Move screen width to AH
    mul ah          ; Do 8-bit multiply AL*AH to AX
    add rdi,rax     ; Add Y offset into vidbuff to RDI
    add rdi,rbx     ; Add X offset into vidbuf to RDI
    rep movsb       ; Blast the string into the buffer
    pop rdi         ; Restore registers we changed
    pop rcx
    pop rbx
    pop rax
    ret             ; and go home!


;-----------------------------------------------------------
; WrtHB:          Generates a horizontal line bar at X,Y
; UPDATED:        5/10/2023
; IN:             The 1-based X position (row #) is passed in RBX
;                 The 1-based Y position (column #) is passed in RAX
;                 The length of the bar in chars is passed in RCX
; RETURNS:        Nothing
; MODIFIES:       VidBuff, DF
; CALLS:          Nothing
; DESCRIPTION: Writes a horizontal bar to the video buffer VidBuff,
;                at th1e 1-based X,Y values passed in RBX,RAX. The bar
;                is "made of" the character in the equate HBARCHR. The
;                default is character 196; if your terminal won't
;                display that (you need the IBM 850 character set)
;                change the value in HBARCHR to ASCII dash or something
;                else supported in your terminal.
```

```
WrtHB:
     push rax          ; Save registers we change
     push rbx
     push rcx
     push rdi
     cld               ; Clear DF for up-memory write
     mov rdi,VidBuff   ; Put buffer address in destination register
     dec rax           ; Adjust Y value down by 1 for address calculation
     dec rbx           ; Adjust X value down by 1 for address calculation
     mov ah,COLS       ; Move screen width to AH
     mul ah            ; Do 8-bit multiply AL*AH to AX
     add rdi,rax       ; Add Y offset into vidbuff to EDI
     add rdi,rbx       ; Add X offset into vidbuf to EDI
     mov al,HBARCHR    ; Put the char to use for the bar in AL
     rep stosb         ; Blast the bar char into the buffer
     pop rdi           ; Restore registers we changed
     pop rcx
     pop rbx
     pop rax
     ret               ; And go home!


;-----------------------------------------------------------------
; Ruler:        Generates a "1234567890"-style ruler at X,Y
; UPDATED:      5/10/2023
; IN:           The 1-based X pos (row #) is passed in RBX
;               The 1-based Y pos (column #) is passed in RAX
;               The length of the ruler in chars is passed in RCX
; RETURNS:      Nothing
; MODIFIES:     VidBuff
; CALLS:        Nothing
; DESCRIPTION:  Writes a ruler to the video buffer VidBuff, at
;               the 1-based X,Y position passed in RBX,RAX.
;               The ruler consists of a repeating sequence of
;               the digits 1 through 0. The ruler will wrap
;               to subsequent lines and overwrite whatever EOL
;               characters fall within its length, if it will not fit
;               entirely on the line where it begins. Note that the
;               Show procedure must be called after Ruler to display
;               the ruler on the console.

Ruler:
     push rax          ; Save the registers we change
     push rbx
     push rcx
     push rdx
     push rdi
     mov rdi,VidBuff   ; Load video buffer address to RDI
     dec rax           ; Adjust Y value down by 1 for address calculation
     dec rbx           ; Adjust X value down by 1 for address calculation
```

```
    mov ah,COLS        ; Move screen width to AH
    mul ah             ; Do 8-bit multiply AL*AH to AX
    add rdi,rax        ; Add Y offset into vidbuff to RDI
    add rdi,rbx        ; Add X offset into vidbuf to RDI

; RDI now contains the memory address in the buffer where the ruler
; is to begin. Now we display the ruler, starting at that position:
    mov rdx,RulerString ; Load address of ruler string into RDX
DoRule:
    mov al,[rdx]       ; Load first digit in the ruler to AL
    stosb              ; Store 1 char; note that there's no REP prefix!
    inc rdx            ; Increment RDX to point to next char in ruler string
    loop DoRule        ; Decrement RCX & Go back for another char until RCX=0
    pop rdi            ; Restore the registers we changed
    pop rdx
    pop rcx
    pop rbx
    pop rax
    ret                ; And go home!


;------------------------------------------------------------------
; MAIN PROGRAM:

_start:
    push rbp
    mov rbp,rsp
    and rsp,-16

; Get the console and text display text buffer ready to go:
    call ClearTerminal ; Send terminal clear string to console
    call ClrVid        ; Init/clear the video buffer

; Next we display the top ruler:
    mov rax,1          ; Load Y position to AL
    mov rbx,1          ; Load X position to BL
    mov rcx,COLS-1     ; Load ruler length to RCX
    call Ruler         ; Write the ruler to the buffer

; Thow up an informative message centered on the last line
    mov rsi,Message    ; Load the address of the message to RSI
    mov rcx,MSGLEN     ; and its length to RCX
    mov rbx,COLS       ; and the screen width to RBX
    sub rbx,rcx        ; Calc diff of message length and screen width
    shr rbx,1          ; Divide difference by 2 for X value
    mov rax,20         ; Set message row to Line 24
    call WrtLn         ; Display the centered message
```

```
; Here we loop through the dataset and graph the data:
    mov rsi,Dataset  ; Put the address of the dataset in RSI
    mov rbx,1        ; Start all bars at left margin (X=1)
    mov r15,0        ; Dataset element index starts at 0
.blast:
    mov rax,r15      ; Add dataset number to element index
    add rax,STRTROW  ; Bias row value by row # of first bar
    mov cl,byte [rsi+r15] ; Put dataset value in lowest byte of RCX
    cmp rcx,0        ; See if we pulled a 0 from the dataset
    je .rule2        ; If we pulled a 0 from the dataset, we're done
    call WrtHB       ; Graph the data as a horizontal bar
    inc r15          ; Increment the dataset element index
    jmp .blast       ; Go back and do another bar

; Display the bottom ruler:
.rule2:
    mov rax,r15      ; Use the dataset counter to set the ruler row
    add rax,STRTROW  ; Bias down by the row # of the first bar
    mov rbx,1        ; Load X position to BL
    mov rcx,COLS-1   ; Load ruler length to RCX
    call Ruler       ; Write the ruler to the buffer

; Having written all that to the buffer, send buffer to the console:
    call Show        ; Refresh the buffer to the console

; And return control to Linux:
Exit:
    mov rsp,rbp
    pop rbp

    mov rax,60       ; End program via Exit Syscall
    mov rdi,0        ; Return a code of zero
    syscall          ; Return to Linux
```

REP STOSB, the Software Machine Gun

Our virtual text display buffer is nothing more than a region of raw memory set aside in the .bss section, using the RESB directive. The size of the buffer is defined by two equates, which specify the number of rows and columns that you want. By default I've set it to 25 rows and 80 columns, but 2023-era console displays can display a great deal larger text screen than that. You can change the COLS and ROWS equates to define buffers as large as 255 × 255, though if your terminal window isn't that large, your results will be (to put it charitably) unpredictable.

Changing the dimensions of your text display is done by changing one or both of those equates. Whatever other changes must be made to the code are handled automatically. Note that this has to be done at assembly time since many of the calculations are assembly-time calculations done by NASM when you build the program.

You do not have to match the size of the terminal window precisely to the ROWS and COLS values you choose, as long as the terminal window is *larger* than ROWS × COLS. If you maximize the terminal window (like Konsole), your text display will appear starting in the upper-left corner of the screen.

Machine-Gunning the Virtual Display

When Linux loads your programs into memory, it typically clears uninitialized variables (like VidBuff from Listing 11.1) to binary zeros. This is good, but binary zeros do not display correctly on the Linux console. To look "blank" on the console, the display buffer memory must be cleared to the ASCII space character. This means writing the value 20h into memory from the beginning of the buffer to its end.

Such things should always be done in tight loops. The obvious way is to put the display buffer address into RDI, the number of bytes in your refresh buffer into RCX, the ASCII value to clear the buffer to into AL, and then code up a tight loop this way:

```
Clear:  mov [rdi],al  ; Write the value in AL to memory
        inc rdi       ; Bump RDI to next byte in the buffer
        dec rcx       ; Decrement RCX by one position
        jnz Clear     ; And loop again until RCX is 0
```

This will work. It's even tolerably fast, especially on newer CPUs. But *all* of the preceding code is equivalent to this one single instruction:

```
rep stosb
```

Really. No, *really*.

The STOSB instruction is the simplest of the Intel string instructions and is a good place to begin. There are two parts to the instruction as I showed it, a situation we haven't seen before. REP is a new type of critter, called a *prefix*, and it changes how the CPU treats the instruction mnemonic that follows it. We'll get back to REP shortly. Right now, let's look at STOSB. The mnemonic means STOre String by Byte. Like all the string instructions, STOSB makes certain assumptions about some CPU registers. It works only on the destination string, so RSI is not involved. However, these assumptions must be respected and dealt with:

- RDI must be loaded with the address of the destination string. (Think: *R*DI, for *d*estination *i*ndex.)
- RCX must be loaded with the number of times the value in AL is to be stored into the string.

- AL must be loaded with the 8-bit value to be stored into the string.
- The Direction flag DF must be set or cleared, depending on whether you want the search to be up-memory (cleared; use CLD) or down-memory (set; use STD). I'll have more to say about DF as used with STOSB a little later.

Executing the STOSB Instruction

Once you set up these three registers, you can safely execute a STOSB instruction. When you do, this is what happens:

1. The byte value in AL is copied to the memory address stored in RDI.
2. RDI is incremented by 1, such that it now points to the *next* byte in memory following the one just written to.

Note that we're *not* machine-gunning here—not yet, at least. *One* copy of AL gets copied to *one* location in memory. The RDI register is adjusted so that it'll be ready for the *next* time STOSB is executed.

One very important point to remember is that RCX is *not* decremented by STOSB. RCX is decremented automatically *only* if you put the REP prefix in front of STOSB. Lacking the REP prefix, you have to do the decrementing yourself, either explicitly through DEC or through the LOOP instruction, as I'll explain a little later in this chapter.

So, you can't make STOSB run automatically without REP. However, if you like, you can execute other instructions before executing another STOSB. As long as you don't disturb RDI or RCX, you can do whatever you want. Then when you execute STOSB again, another copy of AL will go out to the location pointed to by RDI, and RDI will be adjusted yet again. (You have to remember to decrement RCX somehow.) Note that you can change the value in AL if you like, but the changed value will be copied into memory. You may want to do that—there's no law saying you have to fill a string with only one single value.

However, this is like the difference between a semiautomatic weapon (which fires one round every time you press and release the trigger) and a fully automatic weapon, which fires rounds continually as long as you hold the trigger back. To make STOSB fully automatic, just hang the REP prefix ahead of it. What REP does is beautifully simple: It sets up the tightest of all tight loops completely *inside* the CPU and fires copies of AL into memory repeatedly (the reason for its name), incrementing RDI by 1 each time and decrementing RCX by 1, until RCX is decremented down to 0. Then it stops, and when the smoke clears, you'll see that your whole destination string, however large, has been filled with copies of AL.

Man, now *that's* programming!

In the `vidbuff1` program presented in Listing 11.1, the code to clear the display buffer is in the `ClrVid` procedure. The pertinent lines are those shown here:

```
cld                     ; Clear DF so we're counting up-memory
mov al,FILLCHR          ; Put the buffer filler char in AL
mov rdi,VidBuff         ; Point destination index at buffer
mov rcx,COLS*ROWS       ; Put count of chars stored into RCX
rep stosb               ; Blast chars at the buffer
```

The FILLCHR equate is by default set to 32, which is the ASCII space character. You can set this to fill the buffer with some other character, though how useful this might be is unclear. Note also that the number of characters to be written into memory is calculated by NASM at assembly time as COLS times ROWS. This allows you to change the size of your virtual display without changing the code that clears the display buffer.

STOSB and the Direction Flag DF

Leading off the short code sequence shown earlier is an instruction I haven't discussed before: CLD. It controls something critical in string instruction work: the direction in memory that the string operation takes.

Most of the time that you'll be using STOSB, you'll want to run it "uphill" in memory, that is, from a lower memory address to a higher memory address. In ClrVid, you put the address of the start of the video refresh buffer into RDI and then blast characters into memory at successively higher memory addresses. Each time STOSB fires a byte into memory, RDI is incremented to point to the *next higher* byte in memory.

This is the logical way to work it, but it doesn't have to be done that way at all times. STOSB can just as easily begin at a high address and move downward in memory. On each store into memory, RDI can be *decremented* by 1 instead.

Which way that STOSB fires—uphill toward successively higher memory addresses or downhill toward successively lower addresses—is governed by one of the flags in the RFlags register. This is the *Direction flag* DF. DF's sole job in life is to control the direction of action taken by certain instructions that, like STOSB, can move in one of two directions in memory. Most of these (like STOSB and its siblings) are string instructions.

The sense of DF is this: When DF is *set* (that is, when DF has the value 1), STOSB and its fellow string instructions work downhill, from higher to lower addresses. When DF is *cleared* (that is, when it has the value 0), STOSB and its siblings work uphill, from lower to higher addresses. This in turn is simply the direction in which the RDI register is adjusted: When DF is set, RDI is decremented during string instruction execution. When DF is cleared, RDI is incremented.

The Direction flag defaults to 0 (uphill) when the CPU is reset. It is generally changed in one of two ways: with the CLD instruction, or with the STD instruction. CLD clears DF to 0, and STD sets DF to 1. (You should keep in mind when debugging that the POPF instruction can also change DF by popping an entire new set of flags from the stack into the RFlags register.) Because DF's default state is cleared to 0 and all of the string instructions in the vidbuff1 demo program work uphill in memory, it's not technically necessary to include a CLD instruction in the clrvid procedure. However, other parts of a program can change DF. It's always a good idea to place the appropriate one of CLD or STD right before a string instruction to make sure that your machine gun fires in the right direction!

People sometimes get confused and think that DF also governs whether RCX is incremented or decremented by the string instructions. Not so! Nothing in a string instruction *ever* increments RCX. RCX holds a count value, *not* a memory address. You place a count in RCX, and it counts down each time that a string instruction fires until it reaches 0. DF has nothing to say about it. Basically, RDI is where the target is, and RCX is the number of bullets in your clip.

Defining Lines in the Display Buffer

Clearing VidBuff to space characters isn't quite the end of the story, however. To render correctly on the terminal programs that display the Linux console, display data must be divided into lines. Lines are delimited by the EOL character, ASCII 10. A line begins at the start of the buffer and ends with the first EOL character. The next line begins immediately after the EOL character and runs until the next EOL character, and so on.

When text is written piecemeal to the console, each line may be a different length. In our virtual display system, however, the entire buffer is written to the console in one SYSCALL swoop, as a sequence of lines that are all the same length. This means that when we clear the buffer, we also have to insert EOL characters where we want each displayed line to end.

This is done in the remainder of the clrvid procedure. What we have to do is write an EOL character into the buffer every COLS bytes. This is done with a *very* tight loop. If you look at the second portion of clrvid, you may notice that the loop in question isn't *quite* ordinary. Hold that thought—I'll come back to the LOOP instruction in just a little bit.

Sending the Buffer to the Linux Console

I need to reiterate: We're talking a *virtual* display here. VidBuff is just a region of memory into which you can write characters and character strings with ordinary assembly language instructions. However, nothing will appear on your monitor until you send the buffer to the Linux console.

This is easy enough. The procedure Show in Listing 11.1 makes a single call to the sys_write kernel service via SYSCALL and sends the entire buffer to the console at once. The EOL characters embedded in the buffer every COLS bytes are treated as EOL characters are always treated by the console and force a new line to begin immediately after each EOL. Because all the lines are the same length, sending VidBuff to the console creates a rectangular region of text that will display correctly on any terminal window that is at least COLS by ROWS in size. (Smaller windows will scramble VidBuff's text. Try running the vidbuff1 program in various-sized terminal windows, and you'll quickly see what I mean.)

What's important is that your programs call Show whenever you want a screen update. This can be done as often as you want, whenever you want. On modern Linux PCs, the update happens so quickly as to appear instantaneous. With that kind of speed, there's no reason you shouldn't call Show after each and every write to VidBuff, but that's up to you.

The Semiautomatic Weapon: STOSB Without REP

Among all the string instructions, I chose to show you REP STOSB first because it's dramatic in the extreme. But more to the point, it's *simple*—in fact, it's simpler to use REP than not to use REP. REP simplifies string processing from the programmer's perspective, because it brings the entire instruction loop *inside* the CPU. You can use the STOSB instruction without REP, but it's a little more work. The work involves setting up the instruction loop outside the CPU and making sure it's correct.

Why bother? Simply this: With REP STOSB, you can only repeatedly store the *same* value into the destination string. Whatever you put into AL before executing REP STOSB is the value that gets fired into memory RCX times. STOSB can be used to store *different* values into the destination string by firing it semiautomatically and changing the value in AL between each squeeze of the trigger.

You lose a little time in handling the loop yourself outside the CPU. This is because there is a certain amount of time spent in fetching the loop's instruction bytes from memory. However, if you keep your loop as tight as you can, you don't lose an objectionable amount of speed, especially on modern Intel/AMD processors, which make very effective use of cache and don't fetch instructions from outboard memory every time they're executed.

Who Decrements RCX?

Early in my experience with x86 assembly language, I recall being massively confused about where and when the RCX register (actually, way back then, it was simply the CX register) was decremented when using string instructions. It's a key issue, especially when you *don't* use the REP prefix.

When you use REP STOSB (or REP with any of the string instructions), RCX is decremented automatically, by 1, for each memory access the instruction makes. And once RCX gets itself decremented to 0, REP STOSB detects that RCX is now 0 and stops firing into memory. Control then passes on to the next instruction in line. But take away REP, and the automatic decrementing of RCX stops. So, also, does the automatic detection when RCX has been counted down to 0.

Obviously, something has to decrement RCX since RCX governs how many times the string instruction accesses memory. If STOSB doesn't do it—you guessed it—*you* have to do it somewhere else, with another instruction.

The obvious way to decrement RCX is to use DEC RCX. And the obvious way to determine if RCX has been decremented to 0 is to follow the DEC RCX instruction with a JNZ (Jump if Not Zero) instruction. JNZ tests the Zero flag ZF and jumps back to the STOSB instruction until ZF becomes true. And ZF becomes true when a DEC instruction causes its operand (here, RCX) to become 0.

The LOOP Instructions

With all that in mind, consider the following assembly language instruction loop. This is not taken from Listing 11.1, but a cobbled-up example of the "hard" way to do things:

```
     mov al,30h   ; Put the value of character "0" in AL
DoChar:
     stosb        ; Note that there's no REP prefix!
     inc al       ; Bump the character value in AL up by 1
     dec rcx      ; Decrement the count by 1..
     jnz DoChar   ; ..and loop again if RCX > 0
```

Look to see how the loop runs. STOSB fires, AL is modified, and then RCX is decremented. The JNZ instruction tests to see if the DEC instruction has forced RCX to zero. If so, the Zero flag ZF is set, and the loop will terminate. But until ZF is set, the jump is made back to the label DoChar, where STOSB fires yet again.

There is a simpler way, using an instruction I haven't discussed until now: LOOP. The LOOP instruction combines the decrementing of RCX with a test and jump based on ZF. It looks like this:

```
     mov al,30h   ; Put the value of character "0" in AL
DoChar:
     stosb        ; Note that there's no REP prefix!
     inc al       ; Bump the character value in AL up by 1
     loop DoChar  ; Go back & do another char until RCX goes to 0
```

When executed, the LOOP instruction first decrements RCX by 1. It then checks the Zero flag to see if the decrement operation forced RCX to zero. If so, it falls through to the next instruction. If not (that is, if ZF remains 0, indicating that RCX is still greater than 0), LOOP branches to the label specified as its operand.

So, the loop keeps looping the LOOP until RCX counts down to 0. At that point, the loop is finished, and execution falls through and continues with the next instruction following LOOP.

Displaying a Ruler on the Screen

As a useful demonstration of when it makes sense to use STOSB without REP (but with LOOP) let me offer you another item for your video toolkit.

The Ruler procedure from Listing 11.1 displays a repeating sequence of ascending digits starting from 1, of any length, at some selectable location on your screen. In other words, you can display a string of digits like this anywhere you'd like:

```
12345678901234567890123456789012345678901234567890
```

This might allow you to determine where in the horizontal dimension of the console window a line begins or some character falls. The Ruler procedure allows you to specify how long the ruler is, in digits, and where on the screen it will be displayed.

A typical call to Ruler would look something like this:

```
mov rax,1        ; Load Y position to AL
mov rbx,1        ; Load X position to BL
mov rcx,COLS-1   ; Load ruler length to RCX
call Ruler       ; Write the ruler to the buffer
```

This invocation places a ruler at the upper-left corner of the display, beginning at position 1,1. The length of the ruler is passed in RCX. Here, you're specifying a ruler one character shorter than the display is wide. This provides a ruler that spans the full visible width of your virtual text display.

Why one character shorter? Remember that there is an EOL character at the end of every line. This EOL character isn't visible directly, but it's still a character and requires a byte in the buffer to hold it. The COLS equate must always take this into account: If you want an 80-character wide display, COLS must be set to 81. If you want a 96-character wide display, COLS must be set to 97. If you code a call to Ruler as shown earlier, NASM will do some assembly-time math and always generate a ruler that spans the full (visible) width of the text display.

Over and above the LOOP instruction, there's a fair amount of new assembly technology at work here that could stand explaining. Let's detour from the string instructions for a bit and take a closer look.

MUL Is Not IMUL

I described the MUL instruction and its implicit operands way back in Chapter 7. The Ruler procedure uses MUL as well to calculate an X,Y position in the display memory buffer where STOSB can begin placing the ruler characters. The algorithm for determining the offset in bytes into the buffer for any given X and Y values looks like this:

```
Offset = ((Y * width in characters of a screen line) + X)
```

Pretty obviously, you have to move Y lines down in the screen buffer and then move X bytes over from the left margin of the screen to reach your X,Y position. The calculation is done this way inside the Ruler procedure:

```
mov rdi,VidBuff  ; Load video buffer address to RDI
    dec rax      ; Adjust Y value down by 1 for address calculation
    dec rbx      ; Adjust X value down by 1 for address calculation
    mov ah,COLS  ; Move screen width to AH
    mul ah       ; Do 8-bit multiply AL*AH to AX
    add rdi,rax  ; Add Y offset into vidbuff to RDI
    add rdi,rbx  ; Add X offset into vidbuf to RDI
```

The two DEC instructions take care of the fact that X,Y positions in this system are 1-based; that is, the upper-left corner of the screen is position 1,1 rather than 0,0, as they are in some X,Y coordinate systems. Think of it this way: If you want to display a ruler beginning in the very upper-left corner of the screen, you have to write the ruler characters starting at the very beginning of the buffer, at no offset at all. For calculation's sake, then, the X,Y values thus have to be 0-based.

For an 8-bit multiply using MUL, one of the factors is implicit: AL contains the Y value, and the caller passes Ruler the Y value in RAX. We place the screen width in AH and then multiply AH times AL with MUL. (See Chapter 7's discussion of MUL if it's gotten fuzzy in the interim.) The product replaces the values in both AH and AL and are accessed as the value in AX. Adding that product and the X value (passed to Ruler in BL) to RDI gives you the precise memory address where the ruler characters must be written.

Now, there's a fairly common bug to warn you about here: MUL is not IMUL. . .most of the time. MUL and IMUL are sister instructions that both perform multiplication. MUL treats its operand values as unsigned, whereas IMUL treats them as signed. This difference does not matter as long as both factors remain positive in a signed context. In practical terms, for an 8-bit multiply, MUL and IMUL work identically on values of 127 or less. At 128 everything changes. Values above 127 are considered negative in an 8-bit signed context. MUL considers 128 to be. . .128. IMUL considers 128 to be -1. Whoops.

You could replace the MUL instruction with IMUL in Ruler, and the proc would work identically until you passed it a screen dimension greater than 127. Then, suddenly, IMUL would calculate a product that is nominally negative. . .but only if you're treating the value as a signed value. A negative number treated as unsigned is a very large positive number, and a memory reference to the address represented by RDI plus that anomalous value will generate a segmentation fault. Try it! No harm done, and it's an interesting lesson. IMUL is for signed values. For memory address calculations, leave it alone and be sure to use MUL instead.

Ruler's Lessons

The Ruler procedure is a good example of using STOSB *without* the REP prefix. We have to change the value in AL every time we store AL to memory and thus can't use REP STOSB. Note that nothing is done to RDI or RCX while changing the digit to be displayed, and thus the values stored in those registers are held over for the next execution of STOSB. Ruler is a good example of how LOOP works with STOSB to adjust RCX downward and return control to the top of the loop. LOOP, in a sense, does outside the CPU what REP does inside the CPU: adjust RCX and close the loop. Try to keep that straight in your head when using any of the string instructions!

The Four Sizes of STOS

Before moving on to other string instructions, it's worth pointing out that there are four different "sizes" of the STOS string instruction:

- STOSB stores the 8-bit value in AL into memory.
- STOSW stores the 16-bit value in AX into memory.
- STOSD stores the 32-bit value in EAX into memory.
- STOSQ stores the 64-bit value in RAX into memory.

STOSW, STOSD, and STOSQ work almost the same way as STOSB. The major difference lies in the way the destination address RDI is changed after each memory transfer operation. RDI is changed according to the sizes of the quantity acted upon by the instruction. For STOSW, RDI changes by two bytes, either up or down depending on the state of DF. For STOSD, RDI changes by four bytes, again either up or down depending on the state of DF. STOSQ changes RDI by eight bytes, up or down depending on the state of DF.

However, in all cases, with the REP prefix in front of the instruction, the counter register (in x64, RCX) is decremented by *one* after each memory transfer operation. It is always decremented, and always by one. RCX counts *operations*. It has nothing to say about memory addresses nor the size of the value being stored in memory.

Goodbye, BCD Math

This might seem an odd place to talk about machine instructions that are no longer available, but I have a reason. Readers who have seen earlier editions of this book, particularly the 2009 edition, might recall that the vidbuff1 example program (Listing 11.1) used BCD arithmetic to generate the characters that make up the ruler.

To put it bluntly, the architects of x64 removed all BCD math instructions found in the x86 definition. This amounts to six instructions:

```
AAA, DAA, DAS, AAS, AAM, AAD
```

It's outside the scope of this book to explain BCD math (the 2009 edition has some coverage if you're genuinely interested), and I only bring it up because in the 2009 edition, the vidbuff1 program used BCD math. There are use cases for BCD math, mostly in financial calculations, but Intel's BCD instructions go back a long way, and we have better financial calculations techniques these days.

Basically, BCD math allowed you to add an ASCII character to another ASCII character. It's complicated and slow and no longer possible—because the instructions that accomplish it are no longer available.

MOVSB: Fast Block Copies

The STOSB instruction is a fascinating item, but for sheer action packed into a single line of assembly code there's nothing that can touch the MOVS instruction. Like STOS, MOVS comes in four "sizes," for handling bytes (MOVSB), 16-bit words (MOVSW), 32-bit double words (MOVSD), and 64-bit quad words (MOVSQ). For working with ASCII characters as we are in this chapter, MOVSB is the one to use.

The gist of the MOVSB instruction is this: A block of memory data at the address stored in RSI is copied to the address stored in RDI. The number of bytes to be moved is placed in the RCX register. RCX counts down by one after each byte is copied, and the addresses in RSI and RDI are adjusted by one. For MOVSW, the source and destination registers are adjusted by two after each word is copied; for MOVSD, they are adjusted by four after each double word is copied, and for MOVSQ, they are adjusted by eight bytes after each quad word is copied. These adjustments are either increments or decrements, depending on the state of DF. In all cases, RCX is decremented by one each time a data item goes from the source address to the destination address. Remember that RCX is counting memory transfer operations, *not* address bytes!

The DF register affects MOVSB the same way it affects STOSB. By default, DF is cleared, and string operations operate "uphill" from low memory toward high memory. If DF is set, the direction that string operations work goes the other way, from high memory toward low.

MOVSB can operate either semiautomatically or automatically, just as with STOSB. Add the REP prefix to MOVSB, and (assuming you have the registers set up correctly) a block of memory will be copied from here to there in just one instruction, in a tight loop inside the CPU.

To demonstrate MOVSB, I added a short procedure called WrtLn to Listing 11.1. WrtLn copies a string to a given X,Y location in the display buffer VidBuff. It does a job much like Write in Pascal or print in C. Before calling WrtLn, you place the source address of the string in RSI, the 1-based X,Y coordinates in RBX and RAX, and the length of the string in bytes in RCX.

The code that does the work in WrtLn is pretty simple:

```
cld                 ; Clear DF for up-memory write
mov rdi,VidBuff     ; Load destination index with buffer address
dec rax             ; Adjust Y value down by 1 for address calculation
dec rbx             ; Adjust X value down by 1 for address calculation
mov ah,COLS         ; Move screen width to AH
mul ah              ; Do 8-bit multiply AL*AH to AX
add rdi,rax         ; Add Y offset into vidbuff to RDI
add rdi,rbx         ; Add X offset into vidbuf to RDI
rep movsb           ; Blast the string into the buffer
```

The code for calculating the offset into VidBuff from the X,Y values using MUL is the same as that used in Ruler. In the main program section of vidbuff1, some additional calculation is done to display a string centered in the visible buffer, rather than at some specific X,Y location:

```
mov rsi,Message     ; Load the address of the message to RSI
mov rcx,MSGLEN      ; and its length to RCX
mov rbx,COLS        ; and the screen width to RBX
sub rbx,rcx         ; Calc diff of message length and screen width
shr rbx,1           ; Divide difference by 2 for X value
mov rax,20          ; Set message row to Line 20
call WrtLn          ; Display the centered message
```

DF and Overlapping Block Moves

The simple demo program vidbuff1 uses MOVSB to copy a message from the .data section of the program into the display buffer. Although WrtLn uses MOVSB to copy the message "uphill" from low memory to high, you could argue that you could just as easily copy it from high memory "downhill" to low, and you would be right. The direction flag DF doesn't seem to be more than a matter of preference. . .unless and until your source and destination memory blocks overlap.

Nothing requires that RSI and RDI point to entirely separate areas of memory. The source and destination memory blocks may overlap, and that can often be extremely useful.

Here's an example: Consider the challenge of editing text stored in a memory buffer. Suppose you have a string in a buffer and want to insert a character somewhere in the middle of the string. All the characters in the string past the insertion point must be "moved aside" to make room for the new inserted character. (This assumes there is empty space at the end of the buffer.) This is a natural application for REP MOVSB—but setting it up may be trickier than it seems at first glance.

I vividly remember the first time I tried it—which, not coincidentally, was the first time I ever attempted to use MOVSB. What I did is shown schematically in the left portion of Figure 11.1. The goal was to move a string to the right by one position so that I could insert a space character in front of it.

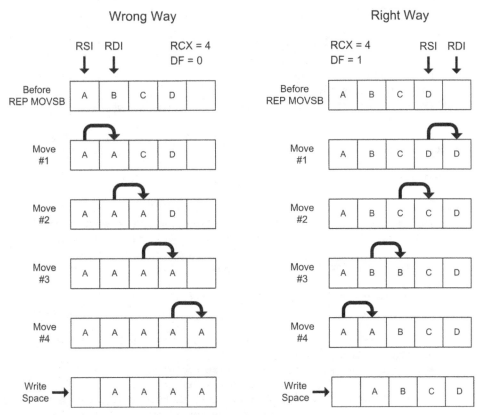

Figure 11.1: Using MOVSB on overlapping memory blocks

I pointed RSI to the first byte in the string and pointed RDI to the position I wanted to move the string. I then executed an "uphill" REP MOVSB instruction, and when the smoke cleared, I discovered that I had replaced the entire string with its initial character. Yes, it's an obvious mistake. . .once you see it actually *happen*. (Yes, when I made this mistake, the registers were 16 bits in size and I was a lot younger, but things work the same in x64 long mode, and the bug is still *very* easy to commit.)

On the right side of the figure is the way such an insert should in fact be done. You must begin at the high end of the string and work "downhill" toward the insertion point. The first character move must take the last character of the string into empty buffer space and out of the way of the next character move, and so on. In this way, two areas of memory that overlap by all but one byte can be copied one to the other without losing any data.

This shows easier than it tells. If you can watch the move happen, it becomes a lot clearer. I've created a sandbox demo of an overlapping block move in Listing 11.2. It's designed for SASM, which is why it has the gcc suffix.

Listing 11.2: movsbdemogcc.asm

```
        section .data
                        ;0000000000111
                        ;0123456789012
        EditBuff: db 'abcdefghijklm '
        BUFFLEN   equ $-EditBuff
        ENDPOS    equ 12 ; 0-based number of last visible character
        INSRTPOS  equ 1


section .text

global main

main:
;    This a "sandbox" program for single-stepping in the SASM debugger,
;    and is not a complete program. Just letting it fly will segfault.

        mov rbp, rsp; for correct debugging

; Put your experiments between the two nops...
        nop

        std                     ; We're doing a "downhill" transfer
        mov rbx,EditBuff
        mov rsi,EditBuff+ENDPOS    ; Start at end of visible text
        mov rdi,EditBuff+ENDPOS+1  ; Bump text right by 1
        mov rcx,ENDPOS-INSRTPOS+2  ; # of chars to bump; not a 0-based
                                ; address but a count
        rep movsb               ; Move 'em!
        mov byte [rbx],' '      ; Write a space at insert point

; Put your experiments between the two nops...
        nop
```

To watch the move in SASM, you have to load the code in Listing 11.2, build it, and then start the debugger. Once you're in debug mode, select Debug ⇨ Show Memory. In the Variable Or Expression field, enter **EditBuff**. In the Type field, select Char from the first drop-down, and b from the second drop-down. EditBuff is 14 characters long (including the trailing space), so enter **14** in the third field. Do not click the Address check box.

Here's how it works: ENDPOS is the 0-based offset of the last nonspace character in the string. Note that this is *not* a count, but an offset from the beginning of EditBuff. The offset of the final character "m" from the beginning of the buffer is 12 bytes. If you start with the address of EditBuff in RSI and add 12 to it, RSI will be pointing at the "m." RDI, in turn, is pointed at the offset of the first buffer position *after* the final character in the string, which is the reason for the ENDPOS+1 assembly-time calculation, which points at the space character at the end of EditBuff.

Deriving the count to be placed into RCX has to take the 0-based nature of the address offsets into account. You have to add 2 to the difference between the string's end position (ENDPOS) and the insert position (INSRTPOS) because both are 0-based, and to get a correct count, you have to add back in the additional two 1s that you would have if ENDPOS and INSRTPOS were both 1-based numbers. (Remember that counts of things are *not* 0-based!)

Note the STD instruction that begins the code block. STD sets the Direction Flag DF to 1, which forces string instructions to work "downhill" from high memory toward low memory. DF defaults to 0, so for this code to work the STD instruction *must* be present!

Single-Stepping REP String Instructions

I should mention here that even though a REP MOVSB instruction appears to be a single instruction, it is actually an extremely tight loop implemented as a single instruction. Single-stepping REP MOVSB in a debugger does *not* execute the whole loop at one blow! Each time you click SASM's Step Into icon, only one memory transfer operation will take place.

If RCX is loaded with a count value of 13, for example, you will have to click Step Into icon 13 times to step your way through the entire instruction. This allows you to watch memory and registers change while the instruction operates. However, for large count values in RCX, that can become a *lot* of clicking. If you're confident of the correctness of your string instruction setup, you may want to place a breakpoint on the next instruction after the REP string instruction and click Continue (or press F5) to execute the string instruction at full speed without pausing after each memory transfer operation. SASM will pause at the breakpoint, and you can inspect the final state of the memory buffer and continue single-stepping from there.

The other issue with watching memory moves with SASM's debugger is the odd way that SASM displays string buffers. If you select Smart from the first drop-down, SASM will display EditBuff as a string of characters in the form "abcdefghijklm" but *without the trailing space*. You can watch the move happen with that display, but it's not the whole picture and might confuse you.

The Char display of EditBuff is how it is in part because it allows you to include nondisplayable characters like EOL. A character is shown as its decimal equivalent and then the actual character in single quotes, like this:

```
{97'a',98'b',99'c',100'd',101'e',102'f'103'g', … 32''}
```

This format will show you the space character at the end of EditBuff, but you'll have to watch closely to see the move as it happens.

My sincere hope is that SASM will one day include a hexdump-style memory display, like the one in Insight.

Storing Data to Discontinuous Strings

Sometimes you have to break the rules. Until now I've been explaining the string instructions under the assumption that the destination string is always one continuous sequence of bytes in memory. This isn't necessarily the case. In addition to changing the value in RAX between executions of STOSB, you can change the *destination address* as well. The end result is that you can store data to several different areas of memory within a single very tight loop.

Displaying an ASCII Table

I've created a small demo program for SASM to show you what I mean. It's not as useful as the Ruler procedure in Listing 11.1, but it makes its point and is easy to understand if you've followed me so far. The showchargcc program uses a lot of the same basic machinery as vidbuff1, including the virtual display mechanism and Ruler. So to save page space in the book, I'm not going to show the whole program here. The complete source code file (as with all the code presented in this book) can be downloaded from my assembly language web page in the listings archive zip file.

The showchargcc program clears the screen, displays a ruler on line 1, and below that shows a table containing 224 of the 256 ASCII characters, neatly displayed in 7 lines of 32 characters each. The table includes the "high" 127 ASCII characters, including foreign-language characters, line-draw characters, and miscellaneous symbols. What it does not display are the very first 32 ASCII characters. Linux treats these as control characters, and even those characters for which glyphs are available are not displayed to the console.

The showchargcc program introduces a couple of new concepts and instructions, all related to program loops. (String instructions such as STOSB and program loops are intimately related.) To save page space, Listing 11.3 presents showchargcc without its procedures. All procedures and macros it invokes are present in Listing 11.1.

Listing 11.3: showchargcc.asm (Minus Procedures)

```
;   Executable name : showchargcc
;   Version         : 2.0
;   Created date    : 10/19/2022
;   Last update     : 5/17/2023
;   Author          : Jeff Duntemann
;   Description     : A simple program in assembly for Linux,
;       demonstrating discontinuous string writes to memory using STOSB
;       without REP. The program loops through characters 32 through 255
;       and writes a simple "ASCII chart" in a display buffer. The chart
;       consists of 8 lines of 32 characters, with the lines not
;       continuous in memory.
;
;   Build using the standard SASM x64 build lines
;

SECTION .data         ; Section containing initialized data
    EOL       equ 10  ; Linux end-of-line character
    FILLCHR   equ 32  ; Default to ASCII space character
    CHRTROW   equ 2   ; Chart begins 2 lines from top
    CHRTLEN   equ 32  ; Each chart line shows 32 chars

; This escape sequence will clear the console terminal and place the
; text cursor to the origin (1,1) on virtually all Linux consoles:
    ClrHome db 27,"[2J",27,"[01;01H"
    CLRLEN    equ $-ClrHome      ; Length of term clear string
    EOL       equ 10             ; Linux end-of-line character

; We use this to display a ruler across the screen.
    RulerString db
"123456789012345678901234567890123456789012345678901234567
8901234567890"
    RULERLEN    equ $-RulerString

SECTION .bss                     ; Section containing uninitialized data

    COLS equ 81                  ; Line length + 1 char for EOL
    ROWS equ 25                  ; Number of lines in display
    VidBuff resb COLS*ROWS       ; Buffer size adapts to ROWS & COLS

SECTION .text                ; Section containing code

global  main                 ; Linker needs this to find the entry point!
```

```
;-------------------------------------------------------------------
; MAIN PROGRAM:
;-------------------------------------------------------------------
main:
    mov rbp, rsp            ; for correct debugging

; Get the console and text display text buffer ready to go:
    call ClearTerminal   ; Send terminal clear string to console
    call ClrVid          ; Init/clear the video buffer

; Show a 64-character ruler above the table display:
    mov rax,1               ; Start ruler at display position 1,1
    mov rbx,1
    mov rcx,32              ; Make ruler 32 characters wide
    call Ruler             ; Generate the ruler

; Now let's generate the chart itself:
    mov rdi,VidBuff         ; Start with buffer address in RDI
    add rdi,COLS*CHRTROW    ; Begin table display down CHRTROW lines
    mov rcx,224            ; Show 256 chars minus first 32
    mov al,32             ; Start with char 32; others won't show
.DoLn:
    mov bl,CHRTLEN        ; Each line will consist of 32 chars
.DoChr:
    stosb                  ; Note that there's no REP prefix!
    jrcxz AllDone          ; When the full set is printed, quit
    inc al                 ; Bump the character value in AL up by 1
    dec bl                 ; Decrement the line counter by one
    loopnz .DoChr          ; Go back & do another char until BL goes to 0
    add rdi,COLS-CHRTLEN   ; Move RDI to start of next line
    jmp .DoLn              ; Start display of the next line

; Having written all that to the buffer, send buffer to the console:
AllDone:
    call Show              ; Refresh the buffer to the console

Exit:
    ret
```

Nested Instruction Loops

Once all the registers are set up correctly according to the assumptions made by STOSB, the real work of showchargcc is performed by two instruction loops, one inside the other. The inner loop displays a line consisting of 32 characters. The outer loop breaks up the display into seven such lines. The inner loop is by far the more interesting of the two. Here it is:

```
.DoChr:
    stosb                  ; Note that there's no REP prefix!
```

```
jrcxz AllDone   ; When the full set is printed, quit
inc al          ; Bump the character value in AL up by 1
dec bl          ; Decrement the line counter by one
loopnz .DoChr   ; Go back & do another char until BL goes to 0
```

The work here (putting a character into the display buffer) is again done by STOSB. Once again, STOSB is working solo, without REP. Without REP to pull the loop inside the CPU, you have to set the loop up yourself.

Keep in mind what happens each time STOSB fires: The character in AL is written to the memory location pointed to by RDI, and RDI is incremented by 1. At the other end of the loop, the LOOPNZ instruction decrements RCX by 1 and closes the loop.

During register setup, we loaded RCX with the number of characters we wanted to display—in this case, 224. (It's 224 characters because the first 32 characters in the full roster of 256 are mostly control characters and can't be displayed.) Each time STOSB fires, it places another character in the display buffer VidBuff, and there is one fewer character left to display. RCX acts as the master counter, keeping track of when we finally display the last remaining character. When RCX goes to zero, we've displayed the appropriate subset of the ASCII character set and the job is done.

Jumping When RCX Goes to 0

JRCXZ is a special branching instruction created specifically to help with loops like this. In Chapter 10, I explained how it's possible to branch using one of the many variations of the JMP instruction, based on the state of one or more of the CPU flags. Earlier in this chapter, I explained the LOOP instruction, which is a special-purpose sort of a JMP instruction, one combined with an implied DEC RCX instruction. JRCXZ is yet another variety of JMP instruction, but one that doesn't watch any of the flags or decrement any registers. Instead, JRCXZ watches the RCX register. When it sees that RCX has just gone to zero, it jumps to the specified label. If RCX is still nonzero, execution falls through to the next instruction in line.

In the case of the inner loop shown previously, JRCXZ branches to the "close up shop" code when it sees that RCX has finally gone to 0. This is how the showchar program terminates.

Most of the other JMP instructions have partners that branch when the governing flag is *not* true. That is, JC (Jump on Carry) branches when the Carry flag equals 1. Its partner, JNC (Jump on Not Carry), jumps if the Carry flag is *not* 1. However, JRCXZ is a loner. There is *no* JRCXNZ instruction, so don't go looking for one in the instruction reference!

Closing the Inner Loop

Assuming that RCX has not yet been decremented to 0 by the STOSB instruction (a condition watched for by JRCXZ), the loop continues. AL is incremented. This is how the next ASCII character in line is selected. The value in AL is sent to the location stored in RDI by STOSB. If you increment the value in AL, you change the displayed character to the next one in line. For example, if AL contains the value for the character A (65), incrementing AL changes the A character to a B (66). On the next pass through the loop, STOSW will fire a B at the screen instead of an A.

After the character code in AL is incremented, BL is decremented. Now, BL is not directly related to the string instructions. Nothing in any of the assumptions made by the string instructions involves BL. We're using BL for something else entirely here. BL is acting as a counter that governs the length of the lines of characters shown on the screen. BL was loaded earlier with the value represented by the equate CHRTLEN, which has the value 32. On each pass through the loop, the DEC BL instruction decrements the value of BL by 1. Then the LOOPNZ instruction gets its moment in the sun.

LOOPNZ is a little bit different from our friend LOOP that we examined earlier. It's just different enough to get you into trouble if you don't truly understand how it works. Both LOOP and LOOPNZ decrement the RCX register by 1. LOOP watches the state of the RCX register and closes the loop until RCX goes to 0. LOOPNZ watches *both* the state of the RCX register *and* the state of the Zero flag ZF. (LOOP ignores ZF.) LOOPNZ will close the loop only if RCX <> 0 *and* ZF = 0. In other words, LOOPNZ closes the loop only if RCX still has something left in it *and* if the Zero flag ZF is not set.

So, what exactly is LOOPNZ watching for here? Remember that immediately prior to the LOOPNZ instruction, we're decrementing BL by 1 through a DEC BL instruction. The DEC instruction *always* affects ZF. If DEC's operand goes to zero as a result of the DEC instruction, ZF goes to 1 (is set). Otherwise, ZF stays at 0 (remains cleared). So, in effect, LOOPNZ is watching the state of the BL register. Until BL is decremented to 0 (setting ZF), LOOPNZ closes the loop. After BL goes to zero, the inner loop is finished, and execution falls through LOOPNZ to the next instruction.

What about RCX? Well, LOOPNZ is in fact watching RCX—but so is JRCXZ. JRCXZ is actually the switch that governs when the whole loop—both inner and outer portions—has done its work and must stop. So, while LOOPNZ does watch RCX, somebody else is doing that task, and that somebody else will take action on RCX before LOOPNZ can. LOOPNZ's job is thus to decrement RCX but to watch BL. It governs the inner of the two loops.

Closing the Outer Loop

But does that mean that JRCXZ closes the outer loop? No. JRCXZ tells us when *both* loops are finished. Closing the outer loop is done a little differently from closing the inner loop. Take another look at the two nested loops:

```
.DoLn:
     mov bl,CHRTLEN          ; Each line will consist of 32 chars
.DoChr:
     stosb                   ; Note that there's no REP prefix!
     jrcxz AllDone           ; When the full set is printed, quit
     inc al                  ; Bump the character value in AL up by 1
     dec bl                  ; Decrement the line counter by one
     loopnz .DoChr           ; Go back & do another char until BL = 0
     add rdi,COLS-CHRTLEN    ; Move RDI to start of next line
     jmp .DoLn               ; Start display of the next line
```

The inner loop is considered complete when we've displayed one full line of the ASCII table to the screen. BL governs the length of a line, and when BL goes to zero (which the LOOPNZ instruction detects), a line is finished. LOOPNZ then falls through to the ADD instruction that modifies RDI.

We modify RDI to jump from the address of the end of a completed line in the display buffer to the start of the next line at the left margin. This means we have to "wrap" by some number of characters from the end of the ASCII table line to the end of the visible screen. The number of bytes this requires is given by the assembly-time expression COLS-CHRTLEN. This is basically the difference between the length of one ASCII table line and width of the virtual screen. (*Not* the width of the terminal window to which the virtual screen is displayed!) The result of the expression is the number of bytes that we must move further into the display buffer to come to the start of the next line at the left screen margin.

But after that wrap is accomplished by modifying RDI, the outer loop's work is done, and we close the loop. This time, we do it *unconditionally* by way of a simple JMP instruction. The target of the JMP instruction is the .DoLn local label. No ifs, no arguments. At the top of the outer loop (represented by the .DoLn label), we load the length of a table line back into the now-empty BL register and then drop back into the inner loop. The inner loop starts firing characters at the buffer again and will continue to do so until JRCXZ detects that RCX has gone to 0.

At that point, both the inner and outer loops are finished, and the full ASCII table has been written into VidBuff. With this accomplished, the buffer can be sent to the Linux console by calling the Show procedure.

Showchar Recap

Let's look back at what we've just been through, as it's admittedly pretty complex. The `showchar` program contains two nested loops: The inner loop shoots characters at the screen via `STOSB`. The outer loop shoots *lines* of characters at the screen, by repeating the inner loop some number of times. (Here, 7.)

The inner loop is governed by the value in the BL register, which is initially set up to take the length of a line of characters. (Here, 32.) The outer loop is not explicitly governed by the number of lines to be displayed. That is, you don't load the number 7 into a register and decrement it. Instead, the outer loop continues until the value in RCX goes to 0, indicating that the whole job—displaying all of the 224 characters that we want shown—is done.

The inner and outer loops both modify the registers that `STOSB` works with. The inner loop modifies AL after each character is fired at the screen. This makes it possible to display a different character each time `STOSB` fires. The outer loop modifies RDI (the destination index register) each time a *line* of characters is complete. This allows us to break the destination string up into seven separate, noncontiguous, nonidentical lines.

Command-Line Arguments, String Searches, and the Linux Stack

When you launch a program at the Linux console command prompt, you have the option of including any reasonable number of arguments after the pathname of the executable program. In other words, you can execute a program named `showargs1` like this:

```
$./showargs1 time for tacos
```

The three arguments follow the program name and are separated by space characters. Note that these are *not* the same as I/O redirection parameters, which require the use of the redirection operators ">" or "<" and are handled separately by Linux.

When one of your programs begins running, any command-line arguments that were entered when the program was launched are passed to the program on the Linux stack. In this chapter, we'll see how to access a program's command-line arguments from an assembly language program. In the process, we'll get to see yet another x86 string instruction in action: `SCASB`.

Displaying Command-Line Arguments from SASM

The fact that Linux places command-line arguments on the stack doesn't mean you have to directly access the stack to get at them. From programs written inside the SASM IDE, your access to the arguments comes to you in registers RSI and RDI. It works like this:

- At program startup, register RDI contains a value, 1 or greater, indicating the number of command-line arguments. The value is always at least 1 because Linux always places the program's command-line invocation text as the first item in its list of command-line arguments.

- At startup, register RSI contains the address of the first item in the list of command-line arguments. Remember that that first item is always the command-line invocation of the program. If there are no command-line arguments, the invocation text is the only thing you can access from RSI. If there are command-line arguments, there will be a list of addresses in memory, with each address pointing to one of the arguments.

Remember that this is true of programs you build with SASM using the default build parameters, or non-SASM programs that you link with gcc. Why? SASM uses the Gnu C compiler gcc as a linker and requires the label main: as the start of the program. All C programs have what's called the *main function*, main(), which is the part of the program that you write. In essence, what SASM builds is a C program for which you write the main() function. The tricky part is that gcc links in a block of code that runs *before* your main() function begins executing.

This "startup" code does a number of things. For this discussion, what matters is that it copies the argument count and the pointer to the argument table from the stack and into registers RSI and RDI. See Figure 11.2. Note that programs linked with glibc but built outside of SASM have the same useful information in RSI and RDI, courtesy of the glibc startup code.

Later I'll explain how assembly programs built without linking with gcc can read the same information off the stack. For now take a look at Listing 11.4, a program that displays command-line parameters for you, written for SASM.

Listing 11.4: showargs1gcc.asm

```
;   Executable name : showargs1gcc
;   Version         : 2.0
;   Created date    : 10/17/2022
;   Last update     : 5/11/2023
;   Author          : Jeff Duntemann
;   Description     : A simple program for Linux, using NASM 2.14.02,
;                   : demonstrating how to access command line
;                   : arguments from programs written/built in SASM.
;
;               Build using SASM standard x64 build setup
;
SECTION .data                   ; Section containing initialized data
```

```
        ErrMsg db "Terminated with error.",10
        ERRLEN equ $-ErrMsg

        MAXARGS equ 5           ; More than 5 arguments triggers an error

SECTION .bss                    ; Section containing uninitialized data

SECTION .text                   ; Section containing code

global  main                    ; Linker needs this to find the entry point!

main:
        mov rbp, rsp            ; for correct SASM debugging

        mov r14,rsi             ; Put offset of arg table in r14
        mov r15,rdi             ; Put argument count in r15

        cmp qword r15,MAXARGS   ; Test for too many arguments
        ja Error                ; Show error message if too many args
                                ; and quit

; Use SCASB to find the 0 at the end of the single argument
        xor rbx,rbx             ; RBX contains the 0-based # (not address)
                                ; of current arg
Scan1:
        xor rax,rax             ; Searching for string-termination 0, so
                                ; clear AL to 0
        mov rcx,0000ffffh       ; Limit search to 65535 bytes max
        mov rdi,qword [r14+rbx*8] ; Put address of string to search in
                                ;         RDI, for SCASB
        mov rdx,rdi             ; Copy string address into RDX for subtraction



        cld                     ; Set search direction to up-memory
        repne scasb             ; Search for null (0) in string at RDI
        jnz Error               ; Jump to error message display
                                ; if null not found.

        mov byte [rdi-1],10     ; Store an EOL where the null used to be
        sub rdi,rdx             ; Subtract position of 0 in RDI from start
                                ; address in RDX
        mov r13,rdi             ; Put calculated arg length into R13

; Display the argument to stdout:
        mov rax,1               ; Specify sys_write call
        mov rdi,1               ; Specify File Descriptor 1: Standard Output
        mov rsi,rdx             ; Pass offset of the arg in RSI
        mov rdx,r13             ; Pass length of arg in RDX
        syscall                 ; Make kernel call
```

```
        inc rbx            ; Increment the argument counter
        cmp rbx,r15        ; See if we've displayed all the arguments
        jb Scan1           ; If not, loop back and do another
        jmp Exit           ; We're done! Let's pack it in!

Error:
        mov rax,1          ; Specify sys_write call
        mov rdi,1          ; Specify File Descriptor 2: Standard Error
        mov rsi,ErrMsg     ; Pass offset of the error message
        mov rdx,ERRLEN     ; Pass the length of the message
        syscall            ; Make kernel call

Exit:
        ret
```

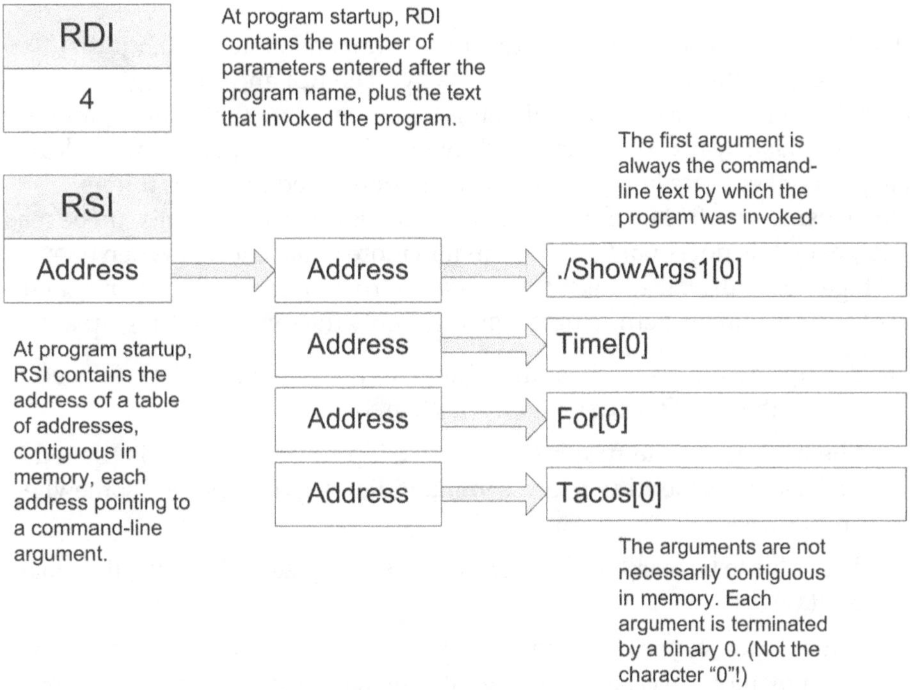

RDI

4

At program startup, RDI contains the number of parameters entered after the program name, plus the text that invoked the program.

The first argument is always the command-line text by which the program was invoked.

RSI

Address → Address → ./ShowArgs1[0]

At program startup, RSI contains the address of a table of addresses, contiguous in memory, each address pointing to a command-line argument.

Address → Time[0]

Address → For[0]

Address → Tacos[0]

The arguments are not necessarily contiguous in memory. Each argument is terminated by a binary 0. (Not the character "0"!)

Figure 11.2: How to access parameters from within SASM

String Searches with SCASB

Because the `glibc` startup code copies the argument count and table pointer into registers for you, getting at the command-line arguments is easy. You have what amounts to a table of addresses on the stack, and each address points to an argument. The only tricky part is determining how many bytes belong to each argument so that you can copy the argument data somewhere else if you need to or pass it to a Linux system call like `sys_write`. Because each argument ends with a single 0-byte, the challenge is plain: We have to search for that 0.

This can be done in the obvious way, in a loop that reads a byte from an address in memory, and then compares that byte against 0 before incrementing a counter and reading the next byte in memory. However, the good news is that the x64 instruction set implements such a loop in a string instruction that doesn't store data (like `STOSB`) or copy data (like `MOVSB`) but instead searches memory for a particular data value. This instruction is `SCASB` (Scan String by Byte), and if you've followed my presentation on the other string instructions so far, understanding it should be a piece of cake.

Listing 11.4 demonstrates `SCASB` by looking at the command-line arguments on the stack and building a table of argument lengths. It then echoes back the arguments (along with the invocation text of the executable file) to `stdout` via a call to `sys_write`.

The first thing to do is copy the argument count and table pointer into different registers, in this case, R14 and R15. Why? The RSI and RDI registers both have secret agendas: RDI is part of using `SCASB` (more on that shortly) and RSI is used to make `sys_write` calls. You'll want the argument count and address table pointer kept safe in registers that will not be used for other things.

We're using a prefix here for the first time in this book: `REPNE`. This can be read as "Repeat while not equal." I'll explain it in more detail shortly. When `REPNE` is used together with `SCASB`, the `REPNE SCASB` instruction can find the 0 byte at the end of each argument. Setting up `SCASB` is roughly the same as setting up `STOSB`:

- For up-memory searches (like this one) the `CLD` instruction is used to ensure that the Direction flag DF is cleared.

- The address of the first byte of the string to be searched is placed in RDI. Here, it's the address of a command-line argument stored somewhere on the stack.

- The value to be searched for is placed in 8-bit register AL. (Here, the binary digit 0.)

- A maximum count is placed in RCX. This is done to avoid searching too far in memory in case the byte you're searching for isn't actually there.

With all that in place, `REPNE SCASB` can be executed. As with `STOSB`, this creates a tight loop inside the CPU. On each pass through the loop, the byte at `[RDI]` is compared to the value in AL. If the values are equal, the loop is satisfied, and `REPNE SCASB` ceases executing. If the values are *not* equal, RDI is incremented by 1, RCX is decremented by 1, and the loop continues with another test of the byte at `[RDI]`.

When `REPNE SCASB` finds the character in AL and ends, RDI will point to the byte *after* the found character's position in the search string. If you want to access the found character, you must subtract 1 from RDI, as the program does when it replaces the terminating 0 character with an EOL character:

```
mov byte [rdi-1],10 ; Store an EOL where the 0 used to be
```

REPNE vs. REPE

It's worth taking a closer look at the REPNE prefix here, along with its partner with the opposite sense, REPE. The SCASB instruction is a little different from STOSB and MOVSB in that it is a *conditional* string instruction. STOSB and MOVSB both repeat their action unconditionally when preceded by the REP prefix. There are no tests going on except testing RCX to see if the loop has gone on for the predetermined number of iterations. By contrast, SCASB performs a separate test every time it fires, and every test can go two ways. That's why we don't use the unconditional REP prefix with SCASB, but either the REPNE prefix or the REPE prefix.

When we're looking for a byte in the search string that matches the byte in AL, we use the REPNE prefix, as is done in the showargs1gcc program. When we're looking for a byte in the search string that does *not* match the byte in AL, we use REPE. You might think that this sounds backwards somehow, and it does. However, the sense of the REPNE prefix is this: Repeat SCASB as long as [RDI] does not equal AL. Similarly, the sense of the REPE prefix is this: Repeat SCASB as long as [RDI] equals AL. The prefix indicates how long the SCASB instruction should continue firing, not when it should stop.

It's important to remember that REPNE SCASB can end for either of two reasons: It finds a match to the byte in AL, or it counts RCX down to 0. In nearly all cases, if RCX is zero when REPNE SCASB ends, it means that the byte in AL was not found in the search string. However, there is the fluky possibility that RCX just happened to count down to zero when [RDI] contained a match to AL. That's not very likely, but there are some mixes of data where it might just occur.

Each time SCASB fires, it makes a comparison, and that comparison either sets or clears the Zero flag ZF. REPNE will end the instruction when its comparison sets ZF to 1. REPE will end the instruction when its comparison clears ZF to 0. However, to be absolutely sure that you catch the "searched failed" outcome, you *must* test ZF immediately after the SCASB instruction ends.

For REPNE SCASB: Use JNZ.
For REPE SCASB: Use JZ.

You Can't Pass Command-Line Arguments to Programs Within SASM

If you build and then run Listing 11.4 inside SASM, what will be shown is the first item in the list, which is the invocation text for the program. However, this invocation text won't include the name showargs1gcc. What you'll see is this or something very like this:

```
/tmp/SASM/SASMprog.exe
```

Why? When you run a program within SASM, what you're running is a temporary binary file called SASMprog.exe. SASM generates this file when it builds a program for you. It's the same filename for any program you write in SASM. The executable file showargs1gcc doesn't exist until you create it by saving the executable to disk. And you can't run it until you open a terminal window, navigate to the folder where the executable program exists, and then run it from the command line.

That leads us to one of SASM's major shortcomings: As best I know, there's no mechanism in SASM for storing command-line arguments that will be passed to a program running within SASM. To get showargs1gcc to actually show arguments, you have to save it as an executable file and run it from the terminal command line.

If you run showargs1gcc from the command line this way:

```
$ ./showargs1gcc time for tacos
```

you will see the following in the terminal window:

```
./showargs1gcc
time
for
tacos
```

Each command-line argument is on a separate line because the program replaces the 0-byte at the end of each argument with an EOL character.

Just a quick reminder: You save an executable file by selecting the File ⇨ Save .exe menu item in SASM and then entering the name you want to give the executable program file. The name doesn't have to be the name of the source code file minus the .asm. You don't have to use the .exe suffix. Most Linux executables are just a name without any suffix at all. You can name it whatever you want. However, I strongly suggest you save the executable file in the same folder where its source code file and makefile live.

The Stack, Its Structure, and How to Use It

The stack is much bigger and more complex than you might think. When Linux loads your program, it places a great deal of information on the stack before letting the program's code begin execution. This includes the invocation text of the executable that's running, any command-line arguments that were entered by the user when executing the program, and the current state of the Linux environment, which is a big to *very* big collection of textual configuration strings that defines how Linux is set up.

This is all laid out according to a plan, and I've summarized the plan in Figure 11.3. First, some jargon refreshers: The *top of the stack* is (counterintuitively) at the bottom of the diagram. It's the memory location pointed to by RSP when your program begins running. The *bottom of the stack* is at the top of the diagram. It's the highest address in the virtual address space that Linux gives to your program when it loads your program and runs it. This "top" and "bottom" business is an ancient convention that confuses a lot of people. Memory diagrams generally begin with low memory at the bottom of the page and depict higher memory above it, even though this means the bottom of the stack is at the top of the diagram. Get used to it; if you're going to understand the literature, you have no choice.

Linux builds the stack from high memory toward low memory, beginning at the bottom of the stack and going down-memory from there. When your program code actually begins running, RSP points to the top of the stack. Here's a more detailed description of what you'll find on the stack at startup:

- At RSP (i.e., the top of the stack) is a 64-bit number, giving you the count of the command-line arguments present on the stack. *This value is always at least 1*, even if no arguments were entered. The text typed by the user when executing the program is counted in with any command-line parameters, and this "invocation text" is always present, which is why the count is always at least 1.

- The next 64-bit item up-memory from RSP is the address of the invocation text by which the executable file was run. The text may be fully qualified, which means that the pathname includes the directory path to the file from your /home directory; for example, /home/asmstuff/asm4ecode/ showargs2/showargs2. This is how the invocation text looks when you run your program from the Insight debugger. (More on Insight in Appendix A.) If you use the "dot slash" method of invoking an executable from within the current directory, you'll see the executable name prefixed by . /.

- If any command-line arguments were entered, their 64-bit addresses lie up-memory from RSP, with the address of the first (leftmost) argument followed by the address of the second, and so on. The number of arguments is obviously variable, though you'll rarely need more than four or five.

- The list of command-line argument addresses is terminated by a null pointer, which is jargon for 64 bits of binary 0.

- Up-memory from the null pointer begins a longish list of 64-bit addresses. How many depends on your particular Linux system, but it can be close to 200. Each of these addresses points to a null-terminated string (more on those shortly) containing one of the definitions belonging to the Linux environment.

■ At the end of the list of addresses of Linux environment variables is another 64-bit null pointer, and that marks the end of the stack's "directory." Beyond this point, you use the addresses found earlier on the stack to access items still further up-memory.

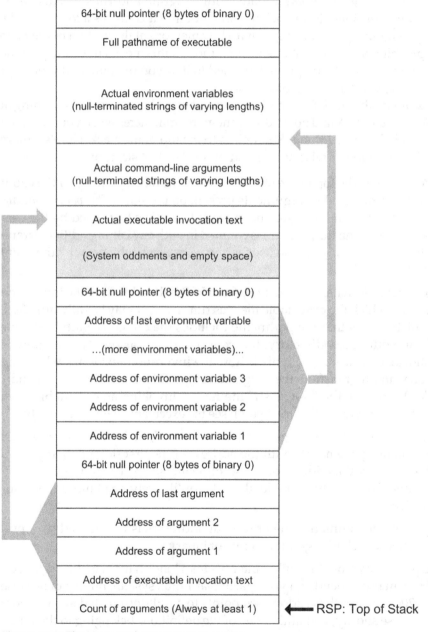

Figure 11.3: The Linux stack at program execution

Accessing the Stack Directly

Listing 11.4 runs in SASM, and the C startup code helpfully copies the argument count and argument table address into registers. If you're not using SASM, that helpful step won't happen. You have to access the stack directly. Listing 11.5 shows how this can be done.

Listing 11.5: showargs2.asm

```
;   Executable    : showargs2
;   Version       : 2.0
;   Created date  : 11/3/2022
;   Last update   : 5/15/2023
;   Author        : Jeff Duntemann
;   Description   : A simple program in assembly for Linux, using
;                   NASM 2.15.05, demonstrating the way to access
;                   command line arguments on the stack. This version
;                   accesses the stack "nondestructively" by using
;                   memory references calculated from RBP rather than
;                   POP instructions.
;
;   Use this makefile to build, with the required tab characters:
;
;   showargs2: showargs2.o
;       ld -o showargs2 -g showargs2.o
;   showargs2.o: showargs2.asm
;       nasm -f elf64 -g -F dwarf showargs2.asm -l showargs2.lst
;

SECTION .data           ; Section containing initialized data

    ErrMsg db "Terminated with error.",10
    ERRLEN equ $-ErrMsg

SECTION .bss            ; Section containing uninitialized data

; This program handles up to MAXARGS command-line arguments. Change
; the value of MAXARGS if you need to handle more arguments than the
; default 10. Argument lengths are stored in a table. Access arg
; lengths this way:
;     [ArgLens + <index reg>*8]
; Note that when the argument lengths are calculated, an EOL char
; (10h) is stored into each string where the terminating null was
; originally. This makes it easy to print out an argument
; using sys_write.

    MAXARGS    equ  10        ; Maximum # of args we support
    ArgLens:   resq MAXARGS   ; Table of argument lengths
```

```
    SECTION .text         ; Section containing code

    global _start         ; Linker needs this to find the entry point!

    _start:
        push rbp          ; Alignment prolog
        mov rbp, rsp
        and rsp,-16

; Copy the command line argument count from the stack and validate it:
        mov r13, [rbp+8]            ; Copy argument count from the stack
        cmp qword r13,MAXARGS       ; See if the arg count exceeds MAXARGS
        ja Error                    ; If so, exit with an error message

; Here we calculate argument lengths and store lengths in
; table ArgLens:
        mov rbx,1                   ; Stack address offset starts at RBX*8

ScanOne:
        xor rax,rax       ; Searching for 0, so clear AL to 0
        mov rcx,0000ffh ; Limit search to 65535 bytes max
        mov rdi,[rbp+8+rbx*8] ; Put address of string to search in RDI
        mov rdx,rdi       ; Copy starting address into RDX

        cld               ; Set search direction to up-memory
        repne scasb       ; Search for null (binary 0) in string at RDI
        jnz Error         ; REPNE SCASB ended without finding AL

        mov byte [rdi-1],10  ; Store an EOL where the null used to be
        sub rdi,rdx          ; Subtract position of 0 from start address
        mov [ArgLens+rbx*8],rdi  ; Put length of arg into table
        inc rbx           ; Add 1 to argument counter
        cmp rbx,r13       ; See if arg counter exceeds argument count
        jbe ScanOne       ; If not, loop back and scan another one

; Display all arguments to stdout:
        mov rbx,1 ; Start (for stack addressing reasons) at 1
Showem:
        mov rax,1         ; Specify sys_write call
        mov rdi,1         ; Specify File Descriptor 1: Standard Output
        mov rsi,[rbp+8+rbx*8]    ; Pass offset of the argument
        mov rdx,[ArgLens+rbx*8] ; Pass the length of the argument
        syscall           ; Make kernel call
        inc rbx           ; Increment the argument counter
        cmp rbx,r13       ; See if we've displayed all the arguments
        jbe Showem        ; If not, loop back and do another
        jmp Exit          ; We're done! Let's pack it in!
```

```
Error:
        mov rax,1        ; Specify sys_write call
        mov rdi,1        ; Specify File Descriptor 2: Standard Error
        mov rsi,ErrMsg   ; Pass offset of the error message
        mov rdx,ERRLEN   ; Pass the length of the message
        syscall          ; Make kernel call

Exit:
        mov rsp,rbp
        pop rbp

        mov rax,60       ; Code for Exit Syscall
        mov rdi,0        ; Return a code of zero
        syscall          ; Make kernel call
```

Program Prologs and Epilogs

Here's a quick note on a tricky subject: stack alignment. I'm going to cover stack alignment in more detail in Chapter 12, but Listing 11.5 contains something interesting: the *alignment prolog*.

```
push rbp         ; Alignment prolog
mov rbp, rsp
and rsp,-16
```

It goes at the beginning of programs that do *not* link with the glibc library. (These are programs that begin at the _start: label. Programs you create with make typically use the alignment prolog.) The x64 ABI standard requires that the stack be aligned on a 16-byte (not bit!) boundary. The AND RSP, -16 is what guarantees that the stack will be aligned. I've discussed AND before; you should catch on quickly that this instruction forces the lower four bits of the stack pointer to 0. It's now aligned to a 16-byte boundary, even if it wasn't before.

Pushing RBP on the stack gives you an anchor from which to address data items such as command-line parameters existing "lower down" (which really means "in higher memory") on the stack. It also helps keep the stack aligned, though how that works will have to wait for the next chapter. The practical consequence of having RBP at the top of the stack is that it contains the original value of the stack pointer. The downside is that you have to skip over it to get to the command-line arguments.

There is also something called an *epilog*, which comes at the end of the program, right before it returns control to Linux. The epilog (again, just for non-SASM programs) comes just before the program exits using SYSCALL:

```
mov rsp,rbp
pop rbp
```

The epilog's purpose is to restore the stack to the state it was on entry to the function. How that happens will have to wait for Chapter 12. Now, you may ask here why we used the alignment prolog in this example and none of the earlier ones. For programs linked with the gcc compiler and glibc library, the stack will be already aligned. So, SASM programs don't need the alignment prolog. SASM does require the MOV RBP,RSP instruction at the beginning of the MAIN: function, or its debugger interface may not work correctly.

Again, I'll take up stack alignment in more detail in Chapter 12. For simple programs that don't use the stack a lot (like most of the examples in this book), stack misalignment may not cause much or any trouble. Still, it's a good idea to get in the habit of placing the alignment prolog at the beginning of your non-SASM programs.

Addressing Data on the Stack

Accessing the stack requires that you know what's on it and where. The "where" begins at what we call the top of the stack, which is the address present in the stack pointer RSP when the program begins running. Note that right after pushing RBP onto the stack, the prolog copies RSP into RBP. This gives you a solid pointer to the stack as it existed when Linux began executing your program. With the original top of the stack safely present in RBP, stack pointer RSP can move up or down as procedures are called and returned from. (The showargs2 program does none of that, for simplicity's sake.) Also, you can push temporary values onto the stack for later use, though with twice as many general-purpose registers in the x64 architecture, this is done less and less often as new code is written. RBP was once BP in the 16-bit era, and the name meant "base pointer." It was created to hold the initial value of the stack pointer, providing a "base" from which to reference other items on the stack.

So what's on the stack as you inherit it from Linux? I've drawn it out in Figure 11.3. This is its state before the prolog pushes RBP onto it. At the top of the stack is an 8-byte value representing the number of command-line arguments. There is always at least 1 item on the stack: the program invocation text. In other words, if the value in [RBP] is 5, there are four actual command-line arguments. The fifth item is the invocation text, which appears first on the stack. The program will display an error message if more than MAXARGS arguments (here, 10) are entered.

Immediately after the argument count is a table of 64-bit addresses pointing to the actual arguments. How many addresses are there depends on how many arguments were entered on the command line. There is always at least one. The first address in the table is the address of the text entered by the user to invoke the program. After that the addresses point to the command-line arguments in the order that they were entered by the user.

Everything read from the stack in `showargs2` is read based on the address in RBP. Testing the number of arguments against a maximum value is done this way:

```
mov r13,[rbp+8]    ; Copy argument count from the stack into R13
cmp r13,MAXARGS    ; See if the arg count exceeds MAXARGS
ja Error           ; If so, exit with an error message
```

Here, the argument count is at the address contained in RBP plus eight bytes, because RBP was pushed on the stack by the prolog and must be "gotten past" to reach the argument count. The fact that RBP holds the address tells the assembler that the value represented by MAXARGS is to be treated as a 64-bit quad word, even if its value is only 10. Remember that equates are values, *not* locations in memory. If the argument count is over 10, the program aborts with a short error message.

Scanning each of the arguments to locate its terminating zero character is done using the most complex effective address calculation possible in x64: Base + (Index x Scale) + Displacement. (See the discussion of effective addresses, especially the figures, in Chapter 9.)

```
mov rsi,qword [rbp+8+rbx*8]
```

The effective address terms here are shown in a different order in the code to make it a little easier to understand how this particular memory reference works. Read it this way:

1. You begin with the "base" address for stack referencing, in RBP.

2. You add 8 to the base to "get past" RBP at the top of the stack. This is the "displacement" term of the effective address.

3. You multiply the 1-based ordinal number of the address being accessed by 8, which is the size (in bytes) of all addresses in x64. In other words, for the second item in the argument list, you would multiply the ordinal number stored in RBX by 8, the size of addresses in x64. The smallest value added is at least 8, which gets you past the argument count.

4. Add the product of RBX and 8 to the base plus displacement, and you have the address of the first argument in the table. This address is copied into RDI, for use with the REPNE SCASB instruction.

If this isn't completely clear to you, go back and read it again. Memory addressing is the single most important concept in assembly language work. If you don't understand memory addressing, knowing the machine instructions and registers will help you little if at all.

Don't Pop!

In the 2009 edition of this book, I presented a version of showargs that accesses items on the stack by popping them into registers. It certainly works, but now in 2023 I recommend that you avoid popping things off the stack unless your own code pushed them there. As you might imagine, popping the argument count into a register like RAX changes the original stack contents by moving RSP. If you can reference stack contents via a single memory address based on RBP, you won't have to worry as much about the bugs that can happen once RSP no longer points to the top of the stack as you originally received it from Linux.

Heading Out to C

Calling External Functions Written in the C Language

There's a lot of value in learning assembly language, most of it stemming from the requirement that you *must* know in detail how everything works or you won't get very far. From the very dawn of digital electronic computing, this has always been true, but from it follows a fair question: *Do I really have to know all that?*

The fair answer is no. It's possible to write extremely effective programs without having an assembly-level grip on the underlying machine and the operating system. This is what higher-level languages were created to allow: easier, faster programming at a higher level of abstraction. It's unclear how much of today's software would exist at all if it all had to be written in assembly language.

That includes Linux. There are some small portions of Linux written in assembly, but overall, the bulk of the operating system is written in C. (These days, post-2022, parts of Linux are starting to be written in a much newer and more memory-secure programming language called Rust.) The Linux universe revolves around the C language, and if you expect to make significant use of assembly language under Linux, you had better be prepared to learn some C and use it when you must.

There is almost immediate payoff: being able to access libraries of procedures written in C. There are thousands of such libraries, and those associated with the Linux operating system are mostly free and come with C source code. There are pros and cons to using libraries of C *functions* (as procedures are called in the C culture), but the real reason for learning the skills involved in calling C functions is that it's part of knowing how everything works, especially under Linux, where the C language has left its fingerprints everywhere you look.

Virtually all the programming examples you'll see for Linux that don't involve interpreted languages such as Perl or Python will be in C or C++. (I won't be touching on C++ in this book—nor up-and-comer Rust.) Most significantly, the C runtime library contains a lot of extremely useful functions but requires that you use the C protocols when making calls to those functions. So if you don't already know the C language, buy a book and get down and bash out some C. You don't need to do a lot of it, but make sure that you understand all the basic C concepts, especially as they apply to function calls. I'll try to fill in the lower-level gaps in this book, but I can't teach the language itself nor all the baggage that comes with it. You may find C a little distasteful (as I did and still do) or you may love it, but what you must understand is that *you can't escape it*, even if your main interest in Linux lies in assembly language.

What's GNU?

Way back in the late 1970s, a brilliant Unix hacker named Richard Stallman wanted his own copy of Unix. He didn't want to pay for it, however, so he did the obvious thing—obvious to him, at least: He began writing his own version. (If it's not obvious to you, well, you don't understand Unix culture.) However, he was unsatisfied with all the programming tools available at the time and objected to their priciness as well. So, as a prerequisite to writing his own version of Unix, Stallman set out to write his own compiler, assembler, and debugger. (He had already written his own editor, the legendary EMACS.)

Stallman named his version of Unix *GNU*, a recursive acronym meaning "GNU's Not Unix." This was a good chuckle and one way of getting past AT&T's trademark lawyers, who were fussy in those days about who used the word *Unix* and how. As time went on, the GNU tools took on a life of their own, and as it happened, Stallman never actually finished the GNU operating system itself. Other free versions of Unix appeared, and there was some soap opera for a few years regarding who actually owned what parts of which. This so disgusted Stallman that he created the Free Software Foundation as the home base for GNU tools development and created a radical sort of software license called the GNU Public License (GPL), which is sometimes informally called "copyleft." Stallman released the GNU tools under the GPL, which not only required that the software be free (including all source code) but prevented people from making minor mods to the software and claiming the derivative work as their own. Changes and improvements had to be given back to the GNU community.

This seemed like major nuttiness at the time, but over the years since then it has taken on a peculiar logic and life of its own. The GPL has allowed software released under the GPL to evolve tremendously quickly because large numbers of people were using and improving it and giving back the improvements without charge or restriction. Out of this bubbling open-source pot eventually arose Linux, the premier GPL operating system. Linux was built with and is maintained with the GNU tool set. If you're going to program under Linux, regardless of what language you're using, you will eventually use one or more of the GNU tools.

The Swiss Army Compiler

The copy of EMACS that you will find on modern distributions of Linux doesn't have a whole lot of Richard Stallman left in it—it's been rewritten umpteen times by many other people over the past 30-odd years. Where the Stallman legacy persists most strongly is in the GNU language compilers. There are a number of them, but the one that you must understand as thoroughly as possible is the GNU C Compiler, gcc. (Lowercase letters are something of an obsession in the Unix world, a fetish not well understood by a lot of people, myself included.)

Why use a C compiler for working in assembly? Mostly this: gcc does much more than simply compile C code. It's a sort of Swiss army knife development tool. In fact, I might better characterize what it does as *building* software rather than simply *compiling* it. In addition to compiling C code to object code, gcc governs both the assembly step and the link step.

Assembly step? Yes, indeedy. There is a GNU assembler called gas, though it's an odd thing that isn't really intended to be used by human programmers. What gcc does is control gas and the GNU linker ld (which you're already using in makefiles) like puppets on strings. If you use gcc, especially at the beginner level, you don't have to do much direct messing around with gas or ld.

Let's talk more about this.

Building Code the GNU Way

Assembly language work is a departure from C work, and gcc is first and foremost a C compiler. Therefore, we need to look first at the process of building C code. On the surface, building a C program for Linux using the GNU tools is pretty simple. Behind the scenes, however, it's a seriously hairy business. While it looks like gcc does all the work, what gcc really does is act as master controller for several GNU tools, supervising a code assembly line that you don't need to see unless you specifically want to.

Theoretically, this is all you need to do to generate an executable binary file from C source code:

```
gcc eatc.c -o eatc
```

Here, gcc takes the file eatc.c (which is a C source code file) and crunches it to produce the executable file eatc. (The -o option tells gcc what to name the executable output file.) However, there's more going on here than meets the eye. Take a look at Figure 12.1 as we go through it. In the figure, shaded arrows indicate movement of information. Blank arrows indicate program control.

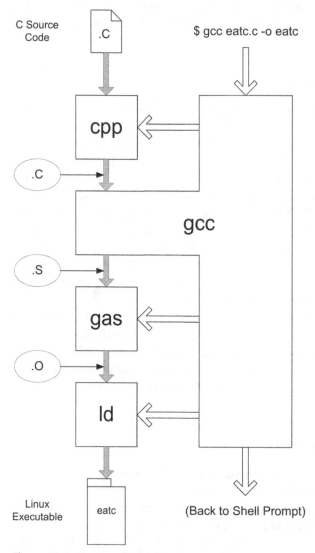

Figure 12.1: How gcc builds Linux executables

The programmer invokes gcc from the shell command line, typically in a terminal window. Then gcc takes control of the system and immediately invokes a utility called the C preprocessor, cpp. The preprocessor takes the original C source code file and handles certain items like #includes and #defines. It can be thought of as a sort of macro expansion pass on the C source code file.

When cpp is finished with its work, gcc takes over in earnest. From the pre-processed C source code file, gcc generates an assembly language source code file with an .s file extension. This is literally the assembly code equivalent of the C statements in the original .c file, in human-readable form. If you develop any skill in reading AT&T assembly syntax and mnemonics (more on which a little later), you can learn a *lot* from inspecting the .s files produced by gcc.

When gcc has completed generating the assembly language equivalent of the C source code file, it invokes the GNU assembler, gas, to assemble the .s file into object code. This object code is written out in a file with an .o extension.

The final step involves the linker, ld. The .o file contains binary code, but it's *only* the binary code generated from statements in the original .c file. The .o file does *not* contain the code from the standard C libraries that are so important in C programming. Those libraries have already been compiled and simply need to be linked into your application. The linker ld does this work at gcc's direction. The good part is that gcc knows precisely which of the standard C libraries need to be linked to your application to make it work, and it always includes the right libraries in their right versions. So, although gcc doesn't actually do the linking, *it knows what needs to be linked*—and that is valuable knowledge indeed, as your programs grow more and more complex.

Finally, ld spits out the fully linked and executable program file. At that point, the build is done, and gcc returns control to the Linux shell. Note that all of this is typically done with one simple command to gcc!

SASM Uses GCC

Some of this may start to sound familiar. We've been using SASM for several chapters now, and SASM has a fundamentally different way of working than we learned with makefiles and the Linux make utility. I alluded early on to the fact that what SASM produces is actually a C program written in assembly language. If you look at the Build tab of SASM's Settings menu, note that gcc (and not ld) is shown in the linker path. This doesn't mean that ld isn't used, as it is when we use makefiles. It means that gcc has full control of the link process, calling ld when necessary to link in precompiled libraries of binary C code.

How to Use gcc in Assembly Work

The process I just described, and drew out for you in Figure 12.1, is how a C program is built under Linux using the GNU tools. I went into some detail here because we're going to use part—though only part—of this process to make our assembly programming easier. It's true that we don't need to convert C source code to assembly code—and in fact, we don't need gas to convert gas assembly source code to object code. However, we do need gcc's expertise at linking. We're going to tap into the GNU code-building process at the link stage so that gcc can coordinate the link step for us.

When we assemble an .asm Linux program using NASM, NASM generates an .o file containing binary object code. As we've seen, invoking NASM under 64-bit Linux is typically done this way:

```
nasm -f elf64 -g -F dwarf eatclib.asm
```

This command will direct NASM to assemble the file eatclib.asm and generate a file called eatclib.o. The -f elf64 part tells NASM to generate object code in the 64-bit ELF format rather than one of the numerous other object code formats that NASM is capable of producing. The -g -F dwarf part enables the generation of debug information in the output file, in the DWARF format. The eatclib.o file is not by itself executable. It needs to be linked. So, we call gcc and instruct it to link the program for us:

```
gcc eatclib.o -o eatclib -no-pie
```

What of this tells gcc to link and not compile? The only input file called out in the command is a .o file containing object code. This fact alone tells gcc that all that needs to be done is to link the .o file with the C runtime library to produce the final executable. The -o eatclib part tells gcc that the name of the final executable file is to be eatclib.

Including the -o specifier is important. If you don't tell gcc precisely what to name the final executable file, it will punt and give the file the default filename for an executable, a.out.

The command line argument -no-pie tells gcc not to link the executable for the position-independent executable (PIE) technology. I'll explain this in detail later in this chapter. It's about reducing the vulnerability of an executable to certain exploits. It's OK to use the -no-pie option in simple, educational programs like those in this book. For production code, you need PIE.

Why Not gas?

You might be wondering why, if there's a perfectly good assembler installed automatically with every copy of Linux, I've bothered showing you how to install and use another one. Two reasons:

- The GNU assembler gas uses a peculiar syntax that is utterly unlike that of all the other familiar assemblers used in the x86/x64 world, including NASM. It has a whole set of instruction mnemonics unique to itself. I find them ugly, nonintuitive, and hard to read. This is the AT&T syntax, so named because it was created by AT&T as a portable assembly notation to make Unix easier to port from one underlying CPU to another. It's ugly in part because it was designed to be generic, and it can be reconfigured for any reasonable CPU architecture that might appear.

▪ More to the point, the notion of a "portable assembly language" is in my view a contradiction in terms. An assembly language should be a direct, complete, one-for-one reflection of the underlying machine architecture. Any attempt to make an assembly language generic moves the language away from the machine and limits the ability of an assembly programmer to direct the CPU as it was designed to be directed. The organization that created and evolves a CPU architecture is in the best position to define a CPU's instruction mnemonics and assembly language syntax without compromise. That's why I will always use and teach the Intel mnemonics.

If it were just this simple, I wouldn't mention gas at all, since you don't need gas to write Linux assembly language in NASM. However, one of the major ways you'll end up learning many of the standard C library calls is by using them in short C programs and then inspecting the .s assembly output files that gcc generates. So having some ability to read AT&T mnemonics can be useful while you're getting comfortable with C calling conventions used under Linux. I'll provide an overview of the AT&T syntax a little later in this chapter.

Linking to the Standard C Library

When you write an all-assembly program using a makefile and the make utility, you write *all* of it. Apart from an occasional dive into Linux kernel services, all the code that runs is only the code that you write. Linking in libraries of external assembly language procedures complicates this picture a little, especially if you weren't the one who wrote those libraries. Linking to functions in the standard C library (which for Linux is called glibc) complicates the picture even more. It may be some comfort to know that linking to glibc routines is easier in x64 assembly language than it was in 32-bit x86 assembly language.

As I've mentioned earlier, writing an assembly program in SASM is much like writing a C program in which you write the program's main body in assembly. SASM's generated programs are a sort of hybrid of C and assembly language. If you create a Linux assembly language program that links in glibc functions, you're doing pretty much the same thing. The structure of this hybrid is shown in Figure 12.2.

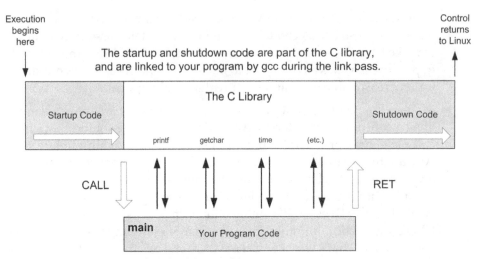

Figure 12.2: The structure of a hybrid C-assembly program

Your program is no longer the simple, start-at-the-top-and-go-down affair that your earlier assembly programs were. glibc is not just a collection of disjoint functions. It's the standard C runtime library, and as part of its standardness, it dictates a certain structure to any programs that link to it. This structure includes a block of code that runs before your program begins, and another block of code that runs after your program ends. Your program is called by the startup code as though your program were a procedure (with the CALL instruction), and it returns control to the C library code using a RET instruction.

Technically, your program *is* a procedure (again, called a *function* in C-land), and it helps to think of it as one. That's how I've drawn it in Figure 12.2. When Linux begins executing your program, it actually starts, not at the top of the code *you* wrote but at the beginning of the startup code block. When the startup code has done what it must, it executes a CALL instruction that takes execution down into your assembly code. When your assembly language program returns control to its caller via RET, the shutdown code begins executing, and it's the shutdown code that actually returns control to Linux via the necessary syscall kernel call.

Once you're linking C code into your assembly programs, it's not a good idea to use SYSCALL service 60 to exit a program and return to Linux. There's some housekeeping to be done, which might include flushing buffers and closing files or closing network connections. The C shutdown code does all this, and if you skip it, bad things may happen. Those bad things probably won't happen when you're working through simple code examples like those presented in this book, but once you start getting ambitious and write thousand-line programs, all that becomes possible and will cause you no end of grief.

Basically, when you're working with C, do things the C way.

In between the startup code and the shutdown code, you can make as many calls into glibc as you like. When you link your program using gcc, the code containing the C library routines that you call is linked into your program. Note well that the startup and shutdown code, as well as all the code for the library functions your program calls, is all physically present in the executable file that you generate with gcc.

C Calling Conventions

The glibc library isn't singling out assembly language programs for special treatment. Pure C programs work almost exactly the same way, and this is the reason that the main program portion of a C program is called the main *function*. It really is a function, the standard C library code for startup calls it with a CALL instruction, and it returns control to the shutdown code by executing a RET instruction.

The way the main program obtains control is therefore the first example you'll see of a set of rules we call the *C calling conventions*. The standard C library is nothing if not consistent, and that is its greatest virtue. All C library functions implemented on x64 processors follow these rules. Bake them into your synapses early, and you'll lose a lot less scalp than I did trying to figure them out by beating your head against them.

First and foremost, your program must begin with the global label main:. Using _start: won't work. The main function is labeled main:, period. SASM programs always begin with main: because SASM uses gcc to link in code from glibc.

That's where you start. The rest gets pretty complicated pretty quickly.

Callers, Callees, and Clobbers

If you've ever studied assembly programming for 32-bit Linux (as I taught in the 2009 edition of this book), you learned that passing parameters to C-style functions was done by pushing the parameters onto the stack before making the call. All gone. (OK, *almost* all gone. I'll come back to this.)

The biggest single difference between 32-bit calling conventions and 64-bit calling conventions lies in how you pass parameters to functions. Passing the first six parameters to an x64 function is done in registers rather than on the stack. If a function has more than six parameters (which is uncommon, and oftentimes bad design) the remaining parameters are passed on the stack.

This was done because we have a lot more registers now than we did in the 32-bit era. Pushing and popping the stack touches memory and is therefore slow. Writing to and reading from registers stays inside the CPU and is therefore much faster. Modern CPU cache technology makes stack usage faster than in ancient times, true, but even memory cache access is slower than register access.

You may remember that in earlier chapters programs passed parameters to Linux function calls using the x64 SYSCALL instruction. All such parameters (at least in the simple programs we worked with) are passed in registers. Furthermore, there is a system to it: The first six parameters are passed in specific registers in a very specific order. This order is as follows:

RDI

RSI

RDX

RCX

R8

R9

The first parameter passed to a function is always passed in RDI. If there are two parameters to be passed to a function, the first is passed in RDI and the second in RSI, and so on. This is true for calls via SYSCALL, and it's also true for calling C library functions.

Parameter order in registers is straightforward. The next part is subtle: Which registers can a function use internally and thus change, and which registers must remain unchanged after the function's execution? To put it in programmer jargon: Which registers can we clobber?

Once again, there's a system to it. These seven registers cannot be clobbered by a function: RSP, RBP, RBX, R12, R13, R14, and R15. This group of registers is called the *nonvolatile* registers, which basically means registers that must be preserved (or left unused) by the callee.

Wait—the *what?*

More jargon. Functions can call other functions. A function that calls another function is the *caller*. The function that is called is the *callee*. There's a sort of trust relationship between the caller and the callee: The callee promises the caller that the values of RSP, RBP, RBX, R12, R13, R14, and R15 will be the same when the callee finishes execution as they were when the callee began execution. The callee can use the nonvolatile registers, but those it uses must first be saved (pushed onto the stack) and restored (popped off the stack) before the callee returns to the caller.

The other registers are called *volatile*, meaning that the callee can use and change them with impunity. These are RAX, RCX, RDX, RSI, RDI, R8, R9, R10, and R11. If you're sharp, you'll notice that all six of the registers used in the C calling convention are volatile registers. This makes sense since the caller is already using them to pass values down to the callee.

But what if the caller is already using some of the volatile registers? If the caller wants any of the volatile registers to survive a trip through the callee, the caller must save them before calling the callee function. After the callee returns to the caller, the caller then restores whatever volatile registers it had saved on the stack by popping the saved values back into the registers.

This implies a lot more pushing and popping than usually happens. One of the challenges facing a good assembly language programmer is simply to stay out of memory, which includes pushing and popping the stack. We have more registers to use now, and cleverness in using those registers pays off, by making access to the stack less frequent.

Save only the registers you must *save, after you've exhausted all other options.*

There were reasons the x64 instruction set eliminated PUSHA and POPA.

Setting Up a Stack Frame

More registers notwithstanding, the stack is still extremely important in assembly language work, and this is doubly true in programs that interface with C, because in C (and in truth most other native-code high-level languages, including Pascal) the stack has a central role.

One low-level mechanism that does bear on Linux assembly work is that of the *stack frame*. Compilers depend on stack frames to create local variables in functions, and while stack frames are less useful in pure assembly work, you must understand them if you're going to call functions written by a high-level language compiler.

A stack frame is a location on the stack marked as belonging to a particular function, including the main() function. It is basically the region between the addresses contained in two registers: base pointer RBP and stack pointer RSP. This draws better than it explains; see Figure 12.3.

A stack frame is created by pushing a copy of RBP on the stack and then copying the stack pointer RSP into register RBP. The first two instructions in any assembly program that honors the C calling conventions must be these:

```
push rbp
mov  rbp,rsp
```

A lot of people call this the program's *prolog*, since it must be included as the start of any program respecting the C calling conventions. Unless the prolog is present, the gdb debugger and its debugger front ends like Insight will not operate correctly.

Once RBP is anchored as one end of your stack frame, the stack pointer RSP is free to move up and down the stack as your code requires for temporary storage. Calling functions in glibc under x64 requires less pushing and popping than it did in the old 32-bit world, now that most parameters are passed to functions in registers.

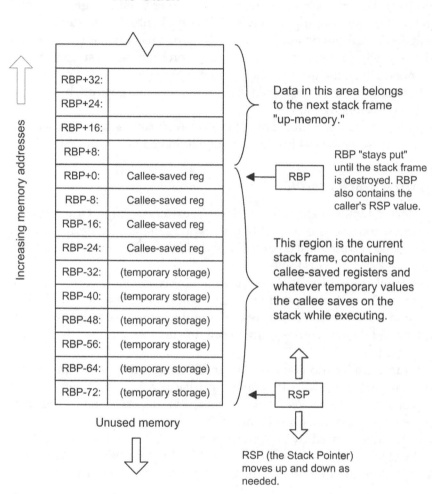

Figure 12.3: A stack frame

Destroying a Stack Frame in the Epilog

Before your program ends its execution by returning control to the startup/shutdown code (refer to Figure 12.2 if this relationship isn't clear), its stack frame must be destroyed. This sounds to many people like something wrong is happening, but not so: The stack frame must be destroyed, or your program will crash. ("Put away" might be a better term than "destroyed" . . . but programmers prefer colorful language, as you'll learn once you spend any significant time among them.)

Your stack must be clean before you destroy the stack frame and return control to the shutdown code. This simply means that any callee-saved registers and temporary values that you may have pushed onto the stack during the program's run must be gone. *Pop what you push!* With that done, we undo the logic we followed in creating the stack frame: We pop the caller's RBP value off the stack and exit, via two instructions that together are often called the *epilog*:

```
pop rbp
ret
```

That's it! The stack frame is gone, and the stack is now in the same state it was in when the startup code handed control to your program. The RET instruction sends control to the C library's shutdown code, so it can do whatever housekeeping must be done before returning control to Linux.

Stack Alignment

The purpose of the prolog and epilog are not immediately obvious, especially if you're coming to x64 for the first time after working in the 32-bit Linux world. It comes down to a new requirement: The x64 stack must be aligned on a 16-byte boundary. What this means is that when you return from a function (including main:), the stack pointer must be pointing at an address evenly divisible by 16. Why is this an issue? Remember that when a procedure (a *function* in C jargon) is called, the caller pushes the return address onto the stack. A return address is 8 bytes in size. But if you access the stack after adding 8 bytes to it (rather than 16) bad things may happen. It's not a guarantee, but it can happen, especially when your code becomes more ambitious than the simple examples in this book.

The prolog pushes RBP onto the stack. This adds another 8 bytes to the stack, for a total of 16. The stack is thus still aligned. In the epilog, you pop RBP's value off the stack. The RET instruction that ends the epilog pops the return address of the stack into the instruction pointer, so you've removed a total of 16 bytes from the stack. The stack was aligned when your main: function took control, courtesy of the glibc startup code, and it had better still be aligned when your program executes the RET instruction that returns control to the glibc shutdown code.

Stack alignment is also required when glibc is not involved, as in programs using a _start: label instead of main: . This time glibc won't help you because it isn't there. A prolog and epilog must still be present, though there is a little more to do than when you link glibc into your program. The required prolog is called the *stack alignment prolog*:

```
push rbp
mov rbp,rsp
and rsp,-16
```

The difference lies in the AND RSP, -16 instruction. This instruction zeros the lowest four bits of the stack pointer RSP. The last hex digit of the address then becomes 0, and the stack is aligned on a 16-byte boundary. If you're careful in your use of the stack, it will remain aligned, as we'll see shortly.

Here's the stack alignment epilog:

```
mov rsp,rbp
pop rbp
```

Another difference when using _start is that the epilog cannot return to Linux by executing a RET instruction. You have to use the Exit service via SYSCALL, as I explained in earlier chapters. After you POP RBP, you can use SYSCALL service 60 to return control to Linux.

So what about the procedures that you write yourself? Ideally, all procedures should begin with the prolog and end with the epilog. You can often get away without using the prolog/epilog in your own functions, especially if they're simple and don't do much with the stack. I've left out the prolog/epilog in some of the example programs in this book for simplicity's sake. Also, I don't take up stack frames in detail until this final chapter, and it's impossible to make sense of stack alignment without knowing how the stack works.

Later in this chapter, in Listing 12.6, randtest, the program passes a seventh parameter to printf() by pushing the parameter on the stack. Keeping the stack aligned on a 16-byte boundary is done a different way: by pushing a "dummy" item onto the stack (here, RAX; its contents are unimportant) and then, after calling printf(), adding 16 to RSP instead of 8. Here's where it's done; don't worry if you don't understand everything in the following snippet:

```
shownums:
    mov r12,qword [Pulls]       ; Put pull count into r12
    xor r13,r13
.dorow:
    mov rdi,ShowArray           ; Pass address of base string
    mov rsi,[Stash+r13*8+0]     ; Pass first element
    mov rdx,[Stash+r13*8+8]     ; Pass second element
    mov rcx,[Stash+r13*8+16]    ; Pass third element
    mov r8,[Stash+r13*8+24]     ; Pass fourth element
    mov r9,[Stash+r13*8+32]     ; Pass fifth element
    push rax                    ; To keep the stack 16 bytes aligned
    push qword [Stash+r13*8+40] ; Pass sixth element on the stack.
    xor rax,rax         ; Tell printf() no vector values coming
    call printf         ; Display the random numbers
    add rsp,16          ; Stack cleanup: 2 item X 8 bytes = 16
```

In this part of the code, pushing RAX decrements the stack by 8. Pushing the seventh parameter onto the stack decrements the stack by another 8, for a total of 16, keeping the stack aligned. So far so good. But that's only half the job. So after the call to printf() is made, we "clean up" the stack with some quick arithmetic: add back the size of both the parameter and the dummy copy of RAX to the stack pointer. In the snippet, pushing two QWORD values onto the stack moved the address in RSP down-memory by 16 bytes. To clean up, we add those 16 bytes back in with an ADD RSP, 16 instruction. The stack will then be both in alignment and "clean" again.

Earlier I told you to "pop what you push." Sometimes popping isn't practical. As long as you restore the stack pointer to the value it had before your push, everything will work out. If you push values onto the stack as local storage, make sure you add back the total size of all those values to RSP to make the stack "clean" again. And if you're not pushing a multiple of 16 bytes onto the stack, pad it by pushing dummy values until the total is a multiple of 16.

Now, why did the x86-64 System V ABI authors mandate a 16-byte aligned stack? Keeping the stack aligned on 16-byte boundaries at all times makes code simpler for a number of things, including the use of SSE vectors when they are stored on the stack. I won't be covering SSE or the other math subsystems in Intel CPUs in this book, so don't worry if that doesn't make sense just yet. Once you get your chops in assembly language, I encourage you to explore the x64 math instructions and vector registers.

One final note on stack alignment: SASM has issues with the prolog and epilog I show here. It needs the mov rbp, rsp instruction at the beginning, but nothing beyond that. The SASM epilog is simply the final RET.

Characters Out Via puts()

About the simplest useful function in glibc is puts(), which sends characters to standard output. Making a call to puts() from assembly language is so simple it can be done in three lines of code. The program in Listing 12.1 demonstrates puts(). The eatlibc program includes the prolog and the epilog. If you knock out the three instructions that set up and make the call to puts(), you can treat the rest as boilerplate for creating new programs that call functions in glibc.

Calling puts() this way is a good example, in miniature, of the general process you'll use to call most any C library routine. Again, in accordance with the general x64 calling conventions, we place the address of the string to be displayed in RDI. We don't need to pass a string length value. The puts() function starts at the beginning of the string at the address passed in RDI and sends characters to stdout until it encounters a 0 (null) character. However many characters lie between the first byte of the string and the first null is the number of characters that the console receives.

Listing 12.1: eatlibc.asm

```
;   Executable name : eatlibc
;   Version         : 3.0
;   Created date    : 11/12/2022
;   Last update     : 5/24/2023
```

```
;   Author          : Jeff Duntemann
;   Description     : Demonstrates calls made into libc, using NASM
;                     2.14.02 to send a short text string to stdout
;                     with puts().
;
;   Build using these commands:
;     nasm -f elf64 -g -F dwarf eatlibc.asm
;     gcc eatlibc.o -o eatlibc -no-pie


SECTION .data               ; Section containing initialized data

EatMsg: db "Eat at Joe's!",0

SECTION .bss                ; Section containing uninitialized data

SECTION .text               ; Section containing code

extern puts                 ; The simple "put string" routine from libc
global main                 ; Required for the linker to find the entry point

main:
    push rbp                ; Prolog sets up stack frame
    mov rbp,rsp

;; Everything before this is boilerplate; use it for all ordinary apps!

    mov rdi,EatMsg          ; Put address of string into rdi
    call puts               ; Call libc function for displaying strings
    xor rax,rax             ; Pass a 0 as the program's return value.

;; Everything after this is boilerplate; use it for all ordinary apps!
    pop rbp                 ; Destroy stack frame before returning
    ret                     ; Return control to Linux
```

Formatted Text Output with printf()

The puts() library routine may seem pretty useful, but compared to a few of its more sophisticated siblings, it's kid stuff. With puts() you can only send a simple text string to a file (by default, stdout), without any sort of formatting. Worse, puts() always includes an EOL character at the end of its display, whether you include one in your string data or not. This prevents you from using multiple calls to puts() to output several text strings all on the same line on the terminal.

About the best you can say for `puts()` is that it has the virtue of simplicity. For nearly all of your character output needs, you're way better off using a much more powerful library function called `printf()`. The `printf()` function allows you to do a number of truly useful things, all with one function call:

- Output text either with or without a terminating EOL
- Convert numeric data to text in numerous formats, by outputting formatting codes along with the data
- Output text to a file that includes multiple strings stored separately

If you've worked with C for more than half an hour, `printf()` will be perfectly obvious to you, but for people coming from other languages, it may take a little explaining.

The `printf()` routine will gladly display a simple string like "Eat at Joe's!"— but you can merge other text strings and converted numeric data with that base string as it travels toward standard output, and show it all seamlessly together. This is done by dropping *formatting codes* into the base string and then passing a data item to `printf()` for each of those formatting codes, along with the base string. A formatting code begins with a percent sign and includes information relating to the type and size of the data item being merged with the base string, as well as how that information should be presented.

Let's look at a very simple example to start out. Here's a base string containing one formatting code:

```
"The answer is %d, and don't you forget it!"
```

The `%d` formatting code simply tells `printf()` to convert a signed integer value to text and substitute that text for the formatting code in the base string. Of course, you must now pass an integer value to `printf()` (and I'll show you how that's done shortly), but when you do, `printf()` will convert the integer to text and merge it with the base string as it sends text to the stream. If the decimal value passed is 42, on the console you'll see this:

```
The answer is 42, and don't you forget it!
```

A formatting code actually has a fair amount of structure, and the `printf()` mechanism as a whole has more wrinkles than I have room to describe in detail in this book. Any good C reference will explain the whole thing in detail. The Wikipedia treatment is excellent:

```
https://en.wikipedia.org/wiki/Printf
```

Table 12.1 lists the most common and useful formatting codes.

Table 12.1: Printf() Formatting Codes

%d	Prints a signed, base-10 integer.
%u	Prints an unsigned, base-10 integer.
%x, %X	Prints an unsigned integer in hex; %x for lowercase, %X for upper.
%s	Prints a null-terminated string.
%c	Prints a single character.
%f	Prints a floating-point number.
%%	Prints a literal "%" character.

The most significant enhancement you can make to the formatting codes is to place an integer value between the % symbol and the code letter:

```
%5d
```

This code tells `printf()` to display the value right-justified within a field five characters wide. If you don't put a field width value there, `printf()` will simply give the value as much room as its digits require.

Remember that if you need to display a percent symbol, you must include two consecutive percent symbols in the string: The first is a formatting code that tells `printf()` to display the second as itself, and not as the lead-in to a formatting code.

Passing Parameters to printf()

Passing values to `printf()` follows the x64 calling conventions. If you're displaying a string with format codes embedded in it, the base string should be the first parameter, with its address passed in RDI. After that, the first value to be merged with the string is passed in RSI, the second in RDX, and so on, in the standard parameter register order. Values are plugged into the codes in the string in order, from left to right.

Listing 12.2 presents a very simple demonstration of `printf()` formatting. One interesting thing to notice is that you can pass numbers either by reference or by value. The first integer is passed by placing its address into RSI. The second integer is passed by copying a literal value into RDX. The third integer is also passed as a literal in RCX. The third value is shown in hexadecimal notation, even though the literal was a simple base-10 integer value loaded into RCX. The `printf()` function can do a lot of conversions like that.

You can merge text strings into the base string in a similar fashion by loading the addresses of the strings to be merged in registers and using the %s code instructing printf() where to plug in the secondary strings.

I've eliminated the comment header to save page space. The makefile for answer.asm is this:

```
answer: answer.o
    gcc answer.o -o answer -no-pie
answer.o: answer.asm
    nasm -f elf64 -g -F dwarf answer.asm
```

Don't forget to insert the required tabs if you type in and save the makefile!

Listing 12.2: answer.asm

```
section .data
    answermsg db "The answer is %d ... or is it %d? No! It's 0x%x!",10,0
    answernum dd 42

section .bss

section .text

extern  printf

global  main

main:
    push rbp                ; Prolog
    mov rbp,rsp

    mov rax,0               ; Count of vector regs..here, 0

    mov rdi,answermsg       ; Message/format string goes in RDI
    mov rsi,[answernum]     ; 2nd arg in RSI
    mov rdx,43              ; 3rd arg in RDX. You can use a numeric literal
    mov rcx,42              ; 4th arg in RCX. Show this one in hex
    mov rax,0               ; This tells printf no vector params are coming
    call printf             ; Call printf()

    pop rbp                 ; Epilog

    ret                     ; Return from main() to shutdown code
```

When you run answer, this is what you'll see:

```
The answer is 42 … or is it 43? No! It's 0x2a!
```

Printf() Needs a Preceding 0 in RAX

There's another small wrinkle to using `printf()`. In almost all cases (and certainly while you're just starting out in assembly), you should place the instruction MOV RAX,0 before the `printf()` call. The 0 in RAX tells the `printf()` function that there are no floating-point parameters in vector registers being passed to it. Once you do start using vector values, you need to place the count of those parameters in RAX before calling `printf()`. Explaining floating-point and vector registers is beyond the scope of this book, so if you're interested, do research it online.

This same requirement also applies to `scanf()`.

You Shall Have –No-Pie

In the makefiles for programs in this chapter that use gcc for a linker, you'll see the gcc option `-no-pie`. The purpose of this option is to prevent gcc from linking your program as a PIE. Explaining PIE in detail would be an advanced topic well beyond the scope of this book. Short form: PIE is a way to prevent certain kinds of code exploits, by placing portions of the executable file in random locations when the executable is loaded. This makes it impossible to predict where a given piece of code will be executing.

Return-oriented programming (ROP) attacks depend on knowing where certain portions of a program are in Linux's virtual memory system. PIE programs are less vulnerable to ROP attacks. The `-no-pie` option directs that the linker will *not* generate a PIE. This theoretically makes the `-no-pie` example programs from this book vulnerable to attacks. Theoretically. Once you're a seasoned programmer producing software for general use (and not simply learning programming), you should know enough to understand the issues and should research it online. PIE complicates debugging some, which is why I don't use PIE in my examples here. But once a program you're writing is debugged and working well, rebuild it as a PIE, which is the default when gcc acts as the linker.

Data In with fgets() and scanf()

Reading characters from the Linux keyboard using the SYSCALL instruction and the sys_read kernel call is simple but not very versatile. The standard C library has a better way. In fact, the C library functions for reading data from the keyboard (which is the default data source assigned to standard input) are almost the inverse of those that display data to standard output.

If you poke around in a C library reference (and you should—there are a multitude of interesting routines there that you can call from assembly programs), you may discover the gets() routine. You may have wondered (if I didn't choose to tell you here) why I didn't cover it. The gets() routine is simplicity itself: You pass it the name of a string array in which to place characters, and then the user types characters at the keyboard, which are placed in the array. When the user presses Enter, gets() appends a null at the end of the entered text and returns. What's not to love?

Well, how big is the array? And how dumb is your user?

Here's the catch: *There's no way to tell* gets() *when to stop accepting characters.* If the user types in more characters than you've allocated room to accept them in an array, gets() will gleefully keep accepting characters and overwrite whatever data is sitting next to your array in memory. If that something is something important, your program will almost certainly malfunction and may simply crash.

That's why, if you try to use gets(), gcc will warn you that gets() is dangerous. It's ancient, and *much* better machinery has been created in the (many) decades since Unix and the standard C library were first designed. The designated successor to gets() is fgets(), which has some safety equipment built-in—and some complications, too.

The complications stem from the fact that you must pass a file handle to fgets(). In general, standard C library routines whose names begin with f act on files. (I'll explain how to work with disk files a little later in this chapter.) You can use fgets() to read text from a disk file—but remember, in Unix terms, your keyboard is already connected to a file, the file called standard input, stdin. If we can connect fgets() to standard input, we can read text from the keyboard, which is what the old and hazardous gets() function does automatically.

The bonus in using fgets() is that it allows us to specify a maximum number of characters for the routine to accept from the keyboard. Anything else that the user types will be truncated and discarded. If this maximum value is no larger than the string buffer you define to hold characters entered by the user, there's no chance that using fgets() will crash your program.

Connecting fgets() to standard input is easy. As I explained earlier in this book, Linux predefines three standard file handles, and these handles are linked into your program automatically. The three are stdin (standard input), stdout (standard output), and stderr (standard error). For accepting input from the keyboard through fgets(), we want to use the identifier stdin. It's already there; you simply have to declare it as EXTERN to reference it from inside your assembly language programs.

So, here's how to use the fgets() function:

1. Make sure you have declared EXTERN fgets and EXTERN stdin along with your other external declarations at the top of the .text section of your program.

2. Declare a buffer variable large enough to hold the string data you want the user to enter. Use the RESB directive in the .bss section of your program.

3. Load the buffer's address into RDI.

4. Next, load the value indicating the maximum number of characters that you want `fgets()` to accept into RSI. Make sure it is no larger than the buffer variable you declare in `.bss`!

5. Load the value of `stdin` into RDX. Note well: Don't pass the address of the external value `stdin`. *Pass the actual value* that the external item `stdin` contains, by using brackets: `[stdin]`

6. Call `fgets`.

As always, the parameters you pass to `fgets()` are entered into registers in the order specified in the x64 calling convention. This is a *lot* more convenient than pushing them onto the stack, as was done in the 32-bit world.

Listing 12.3 is a simple program demonstrating how to obtain text from standard input via `fgets()`. Again, for brevity's sake I've omitted the comment header.

Listing 12.3: fgetstest.asm

```
;   Use this makefile, after adding the required tabs:
;
;   fgetstest: fgetstest.o
;       gcc fgetstest.o -o fgetstest -no-pie
;   fgetstest.o: fgetstest.asm
;       nasm -f elf64 -g -F dwarf fgetstest.asm


SECTION .data        ; Section containing initialized data

message: db "You just entered: %s."

SECTION .bss         ; Section containing uninitialized data

testbuf: resb 20
BUFLEN   equ $-testbuf

SECTION .text        ; Section containing code

extern printf
extern stdin
extern fgets

global main          ; Required so the linker can find the entry point

main:
    push rbp         ; Set up stack frame for debugger
    mov rbp,rsp

;;; Everything before this is boilerplate; use for all ordinary apps!

; Get a number of characters from the user:
    mov rdi,testbuf    ; Put address of buffer into RDI
```

```
    mov rsi,BUFLEN     ; Put # of chars to enter into RSI
    mov rdx,[stdin]    ; Put value of stdin into RDX
    call fgets         ; Call libc function for entering data

;Display the entered characters:
    mov rdi,message    ; Base string's address goes in RDI
    mov rsi,testbuf    ; Data entry buffer's address goes in RSI
    mov rax,0          ; Count of vector regs..here, 0
    call printf        ; Call libc function to display entered chars

;;; Everything after this is boilerplate; use for all ordinary apps!
    pop rbp            ; Epilog: Destroy stack frame before returning

    ret                ; Return to glibc shutdown code
```

The fgetstest program demonstrates embedding a string code %s in the base string. It takes nothing more than placing %s in the base string and then copying the address of the string to be inserted into the next available x64 calling convention register. Here, that's RSI.

From the user side of the screen, fgets() simply accepts characters until the user presses Enter. It doesn't automatically return after the user types the maximum permitted number of characters. (That would prevent the user from backing over input and correcting it.) However, anything the user types beyond the number of permitted characters is discarded.

Using scanf() for Entry of Numeric Values

In a peculiar sort of way, the C library function scanf() is printf() running backwards: Instead of outputting formatted data in a character stream, scanf() takes a stream of character data from the keyboard and converts it to numeric data stored in a numeric variable. The scanf() function works very well, and it understands a great many formats that I won't be able to explain here, especially for the entry of floating-point numbers. (Floating-point values are a special problem in assembly work, and I won't be taking them up in this book.) The Wikipedia entry is very good:

https://en.wikipedia.org/wiki/Scanf_format_string

For most simple programs you may write while you're getting your bearings in assembly, you'll be entering simple integers, and scanf() is very good at that. You pass scanf() the name of a numeric variable in which to store the entered value, and a formatting code indicating what form that value will take on data entry. The scanf() function will take the characters typed by the user and convert them to the integer value that the characters represent. That is, scanf() will take the two ASCII characters "4" and "2" entered successively and convert them to the base 10 numeric value 42 after the user presses Enter.

What about a prompt string, instructing the user what to type? Well, many newcomers get the idea that you can combine the prompt with the format code in a single string handed to scanf(), but alas, that won't work. It seems as though it should—hey, after all, you can combine formatting codes with the base string to be displayed using printf(). And in scanf(), you can theoretically use a base string containing formatting codes . . . but the user would then have to type the prompt as well as the numeric data!

So, in practical terms, the only string used by scanf() is a string containing the formatting codes. If you want a prompt, you must display the prompt using printf() before calling scanf(). To keep the prompt and the data entry on the same line, make sure you *don't* have an EOL character at the end of your prompt string!

The scanf() function automatically takes character input from standard input. You don't have to pass it the file handle stdin, as you do with fgets(). There is a separate glibc function called fscanf() to which you *do* have to pass a file handle, but for integer data entry there's no hazard in using scanf().

Here's how to use the scanf() routine:

1. Make sure that you have declared EXTERN scanf along with your other external declarations at the top of the .TEXT section.

2. Declare a memory variable of the proper type to hold the numeric data read and converted by scanf(). My examples here will be for integer data, so you would create such a variable with either the DQ directive or the RESQ directive. Obviously, if you're going to keep several separate values, you'll need to declare one variable per value entered.

3. To call scanf() for entry of a single value, first copy the address of the format string that specifies what format that data will arrive in into RDI. For integer values, this is typically the string %d.

4. Copy the address of the memory variable that will hold the value into RSI. (See the following discussion about entry of multiple values in one call.)

5. Clear RAX to zero, telling scanf() that no vector register parameters are being passed in the function call.

6. Call scanf().

It's possible to present scanf() with a string containing multiple formatting codes so that the user could enter multiple numeric values with only one call to scanf(). I've tried this, and it makes for a very peculiar user interface. That feature is better used if you're writing a program to read a text file containing rows of integer values expressed as text and convert them to actual integer variables in memory. For simply obtaining numeric values from the user through the keyboard, it's best to accept only one value per call to scanf().

The `charsin.asm` program in Listing 12.4 shows how you would set up prompts alongside a data entry field for accepting both string data and numeric data from the user through the keyboard. After accepting the data, the program displays what was entered, using `printf()`.

Listing 12.4: charsin.asm

```
;   Executable name : charsin
;   Version         : 3.0
;   Created date    : 11/19/2022
;   Last update     : 11/20/2022
;   Author          : Jeff Duntemann
;   Description     : A character input demo for Linux, using
;                     NASM 2.14.02, incorporating calls to both
;                     fgets() and scanf().
;
;   Build using these commands:
;     nasm -f elf64 -g -F dwarf charsin.asm
;     gcc charsin.o -o charsin -no-pie
;

[SECTION .data]          ; Section containing initialized data

SPrompt  db 'Enter string data, followed by Enter: ',0
IPrompt  db 'Enter an integer value, followed by Enter: ',0
IFormat  db '%d',0
SShow    db 'The string you entered was: %s',10,0
IShow    db 'The integer value you entered was: %5d',10,0

[SECTION .bss]           ; Section containing uninitialized data

IntVal   resq 1          ; Reserve an uninitialized double word
InString resb 128        ; Reserve 128 bytes for string entry buffer

[SECTION .text]          ; Section containing code

extern stdin             ; Standard file variable for input
extern fgets
extern printf
extern scan

global main              ; Required so linker can find entry point

main:
    push rbp             ; Prolog: Set up stack frame
    mov rbp,rsp

;;; Everything before this is boilerplate; use for all ordinary apps!
```

```
    ; First, an example of safely limited string input using fgets:
        mov rdi,SPrompt      ; Load address of the prompt string into RDI
        mov rax,0            ; Count of vector regs..here, 0
        call printf          ; Display it

        mov rdi,InString     ; Copy address of buffer for entered chars
        mov rsi,72           ; Accept no more than 72 chars from keybd
        mov rdx,[stdin]      ; Load file handle for standard input into RDX
        call fgets           ; Call fgets to allow user to enter chars

        mov rdi,SShow        ; Copy address of the string prompt into RSI
        mov rsi,InString     ; Copy address of entered string data into RDI
        mov rax,0            ; Count of vector regs..here, 0
        call printf          ; Display it

    ; Next, use scanf() to enter numeric data:
        mov rdi,IPrompt      ; Copy address of integer input prompt into RDI
        mov rax,0            ; Count of vector regs..here, 0
        call printf          ; Display it

        mov rdi,IFormat      ; Copy addr of the integer format string into RDI
        mov rsi,IntVal       ; Copy address of the integer buffer into RSI
        mov rax,0            ; Count of vector regs..here, 0
        call scanf           ; Call scanf to enter numeric data

        mov rdi,IShow        ; Copy address of base string into RDI
        mov rsi,[IntVal]     ; Copy the integer value to display into RSI
        mov rax,0            ; Count of vector regs..here, 0
        call printf          ; Call printf to convert & display the integer

    ;;; Everything after this is boilerplate; use for all ordinary apps!

        pop rbp              ; Epilog: Destroy stack frame before returning
        ret                  ; Return to glibc shutdown code
```

Be a Linux Time Lord

The standard C libraries contain a pretty substantial group of functions that manipulate dates and times. Although these functions were originally designed to handle date values generated by the real-time clock in ancient AT&T minicomputer hardware that was current in the 1970s, they have by now become a standard interface to any operating system's real-time clock support. People who program in C for Windows use the very same group of functions, and they work more or less the same way irrespective of which operating system you're working under.

By understanding how to call these functions as assembly language procedures, you'll be able to read the current date, express time and date values in numerous formats, apply timestamps to files, and do many other very useful things.

Let's take a look at how it works.

The C Library's Time Machine

Somewhere deep inside the standard C library, there is a block of code that, when invoked, looks at the real-time clock in the computer, reads the current date and time, and translates that into a standard signed integer value. This value is (theoretically) the number of seconds that have passed in the "Unix epoch," (or in programmer circles, just "the epoch"), which began on January 1, 1970, 00:00:00 universal time. Every second that passes adds 1 to this value. When you read the current time or date via the C library, what you'll retrieve is the current value of this number.

The number is called `time_t`. For nearly all of its history, `time_t` was a 32-bit signed integer. As years went on, people began to wonder about what would happen when a signed 32-bit integer wouldn't be large enough to contain the number of seconds since 1970. On 3:14:07 UTC on January 19, 2038, computers that treat `time_t` as a 32-bit signed integer will see it roll over to 0, because a 32-bit signed integer can express quantities only up to 2,147,483,647. That's a lot of seconds (and a reasonably long time to prepare), but I'll only be 86, and I expect to be around when it happens. (I remember the whole Y2K panic, heh.)

In truth, it won't happen, just as the infamous Y2K phenomenon didn't bring civilization crashing down, as certain people who should have known better were claiming at the time. A properly implemented C library doesn't assume that `time_t` is a 32-bit quantity at all. So, when the signed 32-bit `time_t` flips in the year 2038, we'll have been using 64-bit values for everything, and the whole problem will be put off for another 292 billion years or so. If we haven't fixed it once and for all by then, we'll deserve to go down with the whole universe in the Big Crunch that cosmologists are predicting shortly thereafter.

Certainly the problem no longer exists in Linux. All 64-bit Linux systems use a 64-bit `time_t`, and since the release of Linux v5.6 in 2020, 32-bit versions of the OS also use a 64-bit `time_t`.

A `time_t` value is just an arbitrary seconds count and doesn't tell you much on its own, though it can be useful for calculating elapsed times in seconds. Another standard data type implemented by the standard C library is much more useful. A tm structure (which is often called a *struct*, and among Pascal people a *record*) is a grouping of nine 32-bit numeric values that express the current time and date in separately useful chunks, as summarized in Table 12.2. Note that although a struct (or record) is nominally a grouping of unlike values, in the current x64 Linux implementation, a tm value is more like an array or a data table, because all nine elements are the same size, which is 32 bits, or 4 bytes. I've described it that way in Table 12.2, by including a value that is the offset from the beginning of the structure for each element in the structure. This allows you to use a pointer to the beginning of the structure and an offset from the beginning to create the effective address of any given element of the structure.

Note that even in a 64-bit Linux instance, the tm fields are 32 bits in size. Why still 32 bits? Easy: None of the elements in tm needs anything near 8 bytes to express. The largest possible value is tm_yday, which contains the ordinal number of the current day, that is, a number from 1 to 366, with 1 being the first day of January. Of course, in a few centuries the number of years since 1900 will exceed 366—but again, don't wait up for it.

Table 12.2:   The Values Contained in the tm Structure

OFFSET IN BYTES	C LIBRARY NAME	DEFINITION
0	tm_sec	Seconds after the minute, from 0
4	tm_min	Minutes after the hour, from 0
8	tm_hour	Hour of the day, from 0
12	tm_mday	Day of the month, from 1
16	tm_mon	Month of the year, from 0
20	tm_year	Year since 1900, from 0
24	tm_wday	Days since Sunday, from 0
28	tm_yday	Day of the year, from 0
32	tm_isdst	Daylight Saving Time flag

The one element that needs a little more explanation is tm_isdst. The value in tm_isdst is positive if daylight saving time (DST) is in effect, and zero if DST is not in effect. If the system cannot tell whether DST is in effect, the value in tm_isdst is negative.

There are C library functions that convert time_t values to tm values and back. I cover a few of them in this chapter, but they're all pretty straightforward, and once you've thoroughly internalized the C calling conventions, you should be able to work out an assembly calling protocol for any of them.

Another cautionary sidenote: The time_t value is not the exact, precise number of seconds since the beginning of the Unix epoch. There are glitches in the way Unix counts seconds, and time_t is not adjusted for accumulated astronomical errors as real-world NIST time is, via "leap seconds." So across short intervals (ideally, less than a year) time_t may be considered accurate. Beyond that, assume that it will be off by a few seconds or more, with no easy way to figure out how to compensate for the errors.

Fetching time_t Values from the System Clock

Any single second of time (at least those seconds after January 1, 1970) can be represented as a 64-bit signed integer in a Unix-compatible system. Fetching the value for the current time is done by calling the `time()` function. Like all functions designed in accordance with the x64 calling conventions, `time()` returns its `time_t` value in RAX.

However, there is a gotcha that sometimes trips up beginners: `time()` can take a parameter. Like all first parameters, it's passed to `time()` in RDI. The gotcha: It's optional.

Sort of.

When you call `time()`, if RDI contains 0, the `time_t` value will be returned in RAX. If RDI contains anything other than 0, `time()` will assume that the value in RDI is an address, and it will attempt to write the `time_t` value to memory at that address. If RDI contains "leftovers" that aren't valid addresses, calling `time()` will usually cause a segmentation fault. I say "usually" because I've heard that on some systems, the implementation of `time()` contains some extra machinery to detect garbage addresses, and if an address in RDI is garbage, it will revert to returning the value in RAX. Still, you can't count on that.

No other parameters need to be passed to `time()`. On return, you'll have the current `time_t` value in RAX. That's all there is to it. Given the possibility of implementation differences, I don't recommend handing `time()` an address. What I do recommend is having the `time_t` value returned in RAX. This *requires* that you clear RDI to 0 before you call `time()`.

Converting a time_t Value to a Formatted String

Again, by itself, a `time_t` value doesn't tell you a great deal. The C library contains a function that will return a pointer to a formatted string representation of a given `time_t` value. This is the `ctime()` function. It returns a pointer to a string buried somewhere in the runtime library. This string has the following format:

```
Wed Nov 28 12:13:21 2022
```

The first field is a three-character code for the day of the week, followed by a three-character code for the month and a two-space field for the day of the month. The time follows, in 24-hour format, and the year brings up the rear. For good measure (though it can sometimes be a nuisance), the string returned by `ctime` is terminated by a newline.

Here's how you call `ctime` and display the time/date string it generates:

```
mov rdi,TimeValue  ; Copy *address* of time_t value into rdi
call ctime         ; Returns pointer to ASCII time string in rax
mov rdi,rax        ; Copy the address in rax into rdi
call puts          ; Call puts to display the ASCII time string
```

This looks pretty conventional, but there is something here that you *must* be aware of, as it departs from our recent experience with `glibc`: You pass `ctime()` the *address* of a `time_t` value, *not* the value itself! You're used to passing integer values to functions by copying those values into RDI, RSI, and so on. Not so here. A `time_t` value is currently, under Linux, represented as an 8-byte integer, but there is no promise that it will always be thus. Older versions of Linux may use a 32-bit `time_t`. Other Unix implementations could be all over the map. So, to keep its options open (and to ensure that Unix can be used for thousands or even billions of years to come, heh), the C library function `ctime()` requires a pointer to the current `time_t` value rather than a `time_t` value itself.

Pass the address of the `time_t` value that you want to represent as a string in RDI, and then call `ctime()`. What `ctime()` returns in RAX is a pointer to the string, which it keeps somewhere inside the runtime library. You can use that pointer to display the string on the screen via `puts` or `printf` or write it to a text file.

Generating Separate Local Time Values

The glibc library also gives you a function to break out the various components of the date and time into separate values so that you can use them separately or in various combinations. This function is `localtime()`, and given a `time_t` value, it will break out the date and time into the fields of a `tm` structure, as described in Table 12.2. Here's the code to call it:

```
mov rdi,TimeValue  ; Pass address of calendar time value in rdi
call localtime     ; Returns pointer to static time structure in rax
```

Here, `TimeValue` is a `time_t` value. Given this value, `localtime()` returns in RAX—much in the fashion of `ctime()`—a pointer to a `tm` structure within the C library somewhere. By using this pointer as a base address, you can access the individual fields in the structure. The trick lies in knowing the offset into `tm` for the individual time/date field that you want, and using that offset as a constant displacement from the address base.

```
mov rdi, yrmsg        ; Pass address of the base string in rdi
mov rsi, dword [rax+20] ; Year value tm_year is 20 bytes offset into tm
mov rax,0             ; Count of vector regs..here, 0
call printf           ; Display string and year value with printf
```

By using the displacements shown in Table 12.2, you can access all the other components of the time and the date in the tm structure, each stored as a 32-bit integer value.

Making a Copy of glibc's tm Struct with MOVSD

It's sometimes handy to keep a separate copy of a tm structure, especially if you're working with several date/time values at once. So, after you use localtime() to fill the C library's hidden tm structure with date/time values, you can copy that structure to a structure allocated in the .bss or .data section of your program.

Doing such a copy is a straightforward use of the REP MOVSD (Repeat Move String Double) instruction, one of a group that I introduced in Chapter 11. MOVSD is an almost magical thing: Once you set up pointers to the data area you want to copy and the place you want to copy it to, you store the size of the area in RCX and let REP MOVSD do the rest. In one operation it will copy an entire buffer from one place in memory to another.

To use REP MOVSD, you place the address of the source data—that is, the data to be copied—into RSI. You move the address of the destination location—where the data is to be placed—in RDI. The number of items to be moved is placed in RCX. You make sure that the Direction flag DF is cleared (for more on this, see Chapter 11) and then execute REP MOVSD:

```
mov rsi,rax    ; Copy address of static tm from rax to rsi
mov rdi,tmcopy ; Put the address of the local tm vartiable in rdi
mov rcx,9      ; A tm struct is 9 dwords in size under Linux
cld            ; Clear df to 0 so we move up-memory
rep movsd      ; Copy static tm struct to local tm copy
```

Why use MOVSD instead of its 64-bit big brother MOVSQ? The tm struct is basically an array of nine 4-byte elements, not 8-byte elements.

Here, we're moving the C library's tm structure to a buffer allocated in the .bss section of the program. The tm structure is nine double words—36 bytes—in size. So, we have to reserve that much space and give it a name:

```
TmCopy resd 9 ; Reserve 9 32-bit fields for time struct tm
```

The preceding code assumes that the address of the C library's already-filled tm structure is in RAX and that a tm structure TmCopy has been allocated. Once executed, it will copy all of the tm data from its hidey-hole inside the C runtime library to your freshly allocated buffer TmCopy.

The REP prefix puts MOVSD in automatic-rifle mode, as I explained in Chapter 11. That is, MOVSD will keep moving data from the address in RSI to the address in RDI, counting RCX down by one with each move, until RCX goes to zero. Then it stops.

One easy mistake you should avoid is forgetting that the count in RCX is the count of data items to be moved, *not* the number of bytes to be moved! By virtue of the *D* on the end of its mnemonic, MOVSD moves double words, and the value you place in RCX must be *the number of 4-byte items* to be moved. So, in moving nine double words, MOVSD actually transports 36 bytes from one location to another—but you're counting double words here, not bytes.

The program in Listing 12.5 knits all of these code snippets together into a demo of the major Unix time features. There are many more time functions to be studied in the C library, and with what you now know about C function calls, you should be able to work out calling protocols for any of them.

Listing 12.5: timetest.asm

```
;   Executable name : timetest
;   Version         : 3.0
;   Created date    : 11/28/2022
;   Last update     : 11/28/2022
;   Author          : Jeff Duntemann
;   Description     : A demo of time-related functions for Linux, using
;                     NASM 2.14.02. Will NOT work in SASM.
;
;   Built using this makefile, after adding required tabs:
;
;   timetest: timetest.0
;        gcc timetest.o -o timetest -no-pie
;   timetest.o: timetest.asm
;        nasm -f elf64 -g -F stabs timetest.asm


[SECTION .data]          ; Section containing initialized data

TimeMsg  db "Hey, what time is it?  It's %s",10,0
YrMsg    db "The year is %d.",10,10,0
PressEnt db "Press enter after a few seconds: ",0
Elapsed
db
"A total of %d seconds has elapsed since program began running.",10,0

[SECTION .bss]          ; Section containing uninitialized data

OldTime  resq 1         ; Reserve 3 quadwords for time_t values
NewTime  resq 1
TimeDiff resq 1
TimeStr  resb 40        ; Reserve 40 bytes for time string
TmCopy   resd 9         ; Reserve 9 integer fields for time struct tm

[SECTION .text]         ; Section containing code

extern ctime
extern difftime
```

```
extern getchar
extern printf
extern localtime
extern strftime
extern time

global main                 ; Required so linker can find entry point

main:
    push rbp                ; Set up stack frame
    mov rbp,rsp

;;; Everything before this is boilerplate; use for all ordinary apps!

; Generate a time_t calendar time value with clib's time function
    xor rdi,rdi             ; Clear rdi to 0
    call time               ; Returns calendar time in rax
    mov [OldTime],rax       ; Save time value in memory variable

; Generate a string summary of local time with clib's ctime function
    mov rdi,OldTime         ; Push address of calendar time value
    call ctime              ; Returns pointer to ASCII time string in rax

    mov rdi,TimeMsg         ; Pass address of base string in rdi
    mov rsi,rax             ; Pass pointer to ASCII time string in rsi
    mov rax,0               ; Count of vector regs..here, 0
    call printf             ; Merge and display the two strings

; Generate local time values into libc's static tm struct
    mov rdi,OldTime         ; Push address of calendar time value
    call localtime          ; Returns pointer to static time structure in rax

; Make a local copy of libc's static tm struct
    mov rsi,rax             ; Copy address of static tm from rax to rsi
    mov rdi,TmCopy          ; Put the address of the local tm copy in rdi
    mov rcx,9               ; A tm struct is 9 dwords in size under Linux
    cld                     ; Clear DF so we move up-memory
    rep movsd               ; Copy static tm struct to local copy

; Display one of the fields in the tm structure
    mov rdx,[TmCopy+20]     ; Year field is 20 bytes offset into tm
    add rdx,1900            ; Year field is # of years since 1900
    mov rdi,YrMsg           ; Put address of the base string into rdi
    mov rsi,rdx
    mov rax,0               ; Count of vector regs..here, 0
    call printf             ; Display string and year value with printf

; Display the 'Press Enter: ' prompt
    mov rdi,PressEnt        ; Put the address of the base string into rdi
    mov rax,0               ; Count of vector regs..here, 0
    call printf
```

```
; Wait a few seconds for the user to press Enter
;    so that we have a time difference:
    call getchar         ; Wait for user to press Enter

; Calculating seconds passed since program began running:
    xor rdi,rdi          ; Clear rdi to 0
    call time            ; Get current time value; return in EAX
    mov [NewTime],rax    ; Save new time value

    sub rax,[OldTime]    ; Calculate time difference value
    mov [TimeDiff],rax   ; Save time difference value

    mov rsi,[TimeDiff]   ; Put difference in seconds rdi
    mov rdi,Elapsed      ; Push addr. of elapsed time message string
    mov rax,0            ; Count of vector regs..here, 0
    call printf          ; Display elapsed time

;;; Everything after this is boilerplate; use for all ordinary apps!

    pop rbp              ; Epilog: Destroy stack frame before returning
    ret                  ; Return to glibc shutdown code
```

If you ever move to other Unix implementations outside the GNU sphere, keep in mind that the time_t value may already have a definition other than a 32-bit integer. At this time, glibc defines time_t as a 64-bit integer, and you can calculate time differences between two time_t values simply by subtracting them. For other, non-GNU implementations of Unix, it's best to use the difftime() function in the libc library to return a difference between two time_t values.

Understanding AT&T Instruction Mnemonics

There is more than one set of instruction mnemonics for the x86 CPUs, and that's been a source of much confusion. An instruction mnemonic is simply a way for human beings to remember what the binary bit pattern 1000100111000011 means to the CPU. Instead of writing 16 ones and zeros in a row (or even the slightly more graspable hexadecimal equivalent 89C3h), we say MOV BX,AX.

Keep in mind that mnemonics are just that—memory joggers for humans—and are creatures unknown to the CPU itself. Assemblers translate mnemonics to machine instructions. Although we can agree among ourselves that MOV BX,AX will translate to 1000100111000011, there's nothing magical about the string MOV BX,AX. We could as well have agreed on COPY AX TO BX or STICK GPREGA INTO

GPREGB. We use MOV BX,AX because that was what Intel suggested we do, and since Intel designed and manufactures the CPU chips, it may know best how to describe the internal details of its own products.

The alternate set of x86 instruction mnemonics that we call the *AT&T mnemonics* came out of the desire to make Unix as easy to port to different computer architectures as possible. However, the goals of instruction set implementers are not the same as those of assembly language programmers, and if your goal is to have a complete and optimally efficient command of the x86/x64 CPUs, you're better off writing code with the Intel set, as I've been teaching throughout this book.

In truth, the AT&T mnemonics look strange and a little opaque, even to me. The reason for that is that they were never intended to be used by humans to write assembly language programs. They were designed to be an easily portable *intermediate language*, that is, a language written by one piece of software to be acted upon by an entirely different piece of software. In Linux, that would generally be the C language compiler gcc, and the Gnu assembler, gas. In fact, the C language was originally considered a "high-level assembler," and compared to other programming languages like COBOL, FORTRAN, or Pascal, it is.

Although there are good reasons for being able to read AT&T mnemonics and syntax, it has grown complex enough that I can't justify teaching it to any depth in a beginner book like this.

AT&T Mnemonic Conventions

So here's the overview: When gcc compiles a C source code file to machine code, what it really does is translate the C source code to assembly language source code, using the AT&T mnemonics. Look back to Figure 12.1. The gcc compiler takes as input a .c source code file and generates a .s assembly language source file, which is then handed to the GNU assembler gas for assembly. This is the way the GNU tools work on all platforms, with all GNU languages, of which there are several beyond C and C++. The assembly step is generally invisible to the programmer, with the .s file discarded after gas converts it to machine code and ld links it. You can have gcc save the AT&T assembly source code file to disk by using the -s option:

```
gcc eatc.c -S -o eatc
```

Note that -s switch uses an *uppercase* S. Nearly everything in Linux and other Unix descendants is case-sensitive.

Now, if you're going to deal with the standard C library and the multitudes of other function libraries written in C and for C, it makes sense to become at least passingly familiar with the AT&T mnemonics. There are some general rules that, once digested, make it much easier. Here's the list in short form:

- AT&T mnemonics and register names are invariably in lowercase. This is in keeping with the Unix convention of case sensitivity. I've mixed uppercase and lowercase in the text and examples to get you used to seeing assembly source both ways, but you have to remember that while Intel's syntax (and hence NASM) suggests uppercase but will accept lowercase, the AT&T syntax *requires* lowercase.

- Register names are always preceded by the percent symbol, %. That is, what Intel would write as AX or RBX, AT&T would write as %ax and %rbx. This helps the assembler recognize register names.

- Every AT&T machine instruction mnemonic that has operands has a single-character suffix indicating how large its operands are. The suffix letters are *b*, *w*, *l*, and *q* indicating byte (8 bits), word (16 bits), long (32 bits), and quad (64 bits). What Intel would write as MOV RBX,RAX, AT&T would write as movq %rax,%rbx.

- When an instruction does not take operands (call, leave, ret), it does not have an operand-size suffix. Calls and returns look pretty much alike in both Intel and AT&T syntax.

- In the AT&T syntax, source and destination operands are placed in the opposite order from Intel syntax. That is, what Intel would write as MOV RBX,RAX, AT&T would write as movq %rax,%rbx. In other words, in AT&T syntax, the source operand comes first, followed by the destination.

- In the AT&T syntax, immediate operands are always preceded by the dollar sign, $. What Intel would write as PUSH 42, AT&T would write as pushq $42. This helps the assembler recognize immediate operands.

- Not all AT&T instruction mnemonics are generated by gcc. Equivalents to Intel's JCXZ, JECXZ, LOOP, LOOPZ, LOOPE, LOOPNZ, and LOOPNE were added to the AT&T mnemonic set not that long ago, and in some versions, gcc does not generate code that uses them.

- In the AT&T syntax, displacements in memory references are signed quantities placed outside parentheses containing the base, index, and scale values. I'll treat this one separately a little later, as you'll see it a lot in .s files, and you should be able to read and understand ATT memory address syntax.

- When referenced, the name of a message string is prefixed by a dollar sign ($) the same way that numeric literals are. In NASM, a named string variable is considered a variable and not a literal. This is just another AT&T peccadillo to be aware of.

- Note that the comment delimiter in the AT&T scheme is the pound sign (#) rather than the semicolon used in nearly all Intel-style assemblers, including NASM.

The displacements will vary, of course, but what this almost always means is that an instruction is referencing a data item somewhere on the stack. C code allocates its variables on the stack, in a stack frame, and then references those variables by literal offsets from the value in RBP. RBP acts as an address starting point, and items on the stack may be referenced in terms of offsets (either positive or negative) away from RBP. The preceding reference would tell a machine instruction to work with an item at the address in RBP minus 16 bytes.

Generating Random Numbers

As our next jump on this quick tour of standard C library calls from assembly, let's get seriously random. (Or modestly pseudorandom, at least.) The standard C library has a pair of functions that allow programs to generate pseudorandom numbers. The *pseudo* is significant here. Research indicates that there is no provable way to generate a truly *random* random number strictly from software. In fact, the whole notion of what *random* really means is a spooky one and keeps a lot of mathematicians off the streets. Theoretically you'd need to obtain triggers from some sort of quantum phenomenon (radioactivity is the one most often mentioned) to achieve true randomness. Such creatures do exist. But lacking a radiation-triggered random-number generator, we'll have to fall back on pseudo-ness and learn to live with it.

A simplified definition of *pseudorandom* would run something like this: A *pseudorandom*-number generator yields a sequence of numbers of no recognizable pattern, but the sequence can be repeated by passing the same *seed value* to the generator. A *seed value* is simply a whole number that acts as an input value to an arcane algorithm that creates the sequence of pseudorandom numbers. Pass the same seed to the generator, and you get the same sequence. However, within the sequence, the distribution of numbers within the generator's range is reasonably scattered and random.

The standard C library contains two functions relating to pseudorandom numbers:

- The srand() function passes a new seed value to the random-number generator. This value must be a 32-bit integer. If no seed value is passed, the seed value defaults to 1.

- The rand() function returns a 31-bit pseudorandom number. The high bit is always 0 and thus the value is always positive if treated as a 32-bit signed integer.

Once you understand how they work, using them is close to trivial.

Seeding the Generator with srand()

Getting the seed value into the generator is actually more involved than making the call that pulls the next pseudorandom number in the current sequence. And it's not that the call to srand() is that difficult: You load the seed value into RDI and then call srand(). That's all you have to do! The srand() function does not return a value. But . . . what do you use as a seed value?

Aye, now there's the rub.

If it's important that your programs *not* work with the same exact sequence of pseudorandom numbers every time they run, you clearly don't want to use an ordinary integer hard-coded into the program. You'd ideally want to get a different seed value each time you run the program. The simplest way to do that (though there are others) is to seed calls to srand() with the seconds count since January 1, 1970, as returned by the time() function, which I explained in the previous section. This value, called time_t, is a signed integer that changes every second, so with every passing second you have a new seed value at your disposal, one that by definition will *never* repeat. (I'm assuming here that the time_t rollover problem that I mentioned in the previous section will be solved by the year 2038.)

Almost everyone does this, and the only caution is that you must make certain that you don't call srand() to reseed the sequence more often than once per second. In most cases, for programs that are run, do their work, and terminate in a few minutes or hours, you only need to call srand() once, when the program begins executing. If you are writing a program that will remain running for days or weeks or longer without terminating (such as a server), it might be a good idea to reseed your random-number generator once per day.

Here's a short code snippet that calls time() to retrieve the current time_t value and then hands the time value to srand() in RDI:

```
xor rdi,rdi   ; Make sure rdi is set to 0 before calling time()
call time      ; Returns time_t value (32-bit integer) in rax
mov rdi,rax    ; Pass the seed value to srand in rdi
call srand     ; Time_t is the seed value for random # generator
```

Setting RDI to 0 before calling time() tells the time() function that you're not passing in a variable to accept the time value. The time_t value you want to keep is returned in RAX.

Generating Pseudorandom Numbers

Once you've seeded the generator, getting numbers in the pseudorandom sequence is easy: You pull the next number in the sequence with each call to rand(). And the rand() function is as easy to use as anything in the C library:

It takes no parameters (so you don't need to pass anything to the function), and the pseudorandom number is returned in RAX.

The `randtest.asm` program in Listing 12.6 demonstrates how `srand()` and `rand()` work. It also shows off a couple of other interesting assembly tricks, and I'll spend the rest of this section discussing them.

Listing 12.6: randtest.asm

```
;   Executable name  : randtest
;   Version          : 3.0
;   Created date     : 11/29/2022
;   Updated date     : 5/24/2023
;   Author           : Jeff Duntemann
;   Description      : A demo of Unix rand & srand using NASM 2.14.02
;
;   Build using these commands:
;      nasm -f elf64 -g -F dwarf randtest.asm
;      gcc randtest.o -o randtest -no-pie
;

section .data

Pulls      dq 36 ; How many nums do we pull? (Must be a multiple of 6!)
Display    db 10,'Here is an array of %d %d-bit random numners:',10,0
ShowArray  db '%10d %10d %10d %10d %10d %10d',10,0
NewLine    db 0
CharTbl
     db '0123456789ABCDEFGHIJKLMNOPQRSTUVWXYZabcdefghijklmnopqrstuvwxyz-@'

section .bss

[SECTION .bss]            ; Section containing uninitialized data

BUFSIZE  equ 70          ; # of randomly chosen chars
RandVal  resq 1          ; Reserve an integer variable
Stash    resq 72         ; Reserve an array of 72 integers for randoms
RandChar resb BUFSIZE+5  ; Buffer for storing randomly chosen characters

section .text

extern printf
extern puts
extern rand
extern srand
extern time


;-------------------------------------------------------------------
;   Random number generator procedures  --  Last update 5/13/2023
;
```

```
;  This routine provides 6 entry points, and returns 6 different "sizes"
;  of pseudorandom numbers based on the value returned by rand. Note
;  first of all that rand pulls a 31-bit value. The high 16 bits are
;  the most "random" so to return numbers in a smaller range, you fetch
;  a 31-bit value and then right-shift it to zero-fill all but the
;  number of bits you want. An 8-bit random value will range from
;  0-255, a 7-bit value from 0-127, and so on. Respects RBP, RSI, RDI,
;  RBX, and RSP. Returns random value in RAX.
;-------------------------------------------------------------------
pull31: mov rcx,0        ; For 31 bit random, we don't shift
    jmp pull
pull20: mov rcx,11       ; For 20 bit random, shift by 11 bits
    jmp pull
pull16: mov rcx,15       ; For 16 bit random, shift by 15 bits
    jmp pull
pull8:  mov rcx,23       ; For 8 bit random, shift by 23 bits
    jmp pull
pull7:  mov rcx,24       ; For 7 bit random, shift by 24 bits
    jmp pull
pull6:  mov rcx,25       ; For 6 bit random, shift by 25 bits
    jmp pull
pull4:  mov rcx,27       ; For 4 bit random, shift by 27 bits


pull:
    push rbp             ; Prolog: Create stack frame
    mov rbp,rsp

    mov r15,rcx          ; rand trashes rcx; save shift value in R15
    call rand            ; Call rand for random value; returned in RAX
    mov rcx,r15          ; Restore shift value back into RCX
    shr rax,cl           ; Shift the random value in RAX by the chosen
                         ;   factor, keeping in mind that part we want
                         ;   is in CL
    pop rbp              ; Epilog: Destroy stack frame
    ret                  ; Go home with random number in RAX

;; This subroutine pulls random values and stuffs them into an
;; integer array.  Not intended to be general purpose.  Note that
;; the address of the random number generator entry point must
;; be loaded into r13 before this is called, or you'll seg fault!

puller:
    push rbp             ; Prolog: Create stack frame
    mov rbp,rsp

    mov r12,[Pulls]      ; Put pull count into R12
.grab:
    dec r12              ; Decrement counter in RSI
    call r13             ; Pull the value; it's returned in RAX
```

```
        mov [Stash+r12*8],rax    ; Store random value in the array
        cmp r12,0                ; See if we've pulled all STASH-ed
                                 ;    numbers yet
        jne .grab                ; Do another if R12 <> 0

        pop rbp                  ; Epilog: Destroy stack frame
        ret                      ; Otherwise, go home!

    ;; This subroutine displays numbers six at a time
    ;; Not intended to be general-purpose...
shownums:
        push rbp                 ; Prolog: Create stack frame
        mov rbp,rsp

        mov r12,qword [Pulls]    ; Put pull count into r12
        xor r13,r13
.dorow:
        mov rdi,ShowArray        ; Pass address of base string
        mov rsi,[Stash+r13*8+0]  ; Pass first element
        mov rdx,[Stash+r13*8+8]  ; Pass second element
        mov rcx,[Stash+r13*8+16] ; Pass third element
        mov r8,[Stash+r13*8+24]  ; Pass fourth element
        mov r9,[Stash+r13*8+32]  ; Pass fifth element
        push rax                 ; To keep stack 16-bytes aligned
        push qword [Stash+r13*8+40] ; Pass 6th element on the stack
        xor rax,rax      ; Passs 0 to show there will be no fp regs
        call printf      ; Display the random numbers
        add rsp,16       ; Stack cleanup: 2 items X 8 bytes = 16

        add r13,6        ; Point to the next group of six randoms in Stash
        sub r12,6        ; Decrement pull counter
        cmp r12,0        ; See if pull count has gone to 0
        ja .dorow        ; If not, we go back and do another row!

        pop rbp          ; Epilog: Destroy stack frame
        ret              ; Done, so go home!

; MAIN PROGRAM:

global main          ; Required so linker can find entry point

main:
        push rbp             ; Prolog: Set up stack frame
        mov rbp,rsp

;;; Everything before this is boilerplate;

; Begin by seeding the random number generator with a time_t value:
```

```
Seedit:
        xor rdi,rdi         ; Mske sure rdi starts out with a 0
        call time           ; Returns time_t value (64-bit integer) in rax
        mov rdi,rax         ; Pass srand a time_t seed in rdi
        call srand          ; Seed the random number generator

; All of the following code blocks are identical except for the size
; of the random value being generated:

; Create and display an array of 31-bit random values
        mov r13,pull31      ; Copy address of random # subroutine into RDI
        call puller         ; Pull as many numbers as called for in [Pulls]

        mov rdi,Display     ; Display the base string
        mov rsi,[Pulls]     ; Display the number of randoms displayed
        mov rdx,32          ; Display the size of the randoms displayed
        xor rax,rax         ; Passs 0 to show there will be no fp registers
        call printf         ; Display the label
        call shownums       ; Display the rows of random numbers

; Create and display an array of 20-bit random values
        mov r13,pull20      ; Copy address of random # subroutine into RDI
        call puller         ; Pull as many numbers as called for in [Pulls]

        mov rdi,Display     ; Display the base string
        mov rsi,[Pulls]     ; Display the number of randoms displayed
        mov rdx,20          ; Display the size of the randoms displayed
        xor rax,rax         ; Passs 0 to show there will be no fp registers
        call printf         ; Display the label
        call shownums       ; Display the rows of random numbers

; Create and display an array of 16-bit random values
        mov r13,pull16      ; Copy address of random # subroutine into RDI
        call puller         ; Pull as many numbers as called for in [Pulls]

        mov rdi,Display     ; Display the base string
        mov rsi,[Pulls]     ; Display the number of randoms displayed
        mov rdx,16          ; Display the size of the randoms displayed
        xor rax,rax         ; Passs 0 to show there will be no fp registers
        call printf         ; Display the label
        call shownums       ; Display the rows of random numbers

; Create and display an array of 8-bit random values
        mov r13,pull8       ; Copy address of random # subroutine into RDI
        call puller         ; Pull as many numbers as called for in [Pulls]

        mov rdi,Display     ; Display the base string
        mov rsi,[Pulls]     ; Display the number of randoms displayed
        mov rdx,8           ; Display the size of the randoms displayed
```

```
        xor rax,rax      ; Passs 0 to show there will be no fp registers
        call printf      ; Display the label
        call shownums    ; Display the rows of random numbers

; Create and display an array of 7-bit random values
        mov r13,pull7    ; Copy address of random # subroutine into RDI
        call puller      ; Pull as many numbers as called for in [Pulls]

        mov rdi,Display  ; Display the base string
        mov rsi,[Pulls]  ; Display the number of randoms displayed
        mov rdx,7        ; Display the size of the randoms displayed
        xor rax,rax      ; Passs 0 to show there will be no fp registers
        call printf      ; Display the label
        call shownums    ; Display the rows of random numbers

; Create and display an array of 6-bit random values
        mov r13,pull6    ; Copy address of random # subroutine into RDI
        call puller      ; Pull as many numbers as called for in [Pulls]

        mov rdi,Display  ; Display the base string
        mov rsi,[Pulls]  ; Display the number of randoms displayed
        mov rdx,6        ; Display the size of the randoms displayed
        xor rax,rax      ; Passs 0 to show there will be no fp registers
        call printf      ; Display the label
        call shownums    ; Display the rows of random numbers

; Create and display an array of 4-bit random values
        mov r13,pull4    ; Copy address of random # subroutine into RDI
        call puller      ; Pull as many numbers as called for in [Pulls]

        mov rdi,Display  ; Display the base string
        mov rsi,[Pulls]  ; Display the number of randoms displayed
        mov rdx,4        ; Display the size of the randoms displayed
        xor rax,rax      ; Passs 0 to show there will be no fp registers
        call printf      ; Display the label
        call shownums    ; Display the rows of random numbers

; Create a string of random alphanumeric characters:
Pulchr:
        mov rbx, BUFSIZE     ; BUFSIZE tells us how many chars to pull
.loop:
        dec rbx              ; BUFSIZE is 1-based, so decrement first!
        mov r13,pull6        ; For random in the range 0-63
        call r13
        mov cl,[CharTbl+rax]  ; Use random # in rax as offset into table
                             ;   and copy character from table into CL
        mov [RandChar+rbx],cl ; Copy char from CL to character buffer
        cmp rbx,0            ; Are we done having fun yet?
        jne .loop            ; If not, go back and pull another
```

```
    ; Display the string of random characters:
        mov rdi,NewLine      ; Output a newline
        call puts            ;  using the newline procedure
        mov rdi,RandChar     ; Push the address of the char buffer
        call puts            ; Call puts to display it
        mov rdi,NewLine      ; Output a newline
        call puts

;;; Everything after this is boilerplate; use for all ordinary apps!

        Mov rsp,rbp          ; Epilog: Destroy stack frame
        pop rbp
        mov rp
        ret                  ; Return to glibc shutdown code
```

Some Bits Are More Random Than Others

Under x64 Linux, the `rand()` function returns a 31-bit unsigned value in RAX as a 64-bit integer. (The sign bit of the integer—the highest of all 64 bits—is always cleared to 0.) The Unix documentation for `rand()` and `srand()` indicates that the low-order bits of a value generated by `rand()` are less random than the high-order bits. This means that if you're going to use only some of the bits of the value generated by `rand()`, you should use the highest-order bits you can.

I honestly don't know why this should be so, nor how bad the problem is. I'm not a deep math guy, and I will take the word of the people who wrote the `rand()` documentation. But it bears on the issue of how to limit the range of the random numbers that you generate.

The issue is pretty obvious: Suppose you want to pull a number of random alphanumeric ASCII characters. You don't need numbers that range from 0 to 2 billion. There are only 127 ASCII characters, and in fact only 62 are letters and numbers. (The rest are punctuation marks, whitespace, control characters, or nonprinting characters such as the smiley faces.) What you want to do is pull random numbers between 0 and 61.

Pulling numbers that range from 0 to 2 billion until you find one less than 62 will take a long time. Clearly, you need a different approach. The one I took treats the 31-bit value returned by `rand()` as a collection of random bits. I extract a subset of those bits just large enough to meet my needs. Six bits can express values from 0 to 63, so I take the highest-order 6 bits from the original 31-bit value and use those to specify random characters.

It's easy: I simply shift the 31-bit value to the right until all bits but the highest-order 6 bits have been shifted off the right end of the value into oblivion. The same trick works with any (reasonable) number of bits. All you have to do is select by how many bits to shift. I've created a procedure for `randtest.asm` with multiple entry points, where each entry point selects a different number of bits to remain from the random value:

```
pull31: mov rcx,0    ; For 31 bit random, we don't shift
    jmp pull
pull20: mov rcx,11   ; For 20 bit random, shift by 11 bits
    jmp pull
pull16: mov rcx,15   ; For 16 bit random, shift by 15 bits
    jmp pull
pull8:  mov rcx,23   ; For 8 bit random, shift by 23 bits
    jmp pull
pull7:  mov rcx,24   ; For 7 bit random, shift by 24 bits
    jmp pull
pull6:  mov rcx,25   ; For 6 bit random, shift by 25 bits
    jmp pull
pull4:  mov rcx,27   ; For 4 bit random, shift by 27 bits

pull:
    push rbp             ; Prolog: Create stack frame
    mov rbp,rsp

    mov r15,rcx          ; rand trashes rcx; save shift value in R15
    call rand            ; Call rand for random value; returned in RAX
    mov rcx,r15          ; Restore shift value back into RCX
    shr rax,cl           ; Shift the value in RAX by the chosen factor
                         ; keeping in mind that part we want is in CL
    pop rbp              ; Epilog: Destroy stack frame
    ret                  ; Go home with random number in RAX
```

To pull a 16-bit random number, call `pull16`. To pull an 8-bit random number, call `pull8`, and so on. I did discover that the smaller numbers are not as random as the larger numbers, and the numbers returned by `pull4` are probably not random enough to be useful. (I left the `pull4` code in so you could see for yourself by running `randtest`.)

The logic here should be easy to follow: You select a shift value, put it in RCX, copy RCX into R15, call `rand()`, copy RCX back from R15, and then shift the random number (which `rand()` returns in RAX) by the value in CL—which, of course, is the lowest 8 bits of RCX.

Why does RCX have to be saved in R15? RCX is not one of the callee-preserved registers in the C calling conventions, and virtually all C library routines use RCX internally and thus trash its value. If you want to keep a value in RCX across a call to a library function, you have to save your value somewhere before the call and restore it after the call is complete. There used to be one place to save a register: the stack. Now, with x64's new general-purpose registers, you may be able to do all your work with registers that `glibc`'s routines don't trash and thus don't have to be saved on the stack.

I use the pull6 routine to pull random 6-bit numbers to select characters from a character table, thus creating a string of random alphanumeric characters. I pad the table to 64 elements with two additional characters (- and @) so that I don't have to test each pulled number to see if it's less than 62. If you need to limit random values to some range that is not a power of 2, choose the next largest power of 2—but try to design your program so that you don't have to choose random values in a range like 0 to 65. Much has been written on random numbers in the algorithm books, so if the concept fascinates you, I direct you there for further study.

Calls to Addresses in Registers

I use a technique in randtest that sometimes gets forgotten by assembly newcomers: You can execute a CALL instruction to a procedure address stored in a register. You don't always have to use CALL with an immediate label. In other words, the following two CALL instructions are both completely legal and equivalent:

```
mov r13,pull8   ; Copy the address represented by label pull8 into r13
call pull8      ; Call the address represented by pull8
call r13        ; Call the address stored in r13
```

Why do this? You'll find your own reasons over time, but in general it allows you to treat procedure calls as parameters. In randtest, I factored out a lot of code into a procedure called puller and then called puller several times for different sizes of random number. I passed puller the address of the correct random-number procedure to call by loading the address of that procedure into RDI:

```
; Create and display an array of 8-bit random values:
mov r13,pull8 ; Copy address of random # subroutine into r13
call puller   ; Pull as many numbers as called for in [pulls]
```

Down in the puller procedure, the code calls the requested random-number procedure this way:

```
puller:
    mov r12,[Pulls]      ; Put pull count into R12
.grab:
    dec r12              ; Decrement counter in RSI
    call r13             ; Pull the value; it's returned in RAX
    mov [Stash+r12*8],rax   ; Store random value in the array
    cmp r12,0            ; See if we've pulled all STASH-ed numbers yet
    jne .grab            ; Do another if R12 <> 0
    ret                  ; Otherwise, go home!
```

See the CALL R13 instruction? In this situation (where R13 was previously loaded with the address of procedure pull8), what is called is pull8—even though the label pull8 is nowhere present in procedure puller. The same code in puller can be used to fill a buffer with all the different sizes of random numbers, by calling the procedure address passed to it in R13.

Calling an address in a register gives you a lot of power to generalize code—just make sure you document what you're up to, since the label that you're calling is not contained in the CALL instruction!

Using puts() to Send a Naked Linefeed to the Console

The randtest program also demonstrates something simple but not obvious: how to send a "naked" newline to the Linux console. I explained earlier that libc's puts() function always ends whatever it displays with a newline—even if you'd rather it not have it display a newline at all. To display things to the console without a newline, you have to use printf().

So what if you want to send a linefeed to the console but nothing else? Easy: Define a variable (I call it NewLine) as a single byte, and put a 0 in it. Then copy the address of the NewLine variable into RDI, and then call puts():

```
mov rdi,NewLine   ; Output a newline
call puts
```

Remember that puts() displays everything from the address passed to it in RDI to the first null (that is, a 0) it encounters. If the only thing at that address is a null, puts() will send a newline to the console and nothing else.

How to Pass a libc Function More Than Six Parameters

If you remember, in the x64 calling convention, the first six parameters passed to a function are passed in RDI, RSI, RDX, RCX, R8, and R9. So what if you want to pass printf() seven parameters or more? Anything beyond six parameters has to go on the stack. I deliberately designed randtest to hand seven parameters to printf(). The action occurs in the procedure called shownums:

```
shownums:
    mov r12,qword [Pulls]     ; Put pull count into r12
    xor r13,r13
.dorow:
    mov rdi,ShowArray         ; Pass address of base string
    mov rsi,[Stash+r13*8+0]   ; Pass first element
    mov rdx,[Stash+r13*8+8]   ; Pass second element
    mov rcx,[Stash+r13*8+16]  ; Pass third element
    mov r8,[Stash+r13*8+24]   ; Pass fourth element
```

```
mov r9,[Stash+r13*8+32]  ; Pass fifth element
push rax                 ; To keep the stack 16 bytes aligned
push qword [Stash+r13*8+40] ; Pass sixth element on the stack.
xor rax,rax              ; Tell printf() no vector values coming
call printf              ; Display the random numbers
add rsp,16               ; Stack cleanup: 2 item X 8 bytes = 16
```

At the label `dorow`: is a sequence of six MOV instructions, all of which pass parameters to be used by `printf()`. The address of the base string goes first (in RDI) followed by the six random numbers making up a row. Once we get to the sixth number we're out of registers to pass things in. So that last parameter value is pushed onto the stack, immediately before we call `printf()`.

Well, *almost* immediately. Earlier in this chapter I covered this same code from a different direction: stack alignment. Although the `glibc` startup code aligns the stack to a 16-byte value, pushing just one item onto the stack adds only 8 bytes to the stack pointer, and thus misaligns the stack. To fix this, push RAX onto the stack just before you push that seventh parameter onto the stack. RAX adds another 8 bytes to the stack, returning it to 16-byte alignment. (What's actually *in* RAX doesn't matter. It's just 8 bytes of padding.)

If there were eight parameters, the eighth would be pushed onto the stack right after the seventh without needing any PUSH RAX instruction at all. Here's why: The gist of **stack alignment** is to grow or shrink the stack only in 16-byte chunks, even if half of one of those chunks is a "dummy" register.

Pushing two parameter values onto the stack grows the stack by 16 bytes, so no dummy value is necessary. In fact, if you forget and add a PUSH RAX anyway, you'll be misaligning the stack!

The `printf()` function knows where to look, and it will find and use all the parameters passed to it. However, `printf()` does *not* clean up after itself. If you push values onto the stack for a `printf()` call, once `printf()` is done with them you have to clean up the stack. This is done not by popping (at least not in this particular case) but by adding the size of the item you pushed onto the stack to RSP. Remember that the stack grows "down" (toward lower addresses). If we push something, RSP gets smaller by the size of the pushed value, in this case, a 64-bit integer. To clean the stack, we add the size of what we pushed back into RSP. In this case, we pushed one 8-byte register plus one 8-byte integer for a total of 16 bytes in size, so we add 16 to RSP. *Voilà!* The stack is now clean—at least from the call to `printf()`.

Keep track of your stack: Pop what you push, or add a pushed item's size back into RSP. Be careful: Mess up the stack, and a segmentation fault is almost inevitable.

How C Sees Command-Line Arguments

In Chapter 11, I explained how to access command-line arguments from a Linux program as part of a more general discussion of stack frames. One of the odder things about linking and calling functions out of the standard C library in `glibc` is that the way you access command-line arguments changes and changes significantly.

The arguments are still on the stack, as is the table of argument addresses. However, you no longer have to go sniffing around up and down the stack to find them.

The key is this: `main()` is a function. It's only one part of a C program. There are also the startup code and the shutdown code. Once the startup code finishes its work, it calls `main()` just as it would call any other function. When `main()` is finished, it returns control to the shutdown code, which does its work, and then returns control to Linux.

What makes the process of finding command-line arguments easier is that the startup code follows the x64 calling conventions when it calls `main()`. The first six parameters are passed to a function in registers. The first register to get a parameter is RDI.

When the startup code calls `main()`, it places the argument count (`argc` in C jargon) in RDI. The only other parameter ordinarily passed to `main()` is the address of the table of pointers on the stack, in C jargon `argv`. Each of the addresses in the `argv` table points to its actual argument text. The pointer to the table of pointers is passed in the second calling convention register, RSI.

Listing 12.7 is functionally equivalent to the `showargs2` program presented in Chapter 11. It is, however, significantly simpler. Take a look, and we'll go through it.

Listing 12.7: showargs3.asm

```
;   Executable name  : showargs3
;   Version          : 3.0
;   Created date     : 10/1/1999
;   Last update      : 5/13/2023
;   Author           : Jeff Duntemann
;   Description      : A demo that shows how to access command line
;                      arguments stored on the stack by addressing
;                      them relative to rbp.
;
;   Build using these commands:
;      nasm -f elf64 -g -F dwarf showargs3.asm
;      gcc showargs3.o -o showargs3
;
```

```
[SECTION .data]    ; Section containing initialized data

ArgMsg db "Argument %d: %s",10,0

[SECTION .bss]     ; Section containing uninitialized data

[SECTION .text]    ; Section containing code

global main        ; Required so linker can find entry point
extern printf      ; Notify linker that we're calling printf

main:
    push rbp       ; Set up stack frame for debugger
    mov rbp,rsp

;;; Everything before this is boilerplate; use for all ordinary apps!

    mov r14,rdi    ; Get arc count (argc) from RDI
    mov r13,rsi    ; Put the pointer to the arg table argv from RSI
    xor r12,r12    ; Clear r12 to 0

.showit:
    mov rdi,ArgMsg ; Pass address of display string in rdi
    mov rsi,r12    ; Pass argument number in rsi
    mov rdx,qword [r13+r12*8]    ; Pass address of an argument in RDX
    mov rax,0      ; Tells printf() no vector arguments are coming
    call printf    ; Display the argument # and argument

    inc r12        ; Bump argument # to next argument
    dec r14        ; Decrement argument counter by 1
    jnz .showit    ; If argument count is 0, we're done

;;; Everything after this is boilerplate; use for all ordinary apps!

    mov rsp,rbp    ; Destroy stack frame before returning
    pop rbp

    ret            ; Return to glibc shutdown code
```

After the prolog, the `argc` count value is copied into R14. The address of the `argv` table is copied into R13. R12 is cleared to 0. At each pass through the `.showit` loop, values are passed to the `printf()` function, all according to the x64 calling convention. The display string's address is passed in RDI, and the argument number is passed in RSI, numbered from 0. The address of the text of each argument is passed in RDX, using an effective address calculated this way:

```
mov rdx,qword  [r13+r12*8]
```

Flip back to Figure 9.9 if you need a quick refresher on effective address calculations. The base term is R13, which is the address of the beginning of the table. Each address in the table takes up 8 bytes, so you treat the ordinal position of the table entries (that is, element 0, 1, 2, 3, etc.) as the index and multiply it by the scale factor, 8 since addresses in x64 are all 8 bytes in size. When the math is done, the effective address of the chosen element in the table is copied into RDX. RDX then carries the address of the argv element to be displayed into printf(). (Note that there is no displacement term in this particular effective address calculation.)

During the .showit loop, R14 counts down the number of arguments, while R12 gives each argument its ordinal number. In other words, R14 counts how many arguments we still have to display, and for each argument R12 gives it an ordinal number that counts up, to be displayed by printf().

All this should be clear from Figure 12.4.

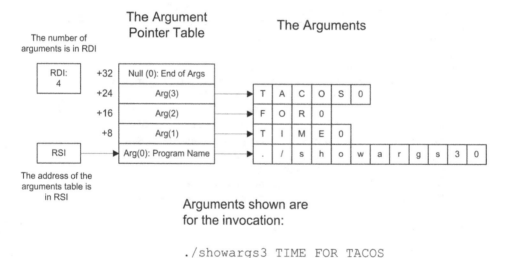

Figure 12.4: Accessing command-line arguments from the x64 main() function

Simple File I/O

The final example program I present in here is nominally about working with disk-based text files. However, it pulls together a lot of assembly tricks and features I've explained earlier and adds a few more. It's the largest and most complex program I've shown you, and if you can read it and follow the flow of the logic, you've gotten everything from this book that I set out to teach you. It's more like a "real" program than anything else in this book in that it works with command-line arguments, writes output to a disk file, and does other useful things that any utility you'll set out to build will likely require.

The program `textfile.asm` in Listing 12.8 creates and fills a text file with text. You can specify the number of lines to be filled in the file, as well as text for the lines. If you don't specify text for the file, the program will generate a line of randomly chosen characters and use that instead. Invoking the program is done like this:

```
$./textfile 50 Time for tacos!
```

This invocation creates a new file (the name of which is fixed in the program as `testeroo.txt`) and write the text "Time for tacos!" to the file 50 times before closing the file. If the file `testeroo.txt` already exists, it will be overwritten from the beginning. If you don't type anything after the line count number, the program will fill the file with random alphanumeric characters. If you don't type an integer as the first argument (for example, the letter Q) `textfile` will display a one-line error message. If you type only the program name and press Enter, `textfile` will display several lines explaining what it is and how to use it.

Converting Strings into Numbers with sscanf()

When you type a number on the command line while invoking a program, you can access that number as one of the command-line arguments, through the mechanisms I described a little earlier in this chapter. However, there's a catch: The number is present *as text*, and you can't just take the textual string "751" and load it into a register or an integer variable. To make use of numeric arguments as numbers, you must first convert their textual expression into numeric form.

The standard C library has several functions to handle this challenge. Some of them, such as `strtod()`, are pretty specific and limited and convert text to only one numeric type. One of them, however, has the ability to convert almost any textual expression of a legal numeric value into an appropriate numeric form. This is `sscanf()`, and it's the one we'll use in Listing 12.8.

The `sscanf()` function takes three parameters, which you must load into the standard parameter registers, in the following order:

1. The first parameter is the address of the text string to be converted to the numeric value that it represents. In `textfile.asm`, we load RDI with the address of `arg(1)`, which is the first command-line argument you type on the command line when you invoke the program.

2. We next load RSI with the address of a formatting code string that tells `sscanf()` what numeric format you want the input text to be converted to. Here the code string is `%d`, which as you may recall from our `printf()` discussion is the code for integers.

3. The third parameter is the address of a numeric variable to contain the numeric value generated by `sscanf()`. This goes in RDX. We're generating

a 64-bit integer here. So, in `textfile.asm`, we pass the address of the variable `IntBuffer`, which is declared as a 64-bit integer.

4. As with `printf()` and `scanf()`, clear RAX to 0 immediately before making the call to `sscanf()`.

Once these three items are loaded into the proper registers and RAX cleared, call `sscanf()`. It returns the converted value in the numeric variable whose address you passed as the third parameter. It also returns a code in RAX to indicate whether the conversion was successful. If the return value in RAX is 0, then an error occurred, and you shouldn't assume that you have anything meaningful in your numeric variable. If the conversion went through successfully, you'll see the value 1 in RAX.

This is the simplest way to use `sscanf()`. It can convert whole arrays of numbers at once, but this is a more specialized use that you're unlikely to need when you're just starting out. Doing those specialized things often requires vector registers, which I'm not covering in this book. It is important, however, to clear RAX to 0 before calling `sscanf()` in the example program to tell the function that no vector registers will be used.

The string passed to `sscanf()` as the second parameter may contain multiple formatting codes, and in that case the string whose address you pass as the first parameter should have text describing numeric values for each formatting code present in the format string. In Listing 12.8, the format text specifies only one value, using the %d format code.

The whole process looks like this:

```
xor rax,rax          ; Clear rax to 0
mov rdi,qword [r13+8] ; Pass address of an argument in rdi
mov rsi,IntFormat    ; Pass address of integer format code in rsi
mov rdx,IntBuffer    ; Pass address of integer buffer for sscanf output
mov rax,0            ; Tell sscanf() that there are no vector arguments
call sscanf          ; Convert string arg to number with sscanf()
cmp rax,1            ; Return value of 1 says we got a number
je chkdata           ; If we got a number, go on; else abort

mov rdi,Err1         ; Pass address of error 1-line message in rdi
mov rax,0            ; Tell printf() that there are no vector arguments
call printf          ; Show the error message
jmp gohome           ; Exit the program
```

Assuming that the user entered at least one argument on the command line (and the program has already verified this before the above excerpt), a pointer to that first argument is located at an offset of 8 from the beginning of the command-line argument pointer table. (The very first element in the table, which we call arg(0), points to the name of the program as the user typed it on the command line.) That's why we load the contents of argument at `[R13+8]` onto the stack; we had already loaded R13 with the address of the argument pointer table. What's located at [R13+8] is the pointer to arg(1), the first actual command-line argument. (The very first argument, arg(0), is the text by which you invoked the program.) See Figure 12.4 if this is still fuzzy.

Creating and Opening Files

By this time you should be pretty comfortable with the general mechanism for making C library calls from assembly. And whether you realize it or not, you're already pretty comfortable with some of the machinery for manipulating text files. You've already used printf() to display formatted text to the screen by way of standard output. The very same mechanism is used to write formatted text to disk-based text files—you're basically substituting a real disk file for standard output. So, understanding text file I/O shouldn't be much of a conceptual leap.

But unlike standard output, which is predefined for you by the C library and always available, you have to create or open a disk-based text file to use it. The fopen() function is what does the job.

There are three general ways to open a file: for reading, for writing, and for appending. When you open a file for reading, you can read text from it via such functions as fgets(), but you can't write to the file. When you open a file for writing, whatever may have been in the file before is thrown away, and new material is written starting at the beginning of the file. When you open a file for appending, you may write to the file, but new material is written *after* any existing material, and whatever was originally in the file is retained.

Ordinarily, when you open a file for writing you can't read from it, but there are special modes that allow both reading from and writing to a file. For text files especially (which are what we're speaking of here) that introduces some complications, so for the most part, text files are opened for either reading or for writing, but not for both at once.

In the Unix file system, if you open a file for either writing or appending and the file does not already exist, the file is created. If you don't know if a file exists and you need to find out, attempt to open it for *reading* and not for writing, or you'll get a file whether it actually existed earlier or not!

To use fopen(), you must set up the following parameters into registers before the call:

1. Place the address of the character string containing the name of the file to be opened in RDI.

2. Place the address of a code indicating which mode the file should be opened for in RSI. The various available modes for Linux are listed in Table 12.3. The ones you'll typically use for text files are r, w, and a. These should be defined as short character strings, followed by a null:

```
WriteCode   db 'w',0
OpenCode    db 'r',0
```

With those two items in registers, you make the call to fopen(). If the file was successfully opened, fopen() will return a file handle in RAX. A file handle is a 64-bit number assigned by Linux to a file during the call to fopen(). If the open was not successful, RAX will contain the value 0 instead of a file handle. Here's how opening a file for reading looks in code:

```
mov rdi,Filename    ; Pass filename to fopen in RDI
mov rsi,ReadCode    ; Pass pointer to write/create code ('r') in rsi
call fopen          ; Open file for reading
cmp rax,0           ; Test for successful file open: failed if 0
je OpenErr          ; Jump to error handling code if open failed
<use opened file>
```

The process of creating a file and then writing to it is identical, except that you must use the w code instead of the r code. We'll see how this works in the program textfile.asm.

Table 12.3:   File Access Codes for Use with fopen()

CODE	DESCRIPTION
"r"	Opens an existing text file for reading
"w"	Creates a new text file, or opens and truncates an existing file
"a"	Creates a new text file, or opens an existing file so that new text is added at the end
"r+"	Opens an existing text file for either writing or reading
"w+"	Creates a new text file, or opens and truncates an existing file for both read and write access
"a+"	Creates a new text file, or opens an existing file for reading or for writing so that new text may be added at the end

Reading Text from Files with fgets()

When fopen() successfully creates or opens a file for you, it returns a file handle in RAX. Keep that file handle safe somewhere—I recommend either copying it to a memory variable allocated for that purpose or putting it in a register you know will not be used for anything else. This is important: If you store it in RAX, RCX, or RDX and then make a call to almost any C library function, the file handle in the register will be trashed, and you'll lose it.

Once a file is opened for reading, you can read text lines from it sequentially with the fgets() function. Each time you call fgets() on an opened text file, it will read one line of the file, which is defined as all the characters up to the next EOL ("newline") character (ASCII 10), which in the Unix world always indicates the end of a text line.

Now, in any given file there's no way of knowing how many characters there will be until the next newline, so it would be dangerous to just turn fgets() loose to bring back characters until it encounters a newline. If you attempt to open the wrong kind of file (a binary code file is one possibility, or a compressed data file), you might bring in thousands of bytes before encountering the binary 10 value that the file system considers a newline. Whatever buffer you had allocated to hold the incoming text would overflow and fgets() would perhaps destroy adjacent data and/or crash your program.

For that reason, you must also pass a limit value to fgets(). When fgets() begins reading a line, it keeps track of how many characters it has brought in from the file, and when it gets to one less than the limit value, it stops reading characters. It then adds an EOL character to the buffer for the final character and returns.

Set up calls to fgets() this way:

1. First, load RDI with the address of the character buffer into which fgets() will store the characters that it reads from the file.

2. Next, load RSI with the character count limit value. This must be the actual integer value, and *not* a pointer to the value!

3. Finally, load RDX with the file handle returned by fopen() when the file was opened.

With all that done, call fgets(). If fgets() returns a 0 in RAX, then either you've reached the end of the file or else a file error happened during the read. Either way, there's no more data forthcoming from the file. But without a 0 returned in RAX, you can assume that valid text is present in the buffer at the address you passed to fgets() in RDI.

I used fgets() to create a very simple disk-based help system for textfile .asm. When the user enters no command-line arguments at all, the textfile program reads a short text file from disk and displays it to standard output. If the disk-based help file cannot be opened, textfile displays a short message to that effect. This is a common and courteous thing to do with command-line programs, and I recommend that all utilities you build for everyday use work this way.

The code for the help system is relatively simple and demonstrates both fopen() and fgets():

```
diskhelp:
    mov rdi,DiskHelpNm ; Pointer to name of help file is passed in rdi
    mov rsi,OpenCode   ; Pointer to open-for-read code "r" gpes in rsi
    call fopen         ; Attempt to open the file for reading
```

```
        cmp rax,0          ; fopen returns null if attempted open failed
        jne .disk          ; Read help info from disk, else from memory
        call memhelp
        ret

.disk:
        mov rbx,rax        ; Save handle of opened file in ebx
.rdln:
        mov rdi,HelpLine   ; Pass pointer to buffer in rdi
        mov rsi,HELPLEN    ; Pass buffer size in rsi
        mov rdx,rbx        ; Pass file handle to fgets in rdx
        call fgets         ; Read a line of text from the file
        cmp rax,0          ; A returned null indicates error or EOF
        jle .done          ; If we get 0 in rax, close up & return
        mov rdi,HelpLine   ; Pass address of help line in rdi
        mov rax,0          ; Tell printf() there are no vector arguments
        call printf        ; Call printf to display help line
        jmp .rdln

.done:
        mov rdi,rbx        ; Pass the handle of the file to be closed in rdi
        call fclose        ; Close the file
        jmp gohome         ; Go home
```

Before procedure diskhelp is called, the caller passes a pointer to the name of the help file to be read in RBX. The code then attempts to open this file. If the attempt to open the help file fails, a very short "fail safe" help message is displayed from strings stored in the .data section of the program. (This is the call to memhelp, which is another short procedure in textfile.asm.) Never leave the user staring at a mute cursor, wondering what's going on!

Once the disk-based help file is opened, we start looping through a sequence that reads text lines from the opened file with fgets() and then writes those lines to standard output with printf(). The maximum length of the lines to be read is defined by the equate HELPLEN.

Why an equate? Instead of being specified at several places all over your source code, the maximum length of your help file lines is defined in only one place, eliminating the chances of accidentally placing multiple values in different parts of your source code. If you need to change it, by using an equate, you can change the value everywhere it's used by changing that one equate only. Equates fight bugs. Use them whenever you can.

Each time a line is read from the file, the address of the line is passed to printf() in RDI and displayed. When no more lines are available to be read in the help file, fgets() returns a 0 in RAX, and the program branches to the function call that closes the file.

Note the `fclose()` function, which in use is quite simple: You copy the file handle of an open file into RDI, and call `fclose()`. That's all it takes to close the file!

Writing Text to Files with fprintf()

Earlier in this chapter, I explained how to write formatted text to the display by way of standard output, using the `printf()` function. The standard C library provides a function that writes the very same formatted text to *any* opened text file. The `fprintf()` function does exactly what `printf()` does, but it takes one additional parameter on the stack: the file handle of an open text file. The same text stream that `printf()` would send to standard output is sent by `fprintf()` to that open file.

So I won't bother re-explaining how to format text for `printf()` using formatting codes and base strings. It's done the same way, with the exact same codes. Instead, I'll simply summarize how to set up a call to `fprintf()`:

1. First (and here's where `fprintf()` differs from `printf()`), copy the file handle of the file to which the text should be written into RDI.

2. Next, copy the address of the base string containing the formatting codes into RSI. Again, just as for `printf()`.

3. Finally, pass pointers to values controlled by the base string in registers, according to the order specified in the C calling convention. There's no difference here from the way it's done for a call to `printf()`. As with `printf()` there can be more than one. In `textfile.asm`, the first is the line number (passed in RDX), and the second is the line of text entered by the user, passed in RCX.

4. As with `printf()`, clear RAX to 0 before calling `fprintf()`.

Then call `fprintf()`. Your text will be written to the open file. Note that to use `fprintf()`, the destination file must have been opened *for either writing or appending*. If you attempt to use `fprintf()` on a file opened for reading, you will generate an error and `fprintf()` will return without writing any data at all.

In that event, an error code will be returned in RAX. However, unlike the other functions we've discussed so far, the error code is a negative number, *not* 0! So, although you should compare the returned value against 0, you actually need to jump on a value *less* than 0—rather than 0 itself. Typically, to jump on an `fprintf()` error condition, you would use the instruction JL (Jump if Less), which will jump on a value less than 0.

Here's the `fprintf()` call from `textfile.asm`:

```
writeline:
    cmp qword r15,0      ; Has the line count gone to 0?
    je closeit           ; If so, close the file and exit
```

```
    mov rdi,rbx         ; Pass the file handle in rdi
    mov rsi,WriteBase   ; Pass the base string in rsi
    mov rdx,r14         ; Pass the line number in rdx
    mov rcx,Buff        ; Pass the pointer to the text buffer in rcx
    mov rax,0           ; Tell fprintf that there are no vector arguments
    call fprintf        ; Write the text line to the file
    dec r15             ; Decrement the count of lines to be written
    inc r14             ; Increment the line number
    jmp writeline       ; Loop back and do it again

;; We're done writing text; now let's close the file: closeit:
    mov rdi,rbx         ; Pass the handle of the file to be closed in rdi
    call fclose         ; Closes the file
```

Notes on Gathering Your Procedures into Libraries

Here's a recap of how to go about gathering procedures together into libraries:

- Create a new source code file and paste the procedure source code into the file, which must have an .ASM file extension.

- Declare the callable entry points to all procedures in the library, as well as any other identifiers that may be used by other programs and libraries, as global. This makes those items visible (and thus usable) by other programs or libraries linked with the new library.

- If the procedures call any C library functions or procedures in other libraries you own or have created, or use variables or other identifiers defined outside the library, declare all such external identifiers as extern.

- When calling library procedures from a program, update the makefile for that program so that the final executable has a dependency on the library.

This last point is the only one that requires additional discussion. The make file shown next builds the textfile.asm demo program, which links in a library called linlib.asm. Note that there is a whole new line specifying how the object file linlib.o is assembled and also that the final binary file textfile depends on both textfile.o and linlib.o.

Because the textfile executable depends on both textfile.o and linlib.o, any time you make changes to either textfile.asm or linlib.asm, the make utility will completely relink the executable file via gcc. However, unless you change both .asm files, only the .asm file that is changed will be assembled again. The magic of make is that it does nothing that doesn't need doing.

```
textfile: textfile.o linlib.o
      gcc textfile.o linlib.o -o textfile -no-pie
textfile.o: textfile.asm
      nasm -f elf64 -g -F dwarf textfile.asm
linlib.o: linlib.asm
      nasm -f elf64 -g -F dwarf linlib.asm
```

The complete file `linlib.asm` is present in the listings archive for this book. The procedures it contains have been gathered from other programs shown in this chapter, so it would be repetitive to reprint them all here.

Finally, the `textfile.asm` program follows, in its entirety. Make sure that you can read all of it—there's nothing here I haven't covered somewhere in this book. And if you want a challenge, here's one for your next project: Adapt `textfile.asm` to read in a text file, and write it out again with line numbers prepended in front of each line of text. Allow the user to enter on the command line the name of a new file to contain the modified text. Keep the help system and write a new help text file for it.

Pull that off, and you can take a bow: You'll be an assembly language programmer!

Listing 12.8: textfile.asm

```
;   Executable name  : textfile
;   Version          : 3.0
;   Created date     : 11/21/1999
;   Last update      : 5/24/2023
;   Author           : Jeff Duntemann
;   Description      : A text file I/O demo for Linux, using NASM 2.14.02
;
;   Build executable using these commands:
;     nasm -f elf64 -g -F dwarf textfile.asm
;     nasm -f elf64 -g -F dwarf linlib.asm
;     gcc textfile.o linlib.o -o textfile -no-pie
;
;   Note that the textfile program requires several procedures
;   in an external library named LINLIB.ASM.


[SECTION .data]       ; Section containing initialized data

IntFormat    dq '%d',0
WriteBase    db 'Line # %d: %s',10,0
NewFilename  db 'testeroo.txt',0
DiskHelpNm   db 'helptextfile.txt',0
WriteCode    db 'w',0
OpenCode     db 'r',0
CharTbl
  db '0123456789ABCDEFGHIJKLMNOPQRSTUVWXYZabcdefghijklmnopqrstuvwxyz-@'
Errl
```

```
    db 'ERROR: The first command line argument must be an integer!',10,0
HelpMsg
    db 'TEXTTEST: Generates a test file. Arg(1) should be the # of ',10,0
HELPSIZE EQU $-HelpMsg
    db 'lines to write to the file.  All other args are concatenated',10,0
    db 'into a single line and written to the file.  If no text args',10,0
    db 'are entered, random text is written to the file.  This msg  ',10,0
    db 'appears only if the file HELPTEXTFILE.TXT cannot be opened. ',10,0
HelpEnd    dq 0

[SECTION .bss]              ; Section containing uninitialized data


LineCount   resq 1         ; Reserve integer to hold line count
IntBuffer   resq 1         ; Reserve integer for sscanf's return value
HELPLEN     EQU 72         ; Define length of a line of help text data
HelpLine    resb HELPLEN   ; Reserve space for disk-based help text line
BUFSIZE     EQU 64         ; Define length of text line buffer buff
Buff        resb BUFSIZE+5 ; Reserve space for a line of text

[SECTION .text]            ; Section containing code

;; These externals are all from the glibc standard C library:
extern fopen
extern fclose
extern fgets
extern fprintf
extern printf
extern sscanf
extern time

;; These externals are from the associated library linlib.asm:
extern seedit              ; Seeds the random number generator
extern pull6               ; Generates a 6-bit random number from 0-63

global main                ; Required so linker can find entry point

main:
    push rbp               ; Prolog: Set up stack frame
    mov rbp,rsp

    mov r12,rdi            ; Save the argument count in r12
    mov r13,rsi            ; Save the argument pointer table to r13

    call seedit            ; Seed the random number generator

    ;; First test is to see if there are command-line arguments at all.
    ;; If there are none, we show the help info as several lines. Don't
    ;; forget that the 1st arg is always the program name, so there's
    ;; always at least 1 argument, even if we don't use it!
```

```
        cmp r12,1           ; If count in r12 is 1, there are no arguments
        ja chkarg2          ; Continue if arg count is > 1
        mov rbx,DiskHelpNm   ; Put address of help file name in rbx
        call diskhelp       ; If only 1 arg, show help info...
        jmp gohome          ; ...and exit the program


;; Next we check for a numeric command line argument 1:

chkarg2:
        mov rdi,qword [r13+8] ; Pass address of an argument in rdi
        mov rsi,IntFormat    ; Pass addr of integer format code in rsi
        mov rdx,IntBuffer    ; Pass addr of integer buffer for sscanf output
        xor rax,rax          ; 0 says there will be no vector parameters
        call sscanf          ; Convert string arg to number with sscanf()
        cmp rax,1            ; Return value of 1 says we got a number
        je chkdata           ; If we got a number, go on; else abort

        mov rdi,Err1         ; Pass address of error 1-line message in rdi
        xor rax,rax          ; 0 says there will be no vector parameters
        call printf          ; Show the error message
        jmp gohome           ; Exit the program

;; Here we're looking to see if there are more arguments. If there
;; are, we concatenate them into a single string no more than
;; BUFSIZE chars in size. (Yes, I DO know this does what strncat
;; does...)

chkdata:
        mov r15,[IntBuffer] ; Store the # of lines to write in r15
        cmp r12,3           ; Is there a second argument?
        jae getlns          ; If so, we have text to fill a file with
        call randline       ; If not, generate a line of random text
                            ; for file. Note that randline returns ptr
                            ; to line in rsi
        jmp genfile         ; Go on to create the file

;; Here we copy as much command line text as we have, up to BUFSIZE
;; chars, into the line buffer Buff. We skip the first two args
;; (which at this point we know exist) but we know we have at least
;; one text arg in arg(2). Going into this section, we know that
;; r13 contains the pointer to the arg table.

getlns:
        mov r14,2           ; We know we have at least arg(2), start there
        mov rdi,Buff        ; Destination pointer is start of char buffer
        xor rax,rax         ; Clear rax to 0 for the character counter
        cld                 ; Clear direction flag for up-memory movsb

grab:
        mov rsi,qword [r13+r14*8]    ; Copy pointer to next arg into rsi
.copy:
```

```
        cmp byte [rsi],0    ; Have we found the end of the arg?
        je .next            ; If so, bounce to the next arg
        movsb               ; Copy char from [rsi] to [rdi]; inc rdi & rsi
        inc rax             ; Increment total character count
        cmp rax,BUFSIZE     ; See if we've filled the buffer to max count
        je addnul           ; If so, go add a null to Buff & we're done
        jmp .copy

.next:
        mov byte [rdi],' ' ; Copy space to Buff to separate the args
        inc rdi             ; Increment destination pointer for space
        inc rax             ; Add one to character count too
        cmp rax,BUFSIZE     ; See if we've now filled Buff
        je addnul           ; If so, go down to add a nul and we're done
        inc r14             ; Otherwise, increment the arg processed count
        cmp r14,r12         ; Compare against argument count in r12
        jae addnul          ; If r14 = arg count in r12, we're done
        jmp grab            ; Otherwise, go back and copy it

addnul:
        mov byte [rdi],0    ; Tack a null on the end of Buff
        mov rsi,Buff        ; File write code expects ptr to text in rsi

        ;; Now we create a file to fill with the text we have:
genfile:
        mov rdi,NewFilename ; Pass filename to fopen in RDI
        mov rsi,WriteCode   ; Pass pointer to write/create code ('w') in rsi
        call fopen          ; Create/open file
        mov rbx,rax         ; rax contains the file handle; save in rbx

        ;; File is open.  Now let's fill it with text:
        mov r14,1           ; R14 now holds the line # in the text file

writeline:
        cmp qword r15,0     ; Has the line count gone to 0?
        je closeit          ; If so, close the file and exit
        mov rdi,rbx         ; Pass the file handle in rdi
        mov rsi,WriteBase   ; Pass the base string in rsi
        mov rdx,r14         ; Pass the line number in rdx
        mov rcx,Buff        ; Pass the pointer to the text buffer in rcx
        xor rax,rax         ; 0 says there will be no vector parameters
        call fprintf        ; Write the text line to the file
        dec r15             ; Decrement the count of lines to be written
        inc r14             ; Increment the line number
        jmp writeline       ; Loop back and do it again

        ;; We're done writing text; now let's close the file:
closeit:
        mov rdi,rbx     ; Pass the handle of the file to be closed in rdi
        call fclose     ; Closes the file
```

```
gohome:                    ; End program execution
    pop rbp                ; Epilog: Destroy stack frame before returning
    ret                    ; Return control to the C shutdown code


;;; SUBROUTINES=========================================================

;---------------------------------------------------------------------
; Disk-based mini-help subroutine  --  Last update 12/16/2022
;
; This routine reads text from a text file, the name of which is passed
; by way of a pointer to the name string in ebx. The routine opens the
; text file, reads the text from it, and displays it to standard output.
; If the file cannot be opened, a very short memory-based message is
; displayed instead.
;---------------------------------------------------------------------
diskhelp:
    push rbp
    mov rbp,rsp

    mov rdi,DiskHelpNm  ; Pointer to name of help file is passed in rdi
    mov rsi,OpenCode    ; Pointer to open-for-read code "r" gpes in rsi
    call fopen          ; Attempt to open the file for reading
    cmp rax,0           ; fopen returns null if attempted open failed
    jne .disk           ; Read help info from disk, else from memory
    call memhelp        ; Display the help message
    pop rbp             ; Epilog
    ret

.disk:
    mov rbx,rax         ; Save handle of opened file in ebx
.rdln:
    mov rdi,HelpLine    ; Pass pointer to buffer in rdi
    mov rsi,HELPLEN     ; Pass buffer size in rsi
    mov rdx,rbx         ; Pass file handle to fgets in rdx
    call fgets          ; Read a line of text from the file
    cmp rax,0           ; A returned null indicates error or EOF
    jle .done           ; If we get 0 in rax, close up & return
    mov rdi,HelpLine    ; Pass address of help line in rdi
    xor rax,rax         ; Passs 0 to show there will be no fp registers
    call printf         ; Call printf to display help line
    jmp .rdln

.done:
    mov rdi,rbx         ; Pass handle of the file to be closed in rdi
    call fclose         ; Close the file
    jmp gohome          ; Go home
```

```
memhelp:
    push rbp            ; Prolog
    mov rbp,rsp
    mov rax,5           ; rax contains the number of newlines we want
    mov rbx,HelpMsg     ; Load address of help text into rbx
.chkln:
    cmp qword [rbx],0   ; Does help msg pointer point to a null?
    jne .show           ; If not, show the help lines
    pop rbp             ; Epilog
    ret                 ; If yes, go home
.show:
    mov rdi,rbx         ; Pass address of help line in rdi
    xor rax,rax         ; 0 in RAX says no vector parameters passed
    call printf         ; Display the line
    add rbx,HELPSIZE    ; Increment address by length of help line
    jmp .chkln          ; Loop back and check to see if we're done yet

showerr:
    push rbp            ; Prolog
    mov rsp,rbp

    mov rdi,rax         ; On entry, rax contains address of error message
    xor rax,rax         ; 0 in RAX says there will be no vector parameters
    call printf         ; Show the error message

    pop rbp             ; Epilog
    ret                 ; Pass control to shutdown code; no return value

randline:
    push rbp            ; Prolog
    mov rbp,rsp

    mov rbx,BUFSIZE        ; BUFSIZE tells us how many chars to pull
    mov byte [Buff+BUFSIZE+1],0 ; Put a null at the end of the buffer
                              ; first
.loopback:
    dec rbx            ; BUFSIZE is 1-based, so decrement
    call pull6         ; Go get a random number from 0-63
    mov cl,[CharTbl+rax]   ; Use random # in rax as offset into char
                          ;  table and copy character from table
                          ;  into cl
    mov [Buff+rbx],cl  ; Copy char from cl to character buffer
    cmp rbx,0          ; Are we done having fun yet?
    jne .loopback      ; If not, go back and pull another
    mov rsi,Buff       ; Copy address of the buffer into rsi

    pop rbp            ; Epilog: Destroy the stack frame
    ret                ;    and go home
```

Conclusion: Not the End, But Only the Beginning

You never really *learn* assembly language.

You can improve your skills over time by reading good books on the subject, by reading good code that others have written, and, most of all, by writing and assembling lots and lots of code yourself. But at no point will you be able to stand up and say, I *know* it.

You shouldn't feel bad about this. In fact, I take some encouragement from occasionally hearing that Michael Abrash, author of *Zen of Assembly Language*, *Zen of Code Optimization*, and his giant compendium *Michael Abrash's Graphics Programming Black Book*, has learned something new about assembly language. Michael has been writing high-performance assembly code for almost 40 years and has evolved into one of the two or three best assembly language programmers in the Western hemisphere.

If Michael is still learning, is there hope for the rest of us?

Wrong question. *Silly* question. If Michael is still learning, it means that *all* of us are students and will always be students. It means that the journey is the goal, and as long as we continue to probe and hack and fiddle and try things that we never tried before, over time we will advance the state of the art and create programs that would have made the pioneers in our field gasp in 1977.

For the point is not to conquer the subject but to live with it and grow with your knowledge of it. The journey *is* the goal, and with this book I've tried hard to help those people who have been frozen with fear at the thought of starting the journey, staring at the complexity of it all and wondering where the first brick in that Yellow Brick Road might be.

It's *here*, with nothing more than the conviction that you can do it.

You can. The problem is not limited to assembly language. Consider my own experience: I got out of school in recession year 1974 with a BA in English, summa cum laude, and not much in reliable prospects outside of driving a cab. I finessed my way into a job with Xerox Corporation, repairing copy machines. Books were fun, but paperwork makes money—so I picked up a tool bag and had a fine old time for a few years before finessing my way into a computer programming position. (How did I do that? I taught myself programming...by reading books and trying things.)

But I'll never forget that first awful moment when I looked over the shoulder of an accomplished technician at a model 660 copier with its panels off, to see what looked like a bottomless pit of little cams and gears and drums and sprocket chains turning and flipping and knocking switch actuators back and forth. Mesmerized by the complexity, I forgot to notice that a sheet of paper had been fed through the machine and turned into a copy of the original document. I was terrified of never learning what all the little cams did and missed the comforting simplicity of the Big Picture—that a copy machine makes copies.

That's Square One: Discover the Big Picture. Ignore the cams and gears for a bit. You can do it. Find out what's important in holding the Big Picture together (ask someone if it's not obvious) and study that before getting down to the cams and gears. Locate the processes that happen. Divide the Big Picture into subpictures. See how things flow. Only then should you focus on something as small and as lost in the mess as an individual cam or switch.

That's how you conquer complexity, and that's how I've presented assembly language in this book. Some might say I've shorted the instruction set, but covering the whole (huge) instruction set was never the real goal here.

The real goal was to conquer your fear of the complexity of the subject, with some metaphors and plenty of pictures and (this really matters!) a light heart.

Did it work? You tell me. I'd really like to know.

Where to Now?

People get annoyed at me sometimes because this book (which has been around in five editions since 1990) does not go more deeply into the subject. I stand firm: *This book is about beginnings*, and I won't short beginnings in order to add more material at the end. (Books can only be so big!) To go further you will have to set this book aside and continue on your own.

Your general approach should be something like this:

1. Study Linux.

2. Study assembly language.

3. Write code.

4. Write more code.

There is no shortage of good books out there on Linux. There are beginner books on most of the popular distributions, including Linux Mint. Check Amazon and your public library. As for your next book on assembly language, here are two I have and recommend.

The Art of 64-bit Assembly by Randall Hyde (No Starch Press, 2022)

If you're looking for your next book on assembly language, consider this one. It's one of the best books out there. (It's also immense, at 1,001 pages!) It covers the complete AVX math subsystem, lots of other intermediate-to-advanced topics, and many more machine instructions. One caution: The book is targeted at Windows and the MASM assembler, and not all of it applies to Linux. The IDE required is Microsoft's Visual Studio. (VS Code won't work.) Nor does this book cover Randy's own High-Level Assembler (HLA) language, which is what his 2003 edition focused on.

Modern x86 Assembly Language Programming by David Kusswurm (Apress, 2018)

I consider this an advanced topics book, but it's a good one. A *huge* chunk of the book is about the AVX math subsystem. Core x64 programming is covered lightly at the beginning. The title is a touch misleading: The book is focused entirely on the x64 processors. If computational math intrigues you, this is the most complete AVX coverage I've seen in one book.

Keep in mind that ebook editions of computer books have a bad habit of scrambling up tables, code snippets, and technical diagrams. As much as I love ebooks, for tech topics I always buy paper.

Stepping off Square One

OK, with a couple of new books in hand and a good night's sleep behind you, strike out on your own a little. Set yourself a goal, and try to achieve it: something *tough*, say, an assembly language utility that locates all files on a specified directory tree with a given ambiguous file name. That's ambitious for a newcomer and will take some research and study and (perhaps) a few false starts. But you can do it, and once you do it, you'll be a real journeyman assembly language programmer.

Becoming a master takes work, and time. Books can take you only so far. Eventually you will have to be your own teacher and direct your own course of study. These days, mastering assembly means understanding the operating system kernel and its low-level machinery, like device drivers. You'll need to learn C well to do that, but there's no way around it. (Looking forward, you may also consider learning a new language called Rust, which might be—and should be—the language that replaces C.) More and more, mastering assembly may also involve writing code to run on high-performance graphics coprocessors like those from Nvidia. The gaming industry drives performance desktop computing these days, and although writing high-performance graphics software is a very difficult challenge, the results can be breathtaking.

But whichever way you end up going, *keep programming*. No matter what sort of code you write, you will learn things while writing it that lead to new challenges. Learning something new always involves the realization that there is a lot more to learn. Study is necessary, but without constant and fairly aggressive practice, study won't help, and static knowledge without reinforcement from real-world experience goes stale in a *big* hurry.

It gets scary at times. The complexity of computing seems to double every couple of years. Still, keep telling yourself: *I can do this.*

Coming to believe the truth in that statement is the essence of stepping away from Square One—and the rest of the road, like all roads, is taken one step at a time.

The Return of the Insight
Debugger

In the 2009 edition of this book, SASM didn't exist yet, and I used a free debugger called Insight for my debugging demos. A few months after the book was published, all of the Linux repositories removed Insight without any explanation.

Yes, Insight is something of an odd bird. It was originally written in an interpreted language called Tcl, with a GUI widget set called Tk. Tcl/Tk (as it came to be known) was first released in 1991. The Tk widgets are modeled on those in Motif, which was one of the very first GUIs and part of the Unix Common Desktop Environment. I've heard grumbles about Tk looking "old," but the real problem with Insight is that the Tcl interpreter was linked right into the executable. This isn't unheard of, but it's kind of a peculiar thing to do.

Insight's source code is open-source and available online. Here and there since 2009, people have put together scripts for building Insight from source. I've tried several, and most of them simply didn't work on recent Linux distros.

Then in 2018, a programmer named antony-jr on GitHub did something remarkable: He created an Insight appimage. An *appimage* is a binary program for Linux created to run without installation. You download the appimage, log into Linux as root, and drop the appimage into /usr/bin. That puts it in your search path, and it can then be run from any folder under your Home folder.

To avoid publishing a link here that might change, I suggest a web search for Insight and antony-jr. In 2023 it's hosted on GitHub.

In this appendix, I will show you how to use the Insight appimage to debug programs that you write outside of SASM. The new Insight has some shortcomings, but for beginner work in Linux it's on point and easy to learn—and if you've already mastered SASM, learning Insight will not be a serious challenge.

Insight's Shortcomings

I need to be honest with you upfront: Insight has some issues. It was created long before 64-bit CPUs existed, and its Memory view window can't show you a quadword at a time. The Registers view, fortunately, has no trouble with 64-bit values. Otherwise, I wouldn't even consider describing it in this book.

Insight's various entry fields don't understand the PC keyboard's navigation keys, apart from backspace. Home, End, PgUp, and PgDn, and the arrows don't come through to Insight. You can backspace over a value in a field and then type a new value. You can also copy and paste address values from the Registers view into the memory view's address field, but for no reason I can discern, Insight places curly brackets around the address value it places on the clipboard. After you paste an address into a field, you have to delete those brackets before pressing Enter, or Insight won't understand the address. You can position the cursor in a field with the mouse and then backspace over the first bracket; then position the cursor at the end of the field and backspace over the other bracket, both before pressing Enter.

Loading a new executable to debug can be fluky. You have to start Insight from a console window showing the working directory of the executable you want to load, or Insight will not be able to find the source code file.

If your program generates a segmentation fault, Insight will crash and vanish. Insight may occasionally crash and vanish anyway, without a segmentation fault. My guess is that running a 30-year-old debugger in 64-bit long mode makes Insight fragile. I don't recommend trying anything exotic with it.

None of this is antony-jr's fault. Absent his work, we wouldn't have Insight at all, and it does fill in a few of the holes in what SASM can do.

These issues are the reason I'm describing the resurrected Insight in an appendix rather than in the book chapters. It's free, and it's fun, especially if you want to look at memory buffers or the stack, neither of which SASM displays well. I've tested it with Linux Mint/Cinnamon. But I don't guarantee that it will work properly on any given Linux distro.

Opening a Program Under Insight

To open an executable program for debugging under Insight, take these steps:

1. Build the software if it hasn't been built for awhile. Make sure that all changes you've made to the source code are reflected in the executable. Insight will complain if your source is newer than your executable.

2. Open a console window in Konsole, or whatever console app you prefer.

3. Navigate to the folder containing the project you want to debug.

4. Launch the Insight appimage from the console window showing the working folder that contains the executable to be debugged. Assuming you placed the appimage in /usr/bin, it should come up from any folder you're working in.

5. Select File ➪ Open. In the Load New Executable dialog, navigate to your working folder and type the name of the binary executable file in your local folder, *not* the source code file!

6. Insight will open the executable and then search the current folder for the source file. It will then open the source code file in its main window.

7. Sometimes Insight will bring up a disassembly of the executable but will not display the source code. Make sure the drop-down list at the right end of the list bar is showing "SOURCE." If it isn't, bring down the list and select SOURCE from the several listed options.

8. If your source code doesn't come up, look at the drop-down list at the left end of the list bar. It should show the name of your .asm source code file. If it doesn't, pull down the list and select it. If it isn't in the drop-down list, make sure your source code file is in the console working directory. If it is but Insight won't show it, exit the program and launch it again.

Insight was designed for high-level languages like C. It can display a number of windows, only a few of which are useful in assembly work. The two windows you want to open are Registers and Memory. Both of these may be selected from the View menu. As with SASM, both windows will be empty until you run the program for debugging.

The Registers view defaults to All, which includes the numerous AVX registers along with the general-purpose registers. If you're working with examples in this book, select General to zero in on the registers you're using in the example programs.

Setting Command-Line Arguments with Insight

Once you have a program and its source code file loaded, but before you run it for debugging, you can load command-line arguments for the program you're working on. Select File ⇨ Target Settings. The Target Selection dialog will appear. In the Connection pane is an Arguments field. Type your command-line arguments into the field, separated by spaces, and click OK. If you step through a program that accepts arguments, the program will take the text you typed into the Arguments field as its arguments.

Running and Stepping a Program

From a single-stepping standpoint, Insight is a great deal like SASM. That shouldn't be a surprise, since behind the scenes Insight and SASM both use the Gnu debugger gdb. If you've become proficient using SASM's debugger interface, you won't have much trouble with Insight.

Theoretically, when Insight loads a program for debugging, it places a breakpoint at the first instruction in the program. A breakpoint is shown as a red square in the left column, beside the line number. I've heard from other users that Insight doesn't always place that breakpoint. You're going to need execution to stop at the first instruction, so if there's no red square beside the line number of the first instruction, click to the left of the line number. Note that breakpoints are set on instructions, *not* data definitions!

Insight breakpoints are toggles. Click beside a line number and a breakpoint appears as a red square. Click the red square, and the breakpoint goes away.

Once you have a breakpoint at the first instruction in the program, click the running man icon at the left end of the icon bar. You can also select Run ⇨ Run from the menu bar. Insight will then run the program.

Yes, it will run the program, but since you set a breakpoint on the first instruction, it will stop there before any instructions execute, with a green highlight showing where execution paused. The highlighted instruction has not yet been executed. As with SASM, when you click Step, the highlighted instruction is executed, and then the next instruction in line is highlighted.

Stepping a program within Insight is a little more involved than with SASM. There are no fewer than six "step" icons. You can hover the mouse pointer over the icons to see what they do. The two you'll use most often are specific to assembly language: Step ASM Instruction and Next ASM Instruction. There are two other icons with similar names: Step and Next. At least for assembly code, they do the same thing as the two ASM Instruction icons. From your experience with SASM, Step is the same as Step Over, and Next is the same as Step Into.

A quick recap from your SASM experience: "Step Into" means "execute the highlighted instruction" even if the highlighted instruction is a CALL instruction. In other words, Step Into will follow the thread of execution into procedures, including procedures linked from glibc. This can be useful. . .sometimes. But if your library procedures are well-behaved and thoroughly tested, you don't need to step through them while you're debugging a new program. Of course, if your new program contains new procedures, you might well want to step into them to see what they do. That's what Step Into is for.

Step Over means just that: Execute the highlighted instruction—but if it's a CALL instruction, don't step through the procedure's instructions. Don't misunderstand the meaning of "Step Over" here: You're *not* skipping the procedure call. You're telling the debugger to execute the procedure and highlight the first instruction after the CALL instruction.

Basically, when you step over a procedure call, the debugger runs the procedure at full speed and meets you at the highlight on the other side.

Again, as with SASM, "Continue" means begin executing at full speed to the next breakpoint. If there are no further breakpoints in the path of execution, Continue will run the program until it exits.

"Finish" has no comparable function in SASM. It simply means, execute at full speed until the program exits.

SASM's Stop icon has no comparable icon in Insight. To stop debugging a program in Insight, select Run ⇨ Kill. That will stop the debugging session without further execution.

The Memory Window

Insight's view of memory is much better than SASM's. Insight gives you a hexdump of memory, similar to that of the hexdump programs I've presented in this book. The difference is that Insight's has a third column on the left side, giving memory addresses for the start of each line in the window.

When you display it, Insight's memory window shows you nothing in particular. To show something, type either a symbolic address or a literal address in the Address field at the left edge of the window. The name of a data item works fine. Figure A-1 shows the memory window displaying memory beginning at the definition of TimeMsg in the timetest.asm program. TimeMsg is the first data definition in the program, so by starting there, you can scroll down to see all of them.

Note that equates do not have addresses and cannot be displayed. Named reserved storage data items in the .bss section can be shown, but until your program stores something in those items, what the window will show are nulls (binary 0s.)

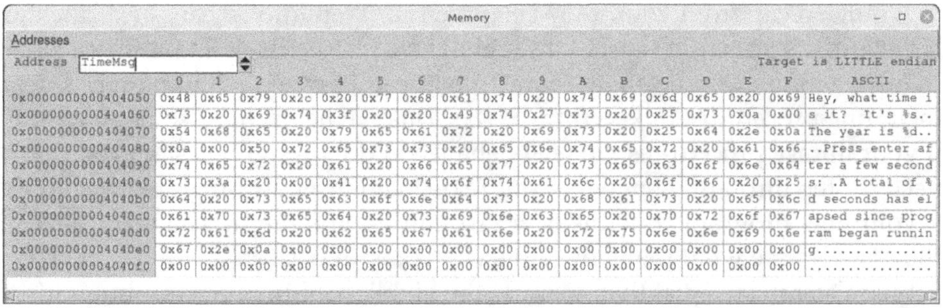

Figure A.1: Insight's memory display of a `.data` section

The arrows to the right of the Address field allow you to move up-memory or down-memory 16 bytes at a time.

Showing the Stack in Insight's Memory View

Insight's memory view can show you any location in your program's memory space. What you may find extremely useful is displaying the stack. The only trick is getting the address of the top of the stack into the address field. Once you've begun debugging a program, the address of its stack is found in either RBP or RSP. The bad news is you can't just type "RSP" into the address field. What you have to do is highlight the address shown for RSP in the Registers window and put it on the clipboard via Ctrl+C. Then highlight and delete whatever is in the address field, and drop the address into the field with Ctrl+V.

There's one peculiar gotcha: Insight inexplicably places curly brackets around the address it places on the clipboard. So a copied address will look something like this:

```
{0x7ffffffffd718}
```

You have to remove those brackets or Insight won't understand the address. Click the mouse pointer into the beginning of the field and delete the left bracket. Click the opposite end of the field and backspace over the right bracket. Note that Insight doesn't understand the arrow keys, Home, End, PgUp, or PgDn.

Once the brackets are gone, press Enter, and the Memory view will show you the stack.

Examining the Stack with Insight's Memory View

The trick in reading a stack display in the Memory view is to remember that numbers and addresses are 64 bits in size and that the display is little-endian. That means the order of the eight bytes is reversed by significance. In other words, the least significant byte of a 64-bit value comes first, followed by the next most significant bytes, and so on. This is why the first eight values on the stack are these:

```
0x04 0x00 0x00 0x00 0x00 0x00 0x00 0x00
```

This is the 64-bit value 4, which is the count of three command-line parameters plus the pathname of the executable file.

The same is true of addresses. The least-significant byte of an address comes first, so the eight address bytes are presented "backwards" from how you're used to thinking of 64-bit addresses. The first address on the stack is that of the invocation text by which the executable was run. It looks like this:

```
0xa0 0xdb 0xff 0xff 0xff 0x7f 0x00 0x00
```

These eight bytes represent the 64-bit address below. With enough practice, you should be able to read an address without manually reversing the order of the bytes.

```
0x7fffffffdba0.
```

You can use the Memory view to "follow" an address to the actual data it points to up-memory. Type the first address on the stack into the navigation control, and the view will move to that address. In this case, that should be the address of the invocation text of the executable file. See Figure A-2.

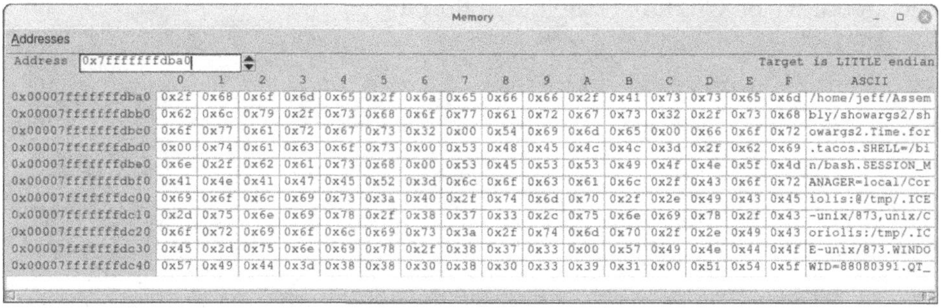

Figure A.2: Command-line arguments in Insight's memory view

Command-line arguments and environment variables are stored nose-to-tail in memory. Each one is terminated by a single 0 byte (a *null*), which is why such strings are called *null-terminated*. Although there's no technical reason for it, command-line arguments and environment variables are stored in the same region of the stack, with the command-line arguments first and the environment variables following.

Most of the effort in learning Insight involves the Memory view window. The rest will seem quite familiar after you've put in some time debugging in SASM.

Learn gdb!

Most Linux debuggers are designed to deal with high-level languages, especially C. It's unusual for a major debugger to be adept at assembly debugging. The debugger behind SASM's and Insight's curtains is gdb. It's completely at home with assembly. Better still, it's almost certainly the most-used debugger in history. If you intend to continue your study of assembly language, I powerfully encourage you to spend the (considerable) time it takes to learn gdb. There are two reasons for this:

- gdb can be very useful all by its lonesome. Yes, you may be impatient with it if you cut your teeth on SASM and Insight. The pure-text interface to gdb can be ponderous. Do it anyway. You will eventually outgrow SASM, and Insight is something of a living fossil. gdb isn't going anywhere.

- There is always the possibility that an assembly-friendly gdb front end something like Insight will be written in the future, and the more you know about gdb, the more effectively you'll be able to use a new front end when it happens.

Yes, there are other front ends for gdb, and I'm sure I've tried them all. None of them deals easily with assembly language. This is no surprise, as nearly all Linux work is done in C. There are online tutorials. Search them out and go through them. A free one-sheet two-sided PDF called gdb Quick Reference is very good. It's on GitHub. Google will find it.

Partial x64 Instruction Reference

Depending on how you count, the x64 architecture now has more than 1,000 machine instructions. Don't panic: A lot of those machine instructions may be used only by operating systems in protected mode. A large number of them implement floating-point math, which for space reasons I can't cover in this book. A fair number are highly specialized for things such as fast encryption and decryption.

In this appendix, I'll present short summaries of the most common machine instructions, the ones you're most likely to use as a beginner to write userspace programs. If you want a more complete (and completely authoritative) instruction reference, see the Intel instruction set documentation:

```
https://software.intel.com/en-us/download/intel-64-and-ia-
32-architectures-sdm-combined-volumes-1-2a-2b-2c-2d-3a-3b-3c-3d-and-4
```

Plan to spend a little time with it: The PDF is 5,060 pages long.

Or if that's a triple handful (it is), a useful web distillation of the Intel docs can be found here:

```
www.felixcloutier.com/x86/index.html
```

This site basically allows you to click around and find the instructions you're looking for and saves you from having to download and hunt through one gigantic document.

What's Been Removed from x64

During the evolution of the x86 CPUs, instructions have been added and removed with each generation. Most of these are fairly arcane, but there are a few that you may have learned as a beginner in the 32-bit era that are no longer available. Most of these now-obsolete instructions date back to the earliest x86 implementations. The following are the most common ones:

- The BCD math instructions: AAA, AAS, AAD, AAM, DAA, and DAS. These instructions haven't been necessary for decades, and they take up valuable space in binary instruction encoding.

- The push-all and pop-all instructions: PUSHA, POPA, PUSHAD, and POPAD. There are 16 general-purpose registers now, each 8 bytes in size. That's a lot of data to move at one time. Registers must be pushed and popped individually now.

- The JCXZ instruction, which jumps when CX=0. This is an ancient 16-bit instruction. Its function is now shared by JRCXZ (jump when RCX=0) and JECXZ (jump when ECX=0.)

- The PUSHFD instruction, which pushes the EFLAGS register onto the stack. Use PUSHFQ now, which pushes the RFLAGS register onto the stack.

- The POPFD instruction, which pops a double word (32 bits) from the top of the stack into the EFLAGS register. Its job is now done with POPFQ, which pops a quadword (64 bits) from the top of the stack into the RFLAGS register.

Flag Results

Each instruction contains a flag summary that looks like this. The asterisks present will vary from instruction to instruction:

```
O D I T S Z A P C   OF: Overflow flag  TF: Trap flag AF: Aux carry
F F F F F F F F F   DF: Direction flag SF: Sign flag PF: Parity flag
*   ? ? * * * * *   IF: Interrupt flag ZF: Zero flag CF: Carry flag
```

The nine most important flags are all represented here. An asterisk indicates that the instruction on that page affects that flag. A blank space under the flag header means that the instruction does not affect that flag in any way. If a flag is affected in a defined way, it will be affected according to these rules:

- **OF:** Set if the result is too large to fit in the destination operand.
- **DF:** Set by STD; cleared by CLD.

- **IF:** Set by STI; cleared by CLI. Not used in userspace programming and can be ignored.

- **TF:** For debuggers; not used in userspace programming and can be ignored.

- **SF:** Set when the sign of the result forces the destination operand to become negative.

- **ZF:** Set if the result of an operation is zero. If the result is nonzero, ZF is cleared.

- **AF:** Auxiliary carry used for 4-bit BCD math. Set when an operation causes a carry out of a 4-bit BCD quantity. Not used in x64 work, as the BCD instructions are no longer available in x64 CPUs.

- **PF:** Set if the number of 1 bits in the low byte of the result is even; cleared if the number of 1 bits in the low byte of the result is odd. Used in data communications applications but little else.

- **CF:** Set if the result of an add or shift operation carries out a bit beyond the destination operand; otherwise cleared. May be manually set by STC and manually cleared by CLC when CF must be in a known state before an operation begins.

Some instructions force certain flags to become undefined. These are indicated by a question mark under the flag header. "Undefined" means *don't count on it being in any particular state*. Until you know that a flag in an undefined state has gone to a defined state by the action of another instruction, do not test or in any other way use the state of the flag.

For a figure showing all flags in detail, see Figure 7.2 in Chapter 7.

Size Specifiers

There is a problem inherent in accessing memory data from assembly language: How much memory data is being acted upon by the instruction in question? Suppose you want to increment a location in memory:

```
inc [rdi+4]
```

So are you incrementing a byte, a word, a double-word, or a quadword? From the instruction as written, there's no way to tell, and NASM will call you on it. But there's an easy way out. NASM recognizes a number of *size specifiers*, which when used with memory data tell NASM the size of the operation. These are BYTE, WORD, DWORD, and QWORD. They specify a data size of 8, 16, 32, and 64 bytes, respectively. The BYTE specifier will treat a memory access as an 8-bit quantity, and so on for the others. The improper INC instruction can be fixed by adding an appropriate size specifier:

```
inc qword [rdi+4]
```

Now we know that we're incrementing a 64-bit value beginning at the effective address RDI+4. This rule applies to all of the x64 instructions taking only a single operand: INC, DEC, NOT, NEG, SHR, SHL, ROR, and ROL. When you're acting on memory, you need a size specifier.

With instructions that take two operands, the issue is more subtle. In any form of a two-operand instruction where one operand is a memory access and the other is a register, NASM infers the size of the access from the size of the register. For example:

```
mov [rdi+rbx*8],rcx
```

Here, NASM sees 64-bit register RCX and thus moves the 64 bits in RCX from RCX to the 8 bytes beginning at [RDI+RBX*8]. Any legal effective address can be used. The same holds true for instruction forms that move data from memory to a register:

```
mov r15,[rbp]
```

Because R15 is a 64-bit register, NASM knows to move the 8 bytes starting at [RBP] to R15. No need to drop in a size specifier, though having an unnecessary size specifier is not always an error.

The only other case in which a size specifier is required is where one operand is in memory and the other operand is a literal constant:

```
mov word [rdi],42
```

This form copies a value of 42 to a word (two bytes) of memory starting at the address in RDI. Of course, a literal constant can't be the destination operand, so in such instruction forms the literal constant must *always* be the source operand.

To save space, I haven't tried to explain this on every instruction's page in this reference. What you should do is stare at an instruction's form and ask yourself, *what here tells NASM the size of the memory access?* If there's a register as either operand, that tells NASM the access is the size of the register. If the source operand is a literal constant, or if the sole operand is a memory reference, you need a size specifier. And if you figure wrong and don't add a size specifier where one needs to go, NASM will tell you.

Instruction Index

INSTRUCTION	REFERENCE PAGE	TEXT PAGE	CPU
ADC			
ADD			
AND			
BT			386+
CALL			
CLC		Here only	
CLD			
CMP			
DEC			
INC			
INT			
IRET			
J?			
JECXZ			x64+
JMP			
JRCXZ			x64+
LEA			
LOOP			
LOOPNZ/LOOPNE			
LOOPZ/LOOPE			
MOV			
MUL			
NEG			
NOP		Here only	
NOT			
OR			
POP			
POPF			

Continues

(continued)

INSTRUCTION	REFERENCE PAGE	TEXT PAGE	CPU
POPFQ			x64+
PUSH			
PUSHF			
PUSHFQ			x64+
RET			
ROL			
ROR			
SBB		Here only	
SHL			
SHR			
STC		Here only	
STD			
STOS			
SUB			
SYSCALL			x64+
XCHG			
XLAT			
XOR			

ADC: Arithmetic Addition with Carry

Flags Affected

```
O D I T S Z A P C   OF: Overflow flag  TF: Trap flag AF: Aux carry
F F F F F F F F F   DF: Direction flag SF: Sign flag PF: Parity flag
*       * * * * *   IF: Interrupt flag ZF: Zero flag CF: Carry flag
```

Legal Forms

```
ADC r/m8,i8
ADC r/m16,i16
ADC r/m32,i32      386+
ADC r/m64,i32      x64+    NOTE: ADC r/m64X,i64 is NOT valid!
ADC r/m8,r8
ADC r/m16,r16
ADC r/m32,r32      386+
ADC r/m64,r64      x64+
ADC r/m16,i8
ADC r/m32,i8
ADC r/m64,i8       x64+
ADC r8,r/m8
ADC r16,r/m16
ADC r32,r/m32      386+
ADC r64,r/m64      x64+
ADC AL,i8
ADC AX,i16
ADC EAX,i32        386+
ADC RAX,i32        x64+    NOTE: ADC RAX,i64 is NOT valid!
```

Examples

```
ADC BX,DI
ADC EAX,5
ADC AX,0FFFFH
ADC AL,42H
ADC RBP,17H
ADC QWORD [RBX+RSI+Inset],5
```

Notes

ADC adds the source operand and the Carry flag to the destination operand, and after the operation, the result replaces the destination operand. The add operation is an arithmetic add, and the carry allows multiple-precision additions across several registers or memory locations. (To add without taking the Carry flag into account, use the ADD instruction.) All affected flags are set according to the operation. Most importantly, if the result does not fit into the destination operand, the Carry flag is set to 1.

```
m8  = 8-bit memory data          m16 = 16-bit memory data
m32 = 32-bit memory data         m64 = 64-bit memory data
i8  = 8-bit immediate data       i16 = 16-bit immediate data
i32 = 32-bit immediate data      i64 = 64-bit immediate data
d8  = 8-bit signed displacement  d16 = 16-bit signed displacement
d32 = 32-bit unsigned displacement NOTE: There is no 64-bit displacement
r8  = AL AH BL BH CL CH DL DH     r16 = AX BX CX DX BP SP SI DI
r32 = EAX EBX ECX EDX EBP ESP ESI EDI
r64 = RAX RBX RCX RDX RBP RSP RSI RDI R8 R9 R10 R11 R12 R13 R14 R15
```

ADD: Arithmetic Addition

Flags Affected

```
O D I T S Z A P C    OF: Overflow flag  TF: Trap flag AF: Aux carry
F F F F F F F F F    DF: Direction flag SF: Sign flag PF: Parity flag
*       * * * *      IF: Interrupt flag ZF: Zero flag CF: Carry flag
```

Legal Forms

```
ADD r/m8,i8
ADD r/m16,i16
ADD r/m32,i32      386+
ADD r/m64,i32      x64+  NOTE: ADD r/m64,i64 is NOT valid!
ADD r/m16,i8
ADD r/m32,i8       386+
ADD r/m64,i8       x64+
ADD r/m8,r8
ADD r/m16,r16
ADD r/m32,r32      386+
ADD r/m64,r64      x64+
ADD r8,r/m8
ADD r16,r/m16
ADD r32,r/m32      386+
ADD r64,r/m64      x64+
ADD AL,i8
ADD AX,i16
ADD EAX,i32        386+
ADD RAX,i32        x64+  NOTE: ADD RAX,i64 is NOT valid!
```

Examples

```
ADD BX,DI
ADD AX,0FFFFH
ADD AL,42H
ADD [EDI],EAX
AND QWORD [RAX],7BH
```

Notes

ADD adds the source operand to the destination operand, and after the operation, the result replaces the destination operand. The add operation is an arithmetic add and does *not* take the Carry flag into account. (To add using the Carry flag, use the ADC Add with Carry instruction.) All affected flags are set according to the operation. Most importantly, if the result does not fit into the destination operand, the Carry flag is set to 1.

```
m8  = 8-bit memory data          m16 = 16-bit memory data
m32 = 32-bit memory data         m64 = 64-bit memory data
i8  = 8-bit immediate data       i16 = 16-bit immediate data
i32 = 32-bit immediate data      i64 = 64-bit immediate data
d8  = 8-bit signed displacement  d16 = 16-bit signed displacement
d32 = 32-bit unsigned displacement NOTE: There is no 64-bit displacement
r8  = AL AH BL BH CL CH DL DH     r16 = AX BX CX DX BP SP SI DI
r32 = EAX EBX ECX EDX EBP ESP ESI EDI
r64 = RAX RBX RCX RDX RBP RSP RSI RDI R8 R9 R10 R11 R12 R13 R14 R15
```

AND: Logical AND

Flags Affected

```
O  D  I  T  S  Z  A  P  C    OF: Overflow flag   TF: Trap flag  AF: Aux carry
F  F  F  F  F  F  F  F  F    DF: Direction flag  SF: Sign flag  PF: Parity flag
*           *  *  ?  *  *    IF: Interrupt flag  ZF: Zero flag  CF: Carry flag
```

Legal Forms

```
AND  r/m8,i8
AND  r/m16,i16
AND  r/m32,i32      386+
AND  r/m64,i32      x64+    NOTE: AND r/m64,i64 is NOT valid!
AND  r/m16,i8
AND  r/m32,i8       386+
AND  r/m64,i8       x64+
AND  r/m8,r8
AND  r/m16,r16
AND  r/m32,r32      386+
AND  r/m64,r64      x64+
AND  r8,r/m8
AND  r16,r/m16
AND  r32,r/m32      386+
AND  r64,r/m64      x64+
AND  AL,i8
AND  AX,i16
AND  EAX,i32        386+
AND  RAX,i32        x64+ NOTE: AND RAX,i64 is NOT valid!
```

Examples

```
AND  BX,DI
AND  EAX,5
AND  AX,0FFFFH
AND  AL,42H
AND  [BP+SI],DX
AND  QWORD [RDI],42
AND  QWORD [RBX],0B80000H
```

Notes

AND performs the AND logical operation on its two operands. Once the operation is complete, the result replaces the destination operand. AND is performed on a bit-by-bit basis, such that bit 0 of the source is ANDed with bit 0 of the destination, bit 1 of the source is ANDed with bit 1 of the destination, and so on. The AND operation yields a 1 if *both* of the operands are 1; and a 0 only if *either* operand is 0. Note that the operation makes the Auxiliary carry flag undefined. CF and OF are cleared to 0, and the other affected flags are set according to the operation's results.

```
m8  = 8-bit memory data             m16 = 16-bit memory data
m32 = 32-bit memory data            m64 = 64-bit memory data
i8  = 8-bit immediate data          i16 = 16-bit immediate data
i32 = 32-bit immediate data         i64 = 64-bit immediate data
d8  = 8-bit signed displacement     d16 = 16-bit signed displacement
d32 = 32-bit unsigned displacement NOTE: There is no 64-bit displacement
r8  = AL AH BL BH CL CH DL DH        r16 = AX BX CX DX BP SP SI DI
r32 = EAX EBX ECX EDX EBP ESP ESI EDI
r64 = RAX RBX RCX RDX RBP RSP RSI RDI R8 R9 R10 R11 R12 R13 R14 R15
```

BT: Bit Test

Flags Affected

```
O D I T S Z A P C  OF: Overflow flag  TF: Trap flag AF: Aux carry
F F F F F F F F F  DF: Direction flag SF: Sign flag PF: Parity flag
                *  IF: Interrupt flag ZF: Zero flag CF: Carry flag
```

Legal Forms

```
BT r/m16,r16    386+
BT r/m32,r32    386+
BT r/m64,r64    x64+
BT r/m16,i8     386+
BT r/m32,i8     386+
BT r/m64,i8     x64+
```

Examples

```
BT AX,CX
BT EAX,EDX
BT RAX,5
BT [RAX+RDX],RCX
```

Notes

BT copies a single specified bit from the left operand to the Carry flag, where it can be tested or fed back into a quantity using one of the shift/rotate instructions. Which bit is copied is specified by the right operand. Neither operand is altered by BT.

When the right operand is an 8-bit immediate value, the value specifies the number of the bit to be copied. In BT AX,5, bit 5 of AX is copied into CF. When the immediate value exceeds the size of the left operand, the value is expressed modulo the size of the left operand. That is, because there are not 66 bits in EAX, BT EAX,66 pulls out as many 32s from the immediate value as can be taken, and what remains is the bit number. (Here, 2.) When the right operand is *not* an immediate value, the right operand not only specifies the bit to be tested but also an offset from the memory reference in the left operand. This is complicated and not covered completely in this book. See a detailed discussion in a full assembly language reference.

```
m8  = 8-bit memory data          m16 = 16-bit memory data
m32 = 32-bit memory data         m64 = 64-bit memory data
i8  = 8-bit immediate data       i16 = 16-bit immediate data
i32 = 32-bit immediate data      i64 = 64-bit immediate data
d8  = 8-bit signed displacement  d16 = 16-bit signed displacement
d32 = 32-bit unsigned displacement NOTE: There is no 64-bit displacement
r8  = AL AH BL BH CL CH DL DH     r16 = AX BX CX DX BP SP SI DI
r32 = EAX EBX ECX EDX EBP ESP ESI EDI
r64 = RAX RBX RCX RDX RBP RSP RSI RDI R8 R9 R10 R11 R12 R13 R14 R15
```

CALL: Call Procedure

Flags Affected

```
O  D  I  T  S  Z  A  P  C    OF: Overflow flag  TF: Trap flag AF: Aux carry
F  F  F  F  F  F  F  F  F    DF: Direction flag SF: Sign flag PF: Parity flag
      <none>                 IF: Interrupt flag ZF: Zero flag CF: Carry flag
```

Legal Forms

```
CALL d16        Not valid in x64
CALL d32        Not valid prior to x64
CALL r/m16      Not valid in x64
CALL r/m32      Not valid in x64
CALL r/m64      Not valid prior to x64
```

Examples

```
CALL DoSomething
CALL RAX
CALL QWORD [EBX+ECX+16]
```

Notes

CALL transfers control to a procedure address. Before transferring control, CALL pushes the address of the instruction immediately after itself onto the stack. This allows a RET instruction (see also) to pop the return address into RIP and thus return control to the instruction immediately after the CALL instruction.

In addition to the obvious CALL to a defined label, CALL can transfer control to an address in a 64-bit general-purpose register (r64) and also to an address located in memory. This is shown in the Legal Forms column as m64. CALL m64 is useful for creating jump tables of procedure addresses. D32 is simply a 32-bit unsigned displacement used in most calls to procedure labels. In 64-bit long mode, a d32 displacement is sign-extended to 64 bits.

There are several more variants of the CALL instruction with provisions for working with the protection mechanisms of operating systems. These are not covered here, and for more information you should see an advanced text or a full assembly language reference.

```
m8  = 8-bit memory data         m16 = 16-bit memory data
m32 = 32-bit memory data        m64 = 64-bit memory data
i8  = 8-bit immediate data      i16 = 16-bit immediate data
```

```
i32 = 32-bit immediate data        i64 = 64-bit immediate data
d8 = 8-bit signed displacement     d16 = 16-bit signed displacement
d32 = 32-bit unsigned displacement NOTE: There is no 64-bit displacement
r8 = AL AH BL BH CL CH DL DH        r16 = AX BX CX DX BP SP SI DI
r32 = EAX EBX ECX EDX EBP ESP ESI EDI
r64 = RAX RBX RCX RDX RBP RSP RSI RDI R8 R9 R10 R11 R12 R13 R14 R15
```

CLC: Clear Carry Flag (CF)

Flags Affected

```
O D I T S Z A P C   OF: Overflow flag  TF: Trap flag AF: Aux carry
F F F F F F F F F   DF: Direction flag SF: Sign flag PF: Parity flag
                *   IF: Interrupt flag ZF: Zero flag CF: Carry flag
```

Legal Forms

```
CLC
```

Examples

```
CLC
```

Notes

CLC simply sets the Carry flag (CF) to the cleared (0) state. Use CLC in situations where the Carry flag *must* be in a known cleared state before work begins, as when you are rotating a series of words or bytes using the rotate instructions RCL and RCR.

```
m8  = 8-bit memory data           m16 = 16-bit memory data
m32 = 32-bit memory data          m64 = 64-bit memory data
i8  = 8-bit immediate data        i16 = 16-bit immediate data
i32 = 32-bit immediate data       i64 = 64-bit immediate data
d8  = 8-bit signed displacement   d16 = 16-bit signed displacement
d32 = 32-bit unsigned displacement NOTE: There is no 64-bit displacement
r8  = AL AH BL BH CL CH DL DH      r16 = AX BX CX DX BP SP SI DI
r32 = EAX EBX ECX EDX EBP ESP ESI EDI
r64 = RAX RBX RCX RDX RBP RSP RSI RDI R8 R9 R10 R11 R12 R13 R14 R15
```

CLD: Clear Direction Flag (DF)

Flags Affected

```
O D I T S Z A P C   OF: Overflow flag  TF: Trap flag AF: Aux carry
F F F F F F F F F   DF: Direction flag SF: Sign flag PF: Parity flag
    *               IF: Interrupt flag ZF: Zero flag CF: Carry flag
```

Legal Forms

```
CLD
```

Examples

```
CLD
```

Notes

CLD simply sets the Direction flag (DF) to the cleared (0) state. This affects the adjustment performed by repeated string instructions such as STOS, SCAS, and MOVS. When DF = 0, the destination pointer is increased, and decreased when DF = 1. DF is set to 1 with the STD instruction.

```
m8  = 8-bit memory data          m16 = 16-bit memory data
m32 = 32-bit memory data         m64 = 64-bit memory data
i8  = 8-bit immediate data       i16 = 16-bit immediate data
i32 = 32-bit immediate data      i64 = 64-bit immediate data
d8  = 8-bit signed displacement  d16 = 16-bit signed displacement
d32 = 32-bit unsigned displacement NOTE: There is no 64-bit displacement
r8  = AL AH BL BH CL CH DL DH     r16 = AX BX CX DX BP SP SI DI
r32 = EAX EBX ECX EDX EBP ESP ESI EDI
r64 = RAX RBX RCX RDX RBP RSP RSI RDI R8 R9 R10 R11 R12 R13 R14 R15
```

CMP: Arithmetic Comparison

Flags Affected

```
O  D  I  T  S  Z  A  P  C   OF: Overflow flag  TF: Trap flag AF: Aux carry
F  F  F  F  F  F  F  F  F    DF: Direction flag SF: Sign flag PF: Parity flag
*        *  *  *  *  *       IF: Interrupt flag ZF: Zero flag CF: Carry flag
```

Legal Forms

```
CMP  r/m8,i8
CMP  r/m16,i16
CMP  r/m32,i32      386+
CMP  r/m64,i32      x64+    NOTE: CMP RAX,i64 is NOT valid!
CMP  r/m16,i8
CMP  r/m32,i8       386+
CMP  r/m64,i8       x64+
CMP  r/m8,r8
CMP  r/m16,r16
CMP  r/m32,r32      386+
CMP  r/m64,r64      x64+
CMP  r8,r/m8
CMP  r16,r/m16
CMP  r32,r/m32      386+
CMP  r64,r/m64      x64+
CMP  AL,i8
CMP  AX,i16
CMP  EAX,i32        386+
CMP  RAX,i32        x64+    NOTE: CMP RAX,i64 is NOT valid!
```

Examples

```
CMP  RAX,5
CMP  AL,19H
CMP  EAX,ECX
CMP  QWORD [RBX+RSI+inset],0B80000H
```

Notes

CMP compares its two operations and sets the flags to indicate the results of the comparison. *The destination operand is not affected.* The operation itself is identical to arithmetic subtraction of the source from the destination without borrow (SUB), save that the result does not replace the destination. Typically, CMP is followed by one of the conditional jump instructions; that is, JE to jump if the operands were equal; JNE if they were unequal; and so forth.

```
m8  = 8-bit memory data            m16 = 16-bit memory data
m32 = 32-bit memory data           m64 = 64-bit memory data
i8  = 8-bit immediate data         i16 = 16-bit immediate data
i32 = 32-bit immediate data        i64 = 64-bit immediate data
d8  = 8-bit signed displacement    d16 = 16-bit signed displacement
d32 = 32-bit unsigned displacement NOTE: There is no 64-bit displacement
r8  = AL AH BL BH CL CH DL DH       r16 = AX BX CX DX BP SP SI DI
r32 = EAX EBX ECX EDX EBP ESP ESI EDI
r64 = RAX RBX RCX RDX RBP RSP RSI RDI R8 R9 R10 R11 R12 R13 R14 R15
```

DEC: Decrement Operand

Flags Affected

```
O D I T S Z A P C   OF: Overflow flag  TF: Trap flag AF: Aux carry
F F F F F F F F F   DF: Direction flag SF: Sign flag PF: Parity flag
*       * * * *     IF: Interrupt flag ZF: Zero flag CF: Carry flag
```

Legal Forms

```
DEC r/m8
DEC r/m16
DEC r/m32          386+
DEC r/m64          x64+
```

Examples

```
DEC AL
DEC AX
DEC EAX
DEC QWORD [RBX+RSI]
```

Notes

DEC subtracts 1 from its single operand and does *not* affect the Carry flag CF. Be careful about that; it's a common error to try to use CF after a DEC instruction as though it were SUB instead.

DEC acting on memory data forms *must* be used with a data size specifier such as BYTE, WORD, DWORD, and QWORD. See the examples given earlier.

```
m8  = 8-bit memory data            m16 = 16-bit memory data
m32 = 32-bit memory data           m64 = 64-bit memory data
i8  = 8-bit immediate data         i16 = 16-bit immediate data
i32 = 32-bit immediate data        i64 = 64-bit immediate data
d8 = 8-bit signed displacement     d16 = 16-bit signed displacement
d32 = 32-bit unsigned displacement NOTE: There is no 64-bit displacement
r8 = AL AH BL BH CL CH DL DH       r16 = AX BX CX DX BP SP SI DI
r32 = EAX EBX ECX EDX EBP ESP ESI EDI
r64 = RAX RBX RCX RDX RBP RSP RSI RDI R8 R9 R10 R11 R12 R13 R14 R15
```

DIV: Unsigned Integer Division

Flags Affected

```
O  D  I  T  S  Z  A  P  C   OF: Overflow flag  TF: Trap flag AF: Aux carry
F  F  F  F  F  F  F  F  F    DF: Direction flag SF: Sign flag PF: Parity flag
?        ?  ?  ?  ?  ?       IF: Interrupt flag ZF: Zero flag CF: Carry flag
```

Legal Forms

```
DIV r/m8     Dividend in AX. Quotient in AL; remainder in AH.
DIV r/m16    Dividend in EAX. Quotient in AX; remainder in DX.
DIV r/m32    386+ Dividend in EAX:EDX. Quotient in EAX; remainder in EDX.
DIV r/m64    x64+ Dividend in RAX:RDX. Quotient in RAX; remainder in RDX.
```

Examples

```
DIV AL
DIV AX
DIV EAX
DIV QWORD [RDI+RSI] Don't use A or D regs in an effective address!
```

Notes

DIV divides the implicit dividend by the explicit divisor specified as DIV's single operand. For dividing by 8-bit quantities, the dividend is assumed to be in AX. For dividing by 16-bit, 32-bit, and 64-bit quantities, the dividend is assumed to be in two registers, allowing a much greater range of calculation. The least significant portion of the dividend is placed in the "A" register (AX / EAX / RAX), and the most significant portion of the dividend is placed in the "D" register (DX / EDX / RDX). Note that even when there is no "high" portion of the dividend, the "D" register is cleared to 0 by DIV and cannot be used to hold independent values while a DIV instruction is executed. For more on DIV, see the Chapter 7 discussion on p. [203].

Remember that when the operand is a memory value, you *must* place one of the type specifiers BYTE, WORD, DWORD, or QWORD before the operand. Also note from the "Legal Forms" section, there is no legal form using an immediate value of any size.

DIV leaves no information in the flags. Note, however, that OF, SF, ZF, AF, PF, and CF become undefined after a DIV instruction.

```
m8  = 8-bit memory data       m16 = 16-bit memory data
m32 = 32-bit memory data      m64 = 64-bit memory data
i8  = 8-bit immediate data    i16 = 16-bit immediate data
```

```
i32 = 32-bit immediate data        i64 = 64-bit immediate data
d8 = 8-bit signed displacement     d16 = 16-bit signed displacement
d32 = 32-bit unsigned displacement NOTE: There is no 64-bit displacement
r8 = AL AH BL BH CL CH DL DH        r16 = AX BX CX DX BP SP SI DI
r32 = EAX EBX ECX EDX EBP ESP ESI EDI
r64 = RAX RBX RCX RDX RBP RSP RSI RDI R8 R9 R10 R11 R12 R13 R14 R15
```

INC: Increment Operand

Flags Affected

```
O  D  I  T  S  Z  A  P  C   OF: Overflow flag  TF: Trap flag AF: Aux carry
F  F  F  F  F  F  F  F  F   DF: Direction flag SF: Sign flag PF: Parity flag
*        *  *  *  *          IF: Interrupt flag ZF: Zero flag CF: Carry flag
```

Legal Forms

```
INC  r/m8
INC  r/m16
INC  r/m32          386+
INC  r/m64          x64+
```

Examples

```
INC AL
INC EAX
INC QWORD [RBP]
INC QWORD [RBX+RSI]
```

Notes

INC adds 1 to its single operand and does *not* affect the Carry flag CF. Be careful about that; it's a common error to try to use CF after an INC instruction as though it were ADD instead.

INC acting on memory data forms *must* be used with a data size specifier such as BYTE, WORD, DWORD, and QWORD. See the two examples given earlier.

```
m8 = 8-bit memory data          m16 = 16-bit memory data
m32 = 32-bit memory data        m64 = 64-bit memory data
i8  = 8-bit immediate data      i16 = 16-bit immediate data
i32 = 32-bit immediate data     i64 = 64-bit immediate data
d8 = 8-bit signed displacement   d16 = 16-bit signed displacement
d32 = 32-bit unsigned displacement NOTE: There is no 64-bit displacement
r8 = AL AH BL BH CL CH DL DH      r16 = AX BX CX DX BP SP SI DI
r32 = EAX EBX ECX EDX EBP ESP ESI EDI
r64 = RAX RBX RCX RDX RBP RSP RSI RDI R8 R9 R10 R11 R12 R13 R14 R15
```

J??: Jump If Condition Is Met

Flags Affected

```
O  D  I  T  S  Z  A  P  C    OF: Overflow flag  TF: Trap flag AF: Aux carry
F  F  F  F  F  F  F  F  F     DF: Direction flag SF: Sign flag PF: Parity flag
        <none>               IF: Interrupt flag ZF: Zero flag CF: Carry flag
```

Legal Forms	Description	Jump If Flags Are
JA/JNBE d8 d32	Jump If Above / Jump If Not Below Or Equal	CF=0 AND ZF=0
JAE/JNB d8 d32	Jump If Above Or Equal / Jump If Not Below	CF=0
JB/JNAE d8 d32	Jump If Below / Jump If Not Above Or Equal	CF=1
JBE/JNA d8 d32	Jump If Below Or Equal / Jump If Not Above	CF=1 OR ZF=1
JC d8 d32	Jump If Carry; synonym for JNAE & JB	CF=1
JNC d8 d32	Jump If Not Carry	CF=0
JE/JZ d8 d32	Jump If Equal / Jump If Zero	ZF=1
JNE/JNZ d8 d32	Jump If Not Equal / Jump If Not Zero	ZF=0
JG/JNLE d8 d32	Jump If Greater / Jump If Not Less Or Equal	ZF=0 AND SF=OF
JGE/JNL d8 d32	Jump If Greater Or Equal / Jump If Not Less	SF=OF
JL/JNGE d8 d32	Jump If Less / Jump If Not Greater Or Equal	SF≠OF
JLE/JNG d8 d32	Jump If Less Than Or Equal/Jump If Not Greater	ZF=1 OR SF≠OF
JO d8 d32	Jump If Overflow	OF=1
JNO d8 d32	Jump If Not Overflow	OF=0
JP/JPE d8 d32	Jump If Parity Set / Jump If Parity Even	PF=1
JNP/JPO d8 d32	Jump If Parity Cleared / Jump If Parity Odd	PF=0
JS d8 d32	Jump If Sign Flag Set	SF=1
JNS d8 d32	Jump If Sign Flag Cleared	SF=0

Examples

```
JB HalfSplit      ;Jumps if CF=1
JLE TooLow        ;Jumps if ZF=1 AND SF=OF
JG NEAR WayOut    ;Jumps to a 32-bit displacement in 32-bit and
                  ; 64-bit protected modes
```

Notes

By default all these instructions make a d8 short jump (127 bytes forward or 128 bytes back) if some condition is true, or fall through if the condition is not true. All legal forms also support a 32-bit displacement (d32) for making a jump to anywhere in the code segment. Most of these jump instructions can also accept a 16-bit displacement, but *not* in 64-bit protected mode. I have left out the d16 tags to make the table simpler. To use a 32-bit displacement, you must follow the conditional jump instruction with the qualifier NEAR, which tells the assembler to use a 32-bit displacement when generating binary code. Remember that there is no 64-bit displacement.

The conditions all involve flags, and the flag conditions in question are given to the right of the mnemonic and its description, under the heading "Jump If Flags Are."

There are often two synonyms for a single conditional jump. For example, JE and JZ are the same instruction, meaning Jump if ZF is set. The synonyms are there to help you understand the code: Jump if the previous comparison showed parameters equal, or jump if the zero flag is set.

```
m8  = 8-bit memory data          m16 = 16-bit memory data
m32 = 32-bit memory data         m64 = 64-bit memory data
i8  = 8-bit immediate data       i16 = 16-bit immediate data
i32 = 32-bit immediate data      i64 = 64-bit immediate data
d8  = 8-bit signed displacement  d16 = 16-bit signed displacement
d32 = 32-bit unsigned displacement NOTE: There is no 64-bit displacement
r8  = AL AH BL BH CL CH DL DH     r16 = AX BX CX DX BP SP SI DI
r32 = EAX EBX ECX EDX EBP ESP ESI EDI
r64 = RAX RBX RCX RDX RBP RSP RSI RDI R8 R9 R10 R11 R12 R13 R14 R15
```

JECXZ: Jump if ECX=0

Flags Affected

```
O D I T S Z A P C   OF: Overflow flag  TF: Trap flag AF: Aux carry
F F F F F F F F F   DF: Direction flag SF: Sign flag PF: Parity flag
        <none>      IF: Interrupt flag ZF: Zero flag CF: Carry flag
```

Legal Forms

```
JECXZ d8          386+
```

Examples

```
JECXZ AllDone     ; Label AllDone must be within +127 or -128 bytes.
```

Notes

Several instructions use ECX as a count register, and JECXZ allows you to test and jump to see if ECX has become 0. The jump may be only a short jump (that is, no more than 127 bytes forward or 128 bytes back) and will be taken if ECX = 0 at the time the instruction is executed. If ECX is any value other than 0, execution falls through to the next instruction. See also the "Jump on Condition" instructions.

JECXZ is most often used to bypass the ECX = 0 condition when using the LOOP instruction. Because LOOP decrements ECX before testing for ECX = 0, if you enter a loop governed by LOOP with ECX = 0, you will end up iterating the loop 2,147,483,648 (2^{32}) times, hence the need for JECXZ. If you use LOOP and it seems to lock up, check this first.

```
m8  = 8-bit memory data         m16 = 16-bit memory data
m32 = 32-bit memory data        m64 = 64-bit memory data
i8  = 8-bit immediate data      i16 = 16-bit immediate data
i32 = 32-bit immediate data     i64 = 64-bit immediate data
d8  = 8-bit signed displacement d16 = 16-bit signed displacement
d32 = 32-bit unsigned displacement NOTE: There is no 64-bit displacement
r8  = AL AH BL BH CL CH DL DH    r16 = AX BX CX DX BP SP SI DI
r32 = EAX EBX ECX EDX EBP ESP ESI EDI
r64 = RAX RBX RCX RDX RBP RSP RSI RDI R8 R9 R10 R11 R12 R13 R14 R15
```

JRCXZ: Jump If RCX=0

Flags Affected

```
O  D  I  T  S  Z  A  P  C    OF: Overflow flag  TF: Trap flag  AF: Aux carry
F  F  F  F  F  F  F  F  F    DF: Direction flag SF: Sign flag  PF: Parity flag
         <none>             IF: Interrupt flag ZF: Zero flag  CF: Carry flag
```

Legal Forms

```
JRCXZ d8          x64+
```

Examples

```
JRCXZ AllDone     ; Label AllDone must be within +127 or -128 bytes.
```

Notes

This instruction operates identically to JECXZ except that the register tested is RCX, not ECX. Because it tests RCX, JRCXZ is available only in x64 processors.

JRCXZ is most often used to bypass the RCX = 0 condition when using the LOOP instruction. Because LOOP decrements RCX before testing for RCX = 0, if you enter a loop governed by LOOP with RCX = 0, you will end up iterating the loop 2^{64} times, hence the need for JRCXZ. (If you use LOOP and it seems to lock up the program, check this first.)

```
m8  = 8-bit memory data          m16 = 16-bit memory data
m8  = 8-bit memory data          m16 = 16-bit memory data
m32 = 32-bit memory data         m64 = 64-bit memory data
i8  = 8-bit immediate data       i16 = 16-bit immediate data
i32 = 32-bit immediate data      i64 = 64-bit immediate data
d8 = 8-bit signed displacement   d16 = 16-bit signed displacement
d32 = 32-bit unsigned displacement NOTE: There is no 64-bit displacement
r8 = AL AH BL BH CL CH DL DH      r16 = AX BX CX DX BP SP SI DI
r32 = EAX EBX ECX EDX EBP ESP ESI EDI
r64 = RAX RBX RCX RDX RBP RSP RSI RDI R8 R9 R10 R11 R12 R13 R14 R15
```

JMP: Unconditional Jump

Flags Affected

```
O D I T S Z A P C    OF: Overflow flag  TF: Trap flag AF: Aux carry
F F F F F F F F F    DF: Direction flag SF: Sign flag PF: Parity flag
        <none>        IF: Interrupt flag ZF: Zero flag CF: Carry flag
```

Legal Forms

```
JMP d8          In 64-bit mode, displacement sign-extended to 64 bits
JMP d16         Not supported in 64-bit long mode
JMP d32         In 64-bit mode, displacement sign-extended to 64 bits
JMP r/m16       Not supported in 64-bit long mode
JMP r/m32       386+; Not supported in 64-bit long mode
JMP r/m64       x64+
```

Examples

```
JMP RightCloseBy   Label ; RightCloseBy must be +127 or -128 bytes.
JMP EAX            ; Not supported in 64-bit mode
JMP RDX
JMP QWORD [RBX+EDI+17]
```

Notes

JMP transfers control unconditionally to the destination given as the single operand. In 64-bit mode, in addition to defined labels, JMP can transfer control to an 8-bit signed offset from RIP, a 32-bit signed offset from RIP, or a 64-bit absolute address (either as an immediate or indirectly through a register or memory). The m64 form is useful for creating jump tables in memory, where a jump table is an array of addresses. For example, JMP [RBX+RDI+17] would transfer control to the 64-bit address found at the based-indexed-displacement address [RBX+RDI+17].

No flags are affected and, unlike CALL, no return address is pushed onto the stack. Note that there are additional JMP forms for other modes and exotic work at higher privilege levels than userspace. See an Intel instruction reference for more details.

```
m8  = 8-bit memory data        m16 = 16-bit memory data
m32 = 32-bit memory data       m64 = 64-bit memory data
i8  = 8-bit immediate data     i16 = 16-bit immediate data
```

```
i32 = 32-bit immediate data        i64 = 64-bit immediate data
d8 = 8-bit signed displacement     d16 = 16-bit signed displacement
d32 = 32-bit unsigned displacement NOTE: There is no 64-bit displacement
r8 = AL AH BL BH CL CH DL DH        r16 = AX BX CX DX BP SP SI DI
r32 = EAX EBX ECX EDX EBP ESP ESI EDI
r64 = RAX RBX RCX RDX RBP RSP RSI RDI R8 R9 R10 R11 R12 R13 R14 R15
```

LEA: Load Effective Address

Flags Affected

```
O D I T S Z A P C  OF: Overflow flag  TF: Trap flag AF: Aux carry
F F F F F F F F F  DF: Direction flag SF: Sign flag PF: Parity flag
      <none>       IF: Interrupt flag ZF: Zero flag CF: Carry flag
```

Legal Forms

```
LEA r16,m
LEA r32,m        386+
LEA r64,m        x64+
```

Examples

```
LEA RBP,MyVariable    ; Loads address expressed by MyVariable to RBP
LEA R15,[RAX+RDX*4+17] ; Loads effective address from calculation to R15
```

Notes

LEA derives the address of the source operand and loads that offset into the destination operand. The destination operand must be a register and *cannot* be memory. The source operand must be a memory operand, but it can be any size. The address stored in the destination operand is the address of the first byte of the source in memory, and the size of the source in memory is unimportant.

This is a good, clean way to place the address of a variable into a register prior to a procedure call or a system call. See SYSCALL.

LEA can also be used to perform register math, since the address specified in the second operand is *calculated* but not *accessed*. The address can thus be an address for which your program does not have permission to access. Any math that can be expressed as a valid address calculation may be done with LEA.

This is one of the few places where NASM does not require a size specifier before an operand providing a memory address, again because LEA calculates the address but moves no data to or from that address.

```
m8  = 8-bit memory data          m16 = 16-bit memory data
m32 = 32-bit memory data         m64 = 64-bit memory data
i8  = 8-bit immediate data       i16 = 16-bit immediate data
i32 = 32-bit immediate data      i64 = 64-bit immediate data
d8 = 8-bit signed displacement   d16 = 16-bit signed displacement
d32 = 32-bit unsigned displacement NOTE: There is no 64-bit displacement
r8 = AL AH BL BH CL CH DL DH      r16 = AX BX CX DX BP SP SI DI
r32 = EAX EBX ECX EDX EBP ESP ESI EDI
r64 = RAX RBX RCX RDX RBP RSP RSI RDI R8 R9 R10 R11 R12 R13 R14 R15
```

LOOP: Loop Until CX/ECX/RCX=0

Flags Affected

```
O  D  I  T  S  Z  A  P  C    OF: Overflow flag  TF: Trap flag AF: Aux carry
F  F  F  F  F  F  F  F  F    DF: Direction flag SF: Sign flag PF: Parity flag
        <none>              IF: Interrupt flag ZF: Zero flag CF: Carry flag
```

Legal Forms

```
LOOP d8            386+ if using ECX for the counter; 64+ if using RCX
```

Examples

```
LOOP AllDone       ; Label AllDone must be within +127 or -128 bytes.
```

Notes

LOOP is a combination decrement counter, test, and jump instruction. It uses CX as the counter in 16-bit modes, ECX in 32-bit modes, or RCX in 64-bit modes. The operation of LOOP is logistically identical in all three modes, and I use 64-bit coding as an example here.

LOOP simplifies code by acting as a DEC RCX instruction, a CMP RCX, 0 instruction, and JZ instruction in one, executed in that order. A loop repeat count must be initially loaded into RCX. When the LOOP instruction is executed, it *first* decrements RCX. Then it tests to see if RCX = 0. If RCX is *not* 0, LOOP transfers control to the 8-bit displacement specified as its operand:

```
      MOV RCX,17     ; Loop 17 times
DoIt: CALL CrunchIt
      CALL StuffIt
      LOOP DoIt
```

Here, the two procedure CALLs will be made 17 times. The first 16 times through, RCX will still be nonzero, and LOOP will transfer control to DoIt. On the 17th pass, however, LOOP will decrement RCX to 0 and then fall through to the next instruction in sequence when it tests CX.

LOOP does *not* alter any flags, even when RCX is decremented to 0. *Warning:* Watch your initial conditions! If you're in 16-bit mode and CX is initially 0, LOOP will decrement it to 65,535 (0FFFFH) and then perform the loop 65,535 times. Worse, if you're working in 32-bit protected mode and enter a loop with ECX = 0, the loop will be performed more than 2 *billion* times, which might be long enough to look like a system lockup. If you're using RCX, well, the loop will go 2^{64} times, which *will* be a system lockup.

```
m8  = 8-bit memory data          m16 = 16-bit memory data
m32 = 32-bit memory data         m64 = 64-bit memory data
i8  = 8-bit immediate data       i16 = 16-bit immediate data
i32 = 32-bit immediate data      i64 = 64-bit immediate data
d8  = 8-bit signed displacement  d16 = 16-bit signed displacement
d32 = 32-bit unsigned displacement NOTE: There is no 64-bit displacement
r8  = AL AH BL BH CL CH DL DH     r16 = AX BX CX DX BP SP SI DI
r32 = EAX EBX ECX EDX EBP ESP ESI EDI
r64 = RAX RBX RCX RDX RBP RSP RSI RDI R8 R9 R10 R11 R12 R13 R14 R15
```

LOOPNZ/LOOPNE: Loop Until CX/ECX/RCX=0 and ZF=0

Flags Affected

```
O D I T S Z A P C   OF: Overflow flag  TF: Trap flag AF: Aux carry
F F F F F F F F F   DF: Direction flag SF: Sign flag PF: Parity flag
        <none>       IF: Interrupt flag ZF: Zero flag CF: Carry flag
```

Legal Forms

```
LOOPNZ d8       386+ if using ECX for the counter; 64+ if using RCX
LOOPNE d8       386+ if using ECX for the counter; 64+ if using RCX
```

Examples

```
LOOPNZ AllDone    ; Label AllDone must be within +127 or -128 bytes.
```

Notes

LOOPNZ and LOOPNE are synonyms and generate identical opcodes. Like LOOP, they use CX, ECX, or RCX depending on the "bit-ness" of the CPU. In 64-bit work, LOOPNZ/LOOPNE decrements RCX and jumps to the location specified in the target operand if RCX is not 0 and the Zero flag ZF is 0. Otherwise, execution falls through to the next instruction.

What this means is that the loop is pretty much controlled by ZF. If ZF remains 0, the loop is looped until the counter register is decremented to 0. But as soon as ZF is set to 1, the loop terminates. Think of it as "Loop While Not Zero Flag."

Keep in mind that LOOPNZ and LOOPNE do not *themselves* affect ZF. Some instruction within the loop (typically one of the string instructions) must do something to affect ZF to terminate the loop before CX/ECX/RCX counts down to 0.

```
m8  = 8-bit memory data        m16 = 16-bit memory data
m32 = 32-bit memory data       m64 = 64-bit memory data
i8  = 8-bit immediate data     i16 = 16-bit immediate data
i32 = 32-bit immediate data    i64 = 64-bit immediate data
d8 = 8-bit signed displacement d16 = 16-bit signed displacement
d32 = 32-bit unsigned displacement NOTE: There is no 64-bit displacement
r8 = AL AH BL BH CL CH DL DH    r16 = AX BX CX DX BP SP SI DI
r32 = EAX EBX ECX EDX EBP ESP ESI EDI
r64 = RAX RBX RCX RDX RBP RSP RSI RDI R8 R9 R10 R11 R12 R13 R14 R15
```

LOOPZ/LOOPE: Loop Until CX/ECX/RCX=0 and ZF=1

Flags Affected

```
O  D  I  T  S  Z  A  P  C    OF: Overflow flag  TF: Trap flag AF: Aux carry
F  F  F  F  F  F  F  F  F     DF: Direction flag SF: Sign flag PF: Parity flag
        <none>               IF: Interrupt flag ZF: Zero flag CF: Carry flag
```

Legal Forms

```
LOOPZ d8          386+ if using ECX for the counter; 64+ if using RCX
LOOPE d8          386+ if using ECX for the counter; 64+ if using RCX
```

Examples

```
LOOPZ AllDone     ; Label AllDone must be within +127 or -128 bytes.
```

Notes

LOOPZ and LOOPE are synonyms and generate identical opcodes. Like LOOP, they use CX, ECX, or RCX depending on the current "bit-ness" of the CPU. In 64-bit work, LOOPZ/LOOPE first decrements RCX and jumps to the location specified in the target operand if RCX is not 0 and the Zero flag ZF is 1. Otherwise, execution falls through to the next instruction.

This means the loop is pretty much controlled by ZF. If ZF remains 1, the loop is looped until the counter register is decremented to 0. But as soon as ZF is cleared to 0, the loop terminates. Think of it as "Loop While Zero Flag."

Remember that LOOPZ/LOOPE do not *themselves* affect ZF. Some instruction within the loop (typically one of the string instructions) must do something to zero ZF to terminate the loop before CX/ECX/RCX counts down to 0.

```
m8  = 8-bit memory data          m16 = 16-bit memory data
m32 = 32-bit memory data         m64 = 64-bit memory data
i8  = 8-bit immediate data       i16 = 16-bit immediate data
i32 = 32-bit immediate data      i64 = 64-bit immediate data
d8  = 8-bit signed displacement  d16 = 16-bit signed displacement
d32 = 32-bit unsigned displacement NOTE: There is no 64-bit displacement
r8  = AL AH BL BH CL CH DL DH     r16 = AX BX CX DX BP SP SI DI
r32 = EAX EBX ECX EDX EBP ESP ESI EDI
r64 = RAX RBX RCX RDX RBP RSP RSI RDI R8 R9 R10 R11 R12 R13 R14 R15
```

MOV: Copy Right Operand into Left Operand

Flags Affected

```
O D I T S Z A P C  OF: Overflow flag   TF: Trap flag AF: Aux carry
F F F F F F F F F   DF: Direction flag  SF: Sign flag PF: Parity flag
        <none>      IF: Interrupt flag  ZF: Zero flag  CF: Carry flag
```

Legal Forms

```
MOV r/m8,r8
MOV r/m16,r16
MOV r/m32,r32      386+
MOV r/m64,r64      x64+
MOV r8,r/m8
MOV r16,r/m16
MOV r32,r/m32      386+
MOV r64,r/m64      x64+
MOV r/m8,i8
MOV r/m16,i8
MOV r/m16,i16
MOV r/m32,i8       386+
MOV r/m32,i32      386+
MOV r/m64,i8       x64+
MOV r/m64,i64      x64+
MOV r8,i8
MOV r16,i16
MOV r32,i32        386+
MOV r64,i64        x64+
```

Examples

```
MOV AX,BP
MOV R14,RDX
MOV [EBP],EAX
MOV RAX,[RDX]
MOV RBP,17H
MOV QWORD [RBX+RSI+Inset],5
```

Notes

MOV is perhaps the most-used of all instructions. The source (right) operand is copied into the left (destination) operand. The source operand is not changed. The flags are not affected.

Note that there are additional forms of MOV that deal with segment : offset addressing, which is not used in x64 userspace and which I am not covering in this book. See the Intel documentation for more information.

```
m8  = 8-bit memory data            m16 = 16-bit memory data
m32 = 32-bit memory data           m64 = 64-bit memory data
i8  = 8-bit immediate data         i16 = 16-bit immediate data
i32 = 32-bit immediate data        i64 = 64-bit immediate data
d8  = 8-bit signed displacement    d16 = 16-bit signed displacement
d32 = 32-bit unsigned displacement NOTE: There is no 64-bit displacement
r8  = AL AH BL BH CL CH DL DH       r16 = AX BX CX DX BP SP SI DI
r32 = EAX EBX ECX EDX EBP ESP ESI EDI
r64 = RAX RBX RCX RDX RBP RSP RSI RDI R8 R9 R10 R11 R12 R13 R14 R15
```

MOVS: Move String

Flags Affected

```
O D I T S Z A P C    OF: Overflow flag  TF: Trap flag AF: Aux carry
F F F F F F F F F    DF: Direction flag SF: Sign flag PF: Parity flag
      <none>         IF: Interrupt flag ZF: Zero flag CF: Carry flag
```

Legal Forms

```
MOVSB
MOVSW
MOVSD
MOVSQ
```

Examples

```
MOVSB          ;Copies byte at [RSI] to [RDI]
MOVSW          ;Copies word at [RSI] to [RDI]
MOVSD          ;Copies double word at [RSI] to [RDI]
REP MOVSB      ;Copies memory region starting at [RSI] to region
               ;  starting at [RDI], for RCX repeats, one byte
               ;  at a time
```

Notes

MOVS copies memory in 8-bit (MOVSB), 16-bit (MOVSW), 32-bit (MOVSD), or 64-bit (MOVSQ) chunks, from the address stored in RSI to the address stored in RDI. The mnemonic that you use from these four is about the size of the chunks, *not* the mode you're using. For example, you can use MOVSB in x64 long mode if you need to move data a byte at a time. If you need to move dwords, use MOVSD, etc.

By placing an operation repeat count (*not* a byte, word, dword, or qword count!) in RCX and preceding the mnemonic with the REP prefix, MOVS can do an automatic "machine-gun" copy of data from a memory region starting at [RSI] to a memory region starting at [RDI].

After each copy operation, RSI and RDI are adjusted (see the next paragraph) by 1 (for 8-bit operations), 2 (for 16-bit operations), 4 (for 32-bit operations), or 8 (for 64-bit operations) and RCX is decremented by 1. Don't forget that RCX counts *operations* (the number of times a data item is copied from source to destination) and *not* bytes!

Adjusting means incrementing RSI and RDI if the Direction flag is cleared (by CLD) or decrementing RSI and RDI if the Direction flag has been set (by STD).

The Direction flag DF thus determines whether your copy operation moves up-memory if DF is cleared (0) and down-memory if DF is set (1).

There are additional forms of the REP prefix (REPE, REPNE, REPZ, and REPNZ) that add the ability to terminate a MOVS operation before the count register goes to 0, by checking the state of the Zero flag ZF. Those additional forms are not covered in this book. See the Intel documentation for details.

```
m8  = 8-bit memory data          m16 = 16-bit memory data
m32 = 32-bit memory data         m64 = 64-bit memory data
i8  = 8-bit immediate data       i16 = 16-bit immediate data
i32 = 32-bit immediate data      i64 = 64-bit immediate data
d8 = 8-bit signed displacement   d16 = 16-bit signed displacement
d32 = 32-bit unsigned displacement NOTE: There is no 64-bit displacement
r8 = AL AH BL BH CL CH DL DH      r16 = AX BX CX DX BP SP SI DI
r32 = EAX EBX ECX EDX EBP ESP ESI EDI
r64 = RAX RBX RCX RDX RBP RSP RSI RDI R8 R9 R10 R11 R12 R13 R14 R15
```

MOVSX: Copy with Sign Extension

Flags Affected

```
O D I T S Z A P C   OF: Overflow flag  TF: Trap flag AF: Aux carry
F F F F F F F F F   DF: Direction flag SF: Sign flag PF: Parity flag
      <none>        IF: Interrupt flag ZF: Zero flag CF: Carry flag
```

Legal Forms

```
MOVSX r16,r/m8     386+
MOVSX r32,r/m8     386+
MOVSX r64,r/m8     x64+
MOVSX r32,r/m16    386+
MOVSX r64,r/m16    x64+
```

Examples

```
MOVSX AX,AL
MOVSX CX,BYTE [EDI]       ; Acts on the byte at EDI
MOVSX ECX,DL
MOVSX RSI,QWORD [RBX+RDI] ; Acts on the doubleword at EBX+EDI
```

Notes

MOVSX operates like MOV but copies values from source operand to the destination operand with sign extension. That is, it carries the sign bit of the smaller source operand to the sign bit of the larger destination operand. This way, for example, a 16-bit signed value in AX will still be a signed value when copied into 32-bit register EDX or 64-bit register RDX. Without sign extension, the sign bit of AX would simply become another bit in the binary value copied into RDX, and the value in RDX would bear no resemblance to the supposedly identical value in AX.

The destination operand must be a register. MOVSX can copy data *from* a memory location, but not *to* a memory location. Also note that the destination operand must be a wider value than the source operand; that is, MOVSX will copy from an 8-bit or 16-bit value to a 32-bit value, but not a 16-bit to a 16-bit, nor 32-bit to 32-bit.

MOVSX is present only in 386 and later CPUs. It does not affect any flags.

```
m8 = 8-bit memory data        m16 = 16-bit memory data
m32 = 32-bit memory data      m64 = 64-bit memory data
```

```
i8  = 8-bit immediate data        i16 = 16-bit immediate data
i32 = 32-bit immediate data       i64 = 64-bit immediate data
d8 = 8-bit signed displacement    d16 = 16-bit signed displacement
d32 = 32-bit unsigned displacement NOTE: There is no 64-bit displacement
r8 = AL AH BL BH CL CH DL DH       r16 = AX BX CX DX BP SP SI DI
r32 = EAX EBX ECX EDX EBP ESP ESI EDI
r64 = RAX RBX RCX RDX RBP RSP RSI RDI R8 R9 R10 R11 R12 R13 R14 R15
```

MUL: Unsigned Integer Multiplication

Flags Affected

```
O D I T S Z A P C   OF: Overflow flag  TF: Trap flag AF: Aux carry
F F F F F F F F F   DF: Direction flag SF: Sign flag PF: Parity flag
*       ? ? ? ? *   IF: Interrupt flag ZF: Zero flag CF: Carry flag
```

Legal Forms

```
MUL r/m8           Dividend in AX. Quotient in AL; remainder in AH.
MUL r/m16          Dividend in EAX. Quotient in AX; remainder in DX.
MUL r/m32   386+   Dividend in EAX:EDX. Quotient in EAX; remainder in EDX.
MUL r/m64   x64+   Dividend in RAX:RDX. Quotient in RAX; remainder in RDX.
```

Examples

```
MUL CH                 ; AL * CH --> AX
MUL BX                 ; AX * BX --> DX:AX
MUL ECX                ; EAX * ECX --> EDX:EAX
MUL DWORD [EBX+EDI]    ; EAX * [EBX+EDI] --> EDX:EAX
MUL QWORD [R14]        ; RAX * [R14] --> RDX:RAX
```

Notes

MUL multiplies its single operand by AL, AX, EAX, or RAX, and the result is placed in AX, in DX:AX, in EDX:EAX, or in RDX:RAX. If MUL is given an 8-bit operand (either an 8-bit register or an 8-bit memory operand), the results will be placed in AX. This means that AH will be affected, even if the results will fit entirely in AL.

Similarly, if MUL is given a 16-bit operand, the results will be placed in DX:AX, *even if the entire result will fit in AX!* It's easy to forget that MUL affects DX on 16-bit multiplies, EDX in 32-bit multiplies, and RDX in 64-bit multiplies. Keep that in mind! Also, if you're multiplying a value in memory, you must add the size specifier BYTE, WORD, DWORD, or QWORD.

Note: It's easy to assume that IMUL is identical to MUL save for IMUL's ability to operate on signed values. Not so: IMUL has more legal instruction forms and is considerably more complex than MUL. For more details, see the Intel documentation.

The Carry and Overflow flags are cleared to 0 if the result value is 0; otherwise, both are set to 1. Remember that SF, ZF, AF, and PF become undefined after MUL.

```
m8  = 8-bit memory data          m16 = 16-bit memory data
m32 = 32-bit memory data         m64 = 64-bit memory data
i8  = 8-bit immediate data       i16 = 16-bit immediate data
i32 = 32-bit immediate data      i64 = 64-bit immediate data
d8  = 8-bit signed displacement  d16 = 16-bit signed displacement
d32 = 32-bit unsigned displacement NOTE: There is no 64-bit displacement
r8  = AL AH BL BH CL CH DL DH     r16 = AX BX CX DX BP SP SI DI
r32 = EAX EBX ECX EDX EBP ESP ESI EDI
r64 = RAX RBX RCX RDX RBP RSP RSI RDI R8 R9 R10 R11 R12 R13 R14 R15
```

NEG: Negate (Two's Complement; i.e., Multiply by −1)

Flags Affected

```
O D I T S Z A P C   OF: Overflow flag  TF: Trap flag AF: Aux carry
F F F F F F F F F   DF: Direction flag SF: Sign flag PF: Parity flag
*       * * * *     IF: Interrupt flag ZF: Zero flag CF: Carry flag
```

Legal Forms

```
NEG r/m8
NEG r/m16
NEG r/m32        386+
NEG r/m64        x64+
```

Examples

```
NEG CH
NEG BX
NEG ECX
NEG DWORD [EBX]
NEG QWORD [R14+RDI*4]
```

Notes

NEG is the assembly language equivalent of multiplying a value by 1. Keep in mind that negation is *not* the same as simply inverting each bit in the operand. (Another instruction, NOT, does that.) The process is also known as generating the *two's complement* of a value. The two's complement of a value added to that value yields zero.

−1 = \$FF; −2 = \$FE; −3 = \$FD; and so forth.

If the operand is 0, CF is cleared, and ZF is set; otherwise, CF is set, and ZF is cleared. If the operand contains the maximum negative value for the operand size, the operand does not change, but OF and CF are set. SF is set if the result is negative, or else SF is cleared. PF is set if the low-order 8 bits of the result contain an even number of set (1) bits; otherwise, PF is cleared.

NEG acting on memory data forms *must* be used with a data size specifier such as BYTE, WORD, DWORD, and QWORD. See the two examples given earlier.

```
m8  = 8-bit memory data      m16 = 16-bit memory data
m32 = 32-bit memory data     m64 = 64-bit memory data
```

```
i8  = 8-bit immediate data      i16 = 16-bit immediate data
i32 = 32-bit immediate data     i64 = 64-bit immediate data
d8  = 8-bit signed displacement d16 = 16-bit signed displacement
d32 = 32-bit unsigned displacement NOTE: There is no 64-bit displacement
r8  = AL AH BL BH CL CH DL DH    r16 = AX BX CX DX BP SP SI DI
r32 = EAX EBX ECX EDX EBP ESP ESI EDI
r64 = RAX RBX RCX RDX RBP RSP RSI RDI R8 R9 R10 R11 R12 R13 R14 R15
```

NOP: No Operation

Flags Affected

```
O D I T S Z A P C    OF: Overflow flag  TF: Trap flag AF: Aux carry
F F F F F F F F F    DF: Direction flag SF: Sign flag PF: Parity flag
      <none>         IF: Interrupt flag ZF: Zero flag CF: Carry flag
```

Legal Forms

```
NOP
```

Examples

```
NOP ;AllDone    ; NOP replaces a jump instruction for debugging purposes,
                ; but the parameter is commented out, since NOP
                ; can't take a label as a parameter.
```

Notes

NOP, the easiest-to-understand of all x86/x64-family machine instructions, simply does nothing. Its job is to take up space in sequences of instructions. The flags are not affected. NOP is used for "NOPing out" machine instructions during debugging, leaving space for future procedure or interrupt calls.

In ancient times, NOP was used for padding timing loops. This makes sense on the surface but can no longer be done. Modern CPUs have the ability to perform various context-sensitive optimizations on executing code inside the CPU. *Precise assembly-time prediction of instruction execution time is no longer possible!*

```
m8  = 8-bit memory data          m16 = 16-bit memory data
m32 = 32-bit memory data         m64 = 64-bit memory data
i8  = 8-bit immediate data       i16 = 16-bit immediate data
i32 = 32-bit immediate data      i64 = 64-bit immediate data
d8  = 8-bit signed displacement  d16 = 16-bit signed displacement
d32 = 32-bit unsigned displacement NOTE: There is no 64-bit displacement
r8  = AL AH BL BH CL CH DL DH     r16 = AX BX CX DX BP SP SI DI
r32 = EAX EBX ECX EDX EBP ESP ESI EDI
r64 = RAX RBX RCX RDX RBP RSP RSI RDI R8 R9 R10 R11 R12 R13 R14 R15
```

NOT: Logical NOT (One's Complement)

Flags Affected

```
O D I T S Z A P C    OF: Overflow flag  TF: Trap flag AF: Aux carry
F F F F F F F F F    DF: Direction flag SF: Sign flag PF: Parity flag
        <none>       IF: Interrupt flag ZF: Zero flag CF: Carry flag
```

Legal Forms

```
NOT  r/m8
NOT  r/m16
NOT  r/m32         386+
NOT  r/m64         x64+
```

Examples

```
NOT  CL
NOT  DX
NOT  ECX
NOT  DWORD [EDI]
NOT  QWORD [RDI+RCX*4]
```

Notes

NOT inverts each individual bit within the operand separately. That is, every bit that was 1 becomes 0, and every bit that was 0 becomes 1. This is the "logical NOT" or "one's complement" operation. See the NEG instruction for the negation, or two's complement, operation.

After execution of NOT, the value FFH would become 0; the value AAH would become 55H. Note that the Zero flag is *not* affected, even when NOT forces its operand to 0.

NOT acting on memory data forms *must* be used with a data size specifier such as BYTE, WORD, DWORD, and QWORD. See the two examples given earlier.

```
m8 = 8-bit memory data          m16 = 16-bit memory data
m32 = 32-bit memory data        m64 = 64-bit memory data
i8  = 8-bit immediate data      i16 = 16-bit immediate data
i32 = 32-bit immediate data     i64 = 64-bit immediate data
d8 = 8-bit signed displacement  d16 = 16-bit signed displacement
d32 = 32-bit unsigned displacement NOTE: There is no 64-bit displacement
r8 = AL AH BL BH CL CH DL DH     r16 = AX BX CX DX BP SP SI DI
r32 = EAX EBX ECX EDX EBP ESP ESI EDI
r64 = RAX RBX RCX RDX RBP RSP RSI RDI R8 R9 R10 R11 R12 R13 R14 R15
```

OR: Logical OR

Flags Affected

```
O D I T S Z A P C   OF: Overflow flag  TF: Trap flag AF: Aux carry
F F F F F F F F F   DF: Direction flag SF: Sign flag PF: Parity flag
*       * * ? * *   IF: Interrupt flag ZF: Zero flag CF: Carry flag
```

Legal Forms

```
OR r/m8,i8
OR r/m16,i16
OR r/m32,i32      386+
OR r/m64,i32      x64+  NOTE: OR r/m64,i64 is NOT valid!
OR r/m16,i8
OR r/m32,i8       386+
OR r/m64,i8       x64+
OR r/m8,r8
OR r/m16,r16
OR r/m32,r32      386+
OR r/m64,r64      x64+
OR r8,r/m8
OR r16,r/m16
OR r32,r/m32      386+
OR r64,r/m64      x64+
OR AL,i8
OR AX,i16
OR EAX,i32        386+
OR RAX,i32        x64+  NOTE: OR RAX,i64 is NOT valid!
```

Examples

```
OR BX,DI
OR EAX,5
OR AX,0FFFFH
OR AL,42H
OR [BP+SI],DX
OR [RDI],RAX
OR QWORD [RBX],0B80000H
```

Notes

OR performs the OR logical operation between its two operands. Once the operation is complete, the result replaces the destination operand. OR is performed on a bit-by-bit basis, such that bit 0 of the source is ORed with bit 0 of the destination, bit 1 of the source is ORed with bit 1 of the destination, and so on. The OR operation yields a 1 if one of the operands is 1; and a 0 only if both operands are 0. Note that the or instruction makes the Auxiliary Carry flag undefined. CF and OF are cleared to 0, and the other affected flags are set according to the operation's results.

```
m8  = 8-bit memory data           m16 = 16-bit memory data
m32 = 32-bit memory data          m64 = 64-bit memory data
i8  = 8-bit immediate data        i16 = 16-bit immediate data
i32 = 32-bit immediate data       i64 = 64-bit immediate data
d8  = 8-bit signed displacement   d16 = 16-bit signed displacement
d32 = 32-bit unsigned displacement NOTE: There is no 64-bit displacement
r8  = AL AH BL BH CL CH DL DH      r16 = AX BX CX DX BP SP SI DI
r32 = EAX EBX ECX EDX EBP ESP ESI EDI
r64 = RAX RBX RCX RDX RBP RSP RSI RDI R8 R9 R10 R11 R12 R13 R14 R15
```

POP: Copy Top of Stack into Operand

Flags Affected

```
O D I T S Z A P C   OF: Overflow flag  TF: Trap flag AF: Aux carry
F F F F F F F F F   DF: Direction flag SF: Sign flag PF: Parity flag
       <none>       IF: Interrupt flag ZF: Zero flag CF: Carry flag
```

Legal Forms

```
POP m16
POP m32    32-bit CPUs only: not valid in x64 mode
POP m64    x64+
POP r16
POP r32    32-bit CPUs only: not valid in x64 mode
POP r64    x64+
```

Examples

```
POP DX
POP RCX
POP QWORD [RDI]
POP QWORD [RDI+RCX*4]
```

Notes

It is impossible to pop an 8-bit item from the stack. Also remember that the *top of the stack* is defined (in 16-bit modes) as the word at address SS:SP, and there's no way to override that using prefixes. In 32-bit modes, the top of the stack is the DWORD at [ESP]. In 64-bit mode, the top of the stack is the QWORD at [RSP]. The 32-bit forms of POP are invalid in 64-bit mode. There is a separate pair of instructions, PUSHF/D/Q and POPF/D/Q, for pushing and popping the Flags register.

POP acting on memory data forms *must* be used with a data size specifier such as BYTE, WORD, DWORD, and QWORD. See the examples given earlier.

There are several forms of POP for popping segment registers, but these forms cannot be used in userspace programming. For details, see the Intel documentation.

```
m8  = 8-bit memory data          m16 = 16-bit memory data
m32 = 32-bit memory data         m64 = 64-bit memory data
i8  = 8-bit immediate data       i16 = 16-bit immediate data
i32 = 32-bit immediate data      i64 = 64-bit immediate data
d8  = 8-bit signed displacement  d16 = 16-bit signed displacement
```

d32 = 32-bit unsigned displacement NOTE: There is no 64-bit displacement
r8 = AL AH BL BH CL CH DL DH   r16 = AX BX CX DX BP SP SI DI
r32 = EAX EBX ECX EDX EBP ESP ESI EDI
r64 = RAX RBX RCX RDX RBP RSP RSI RDI R8 R9 R10 R11 R12 R13 R14 R15

POPF/D/Q: Copy Top of Stack into Flags Register

Flags Affected

```
O I T S Z A P C   OF: Overflow flag  TF: Trap flag AF: Aux carry
F F F F F F F F    DF: Direction flag SF: Sign flag PF: Parity flag
* * * * * * * *    IF: Interrupt flag ZF: Zero flag CF: Carry flag
```

Legal Forms

```
POPF
POPFD           32-bit CPUs only: Invalid in 64-bit mode
POPFQ           x64+
```

Examples

```
POPF            ;Pops 16-bit top of stack into the FLAGS register
POPFD           ;Pops 32-bit top of stack into the EFLAGS register
POPFQ           ;Pops 64-bit top of stack into the RFLAGS register
```

Notes

These instructions pop data at the top of the stack into the flags register appropriate to the mode. POPF pops 16 bits into the FLAGS register. POPFD pops 32 bits into EFLAGS. POPFQ pops 64 bits into RFLAGS. The stack pointer is incremented by 2 after POPF, 4 after POPFD, and 8 after POPFQ. POPF may be used in 64-bit mode, if PUSHF was done earlier. Remember that RFLAGS contains EFLAGS, which in turn contains FLAGS. When you pop the top 16 bits off the stack with POPF, you're popping those bits into the lowest 16 bits of both EFLAGS and RFLAGS.

POPFD is invalid in 64-bit mode.

Pushing and popping the CPU flags is a subtle business and more complex than you might think. It's mostly done by the operating system and isn't often done in userspace programming. For details, see the Intel documentation.

```
m8 = 8-bit memory data          m16 = 16-bit memory data
m32 = 32-bit memory data        m64 = 64-bit memory data
i8  = 8-bit immediate data      i16 = 16-bit immediate data
i32 = 32-bit immediate data     i64 = 64-bit immediate data
d8 = 8-bit signed displacement  d16 = 16-bit signed displacement
d32 = 32-bit unsigned displacement NOTE: There is no 64-bit displacement
r8 = AL AH BL BH CL CH DL DH     r16 = AX BX CX DX BP SP SI DI
r32 = EAX EBX ECX EDX EBP ESP ESI EDI
r64 = RAX RBX RCX RDX RBP RSP RSI RDI R8 R9 R10 R11 R12 R13 R14 R15
```

PUSH: Push Operand onto Top of Stack

Flags Affected

```
O D I T S Z A P C   OF: Overflow flag  TF: Trap flag AF: Aux carry
F F F F F F F F F   DF: Direction flag SF: Sign flag PF: Parity flag
      <none>        IF: Interrupt flag ZF: Zero flag CF: Carry flag
```

Legal Forms

```
PUSH r/m16
PUSH r/m32          32-bit CPUs only; not valid in 64-bit mode
PUSH r/m64          x64+
PUSH i16
PUSH i32            32-bit CPUs only; not valid in 64-bit mode
PUSH i64            x64+
```

Examples

```
PUSH DX
PUSH R13
PUSH QWORD 5
PUSH QWORD 034F001h
```

Notes

PUSH decrements the stack pointer and then copies its operand onto the stack. The stack pointer then points at the new data. (Before the stack is used, the stack pointer points to empty memory.) It is impossible to push 8-bit data onto the stack. Also remember that the *top of the stack* is defined (in 16-bit modes) as the word at address SS:SP, and there's no way to override that using prefixes. In 32-bit modes the top of the stack is the DWORD at [ESP]. In 64-bit mode the top of the stack is the QWORD at [RSP]. The 32-bit forms are not valid in x64. There is a separate set of instructions, PUSHF/D/Q and POPF/D/Q, for pushing and popping the FLAGS/EFLAGS/RFLAGS registers.

PUSH acting on memory data forms *must* be used with a data size specifier such as BYTE, WORD, DWORD, and QWORD. See the examples given earlier.

There are special forms of PUSH for pushing the segment registers, but those forms are not listed here since they cannot be used in ordinary Linux userspace programming.

```
m8  = 8-bit memory data          m16 = 16-bit memory data
m32 = 32-bit memory data         m64 = 64-bit memory data
i8  = 8-bit immediate data       i16 = 16-bit immediate data
i32 = 32-bit immediate data      i64 = 64-bit immediate data
d8  = 8-bit signed displacement  d16 = 16-bit signed displacement
d32 = 32-bit unsigned displacement NOTE: There is no 64-bit displacement
r8  = AL AH BL BH CL CH DL DH     r16 = AX BX CX DX BP SP SI DI
r32 = EAX EBX ECX EDX EBP ESP ESI EDI
r64 = RAX RBX RCX RDX RBP RSP RSI RDI R8 R9 R10 R11 R12 R13 R14 R15
```

PUSHF/D/Q: Push Flags Onto the Stack

Flags Affected

```
O D I T S Z A P C    OF: Overflow flag  TF: Trap flag AF: Aux carry
F F F F F F F F F    DF: Direction flag SF: Sign flag PF: Parity flag
      <none>         IF: Interrupt flag ZF: Zero flag CF: Carry flag
```

Legal Forms

```
PUSHF
PUSHFD               32-bit CPUs only: Invalid in 64-bit mode
PUSHFQ               x64+
```

Examples

```
PUSHF                ;Pushes 16-bit FLAGS register onto the stack
PUSHFD               ;Pushes 32-bit EFLAGS register onto the stack
PUSHFQ               ;Pushes 64-bit RFLAGS register onto the stack
```

Notes

These three instructions push the FLAGS/EFLAGS/RFLAGS register onto the stack. PUSHF pushes the 16-bit FLAGS register. PUSHFD pushes 32-bit EFLAGS. PUSHFQ pushes 64-bit RFLAGS. The stack pointer is decremented *before* the flags values are pushed onto the stack. Remember that RFLAGS contains EFLAGS, which in turn contains FLAGS. When you pop the top 16 bits off the stack with POPF, you're popping those bits into the lowest 16 bits of both EFLAGS and RFLAGS.

PUSHFD is invalid in 64-bit mode.

Pushing and popping the CPU flags is a subtle business, and more complex than you might think. It's mostly done by the operating system and isn't often done in userspace programming. For details, see the Intel documentation.

```
m8  = 8-bit memory data          m16 = 16-bit memory data
m32 = 32-bit memory data         m64 = 64-bit memory data
i8  = 8-bit immediate data       i16 = 16-bit immediate data
i32 = 32-bit immediate data      i64 = 64-bit immediate data
d8  = 8-bit signed displacement  d16 = 16-bit signed displacement
d32 = 32-bit unsigned displacement NOTE: There is no 64-bit displacement
r8  = AL AH BL BH CL CH DL DH     r16 = AX BX CX DX BP SP SI DI
r32 = EAX EBX ECX EDX EBP ESP ESI EDI
r64 = RAX RBX RCX RDX RBP RSP RSI RDI R8 R9 R10 R11 R12 R13 R14 R15
```

RET: Return from Procedure

Flags Affected

```
O D I T S Z A P C    OF: Overflow flag  TF: Trap flag AF: Aux carry
F F F F F F F F F    DF: Direction flag SF: Sign flag PF: Parity flag
        <none>       IF: Interrupt flag ZF: Zero flag CF: Carry flag
```

Legal Forms

```
RET
RETN
RET i16
RETN i16
```

Examples

```
RET
RET 16          ; Removes 2 64-bit (8 byte) parameters from the stack
```

Notes

There are two kinds of returns from procedures: Near and Far, where Near is within the current code segment and Far is to some other code segment. This is not an issue in 32-bit and 64-bit protected mode, for which there is only one code segment in userspace code and all calls and returns are Near. Ordinarily, the RET form is used, and the assembler resolves it to a Near or Far return opcode to match the procedure definition's use of the NEAR or FAR specifier if one is present. Specifying RETN may be done for Near returns when necessary.

RET may take an operand indicating how many bytes of stack space are to be released on returning from the procedure. This figure is subtracted from the stack pointer to erase data items that had been pushed onto the stack for the procedure's use immediately prior to the procedure call. Make sure you calculate the immediate value correctly, or the stack will be corrupted and probably trigger a segmentation fault.

There are additional variants of the RET instruction with provisions for working with the protection mechanisms of operating systems. These are not covered here, and for more information, you should see an advanced text or a full assembly language reference.

```
m8 = 8-bit memory data        m16 = 16-bit memory data
m32 = 32-bit memory data      m64 = 64-bit memory data
```

```
i8  = 8-bit immediate data        i16 = 16-bit immediate data
i32 = 32-bit immediate data       i64 = 64-bit immediate data
d8 = 8-bit signed displacement    d16 = 16-bit signed displacement
d32 = 32-bit unsigned displacement NOTE: There is no 64-bit displacement
r8 = AL AH BL BH CL CH DL DH       r16 = AX BX CX DX BP SP SI DI
r32 = EAX EBX ECX EDX EBP ESP ESI EDI
r64 = RAX RBX RCX RDX RBP RSP RSI RDI R8 R9 R10 R11 R12 R13 R14 R15
```

ROL/ROR: Rotate Left/Rotate Right

Flags Affected

```
O D I T S Z A P C   OF: Overflow flag  TF: Trap flag AF: Aux carry
F F F F F F F F F    DF: Direction flag SF: Sign flag PF: Parity flag
*               *    IF: Interrupt flag ZF: Zero flag CF: Carry flag
```

Legal Forms

```
ROL/ROR  r/m8,1
ROL/ROR  r/m16,1
ROL/ROR  r/m32,1      386+
ROL/ROR  r/m64,1      x64+
ROL/ROR  r/m8,CL
ROL/ROR  r/m16,CL
ROL/ROR  r/m32,CL     386+
ROL/ROR  r/m64,CL     x64+
ROL/ROR  r/m8,i8      286+
ROL/ROr  r/m16,i8     286+
ROL/ROR  r/m32,i8     386+
ROL/ROR  m/m64,i8     x64+
```

Examples

```
ROL/ROR AX,1
ROL/ROR DWORD {EBX+ESI],9
ROL/ROR R14,17
ROL/ROR QWORD [BPI],CL
```

Notes

ROL and ROR rotate the bits within the destination operand to the left (ROL) and the right (ROR), where left is toward the most significant bit (MSB) and right is toward the least significant bit (LSB). A rotate is a shift (see SHL and SHR) that wraps around: For ROL, the leftmost bit of the operand is shifted into the rightmost bit, and all intermediate bits are shifted one bit to the left. Going the other way, for ROR the rightmost bit of the operand is shifted into the leftmost bit, with all other bits moving one bit to the right. Except for the direction that the shift operation takes, ROL is identical to ROR, which is why I treat both instructions on the same page.

The number of bit positions shifted may be specified either as an 8-bit immediate value or by the value in CL—*not* CX/ECX/RCX. (The 8086 and 8088 may only use the forms shifting by the immediate value 1.) Note that while CL may accept a value up to 255, it is meaningless to shift by any value larger than the native word size. The 286 and later limit the number of shift operations performed to the native word size, except when running in Virtual 86 mode.

With ROL, the leftmost bit is copied into CF on each shift operation. With ROR, the rightmost bit is copied into CF on each shift operation. For both ROL and ROR, OF is modified *only* by the shift-by-one forms. After shift-by-CL forms, *OF becomes undefined*. However, if the number of bits to shift by is 0, none of the flags is affected.

ROL or ROR acting on memory data forms *must* be used with a data size specifier such as BYTE, WORD, DWORD, and QWORD. See the examples given earlier.

Although I'm not giving them a separate page here, RCL and RCR work the same way, except that the Carry flag CF is part of the rotation, in essence adding a bit to the rotation.

```
m8  = 8-bit memory data             m16 = 16-bit memory data
m32 = 32-bit memory data            m64 = 64-bit memory data
i8  = 8-bit immediate data          i16 = 16-bit immediate data
i32 = 32-bit immediate data         i64 = 64-bit immediate data
d8 = 8-bit signed displacement      d16 = 16-bit signed displacement
d32 = 32-bit unsigned displacement  NOTE: There is no 64-bit displacement
r8 = AL AH BL BH CL CH DL DH         r16 = AX BX CX DX BP SP SI DI
r32 = EAX EBX ECX EDX EBP ESP ESI EDI
r64 = RAX RBX RCX RDX RBP RSP RSI RDI R8 R9 R10 R11 R12 R13 R14 R15
```

SBB: Arithmetic Subtraction with Borrow

Flags Affected

```
O D I T S Z A P C   OF: Overflow flag  TF: Trap flag AF: Aux carry
F F F F F F F F F   DF: Direction flag SF: Sign flag PF: Parity flag
*       * * * *     IF: Interrupt flag ZF: Zero flag CF: Carry flag
```

Legal Forms

```
SBB r/m8,i8
SBB r/m16,i16
SBB r/m32,i32      386+
SBB r/m64,i32      x64+  NOTE: SBB r/m64,i64 is NOT valid!
SBB r/m16,i8
SBB r/m32,i8       386+
SBB r/m64,i8       x64+
SBB r/m8,r8
SBB r/m16,r16
SBB r/m32,r32      386+
SBB r/m64,r64      x64+
SBB r8,r/m8
SBB r16,r/m16
SBB r32,r/m32      386+
SBB r64,r/m64      x64+
SBB AL,i8
SBB AX,i16
SBB EAX,i32        386+
SBB RAX,i32        x64+  NOTE: SBB RAX,i64 is NOT valid!
```

Examples

```
SBB DX,DI
SBB AX,04B2FH
SBB AL,CBH
SBB BP,19H
SBB DWORD [ESI],EAX
SBB QWORD [RAX],7BH
```

Notes

SBB performs a subtraction with borrow, where the source operand is subtracted from the destination operand, and then the Carry flag is subtracted from the result. The result then replaces the destination operand. If the result is negative, the Carry flag is set. To subtract without taking the Carry flag into account (i.e., without borrowing), use the SUB instruction.

```
m8  = 8-bit memory data          m16 = 16-bit memory data
m32 = 32-bit memory data         m64 = 64-bit memory data
i8  = 8-bit immediate data       i16 = 16-bit immediate data
i32 = 32-bit immediate data      i64 = 64-bit immediate data
d8  = 8-bit signed displacement  d16 = 16-bit signed displacement
d32 = 32-bit unsigned displacement NOTE: There is no 64-bit displacement
r8  = AL AH BL BH CL CH DL DH     r16 = AX BX CX DX BP SP SI DI
r32 = EAX EBX ECX EDX EBP ESP ESI EDI
r64 = RAX RBX RCX RDX RBP RSP RSI RDI R8 R9 R10 R11 R12 R13 R14 R15
```

SHL/SHR: Shift Left/Shift Right

Flags Affected

```
O D I T S Z A P C   OF: Overflow flag  TF: Trap flag AF: Aux carry
F F F F F F F F F    DF: Direction flag SF: Sign flag PF: Parity flag
*       * * ? * *    IF: Interrupt flag ZF: Zero flag CF: Carry flag
```

Legal Forms

```
SHL/SHR r/m8,1
SHL/SHR r/m16,1
SHL/SHR r/m32,1    386+
SHL/SHR r/m64,1    x64+
SHL/SHR r/m8,CL
SHL/SHR r/m16,CL
SHL/SHR r/m32,CL   386+
SHL/SHR r/m64,CL   x64+
SHL/SHR r/m8,i8    286+
SHL/SHR r/m16,i8   286+
SHL/SHR r/m32,i8   386+
SHL/SHR m/m64,i8   x64+
```

Examples

```
SHL/SHR AX,1
SHL/SHR DWORD {EDX+ESI],4
SHL/SHR R12,15
SHL/SHR QWORD [RDI],CL
```

Notes

SHL and SHR shift the bits in their destination operands by a count given in the source operand. SHL shifts the bits within the destination operand to the left, where left is toward the most significant bit (MSB). SHR shifts the bits within the destination operand to the right, where right is toward the least significant bit (LSB). The number of bit positions shifted may be specified either as an 8-bit immediate value or by the value in CL—*not* CX/ECX/RCX. (The 8086 and 8088 are limited to the immediate value 1.) Note that while CL may accept a value up to 255, it is meaningless to shift by any value larger than the native word size. The 286 and later limit the number of shift operations performed to the native word size except when running in Virtual 86 mode.

With SHL, the leftmost bit of the operand is shifted into CF; the rightmost bit is cleared to 0. With SHR, the rightmost bit is shifted into CF; the leftmost bit is cleared to 0. The Auxiliary Carry flag AF becomes undefined after both SHL and SHR. OF is modified *only* by the shift-by-one forms. After any of the shift-by-CL forms, OF becomes undefined.

SHL or SHR acting on memory data forms *must* be used with a data size specifier such as BYTE, WORD, DWORD, and QWORD. See the examples given earlier.

SHL is a synonym for SAL (Shift Arithmetic Left). SHR is a synonym for SAR (Shift Arithmetic Right.) Except for the direction the shift operation takes, SHL is identical to SHR.

```
m8  = 8-bit memory data            m16 = 16-bit memory data
m8  = 8-bit memory data            m16 = 16-bit memory data
m32 = 32-bit memory data           m64 = 64-bit memory data
i8  = 8-bit immediate data         i16 = 16-bit immediate data
i32 = 32-bit immediate data        i64 = 64-bit immediate data
d8 = 8-bit signed displacement     d16 = 16-bit signed displacement
d32 = 32-bit unsigned displacement NOTE: There is no 64-bit displacement
r8 = AL AH BL BH CL CH DL DH        r16 = AX BX CX DX BP SP SI DI
r32 = EAX EBX ECX EDX EBP ESP ESI EDI
r64 = RAX RBX RCX RDX RBP RSP RSI RDI R8 R9 R10 R11 R12 R13 R14 R15
```

STC: Set Carry Flag (CF)

Flags Affected

```
O D I T S Z A P C   OF: Overflow flag  TF: Trap flag AF: Aux carry
F F F F F F F F F   DF: Direction flag SF: Sign flag PF: Parity flag
            *  IF: Interrupt flag ZF: Zero flag CF: Carry flag
```

Legal Forms

```
STC
```

Examples

```
STC
```

Notes

STC changes the Carry flag CF to a known set state (1). Use it prior to some task that needs a bit in the Carry flag. The CLC instruction is similar and will clear CF to a known state of 0.

```
m8 = 8-bit memory data       m16 = 16-bit memory data
m32 = 32-bit memory data     m64 = 64-bit memory data
i8  = 8-bit immediate data   i16 = 16-bit immediate data
i32 = 32-bit immediate data  i64 = 64-bit immediate data
d8 = 8-bit signed displacement   d16 = 16-bit signed displacement
d32 = 32-bit unsigned displacement NOTE: There is no 64-bit displacement
r8 = AL AH BL BH CL CH DL DH      r16 = AX BX CX DX BP SP SI DI
r32 = EAX EBX ECX EDX EBP ESP ESI EDI
r64 = RAX RBX RCX RDX RBP RSP RSI RDI R8 R9 R10 R11 R12 R13 R14 R15
```

STD: Set Direction Flag (DF)

Flags Affected

```
O D I T S Z A P C   OF: Overflow flag  TF: Trap flag AF: Aux carry
F F F F F F F F F   DF: Direction flag SF: Sign flag PF: Parity flag
      *             IF: Interrupt flag ZF: Zero flag CF: Carry flag
```

Legal Forms

```
STD
```

Examples

```
STD
```

Notes

STD simply changes the Direction flag DF to the set (1) state. This affects the adjustment performed by repeated string instructions such as STOS, SCAS, and MOVS. Typically, when DF = 0, the destination pointer is increased and decreased when DF = 1. DF is cleared to 0 with the CLD instruction.

```
m8  = 8-bit memory data          m16 = 16-bit memory data
m32 = 32-bit memory data         m64 = 64-bit memory data
i8  = 8-bit immediate data       i16 = 16-bit immediate data
i32 = 32-bit immediate data      i64 = 64-bit immediate data
d8 = 8-bit signed displacement   d16 = 16-bit signed displacement
d32 = 32-bit unsigned displacement NOTE: There is no 64-bit displacement
r8 = AL AH BL BH CL CH DL DH      r16 = AX BX CX DX BP SP SI DI
r32 = EAX EBX ECX EDX EBP ESP ESI EDI
r64 = RAX RBX RCX RDX RBP RSP RSI RDI R8 R9 R10 R11 R12 R13 R14 R15
```

STOS/B/W/D/Q: Store String

Flags Affected

```
O D I T S Z A P C   OF: Overflow flag  TF: Trap flag AF: Aux carry
F F F F F F F F F   DF: Direction flag SF: Sign flag PF: Parity flag
        <none>       IF: Interrupt flag ZF: Zero flag CF: Carry flag
```

Legal Forms

```
STOS m8
STOS m16
STOS m32
STOS m64
STOSB               ; For 8-bit operations
STOSW               ; For 16-bit operations
STOSD               ; For 32-bit operations
STOSQ               ; For 64-bit operations
```

Examples

```
STOSB               ; Stores AL to [EDI/RDI]
REP STOSB           ; Stores AL to [EDI/RDI] and up, for ECX/RCX repeats
STOSW               ; Stores AX to [EDI/RDI]
STOSD               ; Stores EAX to [EDI/RDI]
REP STOSQ           ; Stores RAX to [EDI/RDI] and up, for ECX/RCX repeats
```

Notes

STOS stores AL (for 8-bit store operations), AX (for 16-bit operations), and EAX (for 32-bit operations) or RAX (for 64-bit operations) to the location at [EDI] / [RDI]. For 16-bit legacy modes, ES must contain the segment address of the destination and cannot be overridden. For 32-bit and x64 protected modes, all segments are congruent, and thus ES does not need to be specified explicitly. Similarly, DI, EDI, or RDI must always contain the destination offset. The STOS form must always have an operand specifying a memory location and size. The STOSB, STOSW, STOSD, and STOSQ forms contain the size of the operation in their mnemonics, and their operands are implicit, with the store operation going to a memory address in EDI or RDI.

By placing an operation repeat count (*not* a byte count!) in CX/ECX/RCX and preceding the mnemonic with the REP prefix, STOS can do an automatic "machine-gun" store of AL/AX/EAX/RAX into successive memory locations beginning at the initial address [DI], [EDI], or [RDI]. After each store, the DI/EDI/RDI register is adjusted (see the next paragraph) by 1 (for 8-bit store operations), 2 (for 16-bit store operations), 4 (for 32-bit store operations), or 8 (for 64-bit store operations, and CX/ECX/RCX is decremented by 1. Don't forget that CX/ECX/RCX counts *operations* (the number of times a data item is stored to memory) and *not* bytes!

Adjusting means incrementing if the Direction flag is cleared (by CLD) or decrementing if the Direction flag has been set (by STD).

```
m8  = 8-bit memory data          m16 = 16-bit memory data
m32 = 32-bit memory data         m64 = 64-bit memory data
i8  = 8-bit immediate data       i16 = 16-bit immediate data
i32 = 32-bit immediate data      i64 = 64-bit immediate data
d8  = 8-bit signed displacement  d16 = 16-bit signed displacement
d32 = 32-bit unsigned displacement NOTE: There is no 64-bit displacement
r8  = AL AH BL BH CL CH DL DH     r16 = AX BX CX DX BP SP SI DI
r32 = EAX EBX ECX EDX EBP ESP ESI EDI
r64 = RAX RBX RCX RDX RBP RSP RSI RDI R8 R9 R10 R11 R12 R13 R14 R15
```

SUB: Arithmetic Subtraction

Flags Affected

```
O D I T S Z A P C   OF: Overflow flag  TF: Trap flag AF: Aux carry
F F F F F F F F F   DF: Direction flag SF: Sign flag PF: Parity flag
*       * * * *     IF: Interrupt flag ZF: Zero flag CF: Carry flag
```

Legal Forms

```
SUB r/m8,i8
SUB r/m16,i16
SUB r/m32,i32      386+
SUB r/m64,i32      x64+   NOTE: SUB r/m64,i64 is NOT valid!
SUB r/m16,i8
SUB r/m32,i8       386+
SUB r/m64,i8       x64+
SUB r/m8,r8
SUB r/m16,r16
SUB r/m32,r32      386+
SUB r/m64,r64      x64+
SUB r8,r/m8
SUB r16,r/m16
SUB r32,r/m32      386+
SUB r64,r/m64      x64+
SUB AL,i8
SUB AX,i16
SUB EAX,i32        386+
SUB RAX,i32        x64+   NOTE: SUB RAX,i64 is NOT valid!
```

Examples

```
SUB AX,DX
SUB AL,DL
SUB EBP,17
SUB RAX,0FFFBH  ; The i32 value is sign-extended to 64 bits
                ;   before the operation
SUB DWORD [EDI],EAX
AND QWORD [RAX],7BH ; The i32 value is sign-extended to 64 bits
                    ;   before the operation
```

Notes

SUB performs a subtraction without borrow, where the source operand is subtracted from the destination operand, and the result replaces the destination operand. If the result is negative, the Carry flag CF is set.

In 64-bit mode, 32-bit source operands are sign-extended to 64 bits before the subtraction operation happens.

Multiple-precision subtraction can be performed by following SUB with SBB (Subtract with Borrow), which takes the Carry flag into account as an arithmetic borrow.

```
m8  = 8-bit memory data          m16 = 16-bit memory data
m32 = 32-bit memory data         m64 = 64-bit memory data
i8  = 8-bit immediate data       i16 = 16-bit immediate data
i32 = 32-bit immediate data      i64 = 64-bit immediate data
d8  = 8-bit signed displacement  d16 = 16-bit signed displacement
d32 = 32-bit unsigned displacement NOTE: There is no 64-bit displacement
r8  = AL AH BL BH CL CH DL DH     r16 = AX BX CX DX BP SP SI DI
r32 = EAX EBX ECX EDX EBP ESP ESI EDI
r64 = RAX RBX RCX RDX RBP RSP RSI RDI R8 R9 R10 R11 R12 R13 R14 R15
```

SYSCALL: Fast System Call into Linux

Flags Affected

```
O D I T S Z A P C   OF: Overflow flag  TF: Trap flag AF: Aux carry
F F F F F F F F F   DF: Direction flag SF: Sign flag PF: Parity flag
      <none>        IF: Interrupt flag ZF: Zero flag CF: Carry flag
```

Legal Forms

```
SYSCALL
```

Examples

```
SYSCALL
```

Notes

SYSCALL makes a fast call to a predefined operating system service routine. (This does *not* include calls into the C library!) It is available only in 64-bit mode. There are currently 335 such service routines. These routines do not have names but are selected by a number. Typically, registers are loaded with the number of the desired service routine and values appropriate to the chosen service routine before SYSCALL is executed.

SYSCALL trashes RCX and R11. All other registers are preserved. For a list of available x64 Linux system calls, see these sites, which were available at this edition's publication date in 2023:

```
https://blog.rchapman.org/posts/Linux_System_Call_Table_for_x86_64
https://hackeradam.com/x86-64-linux-syscalls
```

SYSCALL replaces the INT 80 calling protocol in 32-bit Linux. Remember that the numbers of the x64 system calls are *not* the same as those from 32-bit x86 Linux!

```
m8  = 8-bit memory data          m16 = 16-bit memory data
m32 = 32-bit memory data         m64 = 64-bit memory data
i8  = 8-bit immediate data       i16 = 16-bit immediate data
i32 = 32-bit immediate data      i64 = 64-bit immediate data
d8  = 8-bit signed displacement  d16 = 16-bit signed displacement
d32 = 32-bit unsigned displacement NOTE: There is no 64-bit displacement
r8  = AL AH BL BH CL CH DL DH     r16 = AX BX CX DX BP SP SI DI
r32 = EAX EBX ECX EDX EBP ESP ESI EDI
r64 = RAX RBX RCX RDX RBP RSP RSI RDI R8 R9 R10 R11 R12 R13 R14 R15
```

XCHG: Exchange Operands

Flags Affected

```
O  D  I  T  S  Z  A  P  C    OF: Overflow flag  TF: Trap flag AF: Aux carry
F  F  F  F  F  F  F  F  F    DF: Direction flag SF: Sign flag PF: Parity flag
         <none>              IF: Interrupt flag ZF: Zero flag CF: Carry flag
```

Legal Forms

```
XCHG  r/m8,r8
XCHG  r/m16,r16
XCHG  r/m32,r32      386+
XCHG  r/m64,r64      x64+
XCHG  r8,r/m8
XCHG  r16,r/m16
XCHG  r32,r/m32      386+
XCHG  r64,r/m64      x64+
XCHG  AX,r16
XCHG  EAX,r32        386+
XCHG  RAX,r64        x64+
XCHG  r16,AX
XCHG  r32,EAX        386+
XCHG  r64,RAX        x64+
```

Examples

```
XCHG  AL,AH
XCHG  EAX,EBX
XCHG  R12,[RSI+Offset]
XCHG  [RDI],RDX
```

Notes

XCHG exchanges the contents of its two operands. The two operands must be the same size.

```
m8 = 8-bit memory data          m16 = 16-bit memory data
m32 = 32-bit memory data        m64 = 64-bit memory data
i8  = 8-bit immediate data      i16 = 16-bit immediate data
i32 = 32-bit immediate data     i64 = 64-bit immediate data
d8 = 8-bit signed displacement  d16 = 16-bit signed displacement
d32 = 32-bit unsigned displacement NOTE: There is no 64-bit displacement
r8 = AL AH BL BH CL CH DL DH     r16 = AX BX CX DX BP SP SI DI
r32 = EAX EBX ECX EDX EBP ESP ESI EDI
r64 = RAX RBX RCX RDX RBP RSP RSI RDI R8 R9 R10 R11 R12 R13 R14 R15
```

XLAT: Translate Byte Via Table

Flags Affected

```
O D I T S Z A P C    OF: Overflow flag   TF: Trap flag  AF: Aux carry
F F F F F F F F F    DF: Direction flag  SF: Sign flag  PF: Parity flag
        <none>       IF: Interrupt flag  ZF: Zero flag   CF: Carry flag
```

Legal Forms

```
XLAT
XLATB
```

Examples

```
XLAT            ; 32-bit: Loads AL with byte table entry at EBX+AL
XLAT            ; 64-bit: Loads AL with byte table entry at RBX+AL
```

Notes

XLAT and its synonym XLATB perform a table translation of the 8-bit value in AL. All operands are implicit. The value in AL is treated as the index into a table in memory, located at the address contained in EBX (in 32-bit mode) or RBX (in x64 mode). When XLAT is executed, the value at [EBX+AL] / [RBX+AL] replaces the value previously in AL. AL is hard-coded as an implicit operand; no other register may be used.

The table located at the 32-bit or 64-bit address in EBX/RBX does not have to be 256 bytes in length, but a value in AL larger than the length of the table will result in an undefined value being placed in AL.

```
m8  = 8-bit memory data          m16 = 16-bit memory data
m32 = 32-bit memory data         m64 = 64-bit memory data
i8  = 8-bit immediate data       i16 = 16-bit immediate data
i32 = 32-bit immediate data      i64 = 64-bit immediate data
d8 = 8-bit signed displacement   d16 = 16-bit signed displacement
d32 = 32-bit unsigned displacement NOTE: There is no 64-bit displacement
r8 = AL AH BL BH CL CH DL DH      r16 = AX BX CX DX BP SP SI DI
r32 = EAX EBX ECX EDX EBP ESP ESI EDI
r64 = RAX RBX RCX RDX RBP RSP RSI RDI R8 R9 R10 R11 R12 R13 R14 R15
```

XOR: Exclusive OR

Flags Affected

```
O D I T S Z A P C   OF: Overflow flag  TF: Trap flag AF: Aux carry
F F F F F F F F F   DF: Direction flag SF: Sign flag PF: Parity flag
*       * * ? * *   IF: Interrupt flag ZF: Zero flag CF: Carry flag
```

Legal Forms

```
XOR r/m8,i8
XOR r/m16,i16
XOR r/m32,i32      386+
XOR r/m64,i32      x64+  NOTE: XOR r/m64,i64 is NOT valid!
XOR r/m16,i8
XOR r/m32,i8       386+
XOR r/m64,i8       x64+
XOR r/m8,r8
XOR r/m16,r16
XOR r/m32,r32      386+
XOR r/m64,r64      x64+
XOR r8,r/m8
XOR r16,r/m16
XOR r32,r/m32      386+
XOR r64,r/m64      x64+
XOR AL,i8
XOR AX,i16
XOR EAX,i32        386+
XOR RAX,i32        x64+ NOTE: XOR RAX,i64 is NOT valid!
```

Examples

```
XOR BX,DI
XOR EAX,5
XOR AX,0FFFFH
XOR AL,42H
XOR [BP+SI],DX
XOR [RDI],RAX
XOR QWORD [RBX],0B80000H
```

Notes

XOR performs a bitwise exclusive OR logical operation between its two operands. Once the operation is complete, the result replaces the destination operand. The

XOR operation is performed on a bit-by-bit basis, such that bit 0 of the source is XORed with bit 0 of the destination, bit 1 of the source is XORed with bit 1 of the destination, and so on. The XOR operation yields a 1 if the operands are different and a 0 if the operands are the same. Note that the XOR instruction makes the Auxiliary Carry flag AF undefined. CF and OF are cleared to 0, and the other affected flags are set according to the operation's results.

When XOR is used between a 64-bit value and an immediate value, the immediate value cannot be 64-bits in size. The immediate value may be only 32 bits in size.

Performing XOR between a register and itself is a common way of clearing a register to 0. There is no form to use XOR on a memory value against itself, as only one of XOR's two operands may be a memory value. Therefore, XOR cannot be used to zero a memory location.

```
m8  = 8-bit memory data          m16 = 16-bit memory data
m32 = 32-bit memory data         m64 = 64-bit memory data
i8  = 8-bit immediate data       i16 = 16-bit immediate data
i32 = 32-bit immediate data      i64 = 64-bit immediate data
d8  = 8-bit signed displacement  d16 = 16-bit signed displacement
d32 = 32-bit unsigned displacement NOTE: There is no 64-bit displacement
r8  = AL AH BL BH CL CH DL DH      r16 = AX BX CX DX BP SP SI DI
r32 = EAX EBX ECX EDX EBP ESP ESI EDI
r64 = RAX RBX RCX RDX RBP RSP RSI RDI R8 R9 R10 R11 R12 R13 R14 R15
```

Character Set Charts

The following pages contain summaries of two character sets commonly used on PC-compatible machines. The first is for the IBM-850 character set, commonly available on Linux terminal utilities such as Konsole and GNOME Terminal. The second is the older "Code Page 437" set, which is basically the character set coded into the BIOS ROM of IBM-compatible PCs.

There is one glyph block for each character in each set. Each glyph block includes the following information:

- The three-digit decimal form of the character number, from 000–255. These are in the upper-right corner of each block.

- The hexadecimal form of the character number, from 00–FF. These are in the lower-left corner of each block.

- The character glyph is in the center of the block.

- For control characters from 0–31, the name of the control character (e.g., NAK, DLE, CR, etc.) is printed vertically in the lower-right corner of the block.

Note that the IBM-850 character set is not loaded by default in common Linux terminal utilities and must be specifically selected from the options or settings menu before the character set will be displayed in the terminal window. For more on this, see Chapter 6.

ASCII & PC Extended Characters - IBM-850

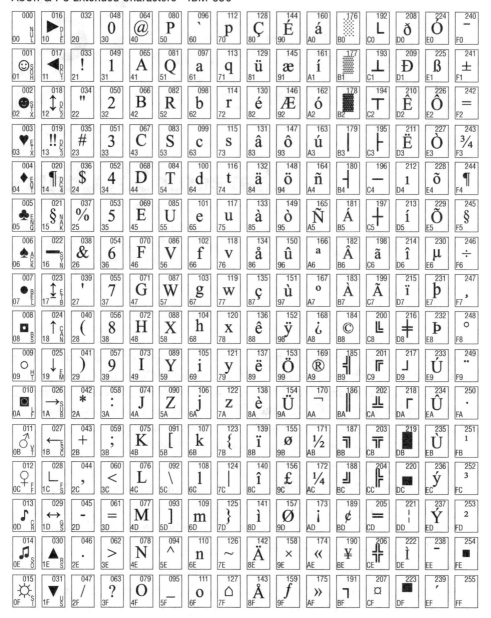

ASCII & PC Extended Characters - Code Page 437

000	016	032	048	064	080	096	112	128	144	160	176	192	208	224	240
NUL 00	► DLE 10	(space) 20	0 30	@ 40	P 50	` 60	p 70	Ç 80	É 90	á A0	▓ B0	└ C0	╨ D0	α E0	≡ F0
☺ SOH 01	◄ DC1 11	! 21	1 31	A 41	Q 51	a 61	q 71	ü 81	æ 91	í A1	▒ B1	┴ C1	╤ D1	β E1	± F1
☻ STX 02	↕ DC2 12	" 22	2 32	B 42	R 52	b 62	r 72	é 82	Æ 92	ó A2	▓ B2	┬ C2	╥ D2	Γ E2	≥ F2
♥ ETX 03	‼ DC3 13	# 23	3 33	C 43	S 53	c 63	s 73	â 83	ô 93	ú A3	│ B3	├ C3	╙ D3	π E3	≤ F3
♦ EOT 04	¶ DC4 14	$ 24	4 34	D 44	T 54	d 64	t 74	ä 84	ö 94	ñ A4	┤ B4	─ C4	╘ D4	Σ E4	∫ F4
♣ ENQ 05	§ NAK 15	% 25	5 35	E 45	U 55	e 65	u 75	à 85	ò 95	Ñ A5	╡ B5	┼ C5	╒ D5	σ E5	∫ F5
♠ ACK 06	▬ SYN 16	& 26	6 36	F 46	V 56	f 66	v 76	å 86	û 96	ª A6	╢ B6	╞ C6	╓ D6	µ E6	÷ F6
• BEL 07	↨ ETB 17	' 27	7 37	G 47	W 57	g 67	w 77	ç 87	ù 97	º A7	╖ B7	╟ C7	╫ D7	τ E7	≈ F7
◘ BS 08	↑ CAN 18	(28	8 38	H 48	X 58	h 68	x 78	ê 88	ÿ 98	¿ A8	╕ B8	╚ C8	╪ D8	Φ E8	° F8
○ HT 09	↓ EM 19	) 29	9 39	I 49	Y 59	i 69	y 79	ë 89	Ö 99	⌐ A9	╣ B9	╔ C9	┘ D9	Θ E9	∙ F9
◙ LF 0A	→ SUB 1A	* 2A	: 3A	J 4A	Z 5A	j 6A	z 7A	è 8A	Ü 9A	¬ AA	║ BA	╩ CA	┌ DA	Ω EA	▪ FA
♂ VT 0B	← ESC 1B	+ 2B	; 3B	K 4B	[5B	k 6B	{ 7B	ï 8B	¢ 9B	½ AB	╗ BB	╦ CB	█ DB	δ EB	√ FB
♀ FF 0C	∟ FS 1C	, 2C	< 3C	L 4C	\ 5C	l 6C	| 7C	î 8C	£ 9C	¼ AC	╝ BC	╠ CC	▄ DC	∞ EC	ⁿ FC
♪ CR 0D	↔ GS 1D	- 2D	= 3D	M 4D	] 5D	m 6D	} 7D	ì 8D	¥ 9D	¡ AD	╜ BD	═ CD	▌ DD	Ø ED	² FD
♫ SO 0E	▲ RS 1E	. 2E	> 3E	N 4E	^ 5E	n 6E	~ 7E	Ä 8E	Pts 9E	« AE	╛ BE	╬ CE	▐ DE	ε EE	▪ FE
☼ SI 0F	▼ US 1F	/ 2F	? 3F	O 4F	_ 5F	o 6F	⌂ 7F	Å 8F	ƒ 9F	» AF	┐ BF	╧ CF	▀ DF	∩ EF	FF

Index

A

$, deriving string length using, 221–222

" (double quote), 219

= (equal) operator, 277

> (greater than) operator, 277

>= (greater than or equal to) operator, 277

< (less than) operator, 277

<= (less than or equal to) operator, 277

<> (not equal) operator, 277

' (single quote), 219

16-bit blinders, 79–80

64-bit long mode, 101–102

ABI, 232, 233–234

Abrash, Michael (author)

Michael Abrash's Graphics Programming Black Book, 211

accidental recursion, 313–314

ADC (arithmetic addition with carry), 507–508

ADD (arithmetic addition), 509–510

adding

multiplying by shifting and, 267–270

one with INC and DEC, 191–192

address pins, 48

addresses, 8–9

addressing

data on Linux stack, 420–421

immediate, 179–181

long mode memory, 279–290

register, 181–183

AF (Auxiliary Carry flag), 189

AND instruction, 253–254

AND logical operation, 511–512

appimage, 493

application programming interface (API), 232

architecture, 63–65

arithmetic, in hexadecimals, 28–33

arithmetic addition (ADD), 509–510

arithmetic addition with carry (ADC), 507–508

arithmetic comparison (CMP), 240, 274, 519–520

arithmetic subtraction (SUB), 568–569

arithmetic subtraction with borrow (SBB), 560–561

ASCII tables, displaying, 402–404